eighth edition

AN INTRODUCTION TO GOVERNMENT AND POLITICS

A Conceptual Approach

MARK O. DICKERSON
University of Calgary

THOMAS FLANAGAN
University of Calgary

BRENDA O'NEILL
University of Calgary

NELSON EDUCATION

NELSON / EDUCATION

An Introduction to Government and Politics: A Conceptual Approach, Eighth Edition
by Mark O. Dickerson, Thomas Flanagan, and Brenda O'Neill

Associate Vice President, Editorial Director:
Evelyn Veitch

Editor-in-Chief, Higher Education:
Anne Williams

Senior Acquisitions Editor:
Lenore Taylor-Atkins

Marketing Manager:
Ann Byford

Senior Developmental Editor:
Linda Sparks

Editorial Assistant:
Jennifer O'Reilly

Photo and Permissions Researcher:
Terri Rothman, M.L.S.

Content Production Manager:
Christine Gilbert

Production Service:
Macmillan Publishing Solutions

Copy Editor:
Kelli Howey

Proofreader:
Dave Luljak

Indexer:
Maura Brown

Production Coordinator:
Ferial Suleman

Design Director:
Ken Phipps

Managing Designer:
Franca Amore

Interior Design:
Dianna Little

Cover Design:
Peter Papayanakis

Cover Image:
© Sergey I / Shutterstock

Compositor:
Macmillan Publishing Solutions

Printer:
Edwards Brothers

Library and Archives Canada Cataloguing in Publication Data

Dickerson, M. O., 1934-
    An introduction to government and politics : a conceptual approach/ Mark O. Dickerson, Thomas Flanagan, Brenda O'Neill.—8th ed.

Includes bibliographical references and index.
ISBN 978-0-17-650042-9

1. Political science—Textbooks.
2. Canada—Politics and government—Textbooks. I. Flanagan, Thomas, 1944- II. O'Neill, Brenda, 1964- III. Title.

JC131.D52 2009   320   C2008-906791-6

ISBN-13: 978-0-17-650042-9
ISBN-10: 0-17-650042-1

BRIEF CONTENTS

PART 4   The Political Process   349

CONTENTS

13   Nationalism   180

14   Feminism   198

20   Parliamentary and Presidential Systems   299

24   Communications Media   390

25   Elections and Electoral Systems   404

PREFACE

The most important revisions in the eighth edition of *An Introduction to Government and Politics* result from adding a new member to the writing team, Brenda O'Neill. Dr. O'Neill's expertise in political engagement, gender and politics, political culture, and democratic procedures is reflected in extensive changes to the chapters on those topics. As always, we have had the benefit of extensive feedback on the text initiated by Nelson Education Ltd. While our conceptual approach remains, the feedback has prompted a number of changes both in content and in format; but, while updating the material and presentation, we have tried to remain faithful to the basic approach that seems to have worked well over the past seven editions.

MAJOR CHANGES FOR THIS EDITION

The text has been updated throughout to take account of recent events, including the wars in Afghanistan and Iraq, changes in Canadian political parties, and the 2008 Canadian and American elections.

- Chapter 5, "Political Culture and Socialization," has been re-written to include the concept of social capital, and a discussion of multiculturalism has been added to Chapter 4, "The Nation."

- Chapter 18, "Transitions to Democracy," has been updated and re-organized.

- Chapter 23, "Political Parties, Interest Groups, and Social Movements: The Organization of Interests," has been expanded and now includes a discussion of contemporary social movements.

- Chapter 24, "Communications Media," has been updated to reflect the newest forms of communication in politics.

- Chapter 25, "Elections and Electoral Systems," has been updated to take account of political events through 2008.

- All end-of-chapter Internet links have been updated and are also available live on the student website at **www.intropolitics8e.nelson.com.**

PEDAGOGICAL APPROACH

The essence of our approach is the pedagogical method E. D. Hirsch calls "selective exemplification." That is, we try to provide readers with "a carefully chosen but generous sampling of factual data that are set forth in a meaningful web of inferences and generalizations about the larger domain."[1] According to Hirsch, educational research shows that this method yields better results than either an abstract discussion of general principles or an encyclopedic recitation of isolated facts. Of course, selective exemplification will work only if the examples make sense to students; so, as with each previous edition, we have taken care to update our examples to make them as current as possible.

This is a text for a first-year course in political science. Although designed for use in Canadian universities and colleges, it does not focus solely on Canadian government. We use Canadian illustrations of general principles together with examples from many other countries, but particularly the British and American political systems—both of which are historically of great importance to Canada.

Historical and Contemporary Perspective

In many years of teaching introductory courses in political science, we have encountered thousands of students. This experience has taught us something about the virtues and vices of the present approach to social studies in Canadian schools. On the positive side, many students come to university with an active curiosity about politics and a healthy scepticism about orthodox opinions. They are eager to learn more about a field that they recognize as important.

At the same time, many students are handicapped by certain deficiencies in the social-studies curriculum:

- They have been offered little historical information and historical perspective on events. History has suffered perhaps more than any other discipline through being integrated into social studies. Students without a historical perspective are adrift intellectually. They lack the important bearings that make sense of Canada's unique history, as well as the development of Western civilization and the rise and fall of other civilizations.

- They have little specific information about the institutions of Canadian government. Most students entering university are unable to say how a judge is appointed or what an order-in-council is. Their knowledge of government is focused more on current affairs, with heavy emphasis on issues as portrayed in the mass media.

- They are accustomed to discussing politics but not to using rigorously defined concepts. They are used to applying looser reasoning than is required for an academic discipline.

Our textbook addresses each of these problems. We can do relatively little about students' lack of historical background, since the course for which this book is designed cannot replace the systematic study of history. However, we do attempt to put important topics in a historical or developmental perspective, and we supply some information about watershed events such as the French and Russian Revolutions. Also, we refer whenever possible to authors, from Plato to Keynes, whose reputations are established and who are important historical figures in their own right.

We can spend only limited time on the details of Canadian political institutions, for those would require a course in Canadian government; we have chosen rather to emphasize concepts. The material in this book follows a careful sequence. Concepts are introduced one at a time, discussed at length, and then used as the basis for explaining further ideas. Important terms are boldfaced where they first occur or where they are thoroughly explained; these terms are used consistently throughout the text and are listed alphabetically at the back of the book for easy reference. We believe that this will equip the student with a comprehensive and logically consistent vocabulary for the study of politics. In the last part of the book we offer a method for conceptualizing the process of politics and for organizing or arranging the many ideas and concepts introduced in the earlier parts. Thinking about politics as a coherent process is an essential first step in becoming a student of politics, evaluating politics, and becoming a critic of one's own political system. We hope that this approach will be of value not only to students who intend to major in political science but also to those who are seeking a shorter path toward becoming informed political observers (and, of course, participants).

Key Terms and Concepts

We are keenly aware that this effort at consistency means simplifying the meaning of some important terms. Political scientists often disagree on the meaning and use of many significant political terms: *politics, nation-state,* and *democracy* are a few well-known examples of this problem. Our experience has been that students at the introductory level cannot absorb all these debates about meaning, especially when they are subjecting these terms to serious analysis for the first time. For this reason we have narrowed the meaning of many terms—without, we hope, departing from the mainstream of current usage. Readers will undoubtedly criticize our handling of this or that concept, but we hope the pedagogical benefit of applying a consistent vocabulary will compensate for any resulting problems. It is a considerable advantage to be able to explain, for example, liberalism in terms of previously established concepts such as society, state, and coercion that the student has already assimilated.

Organization

The book is divided into four parts that together constitute what we believe is a logical way to begin the study of government and politics. Part One defines those terms, ideas, and concepts that are basic to political science. An understanding of terms such as state and society, authority and legitimacy, and law and sovereignty is essential to a systematic study of politics. Part Two discusses the ideological basis of modern political systems. Liberalism and socialism, the fundamental ideological systems in the modern world, are discussed in the context of the political spectrum that runs from communism to fascism. The emergent ideologies of feminism and environmentalism are also discussed here and placed in context. Part Three looks at forms of government. Here we discuss different types of political systems: liberal–democratic, authoritarian, and totalitarian; parliamentary and presidential; federal and unitary. In Part Four we examine government as a process. A complex interaction of individuals and political institutions produces law and public policies for a society, and we try to view this inter-action as a systemic process. The model of politics we offer is hypothetical; however, we draw examples from Canada, the United Kingdom, the United States, and other countries to illustrate how the process works in reality.

Our work is meant to be objective and dispassionate, but that does not mean that it is value-free or without commitment. We consistently try to point out the value of the leading ideas of the Western world's political traditions. We pay particular atten-tion to two different and sometimes conflicting groups of ideas, both of which are of great importance. One group centres on constitutionalism and includes notions such as the rule of law and individual freedom; the other centres on democracy and allied concepts such as majority rule and popular sovereignty. For the past two centuries, the Western world has tried to combine these two clusters of ideas into the system of government known as constitutional or liberal democracy, in which majorities rule within a legal framework intended to prevent the oppression of minorities. This form of government has been most stable and successful in the countries in Western Europe and North America where it originated. In Canada, where liberal democracy seems securely established, we are apt to take it for granted; but it is far from being an obvious or universal form of government. We hope that better understanding of liberal democ-racy will help it to flourish.

UPDATING

This edition of *An Introduction to Government and Politics* went to press in early 2009, just as momentous and unexpected changes were shaking the political world both at home and abroad. The collapse of financial markets meant that governments around the world adopted Keynesian policies that had been largely out of vogue since the 1980s—deficit spending, regulation of markets, and subsidies to threatened indus-tries. At the time of writing, it was too early to tell whether these measures would be short-term and temporary, or whether they signaled a long-term shift comparable to the ascendancy of reform liberalism that began in the 1930s or of fiscal conservatism that began in the 1980s.

In Canada, Stephen Harper's government was almost overthrown in December 2008 over a fiscal update derided by the opposition as inadequate for inadequately responding to the economic downturn and for introducing changes to party finance legislation that would have unduly harmed opposition parties. The Liberals and NDP signed an accord to form a minority coalition also supported by the Bloc Québécois, and the three opposition parties were threatening to vote non-confidence when Harper saved his government, at least for a time, by asking the Governor General to prorogue Parliament. Liberal leader Stéphane Dion then became collateral damage as his party decided suddenly to replace him with Michael Ignatieff. At the time of writing, it was unclear whether Ignatieff would maintain the opposition coalition negotiated by Dion and attempt to defeat the Conservative government quickly, or whether he would play for time.

To cope with all these uncertain but highly significant developments, we will post an update on the text website, **www.intropolitics8e.nelson.com,** in time for use in the fall term of 2009.

ANCILLARIES

- **Instructor's Resource CD (978-0-17-647522-2)** includes the Instructor's Manual, Computerized Test Bank, and PowerPoints in the proceeding listing.

- **Instructor's Manual (978-0-17-640673-8)** includes lecture outlines, teaching tips, discussion questions, student activities, term paper assignments, questions for in-class debate, and much more. The material was developed to help time-pressed teachers more effectively communicate with their students and also strengthen the coverage of course material.

- **Test Bank (978-0-17-640674-5)** Each chapter of the test bank has multiple-choice questions and true/false test items, as well as fill-in-the-blank and short-answer questions.

- **Computerized Test Bank in ExamView®** This computerized testing software helps instructors create and customize exams in minutes. It contains all the questions from the printed test bank. Instructors can easily edit and import their own questions and graphics, change test layouts, and reorganize questions. It is available for both Windows and Macintosh.

- **Microsoft® PowerPoint® Presentation** This presentation features important concepts and key points from the textbook and is provided to professors for classroom use to add colour and interest to lectures. The PowerPoint® presentation is also available on the website. Go to **www.intropolitics8e.nelson.com.**

- **Video (978-0-17-647525-3)** Nelson Education offers a compilation of current CBC news clips covering a wide range of topics. The videos include suggested discussion questions for use in class, making these videos a great enhancement to lectures. Ask your Nelson Education sales representative for more information on how to order the video.

ACKNOWLEDGMENTS

Special thanks are due to Jim Keeley for revising Chapter 8, "International Order." Steve Hobbs gave us indispensable help in updating the text and bibliographies and Evan Wilson revised the glossary. We extend our appreciation to Cara Yarzab, Bram Sepers, Linda Sparks, Christine Gilbert, and Kelli Howey. We would also like to thank the readers retained by Nelson Education to review the seventh edition and give us suggestions for the eighth:

Lavinia Stan, St. Francis Xavier University

Chris Kukucha, University of Lethbridge

Allison Dube, University of Calgary

Visit the Website

For text updates, visit the text's website at **www.intropolitics8e.nelson.com.**

INTRODUCTION
The Study of Political Science

Political science is the systematic study of *government* and *politics,* terms that are defined at greater length in Chapter 1. But before getting into the subject matter, students may find it useful to learn something about the discipline itself.

HISTORY OF POLITICAL SCIENCE

The origins of political science lie in the classical period of Greek philosophy, whose greatest writers were Plato and Aristotle. The Greek philosophers did not approach political science as a specialized discipline in the modern sense, but they thought and wrote systematically about government. They were concerned above all with how politics can contribute to a life of excellence and virtue. The long quotation from Aristotle printed in Historical Perspectives I.1 gives some idea of how this great philosopher saw political science as a moral endeavour committed to the betterment of the human condition. Greek philosophy, and with it the habit of systematic reflection upon government, became part of the cultural tradition of the Western world. Political science continued to exist as a branch of moral philosophy, and important contributions were made by authors who also wrote in other areas of philosophy, such as Thomas Aquinas, Thomas Hobbes, and John Locke. Such writings, extending over more than two millennia, constitute a rich body of wisdom that is still the foundation of political science.

In the eighteenth century, political science started to differentiate itself from moral philosophy—not yet as an independent study, but as part of the new science of political economy. Writers such as Adam Smith, who held the chair of moral philosophy at the University of Glasgow, began to study and write about the workings of the market. They did not do this in a vacuum; in the society of the time, market processes were being freed from mercantilist policies predicated on governmental control of the economy. The study of government was a junior partner in the new science of *political economy,* which emphasized market forces. Government was seen as a limited auxiliary that could carry out a few functions not performed well in the marketplace. In the late eighteenth and early nineteenth centuries, universities established chairs of political economy. During this period, much work that today we would call political science was also done in faculties of history and law, especially under the guise of comparative and constitutional law.

Historical Perspectives I.1

Aristotle on Political Science

"Now it would be agreed that [the Supreme Good, the purpose of human existence] must be the object of the most authoritative of the sciences—some science which is pre-eminently a master-craft. But such is manifestly the science of Politics; for it is this that ordains which of the sciences are to exist in states, and what branches of knowledge the different classes of the citizens are to learn, and up to what point; and we observe that even the most highly esteemed of the faculties, such as strategy, domestic economy, oratory, are subordinate to the political science. Inasmuch then as the rest of the sciences are employed by this one, and as it moreover lays down laws as to what people shall do and what things they shall refrain from doing, the end of this science must include the ends of all the others. Therefore, the Good of man must be the end of the science of Politics. For even though it be the case that the Good is the same for the individual and for the state, nevertheless, the good of the state is manifestly a greater and more perfect good, both to attain and to preserve. To secure the good of one person only is better than nothing; but to secure the good of a nation or a state is a nobler and more divine achievement."

Source: Aristotle, *The Nicomachean Ethics,* I, ii, 4–8, tr. H. Rackham (London: William Heinemann, 1934, rev. ed.; Loeb Classical Library, vol. 19), pp. 5–7.

Economics and political science began to diverge in the second half of the nineteenth century as scholars began to specialize. The discovery of the principle of marginal utility in the 1870s made it possible for economics to become mathematical, and hence more specialized and remote from the everyday concerns of government and politics. Universities in the United States took the lead in establishing autonomous departments of political science, which united the work of professors who might previously have gravitated to political economy, history, and law. Political science in its modern academic form thus stems from developments in the United States in the late nineteenth century. The first American department of political science was founded at Columbia University in 1880; by the outbreak of World War I in 1914, there were 40 such departments in U.S. universities.[1]

Why in the United States? Partly because this rapidly expanding country was opening scores of new universities not bound by old traditions about academic specialties. But the more important reason is that the United States—a nation founded on a political act of revolution—has always been fascinated with government. Political science at the university level was a logical extension of the civics education that was so important in the public schools. Also, these early political scientists tended to be moralistic crusaders for governmental reform—a good example being Woodrow Wilson, the only political science professor ever to become an American president.

In the first half of the twentieth century, political science as an academic discipline remained largely an American phenomenon, with only a few chairs established in universities in other countries. Of course, the substance of political science was pursued elsewhere, but it was usually conducted within departments of law, political economy, economics, and history. However, after World War II, political science was adopted as an independent discipline around the world. This was partly in imitation of the American cultural behemoth. A deeper reason, perhaps, was the tremendous expansion of the scope of government in the second half of the twentieth century. The small state of the *laissezfaire* era could be understood fairly easily within the study of political economy; the large, interventionist state of the present era seems to demand its own specialized discipline.

Political science in Canada must be seen in this historical context. In 1950 there were only about 30 political scientists in Canada, most of them employed in university departments of political economy.[2] Their main periodical was the *Canadian Journal of Economics and Political Science (CJEPS)*. In the 1960s, as enrollments increased and more staff were hired to cope with an unprecedented expansion of universities, these departments began to split into separate departments of economics and political science. In 1967 the *CJEPS* was split into the *Canadian Journal of Economics (CJE)* and the *Canadian Journal of Political Science (CJPS)*, while two separate professional associations also emerged: the Canadian Economics Association (CEA) and the Canadian Political Science Association (CPSA). Some years later, as part of the general movement of Quebec nationalism, political scientists in that province formed their own association, the Société québécoise de science politique, with its own journal, *Politique et Sociétés*. The two associations maintain cooperative relations with one another, and there is a good deal of cross-membership; but in political science, as in so many other areas, the reality of Canada is that Quebec is a "distinct society."

The term political economy no longer embraces the entire territory of economics and politics as it once did. It now has several special uses. In some circles, it refers to the study of certain narrower subjects—such as economic intervention by government—that require information and insights from both disciplines in order to be understood. In other circles, it denotes a historical–materialist approach to the study of politics that draws heavily, though not exclusively, on the thought of Karl Marx and other writers in the Marxist tradition. Within the Canadian political-science community, the practitioners of political economy in this latter sense are a recognized subgroup whose members tend to work together with like-minded historians, economists, and sociologists. Together, they maintain their own academic network and help to support an interdisciplinary journal, *Studies in Political Economy*, which is based at Carleton University in Ottawa.

APPROACHES TO POLITICAL SCIENCE

When political science achieved academic autonomy, its practitioners brought to it the methods of their forebears in philosophy, political economy, law, and history. These methods were chiefly the narrative, chronological, and descriptive study of political institutions, complemented by philosophical reflection about matters of good and evil in the sphere of government. Great changes have taken place since that beginning.

In the 1940s, sociology and social psychology began to exert enormous influence, and political scientists became familiar with methods of research common in those disciplines, such as attitude scales, sample surveys, and statistical analysis. The rapidly increasing use of these methods was closely tied to a shift in emphasis away from formal constitutional structures and toward political parties, pressure groups, elections, and collective behaviour. This transition—often referred to as the *behavioural revolution*—brought political science closer to the other social sciences.

A second phase of the behavioural revolution began in the 1950s and is still far from ending. It is characterized by the influence of rational-choice models of analysis that were first developed in economics and mathematics. Increasingly, some political scientists are using deductive models derived from branches of mathematics such as game theory and information theory to explain the data gathered in their empirical investigations. This phase is more abstract and theoretical in nature than the first and is drawing political science closer to natural sciences such as biology and cybernetics, which often utilize similar mathematical models.

There were acrimonious divisions within the discipline in the 1950s and 1960s between supporters and opponents of the new methods, with many extreme claims being made on both sides. That furor, however, has now largely subsided. Political scientists who use quantitative methods now coexist peacefully with colleagues who rely on the old techniques of description and reflection. It seems to be accepted that political science is inherently pluralistic and is united not by adherence to a single method, but by concern with a common subject. Because different questions of politics and government lend themselves to different approaches, political scientists may resemble philosophers, sociologists, historians, lawyers, economists, or anthropologists in their research methods; yet all feel that they are united in a joint enterprise to understand the many facets of government and politics.

The methodological battles have subsided but have been followed by equally noisy ideological strife. In the late 1960s, political economists and others rooted in the Marxist tradition enunciated a vigorous challenge to what they saw as the capitalist bias of most political science. Their criticism was soon augmented by distinctive new points of view such as environmentalism, feminism, and multiculturalism, each arguing in its own way that fragile and ill-defended assumptions amounting to bias exist in conventional political science. There is no immediate prospect for consensus on such issues, and political science remains what it has always been—an inherently pluralistic discipline in which different points of view clash and final victory is never achieved.

In this respect, political science is very different from the natural sciences. At any given time, probably 99 percent of physicists, chemists, or biologists agree on about 99 percent of the contents of their respective disciplines. They may disagree heatedly about research on the frontiers, but overall the areas of such disagreement are small.

Those who challenge the fundamentals of such disciplines are often regarded as cranks and banished to the periphery. In contrast, political science is an ongoing debate in which honest differences of opinion over fundamental issues are the norm.

Nonetheless, in spite of such deep-seated divisions, there are large areas of agreement. Although feminist and conservative political scientists may disagree profoundly on the larger implications, they should be able to agree on how many women sit in the House of Commons, on what the statistical trend has been over time, and on at least some of the reasons why the percentage (1) used to be extremely low, (2) rose rapidly from the 1960s to the mid-1990s, and (3) has levelled off since the election of 1997 at about 21 percent, still far below the level for men in Canada and also below the level for women in the legislatures of some European countries. Such agreement is important in itself, even if it is immersed in vigorous polemics about whether the trends are good or bad, and whether additional measures ought to be enacted to accelerate the changes.

To introduce some technical terminology, political scientists can hope for agreement on *empirical* (i.e., factual) questions, such as what is the shape of the political world, and how does that world function? Although disagreement on such questions always exists, it can in principle be overcome by more research and better evidence. But disagreement on *normative* (i.e., evaluative) questions is harder, perhaps impossible, to resolve, because it may stem from different value commitments. To go back to the preceding example, even after feminist and conservative political scientists reach agreement on a host of empirical issues relating to the representation of women in the House of Commons, they might continue to disagree on the normative question of whether one *ought* to take steps to increase that level of representation.

Pulling these strands of historical background together, one can identify four leading contemporary approaches within the discipline of political science. These are not the only ones, to be sure, but they are so widespread that everyone studying political science must be aware of them. Few political scientists would maintain that any of these approaches is the only correct one, but in practice most political scientists depend on one of them most of the time in the research that they do. Consequently, the discipline as a whole consists of the aggregate of these different and sometimes conflicting approaches to the study of politics.

Institutionalism

Institutionalism focuses on the detailed, systematic analysis of the working of political organizations, such as legislatures, cabinets, political parties, interest groups, and courts. Obviously, any political scientist has to be an institutionalist to some extent because the political world consists of institutions and you cannot understand politics without knowing what these institutions are and how they work. You could, for example, hardly presume to speak about American politics without understanding that the Congress is divided into two branches called the Senate and the House of

Representatives, that legislation must be approved by both branches, that the president has the right to veto legislation, and that the Congress can override a presidential veto under certain circumstances. Institutionalism, however, is sometimes criticized for being nothing more than formalistic description, devoid of deeper insight into political processes. Dissatisfaction with institutionalism, which was the dominant approach to political science up to the 1950s, led to the development of behaviouralism.

Behaviouralism

Behaviouralism focuses on the behaviour of individuals rather than on the structure of institutions. Behaviouralists typically study topics such as political culture and socialization, public opinion, and voting, where people think and make decisions as individuals, not as cogs in the wheel of an organization. They often use methods such as sample surveys, which allow them to ask people questions and record their responses as individual-level data, after which they use statistical methods to find correlations among variables. This type of research can tell you, for example, which categories of people tend to vote for the candidates of the various political parties—information that is not only interesting in itself but also of great practical importance to the strategists who craft the appeals that parties make to voters during elections.

Behaviouralism has undoubtedly made great contributions to the development of political science, but it has some obvious limitations. Public opinion and elections are interesting and important, but in themselves they do not decide anything except who will fill elected political offices. Those elected officeholders are the ones who actually make decisions, and they do so not as unconstrained individuals but as role-players in institutions. A balanced view, therefore, would see institutionalism and behaviouralism as complementary rather than contradictory approaches to the study of politics, both being necessary for a complete explanation of political outcomes.

Public Choice

Public choice is sometimes called "the economics of politics." It represents the application of assumptions about human behaviour that are standard in economics—rationality and the maximization of individual utility—to the explanation of political phenomena. In its purest form, public-choice analysis begins with abstract reasoning to devise a model of how rational, self-interested, utility maximizers would act in stipulated political circumstances, and of how their behaviour would respond to changes in those circumstances. Would such people vote for Party A or Party B? Would they join a political party? Would they bother to vote at all? The predictions of the model are then tested against data collected from the real world of politics.

One of the great advantages of public choice is its applicability to both individual behaviour and institutional structure. Practitioners of public choice analyze institutions as the aggregation of individual choices. To the extent that this approach works, it has the potential to overcome the split between behaviouralism and institutionalism. Another advantage of public choice is that it operates with a single, explicit theory of human nature, which helps to give it consistency across different applications. However, the critics of public choice believe that interpreting human behaviour as self-interested utility maximization is too narrow and too dependent upon the capitalist theory of economics from which public choice was imported into political science. Many critics denounce public choice as simply an ideological rationalization for a conservative, market-oriented brand of politics.

Even though we admit the significance of some of the criticisms of public choice, the authors of this book have been influenced by it, and one of us has even written a book attempting to interpret Canadian politics in public-choice terms.[3] Public-choice interpretations, therefore, crop up here and there throughout this text. But we do not believe that public choice is the only valid way of doing political science, and the text draws as much, if not more, on the findings of researchers committed to institutionalism and behaviouralism.

Political Economy

Political economy, like public choice, is also an application of economic theory to the explanation of political life, but it mobilizes a different version of economics. Political economy, at least as the term is generally understood today in Canada, derives from the Marxist view that politics is conditioned by and expresses the class struggle, and that the ruling class uses organized government as a tool to maintain its position of dominance. Starting from this premise, practitioners of political economy refuse to analyze politics and government as such; they believe that satisfying explanations can be found only by linking political phenomena to the underlying realities of class conflict.

As part of its Marxist heritage, political economy also rejects the notion of value neutrality that tends to dominate in other contemporary approaches to political science. Political economists do not see themselves merely as value-free analysts of political life; on the contrary, they hope that by exposing the realities of class conflict, they will hasten the approach of a less exploitive, more egalitarian form of economy and society.

The strengths and weaknesses of political economy are in some ways like those of public choice. Political economy transcends the divide between behaviouralism and institutionalism; and its explicit theory of human nature as a product of social circumstances, particularly of the class struggle, gives it rigour and consistency. But as with public choice, those who question the underlying economic premises will have further doubts about the validity of applying them to the interpretation of politics.

ORGANIZATION OF THE DISCIPLINE

Political science, like all academic disciplines, has become so large that internal specialization is necessary. Political scientists typically think of themselves as working in one or two particular fields, and university and college departments of political science organize their course offerings accordingly. The following, most common, way of carving up the discipline is based more on convenience than on any profound intellectual rationale:

- Political philosophy
- Canadian politics
- Comparative politics
- International relations

Political philosophy, which goes back to Plato and Aristotle, is treated as a separate field because it has its own long tradition and because its methods are mainly reflective and conceptual rather than empirical. Yet political philosophy often generates empirical hypotheses that can be tested against evidence in all of the other fields.

Canadian politics is treated as a field simply because we live in Canada and the requirements of citizenship make it important to understand the politics of the country where we live. Each country treats its own national politics as a distinct field. Thus, American and British universities have separate fields of American and British politics and teach Canadian politics (if they do) as part of comparative politics.

It is important to note that Canadian politics does not operate only at the national level. Provincial and municipal governments are important political arenas that for many students are closer to their own experience than the more remote field of national government. Recent developments in aboriginal self-government have further enriched the field of local government. At one time aboriginal communities were simply administered by the Department of Indian Affairs and thus were not of much interest to political scientists; but the more than 600 Indian bands, today usually called First Nations, now have governments that are just as worthy of study as other local governments in Canada.

Comparative politics is the study of politics in different countries. Canadian universities teach American and British politics as part of comparative politics, even though these would be considered separate fields in the United States and Great Britain. This is mainly a matter of convenience. Politics has many similarities and differences all around the world, and everyone understands their own national politics better through comparison with those of other countries. This book, while written for Canadian students, tries to bring in comparative material from many other countries, particularly the United States and Great Britain, to give Canadians a better understanding of their own system.

Comparative politics can also be conceptualized as a method of analysis. Studying multiple cases and looking for both similar and divergent features helps to build a body of knowledge applicable to the entire world, not just to the country in which you happen to live.

International relations studies the way in which independent states relate to one another. As explained at greater length in Chapter 8, international politics is characterized by the absence of overall sovereignty, which makes it a unique field of study. In fact, it is so different that some universities have separate programs or even departments of international relations.

Beyond this traditional fourfold division of political science, still found in almost every university catalogue, there are a variety of fields and subfields that crop up more or less widely. The department of political science in which you are studying may group courses under headings such as public administration, public law, public policy, political behaviour, and research methods. These groupings usually cut across the traditional divisions among the four fields described above. For example, public policy—e.g., the study of government's role in health care—will be both Canadian and comparative. Researchers study the origin and implementation of such policies and also attempt to evaluate their effectiveness in attaining their stated objectives. Policy studies thus have both philosophical and empirical dimensions to the extent that values are involved and evaluations of effectiveness are made. The field of public policy is of particular practical importance because many positions in government are filled by graduates of public-policy programs. A well-known Canadian example of this kind of work is *How Ottawa Spends,* an annual series of volumes produced by the School of Public Administration at Carleton University in Ottawa.

When we debated these matters in our department at the University of Calgary, someone proposed the metaphor of "fields and streams," based on the title of a well-known hunting and fishing magazine. The four traditional areas can be thought of as expansive territorial divisions—the fields—while the special concerns, such as public policy, can be seen as streams meandering through all the fields. Don't take it too seriously; it's just a metaphor. But we have found it helpful in organizing our research and teaching in political science.

HOW SCIENTIFIC IS POLITICAL SCIENCE?

The answer to this question depends upon what you mean by *science.* If you take highly mathematical, theoretical disciplines such as physics and chemistry as the model, political science does not measure up very well. Those sciences operate according to the hypothetical-deductive method, in which hypotheses are logically derived from abstract theories and then tested against real-world data. A famous example is the verification of Einstein's theory of relativity—in itself merely a complex mathematical model—by testing its prediction that the path of light passing close to the sun should be bent by the enormous force of its gravitational field.

Among contemporary approaches to political science, public choice makes the loudest claims to apply the hypothetical–deductive method. Yet many public-choice predictions, including some of the best-known ones, have not been supported very well by empirical evidence.[4] Because of discrepant data, public choice has had to refine its predictions so often that many of them begin to look less like broad generalizations than like specific descriptions of particular cases—in other words, not scientific in the sense of physics or chemistry.

Political science stacks up better against disciplines such as biology and geology, in which systematic observation and careful description still play a larger role than abstract model-building. If biologists can demonstrate how differences in precipitation or soil nutrients affect the growth of plant species, political scientists can show how changes in the electoral system affect the competition of political parties in democracies. If geologists can offer a plausible explanation of many features of the earth's surface in terms of plate tectonics, political scientists can explain elections in terms of the formation and breakup of political coalitions. Geology cannot predict the timing of an earthquake in advance, and political science cannot predict when a realignment of coalitions will take place; but both disciplines can offer enlightening after-the-fact explanations. Political scientists often disagree among themselves about many topics; but meteorologists, geologists, and biologists also sometimes disagree strenuously, for example, about whether global warming is a reality, what its causes might be (if indeed it exists), and how it might be combated (if indeed it ought to be combated).

Political scientists have much to be modest about. The history of the discipline is filled with failed predictions, unsubstantiated claims to scientific rigour, and unproductive ideological controversy. Nonetheless, it is not an unrealistic aspiration for political scientists to build a body of knowledge composed of careful description together with well-tested generalizations about political phenomena.

WHY STUDY POLITICAL SCIENCE?

There are at least four answers to this question.

1. There is no professional category of political scientist, as there is of economist, chemist, or geologist. Nonetheless, the knowledge imparted by political science is highly useful in several professions, and many students major in political science as a sort of pre-professional degree. One can take political science as a preparation for studying law, entering the civil service, or working in party politics. Political science is an obvious springboard for anyone interested in these professions, although other disciplines such as history and economics can also serve the same purpose.

2. Political science is a form of education for citizenship. Everyone in the modern world lives under the jurisdiction of a government and is a potential participant in politics. Even those who are not particularly interested in politics—and not everyone is or needs to be—are required to pay taxes and encouraged to vote. Studying political science can help you become a more effective citizen by enhancing your understanding of the environment in which you operate.

3. The study of political science can be part of a broad liberal-arts education. Political philosophy is particularly useful in this respect. Systematic reflection on government has natural linkages to other liberal disciplines such as philosophy, history, and literature.

4. For a few who have the time, inclination, and ability to go on to postgraduate studies, political science can lead to a career in research and teaching in universities, colleges, and research institutes. Someone who takes this path becomes part of the same type of scientific community that exists for all disciplines. It is a life dedicated to the advancement of knowledge in your chosen field.

All of the above are valid reasons for studying political science. Whatever your own reasons—you probably have more than one—we hope this book provides an entry into the discipline. It's just a first step, not the last word. Take what you learn and build on it. We, as the authors, will be more than compensated if you remember the aphorism of the philosopher Friedrich Nietzsche: "You badly repay your teacher if you always remain a student."

Questions for Discussion

1. Do you agree with Aristotle that politics is not a proper study for young people?

2. Give an example of a normative statement. Do you think that such statements merely reflect personal preferences, or do they have some stronger foundation?

3. Would you personally want to major in political science? Why or why not?

Internet Links

1. Nelson Education Political Science Resource Centre: **www.polisci.nelson.com.** A comprehensive reference site maintained by Nelson Education, the publisher of this book. Includes many links to various topics.

2. Website of the Canadian Political Science Association: **www.cpsa-acsp.ca.**

3. Website of the American Political Science Association: **www.apsanet.org.**

4. The Ultimate Political Science Links Page: **www.rvc.cc.il.us/faclink/pruckman/ PSLinks.htm.** Many links to various topics.

5. Bourque Newswatch: **www.bourque.org.** Gateway to top stories in current events in Canada and around the world.

Further Reading

Archer, Keith, et al. *Parameters of Power: Canada's Political Institutions.* 3rd ed. Toronto: Nelson Canada, 2002.

Baxter-Moore, Nicolas, Terrance Carroll, and Roderick Church. *Studying Politics: An Introduction to Argument and Analysis.* Toronto: Copp Clark Longman, 1994.

Clement, Wallace. *The Challenge of Class Analysis.* Ottawa: Carleton University Press, 1988.

———, ed. *Understanding Canada: Building on the New Canadian Political Economy.* Montreal: McGill–Queen's University Press, 1997.

Dahl, Robert Alan, and Bruce Stinebrickner. *Modern Political Analysis.* 6th ed. Englewood Cliffs, NJ: Prentice-Hall, 2003.

Dyck, Rand. *Canadian Politics: Critical Approaches.* 4th ed. Toronto: Thomson Nelson, 2003.

Goodin, Robert E., and Hans-Dieter Klingemann, eds. *A New Handbook of Political Science.* Oxford: Oxford University Press, 1996.

Guy, James John. *People, Politics & Government: Political Science: A Canadian Perspective.* 5th ed. Scarborough, ON: Prentice-Hall, 1995.

Howlett, Michael, Alex Netherton, and M. Ramesh. *The Political Economy of Canada: An Introduction.* Don Mills, ON: Oxford University Press, 1999.

Johnson, David B. *Public Choice: An Introduction to the New Political Economy.* Mountain View, CA: Mayfield Publishing, 1991.

Jones, Laurence F., and Edward C. Olson. *Political Science Research: A Handbook of Scopes and Methods.* New York: Longman, 1996.

Marsh, David, and Gerry Stoker, eds. *Theory and Methods in Political Science.* London: Macmillan, 1995.

Richter, Melvin. *The History of Political and Social Concepts: A Critical Introduction.* New York: Oxford University Press, 1995.

Shively, W. Phillips. *The Craft of Political Research.* Upper Saddle River, NJ: Prentice Hall, 2002.

Stoker, Gerry, *Why Politics Matters: Making Democracy Work.* New York: Palgrave MacMillan, 2006.

White, Louise G. *Political Analysis: Technique and Practice.* 3rd ed. Belmont, CA: Wadsworth, 1994.

PART 1

Basic Concepts

CHAPTER 1
Society, Government, and Politics

In the Introduction, we used terms such as *politics, government,* and *authority* without attempting to define them or to analyze them carefully. We could do that because everyone knows from ordinary life experience, as well as from attending school, more or less what they mean. But knowing "more or less" what key terms mean is not good enough for students of political science. It is time to take a more systematic and detailed look. Government and politics are features of all human societies; we would not be human without them. Hence, in undertaking a careful exploration of the meaning of key terms, we are not just playing around with words—we are coming to grips with human nature itself.

SOCIETY: LIVING TOGETHER

We are all social beings who need the support of others not merely to live well but to survive. There is no record of a time when human beings lived as isolated individuals, coming together only to mate. As far as we know, people have always lived in groups at least as large as the family or band. The usual term for such groups, large or small, is *society.*

Sociologists usually define **society** as a human group whose members live by common rules of conduct and which has a plausible claim to self-sufficiency. Both of these points need clarification. By rules of conduct we mean not just enforceable commands but also regular and predictable behaviour. All human activities, such as marriage, work, and recreation, are carried on within a framework of such rules. Society exists when people share so many rules of conduct that they are able to understand and predict one another's behaviour.

For example, adults in North America and northern Europe have a clear conception about how close to each other two people should stand or sit. In impersonal business situations, they generally maintain a distance of between one and two metres. But the people of Middle Eastern countries do not use this intermediate spacing; they transact business either closer together or farther apart—the distance depends on factors that would not be immediately apparent to us.[1] Such behavioural differences may cause considerable discomfort and misunderstanding in cross-cultural contact. The physical distance between people is not important in itself, but it is vital that it be understood in the same way by everyone concerned. Understanding and living by the rules that govern interpersonal relations is the essence of social order.

Human beings are not the only social animals. There are social insects (bees, termites, ants) and mammals (hyenas, wolves, chimpanzees, baboons). In recent decades the study of animal societies has grown to become one of the most dynamic scientific fields and has yielded many insights that, with appropriate caution, can sometimes be transferred to the study of human society.[2] The common denominator in both animal and human societies is rules of conduct—predictable, regular patterns of behaviour that integrate the individual with the social whole. The major difference between animal and human societies is this: the vastly greater intelligence of human beings allows them not only to understand social rules of conduct but also to change them by conscious decision.

It is impossible to draw clear lines between societies in the modern world. The international movement of people, commodities, and ideas is so vast that self-sufficiency has almost vanished. Rules of conduct have also become widely diffused. The ascendancy of Western society since the fifteenth century has spread many Western cultural practices around the earth: formal education and literacy, modes of dress, table manners, forms of economic activity, and much more. To a great extent, the world has become one society, with regional differences increasingly blurred. A person can travel to and even work in any major city on any continent without feeling that any profound lines of social demarcation have been crossed. Nonetheless, we often speak of societies as if their boundaries were the same as the legal and territorial boundaries established by governments. Thus, it is common to refer to Canadian society or American society, and even to "Alberta" or "Toronto" society, but for analytical purposes it is essential to remember that societies are not sharply distinguished from one another, certainly not by boundaries of governmental jurisdiction.

GOVERNMENT: MAKING PUBLIC DECISIONS

Society is a field of voluntary interaction. People make their own decisions about whom to marry, how to make a living, who their friends will be, and where to shop. **Government,** in contrast, has to do with compulsion, not voluntary decision making. Government is a specialized activity of those individuals and institutions that make and enforce public decisions that are binding upon the whole community. All effective governments carry out at least the following functions: they protect society from external attack, enforce rules of conduct within society, and settle disputes between members of society. The common denominator of these functions is *order*, both internal and external. Governments selectively use force to maintain a stable and durable social order. Beyond this minimum function, government also provide services for members of society. This is particularly true of modern governments, which deliver mail, pave highways, operate health insurance schemes, and provide old-age pensions. But the essence of government is to maintain peace within the social order by enforcing rules of conduct.

But why do rules of conduct need enforcement? Why do human beings not always obey them spontaneously? The problem of obedience is vastly more complicated in our species than in any other because of our greater intelligence. Humans are able not only to follow rules but also to understand and formulate them, reflect upon them, and manipulate them for their own ends. Because of this, there may be differences of opinion about what rules of conduct apply to particular situations.

Even if we could always agree in the abstract about which rule of conduct to follow, there would still be the problem of enforcement. In many situations, cooperation offers benefits, yet the existence of those benefits creates an incentive for self-interested individuals to cheat. For example, almost all of us benefit from paying taxes if the money is used to pave the roads; yet any one person will benefit still more by evading the taxes while continuing to drive on the roads which others pay to maintain. However, the benefit disappears if enough people default on their taxes, in which case there will not be enough revenue to pay for paving the roads. It is an outcome that no one really wants but that no one can avoid if all are motivated only by narrow self-interest.

THE PRISONER'S DILEMMA

The problem of achieving social cooperation is illustrated by the so-called "Prisoner's Dilemma," which is one of the most widely applied models of game theory. Assume that two men, Mark and Tom, are arrested by the police for possession of illegal drugs and suspected of trafficking. The police interrogate them separately and do not allow them to communicate with each other. The police, furthermore, say the same thing to each prisoner: "We know you are guilty, but we need proof. If you inform on your partner while he remains silent, you can go free, and he will get ten years in jail. But if the situation is reversed—if he informs on you while you remain silent—he will go free and you will get ten years. If you both talk, you will both get eight years. But if neither of you talks, you will each get one year on the lesser charge of possession, which is all that our evidence will sustain without further testimony from one of you."

Mark and Tom will achieve the most favourable outcome if they both keep silent; if they do that, each will escape with a light sentence. But that is not likely to happen in the situation as described; instead, each will probably end up informing on the other and thus both will receive the heavier sentence of eight years. To understand why, consider the following payoff matrix:

Prisoner's Dilemma		Mark	
		Silent	Talk
Tom	Silent	−1,−1	−10,0
	Talk	0,−10	−8,−8

Each cell in the matrix contains a pair of numbers separated by a comma. The first number represents the payoff in a given situation to the row player (Tom), the second number represents the payoff in the same situation to the column player (Mark). The upper right-hand cell, for example, shows that if Mark talks while Tom remains silent, Mark will go free (0) while Tom will get ten years in jail (–10).

Now consider how each player will reason if he has complete information about the game and if he is rational in the sense of caring first about his own self-interest. Tom will say to himself, "I face two possibilities. Mark can either remain silent or talk. If he remains silent, I can either remain silent or talk. If I remain silent, I get one year in jail (–1); if I talk, I go free (0)—so I had better talk (0 > –1). But Mark may talk, in which case I again have two choices. If he talks and I remain silent, I get ten years in jail (–10). If he talks and I also talk, I only get eight (–8)—so in this case also, it is better for me to talk (–8 > –10). No matter what Mark does, I will be better off if I talk." Mark will reason the same way, for his column payoffs are a mirror image of Tom's row payoffs.

This result is both interesting and paradoxical. By a rigorous analysis of his self-interest, each prisoner is led to talk, which ensures that they both achieve the less desirable outcome of eight years in jail (–8). If each could trust the other to remain silent, both could achieve the more desirable outcome of only one year in prison (–1). But in the game as described, if we assume self-interested players, neither has reason to have faith in the other's reliability.

The players might hope to obtain a better joint outcome if the rules of the game were relaxed so they could communicate with each other. They could then agree in advance not to inform on each other. But communication in itself is not sufficient to resolve the prisoner's dilemma, for each player still has an incentive to break the agreement if he believes he can count on the other to keep his side of the bargain. That is, if Tom and Mark agree to keep silent, thus ensuring their best possible joint outcome, Tom (or Mark) can do even better by breaking the agreement and playing the other for a sucker. Thus we may still expect each to betray the other.

The game of Prisoner's Dilemma is a model of the general problem of obtaining social cooperation. In the terminology of the social sciences, a model is a simplified abstraction, often mathematical in character, used to represent a more complex process. No one pretends that a model can capture all the aspects of a situation. Prisoner's Dilemma is an obvious simplification: people are not just individuals but also members of families and communities, and they are not purely self-interested but also care about others and feel obligated to follow general rules of conduct. Nonetheless, a model can illuminate important aspects of a given situation—in this case, the tendency to abandon cooperation in the pursuit of self-interest. Of course, in this particular instance, what is good for the two players is bad for the larger society. But it still shows that voluntary cooperation requires a degree of confidence that the behaviour will be reciprocated.

There are two ways to resolve the Prisoner's Dilemma. One is iteration. If the game is played repeatedly, Mark and Tom can learn from experience how to achieve the best outcome for both. A brilliant study based on computer simulations of iterated

Prisoner's Dilemma has shown that the most effective strategy is tit for tat. Do not be the first to defect; trust the other player as long as he cooperates, but punish him if he defects. At the same time, do not hold a grudge: return to cooperation as soon as he does.[3] Perhaps not surprisingly, this conforms to the working morality of most normal social behaviour: approach others in a cooperative way; cooperate as long as they do, but don't let yourself be played for a sucker. The other way to resolve the Prisoner's Dilemma is to enforce agreements. If Tom and Mark can find some way to ensure—or at least to increase the probability—that both will keep their promises, each will be able to rely on the other and be willing to cooperate to their mutual benefit.

The enforcement of agreements by an external authority is one of the most important things that government does. By promising to serve as an enforcement agency, government promotes social cooperation by overcoming the self-interested logic of the Prisoner's Dilemma game. Remember the example of taxation mentioned earlier in this chapter. The public services paid for by taxation benefit everyone, yet everyone has an incentive to evade taxation and let others carry the burden. It is a multi-sided cooperation problem (*n*-person Prisoner's Dilemma, in the jargon of game theory). By enforcing the payment of taxes, government resolves the dilemma and ensures that resources are made available to provide the public services that people actually want but might not get if all were left to pursue their narrow self-interest.

POLITICS: GATHERING SUPPORT

A concept always associated with government is **politics.** The word comes from the Greek *polis,* usually translated as "city-state." The ***polis*** was the typical Greek form of political community at the time of Socrates, Plato, and Aristotle, the founders of political science. The *polis* consisted of a city, such as Athens or Sparta, plus some surrounding hinterland, including smaller towns and villages. It has given us a number of related words having to do with the idea of the common good, such as *politics* and *police.*

Curiously, politics is one of the most disputed terms in the vocabulary of political science. Almost everyone uses it as an occasional synonym for government, but beyond that it has taken on a wide variety of meanings, some of which are discussed in this chapter. The various definitions tend to emphasize different aspects of politics. We believe that each contains an element of truth and that a satisfactory understanding of politics must be comprehensive and multifaceted. It may seem odd to the student reader to have to slog through a whole range of definitions of a term that is so basic to the discipline, but the reality is that different writers define politics in different ways, so you must be ready for the variety that you will encounter.

One definition comes from a French writer, Bertrand de Jouvenel. According to Jouvenel, "We should regard as 'political' every systematic effort, performed at any place in the social field, to move other men in pursuit of some design cherished by the mover."[4] For him, politics is the activity of gathering and maintaining support for human projects.

Jouvenel's conception of politics emphasizes support. Another common approach is to equate politics with conflict. J. D. B. Miller writes that politics "is about disagreement or conflict."[5] Alan Ball carries this even further; for him, politics "involves disagreements and the reconciliation of those disagreements, and therefore can occur at any level. Two children in a nursery with one toy which they both want at the same time present a political situation."[6]

Ball's definition is not too far from Jouvenel's, for in real life mobilizing supporters for a project almost always involves overcoming conflicts of opinion or desire. Certainly conflicts arise that do not seem political in any usual sense: there is conflict if a mugger tries to take my wallet, but it is a simple crime, not a political action, because no collective project is envisioned. To be political, a crime must be linked to some vision of reordering society. It is thus a political act—as well as a crime—for a revolutionary group to kidnap a politician in the hope of exciting the people to rise against the government.

Yet another conception of politics is expressed in the title of Harold Lasswell's famous book, *Politics: Who Gets What, When, How.*[7] In Lasswell's view, politics is the distribution of the good things of earthly life, such as wealth, comfort, safety, prestige, and recognition. David Easton means the same thing when he says that politics is the "authoritative allocation of values"—values meaning not moral ideals but those things in life that people desire.[8] There is certainly much merit in this approach, in that it draws attention to the fact that the winners in a conflict—that is, those who succeed in mobilizing support for their projects—usually allocate to themselves and their followers a generous share of material and social benefits. At the same time, however, the distributive approach tends to risk merging politics with other activities. Wealth, for example, can be distributed through the impersonal economic transactions of buying and selling, which are not in themselves political acts because they do not involve mobilizing support for a common project. I do not have to be a supporter of Tim Hortons to buy a doughnut and a double-double; I just have to be hungry and have a little money to spend in order to engage in an act of exchange.

Funky Winkerbean © Batom, Inc. North American Syndicate

Having looked at many definitions, we would promote the following, which is a slight variation on Jouvenel's: Politics is a process of conflict resolution in which support is mobilized and maintained for collective projects. Government—which involves making and enforcing rules—is thus laden with politics at every stage. A government cannot carry out its various functions unless it has some popular support. It will probably lose that support if it is unable to maintain internal and external peace and to provide services desired by the population. Government in a democracy must have an especially high level of popular support, and elections are an important way of acquiring it. This is why the term *politics* has come to be associated with elections and related phenomena, such as political parties. The phrase "going into politics" usually implies running for elective office. This popular usage is valid as far as it goes but is only one aspect of politics in the broader sense.

Politics has been called the art of the possible and the art of compromise because it must resolve disagreements among people with different opinions and desires. Compromise is usually necessary if violence and coercion are to be avoided. Political problems rarely have a satisfying solution; usually the best that can be obtained is a settlement—that is, an arrangement that makes no one perfectly happy but with which everyone can live.[9] When this is achieved, politics approximates the definition put forward by the English political scientist Bernard Crick: "The activity by which different interests within a given unit of rule are conciliated by giving them a share in power in proportion to their importance to the welfare and the survival of the whole community."[10] Citing Aristotle, Crick argues that politics is not unity but harmony—that is, the peaceful and cooperative coexistence of different groups, not their reduction to a single imposed pattern. This is a good description of politics as it can be and sometimes is practised; but in reality harmony often breaks down and people resort to coercive measures.

COALITIONS: POLITICS IN ACTION

The fundamental unit of political activity is the **coalition,** defined as "the joining of forces by two or more parties during a conflict of interest with other parties."[11] Coalitions involve both conflict and cooperation. They draw a boundary within which cooperation takes place to defeat or gain advantage over an external opponent. Political coalitions are formed precisely to exclude others and thereby exercise power over them.

There are at least three kinds of coalitions. The first kind has parallels among the primates and the social carnivores, whose coalitional behaviour can be observed both in zoos and in natural settings; the other two are distinctively human because they depend on language and the manipulation of symbols.

1. In small-scale settings, coalitions are based on personal relationships among individuals. For example, in any parliamentary system the prime minister must keep

the support of the party caucus—the party's elected members of parliament—in order to remain in office. Jean Chrétien showed himself to be adept at this while he was prime minister during the 1990s. His caucus contained a so-called "right wing" interested in balancing the budget, reducing taxes, and creating a favourable climate for business, as well as a "left wing" interested in causes such as preserving public health care, expanding publicly funded child care, and promoting gay rights. The prime minister expelled one member from caucus during this period—the Toronto MP John Nunziata—but generally succeeded in keeping these two internal factions cooperative with each other and with the party leadership.

2. Coalitions can also be formal alliances. The North Atlantic Treaty Organization (NATO) is a coalition of 26 European and North American countries that have agreed to defend each other in case of attack. In domestic politics, cabinets are sometimes formed by coalitions when no single party has a majority of seats in the elected legislature. The party caucuses, acting through their leaders, make an explicit agreement to support each other and to divide up the seats in the cabinet. The cabinets of many European democracies—for example, Germany, Italy, Denmark, and the Netherlands—are routinely put together in this way. The most recent Canadian example is the Liberal–NDP coalition cabinet formed in Saskatchewan after the 1999 provincial election left the NDP with exactly half the seats, one seat short of a controlling majority. That coalition lasted until the election of 2003, at which time the NDP won a narrow majority (30–28) over the opposing Saskatchewan Party and the Liberals failed to win any seats at all.

3. Less formally, the building of coalitions is a characteristic of the mass politics of modern democracies. Party leaders form electoral coalitions by proposing policies to attract certain groups of voters. Each party tends to be backed by a distinctive array or coalition of groups defined by geography or demography. For example, major elements in the Republican coalition in American national politics are white Southerners, suburban and rural voters (especially in the Great Plains and Rocky Mountain states), private-sector businesspeople, and (increasingly) Roman Catholics. The Democratic coalition, in contrast, emphasizes blacks, Latinos (except Cubans, who tend to vote Republican), Jews, organized labour (especially teachers and other government employees), and urban voters (especially in the Northeast and on the Pacific coast). Of course, these divisions are not absolute: the Democrats get 90 percent of the black vote in presidential races, while the Republicans get only about 10 percent; but even 10 percent of this large ethnic group is still a lot of people.

The individuals or groups that make up any type of coalition are not necessarily permanent partners. Southern whites and Roman Catholics used to support Democrats in American politics but have changed allegiance over time, as have blacks, who used to vote Republican. In Canada, a dominant coalition virtually monopolized federal politics between 1946 and 1984; as a result, Liberal governments were elected for 32 of those 38 years. Significant groups in this coalition included Quebeckers, both francophone and anglophone; immigrants and ethnic minorities in many parts of the country; Roman Catholics; and many individuals in the media and in the academic community. One factor holding these disparate groups together was a belief in the state's ability to guide change, progress, and economic development in Canadian society. When those years produced expensive bureaucracies and programs that did not always work as intended, the stage was set for the breakup of the dominant coalition, and the Conservatives in 1984 seized the opportunity to create a new one, which in turn fell apart in the early 1990s.

To recapitulate: government and politics are universal aspects of human existence. *Government is the process that makes and enforces rules and decisions for society; politics is the activity of reconciling conflicts and gathering support that makes government possible.* Government and politics both arise from the need for people to live in societies; for a society to succeed, people must settle conflicts and abide by common rules in such a way that the community is not endangered. Government and politics involve coercion, but not for its own sake. One reason why rulers resort to force is to lessen the use of force by private individuals against each other.

Government and politics become more and more indispensable as civilization advances. The more complicated our way of life becomes, the less we can afford to have our plans upset by random intrusions of others on our person, property, or expectations. Government can be the great guarantor of the stability of expectations and the force that makes it possible for other human endeavours, such as religion, art, science, and business, to flourish. When a government is working well, the political process continually and unobtrusively resolves those conflicts that might otherwise tear society apart. In fact, politics may work so well that the ordinary person may take it for granted and have very little need to be concerned with it.

Even though government is essential, we are not always reconciled to it. There is a persistent belief that we may someday attain a perfectly harmonious, conflict-free society in which government will be unnecessary. One form of this belief is the Judeo-Christian tradition of the Kingdom of the Saints or the Kingdom of God on earth.[12] According to this idea, human conflict will cease with the advent (Judaism) or return (Christianity) of the Messiah, and there will be no ruler except this divinely authorized figure. Related ideas in Islam involve the appearance of the Mahdi or the return of the Twelfth Imam—enlightened teachers who presage the coming of the Last Days.

Secular versions of this scenario also exist.[13] The early French socialist Henri de Saint-Simon (1760–1825) wrote that eventually "the government of men" would be replaced by the "administration of things"—a formula later echoed by Lenin.[14] They both hoped that in a future world, where everyone was comfortable and gross inequalities had vanished, people would become so peaceable that governmental coercion would be unnecessary. The same expectation is embodied in the Marxist doctrine of "the withering away of the state," which teaches that government will eventually become obsolete after a communist revolution.[15] But none of these visions has ever come to pass, and still we must rely on politics and government to mediate the conflicts that arise among self-interested individuals.

Canadian Focus 1.1

Conservative Coalition-Building

When Jean Chrétien was prime minister of Canada (1993–2003), the conservative side of the spectrum in federal politics was represented by two political parties, the Reform Party of Canada (later renamed the Canadian Alliance) and the Progressive Conservative Party of Canada. Neither party could get enough votes to wrest control of the government from the Liberals until, in 2003, Alliance leader Stephen Harper invited PC leader Peter MacKay to form a coalition. However the two leaders agreed to go even farther and merge, and large majorities in each of the two parties voted in favour of the merger. The new Conservative Party of Canada went on to bring the Liberals down to a minority in the 2004 election and then win a minority government for themselves in the 2006 and 2008 elections.

These events illustrate coalition-building at all three levels described in the text. First, Stephen Harper and Peter MacKay had to build a personal coalition between themselves before anything else could happen. Then, the members of the two parties had to approve a merger of organizations. Finally, voters who were used to supporting the old merger partners had to play follow-the-leader and support the new Conservative Party in federal elections, thus building a mass electoral coalition.

Questions for Discussion

1. Can you think of examples of political conflicts that you have encountered outside of government, for example, in school, clubs, or athletic teams?

2. Can you think of real-world examples of Prisoner's Dilemma games—that is, situations where everyone involved would like something to happen but no one seems to be willing to contribute to getting it done?

3. Compare the various definitions of politics quoted in this chapter. How different are they, really?

Internet Links

1. Government of Canada home page: **www.gc.ca.** Links to all departments of the government of Canada.

2. Encyclopedia Wikipedia: **http://en.wikipedia.org.** A vast storehouse of information. Search for articles on key terms such as government, politics, primitive government, and so on.

3. Prisoner's Dilemma: **www.princeton.edu/~mdaniels/PD/PD.html.** An interactive site where you can play Prisoner's Dilemma games.

Further Reading

Ball, Alan R., and B. Guy Peters. *Modern Politics and Government.* 7th ed. London: Palgrave Macmillan, 2005.

Bateman, Thomas M. J., Manuel Mertin, and David M. Thomas, eds. *Braving the New World: Readings in Contemporary Politics.* Scarborough, ON: Nelson Canada, 1995.

Blakeley, Georgina, and Valerie Bryson. *Contemporary Political Concepts.* Sterling, VA: Pluto Press, 2002.

Brams, Steven J. *Game Theory and Politics.* New York: Courier Dover Publications, 2004.

Brodie, M. Janine, ed. *Critical Concepts: An Introduction to Politics.* Toronto: Prentice Hall, 2002.

Crick, Bernard. *In Defence of Politics.* Rev. ed. London: Pelican Books, 1964.

Evans, Peter, ed. *State–Society Synergy: Government and Social Capital in Development.* Berkeley, CA: University of California at Berkeley, International and Area Studies, 1997.

Flanagan, Thomas. *Game Theory and Canadian Politics.* Toronto: University of Toronto Press, 1998.

Franks, C. E. S., et al. *Canada's Century: Governance in a Maturing Society: Essays in Honour of John Meisel.* Montreal: McGill–Queen's University Press, 1995.

Hawkesworth, Mary, and Maurice Kogan. *Encyclopedia of Government and Politics.* 2nd ed. London: Routledge, 2004.

Klosko, George. *The Principle of Fairness and Political Obligation.* 2nd ed. Savage, MD: Rowman & Littlefield, 2003.

Lasswell, Harold D. *Politics: Who Gets What, When, How.* New York: Meridian Books, 1958.

Leftwich, Adrian, ed. *What Is Politics? The Activity and Its Study.* Oxford: Blackwell Publishing Ltd., 2004.

McMenemy, John. *The Language of Canadian Politics: A Guide to Important Terms and Concepts.* 3rd ed. Waterloo, ON: Wilfrid Laurier University Press, 2001.

MacLean, George A., and Brenda O'Neill, eds. *Ideas, Interests and Issues: Readings in Introductory Politics.* Toronto: Pearson Prentice Hall, 2006.

Miller, J. D. B. *The Nature of Politics.* Rev. ed. Harmondsworth, UK: Penguin Books, 1965.

Pierson, Paul. *Politics in Time: History, Institutions, and Social Analysis.* Princeton, NJ: Princeton University Press, 2004.

Poundstone, William. *Prisoner's Dilemma: John von Neumann, Game Theory, and the Puzzle of the Bomb.* New York: Doubleday, 1992.

Roninger, Luis, and Ayse Gunes-Ayata, eds. *Democracy, Clientelism, and Civil Society.* Boulder, CO: Lynne Rienner, 1994.

Tansey, Stephen D. *Politics: The Basics.* 2nd ed. London: Routledge, 2000.

Tremblay, Reeta Chowdhary. *Mapping the Political Landscape: An Introduction to Political Science.* Toronto: Nelson, 2004.

Walsh, David F. *Governing through Turbulence: Leadership and Change in the Late Twentieth Century.* Westport, CT: Praeger, 1995.

CHAPTER 2

Power, Legitimacy, and Authority

Power in the broadest sense is the capacity to achieve what you want. The word is related to the French verb *pouvoir,* "to be able." Power can be the physical ability to perform a task such as lifting or running, the intellectual capacity to solve a problem, or the social ability to induce others to do what you want.

In political science, power has this latter meaning. Political science is centred around the study of political power, seeking answers to questions such as the following: Who has power and who does not? Are those who exercise power held accountable in some way to those who do not? Can those who wield power be replaced peacefully or only with violence? What beliefs justify the distribution and exercise of power in political systems?

Power is to politics what money is to economics: the medium of exchange, the universal common denominator. Political power, however, is not a homogeneous quantity like money, and it does not have a simple unit of measurement, such as dollars. There are, in fact, three main forms of power—influence, coercion, and authority—which have to be discussed separately.

INFLUENCE

Influence is the ability to persuade others to do your will, to convince them to want to do what you want them to do. The important point is that the targets of persuasion act voluntarily; they are not conscious of restraints on their will because they have freely chosen to agree. Of course, they may agree either because they have come to think that the action is right and justified in itself or because they think they will reap personal benefit from it. Influence takes many forms, which in the hard light of reality often overlap:

- Appeals to the intellect (i.e., convincing people that a given action is intrinsically best)

- Appeals to the passions (i.e., persuading people to act by playing directly on the emotions)

- Appeals to self-interest (i.e., persuading someone to support a cause because of "what is in it for me")

- Appeals to group solidarity (i.e., persuading people to work on behalf of a community to which they belong)

Because there are so many ways to influence others, there are also many resources that can be deployed in the task. The following list, while by no means exhaustive, enumerates some possibilities:

- Intelligence, knowledge, and research can be used to construct convincing arguments.

- People with money and expertise can produce effective advertising.

- People who control wealth can offer financial inducements (bribes).

- People with organizational connections can offer career prospects (jobs, contracts, patronage in all its forms).

- Officials who control the apparatus of government can offer what political scientists call "policy outputs" (i.e., promises to legislate in ways that will benefit their supporters).

Influence is always at work in government. Candidates for office in a democratic system win elections by persuading their fellow citizens to vote for them. Once in office, they are in turn besieged by individuals and groups who want government to do something on their behalf—for example, to build a road along one route rather than another, or to lower their taxes. For its part, government seeks to influence the behaviour of the electorate. For example, the government of Canada has run extensive advertising campaigns exhorting Canadians to exercise more, stop smoking, drink less alcohol, conserve energy, and support Canadian unity.

Democratic politics is a giant web of influence and persuasion. Consider the position of the Conservative government of Canada elected October 14, 2008. They got to that position by persuading 38 percent of eligible voters to vote for them. In order to accomplish that feat, they had to persuade members to join the party, activists to work during the campaign, and donors to contribute money. Having gotten elected through this exercise of influence, the Conservative government became subject to all sorts of influence from those wanting action of various kinds. Business, labour, and agricultural groups lobby for legislation to benefit their members. Advocacy groups, such as Greenpeace, carry out campaigns to steer public opinion in one way or another, with the ultimate aim of influencing government to do something those groups desire. Moreover, because this was a minority government (i.e., the Conservatives won only 143 of 308 seats in the House of Commons), they had to persuade members of one or more opposition parties to support, or at least not oppose, their legislation if they hoped to get anything passed. At the same time, opposition parties were attempting to persuade the Conservatives to make changes in legislative proposals as the price of such support. And, while all of this was going on, all parties were hoping to influence voters to support them in the next election, whenever that would come.

COERCION

Coercion is the deliberate subjection of one will to another through fear of harm or threats of harm. When coercion is applied, compliance is not voluntary but results from fear of unpleasant consequences.

Coercion can take many forms. **Violence** involves physical harm, such as beatings, torture, and murder. Imprisonment, while not directly violent, is enforced by violence if the prisoner tries to leave custody. Other forms of coercion include monetary penalties (e.g., fines imposed by government) and strikes, in which workers combine to threaten employers with losses in the marketplace. The number of ways of harming or threatening people is infinite, but most methods ultimately rely on violence. We must pay a fine for a traffic violation to avoid imprisonment. Employers must submit to the economic setback of a legal strike. If they repudiated their agreements to bargain collectively with the unions, discharged their workers, and tried to hire a new workforce, they would be breaking the law and could be fined or even imprisoned.

A case that straddles the border between coercion and persuasion involves the manipulation of individuals by means of false or misleading information. Motivating someone to act on false information is tantamount to coercion even though it has the appearance of persuasion. The actions of the one who is persuaded would not have been voluntary had the truth been available, so the result is similar to coercion in that it secures involuntary compliance.

Manipulation is a ubiquitous reality in politics. Political leaders rehearse their statements with professional advisers to test them for effect. Words are chosen, and themes are omitted or included, to achieve a desired result. Statements about future consequences of policies generally emphasize the positive and suppress the negative. Political advertising is even more manipulative than politicians' statements because it is often designed to appeal directly to the emotions.

Modern governments try to control most forms of outright coercion, especially violence. Ordinary people are prohibited from violently assaulting each other or seizing property. They are supposed to refrain from violence except in self-defence and limits are enforced even in such situations. Government uses its near-monopoly on violence to protect society from external attack, and to enforce rules of conduct and punish those who violate them. To these ends, every government has developed a complex apparatus of armed forces, police forces, prisons, and courts.

One partial exception to the governmental control of coercion involves industrial relations. During the twentieth century, governments accepted that collective bargaining is an arena in which employees and employers may resort to economic coercion to achieve their objectives. Yet the exception is perhaps not as great as it seems: collective bargaining was introduced to civilize labour relations, which were for a long time marked by a great deal of overt violence. Governments now try, more or less successfully, to legalize a degree of economic coercion and thus keep both sides from resorting to violence.

Government forbids all individuals or groups to use violence against it. Whatever their other differences, all governments are identical in their resistance to acts of political violence, because such acts undermine the very existence of the state. The use of force and the threat to use force against government are defined as political crimes. A government that cannot resist such threats will not survive long. Liberal democracies define political crimes narrowly as the use of force, or the advocacy of such use, against the state. Totalitarian and authoritarian regimes extend the definition to include peaceful opposition to or criticism of the state. The definition of a political crime is an almost infallible test for the genuineness of liberal democracy.

Coercion is a powerful tool, yet no government can depend on it entirely. Society has so many members engaging in so many different activities that everything cannot be coercively directed. Even if it were possible, it would be too expensive because coercion is so labour-intensive. In any case, it is logically impossible for everything to depend on coercion because there must be a coalition of the coercers to get the job done. What holds them together? More coercion? If so, who provides it? At some point, societies must go beyond coercion to a principle that holds its followers together for joint action and that makes it possible for them to coerce others—in a word, *authority*.

The Chinese communist leader Mao Zedong (1893–1976) expressed this truth when he wrote, "Political power grows out of the barrel of a gun. Our principle is that the Party commands the gun; the gun shall never be allowed to command the Party."[1] (The first sentence of this statement is often quoted out of context, as if coercion were the ultimate reality of politics.) To be sure, the gun is significant, as was demonstrated at Tiananmen Square in 1989, when the Chinese government put down the democracy movement with tanks. But it is noteworthy that the army did nothing until the Communist Party had sorted out its internal disagreements and resolved upon a repressive course of action. Until there was clear direction from the party, the army was unwilling to use its firepower against unarmed civilians. The point is that coercion is not the ultimate form of power but a highly useful adjunct to authority.

AUTHORITY

Authority is a form of power in which people obey commands not because they have been rationally or emotionally persuaded or because they fear the consequences of disobedience, but simply because they respect the source of the command. The one who issues the command is accepted as having a right to do so, and those who receive the command accept that they have an obligation to obey. The relationship between parents and young children is a model of authority. Sometimes the parents will persuade the child to do something, and occasionally they may have to resort to coercion, but most of the time they can command with the expectation of being obeyed.

All governments possess at least some authority and strive to have as much as possible, for obvious reasons. Something more than influence is necessary to guarantee predictable results. Coercion produces compliance, but it is also very expensive and furthermore is possible only if a substantial number of agents of coercion are held together by authority. Clearly, authority is an inescapable necessity of government.

It is safe to say that most people most of the time are acting in deference to authority when they do what their government wishes. They stop at red lights and file tax returns because they realize that such actions have been commanded. (Of course, they may have other motives as well.) Perhaps their consciences bother them if they disobey authority. How else can we explain such obedience even in circumstances where punishment is highly unlikely? Most drivers obey traffic lights even at 3 a.m. on a deserted street, and not solely because they fear a hidden police cruiser—almost certainly, they feel a little uncomfortable about violating an authoritative rule. Nevertheless, not everyone is always deferential to authority; this is why coercion is extremely useful—it motivates by fear those who are not susceptible to feelings of obligation. Coercion is present as a background threat, as with a soldier who may be prompted to obey out of fear of a court-martial. But this coercion, though important, is only a tool of authority. Coercion by itself could not produce the united action necessary to hold a court-martial. On the other hand, authority without powers of coercion to back it up is likely to become ineffectual. We have seen this situation in "failed states" such as Somalia, where the government, though still recognized internationally, has lost effective control. In such cases, authority becomes purely nominal and is no longer a form of real-world power.

We must also distinguish between **natural** and **public authority.** The former exists whenever one person spontaneously defers to the judgment of another. Little children tagging after big children, and students seeking out teachers in the early days of the medieval university, are instances of natural authority. Every individual is always surrounded by numerous natural authorities—friends, relatives, colleagues—and acts as an authority to others on occasion. Natural authority is simply another term for the human tendencies to follow and imitate, as well as to lead and initiate. These are some of the bonds that hold society together.

Public authority, in contrast, is deliberately created by human agreement. The English language recognizes the difference between natural and public authority in an interesting way. We say that an expert on baseball statistics is "an authority" in his chosen field, but not that he is "in authority" in that field. But when we describe, for example, a police officer, we do not say she is "an authority" by virtue of any personal quality, but rather that she is "in authority" by virtue of the power entrusted to her by government. Her uniform is a visible sign of the public or artificial authority that she wields. To be a natural authority, you must have special personal qualities; to hold public authority, you have only to be in a position or office that carries with it rights of command.

What is the relationship between public authority and social order? Power is required to order any society, but it must be more than coercive power if a given society is to be open and free. An advantage of authoritative power over coercive power is that most individuals voluntarily submit to it. But why would people submit to any power that restricts their freedom of action? The answer is not easy to find, and political philosophers have grappled with the question for centuries, searching for the roots of consent to authority. One writer has put the issue this way:

> . . . the authority of government does not create the order over which it presides and does not sustain that order solely by its own fiat or its accredited power. There is authority beyond the authority of government. There is a greater consensus without which the fundamental order of the community would fall apart.[2]

LEGITIMACY

Although we often speak of *having* or *possessing* authority, that usage is misleading because it makes authority sound like a quality some people have, like red hair or a deep voice. In fact, authority is a social relationship; an individual has it only if others respect and obey it. Authority is one pole of a relationship in which the other pole is **legitimacy.** When we emphasize the right to command, we speak of authority; when we emphasize the acceptance of command, we speak of legitimacy. Authority is focused in the one who commands; legitimacy is the feeling of respect for authority that exists in those who obey—it is what makes authority possible. It is the same type of relationship as exists between leadership and "followership." Neither makes sense without the other.

Both authority and legitimacy are moral or ethical concepts; that is, they involve perceptions of right and wrong. We feel that someone in authority has a right to command. Similarly, we feel that it is right to obey, that we have a duty or obligation to do so. Governmental power without legitimacy is only coercion or force; with legitimacy, power becomes authority.

Legitimacy creates a sense of obligation, as illustrated in the following diagram:

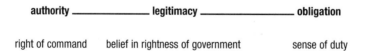

authority ——————— legitimacy ——————————— obligation

right of command   belief in rightness of government   sense of duty

We feel obligated to respond to commands when we are convinced that those who exercise authority are justified in doing so.

Public authority survives only as long as it has some degree of legitimacy in society. It is not necessary that literally everyone, or even a numerical majority, accept the legitimacy of a particular government; but there must be at least a loyal minority, strong and united, to withstand potential opposition. If such a minority exists and is willing to use coercion, it can sustain itself in power for a surprising length of time in the face of widespread popular opposition.

It was obvious for decades that the numerical majorities in the Republic of South Africa and in the communist countries of Eastern Europe would have chosen other rulers if they had been effectively consulted. Yet those governments were in little danger of falling as long as they maintained their weapons monopoly and the political support of a determined minority. All these regimes finally changed when reform movements were established within the governments themselves. In each case, substantial elements of the ruling elite, led by the head of government, decided to break with the past. In each case the system had long ago lost its legitimacy, but this in itself was not sufficient to topple the structure of authority.

Legitimacy rests upon beliefs and values that are not static; these things change over time, and legitimacy is challenged when government actions no longer correspond with them. According to Carl Friedrich:

> The process of aging leadership in consensual power situations is usually associated with the disintegration of authority. The actions of the "old one" are no longer understood, because they make no sense in terms of the altered values and beliefs; his capacity for reasoned elaboration is declining and finally is gone. This often carries with it a decline of power, though just as often the power continues, but it gradually becomes more coercive, less consensual.[3]

Power, authority, and legitimacy are integral components of government and politics. Power without legitimacy represents coercion—naked force. Power combined with legitimacy represents authoritative force—the force required to order a diverse society.

One of the great advantages of democracy is that regular, nonviolent changes of government are possible at periodic intervals. If a government ignores ongoing changes in beliefs and values, it can be voted out of office. Democracy provides a safety valve that enables voters to change governments without having to change the nature of the political system. Legitimacy is maintained for the system as a whole even as authority is transferred within it.

Because authority and legitimacy are so central to political life, they are an important focus of study in political science. One of the most important contributions to understanding them was made by the German sociologist Max Weber (1864–1920), who identified three kinds of authority/legitimacy: *traditional, legal,* and *charismatic.*[4] These "ideal types," as Weber called them, are always found mixed together in political systems. They are intellectual models that never exist in pure form in the real world yet help observers to understand what they see.

TRADITIONAL AUTHORITY

Traditional authority is domination based on inherited position. Hereditary monarchs are a good example of traditional authority. They hold the right of command not because of extraordinary personal qualities or because they have been chosen by others, but because they have inherited a position from a parent or other relative. The arrangement is regarded as legitimate because it has the sanction and prestige of tradition: things have been done that way from time immemorial. The principle of inherited authority also draws support from its similarity to the workings of the family, the most fundamental social institution.

The feudal system of medieval Europe was based mainly on traditional authority. At the apex of authority were the hereditary monarchs. They appointed judges, administrators, and military commanders who owed them personal allegiance; their authority was only an extension of the monarch's. Many governmental functions were performed by members of the nobility, whose social positions also stemmed from right of birth. The system depended on the work of the common people, who were born into a social position out of which it was extremely difficult to rise. Throughout the system, command and obedience were associated with inherited social rank and sanctified by tradition. Similar arrangements characterized much of the rest of the world until very recently; traditional authority still prevails in Saudi Arabia and other Gulf sheikhdoms, where authority is vested in the royal family and a number of related clans.

LEGAL AUTHORITY

The central concept of **legal authority** is that of general rules binding on all participants in the system. Authority is exercised only when it is called for by these rules. It is not associated with individuals who inherit their status, but with legally created offices that can be filled by many different incumbents. It is, to quote an ancient phrase, the "rule of law, not of men." (See Chapter 7 for a further discussion of this phrase.)

In Canada and Great Britain, authority is primarily legal, although the external symbolism is still traditional. A hereditary monarch reigns but does not rule, and actual power is wielded by politicians who are elected to office under a strictly defined system of laws. A prime minister is in authority while in office but has no personal status once dismissed. Those who work for government are no longer the personal servants of the monarch; their allegiance to the Crown means loyalty to the government as a whole, not to a particular person within it. There is no longer a hereditary class of nobles carrying out governmental functions. The House of Lords still survives in Great Britain, but it is mainly a symbolic reminder of the vanished age of traditional authority. The system derives its legitimacy not from the acceptance of status or from loyalty to personal authority, but from loyalty to the constitution, which is a legal system stronger than any individual.

However, some traditional elements still survive within contemporary legal authority. Law itself is hallowed by tradition. As rule-following animals, we quickly build up habits of compliance to those in power. Over time, it begins to seem right to obey, simply because that is the way things have been done in the past. It is undoubtedly true that habit is a powerful source of governmental legitimacy. We obey because we are accustomed to, because we have always done so. Reflective thought is not necessarily involved.

Such habits of obedience are necessary, for if we continually had to reconsider the legitimacy of government we would have time for little else. Those habits break down in times of revolutionary transition, when one form of authority is replaced by another. Yet they quickly re-establish themselves as part of the new government's legitimacy.

The great trend of development in modern political history is for traditional authority to be replaced by legal authority. This long, slow, and painful process began in Great Britain and its American colonies in the seventeenth century, continued in Europe in the eighteenth and nineteenth centuries, and engulfed the entire world in the twentieth century. It is the political aspect of the wider social process known as **modernization.** Social changes gradually and cumulatively modified people's notions of political legitimacy; this process was punctuated at certain times with the dramatic collapse of a traditional regime and its replacement by a new system of legal authority. The great popular revolutions of modern history must be seen in this context:

1688	Glorious Revolution	Stuarts overthrown by English Parliament
1776	American Revolution	American colonies declare independence from British Crown
1789	French Revolution	Bourbon dynasty replaced by a republic
1911	Chinese Revolution	Manchu dynasty replaced by a republic
1917	Russian Revolution	Romanov dynasty overthrown; Russian Empire becomes Soviet Union

These are only a few of the many revolutions that in three centuries have transformed the political face of the globe. Together they make up what is often called the world revolution. The French writer Alexis de Tocqueville, who made an extended tour in 1831–32 of the United States and Canada and noted the great social inequality of the traditional order of Europe, memorably stated the essence of the transition from traditional to legal authority:

> On the one side were wealth, strength, and leisure, accompanied by the refinements of luxury, the elegance of taste, the pleasures of wit, and the cultivation of the arts; on the other were labor, clownishness, and ignorance. But in the midst of this coarse and ignorant multitude it was not uncommon to meet with energetic passions, generous sentiments, profound religious convictions, and wild virtues. The social state thus organized might boast of its stability, its power, and, above all, its glory. But the scene is now changed. Gradually the distinctions of rank are done away; the barriers which once severed mankind are falling down; property is divided, power is shared by many, the light of intelligence spreads and the capacities of all classes are equally cultivated.[5]

This social equalization described by de Tocqueville is inseparable from legal authority, in which individuals are governed by universal rules applicable to all. It cannot coexist for long with the hereditary classes and ranks of traditional authority.

The worldwide transition from traditional to legal authority is the single most important political event of our times, and furnishes the context in which everything else takes place.

The collapse of communism in the Soviet Union and Eastern Europe was a further development in this direction. Communism as an ideology promised the benefits of legal authority and social equalization, but the communist regimes never came close to attaining these goals. In practice, they resembled a kind of bureaucratic feudalism, with great emphasis on the personal authority of the party leaders and disregard for impersonal legal norms. The party leaders constituted an elite as privileged and oppressive as any traditional aristocracy.

CHARISMATIC AUTHORITY

Charismatic authority is based on the projection and perception of extraordinary personal qualities. Weber defined charisma as "a certain quality of an individual personality by virtue of which he is set apart from ordinary men and treated as endowed with supernatural, superhuman, or at least specifically exceptional powers or qualities."[6]

Charisma was originally a theological term, derived from the Greek word for "grace" or "spiritual favour." Generally speaking, charismatic leaders are prophets, saints, shamans, or similar figures. Their legitimacy does not depend on tradition or law but on their followers' belief that they speak to them directly from God. Their transcendental claim to authority often places them in conflict with traditional or legal authorities. Some of our most striking and well-known historical figures were charismatic in this sense: the biblical prophets of the Hebrews, as well as Joan of Arc, whose heavenly visions inspired her to help drive the English from France. (For a Canadian example of charisma, see Historical Perspectives 2.1 on Louis Riel.)

The term *charisma* is also applied to political leaders who base their claim to rule on an alleged historical mission. Adolf Hitler, for example, believed that he had a special mission to restore Germany's greatness. He came to this conviction as he lay in hospital in 1918, having been blinded by a British gas attack on the Western front. His blindness coincided in time with Germany's surrender, and when he recovered his sight he became convinced that he might also be the means of Germany's restoration to greatness. The title he always preferred was *Führer,* the German word for leader; it emphasized that his authority radiated from his personality, not from any office that he happened to occupy.

Charisma is sometimes collectively shared, as in the political thought of the Ayatollah Khomeini (1900–89), the symbol and leader of the revolution that swept the Shah of Iran from power in 1979. Khomeini was a jurist who specialized in the study of the *Shari'a,* the Islamic law. "The jurists," according to Khomeini, "have been appointed by God to rule."[7] The state, he said, must also have secular legislative and executive authorities, but the jurists as a group have an overriding and divinely

Historical Perspectives 2.1

Louis Riel

Louis Riel is Canada's best-known example of a charismatic leader. On December 8, 1875, he experienced a mystical illumination that convinced him he was the "Prophet of the New World." He saw himself as endowed by God with a personal mission to create a new religion in North America in which his own people, the Métis, would be a chosen people like the Hebrews. Riel wanted the Métis to adopt certain Old Testament practices, such as polygamy and the Saturday sabbath; these would eventually be merged with a revised version of Roman Catholicism. Riel preached this novel doctrine to the Métis at Batoche during the North-West Rebellion of 1885. The rebels formed a sort of provisional government, but Riel did not hold office in it—he preferred to be recognized as a prophet. Each morning he assembled the Métis forces to tell them of the divine revelations he had received during the night. He promised his followers that God would work a miracle to defeat the expeditionary force sent by Canada. The miracle did not happen and the uprising was crushed. Riel was later convicted of high treason. He went to the scaffold believing that he, like Christ, would rise from the dead on the third day after his execution. His execution served as a form of martyrdom that ensured his reputation would persist and grow across subsequent generations of history.

In eastern Canada, Riel seemed like a madman, and in fact his friends and relatives in Montreal had him committed to a lunatic asylum in the years 1876–78. But the Métis saw him as charismatic. His inspiration played off the desperation of the buffalo-hunting Métis, as they were increasingly marginalized by the opening of the Canadian West to agricultural immigration and economic development.

given power and responsibility to ensure that all government is carried on within the principles of the *Shari'a*. Khomeini saw himself less as a special individual than as the most prominent representative of a charismatic class. This class of jurists still exercises considerable power in the contemporary Islamic Republic of Iran, though it is also paralleled by a more conventional structure of legal authority based on a written constitution and elections.

The term charisma is also often applied to politicians who have never made claims like those of Louis Riel or Joan of Arc. Two good examples from twentieth-century history in North America were the American president John Kennedy and the Canadian prime minister Pierre Trudeau. Both were young, handsome, athletic, intelligent, and highly educated men who stirred up unusual excitement among the public. Both ran for office under the aegis of idealistic slogans—Kennedy's "New Frontier" and Trudeau's "Just Society." In Canada in 1968, observers referred to Trudeau's first national election campaign as "Trudeaumania." Yet, although both Kennedy and Trudeau enjoyed a type of adulation usually reserved for movie stars, rock musicians, and professional athletes, neither claimed to be anything more than an officeholder in a structure of legal authority. Certainly, neither man claimed a right to rule on the basis of divine inspiration or a world-historical mission. If political leaders such as Kennedy and Trudeau are to be called charismatic, it should be remembered that this is a looser use of the term than when it is applied to genuinely charismatic authorities such as Louis Riel.

Charisma, like authority in general, is not a thing that a leader has; it is a social relationship based on the followers' perception of the legitimacy of the leader's claims. The most important question is not how Joan of Arc, Louis Riel, or Adolf Hitler could utter such extraordinary claims about themselves, but how they could find such a receptive audience. The short answer is that charismatic leaders are accorded legitimacy in times of crisis or grave unrest when other forms of authority appear to have failed. Joan of Arc came to the rescue of France during the Hundred Years' War at a time when England had the upper hand and France was in danger of being conquered. The traditional authority of the French monarch seemed incapable of meeting the challenge. Riel preached his radical gospel to the Métis at a time when the disappearance of the buffalo and the replacement of ox-trains by railways and steamboats threatened to destroy the Metis' way of life. It was a challenge that the traditional Métis authorities, the patriarchs of the clans, were helpless to meet. Hitler came to power during a turbulent phase of German history. The traditional authority of the Kaiser had been destroyed by Germany's defeat in World War I; and the legal authority of the Weimar Republic, never deeply rooted, was gravely shaken by the runaway inflation of the early 1920s and the international depression of the early 1930s. Driven to desperation, the German people, particularly the middle class, listened to Hitler's promises of salvation.

If charisma is a response to crisis, it is difficult to see how it can be very long-lasting. As stability is restored, we would expect a return to traditional or legal authority. Weber was well aware of this tendency, which he called the "routinization of charisma."[8] The more success prophets or leaders have in creating a following, the more either they or their followers find it necessary to create an enduring structure of authority that can exist over generations. If Riel had been successful in the North-West Rebellion, he would eventually have had to take on some role other than prophet. Once the Shah was overthrown, Khomeini approved a new Iranian constitution that institutionalized and regularized the authority of the Islamic jurists, who have carried on since his death. Political history seems to alternate short, intense upheavals of charismatic authority with longer periods of normalcy.

Questions for Discussion

1. Some people talk about hunger, poverty, and disease as forms of violence directed against the poor. Would you agree or disagree with extending the concept of violence to cover these things? Why or why not?

2. The traditional model of authority presents government as a sort of extended family. Based on your experience, what similarities and differences do you perceive between government and the family?

3. Politicians and rock stars can both be charismatic. What do they have in common?

Internet Links

1. Nelson Education Ltd. Political Science Resource Centre: **www.polisci.nelson. com.** Links to studies of political violence.

2. Use "charismatic authority" as a search term. The Internet will give you dozens of discussions of the subject, in both general and specific contexts.

3. Much of this chapter is based on the work of Max Weber. For an informative site on Weber, go to **www.faculty.rsu.edu/~felwell/Theorists/Weber/Whome.htm.** If the link is balky, use "Max Weber" as a search term.

Further Reading

Baldwin, David Allen. *Paradoxes of Power.* Oxford: Blackwell, 1989.

Connolly, William, ed. *Legitimacy and the State.* Oxford: Basil Blackwell, 1984.

Frank, Thomas. *The Power of Legitimacy among Nations.* New York: Oxford University Press, 1990.

Friedrich, Carl J., ed. *Authority.* Cambridge, MA: Harvard University Press, 1958.

Jaffe, Erwin. *Healing the Body Politic: Rediscovering Political Power.* Westport, CT: Praeger, 1993.

Kittrie, Nicholas N. *The War against Authority: From the Crisis of Legitimacy to a New Social Contract.* Baltimore: Johns Hopkins University Press, 1995.

Lukes, Steven. *Power: A Radical View.* 2nd ed. London: Palgrave Macmillan, 2005.

Madsen, Douglas, and Peter G. Snow. *The Charismatic Bond: Political Behavior in Time of Crisis.* Cambridge, MA: Harvard University Press, 1991.

Mumford, Michael D. *Pathways to Outstanding Leadership: A Comparative Analysis of Charismatic, Ideological, and Pragmatic Leaders.* Philadelphia: Lawrence Erlbaum Associates, 2006.

Nelson, Daniel N. *After Authoritarianism: Democracy or Disorder?* Westport, CT: Greenwood Press, 1995.

Raz, Joseph. *Authority.* Oxford: Blackwell, 1990.

Russell, Bertrand. *Authority and the Individual.* Boston: Beacon Press, 1960.

———. *Power: A New Social Analysis.* New York: Routledge, 2004.

Sennet, Richard. *Authority.* New York: Knopf, 1980.

Shaar, John H. *Legitimacy and the Modern State.* New Brunswick, NJ: Transaction Publishers, 1989.

Vidrich, Arthur J., and Ronald M. Glassman, eds. *Conflict and Control: Challenge to Legitimacy of Modern Government.* Beverly Hills, CA: Sage, 1979.

Wrong, Dennis H. *Power: Its Forms, Bases and Uses.* Oxford: Basil Blackwell, 1979.

Zartman, I. William, ed. *Collapsed States: The Disintegration and Restoration of Legitimate Authority.* Boulder, CO: Lynne Rienner, 1995.

CHAPTER 3
Sovereignty, State, and Citizenship

SOVEREIGNTY

The term **sovereign,** derived from the Latin *super,* meaning "above," literally denotes one who is superior. Human beings naturally associate superiority with the physical quality of elevation. We put kings and queens on high thrones to make them taller; and we picture God, the highest of all authorities, as living in the heavens above the earth. Conversely, we lower ourselves to recognize authority. We bow or curtsy when we address royalty, and we kneel or even prostrate ourselves when we pray.

Sovereignty was first used in its modern sense by the French author Jean Bodin toward the end of the sixteenth century. Writing at a time of fierce wars between Catholics and Protestants, Bodin sought to obtain civil peace by establishing the king as the supreme authority whose will could decide such disputes. Bodin's idea was that in any community there ought to be a single highest authority who is not subject to other human authority. He wrote in *Six Livres de la République* (1576) that "sovereignty is the absolute and perpetual power of a commonwealth. The sovereign Prince is only accountable to God . . . Sovereignty is not limited with respect to power, scope, or duration . . . The Prince is the image of God."[1]

Bodin, who was a student of Roman law, was trying to revive the idea of centralized power in an age in which it did not exist or existed only in an imperfect way. To understand why this was so, we must recall some facts about the feudal society of medieval Europe. Everyone was subject to a feudal overlord, but there was no effective pyramid of authority with the monarch at its peak. For all practical purposes, the nobles were often autonomous, as were many city-states in Italy and along the Rhine. The pope exercised a claim to rule in religious matters through his bishops. The Church maintained its own system of ecclesiastical courts; it even had the power to gather taxes, by which means money flowed to Rome. Nowhere was there a single sovereign—a highest authority—and, indeed, except for the authority of God, the concept did not exist. This helps to explain why the religious wars of the Protestant Reformation were so protracted. Various nobles gave their support to one side or the other, and there was no effective central power to keep them all in check. Bodin's idea of the sovereign took hold at a time of revulsion against this warfare and became well established in the seventeenth and eighteenth centuries. This was the age of *absolute monarchs*—so called not because they could do whatever they pleased, but because there was no human authority superior to theirs.

However, it is less the person than the power that is of interest here. **Sovereignty** is the authority to override all other authorities. Family, employer, church—all social authorities—must yield to the sovereign's power when it is turned in their direction. More concretely, sovereignty is a bundle of powers associated with the highest authority of government. One is the power to enforce rules of conduct—by establishing tribunals, compensating victims, punishing offenders, and so on—and includes the power of life and death. Another is the power to make law; that is, to create new law, amend existing law, and repeal old law. Sovereignty also includes the control of all the normal executive functions of government such as raising revenue, maintaining armed forces, minting currency, and providing other services to society. In the British tradition sovereignty also implies an underlying ownership of all land. Private ownership of land "in fee simple" is a form of legal delegation from the sovereign, who can reclaim any parcel of land through expropriation. Compensation to the private owner is customary but not required. Finally, sovereignty always means the power to deal with the sovereigns of other communities as well as the right to exercise domestic rule free from interference by other sovereigns.

Sovereignty was exercised by individual sovereigns in the Age of Absolutism, in the seventeenth and eighteenth centuries, but it can also be placed in the hands of a small group or an entire people. In England, the Stuarts' claims to absolute monarchy were decisively defeated by Parliament in the Glorious Revolution of 1688. This victory ultimately led to the theory of **parliamentary sovereignty,** articulated by William Blackstone in his *Commentaries on the Laws of England* (1765–69). Blackstone held that the supreme authority in England was Parliament, defined as the Commons, Lords, and Crown acting together under certain procedures.

Parliamentary sovereignty is still the main principle of the British constitution. It means that Parliament may make or repeal whatever laws it chooses; one Parliament cannot bind its successors in any way. Parliament is still the highest court in the land and cannot be overruled by the judiciary. The executive authority of government symbolized by the Crown can be exercised only by ministers who are responsible to Parliament.

One hundred years ago, A. V. Dicey, one of the greatest British constitutional experts, claimed facetiously that "Parliament can do anything except make a man into a woman." The invention of sex-change surgery has now removed even that limitation! However, in other ways Parliament has conceded some of its sovereignty in recent years. By entering into the European Union, Britain has voluntarily subjected itself to decisions of the EU bureaucracy and the European Court of Justice. Britain could leave the EU, but as long as it remains a member the sovereignty of Parliament is functionally limited.

While Blackstone was developing the theory of parliamentary sovereignty, the French philosopher Jean-Jacques Rousseau's book *The Social Contract* (1762) set forth the great alternative of **popular sovereignty.** Rousseau taught that supreme authority resided in the people themselves and could not be delegated. Laws should be made by the people meeting in direct-democratic fashion, not by electing representatives to legislate for them (indirect democracy). "The people of England," wrote Rousseau, "deceive themselves when they fancy they are free; they are so, in fact, only during the election of members of Parliament: for, as soon as a new one is elected, they are again in chains, and are nothing."[2]

Because Rousseau's ideal of direct democracy is extremely difficult to attain in a commonwealth of any great size, subsequent writers have kept alive the notion of popular sovereignty by softening the definition. For example, the American Declaration of Independence (1776) states that governments derive "their just powers from the consent of the governed." This moderate formulation of popular sovereignty, which stresses consent rather than direct rule, underlies modern representative democracy.

The three alternatives of personal, parliamentary, and popular sovereignty are not mutually exclusive. All three have to be examined to explain the present reality of, for example, British government. Queen Elizabeth II is still sovereign in the symbolic sense that she represents the power of the state; she "reigns but does not rule," as the saying goes. Parliament is legally sovereign in its control over legislation and all aspects of government, but Parliament does not exist in a political vacuum. The most important part of Parliament is the House of Commons, whose members are elected by the people at large. Interpreters of the British system argue that popular sovereignty exists in the political sense that Parliament depends on public support. If Parliament uses its legal sovereignty in a way that runs counter to public opinion, the people will elect new members to the House of Commons when the opportunity arises. In the long run, popular sovereignty is as much a fact of British politics as is parliamentary sovereignty.

The British situation is complex, the Canadian one even more so. Canada has a heritage of representative democracy based on the British model, and Canadians share the same balance of personal, parliamentary, and popular sovereignty. The Queen is the sovereign of Canada, as she is of Great Britain and of some other members of the Commonwealth, and Canada has a legally sovereign Parliament whose political composition is determined by a voting population. But Canada's political system also divides power among levels of government. The national Parliament and the provincial legislatures each have a share of sovereign lawmaking power. The provinces, for example, have control of education but cannot issue money or raise an army. The government of Canada controls trade and commerce but not property and civil rights, which are provincial matters.

The inevitable disputes between levels of government regarding the precise distribution of powers are settled in the courts, which have a power not needed or possessed by the British courts: judicial review. **Judicial review** is the power of the courts to declare that actions taken by other branches of government violate the Constitution. Canadian courts have the power to nullify legislation passed by one level of government that invades the jurisdiction of the other. The Canadian system is thus a variant of British parliamentary sovereignty, in the sense that sovereignty is shared by a number of parliaments or legislatures and tempered by the courts' power to declare legislation unconstitutional. In other words, Canadian sovereignty is divided, not concentrated.

This arrangement is vastly different from Bodin's original conception of sovereignty as a single, undivided centre of power.

The same is true in the United States, where sovereign power is also divided among levels of government. A further complexity of the American constitution is that the president, the chief executive officer, must cooperate with Congress in order to make law, wage war, and perform other governmental acts.

Sovereignty may also be delegated to administrative agencies or even private bodies. Marketing boards enforcing production quotas, professional associations licensing practitioners, corporations exploiting mineral rights obtained from the Crown, and trade unions requiring all employees to abide by a collective agreement are all exercising a small, delegated share of sovereignty. Much of modern politics consists of a competitive struggle among organized groups to get the government to delegate a share of sovereign power to them, so that they may use it to benefit their members.

Clearly, Bodin's original desire to locate sovereignty entirely in one place has not been fully realized. The bundle of sovereign powers that exists conceptually may be divided among different hands. Some fragmentation of power helps to ensure that sovereignty is exercised within the rules established by the constitution. It is perhaps better for a free society that power be divided in this way, for concentrated, unopposed power is a standing temptation to abuse by those who wield it.

It might even be best to abandon the concept of sovereignty altogether for purposes of domestic politics and to admit that no person or group is sovereign in the original sense of the term. Metaphorically, we might say that the constitution is sovereign; that is, that all political power is constrained by constitutional rules that establish and limit the exercise of public authority. Different authorities exercise sovereign power at different moments in the political process: the people in voting for candidates to office, parliamentarians in voting on legislation, the head of state in giving assent to legislation, the courts in exercising judicial review. Each exercise of power takes place within constitutional limits, so that no one group or person is sovereign in the original sense.

However, even if sovereignty is internally constrained, divided, and delegated within the state, it still makes sense to inquire whether a government is able to control a certain population or a given territory, free from interference by other governments. This is actually the most frequent use of the term today—that is, to denote autonomy from outside control in international affairs. Sovereignty in this sense is claimed by all governments and recognized by international law.

THE STATE

The preceding discussion of sovereignty makes it possible to develop the concept of **state,** which has been mentioned previously but not fully explained. A state is defined by the joint presence of three factors: population, territory, and sovereignty. A state exists when a sovereign power effectively rules over a population residing within the boundaries of a fixed territory. As the sociologist Max Weber put it, "a state is a human community that (successfully) claims the *monopoly of the legitimate use of physical force within a given territory*" [Weber's emphasis].[3]

Canada is a state, as are Great Britain and France. Quebec, on the other hand, is not a full-fledged state in this sense; it has people and territory but not a sovereign government (except to the limited extent in which a province in the Canadian system has a share of sovereignty). It is the program of the Bloc Québécois and the Parti Québécois to turn Quebec into a state by attaining full sovereignty, but that is a project for the future, not a current reality.

The state is the universal form of political organization in the modern world. The earth's entire land mass, with the exception of Antarctica, is divided into territories under the control of sovereign states. At the time of writing, 192 states are members of the United Nations. It is difficult to say precisely how many states there are in total, because of certain anomalous cases. Some mini-states, such as Monaco, Andorra, and San Marino, do not carry on a full range of relationships with other states; their foreign policy is conducted by larger neighbours. Other difficult cases include *governments-in-exile,* states that lack universal recognition—for example, Taiwan—and puppet or buffer states. Various states claim portions of Antarctica, but the claims conflict and have never been resolved. Despite all this, we tend to take the state for granted as the only conceivable form of political organization, even though the combination of people, territory, and sovereignty that we call the state is, historically speaking, a fairly recent invention. The word itself was not widely used before Machiavelli wrote *The Prince* (1513).

Governmental processes in tribal societies are carried on without the state form of organization. Like hunting societies, the earliest agricultural societies were also stateless. Farming took place in autonomous villages that could handle their collective affairs without a specialized machinery of government. How then did the state arise? The answer almost certainly lies in warfare. Armed clashes between hunting tribes do not lead to the formation of a state as long as the losers can migrate to new hunting grounds; roughly the same is true of primitive agriculturalists, as long as arable land is available. But where new land is not readily accessible, warfare produces a social hierarchy of victors and vanquished that is enforced by coercion. A specialized state machinery of armies, courts, tax gatherers, and other officials evolves as the conquerors enrich themselves at the expense of the conquered.[4] When a strong monarch consolidates conquered territory, the state form of organization emerges.

Research in anthropology and human biology has stressed that reproductive competition was interwoven with competition for land and other resources in the rise of the early states.[5] Tribes victorious in warfare commonly killed or enslaved the men seized among their conquered opponents while making wives or concubines of the captured women. Chiefs and headmen used their power to take and support a larger number of wives. Early states were almost all characterized by polygamy in the upper classes, with kings and powerful noblemen maintaining harems of remarkable size. The Hebrew king Solomon reputedly had 700 wives and 300 concubines.[6]

Once created, the state was a powerful and expansive force. It easily prevailed over neighbouring agricultural communities if these had not formed their own states. It found tougher opposition in warlike nomads, who at times overran even territorial states, as happened often in the history of Europe and Asia. Over thousands of years, tribe after tribe of invaders from the steppes of Eurasia descended upon the empires of China, India, the Middle East, and Europe. Often the conquerors did not destroy the state; rather, they took it over and installed themselves as rulers, and were sometimes able to extend the state's territories. At other times, the conquest was such a shock that the state machinery deteriorated and required a long period to be rebuilt.

The modern European states arose from such an interregnum after invasions by Germans and other peoples destroyed the highly developed Roman Empire. The invaders installed themselves as rulers in medieval Europe but did not initially create a full-fledged state system. There were rudimentary specialized structures of government, but territorial boundaries between authorities were not clear. The Norman conquest of England in 1066 led to a situation that seems bizarre by today's standards. For hundreds of years England's Norman kings were nominally feudal vassals of the French kings, because they still had important territorial holdings in France. The Roman Catholic Church in all parts of Europe carried on activities, such as raising revenue and conducting court trials, that today would be considered governmental. The political history of modern times is the history of the emergence of separate, sovereign states out of the overlapping, interlocking jurisdictions of medieval Europe. For more on the development of European states, see Historical Perspectives 3.1.

Historical Perspectives 3.1

The Development of European States

The development of the state runs like a thread through the familiar epochs into which Western history is customarily divided. Although the subject is far too big for a complete discussion here, we can at least mention some of the main stages.

During the Renaissance (in the fifteenth and sixteenth centuries) there was a great revival of interest in classical antiquity. Knowledge of Latin and Greek became more widespread, and many forgotten works of art, literature, and science were recovered. This revival culminated in *humanism,* one of the great contributions of the Renaissance. One consequence of this was a heightened knowledge of Roman law, whose concept of *imperium* helped clear the way for sovereignty. Legal advisers trained in Roman law guided monarchs toward assertion of centralized control over their territories.

The Reformation (in the sixteenth and seventeenth centuries) broke the political power of the Roman Catholic Church. In England and parts of Germany, new Protestant churches

Historical Perspectives 3.1

were created that were firmly subordinated to the state. (The Queen is still head of the Church of England, for example.) In countries such as France and Spain, which remained Roman Catholic, church administration was shorn of independent political power and the pope lost the ability to intervene in internal political disputes. Another aspect of the Reformation, the increased use of vernacular languages rather than Latin, strengthened the developing states of Europe by fostering the notion of a different official language for each state. The dialect of Paris became the language of France, the "King's English" became the standard speech of Britain, and so on.

The Enlightenment (in the eighteenth century) saw a relaxation of religious tensions. Exhausted by more than a century of religious warfare, people turned their energies to secular matters. Science and philosophy flourished under the patronage of kings, who founded institutions such as the Royal Society of London to promote the advancement of learning. Scepticism, science, and individual freedom contributed to the development of the name by which the Enlightenment is best known: the Age of Reason. Hope and optimism became the qualities of a civilization that perceived itself as peaceful and reasonable.

Interestingly, the Enlightenment in its political aspect is often known as the Age of Absolutism. The European continent was now more or less clearly divided into territorial states ruled by strong monarchs, who established standing armies, court systems, and police forces and in other ways developed a virtual monopoly of law enforcement and armed coercion. Further, they founded a professional bureaucracy that was capable of raising money through taxes and of offering public services to the population, such as the construction of harbours and highways and the promotion of agriculture. It was in the eighteenth century that the state first took on a shape we would recognize if we could return to that era.

There was an important contradiction between the political thought of the Enlightenment, which was generally individualistic, and the political practices of that age, which were absolutist and monarchical. "*L'état c'est moi*" ("I am the State"), said Louis XIV, emphasizing his personal sovereignty. In England this contradiction had been partly resolved through the establishment of parliamentary sovereignty in 1688. On the continent of Europe the revolution was delayed for a century and was correspondingly more violent when it came. The year 1789 saw a popular uprising against the French monarchy that proved to be the beginning of the end of personal sovereignty and traditional authority. Since then, all the great royal dynasties have been overthrown or made merely symbolic, as in Britain. Yet the age of popular revolutions did not abolish the states created by the absolute monarchs; on the contrary, it extended and perfected those states. Modern governments control armies, police, and bureaucracies that Louis XIV could never have imagined.

CITIZENSHIP

Remember that the state is defined as a sovereign authority exercising a legitimate monopoly of physical force as it rules over a population inhabiting a fixed territory. Just as the legal boundaries of the state mark the limits of its territory, so the concept of citizenship marks its demographic boundaries. The modern state is not just an organized structure of governmental power, it is also an association of members. **Citizenship** is membership in the state.

When the concept of citizenship first arose in the world of the classical *polis,* its meaning was somewhat different than it is today. Citizenship in the *polis* meant the right to participate in public affairs, to vote and hold public office; it was restricted to a minority of those residing in the city. Only free adult males—not slaves, women, or children—could be citizens. Also, ancient cities typically contained large numbers of resident aliens who lived and worked in the city but did not possess citizenship unless granted as a special favour.

Modern citizenship, in contrast, is universal. Citizens are not a special category within the state; they are the state. The essential feature of modern universal citizenship is the right to live within the territorial boundaries of the state. In Canada this is now protected by Section 6 of the Canadian Charter of Rights and Freedoms: "Every citizen of Canada has the right to enter, remain in and leave Canada." Non-citizens require special permission to become permanent residents; and as long as they do not become citizens, they can be deported for reasons such as having entered the country under false pretences or being convicted of a serious criminal offence.

Beyond this minimal right of residence, modern citizenship has also come to include and universalize the classical notion of the right to participate in politics. This happened in degrees throughout the nineteenth and twentieth centuries as the rights to vote and run for office were gradually extended to women as well as to men who were not property-owners. Today, except in a very few countries where democratic institutions do not exist, political rights are seen as an attribute of citizenship. The relationship is protected in Section 3 of the Canadian Charter of Rights and Freedoms: "Every citizen of Canada has the right to vote in an election of members of the House of Commons or of a legislative assembly and to be qualified for membership therein." Many other imputed attributes of citizenship, both rights and obligations, also appear in public discussion. People often speak of the payment of taxes, military service, reception of economic benefits, and freedom from discrimination as if these things were part of citizenship; but there is in fact considerable variation in these matters among political communities. They are not nearly as universal as the right of residence and the right to participate in politics.

There is also a great deal of variation in the rules that different communities use to determine who is qualified for citizenship, either by birth or by **naturalization,** the procedure by which an adult is granted citizenship. Amidst all the variation, however, one can discern two basic principles known by their Latin names: *jus soli* (right of soil) and **jus sanguinis** (right of blood). According to *jus soli,* which is the basic principle of citizenship law in the United Kingdom, France, Canada, the United States, and most other states in the New World, anyone born within the boundaries of the state automatically becomes a citizen. Thus women from Mexico occasionally go to great lengths to have their baby born during a visit to the United States, so that the child will be able to claim citizenship, including the right of residence, at the age of eighteen. In much of Europe, in contrast, the basic principle is *jus sanguinis* (right of blood), which means that only the children of citizens acquire citizenship by birth.[7] In Germany, which is quite strict in applying the *jus sanguinis,* millions of Turkish and other foreign workers do not have German citizenship even though they were born in Germany. Most states have elements of both *jus soli* and *jus sanguinis* in their citizenship law, but the balance may be tilted quite far toward one side or the other.

The category of Canadian citizenship did not exist until January 1, 1947, when the first Citizenship Act came into effect. Prior to that time, the key status was that of "British subject," which supposedly carried with it not only the right to vote but also the right to live anywhere within the British Commonwealth (in practice, immigration to Canada from non-white countries such as India and Hong Kong was restricted to almost nothing). Before 1947, residents of Britain, Australia, and New Zealand could without limitation immigrate to Canada whenever they chose and could vote or run for office immediately upon taking up residence; Canadians had the same right to move to those countries and exercise political rights. The establishment of a separate Canadian citizenship was an important step in the emergence of a Canadian state distinct from the rest of the British Commonwealth. Canadian Focus 3.1 provides a summary of the types of Canadian citizenship.

As a summary, let us link together the four key concepts that have been discussed thus far: society, state, politics, and government. *Society* is the voluntary, spontaneously emerging order of relationships in which we coexist with and serve the needs of one another. It is what makes possible human comfort and even survival. The *state* is the community organized and armed with coercive power to protect the social order from internal disruption and external attack, and to provide certain public services to the community. *Government* is the decision-making structure and process of the state, while *politics* is the never-ending struggle for support in the public realm. Social factions put pressure on public authorities hoping to influence their decisions in certain ways, and provide support if the desired decisions are made.

Although the concepts of state and government overlap to a considerable extent, there is a subtle distinction of emphasis between them. Government is the process of decision-making and the structure of offices that sustains the process. The state is the entire territorial community, organized for collective action through its government. The state is a more abstract and permanent entity. Governments come and go as politicians and civil servants change in office, but the state remains, unless it is destroyed through civil war, conquest, or annexation by another state.

Canadian Focus 3.1

Canadian Citizenship

According to the Citizenship Act, the following categories of people are deemed Canadian citizens:

- A person born in Canada (*jus soli*).

- A person born outside of Canada if at least one parent is a Canadian citizen (*jus sanguinis*). Such people lose their Canadian citizenship unless they apply for it and live in Canada for a year before they become 28.

- An immigrant who, after living in Canada for three of the last four years, applies for citizenship, demonstrates knowledge of French or English, and passes a simple test of knowledge about Canada (*naturalization*). Dependent children receive citizenship along with their parents.

Questions for Discussion

1. Economists often speak of "consumer sovereignty," by which they mean that, in a competitive market, producers will be able to sell only those goods and services that consumers are willing to pay for. Compare this to the meaning of sovereignty as used in the study of government and politics. Do you see any important differences?

2. Politicians in Quebec routinely refer to their provincial government as "*l'état du Québec*" ("the Quebec state"). How does this way of speaking differ from the definition of state offered in this chapter?

3. Under current law, Canadians can hold dual citizenship. Do you personally favour this? Regardless of your personal view, what advantages and disadvantages do you see in allowing dual citizenship?

Internet Links

1. Bloc Québécois home page: **www.blocquebecois.org.** Parti Québécois home page: **www.pq.org.** These two sites will give you access to documents explaining Quebec separatists' understanding of sovereignty.

2. United Nations home page: **www.un.org.** By following the links, you can get an up-to-date list of member states (192 at time of writing).

3. Citizenship and Immigration Canada home page: **www.cic.gc.ca.** Gateway to information about Canadian citizenship.

4. Dual Citizenship FAQ: **www.richw.org/dualcit.** Highly informative, non-technical source of information about dual citizenship in United States law. This could be of practical significance to you if you are one of the many Canadians who would like to work in the United States or who have an American family background.

Further Reading

Albo, Gregory, David Langille, and Leo Panitch. *A Different Kind of State? Popular Power and Democratic Administration.* Toronto: Oxford University Press, 1993.

Boyer, Pierre, Linda Cardinal, and David Headon, eds. *From Subjects to Citizens: A Hundred Years of Citizenship in Australia and Canada.* Toronto: University of Toronto Press, 2004.

Camilleri, Joseph. *The End of Sovereignty? The Politics of a Shrinking and Fragmenting World.* Aldershot, UK: Elgar, 1992.

Courchene, Thomas J., and Donald J. Savoie. *Art of the State: Governance in a World without Frontiers.* Montreal: Institute for Research on Public Policy, 2003.

Elkins, David J. *Beyond Sovereignty: Territory and Political Economy in the Twenty-first Century.* Toronto: University of Toronto Press, 1995.

Esberey, Joy E., and L. W. Johnston. *Democracy and the State: An Introduction to Politics.* Peterborough, ON: Broadview Press, 1994.

Foisneau, Luc. *Leviathan after 350 Years.* New York: Oxford University Press, 2004.

Gidengil, Elisabeth, André Blais, Neil Nevitte, and Richard Nadeau. *Citizens.* Vancouver: University of British Columbia Press, 2004.

Gill, Graeme. *The Nature and Development of the Modern State.* London: Palgrave Macmillan, 2003.

Godfrey, Sima, and Frank Unger, eds. *The Shifting Foundations of Modern Nation-States: Realignments of Belonging.* Toronto: University of Toronto Press, 2004.

Guehenno, Jean-Marie. *The End of the Nation-State.* Trans. by Victoria Elliott. Minneapolis: University of Minnesota Press, 1995.

Harding, Alan. "The Origins of the Concept of the State," *History of Political Thought 15,* Spring 1994.

Harmes, Adam. *The Return of the State: Protestors, Power-Brokers and the New Global Compromise.* Vancouver/Toronto: Douglas & McIntyre, 2004.

Jouvenel, Bertrand de. *Sovereignty.* Chicago: University of Chicago Press, 1963.

Magocsi, Paul Robert. *The End of the Nation-State? The Revolution of 1989 and the Future of Europe.* Kingston, ON: Kashtan Press, 1994.

McLennan, Gregor. *The Idea of the Modern State/The State and Society*. Milton Keynes, UK: Open University Press, 1984.

Pierson, Christopher. *The Modern State*. New York: Routledge, 2004.

Poggi, Gianfranco. *The State: Its Nature, Development, and Prospects*. Stanford, CA: Stanford University Press, 1990.

Tivey, Leonard, ed. *The Nation State: The Formation of Modern Politics*. Oxford: Martin Robertson, 1981.

Vincent, Andrew. *Theories of the State*. Oxford: Blackwell, 1987.

CHAPTER 4

The Nation

What we described in the previous chapter as the modern, legal, participatory state, many authors prefer to call the **nation-state.** The word *nation* is added to state to emphasize that the state is participatory—that it is an association of citizens, not just an organized system of power within a certain territory. For reasons that will become clear later in this chapter, the term *nation-state* raises all sorts of problems in Canada, and we prefer to use it sparingly. However, the term is widely employed in political science, and you will undoubtedly encounter it many times. Why does the word *nation* have these connotations of voluntary consent and active participation when it is added to *state*?

First of all, *nation* can be almost a synonym for *state*. The United Nations is an organization to which only states can belong, which means that bodies like the Palestine Liberation Organization can have only observer status. Could the United Nations just as well have been called the United States if that name had not already been taken by our southern neighbour? Probably not, for "United States" suggests an association of governments, whereas "United Nations" suggests an association of the peoples of the world. They may communicate with each other through their governments, but if the term means anything they are also involved as peoples.

This brings us to the nub of the issue. There are social realities called nations, which are conceptually distinct from states. Typical nations are the Americans, the French, and the Germans. Who exactly are the Germans? They are not simply those who speak the German language, for German is also spoken in Austria and parts of Switzerland, Luxembourg, and Belgium. Nor can the Germans be identified with reference to a single state, for after World War II there were two German states—the German Democratic Republic (East Germany) and the Federal Republic of Germany (West Germany)—that did not merge until 1990. Nor is religion the explanation, for the Germans are about equally divided between Protestants and Catholics. The French writer Ernest Renan explored this topic in 1882 in a well-known essay, "*Qu'est-ce qu'une Nation?*" ("What Is a Nation?"). He wrote:

> A nation is a soul, a spiritual principle . . . A nation is a great solidarity, created by the sentiment of the sacrifices which have been made and of those which one is disposed to make in the future. It presupposes a past; but it resumes itself in the present by a tangible fact: the consent, the clearly expressed desire to continue life in common. The

existence of a nation is a plebiscite of every day, as the existence of the individual is a perpetual affirmation of life.[1]

In more contemporary language, we would say that a **nation** is an identity shared by a large number of people based upon, but not reducible to, objective factors such as common race, language, religion, customs, and government.

The nation, like the participatory state, is a product of modern European history. It did not exist in medieval Europe. People in that era thought of themselves in both broader and narrower terms: on the one hand as Christians or subjects of the Holy Roman Empire, on the other in terms of limited local identities. The first discernible nations to emerge were the English, French, and Spanish, and in each instance the pattern was approximately the same. A strong monarchy established a stable territorial state within which local identities were merged over centuries into a wider national identity. The language of the royal court became current throughout the realm, while local dialects were marginalized or even suppressed. The monarch's religion was made a state religion, and nonconforming groups were stripped of power or even expelled (Huguenots from France, Jews and Moors from Spain). Social disparities between the nobility and the common people were gradually reduced as the monarchy, employing many commoners in its official service, stripped away the privileges of the aristocracy. The estates of medieval society—nobility, clergy, freemen, and serfs—were levelled into the single category of citizens. Out of this sometimes brutal exercise of state power emerged nations conscious of a common identity and destiny. Events in France after the Revolution of 1789 indicate the emergence of the French nation. With the king overthrown and Austria and Prussia—the traditional enemies of France—threatening war, the French rose to defend *la nation française*. With the introduction of military conscription, huge armies of citizen-soldiers overran Europe, defeating the professional and mercenary armies of other states.

It was the French Revolution more than anything else that awakened the spirit of nationality in Europe. Other peoples began to think of themselves as nations, even though they were not associated with a single strong state like the French or the English. The Italians and the Germans, for example, had lived for centuries divided among many large and small states. Now movements of unification began, which eventually resulted in the formation of the Kingdom of Italy (1861) and the German Empire (1871). Other peoples, such as the Irish and the Greeks, who had long been ruled by foreign masters, began to assert their nationhood in popular uprisings. One of the great themes of European history since 1789 has been the emergence of nations demanding their own nation-states. The process is now largely complete in Western Europe, though a few small groups, such as the Basques, Scots, and Bretons, remain submerged minorities. A striking political phenomenon of recent decades has been the "mini-nationalism" of such small groups—their attempts to assert themselves as full-fledged nations, even to the point of demanding political independence.[2] For a discussion of nation and state in Eastern Europe, see World View 4.1.

Colonization also created new nations elsewhere in the world. European immigrants flocked to the United States, Canada, Australia, New Zealand, and the many

World View 4.1

Nation and State in Eastern Europe

Until World War I, Eastern Europe was controlled by four multinational empires—the German, Russian, Austro-Hungarian, and Ottoman. With the Peace of Versailles (1919), the victorious Allied powers broke up these empires with the announced purpose of creating nation-states. But demographic reality did not correspond to political aspiration. None of the peoples of Eastern Europe lived in neatly bounded territories; centuries of conquest and migration had produced a colourful checkerboard of diverse peoples. Hence all the new nation-states, from Poland on the Baltic Sea through Yugoslavia on the Mediterranean, contained large and often unhappy minorities.

At enormous human cost, World War II led to the "solution" of some of these minority problems, particularly in the northern part of the region. Millions of Jews were killed, and millions of Germans were driven out of Poland and Czechoslovakia. But other minority problems remained unresolved and went into suspended animation when the Soviet Union imposed communism upon its East European satellites.

The struggle to define national identities resumed with a vengeance after half a century of suppression under communist rule. The 1993 break-up of Czechoslovakia into Slovakia and the Czech Republic; the three-cornered war among Serbs, Croats, and Muslims in Bosnia, followed by the fighting between Serbs and Albanians in Kosovo; the war between ethnic Russians and ethnic Romanians in Moldova; the numerous wars in the Caucasus mountains, of which the struggle of Chechnya for independence is one example—these and many other conflicts in the area since the 1990s continue the long process of sorting out nations and boundaries.

states of Latin America. In different ways and at different times, each of these nations gained independence from its mother country, and political autonomy became the focus of new national identities. These are open, synthetic nations composed of immigrants of varied origins, whereas the traditional European nations are more closed, having evolved over centuries of common history.

A major development of the twentieth century was the spread of European-style nationalism to the rest of the world. The rapid pace of global change that continues today has made the nation the chief source of political legitimacy by weakening traditional social institutions such as the family, tribe, and village. It has also meant the destruction of ancient empires and the emergence of new nations from the wreckage. Related to this is the attempt to fuse tribal identities into nationalities. In the nineteenth century most of Africa was divided by the European powers on more or less arbitrary lines that bore little relation to patterns of tribal habitation. The European powers are now gone, but their colonial boundaries remain as the borders between sovereign African states. In most of these states, tribal identities are far more important than national ones. The tragic civil war between Hutu and Tutsi tribes in Rwanda is one example of such tribal conflict; another is the disintegration of the Democratic Republic of the Congo into several warring tribal factions, each receiving some degree of military assistance from neighbouring states. Most recently, the 2008 election in Kenya provoked fighting between the Kikuyu and other tribes. Over time, at least some of these new states may develop viable national identities. In the meantime, many have been devastated by chronic civil war among tribes, and the continent of Africa is troubled with millions of refugees who have been driven from their homes by political violence—the most recent highly publicized example being the genocidal warfare between Arabs and Africans in the southern part of the Sudan.

This brief historical survey confirms that nationality is not tied to any single objective factor. National identity is usually based on some combination of language, race, religion, and government, but none of these is either necessary or sufficient. The Swiss as a nation are divided by religion between Protestant and Catholic, and are linguistically divided among speakers of German, French, Italian, and Romansch; the focus of national identity is government itself. Government is also the focus in the United States, which is a multiracial nation with European, African, Asian, and Native American elements; also, there are now more than 30 million Americans whose first language is not English but Spanish. In contrast to Switzerland and the United States, the small country of Lebanon, where all are of the same race and all speak Arabic, might seem well favoured to develop a coherent nationality; yet that country was torn for much of the 1980s by civil war among Christians and several sects of Muslims. One must look at each case separately to see what factors contribute to or work against the growth of national identity. The only safe generalization is that there is no universal formula. As a form of identity, the nation is a subjective or psychological reality that transcends objective factors. That is what Renan meant when he called it "a plebiscite of every day"—nations are created by human will. Ultimately, identity is a matter of what you wish to call yourself and what you can get others to accept.

Against this backdrop, the contemporary Canadian writer Michael Ignatieff has introduced a useful distinction between ethnic and civic nations.[3] **Ethnic nations** are those in which the national identity depends primarily on objective factors such as language, race, or religion. Where the national identity is ethnic, outsiders may live in the community for decades or even generations without coming to share the identity—think of the Koreans in Japan or the Turkish "Guest Workers" in Germany. **Civic nations,** in contrast, have an identity that depends primarily on acceptance of the political order. In these circumstances, exemplified by Canada or the United States, newcomers may take on the national identity within very few years.

The contrast, however, should not be overdrawn. Civic nations always have ethnic underpinnings; think of the role of American popular culture, expressed in the English language, in reinforcing the American national identity. The Super Bowl and Hollywood movies are arguably as important as the Statue of Liberty and the Star-Spangled Banner in producing the identity of being American. And ethnic nations always have some civic aspects. European nations such as France, Italy, and Germany have, in fact, socialized millions of immigrants and their children to the new national identity, even though the process may be slower than in North America. It is, moreover, not the case that ethnic nations are bad and civic nations are good. Both are valid ways of generating the identity of a political community.

PROBLEMS OF ETHNICITY

Nations are rarely homogeneous; they almost always contain significant minorities whose identity can conflict or overlap with the dominant national identity. Such minorities are often called **ethnic groups,** but that term itself needs further specification. Let us mention three categories of great importance to Canada, all drawn from a more extended classification proposed by the Canadian philosopher Will Kymlicka:[4]

- **Substate nations,** such as the francophones of Canada. Originally the dominant settler group, they were traded by France to the British Empire as part of a complex deal in the Treaty of Paris (1763), and subsequently became outnumbered by new waves of anglophone settlers. Since substate nations could have become sovereign nations if history had turned out differently, it is not surprising that the members of substate nations cling tenaciously to their identities and continue to insist upon their national status, even if they are incorporated into a larger power structure.

- **Indigenous or aboriginal peoples,** such as the North American Indians. Indigenous peoples did not originally describe themselves as nations, for that whole vocabulary is a product of European history. But, once subordinated to a colonial political system, they may adopt that vocabulary and begin to claim national status as a way of obtaining greater political power.

- **Immigrants,** such as Italian Canadians or Chinese Canadians. Immigrants may come from well-established national communities such as the Italians or Chinese, but when they voluntarily move to another country, they are generally thought to have given up any claim to national status in their new homelands. Immigrant groups usually make claims for speedier integration into the nation to which they have moved, rather than recognition of a distinct national status of their own. (African Americans don't fit very well into this tableau because most of them did not come voluntarily to the Americas; their ancestors were brought as slaves.)

Let us look at some North American examples of strategic claims to national status. In the United States the religious movement popularly known as the Black Muslims (their most famous adherent is the boxer Muhammad Ali) maintains that African Americans are a nation—to be precise, the "Nation of Islam."[5] This assertion is tied to the demand that, as a nation with a full-fledged identity, African Americans should have their own sovereign state. Critics of the Black Muslims counter that African Americans are a special group within, but still part of, the American nation. In Canada, the Dene, the indigenous people of the Northwest Territories, elevated themselves to national status in the Dene Declaration of 1975: "We the Dene of the Northwest Territories insist on the right to be regarded by ourselves and the world as a nation."[6] In this they followed the Métis, who have insisted for a century and a half that they too are a nation, the "New Nation." Native Indians in Canada now refer to themselves as "the First Nations";[7] and that position was roundly endorsed by the 1996 report of the Royal Commission on Aboriginal Peoples, which called for "nation rebuilding and nation recognition" of Aboriginal peoples as "a crucial first component" in restructuring Canada as a multinational confederacy.[8] Today, First Nations terminology is routinely used in public not only by aboriginal leaders but also by politicians of all parties.

French Canadians are often regarded by English Canadians as an ethnic group, although, at least in Quebec, they generally regard themselves as the Québécois nation, one of the two so-called "founding nations" of Canada. The issue came to a head in the House of Commons in fall 2006, when Bloc Québécois (BQ) leader Gilles Duceppe introduced a motion recognizing Quebec as a nation. Prime Minister Stephen Harper responded by amending the motion to affirm that "the Québécois form a nation within a united Canada," and all parties supported the amended motion, though the BQ would have preferred the original wording.[9] This was more than just quibbling over words. A nation is potentially a self-governing community, perhaps even potentially a sovereign state.[10] The BQ introduced its original motion precisely to serve as a platform for further efforts to separate Quebec from Canada. Insertion of the phrase "within a united Canada" was meant to derail that plan.

Objectively, there is no precise definition of a nation. It is not a scientific issue but a strategic one relating to whether one social group has the power and the right to assert itself against others. What counts is not objective criteria but the respect and influence that go along with being called a nation.

NATIONS AND STATES

Let us now return to the relationship between nation and state. There are several typical situations. Nation-states exist where the limits of common identity coincide with the boundaries of sovereign authority. Clear contemporary examples are Iceland, Sweden, and Poland, in which the state contains a relatively homogeneous population. Perhaps more numerous are those nation-states where one nation is clearly preponderant but minorities are significant. The United States contains the Nation of Islam and other black nationalists, as well as some Hispanic activists who still dream of reunion with Mexico. Great Britain has to deal with important nationalist movements in Northern Ireland, Scotland, and Wales. Spain contains significant Basque and Catalan minorities, some of whom aspire to independence. When minorities accept the legitimacy of the state, they can be regarded as ethnic groups within the nation, whether as substate nations, indigenous peoples, or immigrant communities. But in many cases the minorities are not content to be ethnic groups and struggle vigorously for national status, union with a neighbouring state, or even a nation-state of their own.

A second situation is that of the **binational** or **multinational state.** In such cases, two or more nations coexist under a single government. From one point of view, Canada is a binational state, a partnership of English Canadians and French Canadians that is enriched by the presence of indigenous peoples as well as immigrant communities. Belgium might also be considered a binational state, a partnership of Flemings and Walloons. India is a vast multinational state, as were the Soviet Union and the Austro-Hungarian, Ottoman, and Russian Empires.

If there are multinational states, there are also multi-state nations. Prime examples are the German people, who were divided into East and West Germany from 1945 to 1990; the Koreans, who are still split into North and South Korea; the Poles, whose state was split up among Russia, Austria, and Prussia at the end of the eighteenth century; and the Basques, who straddle the border between France and Spain. Nations can live submerged for hundreds of years with no state of their own and then suddenly reappear, as the Poles did after World War I when their state was reconstituted.

Overall, it seems safe to say that the world is such a complicated place that homogeneous nation-states are and will continue to be a small minority. Most states comprise multiple identity-groups whose members either have to work out ways of peacefully sharing a government or else will be fated to engage in conflicts that may tear the state apart. The emergence of the nation as the paradigm of political community has not changed the fundamental challenge of politics, which, as Bernard Crick pointed out, is always to achieve a tolerable degree of harmony among people with different interests, identities, and worldviews.

IS CANADA A NATION?

Those who created the Dominion of Canada in 1867, the so-called "Fathers of Confederation," imagined Canada as a single nation. Acutely aware of linguistic, religious, and regional cleavages, they tried to define the new national identity in political terms as allegiance to the government. Quebec's leading spokesman, George-Étienne Cartier, called the new Dominion a "political nationality,"[11] by which he meant that the existence of a common government would create an identity transcending linguistic and regional differences, although these differences would continue to exist and would be reflected in provincial governments. Canadians, like the Swiss, would constitute a single nation, even if they spoke more than one language and worshipped God in different churches.

But there was always a view in Quebec that Canada was a partnership of two nations, French and English; and this view re-emerged forcefully in the 1960s during the Quiet Revolution. Quebec nationalists articulated the *deux nations* view of

Canada, which both the Progressive Conservative Party and the New Democratic Party adopted for a time at the national level. The Liberal Party, however, under the leadership of Pierre Trudeau, continued to insist that Canada was a single nation, albeit bilingual and multicultural. The Meech Lake Accord, proposed but not passed in the late 1980s, referred to Quebec as a "distinct society." Proponents of the Accord saw this as a justifiable accommodation of Quebec's uniqueness, while opponents, including Pierre Trudeau, saw it as code for "two nations." However, that period of Liberal opposition to any talk of "two nations" ended in 2006 when the Liberals supported Prime Minister Harper's motion to affirm that "the Québécois form a nation within a united Canada."

One of the complexities here is that, if Canada consists of two nations, they are of quite different types. The identity of being Québécois is primarily an ethnic one, depending on language, culture, and a common sense of history, whereas the identity of being Canadian is primarily civic, depending on allegiance to the political system. There simply is no English-Canadian nation in the same sense as there is a French-Canadian (or Québécois) nation. English-speaking Canadians have never thought of themselves as a collectivity in opposition to French-speaking Canadians; their identity is intrinsically pan-Canadian and inclusive of Quebec.

In the meantime, while Canada and Quebec were going through this prolonged identity crisis, Aboriginal people started using national terminology to describe themselves. As described above, the Métis, in fact, had long spoken of a "Métis Nation"; and in 1982, the National Indian Brotherhood transformed itself into the Assembly of First Nations. Curiously, politicians who always refused to speak of Quebec as a nation rushed to adopt the new practice of referring to Indian bands as "First Nations." But this was perhaps due more to the weakness than the strength of the Aboriginal position. The more than 630 First Nations are small, with an average population of slightly over 1,000, and scattered across the whole of Canada. Although politically influential in some circumstances, they are not in a position to break up the Canadian state. Quebec, in contrast, is a single province strategically located in the middle of Canada. With more than 7,000,000 people, it is certainly large enough to become a viable state in its own right.

That these are vital political issues, not just conceptual quibbles, was obvious during the Canadian referendum campaign of 1992. Supporters of the Charlottetown Accord (see Chapter 7 for more on the Charlottetown Accord) often spoke of "two founding nations"—English and French—or even three—English, French, and Aboriginal (lumping all Aboriginal peoples together for this purpose). They saw the Accord, with its proposals for special guarantees for Quebec and a "third order" of government for Aboriginal Canadians, as a means of representing these national differences in Canada's political institutions. In contrast, many opponents of the Accord spoke of the "equality" of individuals and provinces within Canada. In their view, Canada was a single nation of equal citizens, and no group required elaborate protections.

The "one Canada" view won the referendum, but that does not mean the debate is over. The view that there are two or three or several hundred nations will remain alive because it articulates the political aspirations of significant social groups with robust identities. Their leaders, like all political leaders, will continue to use words as weapons in their struggle to attain political power.

Questions for Discussion

1. How do you personally think of Canada—as one nation, two nations, or many nations? What is the most important factor in the way you think about Canada?

2. Is Canada truly a political nationality, as G.-E. Cartier maintained, or is the national identity also dependent on aspects of language and culture?

3. Canada has experienced massive immigration in the period since World War II. How do you think this immigration has affected the Canadian national identity(ies)?

Internet Links

1. The Nationalism Project: **www.nationalismproject.org.** Bibliography on nations and nationalism, plus links to other sites.

2. Assembly of First Nations home page: **www.afn.ca.** Information about the main organization of First Nations in Canada.

3. The Nation of Islam Online: **www.noi.org.** Information about a leading black nationalist movement in the United States.

4. Statistics Canada: **www.statcan.ca.** Data about the population of contemporary Canada, including ethnic composition.

Further Reading

Ajzenstat, Janet, Paul Romney, Ian Gentles, and William D. Gairdner, eds. *Canada's Founding Debates.* Toronto: University of Toronto Press, 2003.

Behiels, Michael D., and Marcel Martel, eds. *Nation, Ideas, Identities: Essays in Honour of Ramsay Cook.* Don Mills, ON: Oxford University Press, 2000.

Breuilly, John. *Nationalism and the State.* 2nd ed. Chicago: University of Chicago Press, 1994.

Calhoun, Craig. *Nationalism.* Minneapolis: University of Minnesota Press, 1997.

Conlogue, Ray. *Impossible Nation: The Longing for Homeland in Canada and Quebec.* Stratford, ON: Mercury Press, 1996.

Dahbour, Omar. *Illusion of the Peoples: A Critique of National Self-Determination.* Lanham, MD: Lexington Books, 2003.

Flanagan, Tom. *First Nations? Second Thoughts.* 2nd ed. Montreal: McGill–Queen's University Press, 2008.

Friesen, Gerald. *Citizens and Nation: An Essay on History, Communication and Canada.* Toronto: University of Toronto Press, 2000.

Granatstein, Jack. *Yankee Go Home: Canadians and Anti-Americanism.* Scarborough, ON: HarperCollins Canada, 1996.

Grant, George. *Lament for a Nation: The Defeat of Canadian Nationalism.* New ed. Ottawa: Carleton University Press, 1994.

Halliday, Fred. *Nation and Religion in the Middle East.* Boulder, CO: Lynne Rienner, 2000.

Ignatieff, Michael. *Blood and Belonging.* Toronto: Penguin Books, 1994.

Kohn, Hans, ed. *Nationalism: Its Meaning and History.* New York: Van Nostrand Reinhold, 1965.

Paul, T.V., G. John Ikenberry, and John A. Hall. *The Nation-State in Question.* Princeton, NJ: Princeton University Press, 2003.

Schulze, Hagen. *States, Nations, and Nationalism: From the Middle Ages to the Present.* Translated by William E. Yuill. Oxford: Blackwell, 1996.

Snyder, Louis L. *Global Mini-Nationalism: Autonomy or Independence.* Westport, CT: Greenwood Press, 1982.

Spira, Thomas. *Nationalism and Ethnicity Terminologies: An Encyclopedic Dictionary and Research Guide.* Gulf Breeze, FL: Academic International Press, 1999.

CHAPTER 5

Political Culture and Socialization

National identity, whether predominantly civic or ethnic, or some mixture of these pure types, does not exist in a vacuum; it is part of the wider culture prevailing in the society. Culture, like so many terms used in the social sciences, has a number of different meanings. One writer calls it "one of the two or three most complicated words in the English language."[1] In ordinary speech, it often refers to the realm of the fine arts, including "high culture" (opera, classical music, painting and sculpture, poetry and fiction, live theatre) as well as "popular culture" (network television, Hollywood movies, magazines and comic books, popular fiction). However, when social scientists speak of **culture,** they usually are referring to the pattern of beliefs and behaviour of a people, including the place of the family, the role of religion, and the influence of economics and politics. Culture has become an umbrella term that reflects institutional arrangements as well as the attitudes, beliefs, and values that accompany them.

Observers have long noticed that the different peoples of the world possess cultural traits; such observations lead to cultural stereotypes that, while often exaggerated, usually contain a grain of truth. The Chinese, for example, are thought to be industrious and to maintain close family ties. When Thomas Sowell examined the culture of various ethnic groups after immigration to the United States, he found that the Chinese had become known for their "endurance and frugality" and these characteristics carried over into younger generations in the New World. Even as children, they were "better behaved and more hard working." All this led to a high percentage of people from Chinese immigrant communities entering the professions, so that by 1959 their average income had surpassed the American national average.[2] People of Latin origin are said to be emotional in speech and action. North Americans are probably more egalitarian in their outlook than any other society, yet they are also materialistic and achievement-oriented. Such traits are considered part of the traditions of a society; they reflect national character and persist over long periods of time and even after migration.

The part of culture having to do with government and politics is known, not surprisingly, as **political culture.** It includes the attitudes, beliefs, values, and norms that people have developed toward government and politics. As with culture in general, popular stereotypes, sometimes containing a good deal of truth, exist about different political cultures. Germans, for example, think of themselves as being, and are thought by others to be, respectful of public authority. While such a generalization is interesting and perhaps true, it cannot explain all of German politics. The expectation is, however, that the values and beliefs in a political culture will be widely shared and relatively coherently held among the members of that community. Beyond that, important political subcultures may also exist. Canada has been said to consist of several regional political cultures. The earliest argument along these lines came in the 1970s by Richard Simeon and David Elkins, who argued that the provinces contained political cultures that reflected unique provincial institutions.[3] More recent examinations have confirmed that provincial subcultures remain an important dynamic in Canadian politics.[4]

Political culture represents the psychological dimension of politics.[5] It encompasses how people think about politics and thus can help us to understand differences in how politics is practised across states. Because it includes attitudes, beliefs, values, and norms regarding government and politics, it is simultaneously rational, emotional, and judgmental.

Political culture encompasses ideology—notions about what government is and what it ought to be. An example may clarify the relationship between political culture and ideology. Belief in individual freedom is a fundamental part of the political culture of the Western world. At the same time, within the ideology of liberal democracies, we not only value individual freedom but also believe that maintaining it should be a primary goal of governments. Freedom of political action is the basis on which individuals and groups can become involved in the political process. Without political freedom, there would be little opportunity to participate in politics. Thus the liberal-democratic ideology is an integral part of our political culture. Canadians think it quite reasonable to engage in peaceful protest against a law or policy with which they disagree; such protests are a common and accepted part of democratic governance. They believe that political protest, while never guaranteeing a government response, is worth the effort.

By way of contrast, Latin American political systems are influenced by Iberic–Latin traditions that include, among other things, a society that is hierarchical, stratified, and authoritarian.[6] Although democratization has gained a foothold in the region, recent history is littered with failed attempts at challenging authoritarianism's hold. Public opinion surveys suggest that while there is general support for democracy among Latin Americans, political corruption, heightened crime levels, and lack of trust for governments have led to a loss of support for many of its regimes, which hinders the introduction of democracy.[7]

Political culture researchers grapple with the question of whether a democratic political culture is required for a stable democratic system to take root; many now agree that while democratic values can help in ensuring the success of democracy, it is also the case that a democratic regime itself is integral to instilling those values in citizens.[8] Importantly, political cultures can change, but this occurs only very slowly because values and beliefs adopted early in life are tremendously durable. Generational replacement is generally agreed to be the primary mechanism through which political cultures change.

Studies of public opinion have sought to identify a typology of political cultures, often with a goal of better understanding of their role in the practice of politics. A five-nation empirical study undertaken in the early 1960s by Gabriel Almond and Sydney Verba established three basic categories of political culture: parochial, subject, and participatory.[9] In a **parochial culture,** people hold rather negative views of government and as a result participate little in the political system. In a **subject culture,** people hold more positive evaluations of governments but remain largely uninvolved. In a **participatory culture,** people expect to participate in politics and that government will be responsive to citizen demands. Almond and Verba argued that a "civic culture," one ensuring a stable democracy, consisted of a mix of these three types so as to ensure that challenges to authority could be offset by the obedience of others, and that participation of some could be offset by the apathy of others. Too much participation and too many challenges to authority are as threatening to democratic stability as too little participation and too much deference.

A more modern typology for political culture distinguishes between **polyarchal, fragmented,** and **collectivist cultures.**[10] Polyarchal cultures are unified, which means there is broad agreement on basic social values and active citizen engagement based on a strong sense of efficacy. People in such cultures agree on the key rules of the political game, and participate in it actively, given that such activity is believed to pay off. Disagreements do not lead to violence because they occur at the level of policy (on the goals to pursue), not at the more fundamental level of how to decide on the goals, and because people in these cultures treat others, including political opponents, with respect. Canada, the United States, and France fall into the polyarchal cultures category. Fragmented cultures, on the other hand, are ones that display similarly high levels of citizen engagement, but these are combined with relatively low levels of agreement on the rules of the game. Disagreements and disunity are the norm, as is relative distrust and suspicion of others. Politics in such cultures is often violent, brutal, and deadly, and governments are rarely stable. *Coups d'état,* ethnic cleansing, and political assassinations are commonplace because the lack of trust makes political compromise and accommodation impossible. Two examples of fragmented political cultures are Rwanda and Bosnia. A third type of culture, collectivist, exhibits the broad agreement on social values of polyarchal cultures, but this is combined with little in the way of citizen engagement. The lack of engagement in such cultures stems from the knowledge that engagement is fruitless or even dangerous. Citizens in political systems expressing little support for political and civic freedoms learn to keep quiet or risk imprisonment or worse. Citizen engagement in such states is akin to cheerleading on the sidelines of the real political game, providing moral support to the players but having relatively little effect on the overall outcome of the game. North Korea and Cuba are examples of collectivist political culture. This typology provides a short-hand method for understanding at a basic level why the politics that takes place in a country happens the way that it does: people's political values, beliefs, and norms shape their participation in politics.

TRENDS IN POLITICAL CULTURE

Recent investigations in political culture have focused on trends that affect many societies simultaneously. A prime example is the growth of **post-materialism** in the political culture of the Westernworld. According to Ronald Inglehart, who pioneered research on post-materialism, the years since World War II have seen a gradual but profound shift of values. Relying on two hypotheses—the scarcity hypothesis, which argues that things in short supply are more desirable than things that are abundant, and the socialization hypothesis, which argues that one's values are shaped and set relatively early in life—he argues that recent generations have grown up taking their physical and economic security for granted and, as a result, their priorities differ from those of previous generations. Previous generations are predominantly **materialists,** as Inglehart uses the term, concerned with physical and economic security, whereas more recent generations are **post-materialists,** concerned with self-fulfillment and self-expression. With generational replacement, the electorate is becoming increasingly concerned with self-expression and less inclined to leave politics to politicians and to accept the necessity of pragmatic compromises.[11] There have been several political results. One is a decrease in voter loyalty to particular parties and a corresponding increase in vote switching from election to election. Another is the rise of single-issue movements (feminist, pro-choice, pro-life, environmentalist, ethnic, linguistic, gay-rights, rights for the disabled, and so on) that are reluctant to submerge their causes within a single political party.

An important book by the Canadian political scientist Neil Nevitte, entitled *The Decline of Deference,* examines this process of value change in Canada against the backdrop of similar changes in other liberal democracies in Western Europe and North America.[12] Nevitte's data, as summarized in Figure 5.1, suggest that by 1990 post-materialism had become the dominant value type in Europe and North America among people under 45, whereas older people were more likely to be materialists.

Another important branch of research looking at political culture has identified the importance of social capital for understanding democratic outcomes. **Social capital** consists of the social networks and levels of trust and reciprocity that exist in a community. In a nutshell, the greater the level of community interaction and trust, the greater the democratic health of that community is likely to be. Robert Putnam's book *Bowling Alone* argues that the increasing disconnectedness of Americans has caused a decline in civic health.[13] The importance of this research is in highlighting the role of social activity for determining civic health: political culture does not develop on its own but rather stems at least in part from the day-to-day connections between citizens that may have nothing at all to do with politics. Fewer Americans are joining bowling leagues and similar associations, which means they spend less time with their neighbours and have a smaller social network. One result, argues Putnam, is less trust in others, less willingness to engage in the community, and an overall decline in civic health. Putnam points to a number of factors that help to explain why the current

Figure 5.1 Value Type by Age Group: Europe and North America, 1990

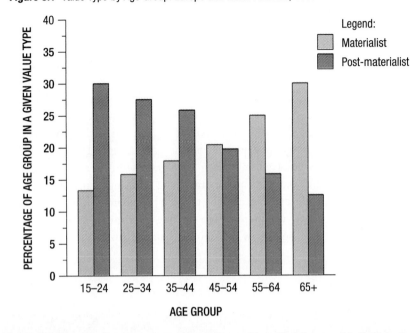

Note: Value type by age group, among the publics of France, Britain, West Germany, Italy, Netherlands, Denmark, Belgium, Spain, Ireland, Northern Ireland, U.S., Canada, and Mexico. (1981, N = 16,043; 1990, N = 20,464.) Value type is not available for U.S. 1981.

Source: 1981 and 1990 World Values Surveys. From R. Inglehart, *Modernization, Cultural Change and Democracy.* (Cambridge University Press, 2005) p. 100.

generation of Americans is more disconnected: increasingly busy lifestyles, two-career families, the spread of suburbia, and the increased use of television and the Internet.

Social connections and networks are central to integration in a community, but so too is where one happens to live. Urban areas, often made up of a mix of ethnic communities, make it more difficult to build stocks of social capital than more rural and less diverse ones. People in diverse communities reveal less trust in others and less willingness to engage with their community; in short, urban residents are more likely to isolate themselves from others in communities that are highly diverse.[14] And while research on this question is still in its early stages, a potential mechanism linking diversity and social capital might be identity: how people identify themselves and others shapes how they behave within their community. Seeing others as like you in some way (as Canadian or American, for example) in spite of other differences likely leads you to trust them more than you otherwise would and to engage in the community with them.

The level of diversity found in communities can be closely linked to immigration patterns: the higher the level of immigration in a community, the greater the level of diversity that it is likely to exhibit. The integration of immigrant and diverse cultures is neither simple to address nor of little consequence for politics; the riots that took place in November 2005 in Paris suburbs mainly populated by African immigrants attest directly to its importance.[15] Multiculturalism policies in Canada have attempted to assist cultural groups in overcoming barriers so as to allow them to integrate more fully into society (see Canadian Focus 5.1). Assistance in learning one of the two official languages has been one of the planks of the policy. With one of the highest levels of per capita immigration in the world—according to the 2006 Census, one in five Canadians is foreign-born—and with 95 percent of immigrants settling in urban areas, integration and national unity are key issues on the political agenda.[16] The challenge is to find a balance between accommodating immigrant cultures and maintaining a strong sense of national unity, while at the same time ensuring respect for key values such as equality, rights and freedoms, and tolerance. The debate in Quebec during the 2007 provincial election over whether women wearing *burqa* and *niqaab* had to reveal their faces in order to vote shows how difficult the balance can be to achieve.

Canadian Focus 5.1

Multiculturalism in Canada

Pierre Trudeau's Liberal government initiated the policy of multiculturalism in 1971. It was a way of dealing with discontent over the report of the Royal Commission on Bilingualism and Biculturalism, which some people saw as focusing so much on English–French issues that it did not pay enough attention to other elements in the Canadian population. Multiculturalism was also recognized in 1982 in Section 27 of the Canadian Charter of Rights and Freedoms: "This Charter shall be interpreted in a manner consistent with the preservation and enhancement of the multicultural heritage of Canadians." Brian Mulroney's Conservative government passed a Multiculturalism Act in 1988 and also created a Department of Multiculturalism, whose functions were later rolled into the Department of Canadian Heritage.

Multiculturalism today is a separate program within that department. It offers grants to ethnic community associations for various kinds of cultural performances, public discussions, English and French language training, and integration into Canadian society. Multiculturalism's declared objective, as part of Canadian Heritage, is not to nourish separate identities but to help immigrants enrich Canadian life by making their own heritage part of the social mainstream.

For further information, go to www.canadianheritage .gc.ca/progs/multi/.

Striking a balance can also be especially difficult when the values in question stem from religious beliefs. Social scientists have argued in the past that the process of **secularization**—that is, the decreasing importance assigned to religion in the modern world—means that religion would cease to be a factor of much importance over time. Recent events have challenged this thinking, however, with the events of 9/11 in particular stimulating renewed interest in the relationship between religion and politics.[17] Unlike a number of countries around the world, Canada and the United States endorse the principle of the separation of church and state, but this does not mean that religion is divorced from politics. That public funding for certain religious schools is found in some Canadian provinces, and the prominent role of religious groups in the American civil rights movement, are but two examples of the interrelationship between religion and politics. Religious beliefs and values directly influence political values and political behaviour. These can reinforce democratic values—equality and freedom—and democratic behaviour—voting—but they can also run up against them, as in the case of the sect of Fundamentalist Latter Day Saints, who practise the subordination of women to men in polygamous marriages. The identity, beliefs, and values stemming from religious beliefs can incite intolerance and lead to violence, terrorist activity, and genocide.

POLITICAL SOCIALIZATION

The means by which a political culture is transmitted from generation to generation is known as **political socialization.** The focus of research on this topic is in determining where and how young people learn about politics, become interested in politics, and decide whether to engage in political and civic life.[18] As one researcher noted, "Good citizens are made, not born."[19] At the macro level, the political system itself will influence learning about politics: how government responds to political events and crises, the importance of and respect shown for human and political rights and freedoms, and the nature of transitions in government necessarily shape political culture. At the individual level, the main agents of political socialization, conveying values, beliefs, and attitudes across generations are the family, schools, friends and peer groups, and the media. Let us say a brief word about each.

It seems intuitively obvious that the family would play an important role in political socialization if for no other reason than that government is a system of authority and the family is where young children first encounter authority. Yet families introduce children to more than simply a system of authority. For many young people, the family setting is where one first learns about politics and government, first hears discussions concerning politics and policy, and first witnesses individual political action. Research shows that families that regularly discuss politics and participate in political activities are likely to produce more politically interested and active children.[20] These early lessons about the importance of politics appear to be crucial for the development of future generations' political engagement.

Schools are also central to learning about government and politics, and in recent years they have significantly increased their efforts to educate students for future citizenship, attempting to stimulate positive attitudes about civic responsibilities such as voting and paying taxes. Part of the spark for this renewed effort at civics education lies in the dropping levels of voter turnout recorded in many Western democracies in recent years; another is research suggesting that citizenship classes can be particularly important for political knowledge. Service learning—sometimes facetiously referred to as mandatory volunteering—has been adopted in a number of schools to develop civic engagement as a lifelong habit.[21]

Although the importance of friends and peer groups for political socialization has always been understood, research in this area has recently begun to re-examine this topic.[22] In line with increased interest in social capital, the importance of social activity for many aspects of political socialization, including civic knowledge and civic attitudes, is now accepted, and how these processes might work during the adolescent years has become a new area of inquiry. Friends and memberships in organizations can play a central role in shaping what we value and what we believe; in adolescence, how many friends we have, who they are, and what and how many groups we have joined are all linked in some way to the attitudes that we possess and to the importance that we assign to civic and political participation throughout our lives. The Boy Scouts and Girl Guides, for example, promote environmental protection when they organize outdoor activities, and they teach lessons about community engagement when they organize bottle drives and cookie sales.

The media, finally, are omnipresent today in all phases of socialization; it would be difficult to overemphasize their importance. Television, radio, newspapers, and magazines are often listed as key sources of information about government and politics. The Internet is fast becoming a rival to these sources, particularly among younger generations.[23] And unlike more traditional sources of news and information, its speed, its ability to facilitate the creation of virtual communities, and its lack of formal gatekeepers sets it apart. Research has yet to determine the precise impact the increased use of Internet sites such as Facebook, MySpace, and YouTube is having on political socialization, but it is clearly having an effect.

Questions for Discussion

1. What are your basic political values and beliefs? How do these shape whether and how you participate in politics?

2. Do you think you are more of a materialist or a post-materialist?

3. How do you think the Internet has changed political socialization?

Internet Links

1. Nelson Education Ltd. Political Science Resource Centre: **www.polisci.nelson.com/ intropc.html.** Links to various sources on political culture and socialization.

2. World Values Survey, Introduction: **www.worldvaluessurvey.org.** A worldwide research project on post-materialism.

3. Environics Research Group: **http://erg.environics.net.** A major Canadian polling company that does a lot of research on values.

4. ThisNation.com: **www.thisnation.com.** An American website on politics with many links to sources on political culture and socialization.

5. Institute for Politics, Democracy & the Internet (IPDI), George Washington University: **www.ipdi.org/About/.**

Further Reading

Adams, Michael. *Fire and Ice: The United States, Canada and the Myth of Converging Values.* Toronto: Penguin Canada, 2003.

Almond, Gabriel A., and Sydney Verba. *The Civic Culture Revisited.* Boston: Little, Brown, 1980.

Bell, David V. J. *The Roots of Disunity: A Study of Canadian Political Culture.* Toronto: Oxford University Press, 1992.

Carpini, Michael X. Delli, and Scott Keeter. *What Americans Know About Politics and Why It Matters.* New Haven: Yale University Press, 1996.

Cristi, Marcela. *From Civil to Political Religion: The Intersection of Culture, Religion and Politics.* Waterloo, ON: Wilfrid Laurier University Press, 2001.

Diamond, Larry Jay, ed. *Political Culture and Democracy in Developing Countries.* Boulder, CO: Lynne Rienner, 1993.

Gibbins, John R., ed. *Contemporary Political Culture: Politics in a Postmodern Age.* London: Sage, 1989.

Hartz, Louis. *The Founding of New Societies.* New York: Harcourt, Brace and World, 1964.

Inglehart, Ronald. *Culture Shift in Advanced Industrial Society.* Princeton, NJ: Princeton University Press, 1990.

Inglehart, Ronald, and Pippa Norris. *Sacred and Secular: Religion and Politics Worldwide.* Toronto: Cambridge University Press, 2004.

Lipset, Seymour Martin. *Continental Divide: The Values and Institutions of the United States and Canada.* New York: Routledge, 1990.

Nevitte, Neil. *The Decline of Deference.* Peterborough, ON: Broadview Press, 1996.

Pierce, John C. *Political Culture and Public Policy in Canada and the United States: Only a Border Apart.* Lewiston, NY: Edwin Mellen Press, 2000.

Putnam, Robert. *Bowling Alone: The Collapse and Revival of American Community.* London: Simon and Schuster, 2000.

Smith, T. Alexander, and Raymond Tatalovich. *Cultures at War: Moral Conflicts in Western Democracies.* Peterborough, ON: Broadview Press, 2003.

Thomas, David M., ed. *Canada and the United States: Differences That Count.* 2nd ed. Peterborough, ON: Broadview Press, 2000.

Woshinsky, Oliver H. *Explaining Politics: Culture, Institutions and Political Behavior.* New York: Routledge, 2008.

CHAPTER 6

Law

Law in the broadest sense means a rule or regularity in the behaviour of any element in the universe. The laws of gravitation describe the motion of falling bodies on the earth or of the planets in the heavens; the laws of evolution describe changes over time in living species; the laws of supply and demand describe human behaviour in dealing with scarce resources. Laws or regularities such as these make the universe intelligible. Law is also the foundation of society, which is essentially a group of people living together under the same laws or rules of conduct.

Although law is all-embracing, it is not monolithic. There is a subtle change in the character of law as one ascends the scale of creation from inanimate objects through plant and animal life to human beings. The higher levels have a greater element of self-guidance or freedom in the way they follow laws. Planets stay in their orbits exactly. Crops grow under certain conditions, but only the average yield can be predicted, not the growth of a particular plant. Animals mate at certain times of year, but not with clockwork regularity. People usually try to buy cheap and sell dear in the marketplace, but any individual may depart from this model for personal reasons.

The variability of human behaviour raises the problem of enforcement (a problem that does not exist for inanimate objects and lower life forms but may have parallels among the higher, social animals). From now on, when we use the term **law,** we shall mean a rule of human conduct that is enforced by the community, by means of coercion or violence if necessary.

Law is only one of several kinds of rules that we follow. Our behaviour is guided by instincts of which we may not even be aware. Innate desires to sleep, find nourishment, and reproduce surely contribute to regularities of human behaviour. However, these basic impulses are always mediated by higher forms of rules. A purely personal rule of conduct is usually called a **habit.** We must all drink, but some of us habitually drink coffee, while others take tea at certain times of the day. Habit gradually merges with **custom** as social forces come more into play. Most adults in the Western world drink either coffee or tea because they see others drink the same beverages. In other spheres, the social element is even more influential. Such things as politeness, appropriate clothing, and table manners are elaborate codes of conduct, learned through imitation and parental instruction, that every society has.

Habits and customs create regularities in human behaviour without coercive enforcement in situations where the incentives to violate or ignore them are small or nonexistent. Language, for example, is primarily what theorists call a coordination game; its purpose is to communicate with others. We suffer a disadvantage if we depart from its rules, because we will not be understood. It does not matter what the rules are; once they exist, it is to our advantage to abide by them. The conventions are more or less self-enforcing. Similarly, we lose out when we flout normal customs of politeness, because others avoid the company of those who create unpleasantness. In these instances there is no true enforcement—only a spontaneous reaction that helps keep our conduct within accustomed channels.

Some things, however, cannot be left to spontaneous self-correction. Typically, enforcement is required when the rules are of primary importance to peaceful cooperation and when the rewards of breaking the rules are attractive relative to the costs. Ordered society demands that, at the very least, we know which family we belong to and which material things are within our control. This is why all societies have rules about the family and property that are coercively enforced. Violating table manners makes one incur heavy social penalties for little apparent gain, so that enforcement is unnecessary; stealing someone's property, on the other hand, can be such an attractive proposition that sanctions against such behaviour become necessary.

The enforcement of law performs a number of functions for society that can be conveniently remembered as the four Rs: retribution, restitution, rehabilitation, and restraint. *Retribution* is the punishment of those who violate the norms of society. *Restitution* is the provision of compensation to those who have been harmed by rule breakers. *Rehabilitation* is a change in conduct that will prevent lawbreaking in the future. And *restraint* is roughly the same as deterrence—the fear we instill in those who cannot be swayed by influence or authority.

Two general points about rules are worth noting. First, we do not need to know what a rule is in order to follow it—we only need to know how to act. Language, for example, is a complex system of rules. We all learn to speak by imitation before we acquire the ability to read those rules in grammar books. Similarly, children learn what kind of behaviour is fair long before they develop a conscious understanding of the rules of justice. A child of three or four, who does not even know the word *justice,* can obey a rule not to grab other children's toys. Second, rules are not necessarily designed by conscious intelligence. They may also grow over time in an evolutionary process of trial and error, as is true of habits, customs, and a great many laws.

CUSTOMARY LAW AND COMMON LAW

These observations help to explain the two main kinds of law. The older kind of law, found in all societies, is evolutionary or **customary law;** this sort of law arises gradually and cannot be traced to an identifiable moment in time. The newer kind of law, **legislation,** is consciously formulated and deliberately constructed. Both kinds of law are equally enforceable and so equally valid. Let us first consider customary law.

All human communities have enforceable rules of conduct. They may not be written down, and no one may be able to articulate them; even so, they exist and are enforced. Such laws are an embodiment of the experience a community has gained in its struggle to survive. With the passage of time, the actors discover methods of cooperation; that is, rules that promote internal order and external strength.

Tribal societies repel or kill external attackers, but their most severe method of enforcement against internal rule breakers is usually ostracism. To be permanently cast out of the small hunting and gathering band, to lose the support of one's family and kin, is tantamount to a death sentence. To be temporarily shunned is usually enough to make the rule-breaker return to accepted norms of conduct.

Laws of this type represent reason—tacit reason—rather than command, because no one has ever issued them. Typically, the community attributes divine origin to them. According to the Old Testament, Moses received the Law on the top of Mount Sinai, enveloped in fire and smoke. God himself wrote the Ten Commandments on two tablets of stone, and the face of Moses shone as he brought the tablets down from the mountain.[1] From the social scientist's point of view, attributing divine origin to law is a way of saying that law does not depend on the will of people alive today and that its importance transcends mere individual preferences.

Society took a step toward assuming conscious control of law when laws began to be written down instead of merely being honoured in practice and entrusted to collective memory. This deliberate recording of laws, however, should not be confused with true legislation. Early legal systems, such as the laws of Hammurabi in Babylon and the Twelve Tables in Rome, were regarded not as a new creation by the sovereign but as a recording of ancient laws that had existed from time immemorial.[2] These laws, said the rulers, had always been valid, but they were now being recorded to avoid misunderstanding and dispute.

A rather similar attitude underlies the **common law** of the English-speaking peoples. Before the Norman Conquest (1066), there were several bodies of law in the different regions of England. The Norman kings set up a unified system of courts throughout the realm that for a time competed with older local courts. The traditional courts gradually fell into disuse as the English found the king's justice to be fairer and more predictable. The king's courts, for their part, continued to interpret the old customary laws, many of which were generally acceptable and became common to all the courts of the realm. Thus there was never a radical break with the past.

Common law is essentially the sum of a vast number of cases decided by English courts since the Middle Ages. Most of these cases were decided not by reference to a written law but by a process of reasoning based on the needs of ordered liberty. Certain principles, such as security of possession of private property and the enforcement of contracts, can be applied to a multitude of disputes. Application yields results, which then serve as models or **precedents** for later cases. The courts generally observe the rule of *stare decisis,* "to stand by what is decided"—that is, to follow precedent. Adherence to the example of past decisions allows the law to grow in an orderly and predictable way. By studying prior cases, one can gain a fair idea of how future disputes will be decided. This is how an enforceable body of law can develop over centuries without ever having been issued as general commands. It is judge-made law, although "made" is perhaps not the best word. It might be better to speak of *finding* the common law, as was done in the Middle Ages. The law, or abstract rule, is gradually discovered through experience with a number of concrete cases.

The great advantage of common law is its flexibility, in the sense that it can forever be applied to new situations. It need never become obsolete so long as judges are reasonably free to follow precedents. For example, the law faced a novel situation when radio waves began to be used commercially early in the twentieth century. Questions arose, such as whether one could broadcast on a frequency already used by another transmitter. Judges immediately began to cope with these problems, reasoning by analogy with other forms of property.

Common law, having been developed in England, was transported to the British colonies and is still very much alive in Canada, the United States, Australia, and New Zealand. It has a big impact on our lives in areas such as personal property, contracts, and family relationships. But, valuable as it is, it has certain inherent limitations. At any given time, it is liable to contain conflicting precedents on unsettled points of law, and conflict means uncertainty. It may become very complex as precedents multiply over the centuries, and complexity is another source of uncertainty. Finally, there is no guarantee that the common-law process will produce desirable results. Judges may box themselves in through a series of undesirable decisions and in doing so create an impasse that may take decades or centuries to resolve.

LEGISLATION

One solution to these problems is to codify an existing body of customary law in a way that reveals its principles in greater clarity. An example of this is Justinian's Code, produced in the sixth century AD by order of Justinian, emperor of the surviving eastern half of the Roman Empire. This code systematized the results of a thousand years of Roman customary law, state practice, and imperial edicts. In the early years of the nineteenth century, Justinian's Code served as a model for the French lawyers whom Napoleon had summoned to codify the complex body of French customary law. The Napoleonic Code is an all-encompassing system that forms the basis of law in France as well as in Italy, Spain, and most other European and Latin American countries.[3]

The production of legal codes is a final step toward deliberate control of law. This conscious creation of law is legislation. It may result in a **statute,** which is a particular piece of legislation, or in a law **code,** which is a comprehensive set of interrelated rules.

As might be expected, Canada, deriving from two colonial powers, has a mixed legal system. The private law of the province of Quebec was systematized in the *code civil* of 1866;[4] private law in the other nine provinces remains an uncodified extension of the common law. In effect, there are two systems of private law in Canada, which is reflected in our constitutional provision that three judges on the Supreme Court of Canada must be from Quebec in order to deal with appeals from that province. The criminal law, in contrast, is unified in the Criminal Code, an Act of Parliament passed in 1892 to replace the common law in those matters.

While the concept of legislation has been understood since antiquity, until the last two centuries it played only a restricted role in governmental affairs. However, the modern state now legislates freely in private as well as public law. The general rule is that common law retains its validity until the state displaces it with statutory law. In Canada, large sections of common law have been replaced by legislated statutes or codes. One good example is labour relations. In the nineteenth century, relations between employer and employee were regulated by the common law of contracts, employment being considered the contractual exchange of money for work. But all the provinces of Canada, as well as the federal government, have now replaced the common law with comprehensive labour-relations codes. They have established a framework for collective bargaining—negotiations, strikes, arbitration, certification of bargaining agents, and so forth—which is far different from what existed under the common law.

The expansion of legislation has certain advantages. Legislators can foresee situations and try to prevent conflicts. In contrast, common law adjudication must wait for conflicts to arise. Also, legislation can be created or changed in a relatively short time; in common law it may take decades for solutions to evolve. As well, legislation may offer greater certainty because the law is not inferred from precedent but is clearly laid down.

This certainty, however, is somewhat illusory. However perfectly designed statutes may be, ambiguity of language can never be completely avoided. Also, statutes are soon overtaken by the course of events and need to be adapted to new situations. Continual legislative amendment is not practical; the statutes must be interpreted in particular disputes as they are brought before the courts. A sequence of cases will arise in which the courts will usually follow precedent according to the rule of *stare decisis*. In this way, legislation becomes subject to the same sort of evolutionary forces that guide the development of common law. See Law Focus 6.1 for a discussion of the development of law through delegated legislation.

NATURAL LAW AND HUMAN RIGHTS

Since the time of the Stoics in late antiquity, many writers on law and government have argued that a **natural law** exists that transcends the **positive law** put in place ("posited") by the state and the will of the sovereign. These writers have held that there is an order in the universe that creates certain principles of conduct binding on all human beings, at all times, wherever they live. There are many versions of natural-law theory. Some have an explicitly religious foundation, like that of the thirteenth-century theologian Saint Thomas Aquinas; others are totally secular, like that of the

Law Focus 6.1

Delegated Legislation

In a democracy, the primary source of legislation is the representative assembly, such as the Parliament of Canada or the provincial legislatures. But many of the statutes they pass set up a framework for other bodies to create legally enforceable rules, known as *delegated legislation*. The main forms of delegated legislation are

- **Orders in Council**—Formal decisions of the cabinet.

- **Regulations**—Rules created by a minister of a government department or by an independent agency, such as the Canadian Human Rights Commission.

- **By-laws**—Rules passed by local governments, for example parking ordinances.

All of these forms of delegated legislation are just as much a part of law as the statutes passed by elected assemblies. The courts will enforce them and levy penalties upon people who flout them. But orders in council, regulations, and by-laws have to be made under a grant of authority from the representative assembly; that is, in conformity to a statute giving subordinate lawmaking authority to cabinet, ministers, agencies, or city councils. Thus the assembly remains the ultimate source of all legislation even when it delegates rule-making authority.

eighteenth-century philosopher David Hume. All versions agree that there exists a higher law that can be used as a criterion to judge laws made by the state, and that in certain cases disobedience to the law of the state can be justified by appeal to this higher law. Thus, Thomas Jefferson invoked "the laws of nature and of nature's God" in the American Declaration of Independence, when he justified the rebellion of the 13 colonies against laws made by Parliament.

The terminology of natural law is infrequently used in twentieth-century political discourse, except at the academic level; however, a very similar idea has taken strong new root in the contemporary field of human rights. **Human rights** are the rights that all human beings are supposed to enjoy simply by virtue of being human. Freedom of religion, freedom to marry and have children, and freedom from torture and arbitrary imprisonment are examples of human rights that are widely accepted in theory (though often violated in practice). These and other such rights are held up in the international community as standards against which the laws and practices of nations are evaluated, and governments that violate them come under pressure to conform. The idea that a constitution is a proper restraint upon the lawmaking ability of the state—this issue will be explored in depth in the next chapter—is also rooted in the tradition of natural law and human rights.

What natural law and human rights have in common is the view that law is not just the command of the sovereign enforced by the machinery of the state, and that the state can be held to account before higher standards of morality.

LAW AND SOCIAL CHANGE

As shown in Figure 6.1, common law and legislation are two different expressions of social ideas about right conduct. The former emerges from conflicts of action, while the latter is created according to deliberate plan, but both rest on the people's conception of what is just.

Should the law lead or follow social change? Any answer must take into account the distinction between judge-made law and legislation. Normally, judges are a conservative force in society, both in developing common law and in interpreting legislation. The rule of *stare decisis* tends to make them look to the past for guidance. While in office they are deliberately (and with good reason) insulated from political pressure and public opinion, and this may partly blind them to social change. For example, the common law acted as a brake on organized labour long after the labour movement had become so powerful that it needed more adequate legal recognition. The solution of collective bargaining finally came through legislation rather than through the evolution of common law. In this instance social change clearly ran ahead of the law until remedial legislation was introduced.

However, the judiciary can also be an innovating force ahead of public opinion. For example, the Ontario Court of Appeal held in 1992 that "sexual orientation" is protected by Section 15(1) of the Charter of Rights and Freedoms, even though these

Figure 6.1 The Social Origins of Law

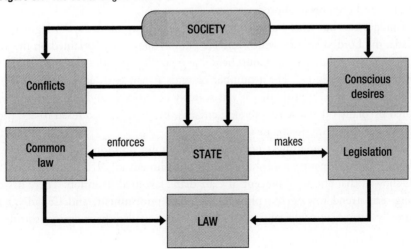

words are not found in the text, and that the Canadian Human Rights Act must be interpreted so as to conform to this reading of the Charter.[5] Section 15(1) reads:

> Every individual is equal before and under the law and has the right to the equal protection and equal benefit of the law without discrimination and, in particular, without discrimination based on race, national or ethnic origin, colour, religion, sex, age or mental or physical disability.

The text does not mention sexual orientation; in fact, the drafters deliberately decided to omit it, fearing that controversy might jeopardize ratification of the Charter. Note, however, that the wording "without discrimination and, in particular, without discrimination based on . . ." is open-ended; that is, the nine explicitly prohibited grounds of discrimination are to be construed as examples, not as an exhaustive list. Gay-rights organizations were successful in persuading the court that sexual orientation is implied in the phrase "without discrimination" even though it is not included in the list of prohibited grounds of discrimination. Groups advocating the rights and interests of gays and lesbians thus won a victory that had long been denied them in Parliament. Political ratification came in 1996, when Parliament passed legislation to make sexual orientation a protected criterion under the Human Rights Act.

Later in the 1990s the courts led again in this area in the province of Alberta, whose human rights act did not mention sexual orientation. In the 1999 *Vriend* case, the Supreme Court of Canada held that sexual orientation must be "read into" the act to make it conform to its previous interpretation of s. 15 of the Charter. Public opinion in Alberta appeared to be opposed to this change before the Supreme Court rendered its decision, but accepting of it afterward. It seems that on many issues an authoritative court ruling is enough to tip public opinion in one direction. The courts have led the evolution of public opinion about gay rights in Canada by generally being one step ahead, most recently by ruling in favour of gay marriage. If, on the other hand, they had been too far ahead, their rulings might have provoked widespread resistance and even been ignored.

If judges can be either behind or ahead of public opinion, so can legislators. In Canada, the Lord's Day Act, which forbade Sunday shopping, remained on the books until 1985, when the Supreme Court held that it conflicted with the Canadian Charter of Rights and Freedoms.[6] For a number of years it had been apparent that the law had become so anachronistic that it was scarcely enforceable and was routinely being ignored by many otherwise law-abiding citizens. But legislators refused to act, preferring to leave this emotional issue to the courts.

Yet legislators sometimes move ahead of public opinion; for example, when Parliament held free votes abolishing capital punishment in 1976 and again in 1987, polls showed that about 70 percent of Canadians favoured retention. There has been a long-term trend toward less physical forms of punishment, and Canadians may eventually turn decisively against the death penalty, as they have against torture and flogging. But in 2001, 52 percent of respondents to an Ipsos-Reid poll still favoured capital punishment in Canada.[7] Yet that majority in public opinion is unlikely to be translated into the restoration of capital punishment because of contrary views among media and political elites. Particularly in cases where the law does not affect the everyday lives of most people, public opinion is less relevant than the views of those who are more influential in making the law.

Experience suggests that law may be a little behind or a little ahead of popular feeling without causing much trouble; but if the discrepancy becomes great, signs of distress will appear. The law will be widely disobeyed, and escalating levels of coercion will be needed for enforcement. This shows that law does indeed come from society and is not just the command of the sovereign. Neither legislators nor judges are immune to the danger of losing touch with citizens; but, in a sense, the two groups can act to balance each other. Legislators can replace outmoded common law, while judges can help adjust legislation to social change.

Questions for Discussion

1. Is natural law an empirical or a normative concept? Why?

2. Changing the law through judicial interpretation is sometimes faster than waiting for legislation to be passed. If that is an advantage of judicial change, can you think of any advantages of legislative change?

3. Can you identify three areas in which you think Canadian law has not kept up with social change?

Internet Links

1. Department of Justice Canada: **http://canada.justice.gc.ca.** By following the links, you can get access to all Canadian federal legislation.

2. Civil Code of Quebec: **www.lexum.umontreal.ca/en/ccq.** Complete text (in English) of Quebec's unique body of civil law.

3. Supreme Court of Canada decisions: **http://scc.lexum.umontreal.ca/en.** You can quickly read recent decisions by typing the name into the search engine. For example, try *Vriend,* the Alberta gay-rights case mentioned in the chapter.

4. United States Department of Justice, Bureau of Justice Statistics: **www.ojp.usdoj.gov/bjs.** Capital punishment is mentioned in this chapter as an area where Canadian legislation seems to have been at variance with public opinion. This site gives statistics about the use of capital punishment in the United States.

Further Reading

Benson, Bruce L. *The Enterprise of Law: Justice without the State.* San Francisco: Pacific Research Institute for Public Policy, 1990.

Bogart, W. A. *Consequences: The Impact of Law and Its Complexity.* Toronto: University of Toronto Press, 2002.

———. *Courts and Country: The Limits of Litigation and the Social and Political Life of Canada.* Toronto: Oxford University Press, 1994.

Bork, Robert. *The Tempting of America: The Political Seduction of the Law.* New York: Simon and Schuster, 1990.

Borovoy, A. Alan. *When Freedoms Collide: The Case for Our Civil Liberties.* Toronto: Lester and Orpen Dennys, 1988.

Boyd, Neil. *Canadian Law: An Introduction.* Toronto: Harcourt Brace, 1995.

Brierly, John E. C. "Quebec's Civil Law Codification Viewed and Reviewed," *McGill Law Journal 14,* 1968, pp. 521–89.

Friedland, Martin L. *A Place Apart: Judicial Independence and Accountability in Canada.* Ottawa: Canadian Judicial Council, 1995.

Hart, H. L. A. *The Concept of Law.* 2nd ed. Oxford: Clarendon Press, 1994.

Hogue, Arthur R. *Origins of the Common Law.* Bloomington: Indiana University Press, 1966.

Horner, Jessie. *Canadian Law and the Canadian Legal System.* Toronto: Pearson Education Canada, 2006.

Leoni, Bruno. *Freedom and the Law.* Los Angeles: Nash Publishing, 1972.

Loughlin, Martin. *The Idea of Public Law.* Toronto: Oxford University Press, 2004.

Marshall, T. David. *Judicial Conduct and Accountability.* Scarborough, ON: Carswell, 1995.

McCormick, Peter, and Ian Greene. *Judges and Judging: Inside the Canadian Judicial System.* Toronto: Lorimer, 1990.

Merryman, John Henry. *The Civil Law Tradition: An Introduction to the Legal Systems of Western Europe and Latin America.* Palo Alto, CA: Stanford University Press, 1969.

Morton, F. L., ed. *Law, Politics and the Judicial Process in Canada.* 3rd ed. Calgary: University of Calgary Press, 2002.

Paciocco, David M. *Getting Away with Murder: The Canadian Criminal Justice System.* Toronto: Irwin Law, 1999.

Roberts, Julian V., and Loretta J. Stalans. *Public Opinion, Crime, and Criminal Justice.* Boulder, CO: Westview Press, 1997.

Tremblay, Luc B. *The Rule of Law, Justice, and Interpretation.* Montreal: McGill–Queen's University Press, 1997.

Waddams, S. M. *Introduction to the Study of Law.* 3rd ed. Toronto: Carswell, 1987.

CHAPTER 7

Constitutionalism

A **constitution** is a set of fundamental rules and principles by which a state is organized. These rules and principles generally:

a. establish the powers and responsibilities of the legislative, executive, and judicial branches of government,

b. allocate powers to different levels of government, such as federal, provincial, and local,

c. enumerate the rights of citizens in relationship to each other and to the government, as in a bill of rights, and

d. stipulate a procedure for amending the constitution.

The term *fundamental rules* is used advisedly, because a constitution comprises not only laws that are enforceable in the courts but also customs, or conventions, that are enforceable chiefly in the sense that a government may lose political support by violating them. A **convention** is a practice or custom that is consistently followed by those in government even though it is not legally required. According to a leading authority, a convention is not just any custom that happens to be observed. To be considered a convention, a practice must exist for a good reason and those who follow it must be aware that they are following a rational rule.[1]

Conventions exist at several different levels; there are strong ones that are essential to the constitution, and weak ones that are really no more than usages. For example, it is essential in a parliamentary democracy that the head of state confide the task of forming a government to a politician who commands a working majority in the representative assembly; otherwise the democratic principle of majority rule would be jeopardized. This convention is of the strongest type. In contrast, there is little or no intrinsic importance to the practice, rigorously followed in Canada, of the Commons adjourning to the Senate to witness royal assent to legislation. The head of state could just as well perform this function in private, as is done in Quebec and Australia. This convention is of the weakest type and could be changed on short notice without damage to the Constitution.[2]

Although useful, the distinction between law and convention is not as solid as it appears, because courts have no power to enforce anything unless judges are obeyed by those who control the coercive apparatus of the state. This obedience is itself no more than a convention (albeit of the strongest type) based upon politicians' belief that public opinion wishes the courts to be obeyed.[3] In the last analysis, law and convention are two related manifestations of the same spirit of constitutionalism and the rule of law.

THE UNWRITTEN BRITISH CONSTITUTION

The older type of constitution, which used to be very common but now survives in only a few countries such as Great Britain and New Zealand, is usually called **unwritten.** It is essential for Canadians to have some understanding of the unwritten British Constitution, for it is the source of our own. The term *unwritten* is not really accurate, for most of the British Constitution is written down. But it is not written down in a single place; rather, it must be pieced together from many different sources. "Unwritten" in this context really means uncodified. Also, there exist as part of the British Constitution many conventions that are not written down at all.

Much of the British Constitution consists of statutes of the King-in-Parliament. The oldest such text is the ***Magna Carta*** (Great Charter), which King John was forced to sign in 1215, before Parliament even existed, and which was later adopted by Parliament in statutory form. It established the principle that the sovereign had to rule within the law of the land. Further restrictions on royal power were established in the Bill of Rights (1689), which, among many other provisions, prevented the Crown from levying taxes without the consent of Parliament. The Act of Settlement (1701), as well as fixing the succession to the throne, protected the independence of judges by making it impossible for the king to dismiss them without cause. The Parliament Act (1911) imposed several restrictions on the powers of the House of Lords and in doing so strengthened the Commons.

These, and many other statutes passed over hundreds of years, make up the legal framework of the British Constitution. But more than statutory law is involved. Since statutes always raise problems of interpretation when they are applied, the body of case law that has developed around the statutes must be considered part of the constitution. Also, the very existence of Parliament rests not on statutes but on the common law or **prerogative** powers of the kings who first established the practice of calling Parliaments for consultation. In an important sense, the statutory structure of the British Constitution has a common-law foundation.

Many of the most important institutions of British government rest not on law but on convention. The cabinet and prime minister are mentioned briefly in some statutes, but the offices have never been deliberately created by legislation. Similarly, it is conventional that the Crown not refuse assent to a bill passed by Parliament, that the leader of the majority party be invited to form a cabinet, and so on.

This short sketch of the British Constitution suggests one of its important characteristics—flexibility. The written part—that is, the constitutional law—is no different from any other type of law; all law, constitutional or otherwise, may be changed by an act of Parliament. An act of Parliament cannot be unconstitutional as long as specified procedures are adhered to, and Parliament could free itself from existing procedures if it chose. Constitutional conventions are even more flexible than constitutional law, since they are essentially usages that are constantly evolving. This peculiar flexibility of the British unwritten constitution has led some observers to say that it is not a constitution at all; and indeed it may be thought of as a synonym for the ensemble of governmental institutions at any given moment.

THE AMERICAN WRITTEN CONSTITUTION

The British Constitution differs strikingly from the American one, which is the world's oldest surviving written constitution. The core of the U.S. Constitution consists of one systematic, deliberately designed document drawn up at the Constitutional Convention in Philadelphia in 1787. In fewer than 6,000 words this text arranges the legislative, executive, and judicial powers of the state; divides government into federal and state levels; and deals with some other necessary matters. The rights of the individual are enumerated in the Bill of Rights, which are the first ten amendments to the Constitution after its adoption. The amending process was intentionally made arduous, so that the Constitution could not be lightly changed by the transitory desire of whoever happened to be in power. Amendments must be approved by a two-thirds majority in both houses of Congress and subsequently ratified by three-quarters of the states. Not surprisingly, this very difficult procedure has been used successfully only 27 times since 1787.

The difficulty of the process is illustrated by the strange history of the proposed Equal Rights Amendment (ERA): "Equality of rights under the law shall not be denied or abridged by the United States or by any State on account of sex." Congress approved the ERA in 1972 and set a period of seven years for ratification by three-quarters of the states. When only 35 of the 50 states had ratified the amendment by 1978, Congress extended the deadline to 1982;[4] but even with the extension, the approval of the requisite 38 state legislatures was never obtained, thus killing the ERA.

This rather rigid amending process has not hampered constitutional evolution in the United States as much as might be expected, because the courts have taken on the function of declaring the meaning of the Constitution in specific applications. A large body of case law has grown up that is indispensable to understanding the Constitution; this case law is flexible in much the same way as common law. For example, the U.S. Supreme Court held in 1896 in *Plessy v. Ferguson* that it did not conflict with the Constitution for states to require racially segregated coaches on railway trains.[5] According to the court, as long as the facilities were "separate but equal," the situation did not violate the equal protection clause of the Fourteenth Amendment. But in 1954, the same court departed from this precedent in the famous case of *Brown v. Board of Education,* holding that segregated schools were necessarily injurious to the minority and thus contrary to the Fourteenth Amendment principle of equal protection of the law.[6] Strictly speaking, the Supreme Court did not overrule *Plessy v. Ferguson;* rather, it distinguished *Brown v. Board* from the earlier precedent because it dealt with education rather than transportation. But the political effect was the same as a change in the constitution. The point here is that the U.S. Constitution is, to a large extent, what the courts say it is.

Although *convention* is not used as a technical term in American constitutional law, there is inevitably something like it in the U.S. Constitution. The power of the courts to declare legislation unconstitutional is not mentioned in the text of 1787. Chief Justice John Marshall first claimed this right in the seminal case of *Marbury v. Madison* (1803); it ultimately rests on the acquiescence of Congress.[7] Another example was the practice established by George Washington, the first president, that no chief executive should serve more than two terms. This precedent was followed until World War II, when Franklin Roosevelt, citing the dangerous international situation, chose to run for a third and then a fourth term. His violation of the practice touched off such a reaction that the Twenty-Second Amendment, ratified in 1951, officially wrote the two-term principle into the constitution. Usage, having proved insufficient, was translated into constitutional law.

The contrast between the British and American Constitutions is instructive. The former is unwritten and flexible, the latter written and rigid. The former can be amended by simple statute, the latter only by an elaborate amending process. Judicial decisions play a role in both but have a far larger role in the American model, where they supply the flexibility that is missing in the constitutional text.

THE CANADIAN HYBRID

The Canadian Constitution may be seen as a blend of the written and unwritten models. Although there is no central, systematic document of the American type, the Canadian Constitution does have a substantial written core. As with the British model, this core consists of a series of statutes enacted over a long period of time; but, contrary to the British Constitution, these statutes can no longer be amended or repealed by a simple act of Parliament. See Canadian Focus 7.1 for a further comparison of the Canadian and American constitutions.

The starting point for finding the written constitution is now the Constitution Act, 1982. Schedule I to the Act lists 30 statutes and orders-in-council (i.e., formal decisions of Cabinet), some Canadian and some British in origin, that are now assured of constitutional status and can therefore be amended only by approved procedures. The most important of these 30 items is the British North America (BNA) Act, 1867, now renamed the Constitution Act, 1867. This British statute created the Dominion of Canada in 1867, and set up the federal system as well as the legislative, executive, and judicial institutions of government, all of which exist today. Many of the 30 items consist of amendments to the BNA Act made by the British Parliament at the request of Canada

Canadian Focus 7.1

Constitutional Preambles

The preambles to the American Constitution and to the Canadian Constitution Act, 1867, give some idea of the differences between the two documents. Note that the American preamble characterizes the making of the Constitution as an act of "the people," whereas the Canadian preamble is an introduction to a piece of British legislation, which is an act of the Crown taken with the advice and consent of Parliament. The people as such do not figure in the British/Canadian model. Also, the American preamble describes a new legal construction, whereas the Canadian preamble emphasizes continuity ("a Constitution similar in Principle to that of the United Kingdom").

Preamble to the American Constitution

We the People of the United States, in Order to form a more perfect Union, establish Justice, insure domestic Tranquility, provide for the common defence, promote the general Welfare, and secure the Blessings of Liberty to ourselves and our Posterity, do ordain and establish this Constitution for the United States of America.

Preamble to the Constitution Act, 1867

WHEREAS the Provinces of Canada, Nova Scotia, and New Brunswick have expressed their Desire to be federally united into One Dominion under the Crown of the United Kingdom of Great Britain and Ireland, with a Constitution similar in Principle to that of the United Kingdom:

And whereas such a Union would conduce to the Welfare of the Provinces and promote the Interests of the British Empire:

And whereas on the Establishment of the Union by Authority of Parliament it is expedient, not only that the Constitution of the Legislative Authority in the Dominion be provided for, but also that the Nature of the Executive Government therein be declared:

And whereas it is expedient that Provision be made for the eventual Admission into the Union of other Parts of British North America. . . .

between 1867 and 1982. These amendments have all been restyled the Constitution Act, 1871, or 1940, or whichever year applies. Other scheduled items include the statutes and orders-in-council by which Canada was enlarged to its present boundaries—for example, the Manitoba Act, the British Columbia Terms of Union, and the Alberta and Saskatchewan Acts. These have all retained their original names. Finally, there is the Statute of Westminster, 1931, a piece of British legislation by which Britain renounced the right to legislate for Canada except to amend the Canadian Constitution—a duty that Britain retained by necessity until 1981, when the federal government and all provinces except Quebec reached agreement on an amending formula.

The Constitution Act, 1982, not only lists and confirms the pre-existing parts of the written Constitution but also introduces important new substance, particularly in the first 34 sections, known as the Canadian Charter of Rights and Freedoms. In establishing limits to the powers of the federal and provincial legislatures and governments, the Charter has radically transformed the nature of the Constitution, which previously did not contain any statement of the fundamental rights of Canadians. Civil liberties such as freedom of religion and speech, and political rights such as the right to vote and run for office, are now enumerated and entrenched in the Constitution. This in turn has enhanced the political power of the courts, which are the natural interpreters of the Constitution.

The rest of the Constitution Act, 1982, addresses aboriginal and treaty rights of Native peoples, future constitutional conferences, ownership and control of natural resources, and—most importantly for this discussion—the process to be followed in amending the Constitution. Before 1982, some parts of the written Constitution could be amended only by the British Parliament. The normal procedure was for a joint address of the Canadian Senate and House of Commons to request that the king or queen have the British Cabinet introduce the needed amendment into the British Parliament—a request that was never refused. Although the mechanics of the procedure were under federal control, it became a matter of convention to seek provincial agreement to amendments affecting the provinces. This usually but not always meant getting the unanimous consent of the provincial governments.

Queen Elizabeth II and Prime Minister Pierre Trudeau sign the Constitution Act, 1982.
The Canadian Press

The Act has transferred constitutional amendment from the realm of convention to that of law. There are now three main ways of changing the Canadian Constitution:

1. For certain fundamental matters, such as the existence of the monarchy and the composition of the Supreme Court, the agreement of all provincial legislative assemblies must be added to that of the Senate and the House of Commons; this is the **unanimous procedure.**

2. Most other questions fall under the **general procedure**—there need only be resolutions of the legislatures of at least two-thirds of the provinces, containing among themselves 50 percent of the population of the provinces, and the consent of the Senate and House of Commons.

3. A third option, sometimes called the **bilateral procedure,** exists for situations that affect only one province. In such a case, approval is required from the legislature of the province in question as well as from the House of Commons and the Senate. The bilateral procedure was used in 1993 to entrench official bilingualism in New Brunswick, in 1997 to remove the constitutionally guaranteed rights of Newfoundland's church-administered schools, and in the same year to change Quebec's school system from a religious to a linguistic basis.

In all three procedures, the Senate has only a suspensory veto. In other words, if the Senate does not agree to the resolution, it can be proclaimed by the governor general if it is passed again by the House of Commons after a waiting period. This happened in the case of the Newfoundland schools amendment. The amendment was rejected in the Senate the first time around, but then passed a second time in the House of Commons after the required six-month waiting period, so it acquired constitutional force without ever being passed by the Senate.

Quebec refused to ratify the 1982 constitutional amendments for several reasons. It was not in the interest of the Parti Québécois, which governed Quebec at the time, to sign on to any form of renewed federalism, for that would have conflicted with its own hopes for separation. But opposition in Quebec went far beyond Parti Québécois circles. At the procedural level, many Quebeckers claimed (although the Supreme Court of Canada disagreed) that their province held a veto under a constitutional convention requiring unanimous provincial consent. At the substantive level, many francophones objected to the fact that the Charter, by guaranteeing certain rights of official-language minorities, reduced traditional provincial powers over education and language.

25 YEARS OF CONSTITUTIONAL POLITICS

Quebec's refusal to ratify the Constitution in 1982 touched off a decade of gruelling constitutional conflict in Canada. In a legal sense, the Constitution Act, 1982, applied to Quebec, but in a political sense Quebec was left "outside the Constitution." The Progressive Conservatives incorporated this fact into their 1984 electoral strategy in

Quebec, offering to obtain further constitutional amendments that would satisfy the demands of the francophone majority for more provincial power. The first result was the Meech Lake Accord of June 23, 1987, which responded to a list of demands submitted by Premier Robert Bourassa of Quebec. Initially, Meech Lake seemed certain to gain the approval of all provinces, but opposition gradually developed, especially after former prime minister Pierre Trudeau condemned it. In the end, the Accord failed when Manitoba and Newfoundland did not ratify it within the required three years.

Premier Bourassa then took several dramatic steps. He announced that Quebec would not participate in further constitutional conferences and demanded that Ottawa and the other nine provinces prepare an offer to Quebec. Then, as a threat to spur the rest of Canada into action, he had the Quebec National Assembly pass a law requiring the province to hold a referendum in 1992. If the offer from the rest of Canada was considered satisfactory by a legislative committee, the referendum could be on acceptance or rejection of that offer; if the offer was unsatisfactory in terms of meeting Quebec's demands, the referendum would be on sovereignty (i.e., some form of separation from Canada).[8]

A long and arduous process of public consultation led to the Charlottetown Accord of 1992, an immensely complicated package of constitutional amendments responding to demands from many regions and special interests within the country as well as from Quebec. In prior decades, ratification by Parliament and the provincial legislatures of the agreement reached at Charlottetown would have been automatic, but one of the main indictments of the Meech Lake agreement was that it had been negotiated without public consultation. It now seemed that the only politically feasible way to approve the Charlottetown Accord was by a national referendum.

The referendum on the Charlottetown Accord was held on October 26, 1992. Quebec held a separate referendum under its own rules on the same day, but the question was the same everywhere. The Accord was defeated in six provinces (British Columbia, Alberta, Saskatchewan, Manitoba, Quebec, and Nova Scotia), with 55 percent of Canadians voting no. This result was surprising, because the Accord was supported by the federal government, the three main federal political parties, all 10 provincial governments, the major Aboriginal organizations, and most of the big corporations, labour unions, and newspapers in Canada.

The Accord was defeated partly because outside Quebec it was perceived as being too generous to Quebec, and in Quebec as being not generous enough. If those had been the only reasons, Canada might now be dangerously polarized and on the verge of breaking apart. But it also seems that many voters, both in and outside of Quebec, were put off by the nature of the Accord. Its length and complexity made it almost impossible to understand; moreover, it was in many respects incomplete—an agenda for further negotiations rather than a conclusive agreement.

One result of these events was the introduction of the popular referendum as an additional means of ratifying constitutional amendments. Although it is not legally required at the federal level, it is now mandatory in the provinces of Alberta and British Columbia; and it seems unlikely that Parliament and the provincial legislatures will ever again attempt to ratify major amendments without first getting approval in a referendum. This will make formal amendment of the Constitution more difficult, because, as shown by the fate of the Charlottetown Accord, even when the political class can agree among itself, the Canadian people will not necessarily accept the results of that agreement. With the formal amending process now in gridlock, it seems likely that Canada will have to rediscover the virtues of the British tradition, which allows for substantial constitutional evolution through legislation, adjudication, and convention.

Indeed, constitutional evolution has continued in an incremental way since the defeat of the Charlottetown Accord. The bilateral procedure has been used three times to pass amendments affecting bilingualism in New Brunswick and the school systems of Newfoundland and Quebec. In 1996 the House of Commons passed resolutions on constitutional amendment and distinct society that gave Quebec some of what it had desired, even if not entrenched in the Constitution. There have also been federal–provincial agreements on employment training and the funding of social programs, again responding in a partial way to some of Quebec's original demands, though not with constitutional amendments as such.

Most recently, the Conservative government of Stephen Harper, first elected in January 2006, has tried to reform the Senate not through a formal constitutional amendment but through legislation to set a fixed term of office for senators and to establish a mechanism of popular election to advise the prime minister on appointing senators. But at the time of writing, the Conservative bills had not got the approval of Parliament, in part because the Liberal opposition, which controls the Senate, insisted that if the Senate was to be reformed, it had to be through constitutional amendment rather than ordinary legislation.

JUDICIAL INTERPRETATION

Whatever happens with the formal amending procedures, the most important mechanism of constitutional change in Canada now is judicial interpretation. This has been true since 1867 with respect to the allocation of powers between the federal and provincial governments as set forth in Sections 91 to 95 of the Constitution Act, 1867. It is only by virtue of court decisions that we know, for example, that the federal government has the power to legislate a national system of wage and price controls under conditions of economic emergency.[9] This is the case even though such power is not specifically mentioned in the Act itself. Since 1982, the interpretive function of the courts in constitutional matters has become much wider because the Canadian Charter of Rights and Freedoms, which is a constitutional text, covers so much territory. The courts now not only allocate power (i.e., rule whether the federal or provincial government has the right to legislate on a particular matter) but also deny power (i.e., rule whether a federal or provincial government may abridge freedom of the press, or take away the right to vote, and so on).[10] Canada is now very close to the United States in the extraordinary importance of the courts in defining what the Constitution means.

In another way, however, we remain close to Great Britain. The Preamble to the Constitution Act, 1867, states that Canada desires to have "a Constitution similar in Principle to that of the United Kingdom." These words have imported into Canada a large body of British constitutional convention relating to the use of the royal prerogative, the appointment of a prime minister and cabinet, the need to maintain support in the House of Commons, and many other matters. The working machinery of parliamentary government in Canada is largely based on these conventions. Because the Constitution Act, 1867, does not even mention the words *prime minister* and *cabinet,* an uninformed reader of the Act might conclude that the governor general and the Queen's Privy Council for Canada were the chief executive authorities in Canada. Even in 1867 that was far from true, and it is not at all true today. But the outmoded language of the written constitution is meaningful because it is supported by many conventions, such as the existence of Cabinet as the working committee of the Privy Council and the reliance of the governor general upon the advice of cabinet ministers.

CONSTITUTIONALISM

All constitutions, whether of the British unwritten, the American written, or the Canadian hybrid type, ultimately manifest an underlying attitude or spirit of **constitutionalism.** This is the belief that government is not the controlling force of society but an instrument within it. It exercises the powers of authority and coercion for the general welfare by doing things that other agencies cannot do; but it is still part of society, not elevated above it. It is, to use another common expression, a **limited state.** The constitution expresses government's limitations by stipulating which powers will be exercised by which person or body. Perhaps more importantly, it also states which powers are not to be exercised by anyone in government but are to be left to the people, such as the power to decide how to worship. The constitution of an unlimited state would be mere camouflage, for if government could do whatever it chose, its actions would not be restricted by rules and its discretion would be complete.

RULE OF LAW

Closely related to constitutionalism and the limited state is the concept of the **rule of law.** This phrase is more readily understood if it is approached as a shortened form of the ancient expression, "the rule of law, not of men." It means that, to the greatest extent possible, people should not be subject to the unhindered discretion of others, but that all—rulers and ruled alike—should obey known, predictable, and impartial rules of conduct. It is a shield that protects citizens against the abuse of power "by laying down a set of procedures governing the use and alleged misuse of coercive power."[11] It has always been part of the Canadian Constitution to the extent that the Constitution was "similar in Principle to that of the United Kingdom," and it has now been made explicit in the short preamble to the Charter: "Whereas Canada is founded upon principles that recognize the supremacy of God and the rule of law." We can distinguish several layers of meaning in the idea of the rule of law.

Maintenance of Law and Order

At the most elementary level, the government must maintain law and order so that people are, as much as possible, prevented from attacking each other. The enforcement of law in this sense allows us to count on security of person and property. Yet it is not enough for sovereigns to restrain us from despoiling each other if they themselves are not so restrained. Simple law and order must be complemented by restrictions upon government itself. The ideal of the rule of law leads logically to constitutionalism and the limited state.

No Punishment without Law

The subject should be liable to punishment by government only for violation of law. "No punishment without law" (*nulla poena sine lege*) is an old maxim of English common law. It prevents rulers from using their coercive power arbitrarily against those who are the object of their dislike. People cannot be punished just for who they are; they must commit specified acts that violate known laws. This aspect of the rule of law is an important safeguard of individual freedoms because it means that people are free to do anything not explicitly forbidden by law. The opposite of this principle is exemplified in the following 1935 law of the German Nazi regime:

> Any person who commits an act which the law declares to be punishable or which is deserving of penalty according to the fundamental conceptions of a penal law and sound popular feeling, shall be punished. If there is no penal law directly covering such an act it shall be punished under the law of which the fundamental conception applies most nearly to the said act.[12]

Under such broadly drawn provisions, one could be punished for any action disliked by someone in authority. The meaning of the rule of law is entirely subverted, even if the form of legislation is preserved.

Discretion

Not all government activity can be reduced to impartial enforcement of rules. There is also the large and important element of **discretion.** This flexibility to decide something within the broader framework of rules appears in law enforcement when the judge assigns a sentence to a convicted offender, and is even more prominent in the service activities of the state. If government is to defend the country from external enemies, it must have discretion to locate military bases in suitable spots, choose effective weaponry, and promote capable officers. If government is to build roads, it must plan their location, acquire land, and let contracts for grading and construction; none of these things can be achieved without discretion.

But discretion need not be complete; it can and must be hedged with limiting rules. Government, for example, must have the discretion to acquire land; but there can be rules ensuring that owners will be compensated at fair market value and that they may appeal to the courts if they are dissatisfied with the state's offer. Similarly, government's discretion in letting contracts can be controlled by requiring contractors to tender bids in an open competition. The rule of law requires that where governmental discretion is necessary, it should be exercised within a framework of rules that discourage arbitrary decisions and offer recourse if such decisions are made.

Government Subject to Law

Government and its employees must be as subject to law as the people who are ruled. This is the great principle that was established in the English-speaking world by the *Magna Carta*. It means today that the powers of government must be founded on either common law or legislation. For example, it may seem necessary in the interests of national security to open the mail of individuals suspected of treasonous or seditious activities; yet this is a power that common law gives neither to government nor to private citizens. If it is to be exercised at all, the rule of law requires that it be explicitly approved by legislation setting forth the appropriate conditions. If postal surveillance is carried on without legislative authorization, government employees are in effect acting outside the law, and this is contrary to the rule of law. See Law Focus 7.1 for a discussion of the Supreme Court's role in the rule of law.

Recognized Procedure

Law must be made by known and accepted procedures and is binding only if these procedures are followed. In the common-law system, if a judge violated accepted rules of procedure—for example, by not allowing one side to speak—the resulting decision would be reversed on appeal and would not become a precedent contributing to the law. Similarly, legislation can be created only if Parliament follows all its rules of procedure. An attempt by the House of Commons to legislate without the assent of

Law Focus 7.1

The Supreme Court and the Rule of Law

The foundational case on the rule of law in Canada is *Roncarelli v. Duplessis*.[13] In 1946, when Maurice Duplessis was premier and attorney general of Quebec, he ordered the Quebec Liquor Commission to revoke the liquor licence of Frank Roncarelli, who owned a small restaurant in Montreal. The only reason given was that Roncarelli, an active Jehovah's Witness, had furnished bail money for other Witnesses who had run afoul of Quebec's laws against distribution of religious literature. The Supreme Court of Canada ultimately concluded that Duplessis had acted without legal authority, because Roncarelli's religious activities were unconnected with the statute under which his liquor licence had been granted. Duplessis was required to pay financial compensation to Roncarelli for the damage caused to his business. His position as premier did not confer on him any immunity for actions taken outside the law.

The 1985 *Operation Dismantle* case extended judicial enforcement of the rule of law even further.[14] A coalition of peace groups known as Operation Dismantle tried to use the courts to prevent testing of cruise missiles in Canadian airspace, arguing that such testing violated the "security of the person" guaranteed by Section 7 of the Charter, in that it made war and attack on Canada more likely. The testing took place under an order-in-council pursuant to Canada's participation in NATO. Although the Supreme Court of Canada refused Operation Dismantle's request for an injunction to halt the cruise tests, it ruled that orders-in-council are governed by the rule of law and must conform to the Constitution, as interpreted in judicial review.

This was an important ruling, for orders-in-council are the chief means by which the political executive acts in a parliamentary democracy. Thousands are passed every year in Canada in the course of meetings of federal and provincial cabinets. Operation Dismantle reaffirmed the principle that those who control the government are not above or beyond the law.

the Senate and the governor general would be contrary to the rule of law. Of course, these legislative procedures are not immutable; they are contained in the Constitution, which can be amended. But amendment itself requires that fixed procedures be followed, as illustrated by the Parliament Act (1911) in Great Britain.

This statute was introduced at the time of a political stalemate created when the Conservative-dominated House of Lords repeatedly rejected economic-reform legislation introduced by the Liberal government and passed in the House of Commons. The Act proposed to reduce the power of the House of Lords in approving legislation to a suspensory veto; this amounted to a fundamental amendment to the British

Constitution. The House of Commons initiated the change, but it could not become effective until it had been approved by the House of Lords itself. If the Lords had not acquiesced, King George V, on the advice of the cabinet, would have appointed to that House enough new members committed to the change to tilt the balance in favour of the Act. In so doing, the king would have been acting legally, as the power of appointment is among the British monarch's discretionary powers. The point is this: a constitution may be changed in virtually any direction, but the rule of law requires that the amendment be made according to recognized procedures.

Freedom and the Rule of Law

The rule of law as described in the preceding passage is tightly connected to individual freedom. A free society is possible only if the rule of law is more or less adhered to. Although it may seem paradoxical, freedom is the consequence of law, not its opposite. "We are all slaves of the law," said Cicero, "that we may be free."[15] Rules of conduct make possible a stable, ordered society in which we can plan our lives with reasonable expectations about how others will respond to our initiatives. Freedom to drive a car depends on a complex set of rules of the road, control of property depends on rules of ownership, and so on.

Normally we think of law in a negative way—as a restraint on our behaviour—but law also has its positive side. It restricts the behaviour of some to violate social rules but enables the rest of us to maximize our freedom of action. If lawbreakers were not restrained, they would use fear and intimidation to limit the freedom of others. A society that lives under the rule of law uses coercion selectively in order to prevent individuals from coercing each other. The result is enhanced freedom for all who abide by the laws.

The protection of liberty under law is not complete until the protecting power, the sovereign, is itself bound by constitutional restraints. James Madison, who drafted the American Constitution, wrote that "in framing a government which is to be administered by men over men, the great difficulty lies in this: you must first enable the government to control the governed; and in the next place oblige it to control itself."[16] Hence, the maintenance of a free society depends ultimately on deference to the constitution and a refusal to amend it except by a procedure that is itself part of that same constitution.

Of course, no society manages to live up to the ideal of the rule of law at all times. Perpetrators of crimes sometimes go unpunished, and innocent people may be punished for actions they did not commit, as happened in Canada to Donald Marshall, David Milgaard, and Guy-Paul Morin—three men accused and convicted of murder but later found to be innocent. The wealthy or the well placed may succeed in skirting the law by exerting personal influence. Those in government may use their position to obtain special privileges for themselves. But an ideal is no less important if it is not fully adhered to; things, after all, would be much worse if no one even tried to live up to it. An ideal still retains its validity as a means of judging the performance of government.

It is also important that the rule of law offer means to redress injustices. Roncarelli finally received payment for damages from Duplessis; Marshall, Milgaard, and Morin were finally released from prison; the Japanese Canadians who were interned during World War II finally received an apology and compensation. It would have been better if these injustices had never taken place, but it is asking too much of human institutions to expect that grave mistakes will never be made. At least, when the rule of law is honoured as a principle, it is possible to correct those mistakes.

CONCLUSION

Constitutionalism can be a forbidding subject. Constitutions bristle with complex clauses and difficult language; and when the courts develop abstruse legal doctrines to tell us what the constitution really means, understanding may get harder rather than easier. Nonetheless, the underlying idea of constitutionalism is simple. The state, which enjoys a monopoly of legitimate violence, must be limited so that those who control the state do not use its power arbitrarily for their own advantage. A limited state makes individual freedom possible. When government is held within the bounds set by the constitution, people can plan their own lives without fear of arbitrary incursions into their own sphere of decision making.

Questions for Discussion

1. Would Canada be better off if our political conventions were written into the Constitution?

2. Can you give an example from current public affairs where you think the rule of law is not being observed?

3. Approving constitutional amendments by means of referendum has the obvious virtue of demonstrating popular consent. Can you think of any possible negative aspects to using the referendum procedure?

Internet Links

1. The Solon Law Archive: **www.solon.org.** A veritable treasure trove, giving access to all Canadian constitutional documents listed in the schedule to the Constitution Act, 1982, plus subsequent amendments; the Meech Lake and Charlottetown Accords; and constitutions of several other countries, including the United States, Mexico, and Australia.

2. Richard Kimber's Political Science Resources: **www.psr.keele.ac.uk/const.htm.** Texts of past and present constitutions of all the world's countries.

3. The Constitution Society: **www.constitution.org.** All sorts of information about the United States Constitution.

4. The Constitution Society: **www.constitution.org/cons/usstcons.htm.** Texts of the constitutions of all the American states.

5. Liberty Library of Constitutional Classics: **www.constitution.org/liberlib.htm.** Large collection of online texts of classic works on constitutionalism and political philosophy.

Further Reading

Ajzenstat, Janet, et al., eds. *Canada's Founding Debates.* Toronto: Stoddart, 1999.

Alexander, Larry, ed. *Constitutionalism: Philosophical Foundations.* Cambridge, UK: Cambridge University Press, 1998.

Beard, Charles Austin. *The Supreme Court and the Constitution.* Mineola, NY: Dover Publications Inc., 2006.

Cardinal, Linda, and David Headon, eds. *Shaping Nations: Constitutionalism and Society in Australia and Canada.* Toronto: University of Toronto Press, 2002.

Cook, Curtis, ed. *Constitutional Predicament: Canada after the Referendum of 1992.* Montreal: McGill–Queen's University Press, 1994.

Cummings, Milton C., Jr., and David Wise. *Democracy under Pressure: An Introduction to the American Political System.* Orlando: Harcourt, 1996.

Dicey, A. V. *Introduction to the Study of the Law of the Constitution.* 10th ed. London: Macmillan, 1959.

Hayek, F. A. *The Constitution of Liberty.* Chicago: Henry Regnery, 1960.

Heard, Andrew. *Canadian Constitutional Conventions: The Marriage of Law and Politics.* Toronto: Oxford, 1991.

Hogg, Peter W. *Constitutional Law of Canada.* 4th ed. Scarborough, ON: Carswell, 1997.

Hurley, James Ross. *Amending Canada's Constitution: History, Processes, Problems and Prospects.* Ottawa: Canada Communication Group, 1996.

Hutchinson, Allan C., and Patrick Monahan, eds. *The Rule of Law: Ideal or Ideology.* Toronto: Carswell, 1987.

James, Patrick, Donald E. Abelson, and Michael Lusztig. *The Myth of the Sacred: The Charter, The Courts, and the Politics of the Constitution in Canada.* Montreal: McGill–Queen's University Press, 2003.

Jennings, W. Ivor. *The British Constitution.* 4th ed. Cambridge, UK: Cambridge University Press, 1961.

Knopff, R., and F. L. Morton. *Charter Politics.* Scarborough, ON: Nelson Canada, 1992.

Licht, Robert A., ed. *Is the Supreme Court the Guardian of the Constitution?* Washington, DC: AEI Press, 1993.

Mandel, Michael. *The Charter of Rights and the Legalization of Politics in Canada.* Rev. ed. Toronto: Thompson Educational Publishing, 1994.

Manfredi, Christopher. *Judicial Power and the Charter: Canada and the Paradox of Liberal Constitutionalism.* Toronto: McClelland & Stewart, 1993.

McIlwain, Charles Howard. *Constitutionalism, Ancient and Modern.* Rev. ed. Ithaca, NY: Cornell University Press, 1947.

McWhinney, Edward. *Constitution-Making: Principles, Process, Practice.* Toronto: University of Toronto Press, 1981.

Milne, David. *The Canadian Constitution.* Rev. ed. Toronto: James Lorimer, 1991.

Monahan, Patrick. *Meech Lake: The Inside Story.* Toronto: University of Toronto Press, 1991.

Russell, Peter H. *Constitutional Odyssey: Can Canadians Become a Sovereign People?* Toronto: University of Toronto Press, 2004.

Sheldon, Charles H. *Essentials of the American Constitution: The Supreme Court and the Fundamental Law.* Boulder, CO: Westview Press, 2002.

Webber, Jeremy H. A. *Reimagining Canada: Language, Culture, Community and the Canadian Constitution.* Kingston, ON: McGill–Queen's University Press, 1994.

CHAPTER 8

International Order

by James F. Keeley

"May you live in interesting times" is an ancient curse. More colloquially, we might say that a good year for creating interest in international relations is like a good year for undertakers. As a coherent thematic unit of time, the twentieth century lasted from the start of World War I (1914) to the end of the Cold War and the collapse of the Soviet Union (1991). It was followed by a hiatus of sorts. With September 11, 2001, the new century burst upon us, and it, too, promises to be interesting. Many of the forces and phenomena now at work are not really new, however, but are ongoing developments partially obscured in the past by a focus on the East–West struggle—the Cold War—as a defining theme of the last 50 years.

This chapter's first section will delineate the concept of international political order, as embodied in the **"Westphalian system"** of international relations. It will then explain how major approaches to thinking about international relations have dealt with this system. The second section will look at phenomena that complicate this thinking and challenge this Westphalian order. The third section will briefly consider some ideas about what this could mean.

THE INTERNATIONAL POLITICAL ORDER

Earlier in this text, "government" was treated as a mechanism for the making of public decisions—decisions binding upon a whole community. If we think of "government" as simultaneously creating, maintaining, changing, and reflecting a given political order—that is, a pattern of who makes decisions, about what, for whom, on what basis, and how—we can readily see that the political order within a state will often be very different from the order between states. Even this phrasing—"the order between states"—itself reflects a certain way of thinking about international relations as the Westphalian system of states.

The Westphalian System

The term *Westphalian system* takes its name from the Treaty of Westphalia. Signed in 1648, this treaty ended the Thirty Years' War among the major European powers. It is often cited as marking the emergence of the modern state system. What are some of the defining features of this order?

First, it inaugurated the domination of the modern, sovereign state as the primary unit of action and analysis in international relations. While other units might exist (city-states, religious groups, and the like), the state, with its central claim of dominant, independent jurisdiction over a defined territory, is taken as the key unit of international relations. Although states will differ significantly in their power—their capability for action—and some (the Great Powers) will play special roles in the **international order** (in essence dominating the decisions taken), all states are nonetheless taken as legal equals, with the same rights and duties within the international system. Since the system is composed of sovereign states, no one state is able to demand, as a matter of law, the subordination of the others. As well, states in the Westphalian system are generally supposed to observe a norm of non-intervention, or non-interference in each other's domestic affairs. In the specific sense that it lacks a centralized government, the Westphalian system of states is by definition an **anarchic** realm ("anarchy" in this context means order arising from mutual coordination rather than central command). This characteristic has given powerful states their central role in the international political order, since there are only limited instruments, including the use of force, to make decisions in this sort of system, or to enforce them. Thus, if the domination of the state, the norm of sovereignty, anarchy, and the role of Great Powers are associated with the Westphalian system, so is a place for the use of force in both enforcing and challenging decisions made in this order.

Within this system, international law, diplomacy, and international organizations and regimes play notable roles as devices for the management of relations among states. **International law** may be defined initially as the body of rules that states observe among themselves. While it is tempting to associate "law" with the mechanisms we observe within a well-ordered domestic society, and to see the concept of international law as self-contradictory, this would be a mistake. Because it is decentralized, the international system must use other means in its legal system than does a domestic society. States create and consent to laws between them, through negotiating and signing treaties and through customary law (practices that are seen as either legally obligatory or legally permitted). There is no central legislating mechanism, though some people think or would like to think that the United Nations fulfills this role. States enforce the law themselves; the international system is one of self-help. However, most states also observe the law most of the time because they have an interest in resolving, or at least controlling, their disputes with each other. Even in time of war, international law may be present; for example, laws of combat try to control the violence that states inflict on each other, and the status of prisoner of war is protected by law.

We often think of law, including international law, as a set of commands, but it is much more than this. International law lends order to the international system by creating formal rules and conditions to govern the relationships and interactions of the actors. Think of playing Monopoly if you had the board, the markers, and the dice, but no rules. International law tells the actors who they are, what capabilities and duties they have (for example, whether and to what degree they might be **"international legal persons"**), and how they are related to other actors of varying types. It indicates to actors what they must do, what they should not do, and what they can do if they wish. It provides a mutually intelligible set of concepts by which disputes may be set forth, and sometimes resolved, and a variety of mechanisms (including negotiations, arbitration, and resort to a court, such as the International Court of Justice) that states might use to try to resolve their differences. Traditionally, by treating sovereign states as the key units in international relations, international law formalized their primacy. Other units, such as groups and individuals, would be treated as subordinate to their states; and states, applying the rule of non-intervention, would not normally interfere in the domestic behaviour of another sovereign state toward its own people. (Nationals of one state in the territory of another might, however, have some protection, and this in the past has given powerful states a means of intervening in other states.) While the twentieth century saw some dramatic developments in the rights given to individuals under international law, and in the development of intervention to defend human rights, the dominance of the sovereign state is still a major foundation principle of the international legal system.

Diplomacy is a system of formal, regularized communication among states that allows them to conduct their business with each other more readily. States exchange diplomatic missions, establish consulates to help their nationals travelling abroad, negotiate treaties, and hold international meetings to discuss common problems and try to reach agreed solutions. Much of this system is enshrined in international law, for example, through the Vienna Conventions on diplomatic relations and on consular relations. These set out in detail the rights (including immunities) and the duties of diplomats and consular officials, and the obligations of states hosting diplomatic missions and consulates of other countries. A violation of these laws is regarded very seriously, since it could strike at the heart of the processes by which states carry on their day-to-day relations with each other.

While the Westphalian system initially stressed states, the twentieth century saw the rise of other mechanisms of international order—international organizations and regimes. An **international organization** is a formal body, usually based on a founding charter or statute (essentially a treaty) signed by member states. These organizations may act within specific issue-areas in accordance with the grant of authority, and through the organs and the processes provided in their charters. The **World Trade Organization** and the World Health Organization are two examples of limited-purpose organizations that operate globally; others, however, such as regional economic development banks, may operate only in a certain part of the world. Other organizations, such as the United Nations, may operate globally but have a broad scope of activities. The Organization of American States similarly undertakes a wide range of activities, but on a regional (Western Hemisphere) basis. While such organizations are not states, and do not enjoy the full range of rights and duties of states under international law (that is, full "international legal personality"), they have at least limited rights and duties, and thus have at least some aspects of "international legal personality."

An **international regime** refers to a broader pattern of cooperation within a specific issue-area. Such regimes may include international organizations, but also may have other components. For example, the nuclear non-proliferation regime, which attempts to stop the spread of nuclear weapons, includes formal organizations such as the International Atomic Energy Agency (IAEA). One of the IAEA's functions is to "safeguard" the peaceful nuclear activities of states, trying to ensure that these are not used to manufacture nuclear explosives. It does this, in part, under the terms of the Non-Proliferation Treaty (NPT), but not all IAEA members have signed the NPT. In addition, some states have formed the Nuclear Suppliers Group (NSG), an informal grouping of states that attempts to coordinate their policies on the export of nuclear goods and services and to establish additional safeguards. And individual states, such as Canada, have their own nuclear export and cooperation policies. All of these various actors and groupings, rules and functions, form the complex whole called the *nuclear non-proliferation regime.* Such complex sets of actors of various types, rules, and agreements exist in a number of other issue-areas as well, marking efforts by some portion of the broader set of states to manage their relations in these various areas.

Thinking about the Westphalian System: Realists, Liberals, and Structuralists

Scholars trying to understand international relations resort to theories to simplify and strengthen their understanding of the basic phenomena, forces, and patterns they see. These theories will differ from each other depending on what aspects of international relations they see as important. In the case of international relations, three broad approaches of this sort are **Realism, Liberalism,** and **Structuralism.** They provide very different views of the nature and future of the Westphalian system.

Realists stress the dominant role of the sovereign state and the anarchic character of the system of states. They view this system as inherently uncertain and threatening, with the threat of force an underlying constant, so that each state is strongly concerned with its own survival and may see any other state as a potentially dangerous competitor. Because the system is one of self-help, no state may rely completely on another for the protection of its interests. Those state interests—above all survival—are assumed to attach to the state as a whole working through its government rather than being simply the interests of more specific groups within the state. States are generally assumed to respond rationally to this environment, and those that do not are assumed to be in danger of disappearing. This view of the world is often traced by Realists to such earlier thinkers as the Greek historian Thucydides, the Italian political philosopher Niccolò Machiavelli, and the English political philosopher Thomas Hobbes. The latter's description of a "state of nature" prior to society, in which the life of man is "solitary, poor, nasty, brutish and short," is sometimes taken (a bit incorrectly) by Realists as applicable to the state system. Leading modern Realists have included Hans Morgenthau, Henry Kissinger, Kenneth Waltz, Joseph Grieco, and Stephen Krasner.

In this sort of world, Realists attach great importance to the distribution of power, especially military power, among states—the "structure" of the international system. They see states as sensitive to gains and losses relative to other states, and to shifts in the distribution of power. Balancing power—trying to prevent any one state from gaining dominance over all the others in the international system—is a fundamental objective of diplomacy according to Realists. So, however, may be seeking to dominate. Sensitivity to the distribution of power and to changes in that distribution may limit the ability of states to cooperate with others even in situations where all might gain from cooperation. Realists question the ability of international law, international organizations, and regimes to limit the fundamental competition of states. For them, the international political order tends to reflect the will of the powerful, and thus changes with the distribution of power. The prevailing order of the world must be agreeable to those most able both to sustain and to challenge it.

The structure of the system may be **multipolar,** indicating that several states are in the ranks of the Great Powers. The pre–World War II world, in which Britain, France, Germany, Italy, the Soviet Union, Japan, and the United States were all considered Great Powers, is an example. If these Great Powers are able to cooperate with each other (as, for a time, occurred in the Concert of Europe in the nineteenth century), then the international order might be relatively peaceful. If they cannot, there is danger of major war among them, as was the case with World Wars I and II. A **bipolar** system is one in which two states clearly stand above the others, and compete (or cooperate) with each other to shape and manage the world. The Cold War between the United States and the Soviet Union is an example. Finally, in a **unipolar** world, one state is dominant. Since the collapse of the Soviet Union, we are often said to be in a unipolar world, with the United States as the dominant power. While this may be the case, events since the end of the Cold War also illustrate the possibility that even a dominant power may be unable simply to do whatever it wants.

Liberals have tended to emphasize those aspects of international relations that maintain order and especially peace—international law, diplomacy, and international organizations and regimes—and that may work more to the benefit of all than the competitive situation seen by Realists. Liberals have also tended to stress developing phenomena they see as strengthening peaceful relations among states, including economic linkages (such as trade and investment) working potentially to everyone's advantage, and transnational non-state actors (of which we will say more below). Liberals also see the spread of democracy as helping to create a more peaceful world. Drawing on the work of the German philosopher Immanuel Kant, they suggest that democracies are less prone to wage war—at least on each other—because the people who will pay the costs of such fighting are those who control the decision for war or peace. They also point to increasing concern with human rights and the environment as requiring and producing greater cooperation among international actors. One prominent Liberal was Woodrow Wilson, president of the United States during World War I. Leading modern Liberal scholars include Charles Beitz, Michael Doyle, and Robert Keohane.

Both Liberals and Realists may see the operation of a **security dilemma** in the interactions of states. It seems obvious that a state should take all necessary measures to protect itself, but the reality is not so straightforward. The actions a state takes in self-protection may alarm others, and lead them to take countermeasures even where no threat to them was intended. Their countermeasures may in turn cause alarm and further action in the first state. This action–reaction cycle may spiral into an arms race, suspicion, preparations for conflict, and even war. This is an example of the prisoner's dilemma game described in Chapter 1, in which the ruthless, short-sighted pursuit of self-interest may make everybody worse off. If the players could break out of this spiral, all could be more secure at lower costs. Liberals see international organizations and regimes as ways of dealing positively with such situations to the benefit of all. They point to arms-control treaties between the United States and the Soviet Union, such as SALT (1972 and 1979), START I and II (1991 and 1993), and multilateral agreements to halt the spread of weapons of mass destruction (the NPT in 1968, and the Chemical Weapons Convention, in force 1997) as examples. Realists may see the possibility, but suggest that states are reluctant to trust each other, so that such spirals are always possible. Moreover, they would point out that, sometimes, "the other guy really is out to get you"—that is, the problem is not simply one of misunderstanding.

Realists think very much within the terms of the Westphalian system, to the point of discounting non-state actors such as international organizations or even the constraining effects of devices such as international law. Liberals, while broadly accepting the state as a major actor, have been more open to the role of other actors and to the beneficial effects of international organizations, international regimes, international law, and increased interdependence (especially economic relations) between states.

The third school of thought, Structuralism, holds that economic relations, not military–security relations, are primary. Reflecting this position's origins in Marxist social and economic theory, Structuralists see relations among states as reflecting both economic competition among them and also the strength of particular economic classes within states. Lenin's theory of imperialism sought to explain both the expansion of the European colonial empires and the outbreak of World War I in terms of struggles for advantage among competing capitalist classes directing their respective state governments. More recently, Structuralist thinking has been dominated by a focus on problems in the economic development of Third World states. It sees the problems these states face as stemming from the way these less developed states have been connected to the world economy (often a reflection of a colonial history), and how these economic relations create social and political conditions within developing states that may hinder or affect their economic development or skew the internal distribution of economic benefits and political power. International economic institutions, such as the World Bank, the International Monetary Fund, and the World Trade Organization—seen by Liberals as part of the solution to world economic problems—are seen by Structuralists as reflecting the domination of rich, capitalist states, and thus as part of the problem. While Structuralist thinking has somewhat gone out of favour with the end of the Cold War, it addresses major recent issues of economic relations between the Third World and developed states, and within the Third World itself. Major recent Structuralist thinkers include Immanuel Wallerstein, Robert Cox, Johan Galtung, and André Gunder Frank.

Differences among these three schools are also found in thinking about the forces driving the foreign policy of individual states. Realists tend to assume an overriding national interest—an interest of the country as a whole—especially in survival. Domestic divisions may threaten the ability of a state to successfully pursue its objectives in a threatening, competitive world. But who defines the national interest, and how? And who selects the instruments used to pursue it? Liberals, aside from seeing greater opportunities for mutually beneficial cooperation among states than Realists do, may be more attentive to the domestic political process that shapes how governments arrive at their definition of policy interests and their selection of policy instruments. Structuralists stress the importance of economic interests—and of powerful domestic economic actors—in shaping the foreign policies of specific governments. They will also argue that the policies pursued by governments—whether domestic or foreign—are likely to reflect the concerns of these powerful domestic interests, rather than some concept of the "true" interest of the country as a whole.

In practice, domestic politics and foreign policy are often closely linked, since any government must have the backing of a significant element of its politically relevant population. This cannot simply be assumed, even in time of war. The Japanese attack on Pearl Harbor in Hawaii united all but the most die-hard American isolationists behind U.S. participation in World War II, but the Vietnam War was bitterly divisive in the United States. As for the U.S.–led humanitarian intervention in Somalia in the 1990s, it took only a few combat deaths before the American public asked why the United States was there, and the U.S. largely withdrew. The same is true in economic affairs: the policy of a particular state toward free trade may reflect not simply a general sense of the economic interest of the country as a whole, but also the strength in domestic politics of particular economic groups and regions that stand to gain or lose by such a policy.

DEVELOPMENTS IN THE INTERNATIONAL SYSTEM

The Westphalian system has evolved over the hundreds of years of its existence, but within the last 50 years it has come under an unprecedented variety of pressures. Some of these developments have already been mentioned as departures from a narrow Realist depiction of the international system. For example, the role of the United Nations, especially in terms of collective security and peacekeeping, introduces a new and sometimes very significant actor—if only a secondary one—into international relations, and also points to other transformations at work. Our three theoretical camps usually respond to these developments in predictable ways. Realists, confronting new actors and assertions of the importance of different dynamics and concerns (e.g., human rights, the environment, economic relations), stress the essential continuity of systemic fundamentals: sovereign states, anarchy, uncertainty, self-help, the dominance of military–security issues, and the importance of power. They argue that states, especially Great Powers, and the competitive character of interstate relations remain dominant. Liberals see these new actors and developments either as additional problems to be overcome or as indicators of new possibilities for a stronger, more peaceful international society. Structuralists stress economic globalization as a challenge to developing states, overlooking to a degree the successes of some newly industrializing states (NICs) such as South Korea, Thailand, and Taiwan.

Collective Security, Peacekeeping, and Humanitarian Intervention

Collective security organizations differentiate the twentieth-century international order from earlier forms of the Westphalian system, in which the balance of power was essentially the only mechanism established on a system-wide basis. The nineteenth-century Concert of Europe, developed after the Napoleonic Wars, tried to preserve the peace of Europe through informal means, allowing the Great Powers to moderate their disputes, constrain their competition with each other, and maintain a balance of power among themselves. World War I, however, made this informal approach seem insufficient to preserve peace; and a new, more Liberal approach was instituted through the collective security mechanism of the League of Nations. The League experiment ended in failure, but was revived in a slightly changed form in the United Nations. The very existence of the UN as a universal international organization charged with preserving international peace and security is a challenge to Realism because it is a conscious effort to coordinate state activity in the interests of peace within an anarchical (decentralized) system, although the UN's failures in this quest reinforce Realist thinking.

Collective security must be distinguished from alliances, or **collective defence** organizations, such as the North Atlantic Treaty Organization. An alliance exists to defend its members from threats from outside their group. A collective security system such as that centred on the United Nations tries to deal with threats to peace arising within the group—the UN membership, which includes almost all the world's states. In theory, all UN members have an interest in restraining any of their number that might threaten international peace and security. In reality, the UN Charter gives special responsibilities and powers to the Security Council, including the veto powers of the five Permanent Members (Britain, China, France, Russia—formerly the Soviet Union—and the United States). Only two instances really saw a collective UN response to aggression: the Korean War (1950–53) and the first Gulf War (1990–91), and in neither case precisely as the UN's founders might have anticipated. The response to North Korea's attack on South Korea was possible only because the Soviet Union, boycotting the Security Council at the time, failed to veto the crucial resolutions. Without American leadership—motivated largely by

Cold War concerns—and American forces, the UN response would have been much weaker. In the Gulf War, a weakened Soviet Union did not block U.S. leadership of a UN–authorized coalition of states, but the UN itself had little control over the course of hostilities.

Peacekeeping, a more frequent and familiar UN activity, developed as a less ambitious sort of operation, though one not really foreseen in the UN Charter. Peacekeeping operations traditionally involved the interposition of symbolic, lightly armed forces between combatants who agreed to stop fighting. Such forces would monitor ceasefires and serve as a buffer between the combatants. They would be present only with the consent of the combatants and would use force only as a last resort and in self-defence. They would not seek to impose a settlement of a dispute on the combatants. Such operations would help to suspend conflicts, keep major powers and neighbouring states from being drawn into direct confrontations, win time for negotiations to settle the underlying dispute, and prevent further bloodshed.

With the end of the Cold War, the UN became involved in many peacekeeping operations not of the traditional state-versus-state kind but rather caused by internal conflicts: civil wars, separatist conflicts, genocidal campaigns, or humanitarian emergencies created or exacerbated by the collapse of a state's government. Such operations (including administering a state or overseeing elections) have been much more complex than simply separating the armies of rival states. In an internal conflict, the factions may be bitter enemies, have little control over their forces, and not control areas easily separable from each other. For these reasons, UN operations in Somalia, Bosnia, and Rwanda were very difficult and widely seen as failures. In some cases, the UN may not wait for permission to intervene—there may be no real government to give permission—but instead may simply declare the situation a threat to international peace and security. In genocidal conflicts, a peacekeeping presence needs to be more willing to use force, not just to defend itself but also to protect innocent civilians. This kind of intervention in a sovereign state without its permission may be the only way to protect its population in a timely and effective manner, but clearly makes weaker states nervous because it overrides the principle of sovereignty, a fundamental element of the Westphalian system, in the name of humanitarian ideals.

The increasing number of internal and humanitarian interventions by the UN and an increased willingness to use force more actively and to ignore the requirement for a state's permission suggest a stronger, more active UN presence. But the Kosovo campaign of NATO states in 1999 and the U.S. invasion of Iraq in 2003 were both undertaken without prior UN authorization, although the Kosovo intervention was effectively legitimized after the fact by the Security Council. The 2003 Iraq War would not qualify as either a collective security operation or a peacekeeping operation.

Both collective security and peacekeeping make heavy demands on the resources and the interests of states. Collective security requires that states be willing and able to mobilize a wide coalition against virtually any state, regardless of their particular or immediate interests. This condition is unlikely to be met—thus the UN's two collective security operations required highly unusual circumstances. Even the demands of peacekeeping can now be considerable, requiring thousands of troops in place in a difficult and dangerous situation for months or even years. Thus, UN forces may be small, slow to arrive, not well-equipped for their particular role, and not readily able to maintain peace in the face of uncooperative local factions. This is one reason why "coalitions of the willing" (as in Kosovo), with or without a Security Council mandate, may become more frequent.

"Globalization," Economic and Otherwise

The term **globalization** refers to the processes and consequences of the increasing ease of movement of goods and services, money, people, and ideas. Here, we look first at the implications of increased economic interdependence among states, and then at some of the other implications of globalization.

In a Realist perspective on international economic relations, the emphasis is on economic capabilities and their contribution to national power: for example, does a state depend significantly on foreign or on domestic supplies of strategic goods such as oil? If it draws primarily on foreign sources, does it have assured supplies or are these readily vulnerable to disruption? A Liberal perspective emphasizes the mutually beneficial properties of economic exchanges, and sees these as presenting powerful incentives for states to preserve peace. Realists stress that economic relations have significant competitive components—states struggle for advantage against each other in the economic as much as the military realm. Structuralists place great emphasis on the economic realm, but question the mutual benefits that Liberals see, and interpret economic relations in terms of class relations. A Structuralist would ask who benefits within a state from its pattern of international economic relations, and which groups across states tend to be favoured by these broad patterns of relations.

Most states are strongly linked to the international economy, a linkage that is becoming more important every year. They export a substantial portion of their overall production, and import a substantial portion of the goods they consume. They borrow from and lend to the world capital market. They are affected by fluctuations in the value of their currencies and the currencies of other states. Repeated financial crises from the oil-price spike of 1973 to the stock market meltdown of 2008 show the importance of the international economy. Participation in the international economy allows states to develop and prosper through mutual exchanges rather than depending solely upon their domestic markets and sources of investment capital. But these international connections complicate the pursuit of legitimate domestic economic policy objectives. For example, if France wishes to stimulate employment by lowering its domestic interest rates—a classic Keynesian policy measure (see Comparative Perspectives 10.1 in Chapter 10)—it may now find that this approach no longer works very well. Increasingly large and fast international movements of capital may negate this policy: French capital may simply move abroad in search of higher rates of return than are available at home. Or domestic political forces may constrain how a state can respond to international conditions. If the Japanese government tries to respond to North American and European pressure to open its market more to foreign goods, it may find itself risking electoral defeat at home. Producer groups seeking shelter from foreign competition—both managements and their workforces—are in effect subsidized by consumers if they enjoy state protection. At the same time, these protected groups may enjoy considerable political power, while removing their protection may create economic dislocations that have political repercussions. These domestic forces and costs of action must be balanced against the pressures that other states, foreign private actors such as multinational corporations, or indeed the international economic system may bring to bear. In the realm of economics, domestic and foreign policies are very strongly connected.

The complex balancing of state interests and domestic and foreign policy objectives is reflected in the institutions of the world economy. The two foundational institutions are the **International Monetary Fund** (created in 1944), and the **General Agreement on Tariffs and Trade** (created in 1947 and replaced in 1995 by the World Trade Organization). The IMF and WTO seek to balance the desires of states to pursue independent domestic economic policies against the benefits of an open international economy. They were formed in large part to avoid repetition of interwar protectionism, which exacerbated the Great Depression and contributed to the outbreak of World War II. A third institution, the International Bank for Reconstruction and Development—known popularly as the **World Bank**—was formed to assist in postwar recovery after World War II, but since then has become a primary source of international aid to developing states.

This balancing of demands and pressures has been a difficult task, with mixed success. Even if states agree on the importance of the world economy, they may not agree on how global economic cooperation should occur. Developed capitalist states tend to favour the freer movement of goods, services, and capital—though with important exceptions (especially in the agricultural sector) where there are strong domestic protectionist forces. Developing states, however, may take another view. Having obtained their independence more recently, they may be sensitive to possible losses of national authority to foreign actors, and so may distrust investment by foreign corporations. Foreign capital can aid development, but the need to pay back foreign loans may bring foreign pressures to follow certain economic policies. Failure to renew those loans at acceptable cost may create a domestic crisis, but the domestic policies necessary to reassure foreign lenders that their money is safe may entail cutting development spending, subsidies, and spending on public services and infrastructure. Third World states may believe that existing patterns of relations hinder development of a more modern manufacturing sector and lock them into a subordinate position as suppliers of raw materials and low-value commodities to developed states.

If states vary in their perceived interests vis-à-vis the international economic system, they also vary in their power to influence it. Here, both Realists and Structuralists emphasize who is best able to exercise power over the choices and policies embodied in the pattern of international economic relations. Realists emphasize states, while Structuralists emphasize classes within and across states. It is probably true that the major buyers and sellers of goods and services, and the major suppliers of international capital, will likely be favoured by the policies adopted in the international economic system—even if the case for broader mutual benefits is strong. As in other areas of international life, the interests and concerns of more powerful actors are more likely to be addressed and acted upon in ways that they find acceptable. Less powerful actors—within states as well as including some states—may not like the results, even where they arguably benefit from them. Just as opening up the domestic economy will create costs and benefits to the advantage of certain favoured groups, the preservation of a more closed economy will favour other privileged groups within a state, who fear the loss of these benefits under more open conditions. While economic globalization complicates the ability of states to pursue their policy objectives, some states, by reason of their international influence and their domestic social, economic, and political character, may be better able to shape and benefit from economic globalization. Indeed, a Realist approach to economic globalization that did not simply dismiss it as irrelevant would expect precisely this.

A number of developing states now find themselves in the ranks of the NICs—the "newly industrialized countries." This creates problems for a Structuralist analysis, for these states have not been locked into a subservient position in the global economy. At the same time, these states have not always followed the Liberal prescription of freeing international economic exchanges and reducing government intervention in the domestic economy. The successes and the problems faced by these states reflect ambitious yet selective government intervention in support of economic development, and also at times a degree of domestic political repression.

Another element of globalization, with implications for economic issues, the distribution of power among states, and the rise of new terrorist threats, is the diffusion of technology. For some kinds of products, this technology is mature, involving no particular innovations in the product or the production process. Access to this technology may require considerable investment to achieve a large scale of production, and it may depend on access to low-wage labour in order to be economically competitive. Textile production is an example of this. For other kinds of products, the technology may be quite new but give some access to relatively small-scale producers. This opens up possibilities for emerging states able to identify and exploit the new technology. Bioengineering might be an example. In still other cases, certain states may be able to offer certain locational advantages—combinations of attractive factors for investment. For example, India has a centre of information technology around Bangalore, exploiting the ready availability of well-trained, English-speaking, computer-literate workers. Malaysia has also encouraged information technology as an engine of national development.

As technology spreads, and as developing states increase their technological capabilities, these states may become more powerful militarily. India and Pakistan, for example, have nuclear weapons production capabilities, and are developing ballistic missile capabilities. This affects their relations not only with each other but also with other states in the South Asia region. Much of the basic technological capability for producing and delivering weapons of mass destruction (WMD) is relatively mature: chemical weapons date from World War I, and biological and nuclear weapons from World War II, while many Third World ballistic missile capabilities are based on 1950s-era Soviet SCUD technology. The production of these weapons and their delivery systems is not a trivial exercise, but it involves problems of engineering and manufacturing, not basic science. Developed states—above all the United States—still have a significant lead in weapons technology, but they have to respect the existence of even a relatively primitive WMD capability.

This maturing of weapons technology has generated fears that WMD could be exploited by non-state actors, such as transnational terrorist groups. In 1995, one quasi-religious cult group in Japan, Aum Shinrikyo, released a form of nerve gas in the Tokyo subway system, causing a few deaths and a large number of other casualties. It is clear that al-Qaeda has been interested in acquiring or producing weapons of mass destruction. To date, the most frequent terrorist use of WMD, whether by domestic or international groups, has been in the form of hoaxes. Where actual use has occurred, it has been on a small scale, and/or the weapons themselves have been relatively primitive—suitable more for causing panic than for inflicting large numbers of deaths. Nonetheless, the prospect of terrorist acquisition of WMD—by their own production, by theft, or by cooperation on the part of sympathetic capable states—has to be taken seriously.

While we often think of globalization in economic terms, other forms of contact across national borders are also increasingly important. People, and especially ideas, may move in high volume, with a considerable impact on other states and on relations between states. This heightens the importance of issues of identity—"who are we?" and "who are they?"—in both domestic and international politics. Realists, emphasizing the state, emphasize also the association of an individual with a specific state; for example, we are all Canadians. Liberals, particularly in the area of human rights, tend to emphasize common humanity; that is, we are all human beings. Structuralists, emphasizing class, may ask whether an individual or a group is proletarian or bourgeois. All three, whether implicitly or explicitly, assume that people do, or should, have a single strong identity that will dominate their interpretation of events. In fact, we all are bundles of differing identities, and varying ones may be invoked in varying situations. We also ascribe identities to others. A woman may see herself as a female professional and parent living in Toronto, whereas others may see her as a left-handed Presbyterian dentist in Ontario who belongs to a curling club. Which identity gets invoked as primary, by whom, how, and what consequences follow, are increasingly questions that theorists of international relations must come to grips with (see International Perspectives 8.1 for an example).

International Perspectives 8.1

An example of the complexities that arise in identity issues both domestically and internationally is found in the 2004 decision by the French government to ban "ostentatious displays" of religious affiliation by French schoolchildren. French Republicanism, as an ideology, is strongly secular in character—to the point of being at times not merely anti-clerical but also anti-religious. This reflects a reaction to the power and privileges of the Church in pre-Revolutionary France. France, in part as a consequence of its imperial past, has a significant Muslim population. This government action responded to fears of some other Frenchmen that the French national identity was being challenged by a growing Muslim population. Many French Muslims objected to it because it would prevent female Muslim students from wearing a headscarf as an act of devotion—a common though not universal practice. They saw the ban as particularly targeting them, and as a sign of their marginalization within French society. The ban, therefore, had a deeply divisive effect in French society, as it touched on basic issues of identity—one's own and that of others. To complicate matters further, some "Islamist" groups outside of France, ostensibly acting to support their French co-religionists, attempted to pressure the French government to rescind the ban, including by terrorist means. Many French Muslims, while they resented the ban and fear the forces of xenophobia, also rejected this foreign pressure as compromising their claim to be good citizens of France.

As populations age in Europe, Japan, and North America, other areas of the world struggle to accommodate rising numbers of young people. Migration from one area of the world to another can help ease both difficulties, as people move from areas with low economic opportunity to areas where their skills and labour might be in short supply. From an economic point of view this may make perfect sense, as does the relocation of jobs from high-wage to low-wage areas. Yet economic rationality is not the only force at work in the world, and its logic may be resisted in the name of preserving jobs at home, or of preserving the ethnic character of a state. Germany has used "guest workers," mainly from Turkey, as a solution to its labour shortage, but there are now many German-born ethnic Turks who need to be more fully brought into German society. Turkey's entry into the European Union could, in the eyes of some Europeans, open the floodgates to large-scale migration, which they see as threatening the current ethnic character of Europe. Nor is Canada free from such concerns, though we have more readily embraced the concept of a multicultural society.

Increased movement of people poses one version of the question "who are we?" However, the increased movement of ideas through enhanced communications systems also challenges local identities. The Internet is the most recent way in which communications systems have increased the ability of people to find out about other people and other places. In some cases, this may pose a threat to the control exercised by local governments and elites because ordinary people now have alternative sources of information and analysis. Governments may seek, therefore, to restrict access by jamming radio signals, attempting to control possession of satellite dishes, or blocking access to certain Internet sites. While the means of communication are new, the response—attempting to control access to information—is not. In some other cases, the inflow of information cannot readily be blocked, but the content is seen as more generally threatening to cultural values. Complaints about the dominance of Western, especially American, media have long been put in terms of the "Coca-Colonization" of the world. So, some states may see themselves as under pressure culturally, if not also politically, from an outside and foreign influence that challenges established ideas of morality and behaviour, ideas of what society and government can and should be like, what is economically possible or desirable, how individuals should think of themselves, dress, and behave, and so on. All of these can create a sense of an identity under attack. Cultures may respond to such pressures in a variety of ways: some may seek to isolate themselves; others may welcome the exchange of ideas as invigorating; still others may resent being challenged and may lash out. Which response predominates will be a matter of internal struggle, but may have significant implications for the international behaviour of a state.

Identity politics within states will also have an indirect influence on interstate relations insofar as identity concerns affect the selection of decision-makers, or influence how decision-makers interpret and respond to international events. Here as well, we must resist the temptation to think of identities within countries as homogeneous. Because we all have multiple identities, a specific policy proposal by our own government, or a specific external event, may invoke a number of responses, and our political elites will have to navigate among these—choosing some, balancing the demands of some, rejecting some—in arriving at an ultimate policy choice.

New Actors—and Some Collapsing Old Ones

Although the core of the Westphalian system is the state, other actors have also been of considerable importance in the international system. The activities of international organizations such as the United Nations and other more specialized or regional organizations of states have already been mentioned. Private actors such as multinational corporations are familiar to us all; significant flows of trade and investment occur through their activities. There are other actors, however, whose presence in the international system is of increasing relevance. These include actors broadly categorized as international civil society, and international terrorist organizations. A list of new actors must also include the European Union. Finally, it is apparent, in the phenomenon of **failed states,** that some old actors, individually if not as a type, are collapsing under the weight of the internal and external challenges they face.

Various **non-governmental organizations** are familiar to us as private charities or aid groups, such as Doctors Without Borders (Médecins sans Frontières), and human rights groups, such as Amnesty International. Taken collectively, such groups are now often referred to as "international civil society"—a group of loosely connected organizations, not set up for profit, operating between the levels of the individual and the government. Such groups are increasingly active on international issues—delivering assistance, lobbying state governments and organizations of states, protesting, and so on. We are by now all familiar with the protests that accompany the meetings of the World Trade Organization and the Group of 8. A significant factor in the creation of the Ottawa Convention, which bans the production, stockpiling, and use of anti-personnel landmines, was the activities of such groups, banded together as the International Campaign to Ban Landmines. Together with other actors such as the Red Cross and some sympathetic governments, and support from highly visible public persons such as Lady Diana, the late Princess of Wales, these groups were able to make the problem of landmines a significant international issue. An important part of their strategy was to redefine the landmines problem from being one of dealing with a conventional military weapon—a typical, if dull, problem in arms control and disarmament—to being a global humanitarian crisis. This was accomplished by stressing the tremendous toll in death and mutilation that civilians suffer from landmines, not only during but even long after the conflicts.

Other transnational non-governmental actors are less benign. International terrorism is not a new phenomenon, though most terrorist activities are directed by persons against their own governments. During the Cold War, some terrorist groups operated internationally, such as the Japanese Red Army. Many domestic groups were supported from abroad, through funding, training, and equipment. Sometimes this support was provided by other states; sometimes it came through the activities of private individuals in other states. In recent years al-Qaeda has emerged as the most notorious transnational terrorist organization. However, it operates through loose association with local groups in various states, essentially in networked fashion, rather than as a highly centralized organization coordinating the activities of its members around the world. Such internationally active organizations may even be seen to be waging "private war." That is, they are engaged in a campaign of violence against others, including possibly states, but they are not themselves a state. This is a basic challenge to the Westphalian system, which has attempted to restrict international acts of major violence—"war"—to states, and to treat all other users of violence as criminals.

A point of particular concern for many Western states is that capable international terrorist organizations such as al-Qaeda might gain access to chemical, biological, radiological, or even nuclear weapons. Such a combination could add substantially to the challenge that "private war" poses to the Westphalian system.

Among new non-state actors, the European Union (EU) is particularly significant. The EU has its origins in the creation of the European Coal and Steel Community in 1952, which integrated those industries in France, Italy, Germany, Belgium, the Netherlands, and Luxembourg. Part of the intention was to deal with the economic power of Germany in a non-threatening way. The solution was to so interconnect the basic industries of coal and steel in the six states that they could never go to war with each other again. Over time, the economic and political partnership established has grown both in terms of member states and the sectors of activity it includes. Now, after the Cold War, the EU extends from the Atlantic Ocean to the eastern borders of Poland, the Baltic States (Estonia, Latvia, and Lithuania), and Finland. The EU has a complex structure of governance, including both a system of courts and the European Parliament. EU laws and regulations can override national legislation in a number of areas of government activity, but the member states of the EU retain some freedom of action in significant elements of their policies. Britain supported the United States with troops in the invasion of Iraq in 2003, but France and Germany were strongly opposed to the American action. The EU has reduced the traditional sovereignty or independence of its member states, yet at the same time it is not simply a larger state. In economic terms, the EU is a major actor in the world. In terms of foreign policy and defence, however, its member states have had trouble achieving and maintaining coordination at the international political level or taking joint military action.

Finally, we must note the phenomenon of failed states. When the European colonial empires retreated after World War II, they left in their wake a large number of newly independent states—their former colonies, now established as independent states. Many of these have become strong, stable, capable units, both domestically and internationally. In other cases, however, the apparatus of the state has had great difficulty in establishing and maintaining itself. It took only a matter of weeks after the Belgian Congo achieved its independence in 1960 for it to slide into crisis. The United Nations was active in the new state for four years, trying to stabilize it. Other states, such as Somalia, Liberia, Yugoslavia, or Rwanda, held together for several years on the basis of strong rule by particular individuals or precarious compromises among domestic groups, only to fall apart when the grip on power faltered or the compromise became unsustainable. In other cases, a state may have a central government, but its ability to provide for the welfare of its people may be diminished by corruption, environmental stress, or other such factors, or its ability to enforce its laws may be uncertain in large portions of its territory. The new central government of Afghanistan, for example, must cope not only with the aftermath of decades of war and internal disorder, but also with powerful tribes and warlords. Its ability to enforce its rules beyond its capital, Kabul, is questionable.

Aside from human costs, state failure also presents security dangers to others—disorderly areas on their borders, flows of refugees that may strain local resources, or cross-border linkages with disaffected local groups. Failed states also present temptations for interference or annexation, which in turn could threaten the security of other states. However, efforts to respond to humanitarian crises in such states through intervention to protect populations from widespread disorder or violations of human rights contradict the fundamental principle of state sovereignty. This may be acceptable to strong states, which are most likely to supply the means of such interventions, but it sits uncomfortably with many new states, or weaker states, which fear being on the receiving end of such actions.

Environmental Pressures

Pressures on the environment from increasing population and demand for resources have long been a matter of international concern, as the implications of environmental degradation become clearer. These pressures do not respect international boundaries: acid rain is not stopped by borders, and polluted water may flow through watersheds and affect the entire ocean. Destruction of the forests in one area of the world may also have repercussions elsewhere. The world is a vast, complex ecological system linked by intricate processes. The environment, then, constitutes a global commons, a resource that everyone shares and depends on.

Some environmental changes may have imminent and grave effects. As plants have a relatively limited tolerance for radiation, depletion of the ozone layer could result in massive crop failures. Global warming, caused by the release of greenhouse gases such as carbon dioxide and methane, changes rainfall and temperature patterns. If sea levels rise, low-lying areas along coasts and some islands (including island states) could be flooded. Desertification and changing weather patterns could create shifts in agricultural zones, stimulating local declines in farm production, hunger, and migration. Melting of the Arctic and Antarctic ice caps could threaten the polar bear in the North, and the krill in the Antarctic Ocean that forms the basis of the food chain there. The movements of global currents, such as the Gulf Stream, could also be affected.

The search for solutions to these problems is complicated by their transnational character. They require cooperation by a number of states, yet states are also differently affected by them, and solutions may impose significant and unwelcome costs. Efforts to restore Canada's East Coast fisheries require the cooperation of other states, which must regulate their catches appropriately. Efforts by states to reduce emissions of chlorofluorocarbons—which contribute to ozone depletion—were unsuccessful until the creation of the Montreal Protocol on Substances that Deplete the Ozone Layer in 1987, which coordinated their actions.

The underlying difficulty is one of coordinating action among a number of states, even though some states may resist cooperation because their contribution to the problem is small, because the costs are considerable, or because powerful domestic interests are affected. In Canada, the Kyoto Protocol to reduce carbon emissions has created concern in oil-producing provinces, such as Alberta, which fear that the costs could fall mainly on them. Similarly, the energy industry has been split, with some questioning the very existence of the problem, others accepting it but questioning the costs as a solution is implemented, and still others moving ahead with their own proposals. The situation is the same globally; differing interpretations of state interests, the distribution of costs of action among states, and competition for resources may all inhibit cooperation. What some states regard as necessary measures to preserve the environment or maintain a certain quality of life, others see as a threat to their development or to their current standard of living. While Liberal analyses properly point out the possibility of cooperation, and to some degree also the undesirable consequences of non-cooperation, Realists have correctly shown that such differences among states make cooperation difficult to achieve.

WHAT LIES AHEAD?

Even when current trends seem clear, uncertainties about their balance and interconnection—not to mention the sheer force of contingency—make all predictions vulnerable. Liberals see in the forces of economic globalization and the spread of ideas of democracy the prospect of a more peaceful world—or at least more peaceful *parts* of the world. But economic globalization, the spread of ideas, and the movement of people may, at least in the short term, bring dislocation, unfamiliarity, and feelings of confrontation; and these may make democratization an uncertain prospect in fragile states with a different history and structure from those in the West. Realists stress the dominance of the state, and the fundamental role that competition, uncertainty, and threat play in the interstate system. Yet many states have learned to cooperate, as the EU suggests, and many now view not states themselves but their failure, or transnational ideas or transnational terrorism, as the sources of a new basic challenge to the world. Structuralists point to class conflict, but now lack even the deeply flawed model of the Soviet Union to suggest a real alternative to capitalism. And environmental pressures continue: Liberals may point to the need for cooperative solutions, and Realists to the problems in achieving these, but can either predict that cooperation will be achieved, or if achieved, whether it will be too little too late?

Following the end of the Napoleonic Wars, the victorious European powers met at Vienna to create a new order, the Concert of Europe. This order lasted about a hundred years, collapsing finally in the outbreak of World War I. At the end of that war, the victorious Allied powers met at Versailles and attempted to create a new order, this time including a key international organization, the League of Nations. That order quickly failed, brought down by the Great Depression, a shifting balance of power in Europe and the Far East, and the rise of Fascism as an ideology. At the end of World War II, the victorious Allied powers again met and planned a new world. Again they included an international organization—the United Nations—in a key role. This time, however, international economic institutions—the International Monetary Fund, the General Agreement on Tariffs and Trade, and the World Bank—were founded to deal with international economic relations. Allied unity soon collapsed into the Cold War and the contest between Communism and capitalist democracy as rival social, economic, and political programs, but these institutions, and an order founded on bipolarity and restrained competition, persisted until the collapse of the Soviet Union.

After the fall of the Soviet Union, there was some adjustment of existing international institutions. Both the EU and NATO expanded eastward, and Russia took the Soviet seat in the UN Security Council. But no large-scale reworking of basic institutions has occurred since the end of World War II except the creation of the

World Trade Organization. The UN itself, after apparently showing its value when Iraq invaded Kuwait in 1990, fell into difficulties in Somalia, Rwanda, and Yugoslavia, and was bypassed more or less in the Kosovo crisis of 1999 and used initially but then bypassed in the 2003 invasion of Iraq. To many observers, the U.S. commitment to multilateral institutions is in question. "Coalitions of the willing" provide flexibility, but not the same assurance of stable rules as more established global institutions. NATO, meanwhile, is also a question mark for some, although it has been active in Afghanistan; again, "coalitions of the willing," put together for specific ventures and purposes, are not the same as the Atlantic Alliance.

Economic institutions seem more relevant than ever in the new global economy, but the huge size of international flows of capital—especially currency trading and other short-term flows—dwarfs the resources of the IMF. The World Trade Organization was successfully created as the successor to GATT, and has made progress even in the difficult area of agricultural subsidies, but the strength of protectionist pressures must also be recognized. A slowdown in the world economy, a huge and persistent U.S. current account deficit, and a persistent American need for foreign investment to cover both its balance of payments deficit and its substantial government budget deficit could all complicate both the trade and the monetary systems. Meanwhile, other states, especially developing states, will have to come to grips with the social and political ramifications of open economies and large, fast capital flows. Open economies are beneficial, but the transitional pain they impose may be considerable, and their effects may disrupt local societies and domestic political compromises.

We can foresee some shifting in the distribution of power among states, but the precise pattern is difficult to predict. India and China, although hampered by their less developed economies, can look forward to playing larger roles in the world. But for China this is conditional in part on whether the Communist Party can reconcile an open economy with continued political control. While India has the advantage of a more responsive, democratic government, it is still hampered by economic under-development and the willingness of some political actors to exploit religious divisions. The EU is not yet sufficiently developed and centralized in its political structures to play the role in security and political affairs that its economic weight might lead one to expect. Russia faces enormous political and economic problems as it treads an uncertain path. It faces a demographic decline as health conditions deteriorate, but it remembers its imperial and superpower past. Elsewhere, Brazil and perhaps South Africa (the latter already a major state in Africa) could anticipate a larger role in the world. But Africa is ravaged by AIDS, the human cost of which could wreak havoc economically, socially, and politically.

What of the United States? It is the dominant power in the world today, but as events in the aftermath of the 2003 Iraq War demonstrate, it may pay high costs for unilateral actions. A stable world order, accepted by others as legitimate, could go far to reduce the costs of wielding American influence, but the prospect for this is not clear. Meanwhile, it must cope with the implications of rising powers elsewhere, especially China. While the overall structure of power in the world is unipolar, the American advantage is not so overwhelming that it can ignore all others, especially regionally significant states. Failure to develop a workable global political structure, complete with functional universal institutions, will hamper, not help, American power.

At the start of this chapter, we took the attacks on New York and Washington, D.C. on September 11, 2001, as opening the new century of international relations. It is conventional to assert that everything changed on that day—but perhaps more so for Americans, now aware of their vulnerability, than for others. What makes things different is the scale of the attack, the nature of the perpetrators, and the scale and determination of the American response. But the forces behind those events had been developing for some time. Their coming to fruition in a transnational terrorist movement marks a significant shift in the set of actors in world politics—the emergence of transnational organizations with a vengeance, so to speak. The development of al-Qaeda is based not only on resentment of outside forces bearing on the Middle East, but also upon the great demographic, political, economic, social, and intellectual pressures at work in many areas of the Muslim world. It reflects, that is, not only resentment of the Western role in Middle East politics, but also strong local dissatisfactions. It also reflects significant splits within the Muslim world over how it should respond to those pressures while remaining true to its varied cultural traditions. The real fate of Islamic fundamentalism will be worked out within the Muslim world, not in its relations with the West. Western actions and policies can influence that path, however.

There have been attempts to project grand patterns for the future. One of these, popular especially in the 1990s, looked to the triumph of Liberalism. At least, it was argued, we could foresee a "zone of peace" among liberal–democratic states, though what would go on outside that would likely not be so benevolent. That liberal–democratic states have not fought against each other has been presented as a major empirical regularity in the study of international relations. But the reason for this is disputed. Liberals argue that liberal democracies have no reason to fight each other. Realists, however, point to the calming effect of the external Soviet threat on rivalries amongst the liberal democracies. Absent this external pressure, will these states retain their peaceful cohesion? Even if this vision is sustainable within the ranks of liberal–democratic states, it leaves open the fate of the rest of the world, where the brutal forces of history presumably continue to hold sway. Nor does it deal adequately with the ramifications of the relations between this "zone of history" and the "zone of peace."

A rival view, especially powerful in the wake of September 11, 2001, is Samuel Huntington's "clash of civilizations." This suggests that the clash of states is no longer the primary force of world politics, but rather lines of conflict between whole cultural groups. Huntington's identification of China (Sinic civilization) and Islam now resonates significantly with those concerned about the future of American power and about the so-called War on Terror. His thesis has been challenged, however, on various grounds, such as his at times peculiar identification of his "civilizations" (the West, Latin America, Africa, Islam, Sinic, Hindu, Orthodox Christian, Buddhist, and Japanese); his tendency to treat internally complex cultural units as if they were monolithic; a tendency to overlook both the extensive interpenetration of cultures and their evolution over time; and fear that his analysis could be a dangerous self-fulfilling prophecy. Two curious aspects of his argument, however, seem to go unnoticed by both those who seize upon and those who criticize it. First, his objective was precisely to prevent or at least mitigate such a clash—for example, by arguing that "the West" must see itself as simply one civilization among many, not as a universal standard. Second, a main driving force of this "clash" seems to be demographic: the availability of large numbers of otherwise unemployed young men, whose fears, discontents, and energies make them a fertile recruiting ground for extremism. As this demographic group declines, he seems to suggest, the problem should abate. Even if a clash of civilizations is one possibility in our current disorderly world, a significant policy objective should surely be to try to avoid it.

Existing theories—especially those drawing too readily on a state-centric, military-security model of international relations—will likely prove insufficient to explain the kind of world that we as scholars, citizens, and policymakers will face. What is coming? We do not know—but it is likely to be interesting!

Questions for Discussion

1. Realists tend to stress the anarchic aspect of world politics, while liberals tend to find significant elements of order. In what senses might both be correct? What would this suggest about international relations?

2. Are states really in decline as the dominant actors in international relations?

3. Would you prefer to see Canada build up its conventional military forces, or put more emphasis on peacekeeping? Are these necessarily incompatible goals?

Internet Links

1. Canada, Department of Foreign Affairs and International Trade: **www.dfait-maeci.gc.ca.**

2. Governments on the World Wide Web: **www.gksoft.com/govt/en.**

3. U.S. State Department: **www.state.gov.**

4. United Nations: **www.un.org.**

5. International Monetary Fund: **www.imf.org.**

6. World Trade Organization: **www.wto.org.**

7. Global Security Organization: **www.globalsecurity.org.**

8. American Society of International Law: **www.asil.org.**

9. Columbia International Affairs Online: **www.ciaonet.org.**

10. BBC: **www.bbc.co.uk.**

Further Reading

Acharya, Amitav, and Alastair Iain Johnston, eds. *Crafting Cooperation: Regional International Institutions in Comparative Perspective.* Cambridge, UK: Cambridge University Press, 2007.

Benhabib, Seyla, Ian Shapiro, and Danilo Petranovich, eds. *Identities, Affiliations, and Allegiances.* Cambridge: Cambridge University Press, 2007.

Burhenne, Wolfgang E., and Nicholas A. Robinson, eds. *International Protection of the Environment: Conservation in Sustainable Development.* Dobbs Ferry, NY: Oceana Publications, 1995.

Damrosch, Lori Fisler, Gennady M. Danilenko, and Rein Mullerson. *Beyond Confrontation: International Law for the Post–Cold War Era.* Boulder, CO: Westview Press, 1995.

Frederick, Howard H. *Global Communication and International Relations.* Belmont, CA: Wadsworth, 1993.

Halliday, Fred. *Rethinking International Relations.* Vancouver: University of British Columbia Press, 1994.

Hay, Robin. *Military and Security Institutions: Challenges in Development and Democratization.* Kingston, ON: Centre for International Relations, Queen's University, 1994.

Howard, Lise Morjé. *UN Peacekeeping in Civil Wars.* Cambridge, UK: Cambridge University Press, 2008.

Jackson, Robert H., and Alan James. *States in a Changing World: A Contemporary Analysis.* Oxford: Clarendon Press, 1993.

Klare, Michael T., and Daniel C. Thomas, eds. *World Security: Challenges for a New Century.* New York: St. Martin's Press, 1994.

Neufeld, Mark A. *The Restructuring of International Relations Theory.* New York: Cambridge University Press, 1995.

Nierop, Tom. *Systems and Regions in Global Politics: An Empirical Study of Diplomacy, International Organization and Trade, 1950–1991.* Chichester, UK: Wiley, 1994.

Palin, Roger H. *Multinational Military Forces: Problems and Prospects.* Oxford: Oxford University Press, 1995.

Smith, Courtney B. *Politics and Process at the United Nations: The Global Dance.* Boulder, CO: Lynne Rienner, 2006.

Sterling-Folker, Jennifer, ed. *Making Sense of International Relations Theory.* Boulder, CO: Lynne Rienner, 2006.

Williams, Howard, Moorhead Wright, and Tony Evans. *A Reader in International Relations and Political Theory.* Vancouver: University of British Columbia Press, 1993.

PART 2
Ideology

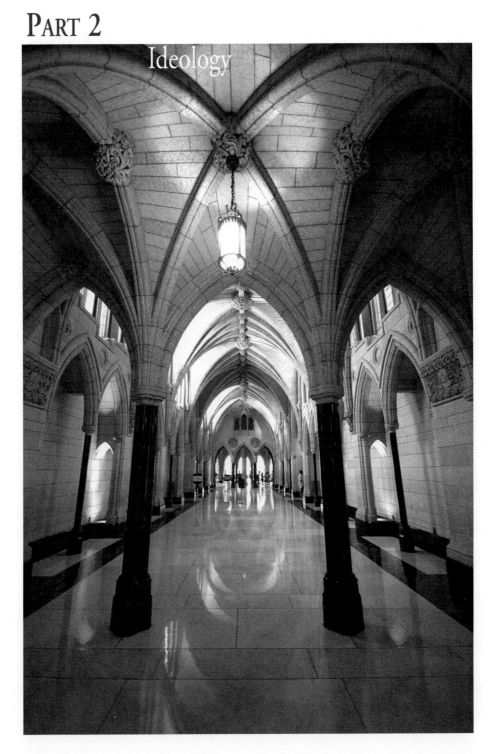

CHAPTER 9
Ideology

Part One showed that government's authority and legitimacy rest on a network of beliefs about human nature, society, and the purpose of government. Speculation about these matters—known as *political philosophy* or *political theory*—was the first aspect of political science to emerge, having been cultivated by the Greek thinkers of classical antiquity. What is said of philosophy in general—that "all philosophy is a footnote to Plato"—is equally true of the special field of political philosophy. All the great issues were already addressed in the writings of Plato and his pupil Aristotle.

Plato (ca. 429–347 BC) made a distinction that is still crucial to the study of political beliefs. He distinguished between *episteme,* which we might translate as true, well-founded knowledge, and *doxa,* or opinion. **Episteme** is knowledge that can be demonstrated by logical argument from first principles; **doxa** is an opinion that may be at least partly true but that believers cannot fully expound. They accept it because they have confidence in its source. To take a nonpolitical example, consider the proposition that the earth revolves around the sun. We all know this to be true, but few of us can justify our belief except by referring to the authority from whom we learned it. Only a scientifically instructed minority can develop the proposition from the first principles of physics; the rest of us accept it as *doxa.*

Political philosophy deals with both *episteme* and *doxa.* It tries to achieve *episteme* by uncovering valid first principles and making deductions from them. It also studies the *doxai* found in society to determine whether they are logically coherent and whether they stem from a more disciplined form of knowledge. The studies of *episteme* and of *doxa* are not wholly separate and generally reinforce each other, since analyzing the opinions that philosophers encounter is a first step in the pursuit of higher levels of understanding.

The usual contemporary word for political *doxa* is **ideology,** which is described in a well-known textbook in the following terms:

> An ideology is a value or belief system that is accepted as fact or truth by some group. It is composed of sets of attitudes towards the various institutions and processes of society. It provides the believer with a picture of the world both as it is and as it should be, and, in so doing, it organizes the tremendous complexity of the world into something fairly simple and understandable . . . An ideology must be a more or less connected set of beliefs that provide the believer with a fairly thorough picture of the world.[1]

Remember that we have defined politics as the activity of gathering and maintaining support for collective projects. Support may be obtained by offering bribes or making threats, but in the long run it has to rest on conviction. Ideology furnishes a basis for political persuasion by providing certain assumptions and values that may be held in common. More specifically, it has the following attributes:

1. Ideology is not a mere personal opinion, but a social belief accepted by large numbers of people and passed on by the normal channels of cultural transmission.

2. Ideology always involves a mixture of factual and moral beliefs. Because governmental legitimacy is an inherently ethical problem, ideology always includes beliefs about how people should act and what they should consider right and wrong.

3. Ideology, as a mass belief, is somewhat simplified. It reduces the infinite complexity of the world to simpler ideas that can be understood by large numbers of people who, after all, must devote most of their time to concerns other than the study of politics.

4. An ideology is not a random collection of opinions but a more or less organized system of beliefs that fit together logically. It is important to say "more or less," for the integration is never perfect. All of us have some surprising contradictions in our opinions. However, there is a big difference between an orderly, interrelated set of ideas and an assortment of unrelated opinions.

In this sense, ideologies are espoused by intellectuals in politics: by lawyers, teachers, journalists, and politicians who carry on public debate in ideological terms. It is doubtful whether many ordinary people, even among a well-educated populace, can be said to have ideologies.[2] They are more likely to believe in an assortment of somewhat conflicting ideological fragments—to be conservative on some points, liberal on others, and socialist on still other matters. It does not bother them to be inconsistent in this way because they probably spend relatively little time pondering social and political questions. Examples of contradictory thinking frequently turn up in public-opinion polls. It is routine, for example, for respondents to say that taxes are too high while simultaneously demanding higher levels of public spending on education and medical care.

One interesting aspect of the term *ideology* is the negative connotations it carries. The word is often used as a weapon to degrade ideas with which one disagrees. Dismissing ideas as "mere" ideology is a common tactic in argument. It is worth knowing why this is possible.

The word *ideology* was coined in 1796 by the French philosopher Antoine Destutt de Tracy, who gave it a meaning quite different from what it bears today. For him, *ideology* was to be the name of a new science—the study of human consciousness in all its aspects. Destutt de Tracy had once supported Napoleon; when he began to criticize him, the emperor responded by ridiculing his new science as an obscure doctrine and branding those who espoused it as ideologues. The concept of ideology probably would have died out if Marx and Engels had not rescued it and redefined it to bolster their theory that all human thought has an economic basis—that art, science, literature, law, and political thought reflect the underlying economic conditions of their creators. Marx wrote that one should always distinguish between the "economic conditions of production," which are the essence of class conflict, and "the legal, political, religious, aesthetic, or philosophic—in short, ideological—forms in which men become conscious of this conflict and fight it out." Economic relations are the "foundation, on which rise legal and political superstructures and to which correspond definite forms of social consciousness."[3]

Marx's view was bound to give the concept of ideology a bad name, because he regarded his own theory not as ideology but as science—scientific socialism. The beliefs of others were ideology, whereas his were science. Marx had a profound, although debatable, reason for thinking this, but it is easy to see how the word could become a mere polemical weapon in the hands of others. Moreover, there is much that is obviously true in Marx's insight. The intellectual world does have some relation to its economic milieu. Marx's insight is so significant that the term he used to express it was bound to become popular.

However, as often happens, the word has become detached from the particular theory that gave it currency. Today, when a belief system is branded an ideology, the detractors might mean any of several things. They might be implying that the beliefs have not really been thought through and would not withstand comparison to a well-developed philosophy (like their own!). Or they might mean that the beliefs are a not very subtle expression of self-interest on the part of some group that is trying to assert itself. Or, following the sociologist Karl Mannheim, they might mean that the beliefs are a rationalization of the status quo, and inherently conservative in function.[4]

Our use of the term is not intended to have any of these special implications. We use *ideology* simply as a convenient, contemporary word for political ideas in action—ideas not as they are found in the philosopher's study but as they motivate large numbers of people. However, students should be aware of the many other connotations of the term that they will certainly encounter elsewhere.

Part Two will emphasize the four main ideologies that dominated politics throughout the nineteenth and twentieth centuries: liberalism, conservatism, socialism, and nationalism. It will also take a briefer look at two more recent ideologies—feminism and environmentalism—that acquired global significance in the latter part of the twentieth century. Ideologies are never static, and it is essential to have some sense of their rise and decline.

Up to a point, it is useful to analyze ideologies as systems of ideas or beliefs. But remember that all ideologies are abstractions. They do not really exist; real people with their individual thoughts, and organizations that adopt statements or programs, are what exist. It is unlikely that the beliefs of any person or organization perfectly fit any of the descriptions given here of particular ideologies. Yet common tendencies and common concerns unite diverse thinkers, even if they do not agree on every point. Think of ideologies as broad tendencies of thought existing over long periods of time. No two people identified as liberals or socialists or feminists think identically, but there are certainly recognizable patterns in their ideas. Above all, do not think of ideologies as fixed creeds, from which a thinker who varies on any point is excommunicated. Ideologies are more like families of ideas; as in any real family, resemblances are strong but disagreements can be heated. When this proviso is kept in mind, the concept of structured ideologies can be a helpful device for showing how ideas are connected to each other.

The six ideological families to be discussed in this book are all peculiarly modern systems of thought. Although they have earlier roots, they have taken on their distinctive forms only in the last two hundred years. The terms liberalism, conservatism, socialism, and nationalism were never used to denote systems of thought before the early decades of the nineteenth century, while feminism and environmentalism only crystallized as worldviews in the last two decades of the twentieth century. These "isms" provide the terms of discourse about politics in the modern world, but they are not a universal and permanent vocabulary of political discourse.

All six ideologies are secular in orientation. Belief in God can be and has been combined with each of them, but it is not essential. All modern ideologies (except for some varieties of environmentalism) are humanistic—not in the sentimental sense of kindness or generosity but in the philosophical sense of being human-centred, taking human happiness on earth as an unquestioned goal. Although each has a different way of arriving there, the goal remains the same. Jeremy Bentham (1748–1832), an early liberal, expressed the goal when he said, "The business of government is to promote the happiness of the society, by punishing and rewarding,"[5] not to fulfill the will of God or to prepare people for the next life. Marx was even more aggressive in his humanism, stating that belief in God was a hindrance to humanity's struggle to create happiness. "Religion," wrote Marx, "is only the illusory sun about which man revolves so long as he does not revolve about himself."[6] The humanism of the other ideologies is not always as forceful as in Marx's teachings, but it is a common trait. This means that the arguments among them focus on the best means of achieving the agreed-upon goal, which is human happiness on earth. On this point, the only dissent among the ideologies is found in the "ecocentric" varieties of environmentalism, which hold that humanity has no special claim to the planet, that all species have equal rights under the principle of "biocentric equality."[7]

Also, all the ideologies we study presuppose that society is something people attempt to change, reform, or mould according to their desires. All except conservatism have programs or agendas of social change for government to undertake. Conservatism differs in that it believes society is too complex to be easily improved by human design. However, conservatism would not exist as a self-conscious ideology except for the challenges posed by the other worldviews. If it had never occurred to anyone that we could take charge of and deliberately improve society, there would have been no occasion to develop a conservative ideology in reaction against such a program. In this sense the modern confidence in social improvement is the backdrop to all contemporary ideologies.

The four older ideologies stem from the same historical situation, symbolized by the French Revolution: the transition from traditional to legal authority and legitimacy. We can see the central values of these ideologies in the famous slogan of that revolution—*liberté* (liberalism), *égalité* (socialism), *fraternité* (nationalism). Broadly speaking, liberalism celebrates the onset of legal authority as human emancipation from bondage. Socialism is ambiguous about it, welcoming the demise of traditional authority, but also fearing that the freedom created by legal authority will produce a new aristocracy of wealth even more oppressive than the old aristocracy of inherited privilege. Nationalism also welcomes the transition to legal authority but seeks to establish a new form of political identity to replace traditional ones. Conservatism is suspicious of pure legal authority, fearing that the accumulated wisdom of the past will be lost if the transition from traditional authority is too abrupt.

It is no accident that the great ideologies of our age appeared on the political scene almost simultaneously at the end of the eighteenth century. The French Revolution and the Napoleonic Wars were the most visible signs of a vast social change. These events in Europe proved to be a rehearsal for similar changes throughout the world. This is the unifying theme of our era, often called the Age of Ideology.

LEFT, RIGHT, AND CENTRE

Are ideologies related to each other in a sufficiently systematic way that we can array them along a single dimension? The answer is a qualified yes as far as conservatism, liberalism, and socialism are concerned; but it becomes much more complicated when nationalism, feminism, and environmentalism are considered. Here we try to relate all these ideologies to each other. You may wish to return to this section after completing Part Two has given you a better idea of what these ideologies mean.

Conservatism, liberalism, and socialism are often depicted as lying along a spectrum whose ends are designated *left* and *right*. Many observers agree more or less on the following construction:

Left		Centre		Right	
	Social	Reform	Classical		
Communism	Democracy	Liberalism	Liberalism	Conservation	Fascism

Although this spectrum corresponds to common perception, it is not easy to say precisely what it means. Is the left for, and the right against, change? That simplistic explanation will hardly do, for everything depends on who is in power. In a communist state, classical liberalism would be an ideology of radical change. In constitutional democracies, both communism and fascism represent radical change. As a yardstick, freedom is not much help either. All ideologies, even fascism, claim to be for freedom, but they define it in different ways. Nor does using democracy as a measure solve the problem, because the democratic centralism of Marxism–Leninism is in reality just as antithetical to popular government as fascism is.

Considering the circumstances in which the words *left* and *right* first began to be used as political labels sheds some light on the subject. The custom arose shortly after 1789 in the French National Assembly. Those factions that favoured retaining substantial powers for the monarchy, such as the right to appoint judges and to veto legislation, sat to the right of the chairman of the Assembly. Those who favoured reducing the monarch to a purely symbolic figure and letting the elected representatives of the people exercise all political power sat to the left of the chairman. The basic issue was popular sovereignty. The left held that all political power emanated from the people, the right believed that God conferred political power upon the king through inheritance, and the centre sought a compromise or balance between these two principles.[8]

This political difference between left and right soon took on an economic dimension as socialism assumed a prominent role in European politics. The term "left" was then applied to those who favoured equalization of property through political action. Socialists proposed to replace the market process, which is not under the control of any identifiable individual or group, with a system of state planning. Socialism thus extended popular sovereignty from the political to the economic sphere.

Many ambiguities of the left–right terminology arise from this double origin. Advocates of popular sovereignty do not inevitably favour socialist planning; they may be sincerely convinced that the market principle will in the long run be of more benefit to ordinary working people. It is also not inevitable that advocates of socialist planning will support popular sovereignty with equal warmth, for the desires of the real, existing people (as opposed to the hypothetical, reformed people) may obstruct the plan. In short, the political and the economic left coincide often but not always.

In contemporary usage, the economic factor predominates, though not entirely. Going back to our commonsense listing of ideologies on the left–right spectrum, we can now give an approximate interpretation in terms of the meanings of equality that will be discussed at greater length in Part Two. Let us now redraw the spectrum, adding the various forms of equality and inequality that the ideologies claim as their own:

Left		Centre		Right	
Equality of Condition	Equality of Opportunity	Equality of Right		Aristocracy	Hierarchy
Communism	Social Democracy	Reform Liberalism	Classical Liberalism	Conservatism	Fascism

This picture is better than the first, but it can still be seriously misleading without appropriate qualifications. Communists advocate long-run equality of result in the sense of the equality of happiness that would be produced by implementing the motto, "From each according to his ability, to each according to his needs." In the short run, they claim to equalize conditions somewhat but not absolutely. Social democrats and reform liberals are not exclusively wedded to equality of opportunity. Their use of the progressive income tax as a levelling measure is also an approach to equality of result.

The classical liberal commitment to equality of right is not especially problematic in this context, but the conservative position easily causes confusion. Early conservatives such as Edmund Burke saw hereditary aristocracy as a socially useful institution. Twentieth-century conservatives no longer defend the hereditary principle but may argue that the wealthy will perform some of the same useful functions as a hereditary aristocracy—philanthropy, public service, and so on. Obviously, this position shades into classical liberalism; the difference is only a matter of whether we emphasize the equality of universal rules or the unequal results arising from them. Finally, fascists tended to think of hierarchy not as social transmission through legal inheritance, but as biological transmission of racial qualities. For Adolf Hitler, Germans were the master race (*Herrenvolk*), while Jews and Slavs were subhuman (*Untermenschen*). This is the most absolute type of inequality that can be imagined, because there is no conceivable way of altering it. Fascists also rejected the constitutional principle of rule of law, which is another formulation of equality of right.

This underlying dimension of egalitarianism is not an absolute scale of measurement that allows us to assign a precise value to an ideology from any time or place. However, it does make a limited amount of sense to say of two ideologies at a certain place and time that one is to the left or right of the other. The same applies to the adherents of ideologies. Thus, it is reasonable to say that in recent Canadian politics the NDP, as a party of social democracy, is usually to the left of the Liberal Party. Yet the difference is chiefly one of degree. Prime Minister Louis St. Laurent said of the CCF, the predecessor of the NDP, that they were only "Liberals in a hurry." That numerous quasi-socialist measures, such as national health insurance and a publicly owned oil company, were proposed by the CCF/NDP and ultimately legislated by the Liberal Party shows the kinship between the two parties. Similarly, the Liberals, as a reformist party, are generally to the left of the Conservatives. But again there is much overlap. In the federal election campaigns of 2004, 2006, and 2008, the Liberals and the Conservatives vied with each other in claiming fidelity to the principles of a public health care system and promising to spend more money on health care. It is, therefore, best to think of parties as occupying overlapping positions on the ideological spectrum:

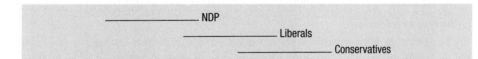

Note that, except for fascism, we have not attempted to place nationalism on the left–right scale. Nationalism can be allied with any one of liberalism, conservatism, or socialism because commitment to the nation-state does not automatically dictate a position on issues of equality. It is worth noting here that in times of war normal political differences are suspended. Parties of the left and right often come together in a coalition government of national unity to carry out the war effort. This illustrates how support for the nation is on a different level than other political issues. When the threat to the nation is past, the distinction between left and right reasserts itself, and governments of national unity soon fall apart (as happened in Canada after World War I and in France and Italy after World War II).

The Bloc Québécois furnishes another example of how nationalism does not fit onto the standard left–right spectrum. The Bloc, formed in 1990 by the former Conservative Lucien Bouchard as a protest against delays in ratifying the Meech Lake Accord, is essentially a single-issue movement devoted to the goal of turning Quebec into a sovereign state. The MPs who joined the Bloc defected from both the Conservative and the Liberal Parties; and they were joined in the 1993 election by candidates who had previously worked for other parties in Quebec, such as the NDP. The present leader, Gilles Duceppe, was at one time a Communist. Although the party takes a generally social democratic position, its true program is the independence of Quebec and it thus attracts many nationalist voters who are not really social democratic in ideology.

The varieties of feminism can be aligned partially, though not completely, with the left–right spectrum. Liberal feminists and socialist feminists can without too much distortion be seen as liberals and socialists who happen to be particularly concerned with a certain set of problems. Overall, their thinking fits into familiar liberal and socialist categories. Radical feminism, however, is much more difficult to place. As a transformation of Marxism, it seems to belong on the left; and when radical feminists get involved in electoral politics, they do so with parties of the left. But their overriding concern with patriarchy is fundamentally different from the concerns with popular sovereignty and economic equality that characterize positions on the left–right spectrum, so that we might think of radical feminism as belonging on a dimension that cuts perpendicularly across the left–right dimension. This helps to explain what otherwise might be seen as some strange political coalitions. For example, radical feminists have frequently worked together with conservatives in law-enforcement agencies on issues such as pornography, sexual abuse, and violence against women. The two groups conceptualize the issues in quite different ways, but they agree on the desirability of harsher criminal penalties. Liberals who are thought of as quite left-wing—for example, members of the Canadian Civil Liberties Association—can find themselves on the opposite side on these issues even though they may think of themselves as favourable to feminism.

The situation with environmentalism is similar. Generally, we can comfortably sort out environmentalists by examining the means they advocate to achieve their ends. Free-market environmentalists clearly belong with the classical liberals, while many advocates of human welfare ecology just as clearly prefer the more interventionist tools of reform liberalism and social democracy. But deep ecology, like radical feminism, is really on a different dimension because it rejects the materialist goals of the other ideologies.

The left–right spectrum, though often useful, is unidimensional. Real-world ideologies are multidimensional—that is, they are concerned not only with inequality and equality but also with many other political values. For example, it would be possible to map ideologies on a continuum according to their views on the scope of state control of society:

Maximum			Minimum
Communism	Social Democracy	Classical Liberalism	
Fascism	Reform Liberalism	Conservatism	Anarchism

Communists and fascists favour the total identification of state and society. Social democrats and reform liberals favour active government regulation and intervention but do not wish to subject all of society to state control. Conservatives and classical liberals desire a very limited state to carry out certain restricted functions; otherwise, they want society to evolve according to its own laws. **Anarchists** believe that society can exist without any government at all.

The above is as valid as the conventional left–right approach, but it expresses another aspect of the reality of ideologies, and thus does not coincide with the conventional left–right spectrum. To speak of left and right is a useful shorthand way of referring to ideologies as long as the limitations of this approach are kept in mind. Left and right are only convenient labels; they are no substitute for a detailed understanding of a point of view. Difficulties quickly become apparent when we try to apply the notion of a left–right continuum to concrete issues. To illustrate, let us look at several issues from the realms of economics, society, and politics.

Among economic issues, the left–right spectrum fits very well the debate about progressive taxation. Those furthest to the left are the most vociferous in their desire to "make the rich pay," as the Communist Party of Canada used to put it. Those in the centre accept the principle of progressive taxation but may worry that the marginal rate is so high as to interfere with productivity; they wish the state to act in a redistributive way, but not to "kill the goose that lays the golden eggs." Those on the right reject progressive taxation in favour of a flat tax; that is, one whose rate is the same for all. The issue of taxation can be readily mapped onto the left–right continuum because the underlying question is one of egalitarianism.

On social issues, the left seems to favour a position of individual libertarianism— abortion on demand, legalization of marijuana, abolition of movie censorship—and the right seems to uphold traditional standards of morality. But this seeming unidimensionality exists only in liberal democracies where the extreme left is weak, as in North America. Communists and other revolutionary leftists are in fact rather puritanical in their outlook on many moral questions. Marijuana and other mind-altering drugs were rigorously forbidden in communist countries, as were many mildly obscene books and movies that would hardly raise an eyebrow in the Western world. Freedom of individual choice is not a high priority for the revolutionary left.

Even with all these nuances and exceptions, the terms *left* and *right* are convenient for categorizing ideological tendencies. Most of the inconsistencies disappear if we restrict the application of the terms to stable constitutional democracies in which the extreme right and left are weak or nonexistent. Under these conditions, left and right stand for relatively coherent ideological positions—reform liberalism and social democracy on the one side, classical liberalism and conservatism on the other. The more moderate forms of feminism and environmentalism can be fitted into this tableau without too much strain; but if radical feminism and deep ecology ever become dominant ideologies, left and right will have to be either redefined or abandoned altogether as practical labels. For more on the multidimensionality of politics, see Concept Box 9.1.

The matrix shows the approximate location of the main political parties in English-speaking Canada as perceived in the 2004, 2006, and 2008 elections. The Conservatives favoured a combination of traditional morality and free-market economics, while the Liberals advocated more government intervention on economic issues, but freedom of choice on social issues. The New Democrats and Bloc Québécois went even further than the Liberals in combining economic interventionism with social libertarianism. The box in the upper-left quadrant was empty, for no political party advocated a combination of traditional morality and interventionist economics.

Concept Box 9.1

Multidimensional Scaling

Many of the difficulties of employing left–right terminology arise from the fact that politics is multidimensional, which is to say that people have different opinions about many different issues and these issues do not all line up neatly on the same dimension. In Canadian politics today there is a cluster of economic issues, including the level of taxation and provision of public services, on which the dimension of difference runs from the free market on the right to government provision on the left. Then there is another cluster of so-called social issues, including abortion and gay rights, on which the dimension of difference runs from traditional morality on the right to individual choice on the left. Combining these into a two-dimensional matrix enables the analyst to make a more accurate classification of where people actually stand.

Note that the New Democrats and the Bloc Québécois seem similarly positioned when we consider only these two dimensions, but they would be much farther apart if we brought in a third dimension of national unity. The NDP favours the continuance of Canada within its present boundaries, whereas the BQ advocates the separation of Quebec from Canada, by unilateral means if necessary. Considering three or even more dimensions of difference brings gains in analytical accuracy, but the resulting diagrams are difficult to reproduce in the two-dimensional world of the printed page.

Concept Box 9.1

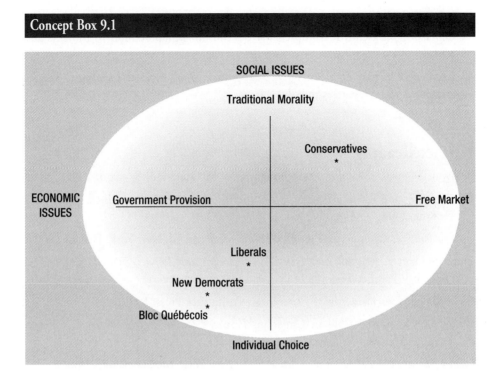

Questions for Discussion

1. Have you ever used one of these ideological labels to characterize your own political views? Based on what you have read thus far, do you think you were using the right label?

2. Can you locate your own views in the two-dimensional matrix shown in Concept Box 9.1? Do you support the political party located nearest to your own views? (Don't worry if there is a discrepancy; there are many other valid reasons for supporting a particular party.)

3. Before reading this chapter, had you ever used the word "ideology" in your own conversation? Can you remember whether you used it as a neutral or a pejorative term?

Internet Links

1. World's Smallest Political Quiz: **www.theadvocates.org/quiz.html.** Measure your own ideological position, using a two-dimensional scheme somewhat similar to that shown in Concept Box 9.1. Compare your results with those of others who have taken the quiz.

2. Keele Guide to Political Thought and Ideology on the Internet: **www.keele.ac.uk/ depts/por/ptbase.htm**. Comprehensive set of bibliographic links to thinkers and topics.

3. Ideology: The War of Ideas: **www.zmangames.com/products/Ideology.** Website associated with a board game.

Further Reading

Baldwin, Douglas. *Ideologies.* Scarborough, ON: McGraw-Hill Ryerson, 1992.

Ball, Terence, and Richard Dagger. *Ideals and Ideologies: A Reader.* 5th ed. New York: Pearson, 2004.

———. *Political Ideologies and the Democratic Ideal.* 3rd ed. New York: Pearson, 2004.

Baradat, Leon P. *Political Ideologies: Their Origins and Impact.* 5th ed. Englewood Cliffs, NJ: Prentice-Hall, 1994.

Boaz, David. *Libertarianism: A Primer.* New York: Free Press, 1997.

Campbell, Colin, and William Christian. *Parties, Leaders, and Ideologies in Canada.* Toronto: McGraw-Hill Ryerson, 1996.

Caute, David. *The Left in Europe Since 1789.* New York: McGraw-Hill, 1966.

Cheles, Luciano, Ronnie Ferguson, and Michalina Vaughan, eds. *The Far Right in Western and Eastern Europe.* White Plains, NY: Longman, 1995.

Desai, Meghnad. *Rethinking Islamism: The Ideology of the New Terror.* London: I.B. Tauris & Co. Ltd., 2006.

Ebenstein, Alan O., William Ebenstein, and Edwin Fogelman. *Today's Isms: Socialism, Capitalism, Fascism, Communism.* 10th ed. Englewood Cliffs, NJ: Prentice Hall, 1994.

Freeden, Michael. *Ideologies and Political Theory: A Conceptual Approach.* Oxford: Oxford University Press, 1996.

Gentile, Giovanni. *Origins and Doctrine of Fascism: With Selections from Other Works.* Piscataway, NJ: Transaction, 2004.

Gibbins, Roger, and Loleen Youngman. *Mindscapes: Political Ideologies Towards the 21st Century.* Toronto: McGraw-Hill Ryerson, 1996.

Holmes, Stephen. *The Anatomy of Antiliberalism.* Cambridge, MA: Harvard University Press, 1993.

Hoover, Kenneth, et al. *Ideology and Political Life.* Fort Worth: Harcourt College Publishers, 2001.

Kaase, Max, and Kenneth Nentin. *Beliefs in Government.* Oxford: Oxford University Press, 1995.

Laponce, Jean. *Left and Right: The Topography of Political Perceptions.* Toronto: University of Toronto Press, 1981.

McLellan, David. *Ideology.* Milton Keynes, UK: Open University Press, 1986.

Minogue, Kenneth R. *Alien Power: The Pure Theory of Ideology.* London: Weidenfeld and Nicolson, 1985.

Plamenatz, John. *Ideology.* London: Pall Mall Press, 1970.

CHAPTER 10

Liberalism

The word *liberal* comes from the Latin *liber,* meaning "free." It was first used as a political term in Spain during the Napoleonic Wars and became common later in the nineteenth century with the establishment of the Liberal Party in Britain. The ideas of liberalism, however, are older than the name. Broadly speaking, liberalism grew out of the English Whig tradition of liberty under law. Prominent Whig thinkers were John Locke (1632–1704) in England, Adam Smith (1723–90) and David Hume (1711–76) in Scotland, and Thomas Jefferson (1743–1826) and James Madison (1751–1836) in America. These men never called themselves liberals, but they elaborated the principles later known as liberalism. They were followed by such writers as John Stuart Mill (1806–73) and his French contemporary Alexis de Tocqueville (1805–59), who consciously thought of themselves as liberals.

THE HISTORY OF LIBERALISM

The history of **liberalism** reveals four principles, all of which relate to the broad concept of freedom: **personal freedom, limited government, equality of right,** and **consent of the governed.** These principles were all mentioned earlier in our discussion of constitutionalism; indeed, political liberalism is really the same thing as constitutionalism:

1. Personal freedom, as understood by liberals, refers to the absence of coercion in the various realms of life. It includes free speech, religious liberty, the right of private property, and the right of political opposition.

2. Limited government means that the state is an instrument serving a particular function in society and is not in general charge of all society.

3. Equality of right implies that all must abide by the same laws, which the state enforces with impartiality.

4. Consent of the governed means that government emanates from the people, is responsible to them, and may be changed by them; it is a moderate and practical statement of the doctrine of popular sovereignty.

These four principles mark the entire liberal tradition from Locke to the present day. Indeed, there is such wide acceptance of these principles today that almost everyone in the Western world at least pays lip service to them. However, there is also a deep division within liberalism that must be carefully examined. From this point on we will distinguish the older classical liberalism from the newer reform liberalism.

Classical liberalism was the dominant ideology in the nineteenth century in North America, Britain, and much of Western Europe. It accepted the four principles in a straightforward and literal way. In particular, it identified personal freedom with a free-market or *laissez faire* economy. **Reform liberalism,** which began as a reform movement within the British Liberal Party at the end of the nineteenth century, was dominant throughout much of the twentieth century. It favours using the state to modify the market system without abolishing it altogether and advocates a larger role for the state in providing equality of opportunity. The differences between classical liberalism and reform liberalism are summarized as follows in terms of the four principles.

Personal Freedom

For classical liberals, freedom is simply the absence of coercion. Without totally rejecting this definition, reform liberals try to add another dimension. They usually think of freedom in terms of our capacity to achieve our goals in life, arguing that freedom from coercion means little unless the means of attaining a decent life are provided. The Canadian journalist Pierre Berton expressed this position in his book *The Smug Minority:*

> A poor man is not free and a destitute man is as much a prisoner as a convict; indeed a convict generally eats better. A man who can't afford a streetcar ticket, let alone real travel, who can exercise no real choice in matters of food, clothing, and shelter, who cannot follow the siren song of the TV commercials, who can scarcely afford bus fare to the library let alone a proper education for himself or his children—is such a man free in an affluent nation?[1]

According to this view, the poor are not really free, even though they are not actively coerced, because the lack of financial means limits their opportunities in life as effectively as if they were kept down by force.

This difference in the understanding of freedom is not a trivial matter; it is at the heart of the difference between the old and the new liberalism. Classical liberals emphasize the absence of coercion—freedom in the sense of being left alone to do what you want, as long as it does not infringe on the freedom of others to do likewise. Reform liberals, on the other hand, wish to use governmental power to reduce the freedom of some in order to provide opportunities for others. They justify this in terms of freedom, arguing that they are increasing the amount of real liberty in society by furnishing people with the means to achieve their goals. The two kinds of liberals use the same words but do not speak the same language. Their differing conceptions of freedom have resulted in differing ideas about the role of the state in economic life. In particular, economic freedom and the market system are not accorded the same primacy in reform liberalism as in classical liberalism.

While reform liberalism now differs significantly from classical liberalism, the former can be seen as a logical outgrowth of the latter. If freedom is the absence of coercion, the individual will—the right to do what you want—must be fundamental to freedom. Reform liberalism purports to be a more effective way of enabling more people to obtain the objects of their desire, using the power of the limited state if necessary. Both versions of liberalism agree (and differ from other ideologies) in celebrating the fulfillment of individual desire as the highest good.[2]

Limited Government

Classical liberals see the state in negative terms: its role is primarily to prevent people from harming each other through force or fraud. To this end, classical liberalism accepts the use of force to protect the community from external attack and to punish those who commit acts of aggression or deception against others. Beyond these functions, the state should do relatively little, leaving people to work out their own destinies within society. The classical liberal idea of government has been caricatured as the night-watchman state, as merely the caretaker of society.

Reform liberals accept that the state has caretaking functions, but wish to add to them the interventionist role of promoting freedom in the additional sense of capacity. They want the state to be a positive force that ensures the availability of leisure, knowledge, and security for those who might not otherwise acquire them. The two different views of freedom lead to two different conceptions of the duties of the state.

Equality of Right

For classical liberals, equality of right means only that all abide by the same rules. It definitely does not imply **equality of result** in the outcomes of social and economic processes. Classical liberals accept that there will always be inequality of wealth, status, and power. One might even say that for them, equality of right is the right to become unequal.[3] Reform liberals, while not committed to a wholesale equalization of results, wish to reduce economic and social differences. They have often adopted what was originally a socialist formula, **equality of opportunity.**

Opportunities, by themselves, are never equal. One child is born to wealthy parents, another to poor ones. One child is born to parents who encourage diligence in school, while another is born to parents who care nothing for learning. Obviously, the state can do little about many such inequalities; but if equality of opportunity is to have any meaning, the state must take positive steps to address those circumstances that cannot reasonably be blamed on the child. Thus, government may provide public schools, trying to ensure that all children start with the same sort of education, and offer low-interest loans to help young people obtain professional training that their parents might not have been able to provide. Such measures go much further than the classical liberal conception of equality of right.

Consent of the Governed

Classical liberals in the nineteenth century often favoured a **property franchise,** which required citizens to own a stipulated amount of property before receiving the right to vote. Viewing government as based largely on the protection of property, they felt it was reasonable to entrust government to those who possessed substantial amounts of property and who paid most of the taxes supporting the state. Reform liberals, in contrast, are strongly democratic. Since they put so much emphasis on using the state positively to provide for the common welfare, they naturally feel it is important that everyone have a share of political power.

Reform liberalism has much in common with democratic socialism. For historical reasons the term *socialist* has been unpopular in North America, whereas it is more respected in Europe. Many who are known as liberals in contemporary North America might be called socialists or social democrats if they lived in Europe.

One final note: the two types of liberalism discussed in this text as ideologies are only loosely connected with the "capital-L" Liberal Party of modern Canada. Over its long history, the Liberal Party has sometimes inclined to one side, sometimes to the other. Under the leadership of Pierre Trudeau (1968–84), the party clearly tilted toward reform liberalism and became quite interventionist in its economic policies; but the Liberal government of Jean Chrétien (1993–2003) moved some distance back toward classical liberalism and downsized or even dismantled some of the interventionist creations of the Trudeau era.

CLASSICAL LIBERALISM

Liberalism grew out of the struggle of Parliament with the Stuart kings in seventeenth-century England. At the level of political power, the Glorious Revolution of 1688 established the supremacy of Parliament over the monarchy. At the level of ideas, the Revolution established that public authority is not derived directly from God, as the Stuarts had tried to maintain, but ultimately resides in the people themselves, who delegate it to the sovereign. Rule is a trust that can be removed if it is abused. The sovereign must rule within the law of the land, as made by Parliament and interpreted by the courts. Arbitrary government is unconstitutional and cause for opposition. The people have a moral right to rise in arms to overthrow an arbitrary government and re-establish the rule of law. In Max Weber's terms, this is the triumph of legal over traditional authority.

The ideas animating the Glorious Revolution were given classic expression by John Locke in *The Second Treatise of Government* (1690). Locke argued that the people deliberately create government by agreement among themselves in order to achieve a reliable, impartial enforcement of law. The purpose of government is fundamentally to protect them in their "life, health, liberty, or possessions."[4] Government is not authorized "to destroy, enslave, or designedly to impoverish the subject."[5] Arbitrary rule by the Stuarts had just this result, so the English were right to resist and depose them:

> Wherever law ends, tyranny begins if the law be transgressed to another's harm. And whosoever in authority exceeds the power given him by the law, and makes use of the force he has under his command to compass that upon the subject which the law allows not, ceases in that to be a magistrate and, acting without authority, may be opposed as any other man who by force invades the right of another.[6]

Locke's arguments were repeated in the American Declaration of Independence of 1776. This text, which was drafted by Thomas Jefferson, is the most concise and memorable statement of the political theory of classical liberalism:

> We hold these truths to be self-evident, that all men are created equal, that they are endowed by their creator with certain unalienable rights; that among these are life, liberty and the pursuit of happiness; that to secure these rights governments are instituted among men, deriving their just powers from the consent of the governed; that whenever any form of government becomes destructive of these ends, it is the right of the people to alter or to abolish it, and to institute new government.[7]

Similar ideals animated the early days of the French Revolution of 1789. In August of that year, the National Assembly adopted the Declaration of the Rights of Man and of the Citizen, which stated:

> The end of all political associations is the preservation of the natural and imprescriptible rights of man; and these rights are liberty, property, security, and resistance of oppression.
>   The nation is essentially the source of all sovereignty; nor can any individual, or any body of men, be entitled to any authority which is not expressly derived from it.[8]

The political theory of classical liberalism called for equality before the law and equality of right in respect to person and property, but not equality of political participation. In the early stages of the French Revolution, a distinction was made between passive citizens (who had full legal and civil rights but not political rights) and active citizens (who could also vote and hold elective office). The incorporation of democracy into liberalism occurred later and will be discussed in the section on reform liberalism.

The demand that government be bound by law was part of a larger concern for freedom of the individual. This was worked out first in the area of religion; many of the disputes between Parliament and the Stuarts had a religious basis. Locke's *A Letter*

Concerning Toleration (1689) held religion to be a private matter: "The care of souls cannot belong to the civil magistrate because his power consists only in outward force; but true and saving religion consists in the inward persuasions of the mind, without which nothing can be acceptable to God."[9] His conclusion was that the state should tolerate all religions as long as they did not disturb civil peace by meddling in politics.

Regarding religion as a private matter was congenial to the increasingly secular outlook of the Enlightenment. It also coincided with a growing feeling that communication ought to be as free as possible. The First Amendment to the American Constitution (1791) established a wide freedom of speech and press:

> Congress shall make no law respecting an establishment of religion, or prohibiting the free exercise thereof; or abridging the freedom of speech or of the press; or the right of the people peaceably to assemble, and to petition the government for a redress of grievances.[10]

At about the same time, the Declaration of the Rights of Man and of the Citizen enunciated an even broader principle: that not only thought and speech, but also conduct, should be left alone by the state as long as it did not coercively invade the rights of others:

> Political liberty consists in the power of doing whatever does not injure another. The exercise of the natural rights of every man, has no other limits than those which are necessary to secure to every other man the free exercise of the same rights; and these limits are determinable only by law.[11]

John Stuart Mill brought all these themes together in his book *On Liberty* (1859), which is perhaps the best-known statement in the English language of the value of freedom. *On Liberty* asserted "one very simple principle": "The only purpose for which power can be rightfully exercised over any member of a civilized community, against his will, is to prevent harm to others. His own good, either physical or moral, is not a sufficient warrant."[12] Mill tried to prove in

John Stuart Mill, 1806–73, one of the most important philosophers of liberalism.

his book that in the long run we would all be better off if the state were restrained from prohibiting "experiments in living," provided they were not coercive of others. Freedom to experiment with new ideas and new ways of doing things would encourage progress through discovery of better alternatives to present practices.

In the economic sphere, classical liberalism is identified with the free market. Locke did not have a fully developed theory of the market, but he helped lay the foundations for one by stressing that a major purpose of government is the protection of private property. The principles of the market were brought to light in the eighteenth century by numerous writers, of whom the most famous was Adam Smith. His book *The Wealth of Nations* (1776) used the metaphorical term "invisible hand" to describe what happens when an individual seeks to promote his own self-interest:

> He intends only his own security; and by directing that industry in such a manner as its produce may be of the greatest value, he intends only his own gain, and he is in this, as in many other cases, led by an invisible hand to promote an end which was no part of his intention. Nor is it always the worse for the society that it was no part of it. By pursuing his own interest he frequently promotes that of the society more effectually than when he really intends to promote it.[13]

Smith articulated in this passage a central belief of classical liberalism: that the common good can be served in the economic sphere by individual initiative without state direction. Much the same thing was meant by Anne-Robert-Jacques Turgot, a French contemporary of Smith, who coined the term **laissez faire** ("let alone"). The terms *invisible hand* and *laissez faire* both imply that human needs are best served by free competition in the economic marketplace. Government has to enforce the rules of property and agreements that make competition possible, but it need not otherwise direct the process.

A more modern exposition of classical liberalism and its leading idea, freedom as the absence of coercion, can be found in the works of two Nobel Prize–winning economists, Milton Friedman and Friedrich Hayek.[14] Their argument for freedom runs approximately as outlined as outlined here.

People must live in communities in order to survive and to live well. The efforts of each contribute to the welfare of all. How can all these individual efforts best be coordinated for the common good? One obvious answer is to set up a central source of direction. But people make better use of their talents if they are left to solve their own problems in their own way. Society is so complex that no central power can direct it efficiently; individuals can do better through mutual adjustment to one another's initiatives. While freedom may seem inefficient, in the long run it is the most effective basis for social life, for there is no intelligence that can look after people's affairs better than they themselves can. This becomes more evident the more advanced and complicated society becomes. A single mind might succeed in directing a small clan or tribe with a few basic wants, but it could hardly begin to cope with the demands of our complex civilization.

Individual initiative does not preclude cooperation. As the eighteenth-century philosopher David Hume pointed out in a famous example, two men would quickly discover how to row a boat across a river. Trial and error would show them how to work the oars together.[15] Society is a great self-regulating order whose parts are continually adjusting to each other through processes of communication and exchange. Cooperation exists, but it is decentralized cooperation achieved through mutual consent, not directed from above. Order emerges as the many members of society, pursuing their own good in their own way, respond to the initiatives of others. Hayek called this emergent, decentralized, voluntary order **spontaneous order.**[16]

The economic marketplace is a spontaneous order since it is not under the control of any one individual or committee. Freely moving prices are the signals by which participants communicate to each other the relative abundance or scarcity of commodities. The science of economics focuses on the ability of the market to clear itself— that is, to bring supply and demand into equilibrium. Producers and consumers use the information conveyed by prices to adjust their expectations so that the quantity produced equals the quantity desired.

This view of markets assumes that there are many buyers and sellers who are trading freely without coercion and who know what they want and what goods and services are available; that entry to the market is relatively open, so that new participants can always undermine any collusion among present participants; and, further, that there is a legal framework to protect property and enforce contracts. Under these conditions, it is argued, all exchanges are mutually beneficial. Because participants have a variety of choices, they do not engage in transactions unless they find them more worthwhile than the available alternatives. As we will see later, those who criticize the spontaneous market order often do so not because they oppose its intrinsic logic but because they believe that one or more of these assumptions are, in practice, false.

The market order requires that behaviour be limited by rules of conduct to prevent mutual coercion. Such rules include respect for individuals and their property as well as the keeping of agreements and contracts. Those who violate rules while expecting others to abide by them are known in the jargon of contemporary economics as **free riders.** Tax evasion, for example, is usually free riding because it is not a protest against government as such, but merely an attempt to enjoy the benefits of government without paying for them. Hence, government is necessary to spontaneous order as the means of enforcing those rules without which order breaks down.

In a large and complex society where most transactions are impersonal, coercion is necessary to discourage and punish free riders. Society can live with a few such individuals, but others may soon imitate them. Once that happens, the rules of conduct collapse and with them goes the possibility of a cooperative spontaneous order. It is the essential role of government to make spontaneous order possible by enforcing those general rules of conduct that are necessary to it. According to classical liberalism, government should otherwise allow people to pursue whatever goals they choose.

Adam Smith offered a succinct classical liberal description of the duties of government:

> According to the system of natural liberty, the sovereign has only three duties to attend to; three duties of great importance, indeed, but plain and intelligible to common understandings: first, the duty of protecting the society from the violence and invasion of other independent societies; secondly, the duty of protecting, as far as possible, every member of the society from the injustice or oppression of every other member of it, or the duty of establishing an exact administration of justice; and, thirdly, the duty of erecting and maintaining certain public works and certain public institutions, which it can never be for the interest of any individual, or small number of individuals, to erect and maintain; because the profit could never repay the expense to any individual or small group of individuals, though it may frequently do much more than repay it to a great society.[17]

Smith's third duty of government embraced certain activities that are not profitable in a free market because it is difficult to charge for them. For example, it would not pay for an entrepreneur to beautify a city because it is difficult if not impossible to charge people for looking; similarly, it seldom pays for an entrepreneur to subsidize basic scientific research because profitable application is so uncertain.

In contemporary economics, such things are known as **collective** (or **public**) **goods.** They are defined as goods and services that are not divisible among individuals but are enjoyed in common, and from which it is difficult to exclude consumers. A traffic light, for example, shines for all who are near the intersection. The fact that one person sees the light does not make it less available for others. Contrast this with food or clothing, which cannot be used simultaneously by more than one person.

Collective goods have an inherent free-rider problem. When people feed and clothe themselves, they have to pay for what they consume; but it is tempting for them to hold back their share of the cost of a collective good, in the hope that others will pay for it and that they will be able to enjoy the benefits free of charge. How many streetlights would there be if they were supported by voluntary contributions?[18] The state helps to provide collective goods through ensuring that we all pay our fair share. The state's monopoly on coercion can be used to collect taxes to pay for harbours, roads, scientific research, urban beautification, and many other desirable things. The liberal justification of this procedure is that, in providing collective goods, government is being used to help people attain what they actually want, not to impose goals upon them that are contrary to their own desires.

Classical liberals have always recognized the category of collective goods, but they have not usually been eager to provide many of them through the state. Adam Smith had only a few such items in mind when he wrote *The Wealth of Nations*. Classical liberals have generally been confident that private ingenuity will find ways to offer in the market the goods and services that substitute for government provision of collective goods. For example, a movie is a sort of collective good, since many people can enjoy it at once, but it can be marketed by the simple expedient of selling the right to a seat.[19]

One crucial tenet of classical liberalism is that, beyond the three functions of government mentioned by Smith, the state has no mandate to correct the results of the marketplace by transferring wealth or income from rich to poor. Classical liberals see a degree of inequality as an inevitable result of free competition. In the long run, they think, it will benefit even the poor, as capital is reinvested to create new opportunities for employment and production. The classical liberal believes that economic advances may initially benefit only a restricted few, but that over time those benefits will become more widely disseminated. Such innovations as television, computers, and cellphones were at first expensive luxuries but eventually became articles of mass consumption.

Classical liberals object to state **redistribution** of wealth and income because they believe it is economically inefficient. For the market to work properly, the agreements made in it must be based on the data about supply and demand that prices furnish. An individual who gains wealth by responding to these price signals is regarded as contributing to the welfare of others, not as taking away from them wealth that must be repossessed by the state. Classical liberals would see nothing untoward in the fact that Bill Gates, perhaps the richest man in the world, has a fortune of more than US$50 billion. Rather, they would emphasize the incalculable benefits that his Microsoft software has conferred upon all who use personal computers.

Classical liberals also object to coercive redistribution for another reason: they believe it clashes with equality of right, which to them means, among other things, that the property of each will be equally protected, regardless of its size. They see the essence of redistribution as taking from the rich because they are rich and giving to the poor because they are poor; and they think such a policy means that the two classes are not equally treated before the law.

Although classical liberalism was not egalitarian in the sense of equality of result, it was an important force for promoting equality before the law. When the ideology crystallized in the seventeenth and eighteenth centuries, there were many grossly unequal institutions, such as slavery, even in the freest countries. Classical liberals fought against both slavery and the privileges of the nobility; against discrimination imposed on ethnic or religious minorities; against monopolies and tariffs that favoured corporations and producer cartels; and against government patronage in employment and public works. Since many of these goals have now been largely achieved in the Western democracies, classical liberalism today seems conservative, a force for preserving the status quo; indeed, classical liberals in this century are often called, and call themselves, conservatives (more on this later). But in the early nineteenth century, classical liberals were a reforming force, and very much in favour of great changes in the existing order.

Although classical liberalism is logically consistent in its views on government, it seems to many observers to lack concern for those not favoured by ability or good fortune. The classical liberal's confidence that, in the long run, free enterprise and the market system will raise the living standards of all does not do much now for those who are less well off. And even if the economic inequalities generated by the market system are no greater than in other systems, many critics object to classical liberalism's willingness to accept these inequalities as inescapable. It should be possible, they say, to do better—to keep the admittedly useful aspects of the market while using government to ensure that all citizens have a decent standard of living, adequate medical care, and education for their children; and that there is financial security for the injured, the sick, the unemployed, and the old. Sentiments like these have encouraged reform-minded liberals to develop a more activist conception of government's role in society.

REFORM LIBERALISM

The American sociologist Paul Starr refers to classical liberalism as "constitutional liberalism," because of its emphasis on constitutional government and the rule of law, and to reform liberalism as "modern democratic liberalism." According to Starr:

> The relationship between liberalism in these two phases has been predominantly cumulative: while rejecting laissez-faire economic policy, modern democratic liberalism continues to take the broader tradition of constitutional liberalism as its foundation. That is why it is possible to speak not only of the two separately, but also of an overarching set of ideas that unites them.[20]

John Stuart Mill, perhaps the best-known exponent of classical liberalism, was also one of the pioneers of reform liberalism. One aspect of his thought that pointed toward the future was its emphasis on democracy. His father, James Mill, had been the first prominent thinker in England to openly espouse representative democracy as the only acceptable form of government. J. S. Mill was somewhat less enthusiastic about democracy than his father, but he still advocated the extension of voting rights to all adults—men and women alike. Fearful that this new mass of uninstructed voters might use the franchise for selfish purposes such as the confiscation of property, he proposed that the educated be entitled to multiple votes; however, in historical perspective his support of democracy was on the whole more politically significant than his reservations about it.

The democratization of liberalism began, but did not end, with the expansion of the right to vote. The ballot has been made secret so that ordinary voters cannot be pressured or intimidated by their employers, creditors, or landlords. Salaries of elected officials have been raised so that one does not have to be independently wealthy to run for office. Entry to careers in the civil service now depends on ability rather than on family connections. Limits have been placed on campaign expenditures by political parties so that a "plutocracy" of big donors cannot simply buy an election.

Democratization of the political system tends to affect the economy. The vote is a form of political power. Once ordinary people gain access to that power, they naturally want to use it to improve their economic status. Though J. S. Mill remained committed to the free market, he was deeply pained by economic inequalities. In 1848 he wrote, in *Principles of Political Economy:*

> If the institution of private property necessarily carried with it as a consequence, that the produce of labour should be apportioned as we now see it, almost in an inverse ratio to the labour—the largest portions to those who have never worked at all, the next largest to those whose work is almost nominal, and so in a descending scale, the remuneration dwindling as the work grows harder and more disagreeable, until the most fatiguing and exhausting bodily labour cannot count with certainty on being able to earn even the necessaries of life; if this or Communism were the alternative, all the difficulties, great or small, of Communism would be but as dust in the balance.[21]

The decisive step toward reform liberalism in Britain was taken by T. H. Green (1836–82), a professor of philosophy at Oxford University. It was Green who redefined the concept of freedom to include not only the absence of coercion but also the presence of means or capacity:

> When we speak of freedom, we should consider carefully what we mean by it. We do not mean merely freedom from restraint or compulsion . . . we mean a positive power or capacity of doing or enjoying something worth doing or enjoying and that, too, something that we do or enjoy in common with others.[22]

Green argued that the state would have to regulate liberty of contract in order to secure a higher standard of living for the less fortunate. Green achieved lasting influence by explaining the quest for equality of result in terms of the attainment of freedom. In doing so, he made it possible for liberalism to incorporate equality of result, which previously had been seen as a socialist issue.

Although Green was an academic philosopher, his ideas had considerable practical effect. He and like-minded professors at English universities educated a generation of students who later rose to prominence within the Liberal Party of Great Britain and laid the foundations of the **welfare state** when they came to power in the first decade of the twentieth century. They adopted the income tax as a means of redistribution; involved the state in unemployment insurance, old-age pensions, and other social-insurance programs; and encouraged, through permissive legislation, the rise of organized labour.

In Canada, William Lyon Mackenzie King was nourished on the same ideas. While he chose to move slowly through the complexities of Canadian federalism, by the time he retired as prime minister in 1948 he had launched the welfare state. Other Liberal prime ministers, notably Lester Pearson and Pierre Trudeau, built on and expanded his reforms. Their governments expanded unemployment insurance and welfare payments and initiated a national medical-insurance scheme. The thrust of these reforms was to guarantee, through state action, the financial security of all residents of Canada.

Another vital player in the development of reform liberalism was the British economist John Maynard Keynes. His *General Theory of Employment, Interest and Money* (1936)

Keynesian Economics

The economist John Maynard Keynes and his followers believed that governments could guarantee full employment without taking over the economy altogether. All that was necessary was to follow what they saw as enlightened fiscal and monetary policies. **Fiscal policy** refers to government spending. **Monetary policy** refers to control over interest rates and the supply of money. In Canada, the Minister of Finance controls government spending through preparation of the annual budget, whereas the Bank of Canada controls interest rates and the supply of money.

To simplify somewhat, the basic idea of Keynesianism was that governments should coordinate both fiscal and monetary policy in a counter-cyclical direction. That is, in times of economic recession government should force down interest rates (monetary policy), thus making it easier for people to borrow money, and spend more than it collected in taxes (fiscal policy). Both measures would tend to put more money in the hands of consumers, which would in turn stimulate business activity. In times of prosperity, government should steer in the opposite direction, raising interest rates and collecting a surplus of taxation over expenditure, thus damping down the economy. In theory, the public budget would be balanced, not necessarily in any one year, but over the course of the business cycle.

The purely economic merits of Keynesianism are still being debated. In practice, however, it was severely contaminated by political considerations. Politicians found it much easier to lower interest rates than to raise them, and to run deficits rather than surpluses. As consumers got used to stimulative measures, they had to be ratcheted upward to have any effect, thus setting off an upward spiral of inflation and deficit spending. Since the 1970s, most economists and governments have renounced Keynesianism as a long-term guide to fiscal and monetary policy.

argued that the spontaneous order of the market had a fatal flaw. Because of this flaw, the economy could fall into a permanent depression characterized by high unemployment of labour and underuse of other resources. Government could compensate for this flaw by applying appropriate fiscal and monetary measures (see Comparative Perspectives 10.1). Keynes did not make government the central planner demanded by socialism, but he did call for it to be much more than the rule enforcer of classical liberalism. It was now responsible for maintaining prosperity and full employment through fiscal and monetary policy, duties that were explicitly accepted by the governments of Britain, Canada, and the United States at the close of World War II.

A striking feature of reform liberalism is that, while it no longer promotes the *laissez faire* economic freedom of classical liberalism, it has preserved and even intensified its commitment to individual choice in other spheres of life—for example, legalizing mind-altering drugs and all sexual relations between consenting adults. Pierre Trudeau's famous remark that "the state has no place in the bedrooms of the nation" is a fair statement of the attitude of reform liberals in these matters.

This apparent paradox in reform liberalism can perhaps be explained as a function of the individualistic character of all liberal thought, classical or reform. All liberals see society as essentially a means for enabling individuals to do what they want without preventing others from doing likewise. Reform liberals believe that their economic interventions will help individuals to satisfy their desires. Their general outlook remains individualistic and libertarian even when they advocate increased state involvement in the economy.

Ideologies do not undergo such profound changes without cause. The rise of reform liberalism was chiefly motivated by concern about the new working class during the Industrial Revolution. The rural poor of Great Britain flocked to cities such as Birmingham, Manchester, and London to work in factories. It is a much-debated question whether their standard of living as industrial workers was lower or higher than it had been as agricultural labourers, but the objective fact is perhaps not as important as the subjective perception.[23] The new working class, concentrated in industrial towns and cities, was far more visible than the rural poor dispersed across the countryside. Extensive urban slums created a widespread belief that the market system caused poverty and wretched living conditions. The new developments in liberalism were an attempt to share the wealth more widely and, in the minds of some, to stave off the socialist revolution that was going to occur if the condition of the working class did not improve.

Another development encouraging the ascendancy of reform liberalism was the growth of large corporations and the reduction of the number of competitors in key markets. Many industries—automobiles, airlines, steel, and petrochemicals, for example—are now dominated by a few giant firms. Reform liberals argue that oligopolies such as these substantially release firms from the constraints of market discipline by weakening competition. Many of them take the position that the factual presuppositions of effective competition no longer exist, and that government must play a regulatory role to protect society from exploitation by corporate giants.[24] Classical liberals dispute this analysis, arguing that, for example, while there may be only a few automobile makers in North America, there are foreign firms able to offer stiff competition now that improved transportation has unified the world market. They also argue that a dynamic and advanced economy offers many alternative products. There may be only a few steel companies, but competition still exists because steel is challenged for many purposes by wood, glass, cement, aluminum, plastics, and other structural materials.[25] This rejoinder does have its supporters, but the reform liberals' attitude toward large corporations has been extremely influential in shaping regulatory legislation.

Reform liberalism was the dominant ideology of the Western world throughout much of the twentieth century, with adherents in parties of all labels. However, the

Because of their belief that government action can improve society, reform liberals are often caricatured as naïve idealists.
By permission of Chip Bok and Creators Syndicate, Inc.

reform liberal consensus that had prevailed since the end of World War II broke down
in the 1980s. Keynesianism became discredited in practice because politicians used it
to legitimize recurrent deficit spending with inflationary effects. There was a revival
of classical liberalism in both the United Kingdom and the United States under the
governments of Margaret Thatcher and Ronald Reagan, respectively. Thatcher and her
advisers were particularly influenced by the writings of Friedrich Hayek; Reagan and
his advisers by the works of Milton Friedman. Both administrations spoke of reducing
the size of government and deregulating the economy, of privatizing government-
owned enterprises, of inaugurating a new era of free-market growth, and of lessening
our preoccupation with social security and equality of result.

The revival of market-oriented classical liberalism came later in Canada and was
enacted less enthusiastically. Pierre Trudeau's last government (1980–84) was highly
interventionist in economic affairs. Brian Mulroney's government (1984–93) took
steps in the direction of deregulating the economy and privatizing or downsizing
government operations, but his initiatives were cautious compared with those in the
United States, the United Kingdom, Australia, and New Zealand.[26] The Liberal government of Jean Chrétien, elected in 1993, returned even further to classical liberalism by accepting that the federal budget must be balanced. Repudiation of deficit

financing caused the Chrétien government to reduce spending on many government programs, such as unemployment insurance (renamed "employment insurance") and social assistance, which reform liberals had previously thought to be untouchable.

The ebb and flow of ideologies has had considerable effect on the taxes we pay because classical and reform liberalism differ in their approach to taxation. Classical liberals generally favoured **proportional taxes,** in which the rate is the same for everyone. We still have many of these taxes in Canada today, for example the federal GST with a rate of 5 percent. The more goods and services you purchase the more tax you pay, but the rate is the same for all payers. Reform liberals, however, generally advocate **progressive taxes,** such as the federal income tax. In a progressive income tax, the rate is graduated so that it rises as the amount of income rises. Reform liberals consider proportional taxes to weigh more heavily on lower income earners who spend a greater proportion of their income on necessities and argue that proportional taxes violate **social justice.** In 2008, the Canadian federal personal income tax had a progressive structure with four rates:

Structure of Canadian Federal Income Tax, 2008

Taxable Income	Applicable Rate
First $37,855	15%
Next $37,884	22
Next $47,415	26
Above $123,184	29

The structure is more steeply progressive than it appears in this table, for the provinces also levy income taxes in tandem with the federal tax. The top federal–provincial combined rate ranges from 39 percent in Alberta to more than 45 percent in some provinces. That is, depending on where they live, Canadians pay tax of 39 percent or more on their taxable income above $123,184. In Canada, as in many other countries, the graduated tax structure used to be steeper but has been flattened somewhat over the last 20 years with the revival of classical liberal thinking. Very steep progressive taxes are generally thought to be a deterrent to work effort (why should I work harder to earn an additional dollar if the government is going to take 70 or 80 percent of it?). On the other hand, there still seems to be wide popular support for some degree of progressivity in the tax system. Progressive income taxes are a means of redistribution because those who earn more pay proportionally more to fund government services that are equally available to all. Such taxes, therefore, mesh with the reform liberal strategy of using the state to promote equality of opportunity.

Classical and reform liberalism are extreme ideal types within the liberal family of ideas. For intellectual purposes, it is useful to organize ideologies into coherent and consistent positions; but in the actual world of politics, many people see merit in both positions and try to combine them in one way or another, or stake out some intermediate position. The portraits of classical and reform liberalism presented in this chapter can be used as tools for analyzing what people say in political discourse, but do not expect to find such clarity and consistency in real life.

Questions for Discussion

1. Critics of reform liberalism often assert that welfare programs such as employment insurance and social assistance create dependency and reduce incentives for self-help. Reform liberals argue, in contrast, that such programs, by giving help when needed, assist people in looking after themselves. Based on your own experience and observations, which view do you think is more accurate?

2. Critics of the progressive income tax often claim that high taxes are a major cause of the so-called "brain drain"; that is, of the tendency of Canadians with high earnings potential to move to the United States. Do you know any Canadians who have made such a move? Do you think tax avoidance was crucial to their decision, or were other factors more important?

3. If you had a magic wand to wave, would you move Canada in a reform-liberal or in a classical-liberal direction? Why? In your mind, is this a question of the values you hold or of your assessment of the best way to attain values that most people hold?

Internet Links

1. Laissez Faire Books: **www.laissezfaire.org.** American bookseller specializing in works with a classical-liberal perspective.

2. Ludwig von Mises Institute: **www.mises.org.** Online editions of the books of the famous liberal economist Ludwig von Mises, who was the teacher of Friedrich Hayek.

3. International Society for Individual Liberty: **www.isil.org.** Large number of links to classical-liberal authors, publishers, and research institutes.

4. Liberal Party of Canada: **www.liberal.ca.**

5. Liberal International: **www.liberal-international.org.** International organization of liberal parties, including the Liberal Party of Canada.

6. Canadian Civil Liberties Association: **www.ccla.org.** Takes an interesting mix of classical-liberal and reform-liberal positions.

7. American Civil Liberties Union: **www.aclu.org.** More consistently reform-liberal (left) than the CCLA.

8. Brookings Institution: **www.brook.edu.** Largest and best-known reform-liberal research institute in North America.

Further Reading

Allen, R. T. *Beyond Liberalism: The Political Thought of F. A. Hayek and Michael Polanyi.* New Brunswick, NJ: Transaction Publishers, 1998.

Amadae, S. M. *Rationalizing Capitalist Democracy: The Cold War Origins of Rational Choice Liberalism.* Chicago: University of Chicago, 2003.

Berlin, Isaiah. *Four Essays on Liberty.* 2nd ed. London: Oxford University Press, 2002.

Bramsted, E. K., and K. J. Melhuish. *Western Liberalism: A History in Documents from Locke to Croce.* London: Longman, 1978.

Girvetz, Harry K. *The Evolution of Liberalism.* New York: Collier, 1963.

Gray, John. *Liberalisms.* Milton Keynes, UK: Open University Press, 1986.

Hartz, Louis. *The Liberal Tradition in America.* New York: Harcourt, Brace, 1955.

Hellsten, Sirkku. *In Defense of Moral Individualism.* Helsinki: Philosophical Society of Finland, 1997.

Higgs, Robert, E. C. Pasour, Carl P. Close, Randal Ray Rucker, eds. *The Challenge of Liberty: Classical Liberalism Today.* Washington, D.C.: Independent Institute, 2006.

Hobhouse, L. T. *Liberalism.* New York: Oxford University Press, 1964. First published in 1911.

Hunter, Albert, and Carl Milofsky. *Pragmatic Liberalism: Constructing a Civil Society.* New York: Palgrave Macmillan, 2007.

Ignatieff, Michael. *The Rights Revolution.* Toronto: House of Anansi, 2000.

Josephson, Peter. *The Great Art of Government: Locke's Use of Consent.* Lawrence: University of Kansas Press, 2002.

Kymlicka, Will. *Liberalism, Community, and Culture.* Oxford: Clarendon Press, 1989.

Laski, Harold J. *The Rise of European Liberalism.* London: George Allen and Unwin, 1936.

Mandle, Jon. *What's Left of Liberalism? An Interpretation and Defense of Justice as Fairness.* Lanham, MD: Lexington Books, 2000.

Minogue, Kenneth. *The Liberal Mind.* London: Methuen, 1963.

Morefield, Jeanne. *Covenants without Swords: Idealist Liberalism and the Spirit of Empire.* Princeton, NJ: Princeton University Press, 2004.

Mulhall, Stephen. *Liberals and Communitarians.* 2nd ed. Oxford: Blackwell, 1996.

Owen, J. Judd. *Religion and the Demise of Liberal Rationalism: The Foundational Crisis of the Separation of Church and State.* Chicago: University of Chicago Press, 2001.

Rawls, John. *Political Liberalism.* New York: Columbia University Press, 1993.

Sandel, Michael J. *Liberalism and the Limits of Justice.* 2nd ed. Cambridge: Cambridge University Press, 1997.

Spitz, David. *The Real World of Liberalism.* Chicago: University of Chicago Press, 1982.

Starr, Paul. *Freedom's Power: The True Force of Liberalism.* New York: Basic Books, 2007.

CHAPTER 11

Conservatism

To *conserve* means to save or preserve. Thus a conservative would be a person who wishes to keep society as it is and who is sceptical about change. **Conservatism** in this sense is a disposition "to prefer the familiar to the unknown . . . the tried to the untried, fact to mystery, the actual to the possible, the limited to the unbounded, the near to the distant, the sufficient to the superabundant, the convenient to the perfect, present laughter to utopian bliss," stated Michael Oakeshott, a twentieth-century British political theorist and well-known conservative writer.[1] Or, as critics of conservatism have said with a touch of exaggeration, a conservative is a person who never wants to do anything for the first time.

This preference for the existing present over the conjectural future rests upon a sober assessment of human nature. The Canadian historian W. L. Morton put it this way:

> To the theologian, this is the belief in original sin, the belief that man is by nature imperfect and may be made perfect only by redemption and grace. In philosophic terms, it is a denial of the fundamental liberal and Marxist belief that human nature is inherently perfectible, and that man may realize the perfection that is in him if only the right environment is created.[2]

According to conservative thinking, the limitations of human nature make it imprudent for society to embark on large-scale ventures of social transformation. Much that is good may be lost with little likelihood of reaching "utopian bliss."

This attitude can also be defended with arguments drawn from social science, particularly from the idea of spontaneous order. The main point is that spontaneous order acts as a vast filter for selecting desirable and discarding undesirable innovations. Such an order consists of millions of intelligences freely cooperating under suitable rules. Any innovation—a new theory in science, a new trend in art, or a new product in business—is subjected to the repeated, independent scrutiny of countless individuals who must decide whether to accept, imitate, or purchase. Any individual may make a poor decision, but there is a strong presumption that in time the right decision or course of action will emerge. This is especially true since the testing process continues over generations.

So there is some reason to assume that the present way of doing things is socially useful. If a better way existed, the chances are that it would already have been adopted.

But this is only a probability, not a certainty. The fact that progress occurs shows that some innovations do have value, even if most do not. This is why the conservative tends to adopt a cautious attitude toward changes, waiting to see their usefulness demonstrated before adopting them. This is not hostility to change or improvement as such, but rather respect for wisdom inherited from the past combined with caution in the face of an unknown future.

Social reformers, whose proposals seem so obviously beneficial in their own eyes, are naturally impatient with this conservative attitude. Conservatives reply in their own defence that existing institutions already have the tacit approval of millions of minds over generations. That is a strong counterweight to reformers' confidence in their own ideas. They may in fact be correct, but they must bear the burden of proof.

An interesting facet of conservatism is respect for habits and customs whose rationale may not be immediately apparent. Conservatives assume that there is tacit wisdom in inherited patterns of behaviour. People may not understand all the reasons for what they do, but they may still be doing the right thing in following custom. Reformers, in contrast, are often quick to condemn what they do not understand, preferring conscious reason over inarticulate habit.

The conservative theory of change is closely associated with the ideas of the Anglo-Irish parliamentarian Edmund Burke (1729–97), who was moved to reflect on change by the outbreak of the French Revolution. In 1789, Louis XVI convened the Estates-General, a medieval type of consultative body that had not met since 1614. The king's goal was to raise new taxes, but events quickly escaped from royal control. The Estates-General converted itself into a National Assembly and declared France a constitutional monarchy. Change followed change with dizzying rapidity. The National Assembly adopted the Declaration of the Rights of Man and of the Citizen, created a form of representative government, abolished the last remnants of feudalism, nationalized the

Edmund Burke, 1729–97, the most important philosopher of conservatism.

property of the Roman Catholic Church, and replaced the old provinces with geometrically drawn *départements*. Even weights and measures were affected: the National

Assembly commissioned the preparation of what became the metric system. All this, as well as much more, was quickly done in an exalted spirit of reform: the rationalism of the Enlightenment, finally put into practice, would remodel society.

The results were not what had been expected. Within four years, France was under the dictatorship of Maximilien Robespierre and the Revolution had entered a phase later known as the Terror. France was also at war with the rest of Europe. Louis XVI and Marie Antoinette had been put to death by the guillotine, a new form of execution. Thousands of other opponents of Robespierre also went to the guillotine, and the dictator himself was finally removed from power in the same way. Political stability was restored only by Napoleon, who ruled at least as autocratically as any of the Bourbon kings had done, though far more effectively.

Burke wrote *Reflections on the Revolution in France* (1790) before the worst excesses began, but he correctly predicted that turmoil and despotism would grow out of such a radical break with the past. We are not wise enough to remake society all at once, he asserted; we must rely on the accumulated wisdom of the past, contained in customs, traditions, and practices:

> We are afraid to put men to live and trade each on his own private stock of reason; because we suspect that this stock in each man is small, and that the individuals would do better to avail themselves of the general bank and capital of nations and ages. Many of our men of speculation, instead of exploding general prejudices, employ their sagacity to discover the latent wisdom which prevails in them. If they find what they seek, and they seldom fail, they think it more wise to continue the prejudice, with the reason involved, than to cast away the coat of prejudice, and to leave nothing but the naked reason; because prejudice, with its reason, has a motive to give action to that reason, and an affection which will give it permanence.[3]

The contemporary reader is struck by Burke's praise of prejudice, which is today a negative word implying unfair discrimination. For Burke, prejudice meant literally the sort of "prejudgment" that contains the latent wisdom of past experience. People are not able to think their way through each new situation, so they must fall back on rules of thumb that have served them well in the past. Take the modern example of a landlord who may refuse to rent to tenants younger than 21 years of age, citing unhappy experiences with young tenants who gave noisy parties, were delinquent in their rent payments, and did not take care of the premises. The landlord's prejudgment against a category of people is, in a sense, unfair and irrational because not all members of the category behave in the same way. Yet, is it irrational for the landlord to rely on prejudice if he has no better way of predicting behaviour? Past experience, limited as it may be, is better than nothing as a guide to the future. The conservative view expressed by Burke is that prejudice is not just an irrational closing of the mind but a necessary way of dealing with a world in which complete information is rarely available.

As the psychologist Gordon Allport has pointed out, "the human mind must think with the aid of categories . . . Once formed, categories are the basis for normal prejudgment."[4] Such prejudgments are necessary and useful; they "become prejudices [in the pejorative sense] only if they are not reversible when exposed to new knowledge."[5] The challenge for conservatism is to combine open-mindedness about new developments with attachment to traditional values.

Burke did not oppose change as such—he had earlier spoken in defence of the American Revolution—but he wanted it to be gradual, so that the inherited wisdom of the past would not be lost:

> We must all obey the great law of change. It is the most powerful law of nature, and the means perhaps of its conservation. All we can do, and that human wisdom can do, is to provide that the change shall proceed by insensible degrees. This has all the benefits which may be in change, without any of the inconveniences of mutation. This mode will, on the one hand, prevent the unfixing old interests at once: a thing which is apt to breed a black and sullen discontent in those who are at once dispossessed of all their influence and consideration. This gradual course, on the other hand, will prevent men, long under depression, from being intoxicated with a large draught of new power, which they always abuse with a licentious insolence.[6]

The conservative attitude toward change is perhaps best expressed in the old adage, "If it is not necessary to change, it is necessary not to change." In the absence of some compelling reason for innovation, it is desirable not to tamper with the status quo, which has at least shown some degree of viability. Alternatives that are attractive in theory may turn out to be much worse in practice. In evaluating proposed reforms, conservatives are aware that they are comparing things that exist and whose faults are therefore apparent with ideas that have not yet been tested and whose faults may be unsuspected.

Conservatism is a prejudice (in Burke's sense) against using the state's coercive power to sponsor large-scale experiments in social change. The conservative will eventually give grudging approval to change that has occurred spontaneously through the cautious accumulation of many individual decisions, but to use the state as an agency of rapid reform short-circuits this process and may commit society to beautiful but unworkable visions.

Conservatism is conveniently described as an attachment to the present or status quo, but that is an oversimplification in one important respect. Conservatives are often highly critical of present trends, comparing them unfavourably with their image of the past. This is not incompatible with their view of gradual change, for the testing period of complex innovations may well extend over decades or generations. Conservatives often feel that we are heading in the wrong direction and should return to the ways of the past before it is too late. Therefore, they can find themselves in the position of making proposals that are themselves innovative vis-à-vis present arrangements. When conservatives refer to the status quo, they mean the present seen not as an isolated moment in time but as an extension of a long past. It is the prolonged experience of the past that the conservative values, not the mere present existence of a custom, practice, or institution.

Burke expressed this unity of past, present, and future by metaphorically speaking of the state as a partnership across generations:

> It is a partnership in all science; a partnership in all art; a partnership in every virtue and in all perfection. As the ends of such a partnership cannot be obtained in many generations, it becomes a partnership not only between those who are living, but between those who are living, those who are dead, and those who are to be born.[7]

No one since has more clearly stated the conservative's sense of continuity. For Burke, this continuity was further buttressed by a belief in divine order as the foundation of social order. Other conservatives have reversed this relationship, seeing religion more as a useful support of society than as its basis. But whatever their differences of religious faith, conservatives all revere the social order as something larger and more important than the individual. They are always mistrustful of the rationalistic intellectual's confidence in individual judgment. Conservatives put more trust in the collective wisdom of society as expressed in customs, usages, and institutions.

As presented here, conservatism is an attitude, not a full-fledged ideology with a whole set of beliefs about human nature, society, and government. By the conservative's own admission, the status quo is always changing and is never the same from year to year. Paradoxically, conservatism's commitment to the status quo entails gradual acceptance of new principles as the present reality changes. In this way, conservatism differs markedly from liberalism and socialism, both of which are built around certain ideas regarded as universal truths. Classical liberals believe that the market is the most effective means of meeting human wants; socialists believe the same of central planning. They defend their systems where they exist and work for their introduction where they do not. They regard the status quo as a secondary factor that merely affects the speed with which desired goals may be achieved; they derive the goals themselves from principles, and have no commitment to what exists simply because it does exist.

All of this means that there is no single unchanging body of doctrine that can be identified as conservative. Nonetheless, conservative thinkers do have certain traits in common. Russell Kirk, a leading American writer on conservatism, lists six such common characteristics:

1. Belief in a transcendent order, or body of natural law, which rules society as well as conscience.

2. Affection for the proliferating variety and mystery of human existence, as opposed to the narrowing uniformity, egalitarianism, and utilitarian aims of most radical systems.

3. Conviction that civilized society requires orders and classes, as against the notion of a "classless society."

4. Persuasion that freedom and property are closely linked: separate property from private possession, and the Leviathan becomes master of all.

5. Faith in prescription and distrust of "sophisters, calculators, and economists" who would reconstruct society upon abstract designs.

6. Recognition that change may not be salutary reform: hasty innovation may be a devouring conflagration, rather than a torch of progress.[8]

Here we must confine our view largely to the Anglo-American tradition.[9] In continental Europe during the past two centuries, conservatism has often referred to the ideology of those who have not accepted the legal type of authority and legitimacy, who have wished to cling to the practices that were widespread in Europe before the French Revolution: a hereditary aristocracy, established religion, and a monarchy unchecked by representative government—in general terms, to a traditional society of inherited status.

Though Anglo-American conservatism also began with the reaction against the French Revolution, that reaction was not as total and violent, because the status quo in England in 1789 was far removed from that in continental Europe. The so-called Glorious Revolution of 1688 had already established parliamentary supremacy and religious toleration in Britain. Although a powerful aristocracy existed, it was closely tied to the business or mercantile class. In the newly independent American colonies, there was no aristocracy at all, the monarchy had been abolished, and religious freedom was nearly absolute. England and America in 1789 already were, to a great extent, what the early reformers of the French Revolution wished to create. Anglo-American conservatism, epitomized by Burke, rejected sudden, state-directed change, but could not have rejected many of the aspirations of these reformers without rejecting itself.

A brief look at some of Burke's opinions suggests the complexities of being a conservative in a society whose traditions are largely liberal. Burke's economic views were almost identical to those of Adam Smith. He praised the market in these terms: "Nobody, I believe, has observed with any reflexion what market is, without being astonished at the truth, the correctness, the celerity, the general equity, with which the balance of wants is settled."[10] Correspondingly, Burke strongly advocated private property and totally rejected the redistributive state. Politically, Burke was a Whig—that is, a member of the party that, in broad terms, supported the rights of Parliament. He revered the memory of the Glorious Revolution, and he spoke in favour of the American colonies in their dispute with England because he thought they were being deprived of the traditional English right of self-government. All of these positions sound very liberal, seeming to support freedom, constitutionalism, and the rule of law. On the other hand, Burke was a strong advocate of hereditary aristocracy, though he himself was not of that class. To ensure that the nobility together with merchants of great property retained control of English government, he opposed any extension of the right to vote, which in his day was quite narrowly restricted. He thought that society was necessarily divided into hierarchical levels and that this was something for government to protect because of the hierarchy's contribution to social stability.

Burke accepted a degree of economic liberalism in combination with his social and political conservatism. The precise nature of that combination is intelligible only in the context of the issues of his day. Since then, Anglo-American conservatives have held various ideas, depending on when and where they lived, but they have generally followed Burke's example in combining market economics with respect for the past. Two of the founders of Canada—John A. Macdonald and George-Étienne Cartier—fit this description well. Both were thoroughly committed to the market system. Macdonald eventually adopted a protective tariff—which violates the concept of free trade—but only because he could not conclude a reciprocity (free trade) agreement with the United States. Both were opposed to universal suffrage and regarded the United States as an instructive example of democracy run amok. Both were strong supporters of the British Empire and the Crown, seeing a constitutional monarchy as a valuable source of social stability. It has been said of these two statesmen:

> It was not that the founders of the Canadian nation despised freedom; indeed, they revered it. But, for them, freedom arises from order, from restraint, not from unconstrained passions. The world they desired was the Burkean world, the world of order, restraint, sterner virtues and prudence.[11]

In comparison with American conservatism, the Canadian variety is less imbued with the virtues of free enterprise and more willing to resort to collectivist economic schemes. By any measure, American society and American thought are more individualistic than their Canadian counterparts, and Canadian conservatism reflects this general difference. Also, there is in Canada a tradition of conservatism that is rather sceptical of the competitive market philosophy of classical liberalism. Thinkers in this vein are often called **Red Tories** because they combine some traditionalist views with others that may seem interventionist or even socialist. The best-known Red Tory is the philosopher George Grant, whose 1965 book *Lament for a Nation* has become a classic of Canadian political thought. Grant was stirred to write his book by the collapse of John Diefenbaker's government over the issue of whether Canada should accept American nuclear warheads on its soil. In Grant's view, Lester Pearson's subsequent decision to accept the weapons showed that Canada had been pulled irretrievably into the American orbit. Grant's objection was not based merely on sentiments of Canadian nationalism but also on philosophical considerations: "The impossibility of conservatism in our era is the impossibility of Canada. As Canadians we attempted a ridiculous task in trying to build a conservative nation in the age of progress, on a continent we share with the most dynamic nation on earth. The current of modern history was against us."[12]

The dynamism to which Grant referred is the individualistic market orientation of American society. He touched here upon a profound truth—that the market is the great dissolver of customs, traditions, and all the things to which conservatives are temperamentally attached. The profit-and-loss psychology of the market tends to promote universal homogeneity and break down local particularity, thus undermining the heritage of the past.

No ideology is ever free of internal contradictions. The characteristic contradiction of conservatism is that in accepting the competitive market, which is really a classical liberal idea, it threatens many of its own values, relating to tradition, stability, and social cohesion. Nonetheless, contemporary conservatism as a practical, real-world ideology tries to ride both horses, so to speak; it accepts the *laissez faire* economic policy of classical liberalism along with a traditionalist view of social customs, morality, and political institutions.

NEOCONSERVATISM

There was a marked conservative (or classical liberal, which in contemporary context amounts to the same thing) tide during the 1980s in the Western democracies. After the Great Depression and World War II, the state had become generally accepted as a force for implementing a more just and equitable society. But a countermovement started with the election of Margaret Thatcher in Great Britain in 1979, Ronald Reagan in the United States in 1980, and Brian Mulroney in Canada in 1984. Parties espousing conservative ideology also governed Japan, Italy, and West Germany for most of the 1980s; and other nominally liberal or social-democratic governments, such as those in Australia and New Zealand, followed economic policies similar to those of conservative governments. It became common to refer to this conservative revival as **neoconservatism,** a term first used in the 1970s by a circle of writers in the United States who had once identified themselves as liberals or even socialists but had become disenchanted with developments in reform liberalism (see Comparative Perspectives 11.1).

Conservatives in power in Britain, Canada, and the United States during the 1980s were convinced that the public sector had become too large and was crowding out the private sector, and that government must therefore be **downsized.** Conservative governments tried to achieve this with wage freezes and rollbacks in the public service, across-the-board cuts in programs, and selective reductions in sectors thought to be particularly over-funded. However, the main obstacle to reducing the size of government is that most of the budget of the modern state consists of either transfer payments or services that are popular with large groups of voters, such as education, pensions, health care, and unemployment insurance. Electors may agree in the abstract that government is too large and may vote for a conservative party that promises to do something about it, but they become irate when they see services cut back.

In spite of attempts at downsizing, the conservative government of Brian Mulroney in Canada made only modest progress in tackling the double challenge confronting politicians in Canada and most other Western governments: the accumulated public **debt** and the annual **deficit.** The promises of the welfare state and reform liberalism, realized in Canada as part of Pierre Trudeau's "just society," proved expensive to keep. The federal government ran a deficit every year from 1975 through 1995—that is, it had to borrow money in order to pay its bills. The biggest expenditures by far were the transfer payments underpinning the welfare state.

A second typical conservative belief is that government controls hamper and restrict the private sector. The typical outgrowth of this line of thought is **deregulation**—that

Comparative Perspectives 11.1

Neoconservatism: The Politics of Naming

Strictly speaking, neoconservatism is an American phenomenon. It refers to a group of writers, mainly from New York City, who derived from various left-wing backgrounds, including communism, Trotskyism, social democracy, and the mainstream of the Democratic Party. Some also claimed to have been influenced by the University of Chicago political philosopher Leo Strauss. Well-known names in the first generation (1970s) include Irving Kristol, Norman Podhoretz, Jeanne Kirkpatrick, and Senator Daniel Patrick Moynihan, writing in journals such as *Commentary* and *Public Interest*. Their main themes were the necessity of offering stiffer resistance to Soviet expansionism, and the desirability of making the American welfare state less expensive, less intrusive, and more effective. Neoconservatives have played important roles in the Republican administrations of Ronald Reagan (1981–88), George Bush (1989–91), and George W. Bush (2001–08). They tend to be associated with East Coast think-tanks such as the Heritage Foundation, Cato Institute, and American Enterprise Institute. The label "neoconservative" was first pinned on them by the socialist writer Michael Harrington, but the neoconservatives accepted it and used it to describe themselves.

The situation is rather different in Canada. No important Canadian writer or political leader has ever described himself as neoconservative. In this country the term has been used exclusively by opponents of conservatism, who have applied it to leaders such as Ontario Premier Mike Harris, Alberta Premier Ralph Klein, Reform Party founder Preston Manning, and Conservative Prime Minister Stephen Harper. The term plays on latent Canadian anti-Americanism. By using an American term to label Canadian political leaders, their opponents imply that their ideas are American and not really Canadian.

is, the lifting of governmental controls on market activity. This was an important theme of the Reagan administration in the United States from 1980 to 1988. During Reagan's two terms in office, the economic (but not safety) aspects of passenger air travel were deregulated, which allowed airlines to determine fares and services competitively, without government approval. Telecommunications were also partially deregulated, creating competition for long-distance telephone services in the United States.

Canadian Conservatives also followed the agenda of deregulation. Shortly after taking office in 1984, they effectively removed the power of the Foreign Investment Review Agency to block or otherwise regulate external takeovers of Canadian businesses. They dismantled the National Energy Program, allowing the price of oil to be set by world markets, and followed the United States in deregulating airline passenger services. In 1992, long-distance telephone services also began to be deregulated.

In the Canadian context, the Free Trade Agreement with the United States might also be considered a form of deregulation. Protective tariffs amount to macro-regulation in that they guide the flow of labour and capital toward protected industries. The decision to lower or even abandon such tariffs is by implication a decision to rely more on market forces to determine patterns of investment and economic growth. Under heavy attack from the Liberals and New Democrats, the Conservatives made free trade their main issue in the 1988 election and renewed their mandate. Whatever their ultimate assessment of its results, historians will probably regard the negotiation of the Free Trade Agreement as the most important event of Mulroney's first term in office. He followed in his second term by negotiating a new agreement including Mexico—the North American Free Trade Agreement (NAFTA).

A third conservative watchword is **privatization**—the sale of government-owned assets or activities to the private sector. The most spectacular steps were taken by the Thatcher government in Great Britain, which organized many sales of previously nationalized companies. One of the most notable was the sale of the entire telephone system through a public share offering. In their first two terms in office (1979–87), the Conservatives in Britain reduced the share of the industrial and trading economy controlled by the state, going from 10 to 5 percent.[13]

In Canada, the Mulroney government completely or partly privatized 16 Crown corporations or other major federally controlled assets in the years 1984–89. Some of these were small and virtually invisible to the public, but others were major economic actors, such as de Havilland Aircraft, Canadair, Air Canada, and the hotel division of Canadian National Railways.[14] After that the pace slowed, although the government did sell 20 percent of Petro-Canada during its second term.

In one sense, the conservative revival of the 1980s petered out in the 1990s. In Britain, Margaret Thatcher was forced to resign in 1990 when she lost the support of her caucus. Her successor, John Major, won a majority Conservative government in the election that followed, but he was much less ideological than Thatcher. He was then defeated in the 1997 British election. In the United States, George Bush, Ronald Reagan's successor, was defeated when he sought re-election in 1992; and the new Democratic president, Bill Clinton, won a second term in 1996. And in Canada, the Liberal Party, led by Jean Chrétien, was returned to power in the election of 1993 and held on to it in the elections of 1997, 2000, and 2004.

But even when conservative parties were out of power, the ideological effects of conservatism were still felt. The Liberals in Canada, the Labour Party in Great Britain, and the Democrats in the United States were all pulled substantially to the right and had to adopt large parts of the conservative agenda in order to defeat their conservative competitors. Bill Clinton showed the way in 1992; many of the themes that carried him to victory that year resonated well with conservatives: cutting the deficit, better education and job training, investment in infrastructure, replacing welfare with "workfare." Conservatives might argue about the methods or the amount of money to be spent, but they had no fundamental quarrel with the objectives.

In this context, the record of the Chrétien government is particularly striking. Although as an opposition party the Liberals had criticized the Mulroney government's initiatives, once they were in power they maintained most of them and indeed took some of them further than Mulroney had done. Specifically, the Chrétien government

- Adhered to the Tories' tight-money, low-inflation policy,

- Left in place the goods and services tax, which is a flat-rate rather than a progressive tax,

- Continued free trade with the United States and extended it to Mexico by signing the North American Free Trade Agreement (NAFTA) negotiated by Mulroney's Conservative government,

- Converted the federal deficit into a surplus,

- Cut 40,000 positions from the federal civil service,

- Reduced fiscal transfers to the provinces for health care, welfare, and advanced education,

- Reduced the generosity of federally controlled social programs such as employment insurance,

- Privatized Canadian National Railways,

- Extended deregulation in the field of telecommunications, and

- Proposed major cuts to personal income tax as part of its 2000 election campaign and enacted them after winning the election.

Of course, the Liberals did not govern in every respect as a conservative party would have done. They took a number of liberal initiatives, particularly in areas where not much money was involved, such as stricter gun control and putting sexual orientation into the human rights code. But they were clearly a much different party from the Liberals of the 1960s and 1970s, who had dramatically expanded the Canadian welfare state. Similarly, Tony Blair's "New Labour" was able to win the 1997 election in Britain only by promising to leave untouched the major policy innovations of the Thatcher years. And in the United States, President Clinton cooperated with the Republican-controlled Congress on measures such as welfare reform and a plan to balance the federal budget.

Some observers think that neoconservatism has run its course, becoming a victim of its own success. Its economic main tenets—stable money, balanced budgets, lower taxes, and competitive markets—have become conventional wisdom, endorsed by most liberals and many social democrats. Its main international opponent, the Soviet Union as leader of the international communist movement, disintegrated in 1991. Neoconservatives had a distinctive agenda when they first surged to power in the 1980s, but it is now rather unclear what they stand for except preserving the accomplishments of the past. Expect a flood of titles similar to the American (originally

Canadian) author David Frum's 2008 book, *Comeback: Conservatism That Can Win Again,* as conservatives grapple with the need to update their political agenda.[15]

CONSERVATISM AND LIBERTARIANISM

As discussed earlier in this chapter, modern conservatism is a not-always-consistent blend of Burkean conservatism and classical liberalism. Virtually all contemporary conservatives agree that the welfare state has become too large and interventionist, so they support the 1980s agenda of downsizing, deregulation, and privatization described in the preceding section. As part of their struggle for smaller government, they also support balancing the budget and reducing the level of taxation. This side of conservatism, often known as **economic conservatism** or **fiscal conservatism,** is non-controversial within conservative political parties and advocacy groups.

Politics, however, is not just about economics. Government also has to deal with many other issues of human conduct that are not reducible to profit and loss. Below are a few examples currently debated in Canada, the United States, and many other countries:

- To what degree should abortion be regulated? Is the fetus merely tissue within a woman's body, over which she should have complete control, or is it an unborn child with rights that the state should protect?

- Should government continue to criminalize possession and sale of drugs such as marijuana, cocaine, and heroin?

- Gambling used to be prohibited or heavily restricted but is now widely available and used as a fundraising tool by governments. Is this trend simply legal recognition of a harmless amusement, or have we gone too far in making it easy for people to squander their savings?

- Television and movies now routinely display levels of violence, profanity, and sexuality that would have been unthinkable 30 years ago. Does this represent laudable progress toward freedom of expression or the degradation of public decency?

Many who call themselves conservatives would answer these and similar questions in the direction of greater restraint on individual behaviour. They believe that abortions should be more difficult to obtain, that mind-altering drugs should be criminally prohibited, that gambling should be severely restricted, and that government should restrain the commercial exploitation of sex and violence. The common denominator in all these positions is a belief that a good society cannot be merely a collection of pleasure-seeking individuals. Social existence demands that human behaviour be restrained by institutions such as the family, the church, the school, and—if all else fails—the state. Conservatives who espouse this Burkean view about the restraint of individual desire in the name of the common good are today often called **social conservatives.**

Other conservatives see things rather differently. While not advocating abortion, drug addiction, gambling, and pornography, they fear the enlargement of the state that may ensue when government is called upon to prohibit or regulate such activities. Some who take this approach prefer to call themselves not conservatives but **libertarians.** They are really classical liberals in the spirit of John Stuart Mill. They follow Mill's argument in *On Liberty* that it is better to leave people alone to make their own mistakes as long as they are not inflicting direct harm upon others. Libertarians might prefer to call themselves "liberals" except that in modern usage that term has become so closely identified with interventionist reform liberalism. Libertarians strive for intellectual consistency around the values of personal freedom and individual choice. They argue that if freedom and choice are essential in the economy, they are just as important in all other areas of social existence.

Struggling libertarian parties exist in Canada and the United States, but they are not really a political force. The importance of libertarianism is more as an intellectual current within the broader political movement of conservatism. For example, several prominent conservative authors have come out in favour of decriminalizing the possession of marijuana and other psychoactive drugs—for example, Milton Friedman, winner of the Nobel Prize in economics and a major source of economic-policy ideas for all conservative thinkers; William F. Buckley, former publisher of the influential conservative magazine *National Review;* and Michael Walker, former president of the Fraser Institute, the largest and most influential conservative research institute in Canada. Meanwhile, however, other conservatives continue to advocate Burkean ideas about the role of government in restraining individual desires.

In a way, this internal split within the conservative camp mirrors the division in the liberal camp between classical and reform liberals. Classical liberals believe in freedom across the board, while reform liberals believe in government restraint of individual choice *within* the economy. Libertarians also believe in freedom across the board, whereas social conservatives believe in government restraint of individual choice *outside* the economy. To see where you fall in this debate, take the World's Smallest Political Quiz at **www.self-gov.org/quiz.html.**

Questions for Discussion

1. Older people are typically more conservative than younger people. Can you explain why this should be so in light of Edmund Burke's theory of conservatism?

2. Many proverbs, such as "A bird in the hand is worth two in the bush," embody a Burkean view of human behaviour. Can you think of other such proverbs and explain the Burkean element in them?

3. Do you think Canada is better off or worse off as a result of the conservative (classical liberal) economic policies adopted during the 1980s and 1990s?

Internet Links

1. Canadian Conservative Forum: **www.conservativeforum.org.** Essays by conservative writers; many links.

2. Fraser Institute: **www.fraserinstitute.ca.** Vancouver-based think tank whose goal is "the redirection of public attention to the role of competitive markets in providing for the well-being of Canadians." Tends toward the libertarian side of conservatism.

3. Centre for Cultural Renewal: **www.culturalrenewal.ca.** Canadian, social conservative orientation.

4. Heritage Foundation: **www.heritage.org.** Large American conservative foundation.

5. American Enterprise Institute: **www.aei.org.** Another large American conservative foundation.

6. Conservative Party of Canada: **www.conservative.ca.**

Further Reading

Betz, Hans-Georg. *Radical Right-Wing Populism in Western Europe.* New York: St. Martin's Press, 1994.

Boaz, David. *Libertarianism: A Primer.* New York: Free Press, 1997.

Cooper, Barry, Allan Kornberg, and William Mishler, eds. *The Resurgence of Conservatism in Anglo-American Democracies.* Durham, NC: Duke University Press, 1988.

Diamond, Sara. *Roads to Dominion: Right-Wing Movements and Political Power in the United States.* New York: Guilford Press, 1995.

Doherty, Brian. *Radicals for Capitalism: A Freewheeling History of the Modern American Libertarian Movement.* Jackson, TN: PublicAffairs, 2007.

Dorrien, Gary. *The Neoconservative Mind.* Philadelphia: Temple University Press, 1993.

Drury, Shadia B. *Leo Strauss and the American Right.* New York: St. Martin's Press, 1997.

Frum, David. *Comeback: Conservatism That Can Win Again.* New York: Doubleday, 2008.

Gairdner, William D., ed. *After Liberalism: Essays in Search of Freedom, Virtue, and Order.* Toronto: Stoddart, 1998.

Harbour, William R. *The Foundations of Conservative Thought.* Notre Dame, IN: University of Notre Dame Press, 1982.

Honderich, Ted. *Conservatism.* London: H. Hamilton, 1990.

Jeffrey, Brooke. *Hard Right Turn: The New Face of Neo-Conservatism in Canada.* Toronto: HarperCollins, 1999.

Kirk, Russell. *The Conservative Mind.* 7th ed. Chicago: Henry Regnery, 1986.

Kristol, Irving. *Neoconservatism: The Autobiography of an Idea.* New York: Free Press, 1995.

———. *Reflections of a Neoconservative.* New York: Basic Books, 1983.

Lakoff, George. *Moral Politics: What Conservatives Know That Liberals Don't.* Chicago: University of Chicago Press, 1996.

Lora, Ronald. *Conservative Minds in America.* Westport, CT: Greenwood Press, 1979. First published in 1971.

Murray, Charles. *What It Means to Be a Libertarian.* New York: Broadway Books, 1997.

O'Sullivan, Noel. *Conservatism.* London: Dent, 1976.

Panichas, George A. *Restoring the Meaning of Conservatism: Writings from Modern Age.* Wilmington, DE: ISI Books, 2008.

Rossiter, Clinton. *Conservatism in America: The Thankless Persuasion.* Rev. ed. New York: Knopf, 1962.

Scruton, Roger. *The Meaning of Conservatism.* 2nd ed. Harmondsworth, UK: Penguin Books, 1984.

Wilson, Francis Graham. *The Case for Conservatism.* Piscataway, NJ: Transaction Publishers, 1990.

CHAPTER 12

Socialism and Communism

Like liberalism and conservatism, **socialism** is not a single ideology. We use the term here as a global concept that includes communism, democratic socialism, social democracy, anarchism, syndicalism, and other ideologies bearing a family resemblance to each other. Four of their common traits are particularly important, although this is not to suggest that there ever has been, or is now, a unified world socialist movement. In particular, communism and social democracy are worlds apart in political orientation, even though they have grown from the same family tree (see Figure 12.1).

COMMON ELEMENTS OF SOCIALIST IDEOLOGIES

Planning

Socialists repudiate the profit-motivated market economy, believing that society can emancipate itself from impersonal market processes and take conscious control of its economic affairs by deliberately planning them to maximize human happiness.

Common Ownership

Socialists condemn private ownership of productive property such as land, factories, stores, and the means of transportation and communication. They believe that such assets should be owned by the community, supposing that the benefits will then flow to all, not just to a restricted circle of private owners. However, they generally accept private ownership of consumer goods.

Equality of Result

Socialists aspire to a high degree of equality of result. While recognizing that people cannot be literally equal in all respects, they believe that much can be done to reduce major inequalities of wealth, income, social position, and political power. They see a planned economy and common ownership as important means to this end.

Figure 12.1 Socialist Family Tree

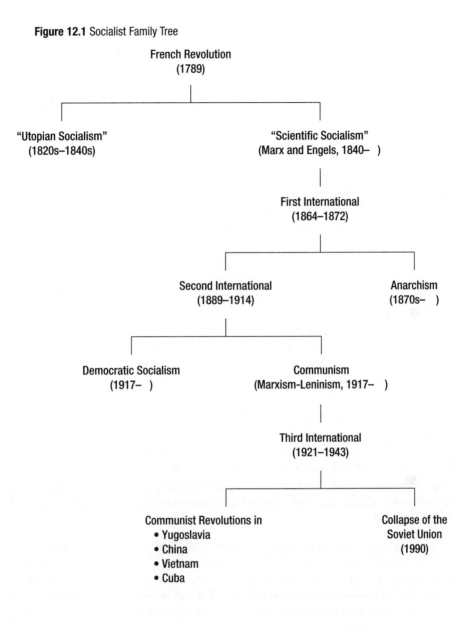

French Revolution
(1789)

"Utopian Socialism"
(1820s–1840s)

"Scientific Socialism"
(Marx and Engels, 1840–)

First International
(1864–1872)

Second International
(1889–1914)

Anarchism
(1870s–)

Democratic Socialism
(1917–)

Communism
(Marxism-Leninism, 1917–)

Third International
(1921–1943)

Communist Revolutions in
• Yugoslavia
• China
• Vietnam
• Cuba

Collapse of the
Soviet Union
(1990)

Selflessness

Socialists regard selfishness not as an innate human characteristic but as the product of flawed social institutions. They are convinced that appropriate social change can produce a new "socialist man" who is less self-interested and more concerned about the welfare of the collectivity.[1] This overall change in human behaviour will result from, and at the same time support, the first three objectives.

HISTORICAL OVERVIEW

Common ownership of property is an ancient topic of philosophical speculation. Plato's *Republic* (ca. 380 BC) portrayed a *polis* in which the intellectual and military classes shared property and wives, although the ordinary people continued to have private property and families. Thomas More's *Utopia* (1516) went further and extended common property to an entire society, but it was a satire on the England of More's day, not a serious proposal for implementation. Other philosophers toyed with socialism from time to time, but it was not viewed as realistic until the nineteenth century.

There is also a long religious history to socialism. The Acts of the Apostles reports that in the first Christian community of Jerusalem, "the whole body of believers was united in heart and soul. Not a man of them claimed any of his possessions as his own, but everything was held in common."[2] Community of goods has repeatedly been reintroduced by Christian sects, particularly those who believe that the second coming of Christ to earth is imminent. In Canada today, this kind of Christian socialism is represented by the Hutterites, who collectively own and operate large farms in the western provinces.

Like so much else in modern politics, secular, political socialism made its debut during the French Revolution, when a journalist named François-Noël Babeuf organized an abortive communist uprising in 1796.[3] Its practical significance at the time was nil because the police broke up the plot and Babeuf was sentenced to death. But the events, and particularly the speech Babeuf made at his trial, begin the story that leads to Marx, Lenin, and the socialist revolutions of our time.

Babeuf's plan was for a short, successful insurrection in Paris on the model of several that had been attempted since 1789. Having seized the French state at the centre, he would institute a provisional government to crush the enemies of the people. Private property would be confiscated, and a "Grand National Economy" would replace the market system of allocation with a central storehouse where goods would be deposited, then distributed to all as needed:

> It will be composed of all in complete equality—all rich, all poor, all free, all brothers. The first law will be a ban on private property. We will deposit the fruits of our toil in the public stores. This will be the wealth of the state and the property of all. Every year the heads of families will select stewards whose task will be the distribution of goods to each in accordance with his needs, the allotment of tasks to be performed by each, and the maintenance of public order.[4]

Babeuf did not desire or expect this system to create great wealth. He quoted with approval the words of Rousseau that "all luxury is superfluous—everything is superfluous above and beyond the sheerest of physical necessities."[5] To ensure that luxury did not creep into this Spartan society, he would have banned money and foreign trade.

Babeuf's conspiratorial and insurrectionary approach survived his death, but was complemented in the first decades of the nineteenth century by the **utopian socialism** of writers like Robert Owen (1771–1858) and Charles Fourier (1772–1837). They proposed not to seize the state by force but to teach by example—to found small-scale communities in which productive property would be jointly owned, all would join in performing necessary labour, and living standards would be more or less equalized. Unlike Babeuf, they did not seek to impose a regime of universal poverty; they believed that their communes would allow everyone to enjoy the luxuries previously reserved for the rich. Literally hundreds of these communes, based on various models, have been tried out. Some of these experiments became quite famous, such as New Harmony, Indiana, run by Robert Owen, and Brook Farm, in Massachusetts, modelled on the ideas of Fourier.[6] The utopian strategy of showing the world the merits of socialism on a small scale has not been fully successful, but neither has it been without effect—the Israeli kibbutz is a lineal descendant of these early experiments.

Karl Marx (1818–83) and Friedrich Engels (1820–95) gave the ideology of socialism its classic formulation. Their greatest innovation was to transform socialism into the doctrine of a single class, the industrial working class, which they renamed the **proletariat.** They labelled their predecessors as utopian for having aimed at the betterment of humanity through appeals to reason. The proletariat, as the "universal class," embodied the future hopes of humanity; its political struggle would furnish the "material weapons" needed by socialist philosophy.[7]

Marx's emphasis on the working class gives the impression that for him the central issues were poverty, equality, and living standards; but the discovery of unpublished manuscripts written in his youth has put the matter in a different light. "An enforced increase in wages," wrote Marx in 1843, "would be nothing more than *a better remuneration of slaves,* and would not restore, either to the worker or to the work, their human significance and worth."[8] To the young Marx, the true issue was what he called alienation. A market system, he argued, reverses the right order of human priorities. Work, which ought to be people's highest activity,

Karl Marx, 1818–83, the most famous philosopher of socialism.

the expression of their creative powers, becomes in such a system merely a means for people to keep themselves alive. Instead of valuing human activity for its own sake, people become acquisitive, obsessed with accumulating purchasing power. They lose control over what they produce as their products are bought and sold on the market. Property owners are equally dehumanized, even if they escape the impoverished condition of the proletariat. The social alienation between owners—the **bourgeoisie,** in Marx's vocabulary—and workers was only one aspect of the larger alienation of all people from their human essence. Of course, that did not make class differentials less odious, and Marx depicted them with all his rhetorical power:

> Labour certainly produces marvels for the rich but it produces privation for the worker. It produces palaces, but hovels for the worker. It produces beauty, but deformity for the worker. It replaces labour by machinery, but it casts some of the workers back into a barbarous kind of work and turns the others into machines. It produces intelligence, but also stupidity and cretinism for the workers.[9]

Marx offered not only a principled critique of society but also an analysis of the course of history. He wanted to show not just that capitalism ought to be destroyed, but that it would destroy itself through its internal contradictions. Marx and Engels called their doctrine **scientific socialism** because they thought it was not only a morally attractive alternative but also an empirically based guide to what was bound to happen.

Although the subject is much too complex to summarize here, we can indicate the main lines of the capitalist breakdown that Marx foresaw.[10] One salient fact was the polarization of society. Capitalism would create a large working class, who would become the "gravediggers" of the system. The proletariat was doomed to impoverishment—perhaps not in absolute terms, but in comparison with the rapidly increasing affluence of the bourgeoisie. The working class, led by socialist intellectuals such as Marx himself, would eventually seize the state and use it to abolish capitalism. Indeed, when the proletariat came to power, it would find that the system had already virtually abolished itself. The market process would have generated industrial monopolies, as only a few giant firms would have survived the rigours of competition. Without many competitors, the market would not work, even on its own terms. The new proletarian state would simply have to confiscate these monopolies from their bourgeois owners and set them to work under central planning.

Marx held that the ultimate victory of socialism was certain but not automatic; it also required a deliberate political struggle. He proposed (and helped to bring about) the representation of the working class by organized political parties. In constitutional states with a parliamentary system, the workers might struggle for the universal franchise. Once the vote was achieved for all, socialists could expect to be elected to power, for the proletariat would be a majority of the electorate; in other words, socialism would be a natural outgrowth of democracy. Simultaneously, Marx also proposed a revolutionary seizure of power, particularly where constitutionalism and the rule of law did not exist. Such a rising would produce a workers' government, the **dictatorship of the proletariat.** In a situation equivalent to civil war, the proletarian dictatorship would have to ignore the niceties of the rule of law, at least until its power was secure. This dual approach to gaining power was to prove fateful for the subsequent history of socialism. The two approaches, united in Marx, would eventually split into the two mutually antagonistic movements known as socialism and communism.

Because of their emphasis on the collapse of capitalism and the proletarian seizure of power, neither Marx nor Engels wrote much about socialism itself. What one mostly finds are abstract and rather enigmatic sayings, such as the dictum that socialism means "the ascent of man from the kingdom of necessity to the kingdom of freedom."[11] However, some scattered passages give a rough idea of what Marx and Engels expected to happen after the workers came to power. It is striking to read the list of transitional measures given in the *Communist Manifesto* (1848), most of which have subsequently been adopted by liberal and even conservative governments (see Historical Perspectives 12.1). The ones marked with an asterisk have been at least partly implemented in most Western democracies.

Historical Perspectives 12.1

Transitional Measures from the *Communist Manifesto*

1. Abolition of property in land and application of all rents of land to public purposes.

2. A heavy progressive or graduated income tax.*

3. Abolition of all right of inheritance.

4. Confiscation of the property of all emigrants and rebels.

5. Centralization of credit in the hands of the state, by means of a national bank with state capital and an exclusive monopoly.*

6. Centralization of the means of communication and transport in the hands of the state.*

7. Extension of factories and instruments of production owned by the state; the bringing into cultivation of wastelands, and the improvement of the soil generally in accordance with a common plan.*

8. Equal liability to all of labour. Establishment of industrial armies, especially for agriculture.

9. Combination of agriculture with manufacturing industries; gradual abolition of the distinction between town and country, by a more equable distribution of the population over the country.

10. Free education for all children in public schools. Abolition of children's factory labour in its present form. Combination of education with industrial production.*[12]

* indicates measures that have been implemented in Western democracies.

Accomplishing these and other measures would supposedly make the state master of the economy, able to conduct central planning. But full equality of result would take a long time to achieve. There would have to be an interim period during which equality would mean, in effect, "equal pay for equal work." All workers would be employed by the state, and ownership of property would no longer allow the wealthy to escape labour; but some would work more effectively and diligently than others, and they would be rewarded for doing so.

Beyond this stage, Marx's thoughts on the future became visionary. The state, even though it would have to be large and powerful in order to conduct central planning, would lose its coercive character. As Engels put it in a biological metaphor, the state would "wither away." Marx preferred to say that the state would be "transcended"— that people would learn to conduct their affairs without a centralized apparatus of coercion.

The transcendence of the state was linked to what Marx called the "higher phase of communist society," where "equal work for equal pay" would give way to a nobler form of equality: "From each according to his ability, to each according to his needs."[13] Work would become a freely creative activity performed for its own sake, not to be bought and sold. People would express themselves in all directions, utilizing their repertoire of human powers; there would be no economic necessity forcing them to be narrow specialists in the socialist "kingdom of freedom." In an almost lyrical passage, Marx and Engels wrote:

> For as soon as the distribution of labour comes into being, each man has a particular, exclusive sphere of activity, which is forced upon him and from which he cannot escape. He is a hunter, a fisherman, a shepherd, or a critical critic, and must remain so if he does not want to lose his means of livelihood; while in communist society, where nobody has one exclusive sphere of activity but each can become accomplished in any branch he wishes, society regulates the general production and thus makes it possible for me to do one thing today and another tomorrow, to hunt in the morning, fish in the afternoon, rear cattle in the evening, criticize after dinner, just as I have a mind, without ever becoming hunter, fisherman, shepherd or critic.[14]

In addition to being theorists, Marx and Engels were also political activists who contributed to the political struggle of the working class. Their first organization, the Communist League, is remembered chiefly because Marx and Engels wrote the *Communist Manifesto* to be its program. More important was the International Workingmen's Association (1864–72), commonly known as the **First International,** in which Marx and Engels were deeply involved. A loose association of socialist parties and labour unions in Western Europe, with headquarters in London, it split into hostile wings in 1872 when old factional differences became too strong to contain. The split was partly a clash of personalities between Marx and the Russian Mikhail Bakunin (1814–76), but there was also an important ideological issue. Bakunin and his followers, who subsequently became known as anarchists, thought that Marx was infatuated with the state. They believed that the state could be destroyed quickly in the aftermath of the workers' revolution, whereas Marx envisioned a period of state socialism leading up to the true classless society and the higher phase of communism. The anarchists feared, with considerable foresight, that the Marxian socialist state might turn out to be permanent rather than temporary.[15]

Although the First International collapsed, socialist parties continued to exist in various European states. They were reunited, excluding the anarchists, in the **Second International,** founded in Paris in 1889 to celebrate the centennial of the French Revolution.[16] Marx having died in 1883, Engels became the elder statesman of the new organization, and Marxism became its ideology. With the Second International, socialism came of age in Europe. Socialist and labour parties thrived by following Marx's evolutionary strategy. None ever won a majority in an election, but all succeeded in electing substantial blocs of representatives wherever liberal and constitutional values kept politics open. The Second International expressed itself in revolutionary rhetoric, but its political practices were overwhelmingly evolutionary and constitutional.[17]

Because the Czar ruled the Russian Empire autocratically, the absence of a parliament and constitution made the evolutionary strategy inapplicable there, forcing the Russian Social Democratic Party to work illegally, secretively, and conspiratorially. Vladimir Ilyich Lenin (1870–1924), leader of the wing of the party known as the Bolsheviks, was led by these conditions, so different from those in Western Europe, to create a new style and a new theory of party leadership. Marx had expected the revolution to grow from the spontaneous class-consciousness of the workers, whereas Lenin, faced with a backward country and a small working class, tended to think of revolutionary consciousness as something transmitted by bourgeois intellectuals to the workers. This seemingly minor difference implied a new approach to the problems of party organization. The party had to be firmly controlled from the top because the leadership could not rely on the workers' spontaneity. Lenin's theory of the disciplined party—**democratic centralism**—moulded the party into an effective revolutionary weapon suited to survival in the autocratic Russian setting.[18]

Lenin, incidentally, is associated with another major innovation in socialist ideology. Marx had always insisted that the socialist revolution would be a world revolution. His view of the world was centred on Western Europe, and he apparently thought that the European nations would drag their empires with them into socialism. Because he emphasized Europe, Marx thought that the revolution would occur soon because capitalism, which was fated to put an end to itself, was well advanced on that continent. But when World War I broke out, he had been dead for 30 years and the socialists still had not come to power anywhere.

Lenin spent most of the war in exile in Switzerland and used this period of enforced leisure to write a pamphlet explaining the delay. *Imperialism: The Highest Stage of Capitalism* (1917) argued that the advanced nations had managed to postpone the revolution by amassing colonial empires. Overseas investments counteracted the falling tendency of the rate of profit, while colonial markets temporarily solved the problem of overproduction. Merciless exploitation of the colonies could buy off the proletariat at home, creating a "labour aristocracy" of well-paid workers at the centre of the empire.

World War I, however, showed that the imperialists had begun to quarrel with each other. The socialist revolution would arise not from a business crash, as Marx had been inclined to believe, but out of the turmoil of war. Lenin thus decisively broadened the scope of socialism from a European to a global movement, and in doing so bolstered his own revolutionary optimism. "Capitalism," he wrote, "has grown into a world system of colonial oppression and of the financial strangulation of the overwhelming population of the world by a handful of 'advanced' countries."[19]

World War I sounded the death knell for the Second International. Most of the workers in the combatant states supported the war effort, effectively pitting the International against itself. In February 1917, the Czar was toppled and a constitutional democracy created. In October of the same year, the Bolsheviks, led by Lenin, seized control of the state through insurrections of armed workers in St. Petersburg and Moscow, creating a dictatorship of the proletariat in which their party played the dominant role. They outlawed political opposition—even socialist opposition. These events were an agonizing test for the socialists of Western Europe, who had yearned for a revolution for generations. Now, as they witnessed a successful one, they were appalled by its undemocratic aspects.

The eventual result of the Russian Revolution was an irreparable split in the world socialist movement. Those who approved of Lenin and his methods formed **communist** parties in every country and gathered themselves in the **Third International,** or **Comintern** (short for "Communist International"). In practice, the Comintern soon became an extension of the Soviet state for foreign-policy purposes. Although Stalin dissolved it in 1943 as a gesture of cooperation with the Allies during World War II, the individual communist parties continued to be closely tied to Moscow. After the end of the war, the organizational emphasis shifted to the Soviet satellite states. In 1947 these were bound together into the **Cominform** (Communist Information Bureau), which in 1956 was in turn replaced by the Warsaw Treaty Organization. The latter was dissolved in 1991 as part of the general decommunization of Eastern Europe. Today, the term *communist* is rarely encountered. The organizations that used to call themselves communist parties still exist, but they have adopted new names emphasizing concepts such as labour or democracy.

Those who opposed Lenin regrouped under the general name of **social democrats,** often merging with Christian and other moderate socialists who had been outside the Marxist consensus of the Second International. These social-democratic parties still exist as the Labour Party of Great Britain, the Social Democratic Party of Germany, and so on. They have kept to the course of constitutionalism and are well integrated into their respective political systems. They form governments when they win elections and resign from office when they lose.

Socialism, in the form of social democracy, is a familiar part of contemporary politics. Its ideology has over decades become considerably diluted, relative to the Marxist thought from which it sprang, so that social democrats today can be hard to distinguish from reform liberals. Both espouse, to a limited degree, the typical socialist goals of central planning, common ownership, and equality of result. Social democrats call for government to guide the economy by pulling the levers of spending, taxation, and regulation. They wish some major enterprises to be publicly owned—that is, they call for a **mixed economy**—but they do not advocate wholesale nationalization of all business.

Several small socialist parties existed in Canada before the great split between communists and social democrats, but none was ever very significant. The first important party of the social-democratic type was the Co-operative Commonwealth Federation (CCF), founded in Calgary in 1932. It drew together remnants of the old socialist parties, trade unionists, farmer activists, and intellectuals who had been educated in Britain or influenced by British socialist thought. The party's first platform was the Regina Manifesto, adopted in 1933. It repudiated "change by violence" and promised to promote the socialist cause "solely by constitutional methods." Although the means would be peaceful, the end was declared to be far-reaching:

> We aim to replace the present capitalist system, with its inherent injustice and inhumanity, by a social order from which the domination and exploitation of one class by another will be eliminated, in which economic planning will supersede unregulated private enterprise and competition, and in which genuine democratic self-government, based upon economic equality, will be possible . . . We aim at a planned and socialized economy in which our natural resources and the principal means of production and distribution are owned, controlled and operated by the people.[20]

The CCF achieved some political successes, most notably the election of the first socialist government in North America in Saskatchewan in 1944, but its electoral support eroded badly during the 1950s. In 1961 it restructured itself as the New Democratic Party, with greatly strengthened ties to organized labour. Tellingly, the word *socialism* did not appear in the New Party Declaration it adopted.[21] As in other countries, social democracy now presented itself not as a full alternative to the market system, but rather as a means of using the state as a reforming agency.

Ed Broadbent expressed the rapprochement of social democracy with the market when he announced his resignation as federal leader of the NDP in 1989:

> The serious debate about the future is not about the desirability of a market economy. For most thoughtful people that debate is now closed . . . We New Democrats believe in the marketplace including private investment decisions, reduced tariffs, private property, the free disposal of assets, the right to make a profit, decentralized decision making . . . As the world evolves so must our policies.[22]

From this perspective, social democracy, like reform liberalism, consists of government efforts to "correct" the market—to change some of its results rather than to replace it outright.

Marx had a grudging admiration for the market system as a means of accumulating wealth but regarded it as a temporary phase of human development. Socialism, he thought, would be able to make much more humane use of the productive powers unleashed by capitalism. But, in fact, socialism has been least successful in precisely those countries that have been most capitalistic and, by Marx's reasoning, most ready for socialism. In the industrialized countries, socialism has been most effective in a diluted form—that is, as social democracy; in such cases it represents a reformist impulse within the system, not a polar alternative. The stronger form of communism came to dominance in the economically backward Russian Empire, and the Soviet Union imposed it by force on the nations of Eastern Europe. Authentic communist revolutions (i.e., not the result of Soviet initiatives) also took place in Yugoslavia, China, and Vietnam. The latter two revolutions were almost the opposite of what Marx would have anticipated: they happened in pre-industrial societies in which capitalism had hardly gotten underway.

We now move on to a more conceptual analysis of socialism as an ideology.

PLANNING

In varying degrees, socialists are generally hostile to the market, condemning it as anarchic, inefficient, and inequitable. Even contemporary social democrats, while accepting the market in principle, think it needs a good deal of correction in practice. Socialists particularly condemn the pursuit of profit; in the words of the Regina Manifesto, the principle of a socialist society "will be the supplying of human needs and not the making of profits."[23] But profit in the market system is not antithetical to need; it is the means by which needs are met. That people need food, clothing, shelter, and recreation and are willing to pay for them induces entrepreneurs to seek a profit by offering these goods for sale. The central issue is not need versus profit, but the most effective means of discovering and satisfying human needs. Is it the market system with competition, floating prices, and the profit motive, or is it a **planning** system, in which a central authority decides what to produce and allocates products to consumers?

The market, while hardly a perfect system, demonstrably performs a job of matching production and consumption across a large number of commodities. Early socialists were quite naïve about how difficult this task is. Babeuf's central storehouses could scarcely have coped with the problem, but he probably would not have cared because he wanted all to live in Spartan simplicity. Marx simply ignored the problem by refusing to speculate on the practical consequences of a socialist society. Through the pain of much trial and error, the Soviet Union and other socialist states developed state planning machinery that was actually a hybrid of the planning principle and the market principle. The State Planning Committee, as it was called in the Soviet Union, developed and updated a national plan that specified tonnes of coal and steel of various grades, kilowatt hours of electricity, litres of oil, tonnes of wheat, and other production quantities to be produced by the various industries. One industry supplied another as part of this plan rather than by market auction. But markets connected the industrial complex to the inhabitants of the country, who purchased the output at retail stores owned by the state and sold their labour to the state as employer. By this partial use of markets, the state refrained from trying to directly control the daily affairs of hundreds of millions of people.

These markets, however, were heavily controlled by the state. The labour market was restricted by lack of mobility; for example, a worker on a collective farm was not allowed to leave that farm to seek work in the city. Also, prices in markets for both labour and consumer goods did not float according to supply and demand but were administered by the state. When price is not used to ration scarce commodities, other forms of rationing must intervene. One is direct assignment by authority, as was used to distribute housing. Another is queuing: the ability to spend time waiting replaced the ability to spend money as a means of acquiring goods. Still another form of rationing was evasion of the law. Those with more money than time frequently resorted to bribery and black markets. Indeed, life in Eastern Europe would scarcely have been possible without the black market, because many goods and services needed in daily life were not available at any price in the state stores.

RETURNING TO A MARKET ECONOMY

Although it produced a low standard of living in comparison with the Western market economy, the communist-planned economy did work after its own fashion and, in the Soviet Union, brought many people a considerable improvement in living standards relative to czarist days. Jobs were guaranteed for all, inflation was repressed, and food, clothing, shelter, and other basic commodities were available at low prices. Education was universal and in some ways of excellent quality; low-tech medical care was generally accessible; and retired people could count on modest state pensions. Taxes were low because the state derived most of its revenue from its ownership of the economy. Daily life was often uncomfortable, inconvenient, and monotonous, but at least it was predictable.

Eastern European communism started to collapse in the late 1980s when the Soviet leader Mikhail Gorbachev attempted to reform the system. Worried that his regime was failing in economic and military competition with the West, he tried to introduce elements of the market economy and individual freedom. But the reform process quickly got out of his control, leading to the fall of all communist governments in Eastern Europe in the late 1980s and early 1990s. Now that marketization is well advanced, people are sometimes nostalgic about the planned economy, for it proved more difficult than anyone had anticipated to make the transition to a market economy.

Analytically, it is easy to specify the main changes that had to take place:

- decontrol or "liberalization" of prices, so that they arise in a competitive market rather than being set by administrative command;

- privatization of the means of production, so that the elements of the economy come under private ownership and control;

- disinvestment in inefficient enterprises that existed for political or military reasons;

- opening of the economy to foreign trade and investment, so that modern techniques of production can be adopted; and

- attainment of a stable currency that is "convertible"; that is, freely exchangeable against other currencies.

The success of marketization has been mixed. East Germany was absorbed by West Germany and entered the market economy by that route; but the cost was higher than anyone predicted and made a mockery of German Chancellor Helmut Kohl's prediction that reunification could be accomplished without raising taxes. The Czech Republic, Slovakia, Hungary, Poland, and Slovenia have made substantial progress, but the Balkan countries—Croatia, Serbia, Albania, Macedonia, Romania, and Bulgaria—have often seemed trapped in a vicious circle of violence, political instability, and corrupt, inefficient government.

Russia, the most important country in Eastern Europe, also has a mixed record. Its crash program of privatization in the early 1990s created a new economic oligarchy, composed of speculators as well as former directors of state enterprises, who got control of the most important state assets. They grew immensely rich by exploiting the peculiarities of the partial liberalization of prices that took place at the same time. They were able to obtain commodities such as oil and minerals at artificially low domestic prices, export them for much higher world prices, and pocket the difference. Russia now has a market economy based on private ownership, but it is fragile. "Civil society is weak and the enforcement of laws is patchy," wrote Chrystia Freeland, a Canadian financial journalist who spent much of the 1990s in Russia. "*Who* you know is still more important than *what* you know or what you can do. No economy built on such weak foundations can flourish, and Russia's hasn't. After a ten-year depression [in which the economy shrank to half its previous size], it managed only anaemic growth of 2 percent in 1999."[24] Since then, however, the economy boomed as international oil prices climbed into the range of US$100 a barrel. Russia has become the world's largest oil exporter, so high prices mean prosperity as long as they last. Some Russians are nostalgic for communism, but hardly anyone in a position of power wants to go back. The debate in Russia is not between capitalism and communism but between crony capitalism and a more open, competitive system.

In the People's Republic of China, the situation is rather different. The Communist Party still exercises firm political control but has largely privatized agriculture, which the majority of China's people are still engaged in. Moreover, it has allowed massive foreign investment in enterprise zones in the provinces bordering on Hong Kong. By some estimates, the economy of China is now more than half capitalist, even though the regime is still nominally communist.[25] At the present time, the Chinese economy continues to enjoy sustained rapid growth.

It may be that China is undergoing a revolution in substance, as opposed to form, and will follow the same path as South Korea and Taiwan, where authoritarian governments backed by overwhelming military force presided over a prolonged period of growth in a capitalist economy. If that is the case, it must be considered encouraging, for both South Korea and Taiwan made progress toward political democracy in the 1980s and 1990s. If the same happens some day in China, it will amount to the reverse of what took place in the Soviet Union. There, political democracy came before economic liberalization, and the result was virtual economic collapse. If China follows the path of South Korea and Taiwan, economic liberalization and rapid growth may pave the way for a degree of democratization. But all countries are unique and there is no way to be certain about China's future. As of 2008, the Communist Party was still firmly in control and there were no signs of political liberalization.

Social democrats in the Western world retreated from full-scale central planning much earlier than the Chinese and Russians. *Social Planning for Canada,* written in 1935 by the leading intellectuals in the CCF, called for a national planning commission modelled on the Soviet example.[26] Today, neither the NDP nor other social democratic parties advocate full-scale planning. Instead, they see the state as a means for guiding the market toward particular objectives such as full employment, location of industry in depressed areas, and advancement of disadvantaged minorities. To achieve these

The Chinese communist regime has launched a campaign of brutal repression against the Falun Gong "cult." Ironically, however, the regime still maintains a public cult of its own authority.
© Chappatte, www.globecartoon.com

goals, the state may employ taxation, subsidies, monopoly concessions, regulatory legislation, price controls, adjustments in interest rates, and other interventionist tools. A program of such interventions is sometimes called a plan, but it is not planning in the original sense of the term.

COMMON OWNERSHIP

Except in times of war or other emergency, central planning cannot work without a high degree of common ownership. Presumably, the central plan will require investment decisions other than those that private owners would spontaneously make; otherwise there would be no need for the plan. To avoid creating a whole new class of potential criminals, productive property has to be publicly owned to remove any conflicts between the plan and property rights.

Common ownership can be achieved in a number of ways. In the Third World, it can be appended to existing communal traditions. If a peasant village already holds grazing, timber, or water rights in common, collective ownership of the surrounding arable land may not be a drastic step. Another approach to common ownership is the voluntary cooperative, utilized to organize either producers or consumers. A great many cooperatives—credit unions, wheat pools, housing co-ops—already exist in Canada, where they function as part of the market economy; but they could also become part of a socialist economy. Another possibility is for the workers to own their own factory or other workplace. A variant of socialism known as **syndicalism** (from the French *syndicat,* "association") takes this approach. No one has ever tried a fully syndicalist economy, but there were elements of syndicalism in the Yugoslavian version of socialism, in which workers' councils had some say in the running of enterprises.

These options are interesting and important, but in the mainstream of socialism, common ownership has meant state ownership. Socialization or nationalization of property means a takeover by the state, which then owns and administers the property as the agent of the people. This ownership can be direct (as in the case of the Canadian armed forces, operated as a government department under ministerial supervision) or indirect (as in the case of Canada Post and the Canadian Broadcasting Corporation, which are Crown corporations owned by the state but operating more or less autonomously under their own boards of directors).

In the Soviet Union, the state owned all factories, railways, and other means of production, as well as all schools, hospitals, and retail stores. It also owned all natural resources and all land, which it leased to entities such as collective farms and housing cooperatives. Private ownership was almost entirely confined to consumer goods.

Social democracy retreated long ago from its commitment to complete nationalization. The Regina Manifesto exempted farms from public ownership but called for nationalization of the entire financial industry, as well as the transportation, communications, and electric-power sectors, "and all other industries and services essential to social planning."[27] The latter would have included many firms in the resource sector. The logic of the list was that these industries represented "the commanding heights of the economy."[28] All other businesses—manufacturing, wholesaling, retailing, personal services, and so on—need access to credit, transportation, communications, energy, and natural resources. If the government owned and controlled these indispensable industries, it would be able to compel or induce other industries to work toward politically chosen goals. Manufacturing firms, for example, could be persuaded to locate in depressed areas by offers of low-interest loans or cheap transportation.

EQUALITY OF RESULT

One of the attractive goals of socialism has been to reduce the material inequalities that are part of a market economy. These inequalities are unseemly to socialists (as well as to many others), who have sought to overcome them through a planned economy and public ownership of property. However, while it is easy to call for equality of result, it is much harder to state precisely what it means. We differ so much in our aptitudes, needs, and desires that it would be absurd to say we should all have the same number of shoes or square metres of housing.

One approach is equality of opportunity: using the state to ensure that everyone can have certain chances in life, but allowing individuals to keep the rewards of their own efforts. This social democratic idea, now widely accepted by reform liberals, fits in well with the contemporary welfare state, which is supposed to educate us as children and protect us against contingencies as adults. Its safety net allows us to bounce back from sickness, accidents, and unemployment but does not in itself guarantee a very desirable standard of living. We have to achieve that on our own initiative.

A related approach to equality is to reduce the range of inequality by raising the floor and lowering the ceiling, so that extremes of wealth and poverty vanish but some variation remains. This partial egalitarianism is widely accepted today, not just by socialists but also by reform liberals and many others who have no definable ideology. It can be attempted in the market system through progressive taxation, redistribution, and the abundant services of the welfare state. Or, as in the Soviet style of planned economy, it can be approached by setting wages and salaries on an egalitarian basis.

By some statistical indices the communist states appeared to equalize living standards. Published data on incomes showed smaller differentials between manual workers and professionals than in the West, and of course large pools of capital no longer existed in private hands. Statistics, however, do not tell the whole story because the communist systems instituted significant forms of non-monetary privilege. For example, high officials of the Communist Party, as well as leading scientists, athletes, managers, and artists, had access to special housing, shopping, and medical care; could often avoid waiting lists for things such as automobiles; and had the privilege of foreign travel.[29]

The ultimate in equality is still as stated in the Marxian slogan, "From each according to his ability, to each according to his needs." This noble sentiment expresses the operating principle of a happy family, one in which parents assess the needs and abilities of their children—but can an entire society of adults operate like a single family? If we let people assess their own needs and set their own contributions, is it not likely that they will estimate the former on the high side, and reduce the latter below what is reasonable? It seems hard to avoid the requirement for a central authority to decide such things (as, indeed, parents are almost all-powerful in relation to their children). This casts serious doubt on the premise that the state will wither away, which is what is supposed to occur in the highest stage of communism.

SELFLESSNESS

The discussion in the preceding paragraph assumes that human behaviour will remain self-interested. The situation would be different if selfishness arose only from the effects of a market economy, which encourages people to put their own interests first. Socialists have often assumed that conflict is typical of capitalism and that cooperation would be typical of a socialist system. However, to contrast cooperation with conflict is misleading. Spontaneous order depends on cooperation voluntarily achieved through mutual pursuit of self-interest, as in Adam Smith's metaphor of the invisible hand. A planned economy calls for cooperation directed from above. The important question is not whether we shall have cooperation, for obviously we must; it is whether mutual coordination is a more effective means of achieving it than authoritative direction.[30]

In contrast to socialism, both liberalism and conservatism accept human beings as they are, with all their flaws, and seek to understand the social order that inevitably follows. They assume that society is and will always be composed of individuals and groups in conflict with one another. They hope to contain that conflict within a peaceful framework, not abolish it altogether. Contemporary socialists, to the extent that they have reduced some of their earlier and more visionary expectations about planning, public ownership, and equality, have also become pessimistic about an easy, quick change in human nature.

GOVERNING

We have discussed at some length the differences between communists and social democrats in their approach to obtaining power. The distinction between constitutional and unconstitutional methods is also reflected in the way socialist states are governed. Social democrats in their rapprochement with liberalism have adopted the constitutional philosophy of the limited state and the rule of law. Communists, in contrast, used constitutionalism only as a means of achieving power.

Central planning and state ownership of the means of production put the entire economy at the disposal of the government. This produced such an unparalleled concentration of power that observers had to invent a new term, *totalitarianism,* to describe the resulting system. This expansion of the state posed thorny problems for the ideologists of Marxism–Leninism. Marx's dictatorship of the proletariat was meant to be a transitional device, even if Marx did not say how long it would last. It was also supposed to preside over the dissolution of social classes, thereby rendering itself unnecessary; a permanent dictatorship of the proletariat would have been a contradiction in terms.[31]

Soviet thinkers maintained that the Soviet state was "a state of the whole people." In the words of Nikita Khrushchev to the Twenty-second Congress of the Communist Party of the Soviet Union (1961):

> With the victory of socialism and the country's entry into the period of full-scale communist construction, the working class of the Soviet Union has on its own initiative, consistent with the tasks of communist construction, transformed the state of proletarian dictatorship into a state of the whole people. That, comrades, is a fact unparalleled in history! Until now the state has always been an instrument of dictatorship by this or that class. In our country, for the first time in history, a state has taken shape which is not a dictatorship of any one class, but an instrument of society as a whole, of the entire people.[32]

This solved one problem but created others, in that it contradicted Marx's view that all states are means by which one class rules over others and undercut his idea of a state that could be unlimited because it was temporary and transitional.

CONCLUSION

As was true of liberalism, the general family of socialism gave rise to a number of different movements, the two most important being social democracy and communism. The definitive split between these two branches of socialism in the 1920s led to very real differences in ideology, of which the five listed below are particularly significant.

Social Democrats

1. See socialism as an evolutionary process.

2. Achieve power through constitutional means; accept the limited state and the rule of law.

3. Advocate a mixed economy.

4. Accept a pluralistic society of self-interested individuals and groups.

5. Advocate the competition of political parties.

Communists

1. See socialism as a revolutionary process.

2. Achieve power unconstitutionally; reject the limited state and the rule of law as a bourgeois mystification.

3. Advocate a state-owned and -directed economy.

4. Envision a future harmonious society of selfless individuals.

5. Advocate a one-party state.

These fundamental differences mean that social democracy and communism amount to separate ideologies in the contemporary world, even though they have grown from common roots.

Questions for Discussion

1. Canada has a mainly market economy, but there are also some sectors, such as public education, that are set up along socialist lines of public ownership and control. Can you think of three other such sectors?

2. Why do you think these semi-socialist sectors were created? What benefits do they offer? Why were Canadians not content just to leave them to the market?

3. What characteristic problems do these socialist sectors face? That is, are there recurrent patterns in the complaints that people make about them?

Internet Links

1. The Socialist International: **www.socialistinternational.org.** Worldwide association of socialist parties, including Canada's New Democratic Party.

2. New Democratic Party: **www.ndp.ca.** Canada's social democratic political party.

3. Canadian Centre for Policy Alternatives: **www.policyalternatives.ca.** Social democratic think tank supported by organized labour in Canada.

4. Albert Einstein, "Why Socialism?" **www.monthlyreview.org/598einst.htm.** The 1949 essay by the great scientist explaining why he was drawn to socialism.

5. Museum of Communism: **www.gmu.edu/departments/economics/bcaplan/ museum/musframe.htm.** Historical information about communism.

6. Marxists Internet Archive: **www.marxists.org.** Online texts of hundreds of Marxist classics, including books by Marx, Engels, Lenin, and so on.

Further Reading

Beilharz, Peter. *Labour's Utopias: Bolshevism, Fabianism, Social Democracy.* London: Routledge, 1992.

Blackburn, Robin. *After the Fall: The Failure of Communism and the Future of Socialism.* London: Verso, 1991.

Cohen, Arthur A. *The Communism of Mao Tse-tung.* Chicago: University of Chicago Press, 1964.

Cole, G. D. H. *A History of Socialist Thought.* 5 vols. London: Macmillan, 1953–1960.

Draper, Hal. *Socialism from Below.* Atlantic Highlands, NJ: Humanities Press, 1992.

Furet, Francois. *The Passing of an Illusion: The Idea of Communism in the Twentieth Century.* Translated by Deborah Furet. Chicago: University of Chicago Press, 2000.

Giddens, Anthony. *A Contemporary Critique of Historical Materialism.* 2nd ed. Basingstoke, UK: Macmillan, 1995.

Gwertzman, Bernard. *The Collapse of Communism.* New York: Times Books, 1992.

Hunt, R. N. Carew. *The Theory and Practice of Communism.* Harmondsworth, UK: Penguin Books, 1963. First published in 1950.

Joll, James. *The Anarchists.* 2nd ed. London: Eyre and Spottiswoode, 1979.

Kitschelt, Herbert. *The Transformation of European Social Democracy.* Cambridge: Cambridge University Press, 1994.

Le Blanc, Paul. *From Marx to Gramsci: A Reader in Revolutionary Marxist Politics: Historical Overview and Selection.* Atlantic Highlands, NJ: Humanities Press, 1996.

McLellan, David. *Karl Marx: His Life and Thought.* London: Macmillan, 1973.

Meyer, Alfred G. *Leninism.* New York: Praeger, 1962. First published in 1957.

Muravchik, Joshua. *Heaven on Earth: The Rise and Fall of Socialism.* Landham, MD: Encounter Books, 2004.

Penner, Norman. *From Protest to Power: Social Democracy in Canada 1900–Present.* Toronto: Lorimer, 1992.

Tucker, Robert. *The Marxian Revolutionary Idea.* New York: W. W. Norton, 1970.

Whitehorn, Alan. *Canadian Socialism: Essays on the CCF-NDP.* Toronto: Oxford University Press, 1992.

Woodcock, George. *Anarchism and Anarchists.* Kingston, ON: Quarry Press, 1992.

CHAPTER 13
Nationalism

The nation, it will be remembered, is a specific type of political community that evolved out of feudal Europe. The decline of universal institutions—the Roman Catholic Church and the Holy Roman Empire—coupled with the erosion of parochial or regional loyalties to manor, village, city, or province—resulted in large aggregates of people sharing a common identity. The nation, which arose in Western Europe, has now become the model of community for the rest of the world as well.

Nationalism, at the level of emotions, is a feeling of loyalty to one's nation, recognizing ties with other members of one's group. The pride Canadians feel when a Canadian wins a medal at the Olympics, and the sense of recognition that Canadians may experience when they happen to meet other Canadians in a foreign land, are manifestations of nationalism. Writing about the *polis,* Aristotle said that "friendship . . . seems to hold states together."[1] Nationalism is the equivalent of friendship in communities that are so large we can never actually know more than a tiny proportion of the other members. A common national identity leads us to care about people with whom we are personally unacquainted.

NATIONAL MYTHOLOGY

Loyalty to a nation rests on the fundamental human need for group identification. It is fostered by national mythology; that is, by stories about the common history and destiny of the nation. The model for such national myths in the Western world is the historical self-awareness of the Hebrews. Their understanding of themselves as a chosen people, bound to God by a special covenant, recurs in the myths by which other nations justify their existence. No nation has a single myth or story; rather, each has a complex mythology or set of stories existing at different levels ranging from folklore to deliberate creations by intellectuals writing history in order to further national consciousness.

A fine example of the latter is the book by Monseigneur Laflèche, Bishop of Trois-Rivières, *Quelques considérations sur les rapports de la société civile avec la religion et la famille* (1866). Laflèche wrote that "Providence has allotted each and every nation its own mission to fulfil."[2] The French-Canadian people, in his view, were a nation among the human family of nations, with their homeland in the valley of the St. Lawrence. Their special calling was "basically religious in nature . . . to convert the unfortunate infidel local population to Catholicism, and to expand the Kingdom of God by developing a predominantly Catholic nationality."[3]

Laflèche's sketch of the history of French Canada emphasized missionary work among the native people. With that period largely past, he wrote, the new calling was to be a devout Catholic enclave in Protestant North America, setting an example that might lead others to Rome. The Catholic faith would be reinforced by adherence to the French language. The historical theory was well suited to preserving the identity of a minority, with its call for an intertwining of language, religion, and customs into a protective whole.

Laflèche did not create French-Canadian nationalism; rather, he articulated historical symbols to express more clearly what the people already felt. His myth entered the wider mythology, to which many other writers also contributed. Of course, mythologies change over time. Today, after the Quiet Revolution of the 1960s secularized Quebec society, Laflèche's religious formulation does not express very well the aspirations of Québécois nationalists, who speak about the unique value of their culture and language rather than about religion. The contemporary version of the Québécois mission is to maintain an island of francophone national culture amidst the anglophone sea of North America; hence the need for provincial legislation to make French the official language of Quebec, to create a "French face" by regulating the language of public signs, and to restrict access to English schools. The mission is now linguistic and cultural rather than religious, but the underlying idea is still the same: the nation has a special role to play in the drama of human history.

This national mythology is likely to be challenged by the effect of current demographic trends in Quebec. As the birthrate has fallen, the government of Quebec has encouraged immigrants from many parts of the Third World to come to the province. Even when they are francophone, as are those from Haiti, they have no natural feeling for the uniquely French-Canadian sense of historical mission. Paradoxically, the new immigration is especially threatening to French-Canadian nationalism because of Quebec's attempt to assimilate the immigrants into the French language and culture. Earlier waves of European immigrants to Quebec—Scots, Irish, Jews, and Italians—largely assimilated into the English community and so did not exercise much influence upon the Québécois. It is possible that present demographic realities may in the long run encourage French-Canadian nationalism to become more open and outward-looking and, in that respect, more similar to English-Canadian nationalism.

The national mythology of English Canada is more diffuse than that of French Canada because the community itself is less well defined. English-speaking Canada is not a single entity but an alliance of several communities founded in different circumstances. Massive immigration has further complicated an already complex situation. However, there is one constant theme in the interpretations Canadians give to their collective existence: to be Canadian is to be not American. Initially, of course, there was no Canada and no Canadian identity, only several British colonies in North America that shared, for ideological reasons, in the rejection of the American Revolution. Indeed, these colonies were largely populated by the descendants of the United Empire Loyalists, who had left the United States during or shortly after the American Revolution. The union of these separate colonies in 1867 was impelled less by positive feelings of friendship for one another than by a collective fear that if they remained separate, they would inevitably fall into the orbit of the United States.

Not surprisingly, statements about the meaning of Canada almost always involve a comparison with the United States. During the nineteenth century and much of the twentieth, these comparisons usually interpreted Canada as a more conservative, orderly, and peaceful country than its neighbour. Common themes of self-congratulation were the superiority of constitutional monarchy over republicanism, the British tradition of social deference, an orderly frontier protected by the North-West Mounted Police, and generous treatment of Canada's Aboriginal peoples. Today, the topics of comparison are different, but the mental process is much the same.[4] Canadians repeatedly stress that they are fortunate to have less crime than the United States, less racial hostility, a more pristine natural environment, and a more compassionate society. They lay particular stress on Canadian public policies (the key one being national health insurance) that do not exist in the United States. Again, it is obvious that the structure of Canadian national mythology serves to protect the group's distinctiveness by discouraging absorption into a larger neighbour. The logic of the situation compels both English- and French-Canadian national mythologies to be defensive in nature.

The character of American nationalism differs from both Canadian nationalisms. The American national identity rests on the political ideas that animated the Revolution of 1776. Ever since that time, Americans have interpreted themselves as participants in a social experiment of vast importance to all humanity—testing the limits of liberty. Thomas Jefferson wrote in 1802:

> It is impossible not to be sensible that we are acting for all mankind; that circumstances denied to others, but indulged to us, have imposed on us the duty of proving what is the degree of freedom and self-government in which a society may venture to leave its individual members.[5]

American national mythology plays endlessly on the theme of freedom and interprets everything else in relation to it. In this perspective, modern mass democracy, which first appeared in the United States, is not just majority rule, and capitalism is not just a form of economic organization; both are the means by which a free people conducts its affairs. The Declaration of Independence, the Constitution, and the Bill of Rights are not just political documents; they are sacred texts for the inspiration of all humanity.

This characteristic of American national mythology perhaps helps to explain why American ventures in international politics often tend to become crusades: in contests with other nations, freedom itself is at stake. Woodrow Wilson brought the United States into World War I "to make the world safe for democracy." Franklin Roosevelt interpreted American participation in World War II in a similar way. Cold War rivalry with the Soviet Union was the defence of the "free world." George W. Bush responded to the September 11, 2001 terrorist attack on New York and Washington, D.C. not just by retaliating against the terrorists but also by denouncing an international "Axis of Evil" composed of Iraq, Iran, and North Korea. He then undertook the invasion of Iraq not just to punish a hostile state but also to bring democracy to the Middle East. In contrast, policymakers in other nations are more likely to see international politics in less moralistic terms.

The point is not that one nation's myths are false while another's are true. It is that each nation worthy of the name has a mythology that supports its national identity by lending meaning to its collective history. Without such a source of meaning, the nation, which is ultimately a psychological reality, an "imagined community,"[6] as Benedict Anderson has called it, could not exist. Space has permitted only a brief look at a few examples, but similar myths exist for all nations.

As shown in Chapter 4, there are two rather different ways of "imagining" the nation. Civic nations are imagined in political terms; the key factor is allegiance to a common government. Ethnic nations, in contrast, are imagined in cultural terms; the key factor is a common background, involving some combination of language, race, religion, and customs. The distinction is not absolute, because civic nations always have some cultural underpinnings, and ethnic nations always have aspects of political allegiance in addition to their emphasis on cultural identity. But distinctions can be useful even when they are not absolute. There is in practice a world of difference between being Canadian or American (primarily civic) and being Lithuanian or Albanian (primarily ethnic).

Nationalism is not a single ideology. The details of each nationalism are unique because each nation is unique. However, there are common factors in the various structures of belief because the national mythologies serve similar purposes for the various nations. Most broadly, nationalism is "the making of claims in the name, or on behalf, of the nation."[7] The claims commonly arise under two headings: loyalty to the nation, and the quest for the nation-state.

LOYALTY TO THE NATION

In the nationalist worldview, loyalty to the nation should transcend other loyalties, such as allegiance to family, region, or ethnic group. The nation is taken to be the primary social group, outranking all others. This presupposition is so deeply entrenched today that we often do not recognize its significance. Why, for example, do we keep economic statistics on a national basis? In fact, economic relationships do not necessarily coincide with national sentiments. To say that the unemployment rate in Canada is 6 percent obscures the fact that it may be 11 percent in Newfoundland and 5 percent in Saskatchewan. What the national figures mean is rather unclear, yet we religiously compute them. Similarly, athletes can compete in the Olympic games only as members of a national team; they cannot represent themselves, a city, or a club. Yet sport has intrinsically as little to do with the nation as does economics.

QUEST FOR THE NATION-STATE

That the nation and the state should coincide in the nation-state is not a universal belief of nationalism. The traditional posture of French-Canadian nationalism, for example, was defence of the French-Canadian nation within the Canadian binational state, which in practice meant heavy emphasis on provincial autonomy. That being said, the demand for the nation-state tends to be a recurring one. Thus, French-Canadian nationalism gave rise to separatism in the early 1960s. Interestingly, René Lévesque, the first separatist premier of Quebec, once defended separatism by saying that it was "natural" for a nation to aspire to statehood. The word "natural" reflects the predominance of the nation-state in contemporary thinking.

Opinion about the inevitability of the nation-state is divided. Because freedom depends on the voluntary acceptance of legitimate authority, John Stuart Mill argued that in the long run a free society is possible only in a nation-state. He wrote in *Considerations on Representative Government* (1861):

> Free institutions are next to impossible in a country made up of different nationalities. Among a people without fellow-feeling, especially if they read and speak different languages, the united public opinion, necessary to the working of representative government, cannot exist.[8]

Mill feared that in a multinational state one nation would always end up coercively oppressing the others. National antagonism would require such a strong government that individual freedom would be impossible. Indeed, the problem that Mill perceived destroyed the Soviet Union. The reform program introduced by Mikhail Gorbachev allowed for the reassertion of national identities that had long been politically suppressed, first by the Russian Empire and then by the Soviet state. Lithuanians, Latvians, Estonians, Ukrainians, and many other nationalities demanded political independence, until nothing was left of the Soviet Union.

A contrary view was maintained by Mill's younger contemporary, Lord Acton (1834–1902), who wrote that "those states are substantially the most perfect which, like the British and Austrian Empires, include various distinct nationalities without oppressing them."[9] The existence of different nationalities was a positive blessing, according to Acton, because it provided a bulwark against too much state domination of society. Smaller nations within the state, fearful that the government would be controlled by the larger nations, would be reluctant to assign too many functions to the central authorities. Sensitive matters such as education and culture would tend to remain with local governments or perhaps even in private hands.

Acton's beliefs greatly influenced the political thought of Pierre Trudeau and formed the philosophical basis of his linguistic and constitutional policies, which had the intention of making Canada a pluralistic state in which neither the French nor the English would feel oppressed by each other. Trudeau's vision of Canada as a culturally pluralistic state was expressed in his often-quoted essay "The New Treason of the Intellectuals":

> Without backsliding to the ridiculous and reactionary idea of national sovereignty, how can we protect our French-Canadian national qualities? . . . We must separate once and for all the concepts of state and of nation, and make of Canada a truly pluralistic and polyethnic society. Now in order for this to come about, the different regions within the country must be assured of a wide range of local autonomy, such that each national group, with an increasing background of experience in self-government, may be able to develop the body of laws and institutions essential to the fullest expression and development of their national characteristics.[10]

Official bilingualism and multiculturalism became for Trudeau the institutional means of allowing Canada's peoples to coexist under a political condominium.

TYPICAL FORMS OF NATIONALISM

The two general concerns of nationalism—loyalty to the nation and the quest for the nation-state—manifest themselves in a bewildering variety of complex phenomena. We will draw attention to a few of the typical situations in which we speak of nationalism, commenting first and at greater length on one—Aboriginal nationalism and the demand for self-government—because of its increasing importance in Canadian politics.

Aboriginal Nationalism

A particular form of nationalism involves Aboriginal peoples, now usually known in Canada as "First Nations." The first stage in Aboriginal nationalism, now largely concluded in Canada, is a redefining of the group as a nation rather than a tribe or ethnic minority. Native people have achieved this and now claim an inherent right of self-government within Canadian federalism. At this point it is not entirely settled whether this legal status will be constitutional or merely statutory—that is, if it will be entrenched in the Constitution or rooted in legislative enactments that are easier to change. Whatever the case, Aboriginal leaders across Canada are pushing for greater political power with which to govern more than 700,000 status Indians in more than 600 bands (now usually called First Nations), as well as almost 400,000 Métis and non-status Indians and about 50,000 Inuit.

One must understand what is meant by **self-government.** The term itself is not new in Canadian politics. In the past, municipal governments have often sought greater powers for self-government vis-à-vis provincial governments. When Alberta and Saskatchewan were seeking provincial status before 1905, this goal was expressed in terms of the power of "self-government" and greater "autonomy."[11] Thus, the basic meaning of the term for Aboriginal peoples relates to the right of greater control over one's own affairs.[12] Self-government involves increasing a group's decision-making powers: giving that group the jurisdiction to deal directly with its problems rather than having them dealt with by federal or territorial administrators.

There are, however, very different ideas about self-government within Aboriginal communities. Some groups seek a great deal of power, equivalent or even superior to that of a provincial government; others are striving for powers very similar to the powers of municipal governments. These differences should not pose an insoluble problem. As Pierre Trudeau said some years ago, "between the unacceptable extremes of assimilation or absolute sovereignty there is a broad range of negotiable possibilities."[13]

Aboriginal peoples want self-government partly so they can break with the paternalism of the past. For a long time, status Indians and Inuit were the responsibility of the federal government; authority had long been vested in a minister and delegated to officials in the Department of Indian and Northern Affairs. This paternalistic system began to change when the Indian Act was revised in 1951. Greater powers were devolved to elected band councils, but in most cases these powers were still not equivalent to municipal government powers in the provinces, and the minister retained the authority to veto band by-laws. Aboriginal peoples, by seeking self-government, are striving for the kind of political power that other Canadians have long enjoyed through their provincial or municipal governments.

A second reason why Aboriginal peoples desire greater self-governing power is to avoid cultural assimilation in order to preserve the traditions and values unique to them. While most Aboriginal peoples see themselves as Canadian, they also see themselves as Canada's first peoples. This is not to say they want to return to some vanished traditional lifestyle—on the contrary, they enjoy as much as any Canadians the amenities of modern life. At the same time, however, they do not want to lose those characteristics that make them Aboriginal. In short, Aboriginal peoples would like to live in two worlds, with one foot in modern Canadian society and the other in Aboriginal society. Whether they can succeed at this is not clear, but it is important that they try. The results will also say much about the effectiveness of the Canadian multicultural experiment.

Aboriginal peoples want to be responsible for themselves. Having more control over decisions concerning education, health care, housing, social services, economic development, and criminal justice is crucial to this goal. In the past, most such decisions were made by administrators far from where the lives affected were lived and far from where the attendant problems occurred. Canada's Aboriginal peoples are now saying they can, if given the power, deal more successfully than can outsiders with the chronic problems that affect them including substance abuse, family violence, high dropout rates among students, and unemployment. It is time, they say, to let Aboriginal people devise their own solutions because the European ones haven't worked.

The federal government, with its fiduciary responsibility for Aboriginal affairs, has taken some steps toward this type of devolution. The Cree and Naskapi people in northern Quebec and the Sechelt band in British Columbia already have forms of self-government, and other Native groups are in various stages of negotiations. In the year 2000, the Nisga'a Treaty in British Columbia created a constitutionally protected form of self-government for the Nisga'a people; but negotiating other treaties in that province has run into many difficulties and none have been fully approved at the time of writing.

Another major experiment in self-government is the case of Nunavut (see Figure 13.1). In 1999 a new territory was created in the central and eastern Arctic, with almost 85 percent of the roughly 30,000 people who live there being Inuit. Formally, Nunavut is not a Native government, but the Inuit majority is so overwhelming that it amounts to almost the same thing.

Figure 13.1 Nunavut Territory

Date of creation: Formally, April 1, 1999
Area: 1,931,511 km² ; approximately 19 percent of Canada
Population: 25,000, almost 85 percent of whom are Inuit
Communities: Population resides in 27 remote communities, with only about 20 kilometres of maintained roads; serviced by air and water transport
Land Claim Agreement: Inuit have title to 354,357 km² and subsurface rights on 35,633 km²
Government: Power of the Nunavut government will be similar to that of the Northwest Territories and Yukon

Except for the Nisga'a Treaty, these steps toward self-government have been taken on a statutory rather than a constitutional basis. An important wing of Aboriginal opinion rejects the statutory approach because it makes Aboriginal governments subordinate to Parliament; these people want to deal with Canada on a "nation to nation" basis. Thus they continue to demand that an "inherent right of self-government" be explicitly entrenched in the Constitution, although they also argue that it is already implied in Section 35 of the Constitution Act, 1982, which says, "The existing aboriginal and treaty rights of the aboriginal peoples of Canada are hereby recognized and affirmed." And a few Aboriginal groups, such as the Iroquois, do not consider themselves part of Canada at all and insist that they possess sovereignty in the full international sense.

Separatism

A substate nation may seek to separate from the state that now rules it in order to establish a nation-state, as illustrated by separatist movements in Quebec and among the Welsh and Scots in Great Britain. Sometimes the minority would have to separate from two or more states; examples of this are the Basques, who are now ruled by France and Spain, and the Kurds, who are divided among Turkey, Iraq, and Iran.

Oppression of Minorities

A national majority that controls the government may use its political power to suppress, assimilate, or expel minorities that do not fit the nation-state's image of itself. In the early 1970s, the African states of Uganda, Kenya, and Tanzania expelled most of their substantial East Indian minorities. These people were vilified as alien exploiters who had been given an unfair position of economic advantage by the British colonialists. More recently, the Albanian-speaking majority of Kosovo has driven out most of the Serbian minority, albeit in retaliation for earlier Serbian oppression of the Albanians.

Irredentism

A nation-state may claim fragments of territory adjacent to its borders on the grounds that they constitute a historical part of the nation. The preamble to the 1978 constitution of the People's Republic of China says, "Taiwan is China's Sacred Territory. We are determined to liberate Taiwan and accomplish the great cause of unifying our motherland."[14] Because of this aspiration, China insisted that Taiwan be expelled from the United Nations before it would join, and it discourages, as strongly as it can, other states from maintaining diplomatic relations with Taiwan. The technical name for this sort of claim is **irredentism.** Another recent example was the unsuccessful Serbian attempt to annex parts of Croatia and Bosnia that had significant Serbian minorities.

Imperialism

A large and powerful nation may create an empire by imposing itself on its neighbours. German nationalism between the two world wars began with irredentist claims to German-populated territories, such as the Sudetenland in Czechoslovakia, which had once been part of the Austrian Empire but had been taken away by the Treaty of Versailles. From there it went on to demand *Lebensraum*, "living space," and to subjugate the neighbouring states of Central and Eastern Europe. Nationalism can thus transcend the nation-state and lead to a multinational empire under the rule of a dominant nation.

Protectionism

The nation-state may try to insulate itself from external influences perceived as threatening it in some way. This can mean blockading ideas—for example, censoring foreign publications or jamming broadcast signals. It can also mean erecting barriers against the movement of goods, such as import quotas or protective tariffs, in the belief that such measures not only stimulate the domestic economy but also protect the integrity of the nation. During the 1988 federal election in Canada, opponents of the Free Trade Agreement with the United States expressed many fears for Canada's future. They claimed that free trade not only would harm Canadian industries but also would reduce the autonomy of the Canadian state, force Canada to adopt American social policies, and destroy Canada's cultural distinctiveness.[15] Such fears were debatable, but they were understandable in the context of the long-term defensive posture of nationalism in Canada.

HISTORICAL OVERVIEW

The relationship between nationalism and other ideologies is complicated. History shows that one can be a nationalist while simultaneously being liberal, conservative, or socialist. This is because nationalism has a different fundamental concern than these three other ideologies. They focus on the question of what the role of government in society should be, whereas nationalism addresses itself to the question of what the proper limits of the political community are. Three French nationalists can agree that France ought to be a sovereign nation-state *une et indivisible,* while adhering otherwise to conservative, liberal, or socialist views about the functions of government. The relationship between nationalism and other ideologies is not merely a matter of chance but is structured, as the historian Hans Kohn has shown, according to the course of historical development in the last two centuries.[16]

Initially, nationalism and liberalism seemed to be natural allies. Great Britain, the first modern nation to emerge, was also the home of liberal constitutionalism. The United States, the first European colony to achieve independence, was constituted in 1776 in a reaffirmation of the principles of the Glorious Revolution. France proclaimed the concept of nationhood in 1789 as part of the liberal freedoms enunciated in the Declaration of the Rights of Man and of the Citizen.

The political situation in the first half of the nineteenth century strengthened the assumption that nationalism and liberalism were two sides of the same coin. Nationalism chiefly meant struggles to liberate small European nations from rule by large empires: the Irish from the British Empire, the Greeks from the Ottoman Empire, the Poles and Finns from the Russian Empire. With the notable exception of the British Empire, all European empires were based on traditional authority rather than legal constitutionalism. Those who struggled for national emancipation had to struggle at the same time for elected parliaments, freedom of the press, religious toleration, and other liberal goals. It was assumed that the peoples of the earth, once liberated from alien rule, would compose a family of nations living side by side peacefully and freely.

The alliance between liberalism and nationalism reached its peak in 1848, when a wave of attempted revolutions swept across Europe, all having the same goal of creating liberally governed nation-states. But the empires were able to reassert themselves, not least by playing the different nationalities against each other, and the liberal nationalist dream did not become reality.

Liberal nationalism continued to exist after 1848, but it was increasingly displaced by a more militaristic, state-oriented kind of nationalism. The national unification of Italy (1861) and of Germany (1871), long a goal of liberal nationalism, was achieved less by liberal methods of voluntary agreement than by military conquest. The new nation-states of Italy and Germany almost immediately began acquiring colonial empires, especially in Africa, where Britain and France, which had long possessed overseas empires, also joined in. Even the United States, which had previously been critical of European imperialism, acquired overseas colonies—Puerto Rico, Cuba, and the Philippines—after a war with Spain in 1898. By the end of the nineteenth century, nationalism had come to imply much less the liberation of small nations than the imperial aggrandizement of powerful nations. Numerous writers extolled the virtues of military service and loyalty to the state. This was also the period when racial theories became allied with nationalism. Writers of the various large nations justified their policies of imperial expansion by claiming biological superiority for Anglo-Saxons, French, or Germans, who had to rule the "coloured" races for their own good as well as that of humanity in general.

This aggressive form of nationalism fostered the growth of anti-Semitism. Jews, who lived dispersed in many European states, were attacked as alien elements in the national community. The German composer Richard Wagner wrote:

> The Jew speaks the language of the nation in whose midst he dwells from generation to generation, but he always speaks it as an alien ... Our whole European art and civilization, however, have remained to the Jew as a foreign tongue; for, just as he has taken no part in the evolution of the one, so he has taken none in that of the other; but at most the homeless wight [an archaic word for "creature"] has been a cold, nay more, a hostile on-looker.[17]

One of the most important expressions of this mood of anti-Semitism was *The Protocols of the Elders of Zion,* a forged document first published in 1903 and often reprinted thereafter.[18] Written by an agent of the czarist secret police in order to encourage anti-Semitism in Russia, it purported to prove there was a Jewish conspiracy to degrade and enslave the entire world. It interpreted Jewish achievements in science, international finance, and the socialist movement not as unrelated developments but as part of a calculated plot to gain ascendancy over the gentiles (non-Jews). The *Protocols* were to have a fateful influence on Adolf Hitler later in the twentieth century. The myth of an international Jewish conspiracy continues to this day to lead a subterranean existence, surfacing from time to time as in the 1980s in Canada, when Ernst Zundel and Jim Keegstra were prosecuted for fomenting hatred against Jews. Both men attracted attention for asserting that the Holocaust—the murder of six million Jews during World War II—had never taken place and was a creation of Jewish propaganda. Holocaust Revisionism, as it is called, is based on the notion of the *Protocols* that there exists a supremely powerful Jewish cabal capable of perpetrating such a massive hoax upon the world.[19]

In the late nineteenth century, European Jews reacted to the growing wave of anti-Semitism by developing their own form of nationalism. **Zionism** taught that the Jews would never achieve respect until they became a nation-state and that the Jewish population must therefore gather itself onto a single territory under the control of a sovereign Jewish state.

The aggressive nationalism of the late nineteenth and early twentieth centuries culminated in World War I, when Britain, France, Russia, and Italy fought in alliance against the German, Austro–Hungarian, and Ottoman Empires. At first, the outcome of this bloody war seemed to be a revival of liberal nationalism. The Treaty of Versailles dismembered the empires that had ruled Central and Eastern Europe and replaced them with nation-states equipped with liberal constitutions. Poles, Czechs, Hungarians, Lithuanians, Finns, and other peoples emerged with their own states for the first time in modern history. But nationalism and liberalism soon parted company. Each of these new nation-states had important national minorities, such as the Germans in Czechoslovakia and the Hungarians in Romania. Nationalistic conflict and irredentism raised the temperature of politics to the point where individual freedoms seemed of minor concern relative to the security of the national community. In the 1920s and 1930s, constitutional government was overthrown in almost all these new states of Europe, from Italy and Germany eastward. Nationalism then made an even more aggressive appearance in the new ideology of fascism.

FASCISM

Fascism arose in the specific conditions of Europe in the years between the two world wars. A communist takeover, as had occurred in the Russian Empire in 1917, seemed like a very real possibility in many of these countries. Liberal constitutionalism appeared unable to combat this threat or to deal with postwar inflation and unemployment. Shortly after World War I, Benito Mussolini—an ardent socialist who had nevertheless rallied to the support of Italy in the war—responded to the crisis by launching a political movement with a unique mixture of ideological themes. Rejection of liberal individualism and constitutional government was paramount. There would no longer be a private sphere of life exempt from governmental intrusion. He extolled the state as the highest expression of the nation and praised war as bringing "all human energies to their highest tension and setting a seal of nobility on the peoples who have the virtue to face it."[20]

The symbol of Mussolini's movement, and the source of its name, was the *fasces,* a bundle of rods containing an axe with the blade projecting, which had been a Roman symbol of authority. The rods and axe represented the threatening power of coercion (i.e., beating or beheading); the fact they were bound together symbolized the unity of the nation. For the third time, Italy would emerge as the leader of humanity. After the Rome of the Caesars and the Rome of the Popes would come the "Third Rome," the "Rome of the People." To these nationalist motifs, Mussolini added elements of socialism. The state, while not nationalizing property, would guide the economy for collective purposes. Mussolini had also learned from Lenin that an elite, disciplined party could seize power in a constitutional state and maintain its hold thereafter by ruthlessly suppressing opposition. Conspicuously absent were the egalitarian ideals of socialism, except in the sense that all were equally exhorted to follow the charismatic leadership of the *duce* (leader).

Although fascism is conventionally placed at the far right of the political spectrum, Mussolini's ideology contained many leftist themes (see Historical Perspectives 13.1).

Like Mussolini's fascism, Adolf Hitler's doctrine of "national socialism" was a combination of left-wing and right-wing motifs, with the substitution of German for Italian nationalism. Hitler's goal was to create the Third Reich, a new German Empire to succeed the medieval Holy Roman Empire and the empire Bismarck had created in 1871. Also, while Mussolini was not anti-Semitic, Hitler made anti-Semitism the centre of his ideology by blaming the German defeat in World War I on the Jews—the "stab in the back" theory, which he arrived at after reading *The Protocols of the Elders of Zion*—and by promising to make Germany *Judenrein* (free from Jews). Similar ideologies sprang up elsewhere in Europe. Their adherents came to power in Spain, with the help of Italian and German intervention, and became influential in such Central European countries as Hungary and Romania.[21]

Fascism is difficult to categorize. The fact that it is certainly not liberal has led some writers to regard it as a form of conservatism; and indeed, it did play on conservative sentiments by promising to prevent the triumph of communism. But futuristic symbols like the Third Rome and Third Reich express an attitude quite foreign to the conservative reverence for continuity with the past. Fascism was in fact a promise of radical change, a conscious break with the past to produce what Mussolini called "fascist man." On balance, fascism is probably best understood as an extreme form of nationalism playing on fears of communism while incorporating certain elements of socialism to strengthen the state.

Fascism survives today in small political parties and movements in many countries. Although nowhere near coming to power, these so-called **neo-fascist** groups can

Historical Perspectives 13.1

Extracts from Benito Mussolini's First Program, 1919

- The minimum age for voters lowered to eighteen years. . . .

- The abolition of the Senate. . . .

- The prompt enactment of a state law sanctioning a legal workday of eight *actual* hours of work for all workers.

- A minimum wage.

- The participation of workers' representatives in industry's technical affairs.

- The management of industries and public services to be entrusted to proletarian organizations that are morally and technically up to the task.

- The forcing of property owners to cultivate their lands under the threat that uncultivated lands will be given to farmers' cooperatives. . . .

- The obligation of the state to provide and maintain schools whose character decisively and soundly shapes a national conscience, impartial in character but rigidly secular. . . .

- A large progressive tax on capital that would amount to a one-time *partial expropriation* of all riches.

- The seizure of all goods belonging to religious congregations and the abolition of episcopal revenues. . . .

- The review of all contracts for war supplies and the sequestration of 85 percent of war profits.

Source: Jeffrey T. Schnapp, ed., *A primer of Italian Fascism* (Lincoln, NE: University of Nebraska Press, 2000), pp. 3–5.

sometimes cause considerable turmoil through street violence, crime, and terrorism. For example, Timothy McVeigh, who blew up the federal building in Oklahoma City in 1995, killing 167 people, was inspired by a novel called *The Turner Diaries*. He followed detailed instructions in the book for constructing a powerful bomb out of fertilizer and diesel fuel. *The Turner Diaries* depicts an all-out race war in the United States between Jews and blacks on one side and a secret order of white super-patriots on the other side. The book is distributed by the National Alliance, which claims to represent the ideological legacy of Adolf Hitler. There are also neo-fascist parties in many European countries, such as the Social Action party in Italy, led by Mussolini's granddaughter Alessandra, and the National Democratic Party of Germany.

WORLDWIDE NATIONALISM

While discrediting fascism, World War II ushered in a historical period in which nationalism became truly a worldwide force. British, French, Italian, Portuguese, American, Dutch, and Japanese colonies all attained independence, leaving the Russian Empire (i.e., the Soviet Union and its sphere of influence) as the last of the great multinational empires until it dissolved itself in 1991. The world is now a society of nation-states, even if many of the new nations are still rather tentative aggregations of tribal, ethnic, and regional groups. The most important new manifestation of nationalism in the postwar period was the struggle of these new nations for independence. In several instances—for example, in Vietnam, Algeria, Angola, and Mozambique—the colonial power was reluctant to surrender its sovereignty and did so only after a prolonged war of national liberation.

In the Third World, the mentality of national liberation is still strong, and its symbolism is still potent. The new nations have achieved political sovereignty, but in economic terms many of them are in difficult straits. They commonly blame their low standard of living not only on the colonial past but also on what they perceive as continuing economic domination by the capitalist nations of the Western world, especially the United States. Not surprisingly, since they believe their problems to be caused by the market system, many of the new nations have turned to socialism (see Chapter 12).

A recent example is the "Bolivarismo" of Venezuelan President Hugo Chavez, named after Simon Bolivar, the "Liberator" whose rebellion led to the emancipation of Latin American nations from the Spanish empire. Chavez's Bolivarismo, combining socialist economics with anti-American nationalism, leads him to make common cause with Cuba, Iran, and any other country that has hostile relations with the United States.

The recurrent alliance between nationalism and socialism in the Third World may prove itself very long lasting because the two ideologies have one important affinity: both see the state as the central institution in society. For socialists it is the planner of society, and for nationalists it is the expression of national identity; in contrast, for liberals and conservatives it is only a limited instrument with special purposes. Socialist and nationalist uses of the state are not incompatible and, indeed, can reinforce each other, as when nationalization of a multinational corporation is touted as an assertion of sovereignty as well as a measure to benefit the local working class.

This rapprochement between nationalism and socialism is mildly ironic, in that the early socialists had little use for the nation-state. Marx sympathized with the national aspirations of the Irish and the Poles not for their own sake, but because he thought national liberation would weaken the political system that helped maintain capitalism. Marx believed that all states, including nation-states, would ultimately disappear. The socialist parties of the Second International were also anti-nationalistic, believing that aggressive nationalism distracted proletarians from the true issue of the class struggle. But the global proliferation of nation-states in this century is a political fact to which ideologies must adjust if they are to survive. Socialists have managed to make the transition by focusing on the state rather than on those parts of their original doctrine that anticipated the passing away of the state.

Nationalism today is critical to the process of building a sense of loyalty and identity among diverse ethnic groups in a given nation-state. At the same time, rabid nationalism can be a destructive force, as can be seen in the series of civil wars in the former Yugoslavia, the repression of the Kurds in Iraq and Turkey, and the ongoing struggle of the Chechens to achieve and maintain independence from Russia. In each case, old animosities have triggered atrocities on all sides. These incidents point out the ugly side of nationalism and the enormous problems involved in reconciling differences through politics.

Questions for Discussion

1. Can you give some concrete examples of how debates about issues of public policy in Canada tend to become debates about Canadian identity and American influence?

2. Belief in a world-Jewish conspiracy, as described in *The Protocols of the Elders of Zion*, is a prime example of conspiracy thinking. Have you encountered any other examples of conspiratorial thinking? What are the common characteristics of this mode of thought?

3. Some authors think that nationalism is becoming less important because of increases in international communication, travel, investment, trade, and immigration. Do you find this to be true of people your own age? Do you think they are less nationalistic than older people, or not?

Internet Links

1. The Nationalism Project: **www.nationalismproject.org.** Literature and links to many sources on nationalism.

2. Institute for Historical Review: **http://ihr.org.** Major purveyor of Holocaust Revisionism, with pretence of academic respectability.

3. Benyamin Neuberger, "Zionism": **www.wzo.org.il/en/resources/view.asp?id=134.** Informative overview of the subject.

4. Italian Life under Fascism: **www.library.wisc.edu/libraries/dpf/Fascism.** Exhibits from University of Wisconsin special collections, with lots of interpretation.

Further Reading

Anderson, Benedict R. O'G. *Imagined Communities: Reflections on the Origin and Spread of Nationalism.* 2nd ed. London: Verso, 1991.

Beiner, Ronald, ed. *Theorizing Nationalism.* Albany: State University of New York Press, 1999.

Bremmer, Ian, and Ray Taras, eds. *New States, New Politics: Building the Post-Soviet Nations.* Rev. 2nd ed. Cambridge: Cambridge University Press, 1997.

Brubaker, Rogers. *Nationalism Reframed: Nationhood and the National Question in the New Europe.* Cambridge and New York: Cambridge University Press, 1996.

Canovan, Margaret. *Nationhood and Political Theory.* Cheltenham, UK, and Brookfield, VT: Edward Elgar, 1996.

Chennells, David. *The Politics of Nationalism in Canada: Cultural Conflict Since 1760.* Toronto: University of Toronto Press, 2001.

Comaroff, John L., and Paul C. Stern, eds. *Perspectives on Nationalism and War.* Amsterdam: Gordon and Breach, 1995.

Cook, Ramsay. *Canada, Quebec, and the Uses of Nationalism.* 2nd ed. Toronto: McClelland & Stewart, 1995.

———. *French-Canadian Nationalism.* Toronto: Macmillan, 1969.

Dahbour, Omar, and Micheline R. Ishay. *The Nationalism Reader.* Atlantic Highlands, NJ: Humanities Press, 1995.

Eley, Geoff, and Ronald Grigor Suny, eds. *Becoming National: A Reader.* New York: Oxford University Press, 1996.

Farnen, Russell F., ed. *Nationalism, Ethnicity, and Identity: Cross National and Comparative Perspectives.* Piscataway, NJ: Transaction Publishers, 2004.

Flanagan, Tom. *First Nations? Second Thoughts.* 2nd ed. McGill–Queen's University Press, 2008.

Goldberg, Jonah. *Liberal Fascism: The Secret History of the American Left from Mussolini to the Politics of Meaning.* New York: Doubleday, 2007.

Griffiths, Richard. *Fascism.* New York: Continuum International Publishing Group, 2005.

Hayes, Carlton J. H. *Nationalism: A Religion.* New York: Macmillan, 1960.

Ichijo, Atsuko, and Gordana Uzelac, eds. *When Is the Nation? Towards an Understanding of Theories of Nationalism.* New York: Routledge, 2005.

Ignatieff, Michael. *Blood and Belonging.* Toronto: Penguin Books Canada, 1993.

Keating, Michael, and John McGarry, eds. *Minority Nationalism and the Changing International Order.* Toronto: Oxford University Press, 2001.

Kohn, Hans. *The Idea of Nationalism.* New York: Macmillan, 1944.

———. *Nationalism: Its Meaning and History.* New York: Van Nostrand Reinhold, 1965.

Minahan, James. *Nations without States: A Historical Dictionary of Contemporary National Movements.* Westport, CT: Greenwood Press, 1996.

Moore, Margaret. *The Ethics of Nationalism.* Toronto: Oxford University Press, 2001.

Motyl, Alexander, ed. *Encyclopedia of Nationalism.* 2 vols. San Diego, CA and London: Academic Press, 2001.

O'Sullivan, Noel. *Fascism.* London: Dent, 1983.

Smith, Anthony D. *Ethnicity and Nationalism.* The Netherlands: Brill, 1992.

Snyder, Louis L. *The New Nationalism.* Piscataway, NJ: Transaction Publishers, 2003.

Tully, James. *Strange Multiplicity: Constitutionalism in an Age of Diversity.* Cambridge and New York: Cambridge University Press, 1995.

Watson, Michael. *Contemporary Minority Nationalism.* London: Routledge, 1990.

CHAPTER 14

Feminism

In the past 40 years the ideological picture has become increasingly complex, with the rise to prominence of new systems of thought, especially feminism and environmentalism. Liberalism, conservatism, socialism, and nationalism are all primarily concerned with questions of power, such as who is going to control human communities, and to what end? **Feminism** adds a new dimension to this debate by focusing on power relationships between men and women.

The current prominence of feminism is probably related to the rise of **post-materialism.** According to the political scientist Ronald Inglehart (see Chapter 5), the years after World War II brought a gradual but profound shift of values in Western societies. While there have been periods of recession and some peripheral military conflicts, the general climate in the Western world since the late 1940s has been one of peace and prosperity. Thus, new generations have grown up taking physical and economic security for granted and have achieved higher levels of formal education, and this has allegedly produced an electorate more concerned with self-expression and other post-materialist values.[1] The result is a favourable climate for ideologies that go beyond concerns of public order and material prosperity to focus on the quality of human relationships.

FEMINISM

The term feminism is derived from the Latin *femina,* which means "woman" or "female." As the name suggests, the ideology is centred on the position of women in human society. It should be noted in passing that the word *feminist* is a label for certain ideas, or for people who hold such ideas. It is not a synonym for woman. Some men are feminists (John Stuart Mill was an influential feminist of the nineteenth century), and not all women are feminists. Younger women, for example, are much less likely to identify themselves as feminist even when they hold attitudes that are consistent with feminism.[2]

Feminism is not an entirely new ideology. Its roots go back to the seventeenth century; and, like liberalism, conservatism, socialism, and nationalism, it belongs to the family of ideologies produced by the French Revolution. It may have seemed new when the contemporary feminist movement burst onto the political stage in the late 1960s, but in fact this was the "second wave" of active feminism. An earlier feminist movement commencing in the second half of the nineteenth century had as one of its main goals women's suffrage, which was attained in most Western countries by the end of World War I. The "new" ideology of feminism is the rekindling of a fire that had once burned brightly and had never gone out.

As with all ideological trends, there were objective reasons for the "second wave" revival of feminism. A crucial factor was the birthrate, which peaked in the late 1950s and declined rapidly throughout the 1960s. This decline was associated with, though not entirely due to, the introduction of effective oral contraceptives. Lower birthrates meant smaller families, which in turn meant that women were starting to spend more of their adult lives working in the paid labour force and engaging in public activities such as politics. These objective developments made it pressing to re-examine sex roles in society because laws and social institutions had traditionally assumed that women's lives would be private and domestic, centred on home and family, while men would predominate in the public sphere of the economy and politics.

Like other ideologies, feminism is a family of belief systems with certain concerns and ideas in common but with many internal differences. The central concern is easily stated: all feminists begin from the belief that society is disadvantageous to women, systematically depriving them of individual choice, political power, economic opportunity, and intellectual recognition. Within this broad perspective are many schools of thought about the causes of and remedies for this situation. We will look at three varieties of feminism often mentioned in the literature: liberal feminism, Marxist feminism, and radical feminism.

LIBERAL FEMINISM

Starting in the late seventeenth century, books and pamphlets began to appear arguing that women had the same intellectual and moral capacities as men and should have the same legal rights. The best known of these early works is *A Vindication of the Rights of Woman* (1792), by Mary Wollstonecraft. A largely self-educated schoolteacher and author, Wollstonecraft is also known for being the mother of Mary Wollstonecraft Shelley, who wrote the novel *Frankenstein.*

The context of the *Rights of Woman* is significant. It was printed very soon after Wollstonecraft's earlier pamphlet *The Rights of Men* (1790), which was an attack on Edmund Burke's *Reflections on the Revolution in France.* Wollstonecraft was an ardent defender of the French Revolution, particularly its egalitarian aspects. In her view, equality for women was the logical corollary of the attempt to create a political system based on equality before the law. She argued that women should have the right to vote, to own property, and to pursue whatever profession they chose, and also to be educated in the liberal arts and sciences like men, not just in the arts of running a household. Like feminists ever since, she argued that political and legal equality had to be rooted in equality within the family. Yet, unlike some contemporary radical feminists, she did not challenge the traditional procreative role of women. "Make women rational creatures and free citizens," she wrote, "and they will quickly become good wives and mothers."[3]

The general theme of **liberal feminism** is equality of rights, or the extension of men's rights to women. This is vividly expressed in the Declaration of Sentiments (1848), drafted by Elizabeth Cady Stanton and modelled closely on the American Declaration of Independence:

> When, in the course of human events, it becomes necessary for one portion of the family of man to assume among the peoples of the earth a position different from that which they have hitherto occupied, but one to which the laws of nature and of nature's God entitle them, a decent respect for the opinions of mankind requires that they should declare the causes that impel them to such a course. We hold these truths to be self-evident; that all men and women are created equal; that they are endowed by their Creator with certain inalienable rights; that among these are life, liberty and the pursuit of happiness; that to secure these rights governments are instituted, deriving their just powers from the consent of the governed.[4]

The underlying presupposition of this text and others in the tradition of liberal feminism is that liberalism would be an adequate ideology if it took itself seriously and extended its view to include both halves of the human race on equal terms.

The liberal feminist view was systematically worked out in John Stuart Mill's essay *The Subjection of Women* (1869), written with the help of his wife, Harriet Taylor Mill. The subordination of women, wrote Mill, "ought to be replaced by a principle of perfect equality, admitting no power or privilege on the one side, nor disability on the other."[5] The dependence of women was nothing but "the primitive state of slavery lasting on";[6] and just as men had been liberated from slavery, so should women. The subjection of women might appear natural, but "was there ever any domination which did not appear natural to those who possessed it?"[7]

The emancipation of women, argued Mill, was in everyone's interest, for "any limitation of the field of selection deprives society of some chances of being served by the competent, without ever saving it from the incompetent."[8] That is, everyone, men and women alike, would profit if women were given a fair chance to develop their abilities and put them to use. Although it might be true that there are natural differences between men and women, Mill claimed that we could not know this for certain because of the dependence in which women had been kept. But that did not matter:

> One thing we may be certain of—that what is contrary to women's nature to do, they never will be made to do by simply giving their nature free play. The anxiety of mankind to interfere in behalf of nature, for fear lest nature should not succeed in effecting its purpose, is an altogether unnecessary solicitude. What women by nature cannot do, it is quite superfluous to forbid them from doing. What they can do, but not so well as the men who are their competitors, competition suffices to exclude them from; since nobody asks for protective duties and bounties in favor of women.[9]

This quotation underscores the liberal character of Mill's approach, which amounts to a kind of *laissez faire* argument applied to the relationship between the sexes.

Mill advocated complete legal equality for women. He also thought marriage should be an equal partnership, and was eloquent about how this would increase the happiness of men as well as women. Yet, typical of early liberal feminists, he seems to have taken for granted that the traditional division of labour between the sexes would continue as the social, although not the legal, norm. Men would continue to be more concerned with public life, married women with the household and private life. Individual women should be perfectly free to devote themselves to the public life of work and government, but it would not be the normal state of affairs:

> When the support of the family depends not on property but on earnings, the common arrangement, by which the man earns the income and the wife superintends the domestic expenditure, seems to me in general the most suitable division of labour between the two persons. If, in addition to the physical suffering of bearing children, and the whole responsibility of their care and education in early years, the wife undertakes the careful and economical application of the husband's earnings to the general comfort of the family; she takes not only her fair share, but usually the larger share, of the bodily and mental exertion required by their joint existence . . . In an otherwise just state of things, it is not, therefore, I think, a desirable custom, that the wife should contribute by her labour to the income of the family.[10]

Mill's words illustrate the paradox of the early phase of liberal feminism: it advocated equality of rights for women in a legal sense and accepted the validity of individual women choosing to pursue careers in the public domain; but it also took for granted a sexual division of labour in which women, even if with exceptions, would freely choose to devote themselves primarily to childbearing and child rearing for most of their adult lives. Thus reappeared the typical classical-liberal tension between equality of right and equality of outcome: men and women would have equal rights, but the conditions of their lives would be very different; and it is men who would continue in fact to have greater control over wealth and power in the public realm, while most women would remain in the private sphere of the household.

When Mill wrote *The Subjection of Women* there was already an active political movement of women, usually known as **suffragism** because of its emphasis on attaining the suffrage, or right to vote, for women. But women's emancipation was much broader than this issue; it included the struggle for legal and political equality in all forms, such as the right to hold public office, to attend university and enter the learned professions, to own property in marriage, and to receive custody of children in cases of divorce or separation. These goals were gradually attained in most Western countries toward the end of the nineteenth and the beginning of the twentieth centuries. Some leading Canadian feminists of that era were Dr. Emily Howard Stowe, Canada's first female physician, who founded the Canadian Women's Suffrage Movement in Toronto in 1876; Emily Murphy, a journalist who was appointed police magistrate in Edmonton in 1916, the first such appointment in the British Empire; and Nellie McClung, also a journalist, who was elected to the Alberta legislature in 1921.[11] Historical Perspectives 14.1 lists some important milestones in the political progress of Canadian women.

Historical Perspectives 14.1

Canadian Women's Political Milestones

1897	Clara Brett Martin is admitted to the Law Society of Upper Canada.
1916	Manitoba, Alberta, and Saskatchewan grant women the right to vote in provincial elections.
1918	Women obtain the right to vote in federal elections.
1929	In the *Persons* case, the Judicial Committee of the Privy Council rules that women are legal persons and may be appointed to the Senate.
1930	Cairine Wilson is appointed to the Senate.
1940	Women get the right to vote in Quebec provincial elections.
1957	Ellen Fairclough becomes the first woman to serve in the federal Cabinet.
1960	Right to vote granted unconditionally to First Nations, including women.
1982	Bertha Wilson becomes the first woman appointed to the Supreme Court of Canada.
1984	Jeanne Sauvé becomes Canada's first female Governor General.
1985	Bill C-31 restores status to First Nations Women who gained status by marrying non-status men.
1989	Audrey McLaughlin is elected leader of the New Democratic Party, the first woman to lead a federal party.
1993	Kim Campbell becomes the first woman prime minister of Canada.
1995	Alexa McDonough succeeds Audrey McLaughlin as leader of the New Democratic Party.
2000	Beverley McLachlin becomes the first female chief justice of the Supreme Court of Canada.
2004	Two new appointments raise the number of women on the Supreme Court of Canada to four out of nine.

The contemporary phase of liberal feminism in North America was signalled by the publication in 1963 of Betty Friedan's best-selling book, *The Feminine Mystique*. Friedan, an American journalist, devoted her book to "the problem that has no name," namely

> . . . a strange stirring, a sense of dissatisfaction, a yearning that women suffered in the middle of the twentieth century in the United States. Each suburban wife struggled with it alone. As she made the beds, shopped for groceries, matched slipcover material, ate peanut butter sandwiches with her children, chauffeured Cub Scouts and Brownies, lay beside her husband at night—she was afraid to ask even of herself the silent question—"Is this all?"[12]

Friedan's answer at that time was unambiguous: no, domestic life was not enough; women had to become complete participants in the public world of politics and the economy:

> There is only one way for women to reach full human potential—by participating in the mainstream of society, by exercising their own voice in all the decisions shaping that society. For women to have full identity and freedom, they must have economic independence.[13]

In her pursuit of these goals, Friedan went on to become a founding member and first president of the National Organization for Women (NOW), an American feminist advocacy group, and a leading figure in the American women's movement.

Her book *The Second Stage,* published in 1981, examined some of the difficulties arising out of women's attempts to play a full role in economic and political life. In the book, she quotes a young woman who is attending Harvard Medical School: "I'm going to be a surgeon. I'll never be a trapped housewife like my mother. But I would like to get married and have children, I think. They say we can have it all. But how? I work thirty-six hours in the hospital, twelve off. How am I going to have a relationship, much less kids, with hours like that? I'm not sure I can be a superwoman."[14] Friedan's answer to this dilemma was "the restructuring of our institutions on a basis of real equality for women and men."[15] Concretely, this would mean changes in sex roles within the family, with both men and women working outside the home while sharing the tasks of housework and child care. It would also require innovations in public policy, such as public support for daycare to facilitate women's participation in the workforce.

This approach sits comfortably within the tradition of reform liberalism. If government can provide old-age pensions and medical care in the name of equality, why not daycare as well? But such demands collided with the conservative revival of the 1980s and the fiscal pressures of the 1990s, and many aspects of the contemporary liberal feminist agenda remain unfulfilled in North America.

MARXIST FEMINISM

Feminism has always been an important theme in socialist thought. Many of the utopian socialists believed in restructuring the relationships between the sexes. Charles Fourier wrote:

> It is known that the best nations have always been those which concede the greatest amount of liberty to women. As a general proposition: Social progress and changes of period are brought about by virtue of the progress of women towards liberty, and social retrogression occurs as a result of a diminution in the liberty of women.[16]

The Israeli kibbutz, remotely based on the ideas of Fourier, tried to revolutionize the status of women by introducing collective housekeeping and child-rearing arrangements. Another early utopian, Robert Owen, also proposed easier divorce and other reforms of the family. Philosophically, Owen's great theme was the malleability of human nature, by which he meant that individual behaviour could be changed by alterations in the social environment:

> the character of man is, without a single exception, always formed for him . . . it may be, and is, chiefly, created by his predecessors . . . they give him, or may give him, his ideas and habits, which are the powers that govern and direct his conduct. Man, therefore, never did, nor is it possible he ever can, form his own character.[17]

If this is true, the relationship between the sexes can be put on the table for social reform along with everything else; there is nothing natural about any particular family structure.

Marx did not write a great deal about the position of women in society, but a few passages show that he made a connection between the family and private property. In *The German Ideology* (1845), he referred to the family as a kind of "latent slavery"—as the first form of property in that it gave the husband "the power of disposing of the labour-power of others" (i.e., of the wife and children).[18] In *The Communist Manifesto*, Marx and Engels predicted that the family would be revolutionized under communism:

> With the transfer of the means of production into common ownership, the single family ceases to be the economic unit of society. Private housekeeping is transformed into a social industry. The care and education of children becomes a public affair; society looks after all children alike, whether they are legitimate or not.[19]

After Marx's death, Engels explored the theme of the family further in *The Origin of the Family, Private Property and the State* (1884), in which he tried to integrate recent anthropological research with his Marxist ideology. Among his conclusions were the following:

> The modern individual family is founded on the open or concealed domestic slavery of the wife, and modern society as a mass is composed of these individual families as its molecules . . . Within the family, he is the bourgeois, and the wife represents the proletariat . . . the peculiar character of the supremacy of the husband over the wife in the modern family, the necessity of creating real social equality between them and the way to do it, will only be seen in the clear light of day when both possess legally complete equality of rights. Then it will be plain that the first condition for the liberation of the wife is to bring the whole female sex back into public industry, and that this in turn demands that the characteristic of the monogamous family as the economic unit of society be abolished.[20]

Thus arose the standard Marxist position on what the nineteenth century called "the woman question": that the legal equality so beloved of liberal feminists like Mill was essential but insufficient. The true emancipation of women could be achieved only through communist revolution. To change the relationship between the sexes in a thoroughgoing way would necessitate socializing the means of production and abolishing the economic system of capitalism. As August Bebel, a leading German Social Democrat, put it in *Women under Socialism* (1883), "the solution of the woman question [would be] identical with the solution of the social question."[21]

There is a somewhat paradoxical quality to Marxist feminism. On the one hand, it is sweeping in its ultimate objectives—far more so than liberal feminism—because it envisions not just legal equality but also major transformations relating to property, work, and the raising of children. On the other hand, it attributes to feminism a secondary role in the revolutionary movement by making women's liberation a consequence of the liberation of the proletariat. So, in practice, while a few women such as Rosa Luxemburg became leading Marxist revolutionaries, there was never an independent women's movement operating on Marxist principles. The female revolutionaries were integrated with, and under the ultimate control of, the male-dominated socialist parties.

Communist regimes in the Soviet Union and elsewhere acted on the implications of Marxist theory. Quickly after coming to power, communist governments legislated legal equality between men and women and also made efforts to destroy "the monogamous family as the economic unit of society." Women were encouraged, indeed virtually required, to take paid employment outside the home. Inexpensive and publicly operated daycare facilities were made easily available to facilitate women's entry into the labour force. Under most communist regimes, divorce, birth control, and abortion were also readily available, which encouraged a sharp drop in the birthrate—this, in what before the revolution had been largely agrarian societies with high birthrates.

These were real and significant changes, and many Western feminists were initially enthusiastic about the effect of communism upon women's lives. Doubts arose, however, as the decades went by. Communism brought women into the labour market, but it did not liberate them from housework, and the lives of ordinary women were filled with overwork and exhaustion. Women entered and even came to dominate certain prestigious professions, such as medicine; but in those professions they earned less than (largely male) factory workers. The climb of women up the administrative and political hierarchies also seemed to stall. No communist regime ever had a female head of state, head of government, or head of the communist party. Women were always represented on the highest committees, but in a token way, never exercising leadership. And while communist states sponsored mass political organizations for women, these were always carefully controlled; no independent women's movement was allowed to emerge.

For all of these reasons, Marxist feminism of the traditional type has little weight today in North America. There are still individual Marxist theorists of feminism, but most of them are academics. While their writings continue to exercise some influence among intellectuals, traditional Marxists do not dominate any of the women's organizations that are so prominent in contemporary politics. Yet Marxist feminism did not die without leaving heirs; a sort of transmuted Marxist feminism, usually called *radical feminism,* is the most provocative force on today's intellectual scene and exercises a remarkable influence on contemporary politics and public policy.

RADICAL FEMINISM

The ideology of **radical feminism** was created by women writing at the end of the 1960s and beginning of the 1970s. Most had participated in the New Left movement of the 1960s, which was a non-communist, anti-authoritarian revival of Marxism. The radical feminists broke with the New Left because they felt that the men in that movement regarded women as subordinate and did not take their concerns seriously. When they departed, they gave up orthodox Marxism but took with them a certain Marxist style of thought that served as a framework for their new categories.

In the radical feminist analysis, women and men constitute separate "sexual classes." History is the story of class struggle between these two sexual classes—not, as the Marxists would have it, between the economic classes of owners and employees. The central concept in radical feminism is not capitalism but **patriarchy.** In the words of Kate Millet, the author of *Sexual Politics:* "When one group rules another, the relationship between the two is political. When such an arrangement is carried out over a long period of time it develops an ideology (feudalism, racism, etc.). All historical civilizations are patriarchies: their ideology is male supremacy."[22]

In one way this was a definite break with Marxism because it no longer saw property relations as the fundamental variable in human history. The New York Radical Feminists stated in a manifesto that "we do not believe that capitalism, or any economic system, is the cause of female oppression, nor do we believe that female oppression will disappear as a result of a purely economic revolution."[23] Another break with Marxists, who see the wage relationship as the chief means of exploitation, comes from radical feminists' focus on personal, face-to-face relationships between men and women. "Women have very little idea of how much men hate them," wrote Germaine Greer in *The Female Eunuch* (1971).[24]

Radical feminists analyze certain behaviours, usually regarded previously as social pathologies, as typical forms of male control over females. In *Against Our Will: Men, Women and Rape* (1975), Susan Brownmiller wrote that rape is "nothing more or less than a conscious process of intimidation by which all men keep all women in a state of intimidation."[25] Radical feminists see rape as well as sexual harassment and violence against women as widespread, almost universal means of social control. Some radical feminists apply a similar analysis to pornography, which they condemn not because it openly portrays sexual conduct but because it degrades and oppresses women. "Pornography is the undiluted essence of anti-female propaganda," in Brownmiller's words.[26] By identifying the harmful impact to women of relationships, activity, and policy within the private sphere, radical feminism introduced the argument that "the personal is the political."

The problem is not just male misconduct but the family itself. "The tyranny of the biological family" must be ended, according to Shulamith Firestone in *The Dialectic of Sex* (1971).[27] For Ti-Grace Atkinson, "the phenomenon of love is the psychological pivot in the persecution of women,"[28] because it leads them to define themselves in relation to men. For a number of leading radical feminists, emancipation from male domination leads directly to lesbianism, which is a political statement, not just a sexual preference. For radical feminists such as Adrienne Rich, the adoption of political lesbianism is essential to feminism in that it requires a commitment to women as an expression of solidarity. Moreover, it directly challenges traditional notions of family and motherhood—both important elements in the oppression of women.

Firestone's *Dialectic of Sex* goes furthest in developing the idea of revolution against supposedly "natural" sex roles. Whereas orthodox Marxists emphasize the importance of production, Firestone makes reproduction the key issue. Women will never obtain their liberation until they can give up the "barbaric" function of pregnancy and reject the myth that children need their mothers. Childbearing must be rejected in favour of a combination of test-tube fertilization and artificial placentas, or perhaps the implantation of human fetuses in an animal host uterus. Responsibility for child rearing must be transferred from biological families to groups of "contracting" adults not necessarily related to the child. With the end of the biological family, the incest taboo could be dropped, and "humanity could finally revert to its natural polymorphous sexuality—all forms of sexuality would be allowed and indulged."[29] Where Marxists argue that freedom requires ending the capitalist mode of production, some radical feminists argue that for women it requires changing the means of reproduction. But other radical feminists, such as Mary O'Brien, have instead identified childbearing and procreation as the source of women's strength, and as a result have advocated reclaiming control of a process which they believe has been captured by a male-dominated medical and scientific community.[30]

Firestone's ideas about reproduction, child rearing, and incest may strike many readers as extreme, as may some other notions of radical feminism, such as equating heterosexual intercourse with rape. Opponents of feminism often cite them in an attempt to discredit the whole ideology of feminism. These views do not represent mainstream opinion on women's place in society, but they have nevertheless powerfully affected the feminist and public policy agendas in the last two decades. Before the rise of radical feminism, discussion mostly revolved around the liberal agenda of legal equality for women who wanted to take their place in the world of work and politics; typical issues were discrimination in employment, admission to professional schools, and nomination as candidates for political parties. While radical feminism did not reject the importance of such issues, it added a new dimension of "sexual politics." The key issues now became rape, violence against women, the sexual abuse of children, sexual harassment, pornography, and the rights of gays and lesbians.

In Canada, as in many other countries, radical feminism has already had a significant impact on public policy. Human-rights law has been amended to incorporate sexual harassment as a form of discrimination—a conceptual merger between the liberal and radical views. Rape-crisis shelters have been established, and Parliament has changed the law and procedures relating to sexual assault to make convictions easier to obtain. The Supreme Court has removed the statute of limitations on incest and child abuse, again increasing the possibility of convictions; and in the *Butler* case (1992), which upheld the criminalization of pornography, it also accepted the radical feminist position that pornography is harmful because it is degrading to women, not because it is sexually explicit. No political observer writing before the emergence of radical feminism would have predicted these legal and political trends.

PERENNIAL QUESTIONS OF FEMINISM

It is typical of ideologies that their most central questions seem to have no final answers. Liberals have disagreed for centuries over what freedom "really" means, and there is no general consensus among nationalists as to which groups are "really" nations. Similarly, certain issues in the feminist movement have never been resolved. Two of these are discussed below.

1. *How different are men and women?* Liberal and socialist feminists have generally emphasized the fundamental similarity of men and women as human beings, arguing that the two sexes have the same mental and moral capacities and can do the same kinds of work. They generally regard physical differences of size and strength as not very important in an increasingly technological world. To the extent that there are more important physical differences associated with reproductive biology, they have often proposed to ameliorate the effects of these differences by changing social arrangements. Relevant examples are the provision of daycare facilities to encourage women's participation in the paid labour force and the policy of some law firms to reduce the "billable hours" expectation for female lawyers in the years when they have young children. The purpose of these and similar proposals is to allow women to compete on as equal terms as possible in occupations that have long been dominated by men. The underlying assumption is that clearing the field of obstacles will allow all players to compete and be judged on the basis of individual performance.

Since the publication of Friedan's *The Second Stage* in 1981, feminists have increasingly emphasized the ways in which women differ from men. Carol Gilligan's *In a Different Voice* (1983) argued that men and women approach moral questions differently (men allegedly think in terms of abstract rights and rules, women in terms of networks and mutual support). Another widely read book is Deborah Tannen's *You Just Don't Understand* (1990), which documents the different conversational styles of women and men. Others go even further in arguing that women are not only different from men, but also morally superior to them, and therefore must develop their differences in a separate "womanculture."

This "feminism of difference," as it has been called, poses difficult problems for the liberal strategy of integration based on the assumption of a fundamental similarity between men and women. If there really are subtle and deep-seated differences in areas such as moral reasoning and conversational style, it may be much harder than liberal feminists originally assumed for women and men to play the same roles in the public world of work and government. Different solutions are conceivable—perhaps women need to change, perhaps men need to change, perhaps the two sexes will become more like each other, perhaps the differences will remain and ways will be found to make them more complementary and harmonious—but this will obviously be more complex than simply legislating equal opportunity.

2. *What is the origin of the differences?* Are they biological or cultural? Feminists have given different answers to these questions. For Shulamith Firestone, the difference is essentially biological, and women can never be emancipated until they no longer have to bear children. Other radical feminists, however, insist that the differences are fundamentally cultural and as such can be overcome by social and political action: "By destroying the present society, and building a society based on feminist principles, men will be forced to live in the human community on terms very different from the present. For that to happen, feminism must be asserted by women, as the basis of revolutionary social change."[31] In this view, women are oppressed by male culture, but they also have their own (now subordinated) "womanculture," which can be asserted through political activism and which will eventually reshape society.

No one would deny that there are cultural differences between men and women related to their upbringing, and the way they are educated in school, depicted in the media, treated by employers, and so on. And no one would deny that these cultural differences are affected by cultural developments. Clearly, women can learn to be plumbers and men can learn to be nurses. But what if men and women tend to learn some things more readily than other things? That is, it may be that the members of either sex can learn to play almost any role; but left to their own devices, they may tend to learn some roles more readily than others. If that is true, any program of eradicating or minimizing gender differences may require degrees of compulsion that will make at least liberal feminists uncomfortable.

WOMEN IN POLITICS

Women make up half or more of the voting-age population in modern Western societies. Thus the extension of the suffrage and other political rights to women at the end of World War I suddenly doubled the size of democracy. What effect has this expansion had upon the political system?

Women do indeed use their political rights; the percentage of women who vote in elections is the same as that of men. Survey evidence reveals, however, that women on average are less interested in and less knowledgeable about politics than men, differences that cannot be explained by differences in education and income, nor by the greater demands that are often made on women's time.[32]

When the working class gained the vote in the nineteenth century, the immediate result was the creation of social-democratic parties largely dependent on the labour vote. In contrast, the entry of women into the political system did not lead to the formation of women's parties. It turned out that women, like men, have a variety of political views and vote for a variety of political parties. There are, however, some interesting differences in the political behaviour of women and men. Up to about 1970, women in most democracies were more likely than men to vote for parties of the centre-right, particularly those with a religious aspect, such as the Christian Democratic parties of Europe and Latin America. But this pattern started to change in the 1970s, first in the United States, then in other countries. Today the general pattern in established democracies is that women are more likely to vote for parties of the centre-left. This is not true, however, of emerging democracies in the Third World or in the post-communist areas of Eastern Europe, although it may evolve that way as time goes on.[33]

This **gender gap** can range from small to quite large. In the 2004 election in the United States, 51 percent of women favoured the Democrat John Kerry for president while only 44 percent of men did the same—a gap of 7 percentage points, slightly smaller than that recorded in the 2000 presidential election. By international standards, this would be considered a moderate difference, but one that was both statistically and practically significant.

Significant gender differences in support for Senators Hillary Clinton and Barack Obama in the 2008 Democratic primaries suggest that gender effects can be primed by the gender of candidates. The situation is somewhat more complicated in Canada because of the existence of five major parties. In recent elections, parties on the right of the electoral spectrum have been less likely to attract the votes of women, while the opposite tends to be the case among parties on the left. In the 1993, 1997, and 2000 elections, the Reform Party and its successor, the Canadian Alliance, recorded gender gaps of roughly 10 percentage points; in the 2000 election, for example, 38 percent of men outside of Quebec supported the party while only 27 percent of women did the same.[34] While the merger between the Alliance and the Progressive Conservatives reduced the gender gap considerably for the new Conservative Party in the 2004 election, a 10-percentage-point gender gap reappeared in the 2006 election. The NDP, on the other hand, has a similarly sized gender gap, although it attracts more support from women than from men.

Explanations for the gender gap include that women in contemporary society are more dependent than men are on government programs and thus more likely to vote for parties that favour the welfare state rather than those criticize it. Due partly to pregnancy, childbirth, and the complexity of the female reproductive system, women visit doctors and hospitals more than men do. In most families, mothers are more directly involved with the health care and education of children than fathers are. In case of divorce, women are more likely to get custody of small children and to be supported by social assistance payments. Finally, women, because of their longer life expectancy, are statistically likely to spend more years supported by old-age pensions. For all these reasons, it is logical for women to be more concerned than men about the generosity and dependability of health care, education, social assistance, and pensions in the welfare state. The gender gap, of course, depends as much on male as upon female voting behaviour. The relative swing of women to the left in the last two decades also reflects the fact that men have been more responsive than women to the appeal of the revival of market-oriented ideology.[35]

The concept of political rights includes not only voting but also holding public office. Women's involvement was slower to develop at this level. Until the end of the

1960s, female legislators were a rarity in most jurisdictions. For example, only one woman, representing 0.4 percent of seats, was elected to the House of Commons in the federal election of 1968. There has been a gradual increase, however, in the following four decades, so that 19 percent of successful candidates were female in the election of 1993. Since then, the percentage of women in the House of Commons has failed to climb any higher than 22 percent. Trends in the Canadian provinces have been similar; and at lower levels of politics, such as city councils and school boards, women have been even more successful. There is much variation across the world in this regard; some democracies have a higher, and some a lower, percentage of female officeholders than Canada. Differences are due to a number of factors including the party system, electoral rules (including the use of quotas and type of electoral system), culture, and women's overall socioeconomic status. Table 14.1 presents the data for a number of countries with which Canada might reasonably be compared.

Table 14.1

Percentage of Women in Elected (Lower) House of Legislature

Country	Year of Last Election	Percentage of Women
Sweden	2006	47
Netherlands	2006	39
Spain	2004	37
Norway	2005	36
New Zealand	2005	33
Germany	2005	32
Switzerland	2007	29
Australia	2007	27
Canada	2008	22
United Kingdom	2005	20
France	2007	18
United States	2006	17
Italy	2006	17
Israel	2006	14
Ireland	2007	13
Japan	2005	9

Source: "Women in National Parliaments, 31 December 2007," Inter-Parliamentary Union, situation as of 31 May 2008, www.ipu.org/wmn-e/classif.htm accessed 3 March 2008. Used with permission of the Inter-Parliamentary Union.

Finally, it should also be emphasized that there is much more to politics than simply voting and running for office. Women are now heavily represented in the media, reporting the news and commenting on developments in public affairs. They have also created important interest groups and advocacy organizations, ranging in Canada from the once strong National Action Committee on the Status of Women on the left to REAL Women of Canada on the right. Given the increasing importance of the judicial process in politics, it is also significant that women now enter the legal profession in more or less the same numbers as men. This means that, with some time lag, they are now frequently appointed to judgeships where they make decisions that can have a significant impact on government and politics. At the time of writing, the Chief Justice of the Supreme Court of Canada and three other members of that court were female, giving women a powerful presence in the highest legal authority in Canada.

Questions for Discussion

1. Think of some difference you have observed in the behaviour of men and women. Think of a possible explanation in terms of inherited genetic differences, and another possible explanation in terms of culture and environment. What kind of evidence would help you decide which explanation is correct?

2. What are some of the main differences between the liberal feminist and radical feminist approaches to workplace issues? Relate these differences to the ideologies themselves.

3. Why do you think women have had more success at being elected to municipal councils and school boards than to provincial legislatures and the federal Parliament?

Internet Links

1. Nelson Education Ltd. Political Science Resource Centre: **www.polisci.nelson.com/women.html.** Many links to sources of information on women in Canadian politics.

2. Nelson Education Ltd. Political Science Resource Centre: **www.polisci.nelson.com/gender.html.** Links to sources on feminism and women in politics in countries around the world.

3. Feminist Theory Website: **www.cddc.vt.edu/feminism.** Bibliography and biographies of feminist writers.

4. Status of Women Canada: **www.swc-cfc.gc.ca.** Federal department responsible for women's issues. Online publications.

5. Feminism and Women's Studies: **http://eserver.org/feminism.** Comprehensive set of links to feminism in the academic world.

Further Reading

Arneil, Barbara. *Politics and Feminism.* Oxford: Blackwell, 1999.

Backhouse, Constance. *Challenging Times: The Women's Movement in Canada and the U.S.* Montreal: McGill–Queen's University Press, 1992.

Baumgardner, Jennifer, and Amy Richards. *Manifesta: Young Women, Feminism, and the Future.* New York: Farrar, Straus, and Giroux Publishers, 2000.

Beauvoir, Simone de. *The Second Sex.* New York: Vintage Books, 1989.

Bryson, Valerie. *Feminist Political Theory: An Introduction.* 2nd ed. New York: Palgrave Macmillan, 2003.

Burt, Sandra, Lorraine Code, and Lindsay Dorney, eds. *Changing Patterns: Women in Canada.* Toronto: McClelland & Stewart, 1993.

Donovan, Josephine. *Feminist Theory: The Intellectual Traditions of American Feminism.* New York: Ungar, 1985.

Faludi, Susan. *Backlash: The Undeclared War Against American Women.* New York: Crown, 1991.

Ferree, Myra Marx, and Aili Mari Tripp. *Global Feminism: Transnational Women's Activism, Organizing, and Human Rights.* New York: NYU Press, 2006.

Friedan, Betty. *The Feminine Mystique.* New York: Dell, 1983.

———. *The Second Stage.* New York: Summit Books, 1981.

Hirsh, Marianne. *Conflicts in Feminism.* New York: Routledge, 1990.

Inglehart, Ronald, and Pippa Norris. *Gender Equality and Cultural Change around the World.* Toronto: Cambridge University Press, 2003.

Jackman, Mary R. *The Velvet Glove: Paternalism and Conflict in Gender, Class, and Race Relations.* Berkeley: University of California Press, 1994.

Jaggar, Alison. *Feminist Politics and Human Nature.* Totowa, NJ: Rowman and Allanheld, 1983.

Lovenduski, Joni, and Pippa Norris, eds. *Gender and Party Politics.* London: Sage, 1993.

MacIvor, Heather. *Women and Politics in Canada.* Peterborough, ON: Broadview Press, 1996.

Mill, John Stuart. *The Subjection of Women.* Arlington Heights, IL: AHM Publishing, 1980.

Newman, Jacquetta A., and Linda A. White. *Women, Politics, and Public Policy: The Political Struggles of Canadian Women.* Toronto: Oxford University Press, 2006.

Phillips, Anne, ed. *Feminism and Politics.* Oxford: Oxford University Press, 1998.

Pinker, Susan. *The Sexual Paradox: Extreme Men, Gifted Women and the Real Gender Gap.* Toronto: Random House Canada, 2008.

Rendall, Janet. *The Origins of Modern Feminism.* London: Macmillan, 1985.

Sharpe, Sydney. *The Gilded Ghetto: Women and Political Power in Canada.* Toronto: HarperCollins, 1994.

Sommers, Christina Hoff. *Who Stole Feminism? How Women Have Betrayed Women.* New York: Simon and Schuster, 1994.

Spender, Dale. *Feminist Theorists: Three Centuries of Women's Intellectual Traditions.* London: Women's Press, 1983.

Sperling, Liz. *Women, Political Philosophy and Politics.* Edinburgh: Edinburgh University Press, 2001.

Steinem, Gloria. *Outrageous Acts and Everyday Rebellions.* New York: Holt, Rinehart and Winston, 1983.

Stetson, Dorothy McBride. *Abortion Politics, Women's Movements, and the State.* Toronto: Oxford University Press, 2001.

Tong, Rosemarie. *Feminist Thought: A More Comprehensive Introduction.* 2nd ed. Boulder, CO: Westview Press, 1998.

Tremblay, Manon, and Linda Jean Trimble, eds. *Women and Electoral Politics in Canada.* Toronto: Oxford University Press, 2003.

Young, Lisa. *Feminists and Party Politics.* Vancouver: University of British Columbia Press, 2000.

CHAPTER 15

Environmentalism

Like feminism, **environmentalism** is not a single belief system but a family of ideologies riven by profound internal differences. Also like feminism, environmentalism has old roots, although it has become a major political force only since the 1970s. Some versions of environmentalism can be traced back about a century. Even older antecedents exist, such as the speculations of Thomas Malthus about the inevitability of overpopulation; but these are probably best interpreted as environmental reflections within a liberal context rather than the beginning of a new ideology. The genuine tradition of environmentalism began about a century ago with the conservationist movement.

CONSERVATIONISM

Conservationism is the attempt to manage natural resources so that human users, including future generations, derive maximum benefit over a long period of time. The emergence of the discipline of forestry in the last century was one important development in conservationism. Another was the national parks movement. In 1872 the U.S. Congress passed the Yellowstone Park Act to create the first national park, and Canada followed suit in 1885 with the creation of Banff National Park. Human use was clearly the driving force in the national parks movement; for example, Banff National Park was established around hot springs and promoted by the Canadian Pacific Railway as a tourist destination and health resort.

Conservationism has continued to be an important political movement. In 1938, for example, the Government of Alberta created the Oil and Gas Conservation Board with the goal of maximizing petroleum output over time by allocating production among producers drawing from the same oilfields. When too much oil is extracted too quickly, pressure drops in the reservoir to the detriment of long-term yields. All producers are better off in the long run when they control their present output. Other aspects of the conservation movement include flood control, reforestation, soil reclamation, and wildlife management and habitat enhancement. The use of resources by humans is the common aim of all these efforts. For instance, many hunters contribute time and money to Ducks Unlimited in an effort to conserve and restore prairie wetlands, with the long-term goal of improving duck hunting. The hunters work to improve wildlife habitat, but they are thinking mainly of human recreation, not of any intrinsic value of wildlife apart from human use.

HUMAN WELFARE ECOLOGY

The rise of **human welfare ecology** began, most observers agree, in 1962, when Rachel Carson's book *Silent Spring* raised alarms about the effects of pesticides, particularly DDT, on the reproduction of birds. This movement began as an extension of conservationism, in that it originally focused on wildlife management. At the same time, it transcended the economic dimension of traditional conservationism by directly addressing the value to human health and happiness of the environment. Since *Silent Spring,* environmental concerns have broadened out till they now embrace an infinity of issues—air and water quality, carcinogens, the ozone layer, global warming, overpopulation, solid-waste disposal, nuclear radiation, and so on—but in all cases the theme is the effect of environmental degradation on human welfare. For example, human welfare ecologists fear that the thinning of the ozone layer may lead to an increase in the incidence of skin cancers, and that global warming may cause flooding of coastal cities as well as desertification of currently productive agricultural lands. Like conservationism, human welfare ecology is basically "anthropocentric" (i.e., human-centred).[1] In practical political terms, the human welfare brand of ecology has led to the passage of environmental legislation, the creation of departments of the environment, and the rise of new regulatory processes, such as environmental impact studies and public hearings on the construction of dams, high-tension power lines, and other major projects.

Both conservationism and human welfare ecology can be understood to some degree as extensions of liberalism. They are chiefly concerned with phenomena that we discussed earlier under the heading of public goods. They typically see problems such as the waste of resources or the pollution of the environment as resulting from "market failure." A famous essay along this line is "The Tragedy of the Commons" (1968) by Garret Hardin. The title comes from an illustration Hardin used: a common pasture that is bound to be overgrazed as long as the livestock owners pursue their individual self-interest without coordination. It is in the interest of each owner to allow his livestock to graze as much as possible on the pasture; a herder who holds his flock back will not get any benefit because others will simply let their animals graze even more. The herders would like to conserve the pasture but cannot do so without a mechanism to prevent free riding. It is in your interest to limit your own herd's grazing only if you can count on others to do likewise. For more on the "tragedy of the commons," see Issues Box 15.1.

The metaphor of the tragedy of the commons places environmental issues squarely within the liberal tradition, with its focus on individual action, profit incentives, and enforcement of rights. The remedies that arise within this perspective correspond roughly to the distinction between classical and reform liberalism.

Issues Box 15.1

The Tragedy of the Commons

Imagine a grazing area owned in common by 10 ranchers, each of whom uses it to pasture 10 head of cattle. The carrying capacity of the pasture is exactly 100 cattle; that is, with that degree of grazing, the grass can renew itself and the cattle can feed indefinitely.

Now put yourself in the position of one of the owners. If you add one more cow to the commons, you increase your personal herd by 10 percent (10 plus 1). True, you degrade the commons, but only by 1 percent (100 plus 1). The costs of the overgrazing, which will be manifested in diminished grass production, will be borne by all owners together, whereas you will get all the benefit of selling the additional cow.

Thus you have an incentive to add livestock beyond the carrying capacity, and so do all the other owners. If all owners follow their incentives for private gain, the result will be the destruction of the commons through overgrazing. With ironical reference to Adam Smith, theorists call this "the back of the invisible hand." In situations of common property, unregulated pursuit of individual interest produces collective loss rather than the common benefit that Smith described in *The Wealth of Nations*.

There are two standard responses to the tragedy of the commons, both of which involve aligning private and collective interest: (1) Privatize the commons and give every owner his own little pasture, which he will then have incentives to preserve. (2) Set up a regulatory regime to ensure that owners do not go beyond sustainable limits. Such a regime can be either formal (government) or informal (social pressure), though informal regimes are likely to work only in stable situations where small numbers of people can get to know each other and monitor each other's behaviour.

The parallel with environmental dilemmas should be clear. The atmosphere, rivers, lakes, and the seas are like commons with many users. Each polluter can benefit by using these commons as disposal dumps; but if too many people act this way, the volume of waste transcends the carrying capacity of the resource, with consequent degradation. Privatization may work in some situations, such as small lakes; but an authoritative management regime seems required for larger resources such as rivers and oceans.

One school of thought, analogous to classical liberalism, is known as **free-market environmentalism.** It argues that the underlying problem in public-goods situations is the failure to assign property rights. There would be no "tragedy of the commons" if the commons were divided up into individually owned pastures. According to this view, a problem such as air pollution arises because no one owns the atmosphere and has an interest in protecting it from degradation. As a result, manufacturers, power producers, drivers of automobiles—indeed, all consumers of goods and services—use the atmosphere as a seemingly free way to get rid of waste products. Free-market environmentalists believe that, while it is not feasible to create literal owners of the atmosphere, a similar result can be achieved by other means. For example, public regulatory authorities could issue licences to emit limited amounts of air pollution, and these licences could subsequently be bought and sold in the market. In this way, atmospheric waste disposal, instead of appearing free as it does at present, would acquire a cost; and as a costly good, it would lead users to seek ways to economize on it. The market's invisible hand would thus produce the "right" amount of air pollution; that is, the amount that can be absorbed without causing unacceptable deterioration of human amenities.

Free-market environmentalism is largely confined to thinkers in universities and research institutes, the main Canadian example being the Fraser Institute. Popular environmentalist movements usually espouse more interventionist approaches. Nonetheless, theories of free-market environmentalism have had some success in influencing policymakers in some countries to adopt tradable pollution quotas and similar quasi-market devices.

Most environmentalists, however, believe that "the tragedy of the commons" can be resolved only by government direction. This view, which is closer to reform liberalism, typically leads to legislation that limits or prohibits certain acts—for example, the production of chlorofluorocarbons (which damage the ozone layer) or the use of chlorine compounds in the production of paper. Environmental debates over issues of this type expand the agenda of liberalism but do not fundamentally break with it. They are similar in principle to the myriad other debates going on all the time about whether human purposes are better served by the market or by governmental provision.

Human-welfare ecology, however, tends to go beyond the liberal tradition to the extent that it is sceptical about the possibility of unlimited economic growth. Many environmentalists in this camp believe that human population and consumption must be stabilized or even reduced. An excellent example of this kind of thinking was the Kyoto Accord (1997), in which the signatory nations pledged to reduce their production of greenhouse gases, including carbon dioxide, below 1990 levels. At the time of writing, Canada had ratified the Kyoto Accord and it had taken international effect among the signatory nations, but it was still unclear how implementation would proceed. Canada has ratified it but not yet done much to implement it unless the United States also ratifies it, which seems very unlikely to happen.

An organizing concept for many human-welfare ecologists is **sustainable development,** defined as follows in the United Nations' Brundtland Commission Report (1987): "a form of development that meets the needs of the present without compromising the ability of future generations to meet their own needs."[2] The implication of the concept of sustainable development is that the present generation may have to sacrifice its material standard of living for the sake of future generations. This goes beyond the classical liberal confidence in economic growth as well as the reform liberal emphasis on redistributing the results of growth along lines of social justice; it questions the very rationale of growth.

Issues Box 15.2

Global Warming as a Tragedy of the Commons

The high-profile issue of greenhouse gas emissions and climate change is another example of a tragedy of the commons. The earth's atmosphere is a classic example of a commons—used by everyone but owned by no one. Ever since human beings discovered fire, they have discharged into the atmosphere carbon dioxide and other gases that capture heat radiated from the earth's surface. At first this hardly mattered, because the number of human beings and their consumption of fossil-fuel energy was small compared to the immensity of the atmosphere. But with the growth of population and the increase of energy-intensive technology, greenhouse-gas emissions have reached the point where they contribute measurably to global warming. Most scientists agree upon the direction of the effect, though there is still much debate over its magnitude and consequences.

Global warming is a particularly difficult tragedy of the commons to deal with because the problem has two levels. Since there is no world government, each of the sovereign states must try to evolve internal policies for restricting the emission of greenhouse gases within its own jurisdiction. This is difficult enough because it means imposing higher costs on consumers as well as on energy-intensive industries such as manufacturing, mining, and petroleum extraction. But even as a government tries to solve its internal problems by introducing new policies, it has to consider its position in the atmospheric commons. A state that introduced strict carbon regulations on its own would damage the competitiveness of its producers in world markets.

The Kyoto Protocol, negotiated in 1997, was supposed to resolve this dilemma by allowing many states to move together when they regulated greenhouse gases, but it fell far short of expectations. Third World countries, including large emitters such as China, India, and Brazil, undertook no obligations, arguing that the problem had been caused by—and should be solved by—the highly industrialized countries of Europe, North America, and Japan. The United States, the world's largest single emitter of greenhouse gases, refused to ratify the Kyoto Protocol. Other nations, such as Canada, ratified it but did not live up to their treaty obligations. The only real cuts in carbon emissions were made in countries such as the United Kingdom, Germany, and former Soviet satellites that, for other reasons, were shutting down obsolete smokestack industries.

It remains a difficult and perhaps impossible challenge to get 192 sovereign states to work together to reduce greenhouse gas emissions for the sake of the global atmospheric commons. If that pessimistic assessment is true, then adaptation to, rather than prevention of, global warming may be the only realistic alternative.

DEEP ECOLOGY

Deep ecology represents a fundamental break with liberalism, and indeed with all other ideologies, because it is "ecocentric"—that is, it posits the entire natural order, not human happiness, as its highest value. As formulated by Arne Naess and George Sessions in 1974, the basic principles of deep ecology are:

1. The well-being and flourishing of human and nonhuman Life on Earth have value in themselves (synonyms: intrinsic value, inherent value). These values are independent of the usefulness of the nonhuman world for human purposes.

2. Richness and diversity of life forms contribute to the realization of these values and are also values in themselves.

3. Humans have no right to reduce this richness and diversity except to satisfy vital needs.

4. The flourishing of human life and cultures is compatible with a substantial decrease of the human population. The flourishing of nonhuman life requires such a decrease.

5. Present human interference with the nonhuman world is excessive, and the situation is rapidly worsening.

6. Policies must therefore be changed. These policies affect basic economic, technological, and ideological structures. The resulting state of affairs will be deeply different from the present.

7. The ideological change is mainly that of appreciating life quality (dwelling in situations of inherent value) rather than adhering to an increasingly higher standard of living. There will be a profound awareness of the difference between big and great.

8. Those who subscribe to the foregoing points have an obligation directly or indirectly to try to implement the necessary changes.[3]

In such an uncompromising form, deep ecology has few adherents. However, two related views have become important political forces. One is **wilderness preservationism,** as manifested in, for example, the movements to save the earth's rain forests, both tropical (the Amazon) and temperate (British Columbia). Adherents of preservationist movements sometimes put forward arguments relating to human advantage (e.g., that the tropical rain forest may be a source of useful medicines); but their case rests mainly on the intrinsic importance of wilderness, whether or not humans use it.

The wilderness preservation movement is older than deep ecology; its roots go back at least to the founding of the Sierra Club in 1892. John Muir, the founder of the Sierra Club, wrote that wilderness preservation would let people "enrich their own little ongoings with Nature . . . washing off sins and cobwebs of the devil's spinning . . . getting in touch with the nerves of Mother Earth."[4] More recently, Monte Hummel, president of the World Wildlife Fund Canada, said, "I believe nature has rights, natural systems have rights."[5] The preservationist perspective, however, is usually anthropocentric to some degree, because it tends to focus on environments that appeal strongly to the human sense of beauty and grandeur, and on "charismatic megafauna," such as lions and grizzly bears, that excite the human imagination.

Wilderness preservation also gives rise to demands for the restoration of wilderness, or "re-wilding." Re-wilding is not a simple concept, because different assemblages of species have dominated regional biospheres at different times in the past. Thus your conception of returning to wilderness conditions depends completely on how far back you want to go. For example, the Great Plains of North America were dominated by mammoths and mastodons, horses, ground sloths, sabretooth tigers, and so on until the end of the last Ice Age, when they disappeared through some combination of climate change and hunting pressure. One author has seriously proposed replacing these North American species, most of which are now extinct, with their closest surviving relatives, such as elephants.[6] Imagine taking marginal crop and grazing land out of production and returning it to range conditions: "Home, home on the range/Where the deer and the elephant play." It is easy to make fun of such novel proposals, but harder to refute them on logical grounds. We have already reintroduced horses to North America; why not elephants, the close cousins of mammoths?

Another variant of deep ecology is the **animal liberation** movement, which proposes to ban hunting, the raising of domestic livestock for food and other economic purposes (although not the keeping of pets), and the use of animals in laboratory experiments. An influential exponent of this movement is the philosopher Peter Singer. In *Animal Liberation* (1975), he argued that all creatures have interests to the extent that they can feel pain, which all the higher animals clearly can do. The cutoff line is difficult to draw, but "somewhere between a shrimp and an oyster seems as good a place to draw the line as any, and better than most."[7] The animal liberation movement is limited because it does not consider the interests of the lower animals, plants, and microorganisms. Using the ability to suffer as a criterion is still anthropocentric, at least by analogy, since it starts from the human desire to avoid pain and extends it to other species. Even so, whatever the logical problems may be, wilderness preservation and animal liberation both point in the direction of deep ecology.

It may be a bit misleading to call deep ecology an ideology, for it is a radical challenge to the civilization that has generated all other ideologies. To the extent that it posits inherent values outside human experience, it has some resemblance to a religious revival; but if deep ecology posits a divinity, it exists in the immanent order of the universe, not in a transcendent God. In fact, deep ecologists are keenly interested in pre-Christian Native religious traditions and have tried to develop political alliances with Native peoples to protest against commercial development of wilderness areas. The alliance, however, is somewhat fragile, because many in the Native community favour commercial development as long as they get an appropriate share of the economic benefits. Aboriginal people, like other sectors of society, are internally divided over environmentalism.

ENVIRONMENTALISM AND POLITICS

One result of the rise of environmentalism as a family of ideologies has been the emergence of environmentalist political parties, usually known as **Green** parties. The first of these parties was the Values Party of New Zealand, founded in 1972. Since that time, a Green party has been founded in virtually every functioning democracy in the world.

Green parties find it almost impossible to elect anyone in countries such as Canada, the United States, and Great Britain, which use the first-past-the-post method of voting (for a further discussion of electoral systems, see Chapter 25). Thus no Green has ever been elected to Parliament or to a provincial legislature in Canada, though a few have been elected to local offices such as school trustee or city councillor. Green candidates, however, sometimes affect the outcome by taking away votes from others. Thus, Ralph Nader's Green candidacy for president of the United States in 2000 may have cost Democrat Al Gore the election. Gore and his Republican opponent, George W. Bush, received almost exactly the same share of the popular vote, but the 2 percent of the vote that went to Nader would probably have broken more for Gore than Bush if the Greens had not run a candidate.

To date, the Greens' biggest success in Canadian politics took place in the British Columbia provincial election of 2001, when they received 12 percent of the vote. The Greens did not win any seats, but their share of the vote caused the defeat of NDP candidates in several ridings, with the result that the NDP, which had previously been in power, did not even win enough seats to be recognized as an official party in the legislature. Playing this "spoiler" role is a form of political power, to be sure, but the Greens would also dearly love to elect representatives. Thus they went unsuccessfully to court to seek a judicial declaration that the Canadian system of first-past-the-post voting violates the guarantees of equality and political rights in the Charter of Rights and Freedoms. The Greens, perhaps more than any other political party in Canada, stand to profit from a move toward proportional representation. In the meantime, they have made breakthroughs in federal politics in Canada by getting 4.3 percent of the vote in the 2004 election, 4.5 percent in 2006, and 6.8 percent in 2008. Under new legislation, this qualifies them for a substantial grant from public funds, which helps them maintain their presence on the federal scene.

In countries that do have proportional representation, Green candidates are frequently elected. Green members sit today in the national parliaments of dozens of countries. There has never been a Green government as such, but under the right conditions Greens may participate in a governing coalition, as has happened in Germany, Finland, Belgium, and France. At the time of writing, Green parties are members of coalition governments in Ireland and the Czech Republic. The Greens also have a presence—and in the 2007 election once again won enough seats to hold the balance of power—in the Australian Senate, which is elected by a form of proportional representation.

Even more influential than Green political parties have been environmentalist advocacy groups, which have proliferated remarkably over the last three decades. Some of these, such as Greenpeace and Friends of the Earth, have a high media profile and operate around the world. Others, like the Canadian Parks and Wilderness Society (formerly the National and Provincial Parks Association of Canada), are organized around issues specific to one country and operate mainly within national boundaries. Still others are local in character, having formed around a specific issue such as the location of a garbage dump or the preservation of wetlands.

Some of these Canadian advocacy groups have conducted highly influential political campaigns. An early success was the Greenpeace campaign to get the European Union to ban the sale of seal furs, thus dealing a major setback to the Newfoundland seal hunt. Greenpeace has also been successful in putting pressure on the forest-products industry by convincing Europeans that British Columbia's forestry practices are environmentally unsound. In a more local example, an *ad hoc* coalition created enough environmental concern to deter Toronto from implementing its plan to use an abandoned mining pit at Elliot Lake as a landfill site for solid waste. It is no exaggeration to say that today virtually any project involving the exploitation of natural resources—mining, forestry, water storage, power generation, highway construction, pipelines—will meet some opposition from international, national, and/or local environmental advocacy groups. Environmentalists do not win all these battles, but the fact that the battles are fought ensures some degree of environmental scrutiny in the decision-making system.

Even beyond the work of political parties and advocacy groups, perhaps the greatest victory of environmentalism is that it has become entrenched in the everyday machinery of government as well as in public opinion. In Canada as in other countries, older government departments with names such as Lands and Forests, Mines, and Natural Resources have long ago been folded into departments of the environment. Both legislation and government policy now require environmental review of government activities as well as major private-sector developments. Public opinion supports this environmental concern and would be outraged at the resumption of practices that were commonplace when the authors of this book were young, such as discharging untreated sewage into rivers, clear-cutting entire mountainsides, and strip mining without reclamation.

Curing such environmental ills costs money, sometimes a great deal of money, but few today would argue that the price is too high. This willingness to pay for higher environmental standards is part of the value shift described earlier as *post-materialism*. When physical security and a high material standard of living seem assured, voters become more concerned about the quality of life, including the cleanliness and beauty of the physical environment.

Questions for Discussion

1. Can you think of an example from your own experience of the "tragedy of the commons"; that is, the degradation of a commonly owned resource by users pursuing their own self-interest?

2. There is much political conflict over national parks in Canada—for example, over the enlargement of ski resorts and town sites. Can you explain how these conflicts

illustrate differences among the various forms of environmentalism discussed in this chapter?

3. As a mental experiment, ask yourself how many cents in additional tax you would be willing to pay on a litre of gasoline in order to reduce the consumption of gasoline and therefore reduce the production of greenhouse gases. How much do you think consumers in general would be willing to pay?

Internet Links

1. Green Parties World Wide: **www.greens.org.** Links to the websites of Green parties around the world.

2. Greenpeace International: **www.greenpeace.org.** Home page of the world's highest-profile environmental advocacy group. Links to national Greenpeace organizations.

3. Great River Earth Institute: **www.greatriv.org.** Deep ecology organization.

4. Canadian Parks and Wilderness Society: **www.cpaws.org.** A Canadian environmental advocacy organization.

5. Ducks Unlimited: **www.ducks.org.** Organization of hunters that helps to protect wetlands and improve waterfowl habitat.

6. JunkScience.com: **www.junkscience.com.** Website devoted to exposing questionable science, including environmental scare tactics.

Further Reading

Anderson, Terry L., and Donald R. Leal. *Free Market Environmentalism.* San Francisco: Pacific Research Institute for Public Policy, 1991.

Bailey, Ronald. *Earth Report 2000: Revisiting the True State of the Planet.* New York: McGraw-Hill, 2000.

Barry, John. *Rethinking Green Politics: Nature, Virtue, and Progress.* London: Sage, 1999.

Beckerman, Wilfred. *Through Green-Colored Glasses: Environmentalism Reconsidered.* Washington, DC: Cato Institute, 1996.

Bliese, John Ross Edward. *The Greening of Conservative America.* Boulder, CO: Westview Press, 2002.

Block, Walter E., ed. *Economics and the Environment: A Reconciliation.* Vancouver: Fraser Institute, 1990.

Conca, Ken, and Geoffrey D. Dabelko, eds. *Green Planet Blues: Environmental Politics from Stockholm to Kyoto.* 2nd ed. Boulder, CO: Westview Press, 1998.

Drengson, Alan, and Yuichi Inoue, eds. *The Deep Ecology Movement: An Introductory Anthology.* Berkeley, CA: North Atlantic Books, 1995.

Dunn, James R. *Conservative Environmentalism: Reassessing the Means, Redefining the Ends.* Westport, CT: Quorum, 1996.

Eckersley, Robyn. *Environmentalism and Political Theory.* Albany: State University Press, 1992.

Ehrlich, Paul R. *Betrayal of Science and Reason: How Anti-Environmental Rhetoric Threatens Our Future.* Washington, DC: Island Press, 1996.

Gore, Albert. *Earth in the Balance: Ecology and the Human Spirit.* Boston: Houghton Mifflin, 1992.

———. *An Inconvenient Truth: The Planetary Emergence of Global Warming and What We Can Do About It.* New York: Rodale, 2006.

Gottlieb, Roger S. *The Ecological Community: Environmental Challenges for Philosophy, Politics and Morality.* New York: Routledge, 1997.

Herndl, Carl G., and Stuart C. Brown, eds. *Green Culture: Environmental Rhetoric in Contemporary America.* Madison: University of Wisconsin Press, 1996.

Lipschutz, Ronnie D., with Judith Mayer. *Global Civil Society and Global Environmental Governance: The Politics of Nature from Place to Planet.* Albany: State University of New York Press, 1996.

Lomborg, Bjorn. *The Skeptical Environmentalist: Measuring the Real State of the World.* Cambridge: Cambridge University Press, 2001.

McKenzie, Judith. *Environmental Politics in Canada.* Toronto: Oxford University Press, 2001.

O'Neill, Michael. *Green Parties and Political Change in Contemporary Europe: New Politics, Old Predicaments.* Aldershot, UK: Ashgate, 1997.

Parson, Edward A., ed. *Governing the Environment: Persistent Challenges, Uncertain Innovations.* Toronto: University of Toronto Press, 2001.

Pepper, David. *The Roots of Modern Environmentalism.* London: Routledge, 1984.

Van Nijnatten, Debora, and Robert Boardman, eds. *Canadian Environmental Policy.* 2nd ed. Toronto: Oxford University Press, 2001.

Worster, Donald. *American Environmentalism: The Formative Period, 1860–1915.* New York: Wiley, 1973.

PART 3
Forms of Government

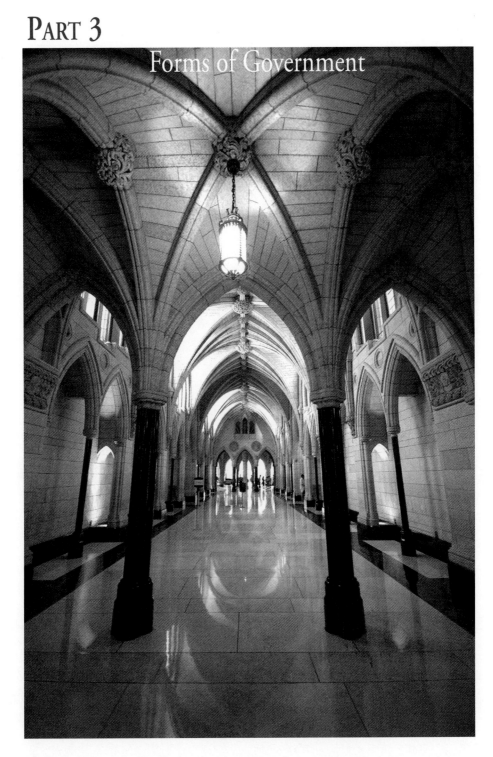

CHAPTER 16

Classification of Political Systems

The review of ideologies completed in Part Two leads naturally to a study of forms of government. Ideologies are not just abstract ideas; they reflect the experience of people who live under one form of government or another. This experience may express itself ideologically as acceptance of a governmental form, or as rejection of it, or as a combination—partial acceptance with proposals for modification. Also, as Marx saw, ideology is at least in part determined by the social milieu, in which government is an important factor. Finally, ideology is a determining factor of government because it establishes goals toward which people strive. For example, liberals try to fashion governmental machinery to enhance individual freedom, however they may define it, while socialists enhance the power of the state through central planning and the nationalization of industry. All this means that government and ideology are reciprocally related—each causes and is caused by the other. Part Three of this book examines the chief forms of government in relation to the ideological climate as it is emerging in the early twenty-first century.

Before one can understand a complicated set of facts, one must be able to classify them—to sort them into groups based on their position along some dimension. This process of organizing factual information about governmental systems produces broad schemes of classification usually known as *typologies*. Once such typologies are formed, one can formulate and test generalizations about the similarities and differences among the various categories.

THE CLASSICAL TYPOLOGY

One of the oldest, and still useful, **typologies** of government dates back to the founders of political science, Plato and Aristotle. They classified governments with two questions in mind: *Who rules?* and *In whose interest?* Possible answers to the first question were simple: rule may be exercised by a single person, by a minority ("the few"), or by a majority of the whole people ("the many"). The second question, concerning whose interests are served, is more difficult and requires a longer answer.

Plato held that there are two basic ways in which rule may be conducted: lawfully and lawlessly. Either the governors are bound by constitutional rules that they are not

Figure 16.1 Platonic/Aristotelian Typology of Government

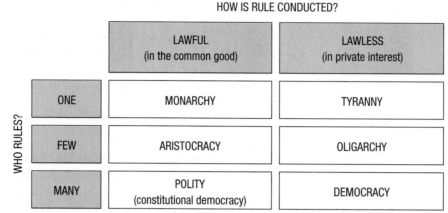

HOW IS RULE CONDUCTED?

		LAWFUL (in the common good)	LAWLESS (in private interest)
WHO RULES?	ONE	MONARCHY	TYRANNY
	FEW	ARISTOCRACY	OLIGARCHY
	MANY	POLITY (constitutional democracy)	DEMOCRACY

free to set aside, or they rule according to unchecked whims and emotional desires. The first possibility corresponds to what we have called the rule of law, the second to the arbitrary rule of individuals. In the words of Aristotle:

> He who bids the law rule may be deemed to bid God and Reason alone rule, but he who bids man rule adds an element of the beast; for desire is a wild beast, and passion perverts the minds of rulers, even when they are the best of men. The law is reason unaffected by desire.[1]

Aristotle added that rule by law is in the general interest of the entire community, whereas arbitrary rule represents exploitation of the ruled for the special interest of the governors. He also pointed out that rule in the common interest tends to be seen as legitimate, and gives rulers authority that the ruled will obey voluntarily, while selfish government does not seem legitimate to those who are oppressed and therefore has to be sustained by coercion and fear. In sum, we have two kinds of regimes: lawful authority seeking the common good, and lawless coercion seeking private interest. Combining these two dimensions of "who" and "how" yields a sixfold typology, illustrated in Figure 16.1.

A **monarchy** for Plato and Aristotle was a regime in which sovereign authority was vested in one person, who ruled within the laws of the *polis*. Its corrupt counterpart was a **tyranny,** in which one person ruled arbitrarily. An **aristocracy** was a system in which political power was held by a restricted class—usually the wealthy and those of noble ancestry—that ruled in the general interest under law. An **oligarchy,** in contrast, was a regime where the wealthy minority used its power to exploit and oppress the impoverished majority. **Democracy,** in the Greek sense of the term, was also an exploitative form of government, in the sense that the many used their political power to obtain for themselves the wealth of the rich—a majority oppressing a minority. It was the rule of the common people unchecked by legal restraints. The positive counterpart of democracy was **polity,** which today we might call **constitutional democracy.**

The word *polity* is derived from *politeia,* the Greek word for constitution. It expresses the idea that the rule of the many is good only if it is exercised within a fixed constitutional framework that prevents the majority from oppressing minorities. It represents the balance of public and private interests through the political process.

This raises a more general point: to the Greek philosophers, democracy or popular government was not necessarily a good thing. They considered any lawful regime preferable to any lawless one. The question of numbers, though not unimportant, was secondary in their minds to the question of lawfulness. This insight—that who rules is less important than how rule is conducted—is sometimes obscured because of the modern habit of regarding democracy as something good in itself. Plato and Aristotle would have said that while a polity or constitutional democracy is a good form of government, unchecked democracy is mob rule, little different in principle from tyranny or oligarchy. The nineteenth-century writers Alexis de Tocqueville and John Stuart Mill made the same point when they expressed the fear that democracy could become a "tyranny of the majority."[2]

Plato and Aristotle left us a body of thought that emphasizes the rule of law—yet paradoxically, Plato believed there was an even higher form of rule. In his famous book *The Republic,* he sketched the ideal of rule by a **philosopher-king,** a man so preeminent in wisdom and moral virtue that he could rule by personal judgment rather than by the constraint of law. He would not be arbitrary or oppressive, because his philosophic wisdom would protect him from the temptations of power. The people would consent to this form of rule because it would be in their own interest.

Plato never completely renounced his belief in the philosopher-king, but he became rather pessimistic about the possibility of finding such a man. In a later dialogue, *The Statesman,* he suggested that the rule of law was an acceptable, second-best alternative in the absence of a philosopher-king. And in his last work, *The Laws,* the philosopher-king is nowhere to be found.

Thus Plato, along with his pupil Aristotle, came to see the rule of law as the best political solution likely to be attained by imperfect human beings. Rule of law is second best in terms of what might be imagined, but best in terms of what human beings, with their limited knowledge, can probably achieve. Yet the image of the philosopher-king, who rules above law in the common good, has never ceased to haunt history. Many autocratic regimes claiming superiority to the law have been based on it.

One other important point must be made. Aristotle was always careful to point out that the conflict between the few and the many was as much one of wealth as of numbers, since in practice the many are usually poor relative to the wealthy few. In his view, the besetting vice of democracy was the tendency of the majority to use the state's power to confiscate the property of the wealthy minority; the parallel failing of oligarchy was the desire of the wealthy few to manipulate the laws to bring about easier exploitation of the masses.

Aristotle's preference was for a polity or constitutional democracy where the rights of property would be protected by law. In the classical view, polity is a balancing act between two negative governmental forms: democracy and oligarchy. If both the wealthy and the poor, the few and the many, hold a share of power in the state, and if neither faction is supreme, they will check each other. Thus, in a negative way, we come back to the desired situation of the rule of law, because the counterpoised factions will watch each other to make sure that neither begins to manipulate the laws to its own advantage. However, Aristotle also pointed out that the balance would probably be unstable if society were polarized into camps of extreme wealth and poverty. It would be best to have a large middle class, as this in a sense would unite numbers and property within itself. Such a class, though not itself rich, would have a stake in protecting the property of the rich—for if the rich could be despoiled, the middle class itself might be next. Aristotle's words have lost none of their wisdom after 2,300 years:

> Great then is the good fortune of a state in which the citizens have a moderate and sufficient property; for where some possess much, and others nothing there may arise an extreme democracy, or a pure oligarchy; or a tyranny may grow out of either extreme.[3]

MODERN TYPOLOGIES

The classical typology of the six forms of government was the beginning of political science and is still useful today, but it is not the only approach to classification. Indeed, there can never be a definitive or final typology, because classification depends on which aspect of reality we wish to emphasize. As forms of government evolve through history, schemes of classification evolve with them (see Figure 16.2 for a summary of the forms of government). The remainder of Part Three uses three different typologies, which correspond to three aspects of government in our own age.

First, we classify governments according to the relationship between state and society. The three types that appear in this classification are liberal democracies, transitional democracies, and autocracies. Second, we classify governments according to the relationship between the executive and legislative powers of government. The chief distinction here is between parliamentary and presidential systems. Third, we classify governments according to their degree of centralization or decentralization. This was not a major concern

Figure 16.2 Modern Typology Summary of Forms of Government

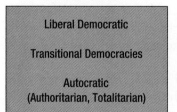

BASIC FORMS	INSTITUTIONS
Liberal Democratic	Parliamentary/Presidential/Hybrid Forms
Transitional Democracies	
Autocratic (Authoritarian, Totalitarian)	Unitary State/Devolution/Federalism/Confederation

of Plato and Aristotle, who thought of government chiefly in the context of the small, independent *polis;* but it is a big problem for the large states of modern times. The major types in this context are the unitary state, devolution, federalism, and confederation.

Our three classification schemes are not mutually exclusive; rather, they can be applied together for a multidimensional description of any particular government. Thus Canada would be described as a liberal–democratic, parliamentary, and federal state, whereas Cuba would be autocratic, presidential, and unitary. There are inevitably many borderline cases that tend to straddle categories; for example, even though political reforms are underway, Mexico still combines certain aspects of both the liberal–democratic and autocratic forms, while France represents a unique combination of parliamentary and presidential systems, and federalism in the former Soviet Union was largely overridden in practice by the overwhelming power of the Communist Party. Also, due to political transitions occurring in many countries today, nation-states can change quickly from one classification to another. For example, Chile moved from an authoritarian military dictatorship to a more liberal–democratic system of government when President Pinochet resigned in 1990. Even though all typologies involve intermediate or ill-fitting cases, we can use these classifications as a first step in understanding how political systems work.

Questions for Discussion

1. What is the problem with "democracy" in the Platonic/Aristotelian typology?

2. What is the benefit of a classification scheme?

3. Why is the scheme devised by Plato and Aristotle no longer fully adequate for classifying the more than 190 nation-states today?

Internet Links

1. *The Economist:* **www.economist.com.** Internet version of the famous magazine. An excellent source of current information on governments all over the world.

2. *Comparative Politics,* Annual Editions: **www.dushkin.com/annualeditions.** More current events.

3. OECD: **www.oecd.org.** Home page of the Organisation for Economic Co-operation and Development. Links to information on governments everywhere.

4. Wikipedia.org, "Form of government": **http://en.wikipedia.org/wiki/Form_of_government,** is an informative article.

Further Reading

Acemoglu, Daron, and James A. Robinson. *Economic Origins of Dictatorship and Democracy.* Cambridge: Cambridge University Press, 2006.

Almond, Gabriel A., G. Bingham Powell, Jr., Kaare Strom, and Russell J. Dalton. *Comparative Politics Today: A Theoretical Framework.* 3rd ed. New York: Longman, 2001.

——. *Comparative Politics Today: A World View.* 7th ed. New York: Longman, 2000.

Andrain, Charles F. *Comparative Political Systems: Policy Performance and Social Change.* Armonk, NY: M. E. Sharpe, 1994.

Brown, Bernard E., ed. *Forms of Government: Notes and Readings.* 9th ed. New York: Harcourt, 2000.

Crick, Bernard. *Basic Forms of Government: A Sketch and a Model.* London: Macmillan, 1973.

Hague, Rod, and Martin Harrop. *Comparative Government and Politics: An Introduction.* 5th ed. London: Palgrave Macmillan, 2001.

Hauss, Charles, and Miriam Smith. *Comparative Politics: Domestic Responses to Global Challenges: A Canadian Perspective.* Toronto: Nelson, 2000.

Jackson, Robert J., and Doreen Jackson. *Comparative Government: An Introduction to Political Science.* 2nd ed. Scarborough, ON: Prentice Hall, 1997.

Kesselman, Mark, Joel Krieger, and William A. Joseph, eds. *Introduction to Comparative Politics: Political Challenges and Changing Agendas.* 3rd ed. New York: Houghton Mifflin, 2003.

Lane, Ruth. *The Art of Comparative Politics.* Boston: Allyn and Bacon, 1997.

McCormick, John. *Comparative Politics in Transition.* 3rd ed. New York: Harcourt College Publishers, 2001.

Moore, Barrington. *Social Origins of Dictatorship and Democracy: Lord and Peasant in the Making of the Modern World.* Boston: Beacon Press, 1966.

Roskin, Michael G. *Countries and Concepts: Politics, Geography, Culture.* 7th ed. Upper Saddle River, NJ: Prentice Hall, 2001.

Tsebelis, George. *Veto Players: How Political Institutions Work.* Princeton, NJ: Princeton University Press, 2002.

Wilson, Frank Lee. *Concepts and Issues in Comparative Politics: An Introduction to Comparative Analysis.* 2nd ed. Upper Saddle River, NJ: Prentice-Hall, 2001.

CHAPTER 17
Liberal Democracy

In today's world, virtually every government claims to be democratic; and when we criticize a government, it is often for not being democratic enough. But democracy was not always so popular. Its universal acceptance stems only from the years of World War I, which was fought, in the famous words of the American president Woodrow Wilson, "to make the world safe for democracy." Despite its popularity, democracy is often misunderstood and, in recent years, has suffered from what many now refer to as "democratic malaise."

Democracy in itself is a technique, a way of making certain decisions by privileging the will of the majority. Democracy is characterized as a system that involves those affected by the decisions in the process of making them. In our view, it becomes a legitimate form of government only when it is united with the traditional Western ideals of constitutionalism, rule of law, liberty under law, and the limited state. And, conversely, it is not the only legitimate form of government. Although only a relatively small number of people could vote, aristocratic rule was not always considered oppressive. Our current democratic government carries on British constitutionalism while bringing the common people into the political realm.

The most basic conceptual problem today is that the two dimensions of the "how" and the "who" of government have become blurred in the single term *democracy*. Its current usage suggests not only majority rule, but also a condition of freedom in which a limited state respects people's rights. Freedoms of speech, religion, and so on are commonly identified as democratic liberties, though they aren't necessarily found in a democracy. To cloud the issue even further, democracy outside the Western world often means government allegedly for the many, but conducted by a ruling elite, such as a vanguard party or a military *junta* (Spanish for a group of individuals forming a government, especially after a revolution), rather than the majority and that faces few constitutional limitations.

All of this raises so many problems that we will restrict ourselves for the moment to a discussion of Western democracy, which in itself is extremely complex. As one writer has stated:

> In the nineteenth century, democratic government was seen mainly in terms of equality of political and legal rights, of the right to vote, to express differing political opinions and to organize political opinion through political parties, of the right of elected

representatives to supervise or control the activities of the government of the day. Today, much more stress is laid upon the need for the State to guarantee to everybody certain economic and social rights, involving the elimination of educational and social inequalities.[1]

During the twentieth century, the concept of democracy expanded. As Giovanni Sartori has written:

> Up until the 1940s people knew what democracy was and either liked or rejected it; since then we all claim to like democracy but no longer know (understand, agree) what it is. We characteristically live, then, in an age of confused democracy. That "democracy" obtains several meanings is something we can live with. But if "democracy" can mean just anything, that is too much.[2]

Democracy has now come to imply freedom—encompassing political, economic, and social rights—as well as the rule of the many.

Brief reflection is enough to show that these two dimensions are quite different and that no inevitable connection exists between them. Freedom is made possible by the rule of law, which minimizes arbitrary coercion and maximizes universal submission to equal laws. Yet the rule of the many, as Aristotle saw, may or may not be lawful. Specifically, a majority might take away the property, language, or religious rights of a minority unless the majority itself is restrained by the constitution. Democracy requires freedom only in the limited and partial sense that a certain amount of political freedom is necessary if the people are to choose officials: they must have a chance to nominate candidates, discuss issues, cast ballots, and so on. But beyond this necessary minimum, democracy in other realms of life could be quite oppressive.

For example, in the southern United States white employers sometimes refused to hire blacks. And in Canada, employers have sometimes refused to hire Aboriginal people. Such job discrimination can limit freedom in that the denial of a job possibility may be the denial of an opportunity to improve one's lot in life. In most democracies today, the definition of democracy includes the assumption that all individuals have an equal legal right to be considered for employment.

From now on, we will use the term *constitutional* or *liberal democracy* to denote a system in which the majority chooses rulers, who must then govern within the rule of law. This is what Plato and Aristotle meant by polity. The term *liberal democracy* refers to liberalism in the broadest sense, without distinguishing between classical and reform liberalism. Whatever their disagreements about *laissez faire,* redistribution, and government intervention, classical and reform liberals are united in their support of constitutional procedures, the limited state, and a private sphere of personal freedom. Liberal democracy, based on this common ground, is broad enough to encompass different experiments in economic policy. The moderate form of socialism that we have called social democracy is also compatible with liberal democracy as a system of government. The limited amounts of nationalization, central planning, and egalitarianism advocated by social democrats are subordinated to majority rule and respect for constitutional procedure.

Communism, however, was never compatible with liberal democracy. In the people's democracies of Eastern Europe, the Leninist theory of democratic centralism, as converted into the operating philosophy of the communist state, did not allow for political freedom and the right of constitutional opposition. The uncontested elections that were the hallmark of communism in power were sharply different from the practice of liberal democracy. When democratization began in Eastern Europe in 1989, those countries repudiated communism and democratic centralism as quickly as they could. From the West they imported the entire apparatus of liberal democracy, including competitive elections, multiple political parties, an executive answerable to an elected legislature, and an independent judiciary. Based on the historical record thus far, we can say that liberal democracies are not easily transplanted, especially in countries with low economic development, or where ethnic and religious interests are strongly entrenched.

Liberal democracy can be briefly defined as a system of government in which the people rule themselves, either directly or indirectly (through chosen officials) but in either case subject to constitutional restraints on the power of the majority. This definition can be expanded through an examination of four operating principles of liberal democracy: equality of political rights, majority rule, political participation, and political freedom. Let us look at these one by one.

EQUALITY OF POLITICAL RIGHTS

Equality of political rights means that every individual has the same right to vote, run for office, serve on a jury, speak on public issues, and carry out other public functions. Obviously, political rights are a matter of degree, and it was only in the twentieth century, when women and ethnic minorities obtained these rights, that full equality was approached in most Western systems. There is no hard-and-fast rule for determining how much political equality is enough for democracy to exist; that being said, universal adult male suffrage was an important threshold because it broke through the barrier of socioeconomic class. Prior to its introduction, suffrage was limited to a small portion of the population, largely made up of affluent men. Another was the extension of the franchise to women, which doubled the electorate.

By these criteria, the United States was the first democracy of modern times. Equality of political rights, however, was not attained all at once because the constitution of 1787 let the individual states determine the franchise. In the first decades of the nineteenth century, the states one by one adopted universal male suffrage, except in the South, where slaves were excluded. The emancipated slaves were theoretically enfranchised after the Civil War, but most were prevented from voting by various tactics until the 1960s. Women received the right to vote in federal elections at a single stroke, through the Nineteenth Amendment (1920).

Figure 17.1 Number of Persons Having Right to Vote per 100 Adults, Britain, 1800–1928

Source: J. Harvey and L. Bather, *The British Constitution,* 2nd ed. (London: Macmillan, 1968), p. 51.

Great Britain was somewhat behind the United States in providing equality of political rights. At the beginning of the nineteenth century, there was still a restrictive franchise that allowed only about 200,000 male property owners to vote in elections for the House of Commons. The parliamentary Reform Acts of 1832, 1867, and 1884 gradually extended the franchise to include the middle class and the more prosperous elements of the working class. The remaining men, as well as women aged 30 and older, received the vote in 1918; women were granted suffrage on equal terms with men in 1928. The growth curve of the British electorate is illustrated in Figure 17.1.

The expansion of the franchise in Canada is more difficult to describe because it was intricately involved in federal–provincial relations. Before 1885, qualifications to vote in parliamentary elections had been determined by the provinces. In that year, Sir John A. Macdonald pushed a uniform Electoral Franchise Act through Parliament, in part because he did not like the tendency of provinces to abolish the property franchise.[3] The Act of 1885 established a moderate property qualification that remained until 1898, when the government of Sir Wilfrid Laurier returned the franchise to the domain of the provinces. Most property qualifications disappeared around that time.

From 1898 to 1917, the provinces controlled the federal franchise, but they could not disenfranchise particular groups of people: if people could vote in provincial elections, they could also vote in federal elections. In other words, provinces could not, through legislation, isolate certain groups demographically and deny them the right to vote in federal elections. In the Military Voters Act and the Wartime Elections Act (1917), the federal government was selective in extending and restricting the suffrage. Under the former, all men and women on active service were permitted to vote. Under the latter, conscientious objectors and those of enemy alien birth were denied the franchise, while wives, widows, and female relatives of men overseas were enfranchised.[4] In 1920, with the passage of the Dominion Elections Act, the federal government resumed control of qualifications for voting in federal elections, while qualifications for voting in provincial elections remained the responsibility of provincial governments. In 1918 women aged 21 and older gained the right to vote in federal elections. Provincially, women were first enfranchised in Manitoba, in 1916; not until 1940, however, were they allowed to vote in Quebec.[5] Registered Indians received the federal franchise in 1960, although they had been allowed to vote in some earlier provincial elections.

Although each country's history is unique, the general pattern in the Western world has been a step-by-step extension of the franchise, with universal adult male suffrage being reached at the end of the nineteenth or beginning of the twentieth century. In most countries, women were given the vote during or shortly after World War I. Switzerland was one exception; women received the right to vote in that country's federal elections only in 1971, and even later in some cantonal (provincial) elections. Indeed, the men of one laggard canton did not agree to grant the franchise to women until 1989.

Today, the franchise can hardly be extended further in most liberal–democratic countries except by giving it to non-citizens, children, prisoners, those with no fixed address, and the mentally disabled. The latter received the right to vote at the federal level in Canada beginning with the election of 1988. The right of prisoners to vote was re-affirmed in 2002 by the Supreme Court of Canada, when it held that the legislation depriving prisoners of the franchise unjustifiably conflicted with Section 3 of the Canadian Charter of Rights and Freedoms, which states that "every citizen has the right to vote in an election of members of the House of Commons or of a legislative assembly."[6] We have virtually reached the end of a process that has transformed the vote from a trust exercised by property owners or heads of families into a universal right of adult citizens.

MAJORITY RULE

Majority rule is the normal working principle of decision-making in democracies. It can be derived logically from the prior principle of political equality. If each vote is to be counted equally, the decision of the majority must be accepted because any other procedure would inevitably weigh some votes more heavily than others.

Yet in some circumstances democracies depart from majority rule. Election to public office in Canada, Britain, and the United States is normally by **plurality** rather than **majority.** In these systems, the winning candidate need only obtain more votes than any other candidate, even if the number fails to reach the "50 percent plus one" requirement for a majority. The plurality criterion is both simple and efficient. If candidates for office were always required to receive a majority, there would have to be an expensive series of runoffs to reduce the candidates to two; only then could it be guaranteed that a plurality would also be a majority of votes cast. In fact, some countries—France, for example—do employ runoff elections. The French president must receive an absolute majority of votes cast, which in practice means a two-stage election.

The majority requirement is also sometimes raised (for example, to three-fifths, or two-thirds, or three-fourths) in what is known as a **qualified majority.** This is done to protect the rights of minorities. Because a qualified majority is obviously harder to obtain than a simple majority, it becomes more difficult for larger groups to act against the rights of smaller ones.

The qualified majority, while a constraint upon democracy, is within the spirit of the rule of law. It is incorporated in most modern democracies as part of the process of constitutional amendment, on the assumption that the fundamental laws of the state are so important that they should not be easily altered by a simple majority. A constitutional amendment in the United States, after being passed by two-thirds of the Senate and House of Representatives, must be ratified by three-fourths of the states. In Canada, amending most parts of the Constitution requires ratification by the Senate, the House of Commons, and the legislative assemblies of "at least two-thirds of the provinces that have, in the aggregate, according to the latest general census, at least fifty per cent of the population of all the provinces." On certain matters of fundamental importance, such as recognition of the monarchy, the consent of all provinces is required.[7]

A variation of the qualified majority is the **concurrent majority,** which was sometimes used in the legislature of the old united province of Canada (1840–67). In that specific case, laws had to receive a majority of votes from representatives of both Canada East (Quebec) and Canada West (Ontario). This was supposed to prevent the two regions, one English and one French, from oppressing each other. A special form of the concurrent majority is **bicameralism,** the practice of dividing the legislature into two chambers. The requirement that a bill be passed in two different houses of the assembly is meant to be a safeguard against precipitous action. John A. Macdonald called the Canadian Senate "the sober second thought in legislation." He also supported the requirement, entrenched in Section 23(4) of the Constitution Act, 1867, that a senator's "Real and Personal Property shall be together worth Four thousand Dollars over and above his Debts and Liabilities," a substantial amount at that time. According to Macdonald, "a large property qualification should be necessary for membership in the Upper House, in order to represent the principle of property. The rights of the minority must be protected, and the rich are always fewer in number than the poor."[8]

While the Senate no longer plays the role Macdonald envisioned for it, its continued existence illustrates the principle that liberal democracy sometimes accepts restraints on the will of popular majorities in order to protect the legal rights of minorities. A requirement for **unanimity** would be the ultimate in protection for minorities, because then no one could be required to do anything against their will. But the practical task of getting unanimous agreement is so formidable that political systems have had to settle for a qualified or concurrent majority as a restraint on popular powers. Balancing majority and minority rights remains one of the major challenges in a democratic system of government.

POLITICAL PARTICIPATION

Democratic institutions are founded on mass participation. The two great varieties of democracy, which differ in the nature of this participation, are **direct democracy,** the only kind known to the ancient world, and **representative democracy** (or *indirect democracy,* as it is sometimes called), the predominant form in modern times.

The city-states of Greece practised direct democracy. The highest authority was the assembly of all male citizens (slaves were not citizens and could not vote). Executive officers were either elected by this body or chosen by lot—a random procedure that was considered superbly democratic because it gave everyone an equal chance of being selected to serve. In either case, terms of office were very short—usually a year or less. Citizens were paid to hold office and even to attend assembly meetings, so that poverty would not prevent participation.

Assembly-style direct democracy faces two obvious problems. One involves the practical difficulty of assembling more than a few thousand individuals to discuss public issues. If direct democracy was just barely possible in the Greek city-state, how could it exist in the modern nation-state, which is so much larger? The other problem concerns the quality of decisions made at large meetings, where emotional rhetoric and appeals to prejudices, emotions, and fears can easily sway votes. The democracy of Athens destroyed itself by enthusiastically voting for a disastrous military campaign against Syracuse. The best minds of antiquity, including Plato and Aristotle, were so unimpressed with direct democracy in action that they turned decisively against it.[9]

Representative democracy tries to address both problems. It overcomes the obstacles of population and distance while providing the means for choosing rulers whose talents are presumably superior to those of the people at large. These rulers are kept in check, and directed by the majority, through the machinery of elections. A ruler elected for life would be effectively insulated from the popular will. This is why democracy requires regular elections that those in power cannot indefinitely postpone: to ensure the accountability of government to its citizens.

The rationale behind representative government was clearly stated in 1825 by James Mill, the first important political philosopher to argue in favour of what we would today call democracy. "The people as a body," he wrote, "cannot perform the business of government for themselves."[10] What was required, he continued, was the creation of a system of "checks" that would induce rulers to act for the general benefit. These checks would be provided by representatives elected by the community for a limited period of time. Limiting the duration of rule was, according to Mill, "an old and approved method of identifying as nearly as possible the interests of those who rule with the interests of those who are ruled."[11]

It cannot be emphasized too strongly that democratic elections do not and cannot decide questions of policy. Citizens vote for representatives but do not make policy decisions; elected representatives make those decisions for the society. Citizens probably agree with some opinions of their favourite candidates and disagree with others.

Also, neither voters nor candidates can be sure of what the future will bring. Politicians are notorious for breaking campaign promises not because they are especially dishonest, but because things may look different a year or two after the election, particularly when seen from the perspective of public responsibility. Elections are much more a judgment on recent policies than a decision about the future. If voters are dissatisfied with the past record of the incumbent government, elections provide an opportunity for installing another party into power.

Many contemporary critics of representative democracy focus on the idea that elected officials have their own political agendas and disregard the wishes of the public. Such critics advocate a move toward some form of direct democracy, or at least more public involvement in the policy-making process. One way to do this would be to institutionalize direct-democratic practices such as the referendum, the initiative, and the recall.

In a **referendum,** electors are asked to vote directly on a constitutional amendment, piece of legislation, or other policy proposal. Some authors use the term **plebiscite** for a nonbinding, advisory referendum,[12] but we will not follow this usage because it is not universal. Both binding and nonbinding referendums are common around the world.

Referendums are used frequently in Switzerland at all levels of government, and in the United States at the state and local levels. They are required in Australia for the approval of all constitutional amendments. All Canadian provinces provide for advisory referendums in some circumstances at the local and provincial level, and there have been three federal referendums: one in 1898 on the prohibition of alcohol, one in 1942 to release Prime Minister William Lyon Mackenzie King from his promise not to send conscripted soldiers overseas, and one in 1992 on the Charlottetown Accord. More recently, three provinces (B.C., Ontario, and PEI) have held referendums on electoral reform; all were defeated (see Chapter 24). Because legislation in Canada is technically made by the Crown with the advice of Parliament or of a provincial legislature, Canadian referendums can be only advisory in a legal sense unless the Constitution is amended; under present conditions, a legally binding referendum would be an unconstitutional restriction on the authority of the Crown.

In Switzerland, however, the vote in a referendum legally determines the legislative outcome of an issue. In France, the president can call a binding national referendum. President Charles de Gaulle (in office 1959–69) used this power on six occasions as a way of circumventing a legislature that would not cooperate on his policy proposals. Not all French presidents have been successful in their use of the referendum. Jacques Chirac called a referendum in 2005 on the proposed Constitution of the European Union expecting victory; instead, the proposal was defeated, which was seen as a devastating blow to his presidency.

The British government has used consultative referendums to clear the air on divisive issues. In 1975 the government called a national referendum on membership in the European Economic Community. It was the first ever held in Britain.

The Conservatives had decided on membership three years earlier, but many Labour Party members remained opposed to the decision. So the newly elected Labour government of Prime Minister Harold Wilson called a referendum in hopes of laying the matter to rest. British voters endorsed membership by slightly more than a two-thirds majority. In 1979, referendums were held in Scotland and Wales as a way of deciding the issue of devolution. Voters in Wales rejected the proposal for a regional parliament. The proposition also failed in Scotland, even though it received the support of 52 percent of voters, because turnout (33 percent) failed to meet the minimum required (40 percent). In 1997, however, voters in both Scotland and Wales accepted regional parliaments in referendums held after Tony Blair's Labour Party came to power.

A second form of direct democracy is the **initiative.** The mechanism is a simple one: if a minimum number of voters sign a petition dealing with a particular issue (the number would be spelled out in legislation), then the government is required to act on it. The required action may be either that the legislative body enact the proposal outlined in the petition or that it submit the proposal to voters in a referendum. A referendum originates in the legislative body and is "referred" to the electorate; in contrast, an initiative moves from the people to the legislature.

In Switzerland, 50,000 voters are enough to force the government to hold a referendum. Initiatives are also popular in California. The famous Proposition 13 was committed to a state-wide referendum in 1978 as a result of an initiative signed by 1.5 million voters. The voters of California proceeded to endorse a forced limit on local property taxes—a move that naturally was unpopular with politicians but very popular with the electorate.[13]

Several standard arguments are made against referendums and initiatives—that legislation is too complex, that voters become fatigued when asked to decide too many issues, and that these instruments can be used to restrict the rights of minorities. There is undoubtedly some truth in these contentions, and, therefore, important reasons for limiting the use of the referendum and initiative. However, voters do not seem to rule out direct democracy as an occasional supplement to representative democracy. Of the arguments in favour of direct democracy, the most interesting comes from former Progressive Conservative MP Patrick Boyer, Canada's leading authority on and advocate for referendums. Boyer argues that referendums are particularly useful in a parliamentary system of disciplined parties where the legislative agenda is controlled by politicians who believe that electoral victory has given them a mandate to legislate as they please.[14] Mechanisms of direct democracy provide a means for testing policy options against the judgment of the public. To date, referendums and initiatives have been used sparingly in Western democracies, but the development of electronic communications may soon make these consultative processes more cost-effective and lead to their increased use.

A third and less common element of direct democracy is the **recall,** which enables voters to remove an elected representative from office.[15] This practice was introduced in the United States at the turn of the century. Its purpose was to rid constituencies of representatives controlled by "political machines" (i.e., party organizations dominated by a few backroom leaders). Provisions for recall usually require a petition signed by a substantial number of voters, and a successful recall vote requires at least a simple majority of those voting. These provisions are designed to protect representatives from a minority of voters who may not like a particular stand. Recall is used in some cities and states in the United States, though less frequently today than in the 1920s. In 2003 California voters recalled Governor Gray Davis and replaced him with Arnold Schwarzenegger; Davis was only the second governor ever to be successfully recalled in the United States.

Venezuela is the only country where the head of the national government is subject to recall. The procedure was tested in 2004 with a recall campaign against President Hugo Chavez, who is considered by his opponents to be too left-wing and too close to Cuban leader Fidel Castro. Forty-two percent voted to recall President Chavez but 58 percent voted to affirm him in office, so he remained president.

In Canada, there is less support for a recall mechanism than for other forms of direct democracy. At the present time only the province of British Columbia has recall legislation, which came into effect in 1995. Since then, 20 recall petitions have been issued but none have been successful. This is due partly to the high bar set for success: the applicant has 60 days to obtain the signatures of 40 percent of registered voters in the previous election in the member's electoral district. The recall may be a fine idea in the United States, where elected officials serve fixed terms and are judged as individuals because party discipline is weak or nonexistent. But in a parliamentary system such as Canada's, elected officials are members of a team that functions collectively—the Cabinet and caucus in the case of the government, the caucus in the case of the opposition. In 1992, Joe Clark spent all his time as a cabinet minister on the constitutional negotiations that led to the Charlottetown Accord, and then on trying to get the Accord passed in the referendum. Now it is clear that the voters in his Alberta riding (Yellowhead) did not like the Accord: almost 70 percent voted no when the referendum was held. But should they have had the right to recall their hardworking MP because he was working on a project whose outcome they eventually disapproved? The answer may be yes if we think of MPs primarily as representatives of their constituencies, but it is probably no if we think of them as members of a team pursuing national policies.

Today, public-opinion polls also play an important advisory role in all democratic countries. An enthusiast for direct democracy will periodically remind us that it is now technically possible to wire all citizens into one computer system and let them decide questions of public policy. But even if such a nonstop referendum were possible, it is doubtful that it would be a good idea. Complex questions of public policy need the attention and deliberation of informed minds, and both legislators and the public need time to digest various views. Representative democracy is not just a second-best substitute for direct democracy, made necessary by the size of modern states; rather, it is a mechanism for seeking the consensus that is essential to good government. However, direct-democratic devices could be a useful supplement when such wisdom does not emerge from representative institutions.

Democratic participation involves far more than the election of representatives. It also involves influencing government policy either through public debate or by making submissions to elected representatives. Governments today often consult extensively with the public before passing major legislation. A general policy statement may be published, followed by a draft of the statute. Often there are public hearings at which interested parties express their views. In fact, participation has expanded so much in recent years, particularly at the level of local government, that it is sometimes seen as unduly slowing decision making and offering too much influence to vocal and well-organized minorities.

Even when they possess a strong parliamentary majority, governments will occasionally withdraw or modify policy proposals in the face of public criticism. Public participation and consultation is now an ongoing process in democratic government. Elections punctuate the process; when governments are not responsive, voters change the participants.

Access to the decision makers is a major problem in contemporary democracies; this issue will be discussed in more detail in Part Four. Critics of democracy say that powerful interests dominate the political process and that groups more marginal to the system have difficulty in influencing decisions. For example, women's and environmental groups claim they have been shut out of the process in the past. However, the existence of elections as open contests at least offers a possibility, if not the certainty, that marginalized groups will be able to exert more influence on decision makers.

POLITICAL FREEDOM

Meaningful participation is possible only if political freedom prevails. Limited participation or directed mobilization of the masses is characteristic not of genuine democracy but of totalitarian pseudo-democracy. An infallible test for political freedom is the legitimacy of opposition: freedom is meaningful only if it extends to those whose opinions differ from the opinions of those in authority. Freedom only to agree is no freedom at all. If freedom does not exist, public support or opposition can only be speculative, and this uncertainty can be very convenient for manipulative rulers. At the same time, the opposition in a liberal democracy must operate within the rule of law. When it resorts to unlawful means—for example, terrorist acts or plotting an insurrection—its actions are not compatible with political freedom in a liberal democracy.

Political freedom has numerous aspects: the right to speak freely, even to criticize the government; the right to form associations, including political parties that may oppose the government; the right to run for office; and the right to vote without intimidation and to choose from a slate of at least two candidates. Without these rights, democracy might be "for the people," but it is certainly not "by the people."

Extensive and important as it is, political freedom is only a part of the whole range of personal freedoms. For instance, it does not include the right to own property or to use one's chosen language. It is quite possible for very wide political freedom to coexist with, and even be the cause of, reduced freedom in other areas. An example can be taken from Quebec: all citizens have full political freedom in that province, but businesses have been restricted by legislation from posting signs in languages other than French. In 1989 the provincial government used its override power, as provided by Section 33 of the Canadian Charter of Rights and Freedoms, to reinstate its language legislation after the Supreme Court of Canada had ruled that the law violated the freedom of expression guaranteed by the Charter.[16] Both the legislation and the use of the notwithstanding clause (as Section 33 is often called) were and remain popular with the francophone majority in Quebec. In this instance, a majority used its political freedom to reduce the linguistic freedom of minorities.

This example highlights what is sometimes seen as a general problem of liberal democracy. Can law restrain the power of the majority so that it does not use its political freedom to take away other freedoms from minorities? The tension between democracy and the rule of law is illustrated in this passage from Xenophon, a pupil of Socrates. It had just been proposed to the Athenian Assembly—the democratic gathering of all male citizens—that certain alleged enemies of the regime be arrested:

> Great numbers cried out that it was monstrous if the people were to be prevented from doing whatever they wished . . . Then the Prytanes [the executive committee of the Assembly], stricken with fear, agreed to put the question [to a vote]—all of them except Socrates . . . he said that in no case would he act except in accordance with the law.[17]

Socrates was ultimately put to death by a democracy that ignored the rule of law and heeded only its own will.

A fear first voiced by Aristotle, and echoed since by countless other writers, is that in a democracy, the many would use their political power to expropriate and distribute the wealth of the few. In the words of John Adams, the second American president, "Debts would be abolished first; taxes laid heavy on the rich, and not at all on the others; and at last a downright equal division of everything be demanded and voted."[18] In fact, the record of liberal democracy does not bear out this gloomy prediction of a dramatic clash of rich and poor. In those countries where liberal democracy has been successful, society has not been polarized into extremes of wealth and poverty.

Political freedom helps to ensure that the interests of citizens are voiced, an important step providing governments with an ability to remain accountable to them. But political freedom, and more specifically the political participation that it encourages, can be argued to be valuable in and of itself. As one political scientist has argued, "good citizens are made, not born."[19] One of the values of democracy is that it encourages citizens to participate in the political process and, in so doing, encourages them to develop the skills, knowledge, and tolerance that can enhance their participation and the quality of collective decision making.

PROBLEMS OF LIBERAL DEMOCRACY

To paraphrase Winston Churchill, liberal democracy is not the perfect form of government, it is only the least worst. For discussion purposes, we will consider three basic problems that have been present since the creation of liberal democracies: elite rule, majority versus minority rights, and public versus private interests.

Elite Rule

One common, and serious, criticism of liberal democracy is that it is elitist—that democracies are, in effect, ruled by elites and therefore undemocratic. It is true that representative democracy is a form of elite rule, if by an **elite** we mean "a minority of the population which takes the major decisions in the society."[20] But to see the place of political elites in modern politics, one must compare them with the elites that were found in traditional societies of earlier centuries. In the latter, a tiny and interlocking group of families dominated the social, economic, and political life of society. In most instances, these families owned large estates, which their children inherited along with all the wealth and responsibilities that went with their status. Traditional societies were highly stratified; that is, there was a large gap between the elite and the masses. This simple, dichotomized society was perpetuated as the children of the elite inherited their positions, while opportunities for the masses were restricted. There was little if any social mobility between the elite and the masses.

In most Western countries this situation has gradually been transformed. The Industrial Revolution broke the hold of the landed aristocracy and created new sources of wealth and employment; mass education created opportunities for many in the lower classes; guilds and unions helped artisans and workers to get better working conditions and wages; urban centres served as the base for dynamic marketing systems; and new attitudes about equality and freedom led to more participatory politics. Modern society is characterized by a large middle class, not by polarization between wealth and poverty. Opportunities for education and jobs are extensive, and this promotes social mobility between classes. Politics is charged with new sources of authority and legitimacy. In short, the old dualism of the traditional society has given way to a complex and dynamic modern social order.

Correspondingly, the old idea of a traditional elite was replaced by the concept of pluralism. New elites began to spring up and challenge the agrarian aristocracy. An industrial elite, a commercial elite, a financial elite, a military elite, and even a political elite emerged; and each had a degree of wealth and power that posed a threat to the old guard with its roots in the land. In modern societies, elites have not disappeared; rather, they have become more numerous and more diverse. Many Marxists tend to deny that this change has really affected societies much. They still see a simple dichotomy—the rulers and the ruled. The two-class situation dominates their frame of reference; except in socialist societies, rulers are thought to exploit the masses. But other observers recognize that modern societies have become pluralistic, and that so have their politics. As the French author Raymond Aron wrote:

> Democratic societies, which I would rather call pluralistic societies, are full of the noise of public strife between the owners of the means of production, trade union leaders and politicians. As all are entitled to form associations, professional and political organizations abound, each one defending its members' interests with passionate ardour. Government becomes a business of compromises.[21]

In democracies, those who aspire to rule must build a power base. They must first of all be chosen by the electorate; then, if they are to remain in office, their policies must be responsive to the needs of some coalition of groups. Contemporary theorists of democracy emphasize the competition of diverse elites. They suggest that the representative system is an instrument for ensuring that no single elite can attain power unless it reflects the desires of some fraction of the ordinary people. While it is true powerful groups may monopolize contemporary politics, if elections are working as they were intended there should be no contradiction between liberal democracy and elite rule.

Majority versus Minority Rights

Liberal democracies operate on the majoritarian principle. Political party nominations, elections to office, and legislative decisions are decided on the basis of a majoritarian vote. But how do minorities fare under majoritarian government? Is it true, as the proponents of liberal democracy claim, that minority rights can be reconciled with majority rule? For example, in a multicultural society, when one or two ethnic groups (or nationalities) occupy a dominant position, can it be guaranteed that the rights of minority cultures will be protected? Can the rights of Native peoples in Canada be protected when they make up less than 4 percent of the total population? How can the rights of cultural minorities such as the Chinese or West Indians, or the political rights of gays and lesbians, be guaranteed when the vast majority of Canadians are European, English- or French-speaking, and heterosexual?

One argument is that all majority and minority rights are protected on the floor of the House of Commons and the Senate. This argument revolves around the assumption that most elected representatives want to be re-elected and so must appeal to a broad coalition of groups in their constituencies. They try not to alienate any voters—and certainly as few as possible, if they have to legislate in a way that will alienate any. But the fact remains that winning coalitions need not be, and probably will not be, all-inclusive. Some minorities, particularly small ones, are likely to be left out, which opens up the possibility that an elected assembly could become a "tyranny of the majority" that consistently votes to override minority rights.

A second way of protecting minority rights is through a constitution and the judicial process. Since the passage of the Canadian Charter of Rights and Freedoms in 1982, individual rights for all Canadians have been spelled out in the Constitution. If the rights of a minority may have been violated by a legislative assembly, representatives of that minority are entitled to challenge the constitutionality of the legislation in the courts. If members of a legislative assembly choose to ignore the rights of a certain segment of society, the citizens affected have recourse through the courts. While there is no guarantee that court rulings will satisfy either the majority or the minority, the judicial system is another possible venue for reconciling majority rule with minority rights.

Public versus Private Interests

Another difficult problem to resolve in liberal democracies relates to the conflict between public and private interests. Ideally, the public interest involves the well-being of all individuals or all groups in society. It is difficult, however, to find an interest that is equally shared by everyone. In practice, therefore, the term *public interest* refers to interests that are relatively broadly shared, such as national defence, enforcement of the law, protection of life and property, stable prices, low taxation, public education, accessible health care, and a social safety net. *Private interests* include the interests of specific groups such as business people, unionized workers, farmers, and students and professors. Most such groups attempt to achieve certain ends through the political process. They may seek concessions of some kind from governments, and these concessions may or may not be in the public interest. For example, postsecondary students may want to have free college or university tuition. Most colleges and universities are public institutions in Canada, so taxes would have to be increased accordingly. Since college and university graduates usually get better-paying jobs than non-graduates, it seems reasonable that these students should pay at least some tuition. However, society (public interest) benefits from the presence of educated young people (private interest), so it pays most of the costs of higher education.

Few conflicts between public and private interest are as easy to reconcile. Often such conflicts centre on definitions of the public interest and the presence or absence of a level playing field. Disputes between developers and environmentalists are notoriously difficult to resolve. Private interests will push for what they see as a healthy economic-development project. It might be a water-storage project for irrigation, or a timber-cutting licence for a pulp mill. In either case, it will be argued that private industrial activity will, through capital investment and job creation, also serve the broader public interest by enhancing the local or regional economy. Developers often make the case, particularly in times of recession, that a softening of environmental regulations would reduce the cost of the project. The argument is usually that increased costs will make the project uncompetitive and that investment and jobs will for that reason be lost.

At the same time, governments are also pressured by those who want to preserve the quality of the air and water in the region. These people argue that poor air and water quality affects the health not only of local residents but also of the environment itself. They argue, as well, that a healthy environment will attract environmentally "clean" industries. In effect, there is a political clash not only between private interests but also between differing conceptions of the public interest. Whichever side the government comes down on, it will claim that its decision is in the public interest.

When legislators write lax environmental regulations, or loosen existing regulations to lure industry, environmentalists claim that private interests have prevailed at the expense of the public interest—that the playing field has been tipped to favour developers. When legislators support strict environmental regulations, industrialists claim that narrow but powerful environmental interests have thwarted the public interest, which is for more jobs and increased investment—that the field was tipped to favour environmentalists. Here again, the challenge facing public decision makers is to balance the demands of conflicting private interests with their different conceptions of the public interest.

These classic problems are not the only ones facing liberal democracies today. Powerful interests, political party responsiveness, influence of the media, voter apathy, representation of the electorate, and the role of the courts are challenges in most current liberal democracies. There is insufficient room in this chapter to discuss these problems individually, so each of these issues will be addressed in chapters on the political process in Part Four.

DIFFERENT PATTERNS OF POLITICS IN LIBERAL DEMOCRACIES

Liberal democracies operate in different ways. For example, within one liberal–democratic system, interest groups such as business organizations, labour unions, or farmers' associations may have a great deal of political **autonomy**—that is, they have a great deal of freedom to pursue political objectives with little interference from the state. In other liberal–democratic systems, political organizations may be highly restricted in their political activity by a powerful regulatory state. Mexico, prior to political reforms instituted after 1994, is a case in point. These different patterns of politics in liberal democracies can be classified as pluralist, corporatist, or consociational (see Concept Box 17.1).

Concept Box 17.1

Liberal Democracies

Pluralist

Liberal democracies in which highly autonomous groups compete freely and openly in the political process are labelled **pluralist.** Robert Dahl's term for this pluralist form of liberal democracy is **polyarchy,** which means many different sources of power. For Dahl, "the characteristics of polyarchy greatly extend the number, size, and diversity of the minorities whose preferences will influence the outcome of governmental decision."[22] In a polyarchy, control of the governmental process may change hands frequently as different groups compete for political power.

Features of pluralist liberal democracies include:

a. a high degree of autonomy for political interests in society to pursue their political ends;

b. equality of all groups in the political process—ideally, there is a level playing field on which political interests compete; and

c. an absence of monopoly control of government or state power by any one group. The power of groups ebbs and flows with societal conditions, as coalitions are accepted or rejected by the voters.

Corporatist

Liberal democracies in which there is a significant lack of autonomy for groups are labelled *corporatist.* In the corporatist pattern, the state is the dominant force in society and the activities of all interests in society are subordinate to that force. One of the principal writers on **corporatism,** Philippe C. Schmitter, has defined corporatism as follows:

> Corporatism can be defined as a system of interests representation in which the constituent units are organized into a limited number of singular, compulsory, non-competitive, hierarchically ordered and functionally differentiated categories, recognized or licensed (if not created) by the state and granted a deliberate representational monopoly within their respective categories in exchange for observing certain controls on their selection of leaders and articulation of demands and supports.[23]

Features of corporatist liberal democracies include:

a. the components of the political process are arranged in a hierarchy and are not equal;

b. the components have limited autonomy, with the state restricting their actions;

c. competition is limited, in the sense that the various components are not free to compete with each other for political ends;

d. the components in the process are dependent on the state; and

(*continued*)

Concept Box 17.1 *(continued)*

e. the relative power of different components may vary, depending on their relationship to the state.

Consociational

Liberal democracies in which elites and organized interests play a special and distinctive role are labelled *consociational*. This form is found in several countries, including the Netherlands, Switzerland, and (to a lesser degree) Canada. Arend Lijphart suggests that the basis for **consociationalism** is a society so sharply divided along linguistic, ethnic, or religious lines that the segments have their own social institutions and live largely apart from one another.[24] The Netherlands is a classic case: although everyone speaks Dutch, the society is divided into Roman Catholic, neo-Calvinist, liberal, and socialist "spiritual families," each of which has its own schools and universities; newspapers and radio and television programs; and labour unions and recreational associations. Switzerland is similarly divided, by language as well as by religion and ideology.

Features of consociational liberal democracies include:

a. each social segment has a high degree of autonomy over its internal affairs, particularly language, culture, religion, and education;

b. a rule of proportionality is followed in allocating government jobs, expenditures, and benefits among the segments;

c. all important segments have the power to veto major changes affecting their vital interests; and

d. government is carried on through a "grand coalition" of political representatives of all the main segments.

Different patterns of politics seem to follow particular cultural attributes of societies. For example, politics in the United States, a country with a strong liberal, anti-state tradition, comes close to the pluralist process that Robert Dahl described as polyarchy. In Canada and Great Britain, where elites have played a greater role in the political process, one finds traces of corporatist and consociational thinking and institutions.[25] And, until the late 1990s, in countries such as Mexico and Brazil the corporatist tradition was very strong—to the point that one can rightly ask how democratic these political systems were. The lines of demarcation between political systems can be just as porous as those between political ideologies.

CONTEMPORARY CRITICISMS OF DEMOCRACY

Up to this point, our discussion of liberal democracy has been mainly theoretical, with a review of some of the traditional problems encountered in this particular form of government. However, we should not give the impression that all is well with liberal democracies. Any perceptive person today knows that nothing could be further from the truth. In most Western democracies, criticisms abound. And most of those criticisms are justified. People feel that political leaders are unresponsive, that they have their own agendas. There is a common perception that the relationship among the cabinet, high administrative officials, and powerful lobbyists is too cozy, that governments are ignoring the demands and expectations of large segments of the population. As a result, there is a great deal of cynicism about modern politics: people feel manipulated by the media and politicians, and powerless in a decision-making process in which, theoretically, citizen participation is valued. Never have people had so many opportunities to participate in politics; yet, paradoxically, never have more people been so critical of the political process. Importantly, there is widespread and overwhelming support around the world for the idea of democracy as a system of governance; there is less, however, for its practice.[26]

The polls verify this sense of disillusionment. In the spring of 1966, in the midst of the Vietnam War and race riots, a survey revealed that 66 percent of Americans disagreed with the statement "the people running the country don't really care what happens to you." When the same question was asked in December of 1997, during a time of relative peace and economic prosperity, 57 percent of the American public *agreed* with it.[27] This trend extends beyond the United States: only one in five British citizens is likely to trust politicians to tell the truth.[28] The public in many Western democracies has simply lost faith in the system and in politicians. We can identify at least three major reasons why: the overall performance of the system, the workings of cabinet government, and the changing nature of society itself.

With respect to the first issue, for the past 50 years Canadian governments have followed a highly interventionist course under the assumption that the state can guide the economy; solve social problems such as unemployment, poverty, and prejudice; care for the aged and infirm; and inspire loyalty to and support for the nation-state. A vast amount of legislation has been passed in those 50 years relating to unemployment insurance, welfare payments, old-age pensions, health care, family allowances, civil rights, and government assistance to businesses. Multiculturalism has been strengthened. Even our flag and our anthem date from this time. In effect, the state has been intervening to regulate society and to provide services to create a more just society. Throughout, most people have supported these actions, in part because most have benefited from them in one way or another.

These programs have been both extensive and expensive. Between the 1960s and the 1990s, government was a growth industry. Budgets and bureaucracies grew, but because public-sector expansion was undertaken at a time when the economy was also expanding rapidly, governments could, and did, increase taxes to pay for the increased services and regulations. Canadians were earning enough discretionary income that most middle-income citizens could pay more taxes and still maintain their standard of living. As government expenditures rose, revenues could be increased to sustain the policies and programs. When the economy faltered, however, and revenues levelled off, governments began to borrow in order to maintain their services and programs, under the assumption that the economy would soon return to a growth cycle, at which time taxes could again be increased. The result was high and rising levels of public debt. The Canadian federal budget now includes an item of $33 billion for debt-service charges, amounting to 15 percent of all tax revenues collected. Although the situation is gradually improving, the necessity to pay so much in interest on past loans still squeezes expenditures on social programs.

The heavy burden of taxation, coupled with the debt legacy that the present generation is leaving for the future, led to an outcry against politicians and their recent performance. Citizens now expect better fiscal management.

Since about 1993 most Canadian jurisdictions responded to this concern and, until the economic problems in 2008–09, were operating with balanced budgets (see Figure 17.2).

Interestingly, at the beginning of the twenty-first century, the debate has shifted from deficits and debt to a growing concern about governments adequately supporting programs such as education and especially health care. Again, this debate also is influenced by ideology. There are those who feel that these vital programs are being underfunded, and at a time when we can ill afford a second-class health and educational system. At the same time, there are those who feel that the state should not try to support all costs involved in education and health care, and that some of this

Figure 17.2 Federal and Provincial–Territorial Budgetary Balances (Public Accounts Basis)

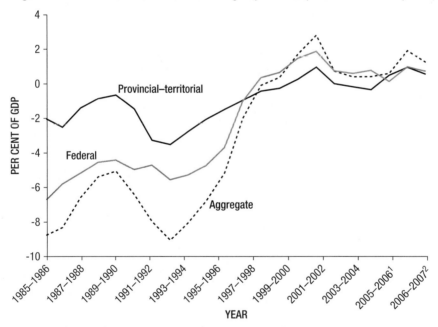

[1]For this and subsequent charts, figures for the combined provincial-territorial sector and the aggregate surplus for 2005–06 are estimates.

[2]Projection.

Source: Department of Finance, Canada "Budget Plan 2007," Chart A1.1, p. 300. http://www.budget.gc.ca/2007/pdf/bkfbsfe.pdf. Reproduced with the permission of the Minister of Public Works and Government Services Canada, 2008.

responsibility should be privatized. This is a contentious debate, and no doubt its outcome has relevance for the question raised by Aristotle about polarization of society along the lines of rich and poor. It will be interesting to see whether resolution of this issue will restore some of the citizens' confidence in government.

A second reason why citizens are criticizing the democratic process relates to the parliamentary process, with its cabinet government and disciplined political parties. This system developed in the nineteenth century, before universal suffrage was introduced and social relationships were democratized. Cabinet ministers still cling to this elitist system; they claim it cannot work without party discipline because changes in government could lead to political instability. Their argument is that a strong executive is vital to the parliamentary system. But this executive-dominated process has now given rise to a populist reaction, as illustrated in the widespread opposition to the Meech Lake and Charlottetown Accords. That opposition did not focus entirely on proposed changes to the Constitution; much of it stemmed from the fact that citizens felt the country's first ministers were imposing these changes on the people. Thus, with the heavy hand of the executive strengthened by political-party discipline, many people question whether their representatives can truly represent them. (More on this in Chapters 23 and 27.)

A third cause of widespread criticism of the present democratic process has to do with changes that have occurred in Canadian society. Many writers and analysts today are talking about a "new politics." What they mean by the phrase is that beliefs and values have changed considerably over the past half century. Among younger generations, there is much less deference toward all social authorities, and especially toward politicians. Many citizens are highly educated; have had a great deal of business, professional, and political experience; and are quite willing to challenge any direction public leaders are embarking on. A symptom of this change is decreased trust in politicians; another is dropping voter turnout levels. Many now view voting as a less than effective use of their time; instead, they prefer to involve themselves in interest groups or community efforts tackling problems and issues directly.

While citizen engagement ought to be applauded, if it comes at the expense of electoral participation then democracy suffers since one of its operating principles is political participation. Democratic legitimacy and the articulation of interests require an informed and engaged voting population.

Can changes be made to restore Canadians' faith in the democratic process? In general, there are two alternatives in this age-old debate: find "better" people to rule, or change the system itself. We believe that systemic change is the better solution to the problem of good government.

As mentioned earlier, mechanisms like referendums and initiatives would involve the public more directly in decision making. While these mechanisms are not without their problems, they do provide a means by which the public, if mobilized, can initiate action. In that sense, they may provide a safety valve when governments become paralyzed and are unable to respond.

Another approach might be to develop more opportunities for the public to influence policymaking earlier in the process and more directly. As mentioned earlier, governments often follow elaborate consultative procedures when formulating policies on particular issues. Cabinets consult with major interests; there are royal commissions; and parliamentary committees sometimes have elaborate cross-country hearings. But these devices, valuable and necessary as they may be, do not appear to be enough. Politicians are now experimenting with new forms of consultation, such as electronic forums, citizen juries, and deliberative dialogues. Such mechanisms require a great deal of time on the part of political leaders, but the dividends in terms of rapport with the people may be great. And given the cynical view people now have about the process, such mechanisms may help to break down the feeling many Canadians have that elected officials are sheltered, unresponsive, and unavailable to the public they are supposed to serve. In short, the public seems to want a more open political process; a process operating from the bottom up rather than the top down. (More on this in Chapter 26.)

Globalization and the reaction to it call into question the actions of the state and protest groups in liberal democracies. Supporters of the idea of globalization argue that free trade among nations will stimulate economic growth, especially in non-industrialized nations. They suggest it is the best way to redistribute wealth. Opponents of globalization in most established democracies argue that it does move manufacturing to non-industrialized nations, but essentially it is a way for multinational corporations to exploit cheap labour in the non-industrialized world, and to be able to do it with few restrictions on working conditions, minimum wages, and environmental protection.

Activities surrounding the concept of globalization have become an issue in a number of Western liberal democracies. Critics of the concept accuse political leaders of negotiating, behind closed doors, world trade deals with multinational corporations. They claim they must protest in the streets in order to open the issue for public debate. Political leaders and supporters of globalization claim discussions of trade arrangements are in a preliminary stage and there will be open debate before agreements are made. Meetings between political and economic leaders and international trade organizations in Seattle; Prague; Davos, Switzerland; Washington, D.C.; and Quebec City did turn violent, with clashes between police and protesters. Thus, the issue of globalization not only raises questions about the idea itself, but also about the conduct of the state and protesters in liberal democracies.

Using the 2001 Quebec City Summit of the Americas trade meetings as an example, note that the Canadian and Quebec governments prepared for the event by constructing a three-metre-high fence around the perimeter of the meeting area to separate protesters and those attending the meetings. The authorities mobilized hundreds of police, claiming the protesters included agitators who intended to provoke violence. Protesters were met with rubber bullets and tear gas.

Whatever one's opinions on globalization, responses by both sides on the issue raise questions of behaviour in liberal democracies. Crises are not new. In the early twentieth century, there were conflicts over legalizing labour unions and over extending the right to vote. As such, one wonders whether they are an inevitable part of life in a free society; if so, liberal democracies ought to do a better job of managing internal conflict. For more on the role of the state in society, see World View 17.1.

World View 17.1

The Third Way

In all democratic systems of government, the role of the state in society is an issue. Whether the state should play a greater or lesser role is at the core of ideological debates. Those on the left of the political spectrum advocate a more interventionist state; those on the right advocate reducing state involvement in society. Anthony Giddens adds to the conceptualization of this debate in *The Third Way:*

> The neoliberals want to shrink the state; the social democrats, historically, have been keen to expand it. The third way argues that what is necessary is to reconstruct it—to go beyond those on the right who say government is the enemy; and those on the left who say government is the answer. (Giddens, 1998, p. 70)

The idea of a "third way" gained credence in academic and political circles with the Clinton administration in the United States (1992 and 1996) and the election of the Labour government of Tony Blair in the United Kingdom (1997). While the Liberal government did not use the term *third way* in Canada,

after their elections in 1993, 1997, and 2000 they did claim their policies were "centralist." They suggested their policies represented a balance between those of the NDP on the left, and the Alliance (known as Reform prior to 2000) and the Progressive Conservative parties on the right.

This pragmatic approach to policy-making has meant many things by those advocating a third way. However, one of their fundamental claims is that government should abandon the old idea of welfare, "the direct provision of economic maintenance" (Giddens, 1998, p. 117), and instead invest in human capital—or *social capital,* as it is frequently called. The claim is that the state's role is to help individuals help themselves; to strengthen policies like education and health care.

For more information on the third way, see Anthony Giddens, *The Third Way: The Renewal of Social Democracy* (Cambridge: Polity Press, 1998) and Anthony Giddens, *The Third Way and Its Critics* (Cambridge: Polity Press, 2000).

CONCLUSION

A liberal–democratic political system, then, is one in which, on the basis of universal adult suffrage, citizens select their governors (representatives); these representatives can be changed by the electorate through periodic elections; individual or group opinions can be discussed freely without fear of retaliation by public officials or private individuals; a legal opposition is free to criticize; and an independent judiciary resolves disputes between citizens, between citizens and government, and between levels of government. If this seems excessively long for a definition, that is because it is not easy to characterize in fewer words a form of government that seeks to reconcile freedom with majority rule.

Liberal democracy is an expression of the political experience of the Western world. It is now practised in every country of Western Europe, although Spain and Portugal did not emerge from authoritarian rule until the 1970s, and Greece underwent a period of military dictatorship in the same decade. Liberal democracy is also strongly entrenched in countries that are essentially transplanted European states; for example, Canada, the United States, Australia, New Zealand, and Israel.

While liberal democracy is a product of Western European traditions and culture, democrats believe that it can be adopted successfully outside that milieu. Two good examples are Japan and India. Both countries have ancient cultural traditions that are quite distinct from those of Western Europe, yet they have successfully operated reasonable approximations of liberal democracy for more than 50 years. There was an initial period of transplantation, to be sure—from the American occupation in Japan, and from the British Raj in India—but since those times, liberal democracy has continued successfully on its own. The economic contrast between Japan and India is also significant. Both countries are heavily populated. Japan is now wealthy, with a standard of living similar to Canada's. India, though now growing more quickly than before, is still poor, with a largely agricultural economy. Nonetheless, in spite of severe religious differences, it has been able to make liberal democracy work. This shows that a high standard of living is not absolutely vital for liberal democracy to work. It is probably true, however, that it is more likely to succeed in countries where the economy is highly developed.

In the beginning of the twenty-first century there is good reason for optimism about liberal democracies. It still remains true that no two liberal democracies have gone to war against each other. The widespread adoption of democracy may be the best available strategy for reducing conflict in the world.

Nevertheless, many analysts still believe that liberal democracies are quite fragile and need to adapt constantly to changing conditions in society. Certainly problems such as human rights, economic inequalities, political alienation, or globalization will provide major challenges for these systems of government. Stand by; politically speaking, the next few decades should be exciting times.

Questions for Discussion

1. How does liberal democracy attempt to reconcile majority and minority rights?

2. What are the responsibilities of citizens in liberal democracies?

3. Which constitutional devices do you see as providing the most effective protection for minority rights?

Internet Links

1. The International IDEA (Institute for Democracy and Electoral Assistance): **www.idea.int.** An intergovernmental organization promoting and supporting democracy around the world.

2. FairVote: The Center for Voting and Democracy: **www.fairvote.org.** American centre; emphasis on elections, voting rights, and electoral systems.

3. Freedom House: **www.freedomhouse.org.** Annual rankings of all nations of the world on indicators of freedom and democracy.

4. World Movement for Democracy: Network of Democracy Research Institutes: **www.wmd.org.** Gateway to centres for the study of democracy all over the world.

5. Rights & Democracy: **www.ichrdd.ca.** Canadian organization promoting democracy around the world.

Further Reading

Ajzenstat, Janet. *The Once and Future Canadian Democracy: An Essay in Political Thought.* Montreal and Kingston: McGill–Queen's University Press, 2003.

Alexander, P. C. *The Perils of Democracy.* Bombay: Somaiya Publications, 1995.

Arthur, John, ed. *Democracy: Theory and Practice.* Belmont, CA: Wadsworth Publishing Co., 1992.

Bachrach, Peter. *The Theory of Democratic Elitism.* Rev. ed. Washington, DC: University Press of America, 1980.

Banting, Keith, Thomas J. Courchene, and F. Leslie Seidle, eds. *Belonging? Diversity, Recognition and Shared Citizenship in Canada.* Montreal: IRPP, 2007.

Barney, Darin. *Communication Technology.* Vancouver: UBC Press, 2005.

Brooks, Stephen. *Canadian Democracy: An Introduction.* 5th ed. Toronto: Oxford University Press, 2007.

Cain, Bruce E., Russell J. Dalton, and Susan E. Scarrow, eds. *Democracy Transformed.* Toronto: Oxford University Press, 2004.

Chapman, John W., and Ian Shapiro. *Democratic Community.* New York: New York University Press, 1993.

Dahl, Robert A. *On Democracy.* New Haven, CT: Yale University Press, 1998.

———. *Polyarchy: Participation and Opposition.* New Haven, CT: Yale University Press, 1971.

Dalton, Russell J. *Democratic Challenges, Democratic Choices.* Toronto: Oxford University Press, 2004.

Di Palma, Giuseppe. *To Craft Democracies: An Essay on Democratic Transitions.* Berkeley: University of California Press, 1990.

Downs, Anthony. *An Economic Theory of Democracy.* New York: Harper and Row, 1957.

Eagles, Munro, Christopher Holoman, and Larry Johnston. *The Institutions of Liberal Democratic States.* Peterborough, ON: Broadview Press, 2003.

Elshtain, Jean Bethke. *Democracy on Trial.* Concord, ON: Anansi, 1993.

Esposito, John L. *Islam and Democracy.* New York: Oxford University Press, 1996.

Evans, Mark, Michael Slovodnik, and Terezia Zoric. *Democracy and Government in Canada: Participating for Change.* Toronto: ITP Nelson, 1996.

Fischer, Mary Ellen. *Establishing Democracies.* Boulder, CO: Westview Press, 1996.

Fishkin, James S. *The Voice of the People: Public Opinion and Democracy.* New Haven, CT: Yale University Press, 1995.

Giddens, Anthony. *The Third Way: The Renewal of Social Democracy.* Cambridge: Polity Press, 1998.

———. *The Third Way and Its Critics.* Cambridge: Polity Press, 2000.

Keane, John. *Democracy and Civil Society.* London: Verso, 1988.

Klosko, George. *Democratic Procedures and Liberal Consensus.* Toronto: Oxford University Press, 2004.

Kymlicka, Will. *Multicultural Citizenship: A Liberal Theory of Minority Rights.* Oxford: Clarendon Press and New York: Oxford University Press, 1995.

Lijphart, Arend. *Democracy in Plural Societies.* New Haven, CT: Yale University Press, 1977.

———. *Patterns of Democracy: Government Forms and Performance in Thirty-Six Countries.* New Haven, CT: Yale University Press, 1999.

Lindsay, A. D. *The Modern Democratic State.* New York: Oxford University Press, 1962.

Mackie, Gerry. *Democracy Defended.* Toronto: Cambridge University Press, 2003.

Manji, Irshad. *Risking Utopia: On the Edge of a New Democracy.* Vancouver: Douglas & McIntyre, 1997.

March, James G., and Johan P. Olsen. *Democratic Governance.* New York: Free Press, 1995.

Mouffe, Chantal. *Democracy and Pluralism: A Critique of the Rationalist Approach.* Toronto: Faculty of Law, University of Toronto, 1995.

Nevitte, Neil. *The Decline of Deference: Canadian Value Change in Cross-National Perspective.* Peterborough: Broadview, 1996.

Parry, Gerraint. *Political Elites.* London: George Allen and Unwin, 1969.

Pateman, Carole. *Participation and Democratic Theory.* Cambridge: Cambridge University Press, 1970.

Sartori, Giovanni. *The Theory of Democracy Revisited: Part I, The Contemporary Debate.* Chatham, NJ: Chatham House, 1987.

————. *The Theory of Democracy Revisited: Part II, The Classical Issues.* Chatham, NJ: Chatham House, 1987.

Saul, John Ralston. *The Unconscious Civilization.* Concord, ON: Anansi, 1995.

Turner, Stephen P. *Liberal Democracy 3.0: Civil Society in an Age of Experts.* Thousand Oaks, CA: Sage, 2003.

Unger, Roberto Magabeira. *Democracy Realized: The Progressive Alternative.* New York: Verso, 1998.

Watson, Patrick, and Benjamin R. Barber. *The Struggle for Democracy.* Toronto: Key Porter, 2000.

CORPORATISM

Cawson, Alan. *Organized Interests and the States: Studies in Meso-Corporatism.* London: Sage, 1992.

————. *Corporatism and Political Theory.* New York: Basil Blackwell, 1986.

Harrison, Reginald James. *Pluralism and Corporatism: The Political Evolution of Modern Democracies.* London: George Allen and Unwin, 1980.

Wiarda, Howard J. *Civil Society: The American Model and Third World Development.* Boulder, CO: Westview Press, 2003.

————, ed. *New Directions in Comparative Politics.* 3rd ed. Boulder, CO: Westview Press, 2002.

Wilensky, Harold, and Lawell Turner. *Democratic Corporatism and Policy Linkages: The Interdependence of Industrial, Labour Market, Incomes and Social Policies in Eight Countries.* Berkeley, CA: University of California Press, 1987.

Williamson, Peter J. *Corporatism in Perspective: An Introductory Guide to Corporatist Theory.* London: Sage, 1992.

Ziegler, L. Harman. *Pluralism, Corporatism and Confucianism: Political Associations and Conflict Resolution in the United States, Europe and Taiwan.* Philadelphia: Temple University Press, 1988.

CONSOCIATIONALISM

Lamy, Steven Lewis. *Consociationalism, Decentralization and Ethnic Group Equalization: The Case of Constitutional Engineering in Belgium.* Ann Arbor, MI: University of Michigan Press, 1980.

Lijphart, Arend. *The Politics of Accommodation: Pluralism and Democracy in the Netherlands,* 2nd ed. Berkeley, CA: University of California Press, 1975.

McRae, Kenneth Douglas, ed. *Consociational Democracy: Political Accommodation in Segmented Societies.* Toronto: McClelland & Stewart, 1974.

CHAPTER 18
Transitions to Democracy

In the previous edition of this text we noted that there was a great deal of optimism about the movement toward democratic systems of government. The collapse of the Soviet bloc and the fall of dictatorships in the Third World allowed democracies to proliferate around the globe. In his book *The Third Wave*,[1] the Harvard political scientist Samuel P. Huntington argued that we are now in the midst of the third great epoch, or "wave," of world democratization, which began in 1974 with the fall of the military regime in Portugal. Larry Diamond, one of the foremost analysts on political transitions, summarized the situation in the mid-1990s:

> Since April of 1974, when the Portuguese military overthrew the Salazar/Caetano dictatorship, the number of democracies in the world has multiplied dramatically. Before the start of this global trend, there were about forty democracies. The number increased moderately through the late 1970s and early 1980s as several states experienced transitions from authoritarian rule (predominantly military) to democratic rule. In the mid-1980s, the pace of global democratic expansion accelerated markedly. By the end of 1995, there were as many as 117 democracies or as few as 76, depending on how one counts.[2]

Freedom House data also furnished grounds for optimism at the time we wrote the previous edition. In 1974, at the beginning of the third wave, their "Annual Survey of Freedom Country Ratings" classified 33 of 146 nations (22 percent) as "free." At the end of 2003, 88 of 192 carried the same classification (46 percent), 55 countries were rated as "partly free" (29 percent), and 49 countries were rated as "not free" (25 percent).[3] Their classification of "free" designates a system of government that this book would categorize as a constitutional or liberal democracy.

Today, however, analysts are more cautious. In their 2007 analysis of 193 countries, Freedom House saw virtually no improvement over 2003, classifying 90 as free (47 percent), 58 partly free (30 percent), and 45 not free (23 percent).[4] Thus, the momentum in favour of democracy has slowed considerably. This levelling off of the trend line has many political observers concerned. Larry Diamond, in a 2008 article entitled "Democracy in Retreat," says that

> . . . celebrations of democracy's triumph are premature. In a few short years, the democratic wave has been slowed by a powerful authoritarian undertow, and the world

has slipped into a democratic recession. Democracy has recently been overthrown or gradually stifled in a number of key states, including Nigeria, Russia, Thailand, Venezuela, and most recently Bangladesh and the Philippines.[5]

Diamond argues that in much of the developing world, abuses of power, corruption, clientelistic political parties, inaccessible judiciaries, contempt for the rule of law, and electoral malpractice have led to "predatory states," in which "the purpose of government is not to generate public goods, such as roads, schools, clinics and sewer systems [but] to produce private goods for officials, their families, and their cronies."[6]

This observation gives rise to a series of questions. Why is it so difficult to build democracies throughout the world? In the transition process, what are those institutions and practices that enhance democratization? And what are the hurdles that impede democratization? After all, most people prefer democracies; in fact, there is a lot of consensus on what democracies have to offer:

> Theorists of democracy have long noted its capacity for peaceful transitions of power and for removing many of the conditions that give rise to violent revolution. It provides for periodic changes in government which effectively prevent a given majority or group of political elites from remaining in power for too long a period.[7]

But the process of democratization is very complex. Democratic transitions involve changing social value systems—moving to values that are compatible with democracy. Conflicts arise because values necessary to democracy may run counter to traditional cultures. At the same time, democratic transitions involve changing the governing institutions of a society, and a change in government can lead to conflict as traditional groups controlling the political process may be removed from their positions of power. So how can democratic values and institutions become embedded in a society? How can democratic practices be consolidated so that they can withstand social, economic, and political pressures? The remainder of this chapter deals with some of the more important factors, both positive and negative, involved in the transition to democracy.

ENHANCING DEMOCRATIC TRANSITIONS
Constitutions and the Rule of Law

In Part Two we spoke of limited government as a component of classical liberalism, but it is also a fundamental principle of all good government. No government's powers should be absolute. Checks and balances have become an essential component of all democratic systems of government. Parliament must answer to the people, cabinets and the prime minister must answer to parliament, and the laws of parliament are subject to review by the courts. These limitations on governments are enshrined in a constitution and in the concept of the rule of law, underscoring the fact that politicians and governmental officials are not above the law as spelled out in a constitution. The principle of *habeas corpus* is an example of limitations placed on governments by the rule of law. Government officials cannot incarcerate individuals and let them languish in prison; they must be charged and tried in the courts or released.

In other words, the constitution provides the rules of the game for governing. It provides for justice and equity in the system; and it provides for freedom of the individual, human rights, and the opportunity to participate as citizens in the political process. Living within these limitations is difficult for many political leaders and does not just occur automatically. The Russian experience in the post-Soviet period is a case in point. Peter Frank notes that in the Soviet Empire (and earlier in czarist Russia) the regime "atomized society . . . to make it terrified and submissive." In addition the Soviet regime provided the "cohesion in a vertically ordered society" through the dictates of the party. Together these factors led to an "unshakable structure."[8] It is not easy for a society to shake hundreds of years of hegemonic cultural tradition and move to a free and more open society. Nor is it easy to establish limits on governing officials when they have never existed. While constitutions and the rule of law are critical to democratic transitions, it may take a long time to nurture a working relationship between democratic values and democratic governance.

Free and Fair Elections

Conducting free and fair elections is another crucial component of democratic transitions. It is an important component because an election is the only peaceful method through which citizens of a polity can change their government.

Between 2003 and 2005, massive street demonstrations led to the removal of authoritarian governments and a turn toward democracy in three states of the former Soviet Union—Georgia, Ukraine, and Kyrgyzstan. While these events showed how widespread the desire for free elections is, and suggest that the movement toward democracy in the former Soviet Union still has momentum, contrary trends are in evidence elsewhere.

For example, after the 2008 elections in Zimbabwe, Robert Mugabe refused to accept what most observers saw as a defeat of his government. While a runoff was scheduled, he and his supporters used violence and intimidation to terrify the opposition. Mr. Mugabe's opponent, Morgan Tsvangirai, eventually withdrew from the runoff because he feared for his own safety and that of his supporters. This refusal to accept the verdict of free elections is a refusal to accept the rule of law and it undermines the confidence of citizens in their governmental process.

For elections to work, they not only have to be free and fair, but citizens must also have confidence that the process is legitimate and that it will make leaders accountable to voters. Elections and accountability are there to "control political power."[9] They contribute to the public's support for the system of governance by creating a sense of legitimacy.

Strong Civil Society

The creation of a strong and viable **civil society** is another important factor in the transition to democracy. Larry Diamond defines civil society as "the realm of organized social life that is open, voluntary, self-generating, at least potentially self supporting, autonomous from the state, and bound by a legal order or set of shared rules."[10] In short, civil society means social pluralism with numerous voluntary, autonomous organizations that seek their own interest, in addition to the public interest as they understand it.

The strength of powerful, autonomous groups can offset the dominating force of a powerful state, a state that may be tempted to arbitrarily use power to suppress opposition. By the same token, a strong civil society can enhance public participation in the political process, and nurture the democratic dialogue essential in a successful transition to democracy. A dynamic deliberative process is one of the cornerstones of democracy.

While civil society is a crucial factor in democratization, Iris Marion Young writes that it can pose a real dilemma for democracies: "Some argue that the fragmentation and plurality of civil society can undermine the trust and solidarity necessary for self-determining democracy. . . ." In other words, powerful associations in society can distort the public interest by overpowering other groups in the political process. Therefore, "democratic state institutions . . . have unique and important virtues for promoting social justice."[11] Therefore, in any transitional process, or in a full-fledged, practising democracy, there must be balance between a strong civil society and the state.

Economic Development

Fifty years ago the American sociologist Seymour Martin Lipset noted a correlation between economic development and democracy in as much as democratic political systems were also the most developed economic systems.[12] Indeed, much of the push for economic development and globalization assumes that these changes will lead to economic growth, and economic growth will enhance democratic transitions:

> While economic growth is systematically associated with poverty reduction, the rate at which growth translates into lower poverty depends on the initial level of income inequality in the distribution of income and how that distribution changes over time. Growth—and its effectiveness in reducing poverty—also depends on sound, stable government. So confronting socioeconomic inequalities and building sound institutions

can be important both for providing a socially sustainable basis for overall growth and for ensuring that poor people gain substantially from that growth.[13]

Developing "sound, stable government," however, may be easier said than done. We now know that entrenching democratic values and institutions in nations in transition to democracy is no easy task. Building a system of governance that individuals see as legitimate and one that they will support requires a lot of political engineering. What is involved in the "consolidation" process by which democracy takes root and becomes formalized? To better understand how economic development may influence democratic consolidation, it is essential to see how different analysts deal with the problem.

One of these analysts is the Finnish scholar Tatu Vanhanen, who has investigated the problem discussed by Lipset; that is, the connection between economics and politics. Vanhanen describes his study as a "resource distribution theory of democratization."[14] In effect he is explaining reasons for a successful democracy as one might explain reasons for one team winning a hockey game. In hockey the explanatory "variables" may be coaching, personnel, financial resources, team spirit, and so on. With democracies, he is seeking a "variable" or "variables" that explain successful democracies:

> If the resources used as sources of power are concentrated in the hands of one group, the same group will be the most powerful group. If the resources used as sanctions are distributed widely among several groups, it is reasonable to expect that power also becomes distributed among several groups.[15]

In an introductory textbook, we cannot provide a complete discussion of Vanhanen's statistical approach, but we can report his major finding: "It was found that the major explanatory factor of the study, the distribution of power resources, explained about 66 percent of the variation in degree of democracy. . . ."[16] In other words, the distribution of power resources in society is strongly correlated with the degree of democratization.

Amartya Sen, a Nobel Prize winner in economics, offers another comprehensive way of examining the process of development. His concept of development includes the social, economic, and political changes occurring in non-industrial societies, connecting the developmental process with freedom of the individual: "The analysis of development presented in this book treats the freedom of individuals as the basic building blocks. Attention is thus paid particularly to the expansion of the capabilities of persons to lead the kind of lives they value. . . ."[17] Sen's argument is that development means "expanding the real freedom that people enjoy," and expanding it for all segments in society. "Human development is first and foremost an ally of the poor, rather than the rich and the affluent."[18]

Sen sees the capitalist system as one of the causes of development in affluent societies:

While capitalism is often seen as an arrangement that works only on the basis of the greed of everyone, the efficient working of the capitalist system is, in fact, dependent on powerful systems of values and norms. Indeed, to see capitalism as nothing other than a system based on a conglomeration of greedy behaviour is to underestimate vastly the ethics of capitalism, which has richly contributed to its redoubtable achievements.[19]

Nevertheless, the use of a capitalist system for development has its limitations, especially in dealing with "economic inequality, environmental protection and the need for cooperation of different kinds that operate outside the market."[20]

For Sen, one critical factor in achieving economic development of a society is the development of "human capabilities." These capabilities are fostered by social development, for example in "education, better health care, finer medical attention and other factors that causally influence the effective freedoms that people actually enjoy."[21] Sen is synthesizing economic growth in society with the development of human capabilities of all individuals of that society. This dual process of development then creates true individual freedom. Thus, an essential step in the fostering of democracy is the development of human capabilities.

Another important work in explaining transitions to democracy is by Hernando de Soto, president of the Institute for Liberty and Democracy in Peru. De Soto makes a straightforward argument about the failure of capitalism in most non-industrial states.[22] He sees capital as a critical component of the developmental process. Capital is the "lifeblood" of capitalism; it provides "the means to support specialization and the production and exchange of assets in the expanded market."[23] In addition, says de Soto, "even in the poorest countries, the poor save. The value of savings among the poor is, in fact, immense—forty times the foreign aid received throughout the world since 1945."[24] However, few in developing systems are able to "transform their assets and labour into capital." They lack "an implicit legal infrastructure hidden deep within their property structure," which Western nations have developed. The key to change in the non-industrial world is to develop the means for converting "property rights" to capital. This legalized, contractual process will, according to de Soto, enable the poor to harness their resources and use the capitalist system to develop freedom and opportunity.[25]

In concrete terms, de Soto is referring to the difficulty that people have in obtaining legal title to land in much of the Third World. Great cities such as Lima, Bombay, and Cairo are thronged with millions of people squatting on publicly owned land. Governments cannot drive these squatters out but also have not created legal procedures for them to regularize their possession. Without proof of ownership, these people cannot use their houses as collateral to borrow money from financial institutions. They also have no legal address and thus often tap into water and electricity services without paying for them. The resulting economic inefficiency and disorder drags down the whole system. De Soto argues that transitional democracies in the Third World should do what the United States and Canada did in the nineteenth century—recognize the titles that squatters acquire by possession so they can enter the economy on a legitimate basis.

World View 18.1

Summary of Hernando de Soto's Argument in *The Mystery of Capital*

1. The situation and potential of the poor need to be better documented.

2. All people are capable of saving money.

3. What the poor are missing are the legally integrated property systems that can convert their work and savings into capital.

4. Civil disobedience and the mafias of today are not marginal phenomena but the result of people marching by the billions from life organized on a small scale to life on a big scale.

5. In this context, the poor are not the problem but the solution.

6. Implementing a property system that creates capital is a political challenge because it involves getting in touch with people, grasping the social contract, and overhauling the legal system.

Source: Hernando de Soto, *The Mystery of Capital* (New York: Basic Books, 2001), p. 277.

For more on de Soto's argument, see World View 18.1.

Obviously, no single factor can fully explain the success of the complex processes of democratization, nation-building, and political development. The difficulties are enormous, as illustrated by attempts to create a new democratic system in Iraq after the United States and its allies conquered that country in 2003 and embarked on the task of "regime change." It is a simplistic assumption that overthrowing autocratic regimes will lead to democracy. Sectarian violence, hate for the U.S. as an intruder in the region, corruption, and the problem of security are only a few of the complications to any transition to democracy in Iraq. At this writing in 2009 there is still no guarantee of a favourable outcome in that struggle.

IMPEDIMENTS TO DEMOCRATIC TRANSITIONS
Ethnic and National Violence

Ethnic and national violence (sometimes referred to as "ethnonational" violence) is an obvious impediment to any democratic transition. The concern for ethnic or national identity preservation engenders strong emotions. Ensuing conflicts, within or between nation-states, can be not only brutal but also self-destructive for emerging democracies. More often than not the loss of life is extensive, the economy is torn to shreds, and the political system becomes dysfunctional. One can look in almost any of the four corners of this world and find examples of destructive violence.

Unfortunately, Africa offers too many examples. The Democratic Republic of the Congo is one of the worst. In the decade prior to 2006, conflicts there involved "three Congolese rebel movements, 14 foreign armed groups, and countless militias; killed over 3.3 million Congolese; and destabilized most of central Africa."[26] An agreement in 2003 and elections in 2006 were supposed to bring peace to the country. "Yet over two million more Congolese have died since the official end of the war."[27]

Ethnonational violence is also a problem in Asia. Sri Lanka gained its independence in 1948, and since that time the country has struggled with the secessionist movement of the Tamil Tigers. There are about 20 million people in the country, with 74 percent of Sri Lankans being Buddhist Sinhalese and about 18 percent Hindu Tamils. The Tamils have been fighting for independence or more autonomy since 1948. A civil war in the 1980s and 1990s took as many as 60,000 lives. The struggle continues and economically it has cost the country in investments and in tourism.

In Eastern Europe, ethnic violence between Serbs and Albanians in the province of Kosovo has been very intense. Before the breakup of Yugoslavia, the violence was so appalling that the North Atlantic Treaty Organisation (NATO) felt compelled to intervene by sending troops to separate the two sides. And even in 2008, when Kosovo, supported by most of the nations of the world, declared independence, Serbs rioted to protest the move.

In fact, the Balkans historically have been one of the world's hotspots. The region contains a highly volatile mix of ethnic groups, nationalities, and religions. Conflict in the area has led to the phrase "the balkanization of politics" (see Comparative Perspective 18.1).

In the Middle East, ethnic and national violence has been one of the problems holding back democracy in the region. The conflict between Israel and the Palestinians has destabilized the region for more than half a century. And the Kurdish minority problem in Turkey has been violent at times and remains a troublesome issue today. And even within the realm of Arabic-speaking Muslims, there are violent clashes between Sunni and Shiite Muslims in Iraq.

In all of these cases one can understand why it is difficult to facilitate a transition to democracy while violence is prevalent. It is almost impossible to entrench constitutional limitations on the state, carry on a public dialogue over policy issues, or administer the construction of roads, schools, hospitals or health clinics when ethnic or national groups are struggling for autonomy or independence.

Religious Fundamentalism and Violence

Religious fundamentalism has emerged as a major difficulty in emerging democracies. This struggle is most obvious in countries with citizens practising the Islamic faith. There are more than one billion Muslims throughout the world. There are more than one billion Muslims throughout the world, and they constitute a majority of the population in many countries from western Africa to Indonesia. Though Arabia was the cradle of Islam, most

Comparative Perspectives 18.1

The Balkanization of Politics

The balkanization of politics means strong and parochial ties between ethnic, religious, and the national groups, and the disintegration of political order due to conflict among the groups. The Balkan peninsula is located in southeastern Europe, between the Black and Aegean Seas in the east, the Adriatic and Ionian Seas in the west, and the Mediterranean Sea to the south. Yugoslavia before and after 1990 is a classic example of balkanized politics. In 1945, Marshal Josip Broz Tito, using the Communist Party, consolidated power in a centralized federal state. There were six

Federal People's Republic of Yugoslavia in 1945

Frontiers between countries that were states in federal Yugoslavia

Other international frontiers

The remaining "Yugoslavia" comprises only Serbia.

Vojvodina and Kosovo are formerly autonomous regions in Serbia.

Source: Adapted from *An Atlas of World Affairs*, 10th ed., Andrew Boyd, © 1998 Routledge, p. 58. Reproduced by permission of Taylor & Francis Books UK.

Comparative Perspectives 18.1

republics: Slovenia and Croatia in the north, Serbia in the east, Bosnia-Herzegovina and Montenegro in the centre, and Macedonia in the south. Vojvodina and Kosovo became autonomous provinces. Within Yugoslavia, three faiths were practised: Roman Catholicism, Greek Orthodox Christianity, and Islam. The federation lasted until 1991, when Croatia and Slovenia declared independence.

Intense and bitter strife in the region can be traced to wars, occupations by the Ottoman and Austro-Hungarian empires, and attempts of the European colonial powers to gain influence in the region. The violence also may be linked to low economic development. The gross national income per capita (2006) was:

Albania	$2,930
Bosnia-Herzegovina	$3,230
Bulgaria	$3,990
Croatia	$9,310
Greece	$27,390
Macedonia	$3,070
Montenegro	$4,130
Romania	$4,830
Serbia	$4,030
Slovenia	$18,666

The Balkan Peninsula Today*

Source: Map from THE WORLD BOOK ENCYCLOPEDIA. © 2005 World Book, Inc. By permission of the publisher. www.worldbookonline.com. All rights reserved.

*Montenegro shift from Serbia in 2006.

Muslims today are not Arabs; rather, they live in countries such as Bangladesh, India, Indonesia, and Pakistan. The problem is not with the Islamic faith itself but with the struggle going on within that faith. The split within the faith is between the fundamentalist and more moderate Muslims. The way this conflict is playing out in Pakistan is an example of how it affects a struggling, transitional democracy.

Pakistan is a country of about 165 million people, of whom about 97 percent are Muslims. Since independence through partition from India in 1947, the country has alternated between democracy and dictatorship, mostly military. In 1988 Benazir Bhutto was chosen as prime minister, the first woman to serve as head of government in an Islamic country. In 1990 her government was dissolved by the president. After the 1993 elections she was returned to power as prime minister, and remained in office until 1996. Again she was forced to resign, and, under questionable accusations of corruption, left the country. In 1999 General Pervez Musharraf led a coup and became president. In 2007 he agreed to return the government to elected officials and elections were scheduled for early 2008. Benazir Bhutto returned to Pakistan to prepare for the election but was assassinated in early 2008. Just before her death she completed a book on the struggle between Muslim factions and explained how this struggle could have profound implications on Pakistan's democracy.

Her book describes the schism within the Islamic faith. "The battle for the hearts and soul of Islam today is taking place between moderates and fanatics, between democrats and dictators, between those who live in the past and those who adapt to the present. . . ."[28] The radical or fanatical Muslims are those

> who claim to speak for Islam who denigrate democracy and human rights, arguing that these values are Western values and thus inconsistent with Islam. These are the same people who would deny basic education to girls, blatantly discriminate against women and minorities, ridicule other cultures and religions, rant against science and technology, and endorse brutal totalitarianism to enforce their medieval views.[29]

These are the people who "attacked America, Spain, Britain, Indonesia, Afghanistan, and Pakistan and then attacked my supporters and me in Karachi on October 19, 2007." And their "ultimate goal: chaos."[30]

Bhutto goes on to suggest that these are not the Muslims she knows, that this is a "caricature" of the Islamic faith she knows. Islam

> is an open, pluralistic, and tolerant religion—a positive force in the lives of more than one billion people across this planet. . . . It is a religion built upon the democratic principals of consultation (*shura*); building consensus (*ijma*); finally leading to independent judgement *(ijtibad)*.[31]

While she argues that radical Muslims, such as the partisans of al-Qaeda, have "twisted the values of a great and noble religion," she does not feel most Muslims agree with their position.[32] Therefore, she is convinced the Islamic religion and democracy can be reconciled.

In commenting on religious conflicts in the Islamic world, we should remember that the development of religious tolerance in Western Europe was a slow and in many cases a brutal process. In writing on religious pluralism in France, Joseph Lecler says,

> All those who were worried about the political unity of the kingdom (France), whether Catholics or Protestants, began therefore to think of granting the dissenters civil tolerance, either provisionally or for good. This solution prevailed, after many a struggle, with the promulgation of the Edict of Nantes (1598).[33]

But in 1685, Louis XIV revoked the Edict of Nantes and expelled the Protestants from France. Religious toleration was not achieved until the nineteenth century.

If our own experience is an indicator, the transition to democracy may be slow and even violent. Religious fanatics can cause terrible disruptions in society, and seriously impede its transformation to democracy. There is little opportunity for peaceful reconciliation of conflicts among different groups in society when little or no tolerance exists.

Strong Military or Para-Military Forces and Corruption

A powerful military or para-military force can totally dominate politics in an emerging society. These forces can make it especially difficult for other societal groups such as labour, peasant farmers, businesspeople, religions, or educators to have any autonomy in the process. Military and para-military groups use the violent power of the gun to create fear and intimidation. As Daron Acemoglu and James A. Robinson suggest, "Many coups" (and most coups are undertaken by the military), "especially in Latin America, had reducing redistribution as one of their major objectives and, in most cases, proceeded to reduce redistribution and change the income distribution significantly."[34] These forces can be used to rig elections, or to so intimidate groups that they fear for their lives and refrain from publicizing their cause or lobbying governments.

Also, corruption can be a significant impediment to democratic transitions. Ronald Inglehart and Christian Welzel note that "the most serious violation of effective democracy is elite corruption." Using corruption,

> elites provide services only to privileged people who can afford to buy them by paying bribes or doing favors. This violates the rule of law and equal rights. Corruption tends to establish conspiratorial networks held together by mutual obligations, fueling nepotism, favouritism, and clientelism. Corruption distributes privileges in highly discriminatory ways disenfranchising the masses.[35]

But in this elaborate study of cross-national cultural values, they see some hope. "If a society's mass culture becomes hostile to favouritism, corruption, and authoritarianism, elite culture is likely to do so as well."[36]

When one reviews the impediments to democratic transitions, it is easy to become pessimistic and think that democracy has no future in the Third World. However, the

North American Leaders' Summit in Montebello, Quebec, 2007. Mexican President Felipe Calderòn, Former U.S. President George W. Bush, and Canadian Prime Minister Stephen Harper.
Source: Saul Loeb/AFP/Getty Images

mass desire for participation in politics, for justice, equity, and the rule of law has had a profound impact upon governance. Democratic values well articulated, plus strong institutions reinforcing those values, are crucial in attempting to overcome the impediments to democracy.

GLOBALIZATION

Globalization obviously has benefited countries like India and China. They have been able to undertake extensive economic growth by rapidly expanding their industrial sector. But the issue of globalization often is interpreted differently in transitional democracies than in established democracies. Many non-industrial nations fear being "thrown into transitional lifestyles that they often neither want nor understand. . . ." They assume that globalization carries with it "waves of cultural transformation" leading to the "convergence" of a global culture, "the McDonaldization of the world."[37] This sort of fear creates a paradox in transitional democracies. Often the countries want foreign investment and the accompanying jobs, but fear the loss of their cultural identity.

Some analysts have argued that these fears are not altogether justified.[38] Ulrich Beck, for example, suggests that globalization is not a "linear convergence." He refers to it as a "dialectical" process whereby international and local forces combine, and the end result is not likely to be a monolithic world culture.[39] This is an interesting thesis, but it may be much later in the twenty-first century before it is verified or refuted.

CONCLUSION

Manipulation of elections, violation of human rights, arbitrary use of force, lack of accountability, rampant nationalism, gross inequalities, and economic stagnation are some of the problems encountered in the transition to democracy. It is clear that developing democratic institutions and procedures, and engendering democratic values and beliefs, is a different process than maintaining established liberal democracies. The transition to democracy may involve destroying old methods of maintaining order and control and eliminating privilege and political immunity based on birthright or force. At the same time, transitions to democracy involve building anew, developing accountability for political leaders, and providing for equity in the system. Transitional systems need to provide opportunity for all so that, as de Soto and Sen advocate, a nation's human capital can be developed.

Will the democracies that emerge from transitions be similar to those that now exist? Will they follow the pattern of Western democracies, or will new forms emerge reflecting indigenous cultures and institutions? Indeed, not all Western democracies follow a single pattern. Democracy in France and democracy in the United States are very different. There are, however, common underlying principles that are followed wherever democracies have been established.

Howard Wiarda addresses this question in *Comparative Democracy and Democratization,* arguing that democracies will inevitably differ: "After all, different cultures and different societies at different levels of development do practice democracy in their own ways, and we should celebrate this diversity. Few countries practice democracy in the same way."[40] He goes on to say that democracy comes in "mixes, gradations, and distinct varieties," and that we should see the transition as a "continuum, a journey, and ongoing process."[41] Because of these differences,

> we need a set of categories—limited democracy, partial democracy, incomplete democracy, and the like—that enable us to comprehend and come to grips not only with the many gradations of democracy but also with the unique, culturally conditioned forms that democracy may take. Not only will that give us a useful and realistic way of measuring the condition and status of global democracy, but it also provides us with a base to encourage further evolution toward democracy in the future.[42]

Specifically, democracy still faces at least five huge challenges:

1. The world's largest country, the People's Republic of China, with an estimated population of 1.2 billion, remains firmly anti-democratic in politics, though it is experimenting with economic liberalization.

2. Democracy is superficial in many of the Soviet successor states in Eastern Europe and Central Asia. In countries such as Russia, Belarus, and Kazakhstan, recycled communists still hold power and the future of democracy is far from certain. In other new states, such as fragments of the former Yugoslavia, democratic elections have established a precedent but the system remains fragile.

3. The world of Islam, from Indonesia through the Middle East to North Africa, has been tentative about embracing liberal democracy. Turkey, with its strong connections to Europe, is the main exception among the 46 Islamic states; and even Turkey's democracy has been broken by periods of military rule and is now challenged by Islamic fundamentalism. Elections have taken place recently in Indonesia, Bangladesh, and Pakistan, but the roots of democracy remain fragile in these countries. The Lebanese democratic experiment has been torn apart by internal religious rivalries and external political hostilities between Israel and the Arab states. However, there has been a promising trend in many Islamic countries to hold elections for local assemblies or for parliaments which, although they may not be able to hold the executive branch of government to account, at least provide a forum for discussion of public issues.

4. Democratic experiments in sub-Saharan Africa are in their earliest stages and are beset with difficulties. One of the largest and wealthiest countries in the region, Nigeria, is under civilian rule but hardly democratic. Tribal rivalries are a deeply rooted problem, and in the worst cases, such as Somalia and the Sudan, civil order has given way to civil war. However, the thus far successful transition of the Republic of South Africa from apartheid to a multiracial, multiparty democracy is a hopeful development. With its large population and (by African standards) highly developed economy, South Africa may be able to help show other countries the way toward liberal democracy. Indeed some of its neighbours, such as Botswana and Namibia, are doing quite well; but another neighbour, Zimbabwe, has been plunged into turmoil by Robert Mugabe's efforts to hang on to power in the face of popular opposition.

5. Liberal democracies do not always "fit" local cultures. Liberal democracy is a value-laden process of government; if it is going to become universal, ways must be found to resolve conflicts between liberal democratic values and existing cultural values. For example, in most of the Islamic world men and women do not enjoy political equality, and in certain societies throughout the world, traditional elites have governed for centuries. Few of these elites will willingly risk giving up power in free and fair elections. We are not arguing that liberal–democratic values, nurtured in the Western world, should be imposed universally. The adoption of such a value system has to be the choice of the people in each society.

Questions for Discussion

1. What is the role of civil society in stabilizing democratic government?

2. Is it inevitable that one day all systems of government will be democratic? Why or why not?

3. Which writer discussed in this chapter do you feel offers the most insight into the consolidation of transitional democracies?

Internet Links

1. Democracy Program, The Carter Center: **www.cartercenter.org.** Foundation established by former U.S. president Jimmy Carter to promote democratization.

2. Freedom House: **www.freedomhouse.org.** Annual rankings of freedom and democracy in all nations.

3. Institute for Liberty and Democracy: **www.ild.org.pe.** Hernando de Soto's foundation, based in Lima, Peru.

4. Gorbachev Foundation of North America: **www.gfna.net.** Established by Mikhail Gorbachev, the last leader of the Soviet Union, in order to promote worldwide democracy.

Further Reading

Acemoglu, Daron, and James A. Robinson. *Economic Orgins of Dictatorship and Democracy.* Cambridge: Cambridge University Press, 2006.

Badie, Bertrand. *The Imported State: The Westernization of the Political Order.* Trans. by Claudia Royal. Palo Alto, CA: Stanford University Press, 2000.

Baker, Randall, ed. *Transitions from Authoritarianism: The Role of the Bureaucracy.* Westport, CT: Greenwood Publishing Group, 2002.

Baylis, John, and Steve Smith, eds. *The Globalization of World Politics.* 4th ed. Oxford: Oxford University Press, 2007.

Beck, Ulrich. *What Is Globalization?* Trans. by Patrick Camiller. Cambridge: Polity Press, 2000.

Bhutto, Benazir. *Reconciliation: Islam, Democracy, and the West.* New York: HarperCollins, 2008.

Clark, Terry D. *Beyond Post-Communist Studies: Political Science and the New Democracies of Europe.* Armonk, NY: M. E. Sharpe, 2002.

Devins, Neal E. *The Democratic Constitution.* Toronto: Oxford University Press, 2004.

Diamond, Larry. *Developing Democracy: Toward Consolidation.* Baltimore: The Johns Hopkins University Press, 1999.

Fairfield, Paul. *Why Democracy.* Albany: State University of New York Press, 2008.

Feldman, Noah. *What We Owe Iraq: War and the Ethics of Nation Building.* Princeton, NJ: Princeton University Press, 2004.

Giddens, Anthony, ed. *The Global Third Way Debate.* Malden, MA: Blackwell, 2001.

Haggard, Stephen, and Robert R. Kaufman. *The Political Economy of Democratic Transitions.* Princeton, NJ: Princeton University Press, 1995.

Handelman, Howard, and Mark Tessler, eds. *Democracy and Its Limits: Lessons from Asia, Latin America, and the Middle East.* Notre Dame, IN: University of Notre Dame Press, 1999.

Hollifield, James Frank, and Calvin C. Jillson. *Pathways to Democracy: The Political Economy of Democratic Transitions.* New York: Routledge, 2000.

Huntington, Samuel P. *The Clash of Civilizations and the Remaking of World Order.* New York: Simon and Schuster, 1996.

———. *The Third Wave: Democratization in the Late Twentieth Century.* Norman: University of Oklahoma Press, 1991.

Inglehart, Ronald, and Christian Welzel. *Modernization, Cultural Change and Democracy: The Human Development Sequence.* Cambridge: Cambridge University Press, 2005.

Keane, John. *Democracy and Civil Society.* London: Verso, 1988.

———. *Violence and Democracy.* Toronto: Cambridge University Press, 2004.

O'Donnell, Guillermo, and Philippe C. Schmitter. *Transitions from Authoritarian Rule: Tentative Conclusions about Uncertain Democracies.* Baltimore: Johns Hopkins University Press, 1986.

Pridham, Geoffrey, ed. *Transitions to Democracy: Comparative Perspectives from Southern Europe, Latin America and Eastern Europe.* Aldershot, UK: Dartmount, 1995.

Przeworski, Adam. *Democracy and the Market: Political and Economic Reforms in Eastern Europe and Latin America.* Cambridge: Cambridge University Press, 1991.

Przeworski, Adam, et al., eds. *Democracy and Development: Political Institutions and Well-Being in the World, 1950–1990,* New York: Cambridge University Press, 2000.

Reynolds, Andrew. *The Architecture of Democracy.* Toronto: Oxford University Press, 2002.

Schedler, Andreas, Larry Diamond, and Marc F. Plattner, eds. *The Self-Restraining State: Power and Accountability in New Democracies.* Boulder, CO: Lynne Rienner, 1999.

Sen, Amartya. *Development as Freedom.* New York: Anchor Books, 1999.

Shapiro, Ian, and Casiano Hacker-Cordon, eds. *Democracy's Value.* Cambridge: Cambridge University Press, 1999.

Sharansky, Natan. *The Case for Democracy: The Power of Freedom to Overcome Tyranny and Terror.* New York: Public Affairs, 2004.

Soto, Hernando de. *The Mystery of Capital: Why Capitalism Triumphs in the West and Fails Everywhere Else.* New York: Basic Books, 2000.

Sunstein, Cass R. *Designing Democracy.* Toronto: Oxford University Press, 2002.

Tilly, Charles. *Democracy.* Cambridge: Cambridge University Press, 2007.

Vanhanen, Tatu. *Prospects of Democracy: A Study of 172 Countries.* London: Routledge, 1997.

Whitehead, Laurence. *Democratization.* Toronto: Oxford University Press, 2002.

Wiarda, Howard J., ed. *Comparative Democracy and Democratization.* Orlando: Harcourt College Publishers, 2002.

CHAPTER 19

Autocratic Systems of Government

While there is much hope about the transition to democracy, there remain many non-democratic systems of government. In the previous chapter, Freedom House data for 2007 classified 45 of 193 nations as "not free"; that is, 23 percent.[1] Most of these states manifest some form of autocratic rule. The term **autocracy** is formed from two Greek stems: *auto-,* meaning self, and *-kratia,* meaning power or rule. It means, literally, self-rule—that is, doing whatever you want if you have the power. It represents absolute government, by an individual or a group that possesses unrestricted power, ruling according to their own desires rather than the rule of law. Such rulers are not responsible to anybody or any institution.[2]

Autocracy is essentially the same thing as tyranny or despotism. Aristotle defined tyranny as "the arbitrary power of an individual which is responsible to no one, and governs all alike . . . with a view to its own advantage, not to that of its subjects, and therefore against their will."[3] Montesquieu (1689–1755) said much the same thing when he defined **despotism** as one man ruling through fear without regard to law.[4] Such definitions of autocracy, tyranny, and despotism always point to certain similar and interrelated characteristics:

- Rule is arbitrary and not bound by law.
- Rule is exercised in the interest of the rulers and not in the common interest.
- Rule is based on coercion and fear.

These ideas are logically interlocked. People willingly submit to authority if it is exercised under genuine laws that are universal rules of conduct, and if these rules are binding on government and citizens alike for the common good. When these conditions are not met, fear must substitute for voluntary compliance.

Note that the essence of autocratic or tyrannical rule is found in the "how" of government, not in the "who." It is not a question of numbers. A single individual who rules under law is a constitutional monarch; someone who rules arbitrarily, according to caprice, is a tyrant.

Autocracies can be further classified as either authoritarian or totalitarian. Even though these forms of government are decreasing in numbers, they are not likely to disappear from the globe, so it is important to understand their basic characteristics.

AUTHORITARIANISM

The concept of **authoritarianism** implies authority that may or may not rest on wide popular support but that is not put to the test of free elections. While that seems clear enough, a problem in speaking of authoritarian regimes is that the category includes such a wide diversity of types. Some regimes are civilian (Syria), others military (Myanmar); some are secular (Turkey has been but faces pressures from Islamic fundamentalists), others avowedly religious (Iran); some are capitalist (Algeria), others socialist (Vietnam); some are traditional monarchies with few or none of the institutions of modern democracy (the Gulf sheikhdoms); others appear to have all the machinery of modern democracy, but it is manipulated in such a way that there is no real democratic choice (Zimbabwe).

We cannot pursue all these differences here, but we will draw a distinction between right-wing conservative regimes that interpret their mission as protecting society from harmful influences, and left-wing revolutionary regimes that claim to be building a new society. Right-wing authoritarianism, for example the government of General Pinochet in Chile (1973–90), originally consisted of anti-communist regimes whose ostensible mission was to prevent a Marxist revolution. More recently, however, many conservative authoritarian regimes in Africa and the Middle East—for example, Morocco and Algeria—are directed not against communism but against Islamic radicalism. Similarly on the left, authoritarian regimes used to be mainly socialist, and that type still exists, as in the contemporary government of Hugo Chavez in Venezuela (1999–); but there also are Islamic radical regimes, such as the Islamic Republic of Iran, founded in 1979, or the Taliban regime in Afghanistan (1996–2001).

Right-Wing Authoritarianism

Drawing heavily on the example of Spain under Francisco Franco (in office 1936–75), Juan Linz developed a model of right-wing authoritarian system of government that emphasized the following characteristics:

- limited political pluralism,
- no elaborate or guiding ideology,
- no extensive political mobilization, and
- leaders who exercise power within ill-defined yet predictable limits.[5]

One might add to these a bias toward statism and a major political role for the military.

In most right–authoritarian systems there is no idea of a classless society or a master race. A substantial degree of social pluralism is tolerated. As the society grows more complex, a variety of organizations—business associations, labour unions, churches, peasant groups—can function with a minimum of interference by government. In fact, an authoritarian regime may use these organizations to achieve certain goals, such as the production of goods and services, or look to them for political support. These organizations can survive as long as they offer political support or at least remain neutral politically. If, however, they become too critical of government policy or suggest fundamental societal change or a change in political leadership, they are expendable.

Right–authoritarian systems do not have an elaborate blueprint for utopian order. While the authoritarian ruler always advocates economic development, there is usually no doctrinaire plan to totally transform society to achieve this growth. Rather, economic development (the most common objective) is defined in terms of doing more of what is already being done and doing it within the existing structures of society.

The military regime that ruled South Korea from 1961 to 1988 is an excellent example. The government encouraged industrialization by creating favourable conditions for large companies to operate. Within two decades, South Korea became an international force in steel, shipbuilding, automobiles, clothing, electronics, and other industries. The country transformed itself in a very short period of time from a backward agricultural economy into a modern industrial power. Standards of living also rose dramatically, and continue to do so, although they are still below those in Japan or North America.

During these years of rapid development, the government tolerated token political opposition but manipulated elections to ensure its continued dominance. Social pluralism was allowed, but organizations that challenged government policy, such as labour unions, were severely repressed. The government often equated opposition to itself with communism—a tactic that retained some credibility because of the belligerence of North Korea. Right-wing authoritarianism in South Korea was typical in its political methods but exceptional in the success of its economic policies; few governments of this type have presided over such rapid and sustained industrial growth.

Another characteristic of the authoritarian model is that there is no great drive to mobilize the society in order to achieve utopian ends. In Chile, for example, all political parties were banned from 1973 until the closing years of General Pinochet's regime; the military government did not even maintain a party of its own, so great was its distaste for mass participation in politics. Mobilizing large numbers of people can nurture political instability by breaking down old patterns of living and stimulating the growth of new institutions. Unless the effects of these changes can be channelled or contained, they can be disastrous for a political leader. Few authoritarian leaders are willing to risk the consequences of drastic change. On the contrary, most cling to the stability of the status quo. However, they may undertake certain reforms, particularly in the interest of economic efficiency. South Korea redistributed much agricultural land—large holdings were appropriated from their owners, divided into smaller pieces, and given to peasants; and the late Shah of Iran confiscated large landholdings of the Islamic clergy. Improvements in nonpolitical areas (for example, technical education) are also not uncommon in conservative authoritarian regimes. However, reform generally stops short of upsetting the balance of political power.

Rightist authoritarianism, even though broadly opposed to socialism, often leans toward **statism.** Rulers are usually unwilling to leave the process of economic development entirely to the private sector. While they may not impose state ownership of the economy, they see the state as a principal instrument in expanding the production of goods and services. The state becomes the driving force, influencing wages, employment, investment, and the development and management of natural resources and international trade. South Korea, for example, controlled exchange rates and restricted imports during its period of highest industrial growth, thus restricting opportunities for consumption and channelling savings into investment.

This particular role of the state seems to be a significant characteristic of many authoritarian systems. Numerous authoritarian governments have used their concentrated political power to control many, if not all, aspects of a market economy. Examples are Taiwan, South Korea, Kenya, Brazil, and Chile. The last case is particularly instructive.

In 1973 a military revolt overthrew the socialist government of President Salvador Allende. The government of General Pinochet, tacitly supported by the United States, soon reversed many of Allende's socialist policies—most notably in the monetary field, where rampant inflation was reduced through application of conservative economic theories. Relative monetary stability resulted in an improved climate for business investment and the development of new industries, such as the production of fruit and wine for export. Yet the military government did not reverse Allende's decision to nationalize the copper industry. This illustrates the general rule that authoritarian rulers are often eclectic with respect to ideologies. They choose ideas from several sources; they don't commit themselves to a doctrine. In this sense, their approach remains statist, for the ultimate choice of policy is determined by the needs of the rulers rather than being left to spontaneous social evolution.

The military is usually the dominant institution in right-wing authoritarianism. Given its weapons and organizational capability, the military can intimidate political parties, interest groups, and the courts. Because authoritarian leaders have to rely on coercion rather than popular support, the military becomes the decisive force in the struggle for power. It often promises a return to civilian rule, but usually the date of free elections is repeatedly postponed until it vanishes into the indefinite future.

There are, however, cases in which military regimes have voluntarily relinquished power. In Brazil (1964), Uruguay (1973), and Argentina (1976), authoritarian military regimes ousted elected civilian governments. In each case they accused the civilian politicians of creating economic chaos and pledged economic stability and development through efficient management. In 1984, each regime took steps to return the government to elected civilians. Interestingly, in each case the economy was in no better shape than it had been when the military seized power. These examples do not support the "efficient authoritarian" hypothesis; generals, like other mortals, do not necessarily have a quick fix for the complex economic problems of development.

That being said, the record of military regimes is not totally devoid of economic success stories. Pinochet's regime in Chile (1974–90) had a poor record on human rights; horrifying measures were used by the government in trying to eradicate the socialist movement as a political force. At the same time it liberalized trade, reduced inflation, and reformed social programs. The result, after some years of austerity, was an export boom that continued through the transition to democracy and gave Chile one of the most dynamic economies in South America. Chile subsequently signed free-trade agreements with Canada, Mexico, and the United States, helping to lock in its internal reforms by tying them to external treaty commitments.

Using the South Korean and Chilean examples, it may be tempting to subscribe to the argument that dictatorships are efficient economically. However, the evidence is to the contrary. Adam Przeworski and others examined more than one hundred regimes, authoritarian and democratic, between 1950 and 1990. Their findings:

> The main conclusion of this analysis is that there is no trade-off between democracy and development, not even in poor countries. Although not a single study published before 1988 found that democracy promoted growth, and not one published after 1987 concluded in favour of dictatorships (Przeworski and Limongi, 1993), there was never solid evidence that democracies were somehow inferior in generating growth—certainly not enough to justify supporting or even condoning dictatorships. We hope we have put that issue to rest.[6]

They go on to say, "The few countries that developed spectacularly during the past fifty years were as likely to achieve that feat under democracy as under dictatorship." Moreover, "per capita incomes grow faster in democracies." Finally, "These findings add up to a bleak picture of dictatorships. Although democracies are far from perfect, lives under dictatorships are grim and short."[7]

Left-Wing Authoritarianism

Left–authoritarian regimes seem very different from their right-wing counterparts, at least at first glance. They have an official ideology—either radical Islam, or some variety of socialism other than orthodox Marxism–Leninism, combined with a strong element of nationalism. Tanzania had Nyerere's *ujamaa* socialism—a blend of British Labour ideology and indigenous African traditions. Iraq under Saddam Hussein and Syria under Hafiz al-Assad (who died in 2000) were mortal enemies, but both professed *ba'ath* (renaissance) socialism. In Libya, Colonel Kaddafi has propounded a unique mixture of revolutionary socialism and Islamic fundamentalism. His *Green Book,* like the *Little Red Book* of Chairman Mao, is prescribed ideological reading for a whole nation. In Afghanistan from 1996 to 2001, the Taliban took a certain interpretation of the Koran as their official ideology (see Historical Perspectives 19.1).

Historical Perspectives 19.1

The Taliban in Afghanistan

The Taliban regime in Afghanistan (1996–2001) manifested many totalitarian characteristics. In effect, they established a theocratic state. Religious leaders' interpretation of the Koran served as an ideological basis for remaking society. Public punishment for violations of a strict form of Sharia law was used to terrorize the people. Anything "Western," such as clothing, music, or communication devices, was prohibited. There were no schools for girls and part of the training for boys included indoctrination against Western culture. The idea was to use Afghanistan as the base for the true Islamic state from which to combat the evils of the Western world. That included providing shelter and assistance to al-Qaeda, which organized the attacks against New York City and Washington, D.C., on September 11, 2001.

With the approval of the United Nations Security Council, NATO invaded Afghanistan in late 2001 and quickly overthrew the regime. The Taliban, however, were not totally defeated because they could seek refuge in neighbouring parts of Pakistan. Canada, along with many other Western nations, continues to have troops in Afghanistan helping to prevent the return of the Taliban, but the ultimate outcome of the operation remains unclear. Western nations cannot prop up a government in Afghanistan forever, but neither can they tolerate a regime in that country that organizes attacks against them. Sooner or later there must be a political settlement, but how do you arrive at a political settlement with a theocratic opponent determined to destroy your civilization? For more information, see the so-called "Manley Report," the *Report of the Independent Panel on Canada's Future Role in Afghanistan* (Ottawa, 2007), http://dsp-psd.pwgsc .gc.ca/collection_2008/dfait-maeci/ FR5-20-1-2008E.pdf.

Though they differ in detail, the ideologies of all these regimes called for a fundamental social transformation and referred to revolution in all public discussion. In certain other ways, too, they seemed more totalitarian than authoritarian, at least at the rhetorical level. Political mobilization of the masses was a continuing theme, as was centralized economic planning under the control of a vanguard party.

Perhaps the difference between these left–authoritarian regimes and true totalitarianism is one of degree rather than of kind. If they lived up to their stated goals, they might well become totalitarian. But their revolutions have not been as thoroughgoing or single-minded in the pursuit of the stated utopian goals; there has been more compromise with present reality, and more autonomy for groups in the society that do not oppose the leadership. In Libya, for example, Kaddafi nationalized the oil reserves previously owned by foreign oil companies, but he did not take the country out of the international network of the oil industry. Large numbers of managers and workers from other countries continue to operate the extraction and refining systems, and the products are exported to Western purchasers. Compare that to the autarchic policies of totalitarian states such as Albania and Cambodia, which excluded Western influences altogether; or to the Soviet Union, which tried to develop major industries, including a petroleum industry, without outside help, although it was willing to export surpluses for hard currency.

Lacking the full intensity of totalitarian regimes, left–authoritarian governments in practice often resemble right–authoritarian ones. Some social pluralism may be tolerated as long as it does not become politically dangerous. Police terrorism is used chiefly as a way of retaining power rather than as a means of inducing social change. The rigours of central planning are softened by bribery and corruption. Lip service is paid to ideological goals, but the government does not enforce a monopoly of ideas. Foreign travel is allowed, as are foreign publications, and these things lead to some ideological diversification.

Whether of the left or right, authoritarian leaders tolerate little or no opposition and may do almost anything to remain in power. In virtually every case, they reject the principles of liberal democracy, regarding it as too inefficient for the needs of developing nations. They argue that democracy promotes factions and that a faction-ridden society is unable to attain the mass unity required for social and economic development.

There is, no doubt, a great deal of truth in these criticisms. Liberal democracies are clumsy in their response to crisis and slow to implement public policies when a variety of interests must be considered. Yet the alleged efficiency of authoritarian rulers is often illusory. Their statist mentality often leads them to impose on society vast projects that seem no more productive than the pyramids of the Pharaohs. Or they may embark on reckless international adventures: Iraq's invasion of Iran in 1981 was one of these, as was Argentina's attempt to take the Falkland Islands by force in 1982. When only one will is obeyed, the chances of dramatic error are heightened. The presumed inefficiency of a liberal government is in the long run actually one of its virtues. By fragmenting power, it allows many projects to compete with each other. Some will inevitably fail, but diversity increases the likelihood that solutions to the unexpected problems of the future will be found.

While liberal democracies have worked well for most Western societies, they are not easy to manage, and a certain democratic tradition may be required to make them work. The fact remains, however, that they are not designed to run efficiently. Internal checks are built into them to impede a takeover by a powerful military leader. The processes are set up in such a way that a political leader cannot set a blind course and refuse to hear criticism or consider alternative courses. What seems like inefficiency in the short run may be the most efficient long-run method of governing in an ever-changing and unpredictable world.

Evidence of this can be seen in the fact that many authoritarian rulers enjoy power for only a short time, even when they were first greeted as saviours and later employed various tactics to maintain popular support. Leaders like this are frequently charismatic and often articulate nationalist goals (mostly economic) that have mass appeal. In time, however, enthusiasm wanes as the leader is unable to perform economic miracles. Time seems to erode initial support for authoritarian dictators; to remain in power they begin to rely more on coercion than on popular support. Often they are overthrown in a ***coup d'état*** organized by a faction within the military or the ruling party. In many authoritarian systems, the *coup d'état* has been virtually institutionalized as a means of changing officeholders and plays a role analogous to elections in a liberal democracy. The system remains authoritarian, but there is rotation of personnel at the top. The distinction between authoritarian and totalitarian rule will be clearer after the discussion of the fundamental characteristics of the totalitarian system.

TOTALITARIANISM

Many scholars argue that the twentieth century witnessed a new form of autocratic rule: totalitarianism. The word was coined by Mussolini to describe his system of government. He summarized his views in a speech in 1925: "Everything in the state, nothing outside the state, nothing against the state."[8] The term was soon accepted by the Nazi regime in Germany and later applied by external observers to the Stalinist regime in the Soviet Union and to the People's Republic of China under Mao Zedong.

Totalitarianism is a way of organizing tyrannical or despotic rule in a modern society. In a perceptive analysis of the way totalitarian leaders manipulate the masses, use political organization and the power of the state, and apply ideology and terror, Hannah Arendt noted that

> totalitarianism differs essentially from other forms of political oppression known to us such as despotism, tyranny, and dictatorship. Wherever it rose to power, it developed entirely new political institutions and destroyed all social, legal, and political traditions of the country.[9]

As a term, totalitarianism was most used immediately after World War II. Usage began to fall as Hitler and Mussolini faded from public memory, as the Soviet regime moderated its practices in some respects after Stalin's death in 1953, and as communist China began to open itself to the rest of the world after the death of Mao in 1976. Some scholars have held that the concept is merely propaganda—that totalitarianism exists more in the minds of analysts who are anticommunist or antifascist than as a real political system. This issue could be debated forever. That being said, the term is still used by politicians, journalists, and scholars; and, because totalitarian regimes may arise again in the future, it is important to analyze the principles on which they operate.[10]

Arendt restricts the term *totalitarian* to a small number of regimes—to those that combine an all-powerful political leader and an almost messianic sense of historical mission. Two distinguishing features of totalitarianism are, first, the existence of a revolutionary movement that claims to base itself on nature or history, and, second, the use of terror as an integral tactic in maintaining the momentum of a society in transformation. The leader uses systematic terror as a means of atomizing individuals and keeping the entire population off-balance. Arendt describes this use of terror:

> Under conditions of total terror not even fear can any longer serve as an advisor of how to behave, because terror chooses its victims without reference to individual actions or thoughts, exclusively in accordance with the objective necessity of the natural or historical process.[11]

In Arendt's analysis, the arbitrary use of terror on any and all segments of the population becomes an institutionalized way of preventing the development of political forces opposed to the leader's vision of a new society.

Carl Friedrich and Zbigniew Brzezinski offer a broader definition of totalitarianism. To them it is a "syndrome," or "pattern of interrelated traits," which includes the following six elements:

1. an official ideology

2. a single party typically led by one man

3. a terroristic police

4. a communications monopoly

5. a weapons monopoly

6. a centrally directed economy.[12]

One or more of these elements may be found individually in other forms of government; totalitarianism exists when they all come together.

The analysis of totalitarianism presented here is based on the historical reality of fascist regimes (Italy and Germany) and communist regimes (the Soviet Union and its East European satellites; the People's Republic of China; and the smaller communist states of Yugoslavia, Albania, North Korea, Vietnam, Cambodia, Laos, and Cuba). Of course, with the collapse of international communism, much of this description is recent history rather than current politics. The Soviet Union and Yugoslavia no longer exist as multinational communist states. China and Vietnam are still nominally communist, but they are encouraging a market economy and foreign investment to such an extent that it is questionable whether the state still exercises total control over society. With the retirement of Fidel Castro in 2008, Cuba is starting to evolve away from the "totalitarian syndrome," leaving North Korea as the only full-fledged representative of totalitarianism in the contemporary world. But even if it is temporarily in eclipse, totalitarianism is a real and recurrent possibility and as such cannot simply be tucked away into the history books along with the descriptions of the Greek *polis* and the Mongol Empire.

Below we describe the "totalitarian syndrome" under eight headings derived from Friedrich and Brzezinski, Arendt, and other writers on the subject.

Attempt to Remake Society

Central to totalitarianism, and distinguishing it from simple tyranny, is the attempt to remake society on a grand scale, to produce a condition of utopian perfection. These blueprints for the future are usually a part of the official ideology. Communists, for example, claimed to be working toward the classless society and the withering away of the state. This transformational view of history was enshrined in the Soviet constitution, the preamble of which asserted that the Soviet Union was "a developed socialist society" that was "a logically necessary state on the path to communism."[13] Hitler envisioned a new order in which the German master race would create a new empire (the Third Reich) that would last a thousand years. Mussolini proclaimed the age of the Third Rome (the first two being the Roman Empire and the Roman papacy), during which modern Italy would again lead the world to new heights of civilization. Both the communist and fascist visions of the future were sweeping, radical, and above all **monistic** in the sense that they reduced everything to a single factor—class (communism), race (Nazism), or state (Mussolini's fascism). Such monism gives rise to terror as a principle of government because pluralistic societies must be forcibly remoulded to fit the monistic image.

Thus arises the enormous scale of violence that has marked totalitarianism. Hitler was responsible for the death of six million Jews, half a million Gypsies, and several million Slavs—all of them members of allegedly inferior races. As part of the collectivization of agriculture in the early 1930s, Stalin eliminated perhaps 14 million Ukrainian *kulaks* (independent peasants) through famine and deportation.[14] Between 1975 and 1979, in an attempt to purify the country of Western and bourgeois influences, the Khmer Rouge of Cambodia are said to have killed one-sixth of the population (over one million people). In 1958, at the time of the Great Leap Forward, which was a disastrous attempt to industrialize China almost overnight, Mao expressed the totalitarian outlook in an unforgettable way:

> Apart from their other characteristics, China's 600 million people have two remarkable peculiarities; they are, first of all, poor, and secondly, blank . . . A clean sheet of paper has no blotches, and so the newest and most beautiful pictures can be painted on it.[15]

Society, to vary the metaphor, is viewed by totalitarian regimes as raw material to be moulded by the state according to ideological design.

One-Party State

Totalitarianism imposes a single mass political party that penetrates all aspects of state and society, including the army, schools, trade unions, churches, and leisure organizations. This disciplined party, controlled from above, coordinates all sectors of society. Social organizations may be formally distinct from government, but the leaders of all institutions are either members of the party or acceptable to it. All other political parties are either outlawed, as was the case in the Soviet Union, or carefully manipulated in a common front, as was done in East Germany. Never is real opposition tolerated.

The rejection of political pluralism is linked to the transformation of society. If, as in Mao's metaphor, a picture is being painted, the artist must be in control of the materials and cannot allow other artists to sketch rival conceptions on the same canvas. The fundamental difference between this approach and that of liberal democracy lies in the totalitarian assumption that society is united in a single common project directed by the party through the state. In contrast, liberal democrats see society as the field in which individuals and groups pursue projects of their own choosing.

This leading role of the party was a central tenet of communism from the time the Bolsheviks came to power in 1917. The Soviet Union intervened in Czechoslovakia in 1968 precisely because it feared that the Communist Party there was losing its monopoly of political power. The watershed event in the movement away from totalitarianism in Eastern Europe was the decision by the Polish authorities to allow the Solidarity labour movement to contest the parliamentary elections of 1989. The system was still rigged against Solidarity in that large numbers of seats were effectively reserved for the Communists; but the very fact that another party was allowed to contend for power broke the totalitarian mould. Within three years, the rest of Eastern Europe and the Soviet Union had followed the Polish example and legalized political opposition.

All-Powerful Leader

At one time, it seemed that domination of the party by an all-powerful, charismatic leader was an integral part of totalitarianism. However, Lenin, Stalin, Mao Zedong, Ho Chi Minh, and Tito passed away without leaving replacements of comparable stature, yet their regimes endured, at least for a time. The only totalitarian leader today that one might call omnipotent or charismatic is Kim Jong Il of North Korea, now that Cuba's Fidel Castro has retired. It may be that charismatic leadership is a phenomenon of the early stages of totalitarianism, a requirement for transmitting the energy necessary to seize and consolidate power. The routinization of charisma described by Max Weber in other contexts applies here as well: after the death of the revolutionary leader, power passes into the collective leadership of the party. There may be a reaction against the departed leader, as occurred in the Soviet Union after Stalin's death in 1953, when a new generation of leaders criticized the cult of personality and vowed that it would never arise again. Or, as has taken place in China, the memory of the leader may be revered, while at the same time there is an effective break with many of his policies. In either case, the evidence is that totalitarianism seems able to carry on without charismatic leadership.[16] However, the loss of charismatic authority tends to release demands for democratic reform.

Pseudo-Democratic Rule

The leader and party maintain their power by force but rationalize their rule with pseudo-democratic arguments. Hitler argued that he represented the people (*Volk*) in such a special way that elections were unnecessary. Communism relied on Lenin's theory of democratic centralism. Elections took place, but the party nominated or approved all candidates. Usually there was only one candidate per position, and voting was more ratification than selection. The role of an elected representative was not to contest the policies of the leadership but to increase and maintain society's support for the leadership and its policies.

Authoritarian regimes may also use pseudo-democratic devices to legitimize their authority; but when they do so, it is usually in a cynical and transparently obvious way. In contrast, pseudo-democracy is an intrinsic part of totalitarianism. Because society is being remade, it is important to create popular participation while at the same time making sure the people cannot change their rulers. Thus arises the curious situation that political participation, though ineffective and meaningless from a liberal–democratic point of view, is energetically promoted by the state. Voting is made a legal duty. School and university courses in political education are mandatory. Attendance at political meetings and discussion groups is encouraged or even required. Parades and demonstrations are arranged as needed for specific purposes. In contrast, authoritarian regimes are usually happiest if their subjects refrain from criticism and stay out of politics altogether.

Control of Communications

The totalitarian state seeks to monopolize the flow of ideas. This means that the physical bases of communication—newspapers, radio stations, publishing houses— are either owned or completely controlled by the state. Before Mikhail Gorbachev's attempt at reform in the final years of communism, prepublication censorship in the Soviet Union was rigidly enforced to ensure that public statements followed what communists called "the party line." Photocopying machines and personal computers were considered a potential threat, and access to them was carefully restricted. Foreign books, newspapers, and magazines were not sold freely but were confined to special libraries used by trustworthy researchers. With the means of mass communication so much under state control, dissenting opinions could circulate only by word of mouth or by the laborious process of *samizdat* (self-publication), which involved dissidents typing and retyping their treatises.

The purpose of control over communications is to support an official ideology. In totalitarian states, political doctrine amounts to an official religion. Fascism or Marxism–Leninism is taught in the schools and otherwise made the only publicly acceptable system of belief, while proponents of competing ideologies are subject to persecution.

An important aspect of totalitarianism is that it takes a political doctrine and forces it deep into nonpolitical activities, even into the fine arts and natural sciences. Because of Albert Einstein's Jewish origin, the Nazis rejected the theory of relativity and did not allow it to be taught in German universities. They also banned works of art and literature by Jewish artists and authors. In the Soviet Union in the 1930s, an obscure agronomist named T. D. Lysenko attracted Stalin's attention with the Lamarckian theory of the inheritance of acquired characteristics, a theory long discredited among biologists. Lysenko promised a shortcut to breeding better strains of wheat and cattle; instead of the patient work of selective breeding over generations, he believed that it was necessary to nourish only one generation exceptionally well and let it pass on its vigour to its progeny. This doctrine was officially ratified by the Central Committee of the Communist Party in 1948 and was not repudiated until after the fall of Nikita Khrushchev in 1964. It dealt Soviet agriculture a blow from which it never fully recovered. In China the expansion of ideology merged with the charismatic leadership of Mao Zedong to produce the almost magical "thought of Chairman Mao":

> The thought of Mao Tse-tung is the sun in our heart, is the root of our life, is the source of all our strength. Through this, man becomes unselfish, daring, intelligent, able to do everything . . . The thought of Mao Tse-tung transforms man's ideology, transforms the Fatherland.[17]

Use of Terror

Totalitarian rule is supported by the terroristic activities of a special political police. The Nazi Gestapo and the Soviet KGB were two such forces. A political police reports directly to the leader and is under no legal restraint. It may use intimidation, arbitrary arrest, torture, and execution. It infiltrates other coercive agencies of the state, such as the regular police and the armed forces, to ensure their compliance. Stalin and Hitler even used their political police against the party to ensure their personal control of the apparatus. A political police operates as an empire in itself, maintaining its own prisons, mental hospitals, and labour camps outside the supervision of the legal agencies of the state.

Authoritarian regimes also make use of political police, and their methods are equally grim. Brutality, torture, and summary execution are international phenomena, not confined to a single ideology or system. But there is usually a difference in the scale of operations. Authoritarian governments tend to single out overt political opponents for mistreatment; totalitarian regimes may use the political police against almost anyone. This is a logical consequence of remaking society: anyone who does not wholeheartedly embrace the state-sponsored monistic society of the future is a political opponent. The difference could be formulated this way: in a liberal democracy, the only political crime is to attempt or advocate the violent overthrow of the government; in an authoritarian regime, even criticism or peaceful opposition becomes a political crime; in a totalitarian state, literally any word or action that suggests less than complete commitment to the regime can become cause for detention by the political police.

Subordination of the Law to the State

In a totalitarian state, law is a tool. It is only what the state says today, and it may speak differently tomorrow. Law is subordinate to the state, not the other way around; there are no rights in the proper sense of the term, for rights exist only under law.

In the enthusiasm of the first years after the revolution of October 1917, which brought the communists to power, Soviet theorists held that law would disappear altogether in a communist society. Enforceable rules of conduct were required only because of the antagonisms of class society and would no longer be necessary in the classless society of the future. These early notions were soon replaced by the concept of socialist legality, which is a particular form of legal positivism. It holds that the state should follow regularized procedures in dealing with citizens. These legal norms, however, arise less from an existing consensus in the present society than from the desired shape of the future society that is under construction. Because the state, guided by the party, is the only legitimate interpreter of the goal of evolution, it is for all practical purposes the source of all law.

One illustration of this relates to the status of constitutional documents in totalitarian states. All the communist states had constitutions that spelled out civil liberties in admirable terms. What could be clearer than Article 45 of the 1978 Chinese constitution (no longer in force): "Citizens enjoy freedom of speech, correspondence, the press, assembly, association, procession, demonstration and the freedom to strike, and have the right to speak out freely, air their views fully, hold great debates and write big-character posters."[18] In fact, periods of freedom of speech were announced several times in China with great fanfare, for example in Mao's Hundred Flowers campaign of 1957 ("Let a hundred flowers bloom, let a hundred schools of thought contend"); after Mao's death in September 1976, when the new leadership suggested the virtue of "four freedoms"; and in 1986, when General Secretary Hu encouraged open criticism of party policies. In each case, the state quickly intervened to suppress discussion when it threatened to become critical. The tragic events of 1989, when after having encouraged freer speech for a time the government used tanks to crush student demonstrations at Tiananmen Square, were part of a pattern stretching back more than four decades. For information on one woman's experience under a totalitarian regime in China, see Comparative Perspectives 19.1.

The status of law is a crucial issue in the internal reform of totalitarian regimes. Initially, citizens may be grateful merely to enjoy freedom of speech and voluntary political participation, but they will soon want to see these rights entrenched in the constitution and protected by an independent judiciary. Legal theorists in post-communist Eastern Europe have adopted the liberal idea of rule of law. Movement in this direction is less visible than highly publicized electoral reform, but it is at least as important in restricting the arbitrary power of the state.

Comparative Perspectives 19.1

Life and Death in Shanghai

The nature of totalitarian regimes is expressed most vividly not in textbooks but in the memoirs and autobiographies of people who have lived under such governments. A fine example of this type of literature is Nien Cheng's best-selling book, *Life and Death in Shanghai*.

Madame Cheng was born in Beijing in 1915, studied at the London School of Economics, married a Chinese diplomat, and lived in Australia from 1941 to 1948. After the communist revolution, she and her husband returned to China because they supported the new regime. The government found it in its interest to let a few Western corporations continue to operate in China, so her husband became the local manager for Shell Oil in Shanghai. After his death, Madame Cheng took over as an adviser to the company, until she was caught up in the Cultural Revolution in 1966.

The Cultural Revolution was a complex series of events—partly a youth protest movement unleashed by Chairman Mao Zedong in an attempt to renew the Communist Party, partly a naked power struggle among different factions within the party. Madame Cheng, though not a political activist, quickly became suspect because of her association with a Western corporation. After the Red Guards youth militia invaded her house and destroyed most of her possessions, she was accused of being a British spy and locked up in solitary confinement for six and a half years. She was cruelly mistreated through denial of proper food, clothing, and medical care, amounting in effect to severe torture. Although repeatedly interrogated for months at a time, she never confessed to anything.

When she was finally released after internal changes in the political power structure, she learned that her only child, an actress not involved in politics, had also been arrested by the Red Guards and had died in custody after being pressured to incriminate her mother. The death had been falsely reported as suicide.

With incredible courage, Madame Cheng worked to expose the truth about her daughter's fate. She then took advantage of a temporary political thaw in 1980 to leave China and go to the United States, where two of her sisters lived. Her book, first published in 1986, is not only a moving account of one woman's suffering and heroism, but also an incisive portrait of a political system not subject to the rule of law.

Planned Economy

The totalitarian state aspires to control a planned economy. This may entail public ownership, as in communism, or state supervision of private enterprise, as in Nazi Germany or fascist Italy, where the state took a vigorous role in setting prices and production quotas. A controlled economy is vital to the totalitarian state. It cannot allow a liberal economy, in which each individual or group pursues private interests and coordination is left to the undirected market process symbolized by Adam Smith's "invisible hand." Individual interests and goals must be subordinated to the imposed goal of social transformation.

This helps to explain the position of labour unions in totalitarian states. All such states foster unions by making membership compulsory, but these organizations are not autonomous associations of workers. Collective bargaining in the Western sense does not take place. The union, itself controlled by the dominant political party, is a control over the workers rather than an expression of their interests. This is not surprising; in any economy, labour is the most important factor of production. If the state could not set wages and otherwise direct labour, central planning would be meaningless. This is why the emergence in Poland in 1980 of the Solidarity union as an autonomous force was an event of the highest significance. In December 1981, the Polish government declared martial law, which restricted the activities of Solidarity. Then, in October 1982, it banned all unofficial unions and thereby re-established the supremacy of the Communist Party. These moves demonstrated the reluctance of Poland's leaders to accept a relatively autonomous organization in society. Thus the legal recognition of Solidarity in 1989 was a landmark in Poland's gradual rejection of totalitarian rule.

China is now attempting to combine elements of a market economy with the totalitarian apparatus of rule. (On a smaller scale, so is Vietnam.) The initial results of this experiment have been encouraging from the rulers' point of view: production has soared while the Communist Party continues to control the state. However, one may question whether this will be a stable combination in the long run. A rapidly growing market economy will bring about all sorts of challenges to the "totalitarian syndrome," such as ever-increasing exposure to foreign influences; the proliferation of faxes, cell-phones, and e-mail outside state control; and an ethic of individual self-fulfillment and self-expression rather than subordination to the collective good as defined by the state. Such sweeping economic change will probably result in political transformation sooner or later.

CONCLUSION

Totalitarianism makes use of the vastly improved technical apparatus of rule that has become available in this century. Innovations in mass communication make it possible to saturate the population with propaganda to an unprecedented degree. Inventions in weapons and new forms of organization provide a means to coerce people on a much vaster scale. Totalitarianism is in one sense a bigger and better despotism, implemented by the most up-to-date means. But it differs from authoritarianism in the importance it places on ideology and in its single-minded urge to remake society according to a utopian vision. At the heart of all forms of autocracy is the repression of the people of a society.

Questions for Discussion

1. Why do authoritarian systems sometimes have a certain popular appeal?

2. What is the fundamental difference between authoritarian and totalitarian systems?

3. What is the most common way in which authoritarian systems try to build political legitimacy?

Internet Links

1. Hoover Institution, Stanford University: **www.hoover.org.** Famous research institute that has sponsored many studies of totalitarian governments.

2. Internet Guide for Chinese Studies, Institute for Chinese Studies, Heidelberg University: **http://sun.sino.uni-heidelberg.de/igcs.** Gateway to information about the world's largest remaining quasi-totalitarian system.

3. Use *Black Book of Communism* as a search term. This large book, originally published in France in 1997, documents totalitarian atrocities in great detail. Using the title as a search term will lead you to useful reviews and discussions.

Further Reading

AUTHORITARIANISM

Acemoglu, Daron, and James A. Robinson. *Economic Origins of Dictatorship and Democracy.* New York, Cambridge University Press, 2006.

Angell, Alan, and Benny Pollack. *The Legacy of Dictatorship: Political, Economic and Social Change in Pinochet's Chile.* Liverpool, UK: University of Liverpool, Institute of Latin American Studies, 1993.

Boron, Atilio C. *State, Capitalism, and Democracy in Latin America.* Boulder, CO: Lynne Rienner, 1995.

Casper, Gretchen. *Fragile Democracies: The Legacies of Authoritarian Rule.* Pittsburgh: University of Pittsburgh Press, 1995.

————. *Negotiating Democracy: Transitions from Authoritarian Rule.* Pittsburgh: University of Pittsburgh Press, 1996.

Dominguez, Jorge I., ed. *Authoritarian and Democratic Regimes in Latin America.* New York: Garland, 1994.

Germani, Gino. *Authoritarianism, Fascism and National Populism.* New Brunswick, NJ: Transaction Books, 1978.

Hogman, David E. *Neo-Liberalism with a Human Face? The Politics and Economics of the Chilean Model.* Liverpool, UK: University of Liverpool, Institute of Latin American Studies, 1995.

Huntington, Samuel P., and Clement H. Moore, eds. *Authoritarian Politics in Modern Society: The Dynamics of Established One-Party Systems.* New York: Basic Books, 1970.

Jalal, Ayesha. *Democracy and Authoritarianism in South Asia: A Comparative and Historical Perspective.* New York: Cambridge University Press, 1995.

Linz, Juan J., and H. E. Chehabi. *Sultanistic Regimes.* Baltimore: The Johns Hopkins University Press, 1998.

Moore, Barrington, Jr. *Social Origins of Dictatorship and Democracy.* Boston: Beacon Press, 1967.

Nelson, Daniel N., ed. *After Authoritarianism: Democracy or Disorder?* Westport, CT: Greenwood Press, 1995.

Neumann, Frantz. *The Democratic and Authoritarian State.* New York: Free Press, 1964.

Ottaway, Marina. *Democracy Challenged: The Rise of Semi-Authoritarianism.* Washington DC: Carnegie Endowment, 2003.

Roller, Matthew B. *Constructing Autocracy: Aristocrats and Emperors in Julio-Claudian Rome.* Princeton, NJ: Princeton University Press, 2001.

Scott, James C. *Seeing Like a State: How Certain Schemes to Improve the Human Condition Have Failed.* New Haven, CT: Yale University Press, 1999.

Seligman, Adam B. *The Transition from State Socialism in Eastern Europe: The Case of Hungary.* Greenwich, CT: JAI Press, 1994.

Shain, Yossi, with Juan J. Linz. *Between States: Interim Governments and Democratic Transitions.* Cambridge: Cambridge University Press, 1995.

Shapiro, Ian, and Russell Hardin, eds. *Political Order.* New York: New York University Press, 1996.

Wittfogel, Karl A. *Oriental Despotism.* New Haven, CT: Yale University Press, 1967.

TOTALITARIANISM

Arendt, Hannah. *The Origins of Totalitarianism.* Rev. ed. Cleveland: World Publishing, 1958.

Aron, Raymond. *Democracy and Totalitarianism.* New York: Praeger, 1969.

Beilharz, Peter, Gillian Robinson, and John Rundell, eds. *Between Totalitarianism and Postmodernity: A Thesis Eleven Reader.* Cambridge, MA: MIT Press, 1992.

Boesche, Roger. *Theories of Tyranny, From Plato to Arendt.* University Park, PA: Pennsylvania State University, 1996.

Brooker, Paul. *Non-Democratic Regimes: Theory, Government, and Politics.* New York: St. Martin's Press, 2000.

————. *Twentieth-Century Dictatorships: The Ideological One-Party States.* New York: New York University Press, 1995.

Conquest, Robert. *Reflections on a Ravaged Century.* New York: W. W. Norton, 2000.

Curtis, Michael. *Totalitarianism.* New Brunswick, NJ: Transaction Books, 1980.

Friedrich, Carl J., and Zbigniew K. Brzezinski. *Totalitarian Dictatorship and Autocracy.* 2nd ed. New York: Praeger, 1965.

Friedrich, Carl J., Benjamin Barber, and Michael Curtis. *Totalitarianism: Its Changing Theory and Practice.* New York: Praeger, 1969.

Gleason, Abbott. *Totalitarianism: The Inner History of the Cold War.* New York: Oxford University Press, 1995.

Howe, Irving, ed. *1984 Revisited.* New York: Harper and Row, 1983.

Linz, Juan J. *Totalitarian and Authoritarian Regimes,* Boulder, CO: Lynne Rienner, 2000.

Menze, Ernest A. *Totalitarianism Reconsidered.* Port Washington, NY: Kennikat Press, 1980.

O'Kane, Rosemary H. T. *Paths to Democracy: Revolution and Totalitarianism.* New York: Routledge, 2004.

Pauley, Bruce F. *Hitler, Stalin, and Mussolini: Totalitarianism in the Twentieth Century.* Wheeling, IL: Harlan Davidson, 1997.

Rousso, Henry, and Richard Joseph Golsan, eds. *Stalinism and Nazism: History and Memory Compared.* Lincoln, NE: University of Nebraska Press, 2004.

Soper, Steven Paul. *Totalitarianism: A Conceptual Approach.* Lanham, MD: University Press of America, 1985.

Talmon, J. L. *The Origins of Totalitarian Democracy.* New York: W. W. Norton, 1970.

Thurston, Robert W. *Life and Terror in Stalin's Russia, 1934–1941.* New Haven, CT: Yale University Press, 1996.

CHAPTER 20
Parliamentary and Presidential Systems

Of the many possible models for organizing the apparatus of representative government, the two most important are the parliamentary and presidential systems. Both trace their origins to Britain in the seventeenth and eighteenth centuries and are now found everywhere in the world, even in societies that owe relatively little to Anglo-American traditions. They exist in their pure form only in liberal democracies, though many autocratic systems have "borrowed" them to create a veneer of legitimacy.

The difference between the parliamentary and presidential systems can be understood only in the context of **separation of powers,** a doctrine that has a long history in political science. All governments, no matter how they are organized, have to perform certain functions and exercise certain powers. The most common approach is to divide these powers into three categories: legislative, executive, and judicial. The **legislative** power makes general laws of conduct for members of the community and establishes policies such as health care and education. Included are matters of both **private law** (such as rules about property, contracts, and marriage) and **public law** (such as rules governing voting, military service, and payment of taxes). The **executive** power does not make general rules but proposes policies and administers the state's resources. For example, the executive commands the army (which was created by the legislative power), oversees the monetary system, and raises and spends taxes that the legislative power has authorized. This entails making many discretionary decisions, such as where to locate post offices and military bases. The executive power enforces the rules of conduct by administering police forces and prisons to ensure that laws are obeyed. The *judicial* power, or **judiciary,** resolves conflicts that arise when laws are not obeyed or when there is disagreement over what the law means.

Early liberal thinkers such as John Locke argued that these powers of state should be distributed among different hands rather than concentrated in one institution, because dispersion lessens the temptation to use power arbitrarily: "In all moderated monarchies and well-framed governments," wrote Locke, "the legislative and executive power are in distinct hands."[1] In its simple form, this view tends to equate each power with one branch of government, which specializes in it. In *The Spirit of the Laws* (1748), Montesquieu analyzed British government in this way. He wrote that Parliament constituted the legislative branch, the monarch and ministers the executive branch, and the courts the judicial branch. The separation of powers into distinct branches of government was, in Montesquieu's opinion, the secret of the excellence of the British constitution, which made Britain the freest and most enviable country in Europe. Soon after, the doctrine of separation of powers became an integral part of liberal thinking, providing a structural and legal way of limiting the power of government.

Although certainly true in part, Montesquieu's analysis was too simple. He overlooked the fact that the courts had a large share of legislative power to the extent that the common law evolved through their decisions. This was not deliberate making of law (which was Parliament's function), but it was equally significant as a source of rules of conduct. Even more importantly, Montesquieu did not fully appreciate the custom—increasingly observed since the Glorious Revolution—that ministers of the Crown had to be members of parliament, in either the Commons or the Lords. The executive and legislative branches were more closely connected than Montesquieu thought.

Since the publication of *The Spirit of the Laws,* British-style representative government has evolved in two different directions. In the United States, where Montesquieu's philosophical authority was very great at the time of the constitutional convention, the Americans retained institutions modelled on those of Britain, but the division between the president and Congress was made sharper than the one between the Crown and Parliament. This American model is the source of most contemporary presidential systems, in which the separation of powers is still maintained. In Britain, however, and in colonies such as Canada that stayed within the Empire, political evolution has brought the legislative and executive branches closer together. In modern parliamentary systems, the executive (cabinet) and the legislature work closely together because of the practice of political party discipline. We will discuss the parliamentary system first and then return to the presidential model.

THE PARLIAMENTARY SYSTEM

After the Norman Conquest, all three powers of government were united in the monarchy. The king was the "font of justice" and the supreme military commander and could also legislate by royal proclamation. Parliament, which was first convened by Edward I in 1295, was originally not a legislative body at all. Its major functions were to advise the monarch and to approve the taxes necessary to support government. Over time, Parliament increased its power by refusing to grant revenue unless the monarch fulfilled its desires, which were drawn up in "bills," or lists of requests. This ancient practice is the reason why a statute under consideration by Parliament is known today as a **bill.** Another reminder of this early period is that all legislation is still proclaimed by the monarch "with the advice and consent" of Parliament. Though Parliament long ago captured the legislative power, this verbal formula shows that it once belonged to the Crown.

The Glorious Revolution brought about a separation of powers that had until then been united. Parliament made itself a legislative body and also created an independent judiciary by forcing the Crown, which appointed judges, to respect the tenure of those judges. But the settlement of 1689, although it made Parliament supreme, still left the monarch with considerable prerogative powers. The King or Queen remained a true chief executive, with the discretionary right to appoint and dismiss officials, declare war, conduct foreign relations, command the armed forces, pardon convicted criminals, and (as a remnant of lost legislative power) withhold assent to legislation.

Further political evolution reunited the legislative and executive powers under the control of a new executive: the prime minister and cabinet. At first this trend seemed to be a further victory of Parliament over the Crown, as the custom grew that ministers had to be members of parliament and had to have the political support of a working majority in the House of Commons. This mechanism of **responsible government** meant that the Crown could act only on the advice of those who had the confidence of Parliament. Parliament, by the middle of the nineteenth century, appeared to have captured the executive power as it had previously captured the legislative. But before long, the new practice of **party discipline** made it clear that the cabinet, led by the prime minister, was the real victor. As long as the supporters of the prime minister in the House of Commons vote as directed, the executive and legislative powers are fused, and separation of powers no longer acts as a check. The check in a parliamentary system comes when the prime minister loses majority support and the opposition can withdraw confidence from the government.

The Westminster Model

The political machinery of the British parliamentary system, referred to as the Westminster model, consists of the Crown, the Cabinet, the House of Commons, and the House of Lords. The Crown requests the leader of the majority party, if there is one, to form a government, which consists of cabinet ministers sitting in either house; they govern as long as they are not defeated in the House of Commons. If no party holds a majority of seats and there is no formal coalition of parties to create a majority, a party leader with a large bloc of seats will be asked to form a government. Such a situation is referred to as a minority government, and this government is entitled to govern as long as a majority in the Commons supports it, or at least does not defeat it.

Parliament is a bicameral institution consisting of the House of Commons and the House of Lords. The Commons is structured in a pyramidal fashion. The prime minister, who is leader of the majority party, was originally thought to be ***primus inter pares***—"first among equals." Now, however, he or she is much more: the first minister of Cabinet, the party leader, and the leader of government. Cabinet ministers of the governing party manage the legislative process with some cooperation from opposition parties. Those who do not belong to the Cabinet are referred to as **private members,** whether they sit on the side of the government or in the opposition. They are the rank and file: the elected parliamentary members who are not part of the governing party's leadership. Their influence is not substantial. While they may introduce **private members' bills,** few of these bills are ever passed by Parliament. There are 646 members of the British House of Commons: 529 English constituencies, 40 Welsh, 59 Scottish, and 18 from Northern Ireland.

The House of Lords began as a largely hereditary body of more than 1,000 members, but recent reforms have reduced that number. Of the 746 members today, 628 are life peers—distinguished men and women appointed by the Crown on the recommendation of the prime minister, who in turn is advised by an appointments commission. There are also 26 archbishops and bishops of the Church of England, plus 92 hereditary peers. The powers of the two houses of Parliament were originally equal, but since the Parliament Acts of 1911 and 1949 were passed, the Lords have become subservient to the Commons. They may initiate and amend legislation but cannot veto acts of the Commons and can only delay bills for approximately one year. As of 2008, the government is seriously considering reforms for the Lords. The issues include the power of the House as well as what percentage of its members is to be elected. One proposal is to have 80 percent elected and 20 percent appointed.

With all of these changes, the parliamentary system today has become what some observers refer to as *prime-ministerial government;* for no one—not the monarch, not private members in the Commons, not members of the House of Lords—is as powerful as the prime minister, supported by the cabinet whose members he or she chooses.

Canada was one of the first colonies in modern history to peacefully attain independence from a colonial power. Its Parliament developed within the British tradition. Before 1867, colonial governors representing the Crown existed alongside locally elected legislatures. The Constitution Act, 1867, finally implemented one recommendation from Lord Durham's report of 1839. Durham had been appointed governor in 1838 to reform the colonial system so as to prevent further rebellions like the ones of 1837. He called for the eventual union of the colonies of Upper and Lower Canada, Nova Scotia, and New Brunswick, based on the assumption that a larger polity would be better able to assimilate the restive French-Canadian population.

At the national or federal level, one Parliament was created for all the colonies in 1867. This institution, like the British Parliament, was a bicameral legislature containing two houses, the Senate (which now has 105 seats) being the upper house and the Commons (which now has 308 members) being the lower one. Canada is a federal system; otherwise, the Canadian Parliament operates in principle like the British. The British monarch is our **head of state.** The Crown's representative in Canada is the governor general, who is appointed by the monarch on the advice of the prime minister of Canada. Lieutenant governors, who are appointed by the governor general (also on the advice of the prime minister), play the role of head of state in provincial governments. The Queen, governor general, and lieutenant governors together represent the Crown in Canada. The prime minister and the provincial premiers are the **heads of government.**

The heads of state normally do not exercise actual political power; they "reign rather than rule." Most functions of a head of state are symbolic in nature. The duties include selecting or dismissing a head of government; performing certain ceremonial functions—for example, greeting foreign dignitaries; assenting to and proclaiming legislation; formally appointing judges and other public officials; dissolving Parliament and calling elections; and exercising certain emergency powers if and when there is a leadership crisis or when government is deadlocked. In normal circumstances, the representative of the Crown carries out these functions without making real prerogative choices. The monarch or governor general must take the advice of the cabinet as long as there is a government in office. No executive action is taken without the signature of one or more ministers. Even in selecting a new government, the head of state normally has no real choice, because the person to become head of government has already been determined by the voters.

By constitutional convention, the leader of the political party with a majority of seats in the House of Commons is asked by the governor general to form the government of Canada. The prime minister then nominates the rest of the cabinet for appointment by the governor general. If there is no single party with a majority of seats, the party leader with the largest plurality of seats or which has received sufficient indications of support from other parties is asked to form a government.

In 2004 Paul Martin's Liberals carried on as the government even though they won only 135 seats in the election of June 28. They did not have the 155 seats needed for a clear majority, but they had more seats than any other party and a hope of being able to get support from other parties on specific measures. In short, they were entitled to form a government as long as they could keep the **confidence** of the House; that is, as long as they could continue to win votes in the House. The election of January 23, 2006 again yielded a minority result, this time in favour of the Conservatives, who won 124 seats compared to 103 for the Liberals. Thus, Paul Martin resigned as prime minister and Conservative leader Stephen Harper was invited to form a government. After the election on October 14, 2008, the Conservatives won 143 seats, Liberals 77 seats, and again Stephen Harper formed a minority government.

An interesting development occurred in Ontario in 1985. The Conservatives, who had been in power since 1943, won only 52 of the 124 seats in the provincial legislature in the April election. The Liberals won 47 seats and the New Democrats 25. Conservative premier Frank Miller continued to govern until June, when he was defeated in the legislature by the Liberal and NDP opposition on a non-confidence motion. David Peterson, leader of the Liberals, then formed a government supported by the NDP. It was not a coalition, because no ministerial positions were allocated to the NDP. Rather, the two parties signed an "accord," a written agreement that for two years the Liberals would not call an election and the NDP would not defeat the government on a non-confidence motion. There is a long history in Canada of informal understandings being reached for the purpose of supporting a minority government, but this was the first formal, written agreement. In 1999, the NDP and Liberals in Saskatchewan signed another formal agreement in order to create a coalition government.

The Crown

The constitution almost always dictates the actions of the Crown. In rare circumstances, there might not be a constitutionally clear course of action—for example, if a prime minister were to unexpectedly die in office and the party had not agreed on a successor. Then the head of state might have to use discretion in asking someone to form an interim government until the majority party could sort out its affairs. In general, the Crown acts unilaterally only if a crisis immobilizes responsible political institutions. In times of emergency, there is a role to be played by the head of state; this has been one of the principal arguments made by those who favour retaining the Crown as an integral part of Canadian government.[2]

A case in point was the course of action taken following the crisis that provoked the American intervention in Grenada in October 1983. Prime Minister Maurice Bishop had seized power in 1979, backed by the New Jewel Movement, which initially enjoyed a great deal of popular support on the island. In October 1983 Bernard Coard, an official in the Bishop government, staged a *coup d'état*. Bishop was ousted and later shot by forces supporting Coard. The United States then intervened militarily at the request of several neighbouring islands. With the prime minister dead and Coard in custody, Governor General Sir Paul Scoon assumed responsibility for governing the island and scheduled national elections for 1984. Thus the head of state governed until the people had an opportunity to choose new leaders to form a government.

The House of Commons

The second major component of the parliamentary system is the House of Commons. The House is to the machinery of government what an engine is to an automobile. The government of the day is formed mostly from the House. The leader of the majority party, or of a party that has a working majority, becomes prime minister and chooses ministers from among members of the House or the Senate. Technically, a prime minister may choose an individual who is not a member of either house to become a member of the cabinet, but the practice is rare, and when it is followed that person is expected to obtain a seat in the House or the Senate within a matter of months. Under modern practice, almost all cabinet members come from the House of Commons, with only one or two senators. Cabinet ministers, supported by members of their party, have legitimate and legal powers to govern as long as they can command the confidence of the House.

The Senate

The third component of the Canadian parliamentary system is the Senate. Under the Constitution Act, 1867, the passage of legislation requires the approval not only of the House of Commons but also of the Senate. The Senate has exactly the same legislative power as the House of Commons except that bills involving taxes or expenditures must originate in the House.[3] The Senate, however, is not a confidence chamber. When it rejects a bill from the Commons, the government does not have to resign.

It was long thought that the Senate had faded into insignificance in the Canadian parliamentary system, but events since 1984 have forced observers to modify that view. During the Mulroney years, the large Liberal majority in the Senate repeatedly obstructed the plans of the Conservative government. By refusing to pass legislation until it was amended, the Senate forced several important bills to be changed. The Senate's refusal to pass legislation to implement the Free Trade Agreement in the fall of 1988 led Prime Minister Mulroney to request a dissolution of Parliament and an election—an election that turned into a virtual referendum on free trade. After the Conservatives won the election, the Senate passed the free-trade legislation, even though it still had the constitutional right to reject it.

Senators are chosen by personal decision of the prime minister, and this method of appointment tends to produce a Senate dominated by the opposition party when, as in 1984, power shifts in the House of Commons after one party has been in power for a long period of time. Because the Liberals had been in power almost continuously from 1935 to 1984, Liberal prime ministers had chosen almost all those sitting in the Senate by the time Brian Mulroney became prime minister. Since senators serve until the age of 75, Mulroney had no standard means available to install a Conservative majority in the upper house. In 1989, in order to ensure passage of the GST legislation, which the Liberals were blocking in the Senate, he resorted to an obscure provision of the Constitution that allows the governor general, with the prior approval of the queen, to appoint eight extra senators.[4]

The shoe was on the other foot when the Liberals returned to power in 1993. Prime Minister Chrétien at the time had to deal with a holdover Conservative majority in the Senate, which succeeded in blocking several pieces of Liberal legislation. By 1996, however, Chrétien had restored the Liberal majority in the Senate by appointing a Liberal every time a vacancy occurred.

Because the Conservative Party of Canada advocates election of senators, Prime Minister Stephen Harper has appointed only two senators since coming to power in 2006—Michael Fortier (temporarily), so that someone from Montreal could be in the cabinet; and Bert Brown, who had previously been chosen by an advisory election in Alberta. By refusing to make appointments, Mr. Harper is trying to gain support for the idea of electing senators, but it is not clear how long this moratorium on appointments can last. Given the scheduled pace of senatorial retirements, it will not take long years before the remaining members of the Senate will find it difficult to carry out responsibilities such as committee work.

Canada's difficulties with the Senate are unique because it is a centrally appointed upper house in a federal system of government, but other parliamentary systems have also experienced problems with an upper house. In 1975, Australia's House of Representatives passed a money bill that the Senate refused to approve. The conflict evolved into a fiscal and constitutional crisis. The government would not budge, nor would the Senate, which is popularly elected in Australia. Finally, the governor general dismissed the prime minister, dissolved both houses, and issued the writs for a new election. The prime minister was furious and accused the governor general of overstepping his powers and precipitating a constitutional crisis by permitting the upper house to bring down the government. The election that followed resolved the political issue with the defeat of the government, which vindicated the governor general to some degree.

There is general agreement that an upper house with equal power can obstruct the legislative proceedings of a parliament. There is little agreement, however, on the validity of such obstruction. Advocates of unicameralism argue that the final say on bills should rest with a single house in which representation is based on population. They see obstruction by another house as a violation of parliamentary principles. Many advocates of bicameralism in Canada, supporting the principal of separation of powers, reply to this that an elected second house, with representation based on regions, should be able to veto the bills of a lower house. They claim their argument is underscored when representation in the lower house may reflect a majority of the population concentrated in a single region, which then controls a majority of seats in the legislature. This is the argument Western Canadians often make for a "triple-E" Senate: an elected, equal, and effective Senate would safeguard regional interests.

Fusion of Powers

To understand how Parliament actually runs, one must understand the fusion of powers between the executive and the legislature. As Figure 20.1 indicates, the prime minister cannot function without support in the House of Commons, and ultimately it is the electorate that provides this support by determining the balance of partisan power in the House of Commons. Three election outcomes are possible. One party may win a majority of seats in the House, in which case its leader will form a **majority**

Figure 20.1 The Canadian Parliamentary System

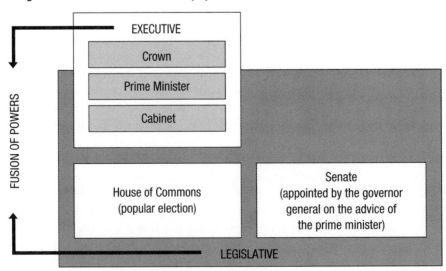

government. If no party wins a majority, the leader of one party—usually but not necessarily the party with the largest number of seats—can form a **minority government.** Such a minority government can stay in office only if the other parties refrain from defeating it. Finally, two or more parties may join forces to form a **coalition government,** dividing ministerial appointments between them. The leader of the larger partner in the coalition normally becomes prime minister.

There has never been a true coalition government at the national level in Canada. The "Union Government" that ruled during World War I under Robert Borden consisted of breakaway Liberals who joined with the Conservatives; it was not a genuine coalition of the two parties. However, there have been a number of coalitions at the provincial level, including most recently an NDP–Liberal coalition in Saskatchewan (1999–2003).

Cabinet and the Legislative Process

In forming the federal cabinet, the prime minister chooses the other ministers from MPs in his or her political party, who are then officially appointed by the governor general. The governor general would also dismiss them on the advice of the prime minister, although the usual course is for the prime minister to request and receive a resignation from a minister whose presence is no longer desired in the cabinet. The prime minister and the cabinet ministers, along with the Crown, form the political executive. Including Prime Minister Harper, the cabinet in 2008 consisted of 27 ministers, plus eleven junior ministers who do not attend meetings of the full cabinet but may serve on cabinet committees.

The cabinet determines legislative priorities and sets the legislative agenda. Cabinet ministers initiate almost all legislative proposals, using the civil service as a primary source of information and ideas. The cabinet has aptly been called "a combining committee—a hyphen which joins, a buckle which fastens, the legislative part of the state to the executive part."[5] It is the institution that most clearly distinguishes the modern parliamentary system from the presidential form of government. It is a collective decision-making body, but dominated by the prime minister (see Canadian Focus 20.1). After extensive discussion, the prime minister usually summarizes the arguments and announces the action to be taken. Once a course is set, the principle of **cabinet solidarity** prevents ministers from differing with government policy in public, whatever their private reservations.

Private members' bills, which are introduced by members of parliament who are not ministers, may be numerous but are seldom passed. Significant legislation is almost invariably initiated by cabinet ministers. The prime minister, the cabinet, and the leaders of the opposition parties, together with their chief advisers, are the dominant figures in the parliamentary process. However, various changes in the rules of procedure of the House of Commons adopted since 1986 have eased the way for private members' bills, and more are now passing than used to be the case.

Canadian Focus 20.1

How Cabinet Worked under Prime Minister Jean Chrétien

"He [Chrétien] was comfortable knowing that Cabinet decisions are the sole prerogative of the prime minister; there are no votes taken in Cabinet, and decisions aren't dependent on the number of ministers who have spoken on one side or an issue or another. As soon as discussion ended on an issue, he usually called his decision and moved onto the next item. Occasionally, where there was no apparent consensus and where he had no strong views, Chrétien would take an issue under advisement and would decide at a later date."

Source: Eddie Goldenberg, *The Way It Works: Inside Ottawa* (Toronto: McClelland & Stewart, 2006), p. 99.

The House functions within strict procedures and rules that are observed most of the time by all parties and enforced by a Speaker who is elected by the House. Until recently, it was customary for the prime minister to nominate the Speaker, and party discipline turned the election into a foregone conclusion. Now, however, the Speaker is chosen by free election, without prime-ministerial nomination and party discipline.[6] In Great Britain the Speaker becomes an impartial figure who completely withdraws from party affiliations, runs unopposed for re-election, and serves as Speaker until retirement from the House. In Canada the Speaker is also supposed to conduct the affairs of the House impartially, but the divorce from partisan politics is not so complete. The opposition parties generally field candidates in the Speaker's constituency at election time, and a Speaker is selected each time a new Parliament convenes.

A proposed bill must go through three **readings** in both chambers. At the first reading, the bill's title is introduced; the text of the proposed legislation is then printed and distributed to members. After the second reading, there is a full debate on the bill, with the opposition and government backbenchers having a specified time to address different aspects of it. It may then go to a standing committee—or, more commonly, to a special legislative committee of the House. **Standing committees** are permanent committees appointed to study particular areas of public policy; their membership is proportional to party strength in the House. Examples include committees on finance, health, and citizenship and immigration. **Special (or ad hoc) committees** are established to deal with specific problems and are dissolved when their assignment is finished.

Backbenchers become involved in the legislative process by serving on parliamentary committees. Their power is very limited in a majority Parliament because the government party will have a majority on all committees and bloc voting will prevail. But in a minority Parliament, opposition members will outnumber government members on committees and may use their voting power to harass and frustrate the government. Committees sometimes produce amendments to government bills, but they do not reject them altogether. The bill then goes through the **report stage,** at which time the House receives the committee report and votes on any proposed amendments.

The bill as amended is then received and voted on by the House in the third reading; no amendment is allowed at this final stage. The bill is then introduced in the Senate, whose deliberations also may involve committee action. The Senate may suggest changes and send its version of the bill back to the House. Occasionally, the Senate tries to block legislation coming from the House, as described above, but more frequently it functions as a source of technical amendments. It may even finish considering a bill before the Commons does. When this happens, its suggested amendments may be incorporated by the Commons at third reading.

A bill passed by the Commons and the Senate then goes to the governor general for **royal assent** and **proclamation.** *Royal assent* means that the governor general approves the bill; *proclamation* involves setting the date on which the new law will take effect. There is generally a period of weeks or months—sometimes even years—between royal assent and proclamation.

Throughout the legislative process, the **opposition** parties (i.e., those parties that do not share ministerial appointments) criticize the government and sometimes win concessions from it even if they do not have the voting strength to make their views prevail. The government may feel that points raised by the opposition have merit or public support, or it may yield in order to avoid obstructive or disruptive behaviour.

The seats in the Canadian House of Commons, following the British model, are placed on two sides of a central aisle in order to emphasize the difference between government and opposition.
The Canadian Press (Fred Chartrand)

In Canada and Britain, the largest of the opposition parties is singled out as the **Official Opposition** (or simply the Opposition). Such status entitles the party to preferential funding and certain privileges during debate. The leader of the Opposition assigns various party members to follow the activities of one or more cabinet ministers with particular attention. For example, there will be an agriculture critic among the Opposition to watch the minister of agriculture. In Britain, the leader of the Opposition and these specialist critics form a cohesive group known as a **shadow cabinet,** ready to assume office if invited to do so by the head of state; but Canadian Opposition parties have not always had this degree of organization. Indeed, it is inconceivable that the Bloc Québécois, which formed the Official Opposition from 1993 to 1997, would ever have been invited to form the government of Canada.

Confidence, Party Discipline, and Responsible Government

In the parliamentary process, the lifeblood of the government is party loyalty. For its tenure, the government depends not just on the support of the electorate at election time but also on its ability to maintain a majority on the floor of the House of Commons. In other words, the exercise of power hinges on the government's ability to maintain the **confidence** of the House. The idea of confidence is rooted in the principle of responsible government, which makes the cabinet responsible to the House of Commons. Every legislative proposal made by the government must go to the floor of the House. As long as these proposals are supported by a majority of those voting, the government enjoys the confidence of the House and is ruling "responsibly."

Note that the term **responsible government** (meaning that the cabinet must enjoy the continued support of the popularly elected house of the legislative assembly in order to remain in office) is a concept associated with parliamentary government. It is an essential aspect of the parliamentary form of representative democracy, but not of representative democracy in general. In the governments of Switzerland and the United States, the cabinet does not need legislative support to remain in power; but these governments are just as democratic as parliamentary ones because they are equally responsible or accountable to the people through elections. This broader sort of accountability should not be confused with the precise form of responsible government that characterizes the parliamentary system.

Budgetary bills are always treated as confidence motions, but beyond that the prime minister is free to decide whether any legislation or other motion should be a matter of confidence. Typically, a majority government will treat all votes as confidence votes, but a prime minister in a minority situation will often declare that legislation (except the budget) is not a matter of confidence, meaning that his government does not need to resign or ask for an election even if its legislation does not pass.

The necessity of maintaining a majority has led to the strengthening of party discipline in all parliamentary systems. A member's loyalty to the party may take precedence over personal views or loyalty to constituents. A member who does not support the party position on the floor of the House or in committee can be punished in various ways; for example, travel opportunities or choice committee assignments may be denied. At the extreme, a recalcitrant member may even be expelled from caucus, and the party may deny that individual the right to run in the next election under the party label. However, the role of coercion should not be overestimated. Caucus members vote together most of the time more or less voluntarily for three reasons: they want to remain in the good graces of the party's leadership; they would like to benefit from political patronage; and they see themselves as part of a team, and understand that the parliamentary system of responsible government will not work unless parties exhibit some coherence. Contemporary Canadian practice allows members of parliament to deviate from the party line occasionally but not too often, especially if it might unseat the government.

One other variation should be noted. Occasionally the government may allow a **free vote** on certain bills that are of a controversial nature. In this situation, all members of the caucus do not have to vote with the party; they are free to "vote their conscience." The Mulroney government held free votes on the morally supercharged issues of capital punishment and abortion, the Chrétien government allowed free votes on religious educational rights in Newfoundland and Labrador and Quebec, and the Martin and Harper governments both held free votes on same-sex marriage.

Party Caucus

Critics of the parliamentary system often complain that members do not have the freedom to vote either their conscience or the will of their constituents. This is true if party discipline is effective, but it does not necessarily mean that **backbenchers**— those who are not in the cabinet or the shadow cabinet and who therefore sit on the rear benches in the House—have no influence on their party leadership. One primary function of the party **caucus** is to give party members an opportunity to be heard by their leaders. A party caucus is a closed meeting of the members of a parliamentary party in the House and Senate. Every party in Parliament has a caucus. At caucus meetings, backbenchers can question their own leaders and suggest alternatives to the party's policies. During these meetings, MPs within a party can argue policy with each other and the leadership can test the pulse of the backbenchers on particular proposals. Party leaders know that the support of backbenchers is required to maintain a majority position and they must therefore take into account the nature and strength of backbench opinion. In caucus meetings an attempt is made to arrive at a consensus on issues. Unanimity seldom exists, so these meetings can be raucous affairs. However, once a given issue is settled and goes to the House, all members are expected to support the government's position. The backbenchers of a majority party can bring down a government by failing to support their own leaders. Although this rarely happens, it does mean that the government's own party can provide an important check on political power.

A second check on government is the activity of the opposition parties. The development of an institutionalized practice of loyal opposition in which one can legally challenge the government without fear of repression is one of the significant achievements of liberal democracy. The rationale for an opposition is the liberal view that everyone has limited knowledge and that no government or governor is infallible. The mighty also make mistakes, and there should always be an opportunity to air them in public.

The essence of the parliamentary process is the formal duel between the government and those forces unable to muster sufficient legislative seats to form a government. This opposition has three basic functions: to offer an alternative government, to offer alternative policies, and to question and call attention to controversial legislative proposals or government actions of any kind. If the opposition is a minority, it cannot by itself defeat the government; it does, however, have important opportunities to object to legislation to which it is opposed and to delay and obstruct legislative proposals it wants altered. Time is limited in the House, and parliamentary procedures protect the role of the opposition. Proceedings can be immobilized until the opposition and government come to a compromise agreement. A government that tries to run roughshod over the opposition parties may succeed in passing a particular piece of legislation, but may well find other aspects of its program jeopardized by delaying tactics.

A final check on the government is the electorate. At least every five years, voters have the opportunity to pass judgment on the record of the party in power. This serves to remind us of the liberal–democratic principle that political power emanates from the people and rests upon the consent of the governed. Ideally, the check exercised by elections ensures that government legislation is responsive to the needs of the people. However, in the liberal tradition, there is an unwillingness to assume that governments will automatically act in the best interests of their citizens. So checks also come into play when an unresponsive system needs prodding.

In times of minority government, such as ensued after the elections of 2004, 2006, and 2008, the government's power to control the House of Commons is considerably reduced. See the description in Canadian Focus 20.2.

Variations on the Westminster Model

We have used the British and Canadian examples in describing the parliamentary system of government. While there are a number of structural differences between our process and Britain's (federalism, for instance), both systems exemplify the Westminster

Canadian Focus 20.2

Majority vs. Minority Government

The first critical change in a transition from a majority government to a minority is the centrality of Parliament itself. [Prime Minister Paul] Martin has made much of the "democratic deficit" and the need to restore the influence of backbench members. Nothing will erase the democratic deficit faster than the election of a minority Parliament. The House of Commons becomes king— power slips away from the executive toward the legislature. In a majority government, Parliament is like a production line. How many bills can we get through, how do we organize the committees, what information should we provide to MPs, how can the requirements of Parliament be balanced against all the other tasks of government, etc.? The demands of the executive almost always win out over the needs of the House.

Not so in a minority Parliament. Policy actually gets made on the floor of the Commons. The House leader and the chief whip, not the minister of Finance or the minister of Foreign Affairs, become the critical colleagues of the prime minister. The whole focus of Ottawa shifts from quiet discussions between deputy ministers to the public and noisy negotiations between politicians in the cockpit of Parliament.

Source: Thomas S. Axworthy, "Is There an Angel to Ride the Ottawa Whirlwind?" *Policy Options* 25 (September 2004), pp. 23–24.

model. In other countries, that basic model has been modified to meet the needs of different political environments. The parliamentary process can easily result in minority government; and without a majority, governments may change frequently, the result being political instability.

Under the Weimar constitution of 1919, Germany had something close to the Westminster model of parliamentary government. But representation in the legislative body was badly fragmented among a number of political factions so that no political party commanded a majority. Weak coalition governments, many of them dependent on the support of extremist or splinter parties, proved unable to deal effectively with political crises. The system found itself unable to combat the economic crash of 1929, with the result that Hitler established the Third Reich in 1933.

After World War II, the Germans modified the parliamentary system in order to deal with the problem of instability. The constitution of the Federal Republic of Germany, known as the Basic Law, was adopted in 1949. Those who drafted the document instituted a positive or **constructive vote of confidence.** The chancellor, or prime minister, is the leader of the majority party, or a coalition of parties making up a majority, in the *Bundestag* (the lower house of Parliament). The government can be defeated on a non-confidence vote in the *Bundestag;* however, the vote defeats the government only if the chancellor's successor is chosen at the same time. In other words, a majority in the *Bundestag* can bring down the government, but not until that majority approves another government. This breaks with the British and Canadian custom of holding an election or forming a new government after defeat on a matter of confidence.

Israel has found yet another way of coping with cabinet instability. Because that country uses a pure form of proportional representation (see Chapter 25), there are so many political parties that all governments have to be coalitions. Israeli governments take coalitions as a fact of life and treat cabinets almost as if they were legislatures. Cabinet secrecy has been abandoned, as has cabinet solidarity; formal votes are taken in cabinet on important issues, and the results are announced to the public. The result is that, having made their opposition to a policy known, coalition partners do not necessarily feel obliged to break up the coalition. Thus, coalitions can survive tensions that would destroy cabinets operating on the Westminster model, and political instability can be avoided despite the proliferation of parties. From 1992 to 2003, in a further attempt to avoid executive instability, Israel adopted a unique procedure for direct popular election of the prime minister. Under this system, Ariel Sharon was named prime minister in a popular election held in early 2001, while the other members of the Knesset (legislature) remained in place. Sharon then had to build a coalition with existing party groups in the Knesset in order to form a cabinet. The innovation, however, was widely considered a failure, and in 2003 Israel abolished the separate election of a prime minister.

Different modifications have been made in other parliamentary systems, adapting the process to societal needs in different nation-states. However, the basic principle of these systems remains responsible government. A government is not entitled to govern unless it commands a working majority of the seats in the elected portion of the legislature. Regardless of the way in which the machinery is adjusted, this principle remains essential to the parliamentary apparatus.

Assessing Parliamentary Systems

Critics often argue that the problem with the parliamentary process is that the executive has become too powerful. In using strong party discipline, the executive has created an imbalance in the legislative process. As the dominant institution in the legislative process, the executive is denying other members of parliament their role as representatives of the people. Some analysts would go so far as to say now we have prime-ministerial government. With reference to executive federalism (i.e., federal politics monopolized by first ministers), Stephen Brooks suggests that "it is a process from which legislatures are almost entirely excluded, except when called upon to ratify an agreement reached between executives of the two levels of government."[7]

And, in regard to the policymaking process of the federal government, he says:

> The popular identification of "government" with the individual who occupies the position of prime minister and his team of cabinet colleagues entails an accurate assessment of where the centre of power lies in the state system. In parliamentary systems as different as those of Canada, Belgium, and France the political executive is that part of the state system best able to shape the direction of public policy.[8]

When the executive initiates party policy and caucus members are expected to support it, the executive has become in effect an almost autonomous force at the expense of the legislature.

This is certainly how most of the electorate perceives the process. The cabinet is seen as being cloistered in Ottawa together with top bureaucrats, making public policy for the country with little regard for alternative proposals. Backbenchers are expected to support the party's objectives regardless of the feelings of their constituents. Elected MPs not in the inner circles of government do not have the opportunity to advocate the views of their constituents; they are expected to toe the party line. Such perceptions may not be altogether true, but they exist and have led to a great deal of frustration in the electorate. Many voters are claiming that their representatives have been stifled by party discipline and are calling for reforms of parliament. Some have become supporters of anti-establishment political parties.

All of this highlights one of the paradoxes of the parliamentary system. With a strong majority in the House of Commons, the leadership of a political party can override the petty bickering and the powerful special interests that attempt to thwart the interest of the entire nation. In short, a government with a substantial majority in a parliamentary system represents an extremely powerful liberal–democratic government. If, however, the governing majority pursues its own legislative agenda without regard for popular feeling, a large portion of the public may come to feel alienated from the process of government; and, if the government continues on its course, voters may shift to the opposition or to minor parties that they feel represent their interest.

In the system there is thus a need to balance the roles of the legislature and the executive. The executive must not operate as an autonomous force, and there must be a way to involve backbenchers—and the public for that matter—in the process of formulating policy. The question is, how can this be accomplished without rendering the legislative process impotent? How can the process be made more open to differing points of view without bringing it to a grinding halt?

If party discipline does in fact undermine representation, there are ways to relax that discipline, such as increasing the number of free votes, or permitting party members to oppose the government on votes. The result might well be a more open debate on issues within the governing party itself. A reduction of party discipline might also show the electorate that backbenchers are not just puppets of the leadership; the party's rank and file would in fact have an opportunity to more openly represent constituents. Yet too much autonomy of the legislature could lead to gridlock, as is sometimes the case in the presidential system.

THE PRESIDENTIAL SYSTEM

The presidential system of government was first devised in the United States, as an alternative to the monarchical system. It is chiefly used today in areas of the world where American influence has been particularly strong, as in Latin America and the Philippines. In some cases, it may simply be a guise for an autocratic dictatorship. Nevertheless, the basic model is distinctive; the principle of separation of powers and the lack of responsible government set it apart from the parliamentary system.

After 1776, the new United States reacted to their experience of a strong British executive by granting an extraordinary amount of political power to the legislative body. This was logical, given their suspicion of strong government as exercised by the British Crown. They felt that the danger of abuse could be minimized if governors were elected and periodically held responsible to the people. These sentiments were demonstrated in the adoption of the first constitution for the new republic—the Articles of Confederation of 1781, which almost eliminated the executive. The legislatures of the several states were supreme. In time, however, it was realized that an executive to supervise the work of government was essential. The fault was corrected with the adoption of the Constitution in 1789. A president was made the chief executive officer of the government, answerable to the legislative branch in certain respects, but not dependent on it for continuation in office.

While the parliamentary system is known for the fusion of powers and for cabinet government, the presidential system is known for the separation of powers and for the congressional committee system. The executive branch, although instrumental in the legislative process, is physically separated from the legislative branch. While the separation is real (each branch has veto powers), cooperation is required to pass legislation. In this system of government, the committees of both houses of Congress dominate the legislative process. Figure 20.2 depicts the presidential system of the United States.

Figure 20.2 The United States Presidential System

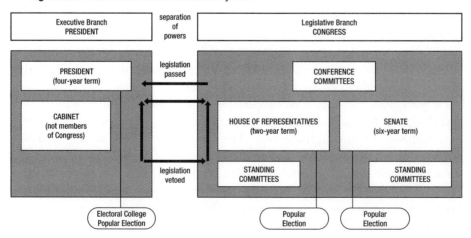

Figure 20.3 Balance of Powers in the American Presidential System

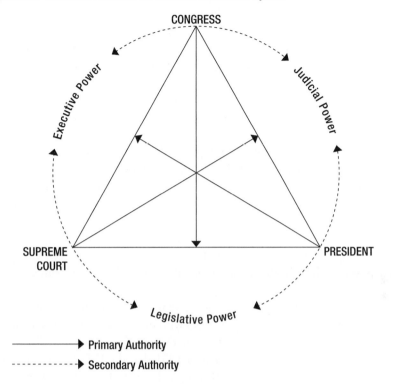

The customary term used to describe the presidential system—separation of powers—is somewhat misleading. James Madison, the chief draftsman of the American Constitution, explicitly criticized the oversimplified view that the legislative, executive, and judicial powers of government ought to be absolutely separated among the distinct institutions or branches of government. In No. 47 of *The Federalist,* a series of essays he wrote with Alexander Hamilton and John Jay to persuade the American public to ratify the new constitution, Madison outlined the ideal of placing each power in the custody of a branch of government primarily concerned with it, while allowing the other two branches a secondary role in exercising it. This delicate balance of institutions would diminish arbitrary government by preventing unilateral actions. Neither the president, nor Congress, nor the courts would be able to follow a course of action for very long without the cooperation of the other branches. A modern scholar has suggested that "separated institutions sharing powers" is a more apt description of the Madisonian system than "separation of powers."[9] Figure 20.3 illustrates this complex balance.

The President

The president, the only elected official on the ballot throughout the nation, is elected for a four-year term and is both head of state and head of government. As head of state, the president greets foreign dignitaries and performs other ceremonial functions. As head of government, the president is the chief executive officer. The constitution grants the president powers that are, on the whole, rather similar to the ancient prerogative powers of the British Crown. In Britain, these are now wielded by the prime minister with relatively little interference by Parliament as long as party discipline holds; in the United States, the president's powers are restricted by not being a member of Congress and as a result, limited to exercising influence rather than authority over its members. Let us look at this complex balance of power in some detail.

The president has the power to appoint the highest officials of government: cabinet secretaries, ambassadors, federal judges, senior civil servants, and members of regulatory commissions. But all these appointments must receive the advice and consent of the Senate, the upper house of Congress. A simple majority suffices. As chief executive, the president directs the manifold business of government, yet this power is dependent for revenue on appropriations from Congress. Although the president submits a budget to Congress, that body can and does alter it freely. Congress also has the power to investigate the administrative activities of government in either closed or public hearings.

The president is responsible for the general conduct of foreign affairs and, in particular, is authorized to negotiate treaties with other states. But these treaties must also receive the advice and consent of the Senate—in this instance a qualified majority of two-thirds. Canadians were reminded in 1981 that the U.S. Senate can and does reject treaties when President Ronald Reagan had to withdraw a Canadian–American fisheries treaty because he knew the Senate would not ratify it.[10] The power of the president to appoint officials and to initiate policy, and the power of the Senate to approve or reject appointments and the power of Congress to pass legislation, creates the push and pull of the legislative process. The essence of the dynamic of the presidential system is that the president checks Congress and Congress checks the president.

The president is the commander-in-chief of the armed forces, but this coercive power is also subject to congressional limitation. The armed forces can be paid only with revenue voted by Congress, and a declaration of war requires approval in both houses of Congress. This constitutional provision has not been invoked since 1941. The Korean and Vietnam wars were waged as "police actions" under presidential authorization and were not declared by Congress. The war in Afghanistan (2001) and the two wars with Iraq (1990 and 2003) were approved by majority resolutions in both houses of Congress, but these were not official declarations of war.

Technically, the president is chosen by the **Electoral College.** Some delegates to the constitutional convention of 1787 wanted the president to be elected by Congress. Others, fearing the demise of state power in the federal system, wanted the president to be chosen by state legislators. A few others considered a more radical move—direct election by all voters. The Electoral College was the compromise. This was a group of electors, each supposedly an upstanding and respected individual of independent mind. They would be chosen by voters within the states and would in turn formally elect the president. The number of electors from each state was determined by adding the number of representatives from the state in the federal House of Representatives (determined by the population of the state) and the number of senators from the state (two). The total Electoral College vote in the United States is now 538: 435 for the number of members of the House, 100 for the number of senators, and an additional three electors from the District of Columbia.

In each state, the political parties select slates of electors who are pledged to cast their votes in the Electoral College for their party's candidate. When voters cast their ballot for president on election day in November, they are, strictly speaking, voting for one of these slates. The electors assemble in their respective states in December to cast their votes. Technically, the vote remains secret until January, when votes are counted by the vice president in the presence of the Speaker of the House of Representatives.

In fact, usually everyone knows the outcome of the race on election night because the popular vote in each state on election night determines the Electoral College vote. Members of the Electoral College usually vote according to the popular vote in the state. In some states this is a legal requirement, but in most states it is merely a well-observed practice. For a discussion of the importance of the Electoral College on the outcome of the 2000 presidential election, see Comparative Perspectives 20.1.

The Congress

Congress, like the Canadian Parliament, is a bicameral legislature. The House of Representatives has 435 members, all elected in constituencies based on population. Each elected member represents a constituency called a *congressional district*. The boundaries of these districts are redrawn periodically to reflect population shifts, and attempts are made to keep these districts approximately equal in size. Each state, no matter how small, gets at least one representative.

The term of office of a member of the House is two years. Unlike the parliamentary system, the presidential system does not provide for the government to call elections. Rather, the dates are fixed. Election day in the United States is on the Tuesday after the first Monday in November. At that time, voters select all elected officials at the federal and state levels, as well as many at the local level. This system of fixed dates for elections prevents the president from dissolving the Congress at a politically opportune time and going to the people for a new mandate.

The Senate has 100 members (two from each state), each elected for a six-year term. Senators were originally chosen by state legislatures, but this process was changed in 1913 by the Seventeenth Amendment, so they are now directly elected. At the

Comparative Perspectives 20.1

The 2000 Presidential Election in the United States

Since the candidate who gets a plurality of popular votes in a state gets all of that state's electoral votes, there is often a marked difference between the percentage of popular votes and the percentage of electoral votes that candidates obtain. Table 20.1 shows how 55 or 60 percent of the popular vote can translate into 80 or 90 percent of the electoral votes.[11]

However, the November 2000 election between George W. Bush (Republican) and Al Gore (Democrat) was very close, both in the popular vote and in the Electoral College. Of the approximately 103 million voters, Gore won the popular vote by 540,000. But Bush received a majority of the Electoral College vote, 271 to 267. The result was not decided until weeks after the election, after the Supreme Court of the United States rejected appeals from Florida courts.

The Florida dispute reflected two important points. First, state governments are responsible for conducting federal elections. This fact goes back to the original compromise on adopting the 1789 Constitution when the states held out for a strong role in the governing process. Second, states may not have rigid standards for conducting elections; the quality of voting machines, for example, varied considerably from county to county in Florida. Old voting machines led to a high number of spoiled ballots, or ballots that could not be counted. Vice President Gore tried to get the courts to order a recount in counties where disputes were obvious. In the end, the Supreme Court rejected the appeal and Governor Bush was elected president. Ultimately, it was the courts that decided the outcome.

Electoral College Votes, American Presidential Election, 2000

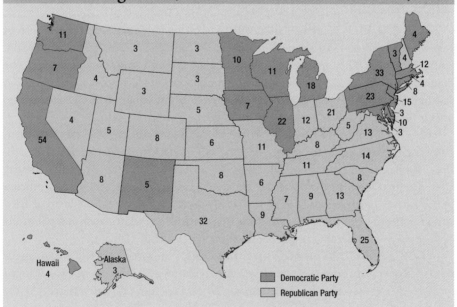

Democratic Party
Republican Party

Comparative Perspectives 20.1

Table 20.1 Landslide Presidential Elections in the United States

Winner	Year	Popular Vote (%)	Electoral Vote	States Won
Warren G. Harding (R)	1920	60.3	404 (76.1%)	37
Franklin D. Roosevelt (D)	1936	60.8	523 (98.5%)	46
Lyndon B. Johnson (D)	1964	61.1	486 (90.3%)	44
Richard M. Nixon (R)	1972	60.7	520 (96.7%)	49
Ronald Reagan (R)	1984	58.9	525 (97.6%)	49

In the November 2008 election, Senator Obama won 52 percent of the popular vote and 364 electoral college votes; Senator McCain won 46 percent of the popular vote and 163 electoral college votes. The Democrats also increased their majorities in the House of Representatives and the Senate.

constitutional convention in 1787, equal representation of states in the Senate and representation by population in the House represented a compromise. It was a trade-off between the populous states (which wanted to emphasize numbers as the basis of representation) and the thinly populated states (which wanted to emphasize territory). The Senate is considered the upper house and has more functions than the House of Representatives; most notably, it confirms presidential appointments and ratifies treaties. However, all money bills (i.e., those involving revenue or appropriations) must originate in the House of Representatives. This echoes the ancient British practice whereby revenue bills must originate in the House of Commons.

Congress is the chief repository of legislative power; but as Congress checks the president in the executive area, so the president checks Congress in the legislative area. All bills passed by Congress are sent to the president, who then has three options: to sign the bill, at which time it becomes law; not to sign the bill (after ten days it becomes law without the signature); or to **veto** the bill. In the event of a veto, the bill returns to Congress. If the bill passes again with a two-thirds majority in each house, the president's veto is overridden and the bill becomes law. This latter contingency is rather rare; the president's veto is usually final except on occasional highly charged issues.

The veto power is especially important because the president must approve or veto a bill as a whole. Most American state constitutions give the governor an **item veto**—the power to reject only certain clauses within a bill—but the president must approve or reject an entire package. Knowing this, Congress often puts together omnibus legislation, which contains items that the president is known to oppose along with those he is known to like. Such tactics, coupled with the inevitable shortage of legislative time, often manoeuvre the president into signing legislation that he would not otherwise sign.

The president cannot actually introduce a bill into Congress—that task must be performed for him by a senator or representative—but can have legislation drafted to submit to Congress; and, in fact, a large majority of American legislation originates this way. However, it is subject to amendment as it goes through Congress, and the final result may differ greatly from the original draft.

There are other important ways in which the presidential machinery of government differs from the parliamentary model. Neither the president nor the cabinet secretaries may hold a seat in Congress. In fact, if the president chooses a member of the House or Senate to be a cabinet secretary, the member must resign from Congress. The American cabinet, furthermore, is not a collective decision-making body. The main relationship is between the president and the secretaries individually. Under some presidents, the cabinet seldom or never met as a group. The number of cabinet secretaries varies with the administration, between 14 and 16 in recent decades.

Another essential feature of the presidential system is that there is no vote of confidence and thus no principle of responsible government. The tenure of office of the president and members of Congress is specified in the constitution. No matter how votes go on the floor of either house, there is nothing comparable to the non-confidence motion or the dissolution of Parliament. Barring death, resignation, or removal for misconduct, the president is in office for four years, members of the House of Representatives for two years, and senators for six years. Since the executive is not responsible to the legislature, there is less need to practise party discipline, and party solidarity is not crucial for survival. A member who chooses to vote against the party's position on a bill will not be disciplined. In such a system, the individual's first loyalty can be to the constituency rather than to the party. Party leaders in Congress try to invoke party discipline on votes, but they simply do not have the power that they would in the parliamentary system.

This generalization admits certain exceptions. Appointments to congressional standing committees are made along party lines at the opening of each session. If, for example, 60 percent of the membership of a chamber is Republican, the partisan division of members constituting committees will be 60 to 40, Republicans to Democrats. Party positions often, though not invariably, count in these committees. Still, the necessity for strong party ties that exists in the parliamentary system does not hold in the presidential system.

A final feature of the presidential system is the importance of congressional committees. The number of committees may vary slightly, but it is usually around 20 in each house of Congress. These committees are almost little legislatures in themselves. After a bill is introduced in either house, it goes immediately to a committee. In most instances, if a bill is to reach the floor of either house it must first be approved by the committee.

Congressional committees, like the cabinet in the parliamentary system, are powerful organizations for managing the legislative process. A bill that has successfully passed through a committee usually passes on the floor vote in the House or Senate.

Conversely, bills can sometimes be bottled up in committee by influential members such as the chairman of the whole committee or of a powerful subcommittee. A great deal of vote trading, or **logrolling,** develops among committee members in the process of getting legislation passed. Deals arise in committee that in the parliamentary system would be hidden in cabinet proceedings.

Judicial Review

Although the American constitution does not explicitly mention **judicial review**— the power to declare legislation or executive action unconstitutional—the U.S. Supreme Court quickly asserted this role for itself and the lower courts. Judicial review means that in constitutional matters the courts have, in effect, the power to veto legislation, which amounts to a share of legislative power. As well, they share executive power to the extent that they rule on the legality of administrative actions when these are challenged. This power helps keep executive discretion within the bounds of the law.

Court decisions are final in the short run; in the long run, the judiciary is balanced by the other branches of government. Because federal judges must be appointed by the president and confirmed by the Senate, the political complexion of the courts can be changed gradually as retirements open vacancies on the bench. During his years in office, President Reagan had the opportunity to appoint three new members to the Supreme Court out of a total of nine, and to elevate William Rehnquist from associate justice to chief justice. Even more strikingly, he had appointed more than half of the lower federal judges by the end of his second term. All of this had a noticeable effect on judicial decision making because Reagan, like other presidents, appointed judges whom he considered sympathetic to his own ideology. The result, through the use of judicial review, was a shift in the American federal courts toward conservative judicial restraint and away from liberal judicial activism that has prevailed up to the present.

Even when the courts declare a piece of legislation unconstitutional, their ruling may not be the end of the story. Congress can introduce an amendment to the constitution. The amending process is complex: an amendment must be approved by two-thirds of the members of Congress, then ratified by three-quarters of the state legislatures. Nevertheless, the amending process serves as a potential check on the judiciary by the legislative branch.

In managing the legislative process a president must be concerned with all three branches of government. He must first of all have consensus on legislative proposals within the cabinet (executive branch); he must have support in Congress (legislative branch); and he must hope the courts (judicial branch) do not contest the constitutionally of the legislation once passed. And because of the latter, judicial appointments are a very important issue in politics. This issue will be discussed in more detail in Chapter 29.

Checks and Balances

The system of **checks and balances,** as the Americans call it, gives the many interest groups of a pluralistic society marvellous opportunities to find friends in government. Cotton growers, to select an example at random, make a special effort to have good relations not only with the chairs of the Senate and House agriculture committees but also with the chairs and members of the subcommittees that deal primarily with fibre crops. Even if the president or a congressional majority has pledged to do something that may reduce cotton growers' incomes—for example, end a price-support program—they may be able to hold their ground by getting a strategically placed senator or representative to arrange for the bill to die a lingering death in committee. Or if a group cannot get Congress or the president to act upon its demands, as was true of blacks seeking civil rights in the 1950s, it may turn to the courts to accomplish by litigation what it could not achieve by legislation. In the more narrowly focused power configuration of the parliamentary system, it is much harder to influence government in this manner.

Clearly, the presidential system is highly decentralized, almost fragmented. Power, instead of being concentrated in the hands of a prime minister and cabinet, is divided among many offices. The reason for this was explained by James Madison in *The Federalist* No. 51:

> Ambition must be made to counteract ambition . . . If men were angels, no government would be necessary. If angels were to govern men, neither external nor internal controls on government would be necessary. In framing a government which is to be administered by men over men, the great difficulty lies in this: you must first enable the government to control the governed; and in the next place oblige it to control itself.[12]

Separation of the legislative, executive, and judicial branches is one way of organizing government so as to "oblige it to control itself."

Assessing Presidential Systems

The presidential system is founded on different principles than the parliamentary system. The executive initiates policy proposals, but the House of Representatives and the Senate deal with those proposals in their own way. When the Congress and the president are in accord on proposed legislation, the system can work very smoothly in passing bills; but when the president and the Congress are at loggerheads over an issue, the system can go into gridlock. A great deal of vote trading can be done to develop grounds for a compromise; but if the Congress can muster a majority in opposition to the president's policy proposals, there is no way the executive will get what it wants. Inevitably the legislature is much more autonomous in the presidential than in the parliamentary system.

The presidential forms of government used around the world today are not mere carbon copies of the American one. Structural as well as cultural factors influence the way in which forms of government work in other countries. In Mexico, for example, the equivalent of today's PRI (Institutionalized Revolutionary Party) first elected a president in 1929. Over the years this party did become "institutionalized." In the view of its critics, a populist party became unresponsive, non-democratic, and even authoritarian. The party and the president were able to use patronage, legislative programs, electoral intimidation, coercion, and corruption to dominate most facets of the Mexican political process—the Congress, the bureaucracy, the courts, and even the governments of the states and municipalities. To his credit, the last PRI president Ernesto Zedillo (1994–2000) initiated political reforms that bore fruit in the 2000 elections. In that year Vicente Fox of the National Action Party (PAN) was elected president—the first opposition win in that office in 71 years.

PARLIAMENTARY VERSUS PRESIDENTIAL SYSTEMS

Whether the parliamentary system is preferable to the presidential system as a form of liberal democracy is one of those questions that is interesting to debate in the abstract but not of much practical relevance unless a new constitution is being designed. Ongoing systems have so much momentum that it is not feasible to flip from one model to the other. Interestingly, those who live under one system and become critical of it usually wish to make it more like the other. For example, it is often said in Canada that the prime minister's power of appointment is too unrestricted and that there should be a body, like the American Senate, to confirm appointments to the bench or other high office. Or it is suggested that party discipline is too strict, and that members of parliament should be free to vote their conscience or the wishes of their constituents.

But the separation of powers creates problems of its own, as illustrated by the collision that occurred between President Clinton and the Republicans, who had a majority in both houses of Congress in the years 1995–96. Clinton vetoed the Republicans' budget because, he said, the spending cuts were too severe. When the Republicans refused to pass Clinton's budget, the federal government ran out of money; it did not quite shut down, but it had to curtail some activities for several weeks. Canadians are quite unaccustomed to such a degree of disorganization in their national government.

Because of the logic of the presidential system and the lack of party discipline, cooperation can never be taken for granted but must always be maintained through careful practise of the art of politics. Both parties seem to have drawn this conclusion after the 1996 election, in which the Republicans retained control of Congress while

President Clinton was also re-elected. In the spring of 1997, the two sides reached agreement on a multiyear plan to bring the budget into balance early in the next century.

Perhaps the conclusion must be drawn that "the grass is always greener" elsewhere. Once a system is solidly established, it has so much inertia and weight of tradition behind it that the benefit of a wholesale change is unlikely to be worth the cost, although piecemeal reforms may transfer to one system some of the advantages of the other.

The two systems, while more or less equally viable, have different strengths and weaknesses, which can be summarized as follows. Overall, it might be said that, while both are effective forms of liberal democracy, the presidential system is more liberal and the parliamentary system is more democratic. By "more liberal," we mean that the presidential system has more internal checks on the exercise of power, which is in line with the classical liberal fear of excessive state control of society. By "more democratic," we mean that the parliamentary system is more effective in expressing the will of the majority because it allows the electorate to choose a government that can govern with relatively little hindrance from countervailing power.

This democratic potential of the parliamentary system raises problems for a country such as Canada, in which a national majority is often difficult to form because of regional or linguistic fragmentation. In such situations, the parliamentary system may confer tremendous power on the governing party even though it represents not a true majority, but only the largest single minority. For example, the Conservatives won a solid majority of 169 seats in the House of Commons in the 1988 election, but with only 43 percent of the popular vote. They then used their majority to push through the Free Trade Agreement and the goods and services tax (GST), even though the former might well have been defeated, and the latter certainly would have been defeated, in a popular referendum. Although the government was much criticized by the opposition parties for legislating contrary to the "will of the people," it was not acting any differently than have other governments in the past. It is part of the logic of the parliamentary system that the representatives of the largest voting minority act as if they represented a majority, at least for a period of time. For a comparison of the strengths and weaknesses of parliamentary and presidential systems, see Comparative Perspectives 20.2.

One of the recurrent themes of Canadian politics is protest by minorities who feel that their rights have been ignored or curtailed by overwhelming parliamentary majorities. One thinks immediately of the resistance of French Canadians against conscription in the two world wars, the demands of Aboriginal peoples for self-government, and the constant struggle of the Western provinces against Ottawa during the Trudeau years. Parallels at the provincial level are the attempts of anglophones in Quebec and francophones in Manitoba to assert linguistic rights in the face of legislation supported by large majorities in the provincial electorate and legislature. These considerations lead to the discussion of the centralization and decentralization of government in Chapter 21.

Comparative Perspectives 20.2

Comparing the Parliamentary and Presidential Systems

Parliamentary	Presidential
Strengths	
1. With a majority, the government has the power to govern.	1. Separation of powers discourages concentration of power.
2. The non-confidence vote provides a check on the government.	2. Checks and balances limit the power of branches of government.
3. The lines of responsibility for passage or defeat of legislation are clear. A voter can make decisions on the basis of party stance.	3. Without strict party discipline, members can be more constituency-oriented.
Weaknesses	
1. The system may be unstable if a majority is not obtained.	1. Separation of powers fragments the system, often rendering it immobile.
2. The power of a government with a large majority is very great—it is possibly insensitive to public desires.	2. Voters cannot pin responsibility on any one party.
3. Because party loyalty is necessary, individual members may have to vote against the wishes of their constituents.	3. Without a non-confidence vote, the electorate must wait for an election to unseat an unpopular president or member of Congress.

SEMI-PRESIDENTIAL SYSTEMS

That parliamentary and presidential systems operate differently has inevitably led constitution-makers to try to combine the advantages of both in the so-called **semi-presidential system.** The prototype of the semi-presidential system is France, which experienced extreme political instability during the Fourth Republic (1946–58). Numerous political parties were represented in the National Assembly, but none could command a majority of the seats, and governments were founded on loose and generally short-lived coalitions. In the constitution of the Fifth Republic (1958), General Charles de Gaulle remedied the instability by modifying the political executive. To the prime minister and the cabinet, he added a president who is elected directly by the people for a seven-year term of office. The president is the actual head of government, not just a titular head of state. One responsibility is to appoints the prime minister, who is traditionally the leader of the majority party or of the senior party in a coalition in the National Assembly. The president also appoints the cabinet, although the prime minister can propose candidates for the positions. The National Assembly can still pass a non-confidence motion—or **vote of censure,** as it is called—and defeat the government, but this right can be exercised only once in a year. When the government is censured, only the prime minister and the cabinet must resign; the president remains because the incumbent has been popularly elected for a specific term of office.

Because the president remains in office in spite of government turnovers, the executive branch of government is stabilized; however, the value of this stability should be weighed against the possibility of deadlock. A French president may belong to a different party than the majority in the National Assembly. Under these circumstances, which the French call *cohabitation,* the president and the majority in the National Assembly must each put a little water in their wine and arrive at compromises in order to get anything done. Although such power-sharing seems awkward, the French have made it work.

The French semi-presidential model has been widely imitated in countries making a transition to democracy after long periods of authoritarian or totalitarian rule. A 2008 Wikipedia.org article listed 39 semi-presidential systems, including important countries such as Russia, South Korea, Taiwan, and Pakistan.[13]

Questions for Discussion

1. Would you rather live under a parliamentary or presidential system? Why?

2. If you were a political engineer advising a transitional democracy in a non-industrial society, would you recommend the parliamentary or presidential system of government?

3. What are the advantages and disadvantages of a disciplined party system in a parliamentary democracy?

Internet Links

1. The Parliament of Canada: **www.parl.gc.ca.** Gateway to both the Senate and the House of Commons; information on members, bills, procedures, and so on.

2. The United States Senate: **www.senate.gov.**

3. The United States House of Representatives: **www.house.gov.**

4. Commonwealth Parliamentary Association: **www.cpahq.org.** The Canadian Region of this international organization publishes the *Canadian Parliamentary Review.*

5. Parliament of the United Kingdom: **www.parliament.uk.**

Further Reading

PARLIAMENTARY SYSTEMS

Aydelotte, William O., ed. *The History of Parliamentary Behavior.* Princeton, NJ: Princeton University Press, 1977.

Beyme, Klaus von. *Parliamentary Democracy: Democratization, Destabilization, Reconsolidation, 1789–1999.* New York: St. Martin's Press, 2000.

Bowler, Shaun, David M. Farrell, and Richard S. Katz, eds. *Party Discipline and Parliamentary Government.* Columbus, OH: Ohio State University Press, 1998.

Docherty, David. *Legislatures.* Vancouver: UBC Press, 2004.

Dodd, L. C. *Coalitions in Parliamentary Government.* Princeton, NJ: Princeton University Press, 1976.

Franks, C. E. S. *The Parliament of Canada.* Toronto: University of Toronto Press, 1987.

Goldsworthy, Jeffrey. *Parliamentary Sovereignty.* Toronto: Oxford University Press, 2001.

Herman, V. *Parliaments of the World.* London: Macmillan, 1976.

Jennings, W. Ivor. *Parliament.* 2nd ed. Cambridge: Cambridge University Press, 1957.

Laver, Michael, and Kenneth A. Shepsle. *Making and Breaking Governments: Cabinets and Legislatures in Parliamentary Democracies.* Cambridge: Cambridge University Press, 1996.

MacKinnon, Frank. *The Crown in Canada.* Toronto: McClelland & Stewart, 1976.

Mackintosh, John P. *The Government and Politics of Great Britain.* 5th ed. London: Hutchinson, 1982.

March, Roman R. *The Myth of Parliament.* Scarborough, ON: Prentice-Hall Canada, 1974.

Marleau, Robert, and Camille Montpetit. *House of Commons Procedure and Practice.* Ottawa: House of Commons, 2000.

Marshall, Edmund. *Parliament and the Public.* London: Macmillan, 1982.

Rose, Richard, and Ezra N. Suleiman, eds. *Presidents and Prime Ministers.* Washington, DC: American Institute for Public Policy Research, 1980.

Rush, Michael. *The Cabinet and Policy Formation.* London: Longman, 1984.

Russell, Peter H. *Two Cheers for Minority Government: The Evolution of Canadian Parliamentary Democracy.* Toronto: Emond Montgomery, 2008.

Seidel, F. Leslie, ed. *Rethinking Government: Reform or Reincarnation?* Institute for Research on Public Policy. Ottawa: Renouf Publishing, 1993.

Smith, David E. *The Invisible Crown: The First Principle of Canadian Government.* Toronto: University of Toronto Press, 1995.

———. *The People's House of Commons.* Toronto: University of Toronto Press, 2007.

PRESIDENTIAL SYSTEMS

Barilleaux, Ryan J. *The Post-Modern Presidency: The Office after Ronald Reagan.* New York: Praeger, 1988.

Bessette, Joseph M., and Jeffrey Tulis, eds. *The Presidency in the Constitutional Order.* Baton Rouge: Louisiana State University Press, 1981.

Burns, James MacGregor. *Presidential Government.* Boston: Houghton Mifflin, 1965.

Califano, Joseph A., Jr. *A Presidential Nation.* New York: W. W. Norton, 1975.

Cheibub, José Antonio. *Presidentialism, Parliamentarism, and Democracy.* New York: Cambridge University Press, 2007.

Cronin, Thomas E., and Michael A. Genovese. *The Paradoxes of the American Presidency.* 2nd ed. Toronto: Oxford University Press, 2003.

DiBacco, T. V. *Presidential Power in Latin American Politics.* New York: Praeger, 1977.

Edwards, George C. *Presidential Leadership: Politics and Policy Making.* Toronto: Thomson Nelson, 2003.

Fisher, Louis. *Constitutional Conflicts between Congress and the President.* 3rd ed. Kansas: University Press of Kansas, 1991.

Genovese, Michael A. *The Presidential Dilemma: Leadership in the American System.* White Plains, NY: Addison-Wesley Longman, 1997.

Gilmour, Robert S., and Alexis A. Halley, eds. *Who Makes Public Policy? The Struggle for Control between Congress and the Executive.* Chatham, NJ: Chatham House, 1994.

Goldwin, Robert A., and Art Kaufman. *Separation of Powers: Does It Still Work?* Washington, DC: American Enterprise Institute, 1986.

Heclo, Hugh, and Lester M. Salamon, eds. *The Illusion of Presidential Government.* Boulder, CO: Westview Press, 1981.

Henderson, Phillip G., ed. *The Presidency Then and Now.* Landham, MD: Rowman and Littlefield, 2000.

Lijphart, Arend, ed. *Parliamentary versus Presidential Government.* Oxford: Oxford University Press, 1992.

Linz, Juan J., and Arturo Valenzuela, eds. *The Failure of Presidential Democracy.* Baltimore: Johns Hopkins University Press, 1994.

McDonald, Forrest. *The American Presidency: An Intellectual History.* Lawrence, KS: University Press of Kansas, 1994.

Nwabueze, B. O. *Presidentialism in Commonwealth Africa.* New York: St. Martin's, 1974.

Pfiffner, James P. *The Modern Presidency.* New York: St. Martin's Press, 1994.

Schneier, Edward V. *Congress Today.* New York: St. Martin's Press, 1993.

CHAPTER 21

Unitary and Federal Systems

Governments can also be classified according to the degree of centralization they exhibit. The two main types applicable to modern circumstances are the **unitary system,** in which a single sovereign government controls all regions of the country, and **federalism,** in which sovereignty is divided between a central government and several regional or provincial governments. Two other types of less practical significance are **devolution** and **confederation.**[1] The former is a variant of the unitary state in which the central government creates regional governments but can override them as it wishes, even to the point of abolishing them. The latter is an inherently unstable arrangement in which sovereign constituent governments create a central government without sovereign power of its own.

These types can be arranged as follows on a continuum of centralization:

Sovereign States	Confederation	Federalism	Devolution	Unitary State
No central government	Central government exists, but sovereignty retained by constituent governments	Sovereignty shared between central and constituent governments	Constituent governments exist, but sovereignty monopolized by central government	No constituent governments

As with most other classifications, the types represent points on a continuum, and existing political systems may fall between types. One federal system may be so centralized as to approach devolution, while another may be so decentralized that it almost amounts to a confederation. With this qualification in mind, let us discuss the major types.

THE UNITARY SYSTEM

In a unitary system, powers and responsibilities are concentrated within central governmental authorities. Constitutionally, the central government is sovereign. Municipal or county governments may exist, but their responsibilities are delegated by statute from the central government. Their functions are more administrative than legislative, much of their revenue comes from grants made by the central government, and in general they depend heavily on the central government. In a unitary system, no attempt is made to create provinces or states with specific powers established in a constitution. Ireland, France, Colombia, Japan, Sweden, Denmark, and almost 150 other contemporary states are unitary. In each case, a National Assembly, Congress, Parliament, or Diet is responsible for governing the entire nation. The power of local governments varies considerably, depending on the extent to which central authorities have delegated responsibilities of government and administration.

Devolution—the granting of governmental responsibilities, including limited legislative responsibilities, to regional governments—is a step toward decentralization. The powers of regional governments, however, are not entrenched in the constitution. They are created by statute of the central government and may be modified or abolished in the same way. An example would be the government of Northern Ireland from 1921 to 1972. Under the Government of Ireland Act of 1920, the British established at Stormont Castle a Parliament with local responsibilities. This legislative body had a great deal of autonomy in domestic matters such as housing, services, and public employment. The experiment was terminated in 1972 because violence between the Protestant majority and the Roman Catholic minority made regional government unworkable.[2] This example illustrates the utter dependence of regional governments upon the central government in a devolved system. There was no constitutional barrier to the British cabinet's unilateral decision to dissolve the Stormont Parliament and put Northern Ireland under the direct control of a Secretary of State for Northern Ireland. For a description of devolution in Britain today, see Comparative Perspectives 21.1.

FEDERALISM AND CONFEDERATION

In a federal system, powers and responsibilities are divided between a federal (or national) government and various regional governments. The federal government, for example, may be responsible for minting money and raising an army, while the provinces (or states, or cantons, or departments) may be responsible for education and public works. Constitutionally, sovereignty is divided between different levels of government instead of being concentrated in one government. Both levels of government are mentioned in a constitutional document, and neither level can unilaterally modify or abolish the other. In reality, however, it is virtually impossible to divide powers neatly so that the responsibility of one level of government is totally independent of the other. This means that disputes, overlapping jurisdictions, and joint efforts are commonplace in any federal system.

Although Switzerland has a history of confederation dating back to 1291, it was the American constitution of 1789 that created the world's first modern federal system. The model has since been imitated in about 20 states, including Brazil, Mexico, Venezuela, Canada, Switzerland, Australia, Indonesia, India, Germany, and Russia.

Comparative Perspectives 21.1

The Evolution of Devolution

When the first edition of this textbook was published in 1982, devolution appeared to be pretty much a thing of the past. The Stormont Parliament in Northern Ireland had been dissolved in 1972, and Scottish voters had rejected devolution in a 1979 referendum. But things change.

Tony Blair's Labour government was elected in 1997 on a program that included modernizing the British constitution, which in turn included consideration of devolution for Scotland, Wales, and Northern Ireland. Later that year, referendums were held in Scotland and Wales. Devolution passed with enthusiasm in Scotland (almost 75 percent) and barely in Wales (just over 50 percent). Scottish voters also approved giving their new Parliament the ability to levy taxes.

In 1998, the Parliament of the United Kingdom passed the Scotland Act and the Government of Wales Act to create the Scottish Parliament and the National Assembly for Wales. Both bodies have a legislature and a cabinet, but in other respects their powers are somewhat different, reflecting different political aspirations in the regions.

The Northern Ireland Assembly, created after the 1998 Good Friday agreement among the various political forces, was created by British legislation and also approved by referendum. It was suspended in 2002 because of continuing communal violence but was restored in 2007 after the Belfast Agreement made free and peaceful elections possible.

Representing a pragmatic British tradition of politics, devolution is a complex system of different arrangements for different parts of the United Kingdom. There are now three regional governments, each with different powers, while the main region—England—has no regional government of its own. The residents of the regions still elect members to the Parliament at Westminster, and Parliament is still sovereign; that is, it still retains unilateral legal authority to amend or abolish devolution. There will undoubtedly be further changes as conditions evolve, particularly in Northern Ireland, which may some day want closer relations with the Republic of Ireland.

The invention of federalism was precipitated by the inadequacy of confederation as a form of government. After winning its independence from Britain, the United States in 1781 adopted the Articles of Confederation, the first American constitution. The states retained sovereignty, and the federal Congress was little more than a meeting place for ambassadors of these state governments. Congress could not levy taxes, raise an army, regulate commerce, or enforce law within the states, nor was there a national executive authority. General recognition that this system could not last very long led to the constitutional convention of 1787.

As with many important political innovations, the invention of modern federalism was almost accidental. According to the conventional wisdom of the eighteenth century, sovereignty was indivisible. Those who supported the Articles of Confederation saw sovereignty as lodged in the 13 sovereign states; those who criticized the Articles wanted to create a new unitary state possessing sovereignty at the centre. Both sides agreed that sovereignty had to be in one place or the other. James Madison broke the deadlock by suggesting that two levels of government could each have legislative authority secured by the constitution. The logical puzzle about sovereignty was solved by declaring that the people were sovereign, and that the state and federal governments were their instruments, created and restrained by the constitution, which the people could alter according to prescribed methods. Few people at the time saw this as a new type of government; most thought of it as a constitutional marriage of two existing and well-understood forms of government: confederation and the unitary state. But it subsequently became conventional in political science to emphasize the division of sovereignty and to speak of federalism as a distinct form of government rather than a combination of other types.

The rise of federalism has largely driven confederation from the field as a serious alternative, though it still appears occasionally, as in the proposal for sovereignty-association between Quebec and the rest of Canada—which, depending on the details of implementation, might not even reach the level of a confederation. According to the official proposal by the Parti Québécois, Canada and Quebec would be sovereign nations cooperating in selected areas. For example, there might be a common currency supervised by a central bank in which both partners would hold shares. But there would be no central legislature of any kind, not even one like the very weak American Congress of 1781–87.

We may also see a resurgence of confederations as the world economy becomes more tightly interconnected. When the European Union was founded in 1956, it was little more than a free-trade zone. In governmental terms, it represented six sovereign states agreeing to specific forms of cooperation under the Treaty of Rome. Today, there are 27 member states (as of 2008), and the cooperation has become so massive and complex that use of the term *confederation* may one day be justified. There is as yet nothing resembling a European cabinet or head of state, but there are European prototypes of the other main governmental institutions—for example, the European Parliament at Strasbourg, a European bureaucracy at Brussels, and a European Court of Justice in Luxembourg—as well as regular meetings of first ministers. There have been so many attempts to harmonize policy in so many areas, such as labour codes, human rights, consumer standards, and the environment, that the legislative discretion of member states is now substantially reduced, particularly now that the euro has been adopted as a common currency for most member nations. Whether or not we call the European Union a confederation may be only a semantic quibble.

Because of its special relevance to Canadians, let us return to a more extended discussion of federalism. Federal systems have emerged for at least three important reasons. First, it has been said that "federalism is one way to resolve the problem of enlarging governments."[3] Federal systems are alternatives to large empires established by imperial force. Decentralization allows far-flung regions to feel that not all decisions are made for them in a distant capital. Not surprisingly, most federal states are geographically large, such as Russia, Mexico, Australia, and India. Second, federal systems are often established in societies where a substantial degree of linguistic, religious, or cultural diversity exists. This explains the development of federalism in Switzerland, which is geographically small but linguistically and religiously diverse. Linguistic division is not a factor in Germany, but the circumstances of history have promoted federalism there. Because Germany was not fully united until 1871, some of the German *Länder* (provinces), such as Bavaria, were sovereign states until relatively recently and still have important historical traditions of their own. Federalism can accommodate this sort of diversity. In practice, a large land area and cultural pluralism often go together, which means that federalism has a double *raison d'être* in such countries as India and Canada. Third, federal systems provide one way of checking governmental power. When powers are divided among levels of government, absolute power is not concentrated within a single unit. The logic is much the same as in Madison's justification of the separation of powers—in a federation, government in effect "controls itself" because the ambitions of one group of politicians can never entirely defeat the ambitions of another. When the provinces check the federal government and the federal government checks the provinces, a balance may well result.

There are other advantages to the federal system of government. A larger state probably has greater human and natural resources with which to defend itself against foreign enemies. Also, the larger the nation-state, the greater the economies of scale. It should be cheaper to administer public services on a large scale where costs can be spread among more people. As well, when governments are located at a regional level, people tend to feel closer to the decision-making process, and the decision-makers tend to be more aware of local needs and better able to respond to them. Finally, constituent governments can often establish innovative programs and policies aimed at particular problems. These experiments may prove valuable for the entire country once they are tested. For example, Saskatchewan enacted hospital insurance in 1946 and medical-care insurance in 1961; in each case that province anticipated federal legislation by a decade.

In spite of these advantages, as Garth Stevenson states, "One is tempted to conclude that both the arguments against federalism and the arguments in its favour can be as easily refuted as supported."[4] "Layered" government has financial costs that may outweigh any economies of scale. And while governments at the local or provincial level are closer to the people, this is no guarantee that they are any more responsive to local needs than a federal government would be. Moreover, the federal system may foster divisive intergovernmental conflict.

Obviously, the division of sovereignty in a federal system reduces the power of the central government, thus taking away some of its ability to oppress the people. Less obvious, but equally true, is that the existence of two levels of government is a check on tyrannical tendencies in the constituent governments. This was brilliantly pointed out by James Madison in his contributions to *The Federalist*. He showed that in a small democracy there is a strong likelihood of some group gaining the upper hand and practising a tyranny of the majority. A small jurisdiction is usually homogeneous in social composition, and this makes it easy for a majority to form. But in a large country, there is such a diversity of classes and interests—farmers, workers, merchants, and so forth—that there is "in the society so many separate descriptions of citizens as will render an unjust combination of a majority of the whole very improbable."[5] While the following example dates from 150 years later, it indicates that Madison may have had a point. In the 1930s in Alberta, William Aberhart's Social Credit government, elected by a majority including many debtors, passed laws against banks that amounted to confiscation of property. When the newspapers criticized Aberhart harshly, he tried to impose a form of censorship on them. The federal government protected the rights of banks and newspapers by disallowing provincial legislation and exercising judicial review.

The situation with blacks in the American South is also a case in point, but from a different perspective. For almost 100 years, state governments in the decentralized American federal system had been able to pass laws that discriminated against blacks. For instance, laws were passed limiting voting rights and segregating schools. By 1965, with the U.S. Supreme Court leading the way, the federal government was finally able to override the legal structure of racial segregation. The point is that in a decentralized federal system, power at the constituent level (in this case, the state level) can be used to restrict the social, economic, and political rights of minorities. Although it took about a century and a great deal of grief for blacks and some whites, Madison's idea of justice finally prevailed. The genius of federalism lies in its recognition that power at any level is subject to abuse and in the way it establishes layers of government with enough power to balance each other.

Structural Features of Federalism

Although each federal system must be uniquely adapted to the pluralistic conditions of its society, certain structural features are universal, or very nearly so. First, there must be a written document that explicitly assigns powers to the two levels of government. In Canada, Section 91 of the Constitution Act, 1867, grants power to the federal government, while Sections 92 and 93 spell out the powers of the provinces. Section 95 assigns concurrent jurisdiction to the two levels of government over agriculture and immigration. The powers of the federal or national Parliament include, for example, control of trade and commerce, maintenance of a postal service, and responsibility for navigation and shipping. Provincial powers under Section 92 include control of the sale of alcoholic beverages, responsibility for the solemnization of marriage, and management of hospitals. Section 93 makes provincial governments responsible for education "in and for each province"; this wording is open enough to allow the federal government to help support universities, whose research role transcends provincial boundaries.

The constitution of a federal system also has to say something about **residual powers**—that is, those powers of government that are not specifically mentioned in the text. No list of functions can ever be complete, if only because situations unforeseen at the time of drafting are bound to arise. In Canada, residual powers were given to the federal government by Section 91 of the Constitution Act, 1867:

> It shall be lawful for the Queen, by and with the Advice and Consent of the Senate and House of Commons, to make Laws for the Peace, Order, and good Government of Canada, in relation to all Matters not coming within the Classes of Subjects by this Act assigned exclusively to the Legislatures of the Provinces. . . .

In contrast, the Tenth Amendment to the American Constitution took the opposite approach: "The powers not delegated to the United States by the Constitution or prohibited by it to the States, are reserved to the States respectively, or to the people."

Almost all federal systems have bicameral legislatures in the central government, although in some the powers of the upper house have atrophied over the years. The rationale behind federal bicameralism is to provide the provinces or regions with a special form of representation within the central government. This is supposed to ensure that regional voices are heard in the capital and to prevent regional interests from being overridden by a numerical majority in the nation as a whole. It is quite frankly a restraint upon the pure democracy of majority rule.

Germany is a good example of federal bicameralism. The upper house or *Bundesrat* is composed of delegates chosen by and responsible to the governments of the *Länder,* with the number of delegates being roughly in proportion to the size of the *Land* ("province"). The federal cabinet is responsible only to the lower house, or *Bundestag,* but the *Bundesrat,* unlike the Canadian Senate, often exercises its power of refusing to pass legislation. The American Senate is another good example. Senators, now democratically elected, were once chosen by state legislatures and still feel responsible for seeing that their states' interests are respected in Washington. Having two senators per state, regardless of the state's size, guarantees equal state representation.

In comparison, Canada has a weaker form of federal bicameralism, because the power of the Canadian Senate is quite limited in practice. Section 22(4) of the amended Constitution Act, 1867, specifies a certain regional distribution of senators (24 each from Quebec, Ontario, Western Canada, and the Maritimes; 6 from Newfoundland and Labrador; and 1 each from Yukon, the Northwest Territories, and Nunavut); but this distribution does not make senators true regional representatives, since they are appointed by the governor general on the advice of the prime minister. From the beginning, the cabinet, which has traditionally included ministers from most provinces, has been a stronger instrument of federalism in Canada than the Senate.

Not surprisingly, most of the recent proposals to reform the Canadian constitution involve changing the Senate to make it a more active representative of provincial interests. The Meech Lake Accord would have required the prime minister to choose senators from among names submitted by the governments of the provinces, and the

Charlottetown Accord would have gone even further by giving each province an equal number of popularly elected senators.

Without reform, Canada's upper house will never really do the job that such bodies in most federal states perform. Even when it is active, as in recent decades when Liberals and Conservatives have taken turns in using the Senate to block or delay legislation coming from the House of Commons, it does not effectively represent regional or provincial interests. The fact that the Senate does not speak for the regions undoubtedly contributes to the feeling among such provinces as Alberta and Newfoundland and Labrador that their interests are not effectively represented in Ottawa. Residents of these provinces often feel they are repeatedly overridden by the majority power of the electors in Ontario and Quebec. By the same token, Ontario consistently voting with the West could dominate Parliament. To this, many members of parliament and some analysts of the Canadian federal system would answer that all provinces are represented in the House of Commons and that, regardless of whether the MP is on the government or the opposition side, this representation is adequate.

Many critics, however, argue that federalism requires, by definition, a dual basis for representation. Their position is that an upper house is an integral part of any federal system and should represent the interests of the regions. There have been many suggestions over the past 15 years relating to how regional interests can be better represented in Ottawa. They range from the "triple-E" proposal (see Chapter 20) to the compromise in the Charlottetown Accord (see Figure 21.1).

Although the abolition of the Senate has been suggested, this position seems a bit facile in that Canada would then be the only federal system in the world without an upper house. Most federalists argue that an upper house is an integral part of our federal system, and that what we need is a Senate that is democratic, has real power vis-à-vis the House of Commons, and represents all provinces and territories without entirely disregarding population differences.

The weakness of regional representation in Ottawa has encouraged Canadian federalism to develop an *interstate* (activity between provinces and the federal government) rather than an *intrastate* (activity within the nation-state) character.[6] Provincial governments have become the main advocates of regional interests and now deal with each other and with the federal government in quasi-diplomatic fashion. The most visible manifestations of this **executive federalism** are the periodic first ministers' conferences, which are conducted very much like international conferences; that is, with public posturing, secret negotiations, and final communiqués. These sessions are only the most visible meetings in the ceaseless round of federal–provincial talks at various levels among cabinet ministers, deputy ministers, and officials. This cycle of negotiations and meetings occurs outside parliamentary government in Ottawa. There is nothing like it in other major federal polities such as Australia, the United States, and Germany.

In federal systems, constituent governments often clash with each other and with the national government, and the courts often become the arbiters of these conflicts. Judicial review, the power to declare legislation unconstitutional, is an important feature of most federal constitutions. Curiously, judicial review in federalism issues

Figure 21.1 Proposed Geographical Distribution of Senate Seats

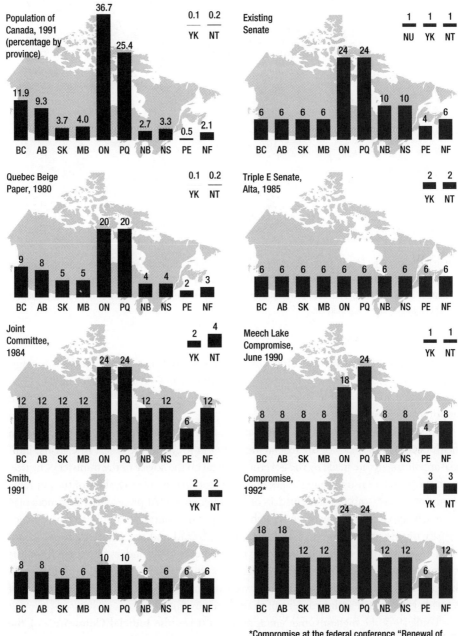

*Compromise at the federal conference "Renewal of
Canada Institutional Reform," Calgary, January 1992.

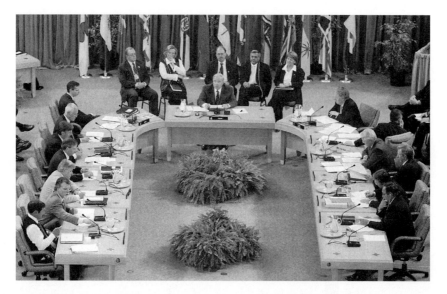

Prime Minister Paul Martin along with his provincial and territorial counterparts takes part in a session of the First Ministers Conference on Health in Ottawa in September 2004. The Conservative government of Stephen Harper has held fewer of these meetings since coming to power in February 2006.
The Canadian Press (Fred Chartrand)

is now said to be relatively unimportant in the United States, where federalism originated.[7] But it is still generally true, and certainly true in Canada, that federalism gives the courts a higher profile than in most unitary states. This in turn makes judicial appointments politically sensitive.

In the United States, Senate confirmation of presidential appointments to the bench helps raise the legitimacy of the federal judiciary in the eyes of the states. In Canada, judicial appointments are made by the governor general on the advice of the minister of justice, with the prime minister playing a special role by nominating the members of the Supreme Court of Canada and the chief justices of the other courts. At present, the provinces play no role in appointing judges, even though the Supreme Court's decisions can have a major impact on provincial powers. The Meech Lake Accord and the Charlottetown Accord tried to address this problem by providing that Supreme Court judges be chosen from lists submitted by the provinces. Since the defeat of both amendment packages, the status quo has prevailed; undoubtedly the provinces will continue to feel that the Supreme Court of Canada is too much an instrument of the federal government.

Until 1949 the highest Canadian appeals court was the **Judicial Committee of the Privy Council (JCPC),** a special British court that heard appeals from the whole empire. The provinces had never considered this a problem because, in fact, the JCPC rendered a long series of decisions favourable to the provinces in their disputes with Ottawa. But when appeals to the committee were abolished in 1949, the Supreme Court of Canada, appointed solely by federal authorities, became the ultimate interpreter of the Constitution.

Since that time, the provinces have increasingly desired a role in choosing judges, and something in this direction will probably happen sooner or later.

Constitutional amendment is another contentious subject in federal systems. There must be some sort of balance between the two levels of government. If the central government can change the constitution at will without the consent of the regional governments, the system is tantamount to devolution, because the central government could modify or even abolish the regional governments by unilateral constitutional amendment. Before 1982, the legal method for amending the Canadian Constitution was for the British Parliament, acting on a joint address from the Canadian Senate and House of Commons, to amend the British North America Act (as it was then called). In most, but not all, instances in which provincial rights were affected, the federal government obtained the prior consent of all the provinces before requesting constitutional amendments. An all-Canadian amending formula was introduced as part of the Constitution Act, 1982. Under the general procedure of Section 38, amendments must be passed by the House, the Senate, and the legislative assemblies of two-thirds of the provinces that have at least 50 percent of the population of all the provinces; amendments in certain matters require the agreement of all provinces. These provisions institutionalized the roles of the federal and provincial governments in amending the Constitution and excluded Great Britain altogether. In the United States, all constitutional amendments must receive approval from two-thirds of both houses of Congress and three-quarters of state legislatures. Again there is a balance of power between the central and constituent governments.

At the time of Confederation, the Canadian system had a feature that is unusual in federal states: the right of the central government to nullify the legislation of the constituent governments, even when they were acting within their proper constitutional sphere. There are two mechanisms by which this can happen. In the first, known as **reservation,** the lieutenant governor of a province can refuse royal assent to a bill and refer it to the federal cabinet for a final decision. In the second, known as **disallowance,** the federal cabinet can nullify a provincial act within one year of passage, even though it has received royal assent from the lieutenant governor of the province. These powers of the federal government were used frequently in the early years of Confederation, and are still constitutionally alive, though they are now in abeyance. No provincial act has been disallowed since 1943, although Ottawa has sometimes threatened such action. In 1961, Saskatchewan's lieutenant governor reserved a bill without seeking prior advice from Ottawa, much to the embarrassment of Prime Minister John Diefenbaker. In practice, court challenges have replaced reservation and disallowance in Canada. In the United States, as in most federal systems, there is no parallel to this constitutional dominance by the central government.

This review shows that Canadian federalism was originally so highly centralized as to border on devolution. In other words, a very centralized federal system may resemble a unitary system that has undergone devolution. The federal right to appoint judges and senators, nullify provincial legislation, amend the constitution, and exercise residual powers far outweighed the provincial powers. This was by design. The Fathers of Confederation could not ignore the American Civil War (1861–65). Most believed that the American constitution had granted too much power to the states.

Sir John A. Macdonald would have preferred a unitary state, then known as a *legislative union* (only one legislature for all of Canada); but he realized that some form of federalism was required to entice Quebec and the Atlantic provinces into association with Ontario. The solution that emerged was, in legal terms, a strong central government with minimal concessions to the provinces.

The subsequent evolution of Canada has undone much of this work. The forces of decentralization were too strong to be contained within the centralizing constitution of 1867. The JCPC rendered a long series of decisions that circumscribed the legislative powers given Ottawa under Section 91 and expanded provincial powers under Section 92. Ottawa also gradually relinquished the use of centralizing powers such as reservation and disallowance.

There was, to be sure, a centralizing trend that began in World War II and carried on into the postwar period. The federal government acquired the important new jurisdictions of unemployment insurance and old-age pensions through constitutional amendment. It also used its extensive revenues to create national welfare programs such as health-care insurance and the Canada Assistance Plan. But this centralizing thrust in turn gave rise to a counter movement of decentralization. As the provinces expanded their tax base in the late 1950s and 1960s, they became less dependent on the federal government for financial support, which encouraged a new dynamic in the federal system. The Meech Lake and Charlottetown Accords contained provisions that would have enhanced provincial at the expense of federal jurisdiction. Quebec, motivated by linguistic and cultural factors, is at the forefront of provinces seeking more power, but it is not the only such province. The decentralizing trend is likely to continue, as the provinces aggressively seek greater health care transfers from the federal government, arguing that Ottawa has not lived up to its commitment to fund a greater portion of medical care expenses under the Canada Health Act.

There have been many proposals for reforming the federal system, of which the Meech Lake and Charlottetown Accords, arrived at by the first ministers, received the most attention. Proposals have dealt with almost every conceivable topic, including multiculturalism, Senate reform, immigration policy, Supreme Court nominations, and the use of referendums. Almost invariably there has been a clear recommendation to expand the role of the provinces in the federation.

One interesting product of these constitutional discussions was the concept of **asymmetrical federalism,** a term used to convey the idea of powers being divided unevenly among provinces, of some provinces choosing to have greater responsibilities or more autonomy than others. Of course, a degree of asymmetry already exists in Canadian federalism. Quebec, for instance, collects its own income tax, operates its own provincial pension plan, and exercises more control over immigration than do the other provinces, which have been content to let Ottawa perform these functions. The transfer of powers to the provinces envisioned in the Meech Lake and Charlottetown Accords would have led to more of these asymmetrical arrangements. Many Canadians feared that, as a result, Canada would be "balkanized"; that is, reduced to a patchwork of different programs in different jurisdictions across the country.

Proponents of asymmetrical federalism are willing to run this risk. They believe that greater flexibility in federalism will accommodate the differing needs of the provinces, especially those of Quebec, and thus reduce the threat of separatism. Opponents question whether pushing asymmetry too far might not lead to the disintegration of federalism as we know it. They fear that too much decentralization would so weaken the federal government that Canada would be left with only a very loose confederation. This debate was not really resolved with the rejection of the Charlottetown Accord and continues to bubble beneath the surface of Canadian politics. See Canadian Focus 20.1.

Curiously, American political evolution has moved in the direction of greater centralization, with power shifting steadily toward the federal government. International crises—two world wars, the Cold War, and the Korean, Vietnam, and Gulf Wars—and the nationalization of domestic issues, such as racial disparities and inflation, have tended to make all eyes focus on Washington for solutions. The federal government totally overshadows any state or group of states in its ability to confront national issues. An abstract reading of the American and Canadian constitutions would suggest that American states are far more powerful than Canadian provinces, but this is in fact a highly distorted picture of the current reality.[8] The constitutional allocation of residual powers to the federal government in Canada and to the states in the United States has had little long-run, practical effect.

Canadian Focus 21.1

Quebec and Canadian Federalism

In November 2006, the House of Commons passed a motion introduced by Prime Minister Stephen Harper to "recognize that the Québécois form a nation within a united Canada." This motion rekindled old, emotional feelings about Canada's federal system and Quebec's place in it.

Many "nationalists," particularly in English Canada, have argued that Canada is "one nation" with predominantly a symmetrical, federalist structure, and for the most part granting equal powers to all provinces. This model of federalism was reinforced with the Charter, which granted equality individually for all Canadian citizens. But there was no official recognition of the distinctness of Quebec or of aboriginal First Nations. The idea was, and has been, that the concept of one nation provided for unity within a diverse Canadian society. There was no adherence to the notion of dualism; individual rights, not collective rights, were of primary importance. No formal recognition of a dual society or a distinct society was needed; in fact, this kind of recognition could threaten unity or even break up the Canadian nation. Symmetrical federalism within one nation was the model for a successful system of government.[9]

(continued)

Canadian Focus 21.1   *(continued)*

On the other hand, many "federalists," particularly in Quebec, have argued that our federal system of government should reflect our multinational character. These people argue that the Meech Lake and Charlottetown Accords were attempts to create a more dynamic federal system—an experiment unique to Canada. It is worthwhile to examine the basis for this argument as articulated by three prominent political analysts.

Charles Taylor suggests the importance of a "unique identity" for "French Canadians, and particularly Quebeckers . . . and aboriginal peoples." The "survival" of this identity is important so that the society will not lapse into uniformity and all people assimilated into a single culture. Thus there is a threat to recognizing "the equal value of different cultures" under the idea of one nation.[10]

Guy Laforest argues that Trudeau's constitutional changes represented the end of a Canadian dream. Part of the dream for the Québécois was a belief in the "duality" of Canadian society; that the sense of a distinct "nationalism" in Quebec was the basis for a belief in "two majorities" in Canada.[11] And for him, the idea was to have asymmetrical powers in a federal constitution where national differences could be enshrined.[12]

Kenneth McRoberts claims that for French Canadians, "federalism had a different purpose, the defence of culture as opposed to regional or economic interests." He noted that asymmetry was started under Prime Minister Lester Pearson's government but halted by Trudeau.[13] McRoberts sees an option for accommodating Quebec: "an alternative strategy based on constitutional recognition of duality . . . ; asymmetry in federal-provincial relations; and territoriality in language policy." And the strategy could be modified to "incorporate the objectives of aboriginal peoples."[14]

One can see that the place of Quebec in Canadian federalism is an emotional issue—for nationalists and for federalists. No one knows whether the Harper motion is an indication of movement toward a more flexible federal system for Canada. But one of the strengths of a federal system is that it can adapt to diversity and at the same time retain unity. It can adapt to regional differences as well as multinational, multiethnic, and multireligious differences. It is a supple form of government for large and diverse societies.

Assessing Federal Systems

While federal systems have enabled the building of large nation-states, they have not provided the cure for all political ills. Indeed, separatist movements have plagued many countries with a federal form of government. The Civil War in the United States was fought over the South's claim of a right to secede from the Union. In Nigeria, Biafrans with their strong tribal identity and oil resources tried in 1967 to secede from the federation. The Chechens are still fighting Russia in their attempt to found an independent republic. Separatists in the Parti Québécois still vow to establish sovereignty in Quebec.

A basic problem with all federal systems is to establish a workable balance acceptable to all levels of government. It was once believed that a central government was best suited to cope with national problems. Over the last 60 years there have been two conflicting trends: one toward centralizing power at the national level because governments have expanded their functions to meet economic crises and have become involved in international conflicts, and the other toward decentralizing power because national and ethnic feeling are running strong and because many people feel that regional governments can best deal with individual citizens. There seems to be much appeal in the thesis that "small is beautiful." Indeed, many federal systems of government are using decentralization as a way of countering separatist movements.

In Canada we are also getting mixed signals about our federation. The provinces have become more powerful in the federal system, and the Meech Lake and Charlottetown Accords were proposals to institutionalize that trend. However, for a variety of reasons, both accords failed to pass. With Quebec separatism at least temporarily in eclipse, the most important contemporary debate is over who pays for program responsibilities. The Conservatives campaigned in 2006 on a promise to end the "fiscal imbalance" by transferring more money to the provinces, a pledge that was redeemed to some extent in their 2007 budget; but the squabbling over money continues as strongly as ever; it seems to be rooted in the DNA of Canadian federalism.

Questions for Discussion

1. In your opinion, is federalism properly balanced in Canada today, or do you see the provinces or the federal government as having too much power?

2. Why do you think there are many more unitary than federal states in the world?

3. Compare British devolution to Canadian federalism. Does federalism or devolution tend more to asymmetry?

Internet Links

1. *Publius, The Journal of Federalism*: **www.oxfordjournals.org/our_journals/pubjof/index.html.**

2. Institute of Intergovernmental Relations, Queen's University: **www.queensu.ca/iigr.**

3. European Union: **http://europa.eu.int.**

Further Reading

Bakvis, Herman, ed. *Canadian Federalism.* Toronto: Oxford University Press, 2001.

Bakvis, Herman, and William M. Chandler, eds. *Federalism and the Role of the State.* Toronto: University of Toronto Press, 1987.

Bogdanor, Vernon. *Devolution in the United Kingdom.* Toronto: Oxford University Press, 2001.

Burgess, Michael, and Alain G. Gagnon, eds. *Comparative Federalism and Federations: Competing Traditions and Future Directions.* Toronto: University of Toronto Press, 1993.

Cairns, Alan C. *Charter versus Federalism: The Dilemmas of Constitutional Reform.* Kingston: McGill–Queen's University Press, 1992.

Conlan, Timothy J. *From New Federalism to Devolution: Twenty-Five Years of Intergovernmental Reform.* Washington, DC: Brookings Institution Press, 1998.

Courchene, Thomas J. *In Praise of Renewed Federalism.* Toronto: C. D. Howe Institute, 1991.

Elazar, Daniel J., ed. *Federal Systems of the World: A Handbook of Federal, Confederal and Autonomy Arrangements.* Harlow, UK: Longman, 1991.

Gibbins, Roger. *Regionalism: Territorial Politics in Canada and the United States.* Toronto: Butterworths, 1982.

Gutmann, Amy. *Multiculturalism.* Princeton: Princeton University Press, 1994.

Harrison, Kathryn. *Passing the Buck: Federalism and Canadian Environmental Policy.* Vancouver: University of British Columbia Press, 1996.

Hobson, Paul A. R., and France St. Hilaire. *Toward Sustainable Federalism: Reforming Federal–Provincial Fiscal Arrangements.* Montreal: Institute for Research on Public Policy, 1993.

Hueglin, Thomas O. *Early Modern Concepts for a Late Modern World: Althusius on Community and Federalism.* Waterloo, ON: Wilfrid Laurier University Press, 1999.

———. *A Political Economy of Federalism: In Search of a New Comparative Perspective with Critical Intent Throughout.* Kingston, ON: Institute of Intergovernmental Relations, Queen's University, 1990.

Knop, Karen, et al., eds. *Rethinking Federalism: Citizens, Markets, and Governments in a Changing World.* Vancouver: University of British Columbia Press, 1995.

Laforest, Guy. *Trudeau and the End of a Canadian Dream.* Translated by Paul Leduc and Michelle Weinroth. Montreal: Mcgill-Queen's University Press, 1995.

LaSelva, Samuel V. *The Moral Foundations of Canadian Federalism: Paradoxes, Achievements, and Tragedies of Nationhood.* Montreal: McGill–Queen's University Press, 1996.

McRoberts, Kenneth. *Misconceiving Canada: The Struggle for National Unity.* Don Mills, ON: Oxford University Press, 1997.

Murphy, Michael, ed. *Canada: The State of the Federation, 2005: Quebec and Canada in the New Century.* Montreal: Mcgill-Queens University Press, 2007.

Nagel, Robert F. *The Implosion of American Federalism.* New York: Oxford University Press, 2001.

Randall, Stephen J., and Roger Gibbins. *Federalism and the New World Order.* Calgary: University of Calgary Press, 1994.

Riker, William H. *Federalism: Origin, Operation, Significance.* Boston: Little, Brown, 1964.

Rocher, François, and Miriam Smith, eds. *New Trends in Canadian Federalism.* 2nd ed. Peterborough, ON: Broadview Press, 2003.

Saywell, John T. *The Lawmakers: Judicial Powers and the Shaping of Canadian Federalism.* Toronto: University of Toronto Press, 2002.

Simeon, Richard, and Ian Robinson. *State, Society, and the Development of Canadian Federalism.* Toronto: University of Toronto Press, 1990.

Smiley, D. V. *The Federal Condition in Canada.* Toronto: McGraw-Hill Ryerson, 1987.

Smith, Jennifer. *Federalism.* Vancouver: University of British Columbia Press, 2004.

———. *The Meaning of Provincial Equality in Canadian Federalism.* Kingston, ON: Institute of Intergovernmental Relations, Queen's University, 1998.

Stevenson, Garth. *Unfulfilled Union: Canadian Federalism and National Unity.* 3rd ed. Toronto: Gage, 1989.

Ter-Minassian, Teresa, ed. *Fiscal Federalism in Theory and Practice,* Washington, DC: International Monetary Fund, 1997.

Watts, Ronald L. *Comparing Federal Systems.* 2nd ed. Kingston, ON: Institute of Intergovernmental Relations, Queen's University, 1999.

———. *The Spending Power in Federal Systems: A Comparative Study.* Kingston, ON: Institute of Intergovernmental Relations, Queen's University, 1999.

Westmacott, M. W., and Hugh Mellon. *Challenges to Canadian Federalism.* Scarborough, ON: Prentice Hall, 1998.

Wheare, K. C. *Federal Government.* New York: Oxford University Press, 1964.

Wildavsky, Aaron B., Brendon Swedlow, and David Schleicher, eds. *Federalism and Political Culture.* Piscataway, NJ: Transaction Publishers, 1997.

PART 4
The Political Process

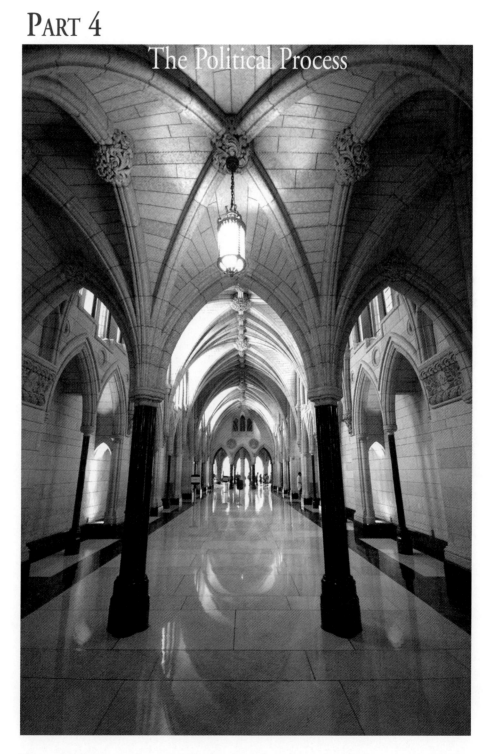

CHAPTER 22

The Political Process

In Part One we discussed politics in abstract terms, associating it with functions such as the exercise of authority, the allocation of values, and the settling of disputes. In Part Four we want to move from the level of abstraction to the level of concrete reality and be much more specific about the political process. Our objective is to explain politics as an institutionalized process for making public decisions. Our hope is that politics and the political process become a vivid and concrete idea in your mind.

It is important for all citizens of a polity to be able to conceptualize the process of politics in some way. When one speaks of the game of hockey, for example, there is no problem visualizing the sport and understanding all its complexities. When one thinks of politics, however, many things come to mind: a parliament, a prime minister or premier, corruption, lobbying, or perhaps elections. In fact, all these impressions can be part of the political process. The problem is we need some way to pull all of these impressions together—and that is what a concept does for us. Therefore, if as citizens we talk politics, evaluate it, criticize it, or even participate in it, it is important to be able to see the whole process, all its actors and institutions, and understand how they interact in the process. In this chapter, we offer two different ways of conceptualizing politics: politics as a comprehensive systemic process and politics as a "problem-oriented" policy process. Understanding either, or hopefully both, will be a first step in understanding the complexities of the political process.

The task may be easier to state than to accomplish. While all of us know that the process exists and that it works, it is still difficult to describe in precise terms. The political process is the complex activity of making public decisions for a society. It involves the interaction of organized political structures such as interest groups, political parties, executives, legislatures, and the courts. Politics is the interplay of all these components in devising public laws and policies, selecting and rejecting rulers, and shaping public opinion. Finding a successful course of action that can withstand the scrutiny of public dialogue is an art that requires a particular intuitive sense. It is probably true that the greater the freedom in society, the greater the participation in politics; and the greater the participation in politics, the more complex the political process. It is, then, a challenge to be able to understand this dynamic aspect of public life in an open society.

There is in all societies an endless and ongoing **political process** by which public decisions are made in response to claims and counterclaims from elements of that society. This political process produces not only decisions but also patterns of support for and resistance to these decisions. The process can be conceived as a system. In the cybernetic sense, a system is a connected set of functions that converts inputs into outputs and feeds the results back as data for future rounds of decision making.[1]

POLITICS AS A SYSTEMIC PROCESS

David Easton specifically applied systems analysis to politics in a well-known book, *A Systems Analysis of Political Life* (1965). He showed that the political system in its simplest form was a process of authoritative decision making,[2] as illustrated in Figure 22.1. Consider politics as a systemic flow. Specific inputs (demands and supports) are generated in society. Demands are what people would like government to do for them; supports are the approbation they bestow on a government they consider legitimate. These demands and supports are transformed or converted into outputs: laws and policies. This conversion takes place in what Easton calls the "black box," which is made up of the various branches and layers of government. He calls it the black box because at this point he is not concerned with the internal mechanisms by which conversion is accomplished; he is just noting that conversion occurs and is trying to situate it in a systemic context. The box is black because he does not yet look inside it. The impact of laws and policies on society takes place through feedback, which generates new demands and supports. Easton was one of the first to apply the term *political system,* which is now used extensively in the political science literature to refer to the process of government and politics in any state.

An influential book by Gabriel Almond and G. B. Powell, *Comparative Politics* (1966), took a similar approach.[3] Almond and Powell also adopted the fundamental notions of input, conversion, output, and feedback. However, they provided a more

Figure 22.1 The Systemic Flow of Politics

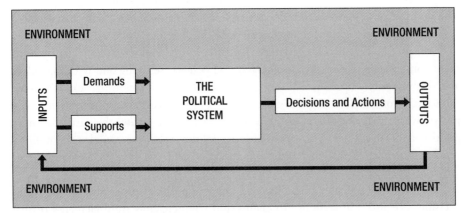

Figure 22.2 The Political Process

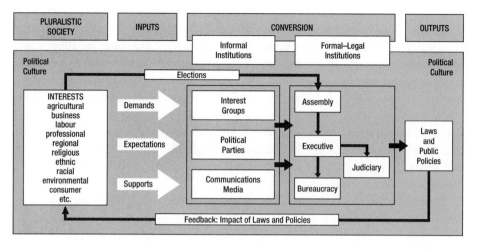

detailed analysis of the conversion process in the modern democratic state—an analysis that is at the same time compatible with traditional ideas in political science, such as the separation of powers into legislative, executive, and judicial branches. They pointed to six important **structures** that carry out necessary functions: interest groups, political parties, the mass media, legislatures, executives, and the judiciary. The corresponding **functions** in the political process are interest articulation (making the position of the group known), interest aggregation (combining the positions of a number of interests), communication, making laws, administering laws, and adjudicating disputes.

Our model, shown in Figure 22.2, portrays politics as a process in which information flows from left to right. The process begins with the plural society (one composed of many interests) and converts political inputs (demands, expectations, and supports) into political outputs (laws and policies). Institutions, both formal and informal, interact to achieve this conversion and produce laws and public policies. Laws and policies can be classified as **regulative, extractive, distributive,** and **symbolic.** They are *regulative* when they control individual and group behaviour in society; speed limits are a regulative law. They are *extractive* when taxes are taken from citizens to pay for government; requirements to pay personal and corporate income taxes are extractive laws. They are *distributive* when they extend payments and services to individuals; public education, health care, and even garbage collection exemplify distributive policies. They are *symbolic* when they represent the community with images such as a flag or national anthem. Feedback allows the system to adjust spontaneously to ever-changing conditions as outputs are evaluated and give rise to new inputs.

In society, conflicts inevitably develop among groups with different interests, goals, and expectations. For example, environmentalists have been demanding the reduction of greenhouse gas emissions. One of the methods to achieve that goal, supported by both the Liberal government of Paul Martin and the Conservative government of

Stephen Harper, was to require gasoline sold at the pump to contain 5 percent ethanol, which is manufactured from corn or other grains. The regulation was accompanied by special tax incentives for ethanol producers. Farmers liked the policy because it created new markets and higher prices for the grains they grow, but by 2008 it was also becoming apparent that consumers might pay higher prices for food as a result of diverting grains into fuel production. That might not matter too much in a wealthy country such as Canada, but could have serious consequences in famine-prone Third World countries, where many people live on the edge of hunger. Environmentalists, farmers, and consumers represent different groups with partially conflicting, partially overlapping interests. In such circumstances, any governmental decision is an output that affects these groups. Even a decision to postpone a decision is in effect an output that ratifies the status quo.

Nothing in the model assumes that all groups will be equally powerful or have an equal chance of advancing their interests. Depending on the social structure, some groups will have command over greater resources or will be more strategically positioned. Rather than being egalitarian, the outcomes of the political process tend to reflect the inequalities of the existing social structure.

Not all political activity is necessarily conflict-oriented; many actions by individuals and groups support the political process. Taxes are paid and speed limits are observed. For society to be orderly, there must be compliance with authority. In fact, without compliance, the entire process would become oppressive. The point is that the political behaviour of individuals and groups involves both demands and supports. For example, people usually pay taxes voluntarily. If, however, tax rates go beyond what people consider a just proportion, tax avoidance and evasion may reduce the amount of revenue collected. Clearly, government cannot function without a basis of support.

Public participation by individuals and groups in the political process follows certain patterns. Most of it is organized around the various intermediate institutions that link people and their governors: interest groups, political parties, and the media. These are frequently referred to as the **informal institutions** of government. While they are an integral part of the process, they are informal (as opposed to formal–legal) because they are not established by a constitution. Yet they have power because they tend to coordinate and channel the activities of people in a concerted way. The development of these intermediate institutions has facilitated participation by large numbers of people in the modern political process.

Other institutions are **formal–legal.** That is, they are created explicitly by a constitution, which provides the rules of the political game. One of the primary functions of a constitution is to grant power to various institutions that formalize laws and policies for a society. These institutions include elected assemblies, executives, and the judiciary. A final formal–legal institution is, of course, the election—the means by which society's members choose their governors and express their opinion of past governmental performance. The activities of these formal–legal organizations are the most visible part of the political process.

The systemic view of politics is one way of conceptualizing the process of politics. While it includes most political institutions and suggests the interaction of these institutions creates a "political flow" (from input to output), it can never capture the dynamic of a charismatic leader and his/her influence on the process, or the impact of corruption on the system. Nevertheless, a systemic view of politics does offer a way of pulling together a complex process of public decision making.

POLICY COMMUNITIES AND NETWORKS

The political process can also be examined in the context of public policy. Political scientists study topics such as the politics of energy, health care, unemployment insurance, transportation, and defence. Instead of focusing on the role of particular institutions such as interest groups, political parties, the cabinet, the bureaucracy, and the courts, political scientists may analyze the interactions of the major players involved in enacting or rejecting a specific policy or set of policies.

Paul Pross enhanced this approach to political analysis by formulating the idea of a **policy community.** William Coleman and Grace Skogstad suggest that the policy community includes "all actors or potential actors with a direct or indirect interest in a policy area or function who share a common 'policy focus,' and who, with varying degrees of influence shape policy outcomes over the long run."[4] The policy community forms once a particular policy becomes an issue. Within the policy community there are sub-government groups and the attentive public. Sub-governments include "government agencies, interest associations, and other societal organizations such as business firms." The attentive public includes "relevant media and interested and expert individuals."[5]

The policy community is interactive and dynamic (see Figure 22.3). For example, once the federal government begins to consider a clean-air standards act, an environmental policy community emerges. Agencies of the state involved in this policy decision will include the cabinet, the departments of environment and industry, agencies concerned with interprovincial and international trade, parliament, and perhaps the courts. Other groups with a stake in this process will also become involved: environmental groups and provincial governments, as well as actors in the private sector such as business firms and labour unions. Presumably the interaction of these organizations will produce some kind of policy.

Thus, the policy approach to politics is, according to Les Pal, a "problem"-oriented approach: "Existing policies therefore contain some definition of a problem; designing new policies depends initially on recognizing and defining public problems."[6] Focusing on societal problems offers another way of conceptualizing the process of politics. And we feel it is important for everyone to have some way of visualizing the process of politics, especially if one is to discuss, evaluate, and criticize politics.

Figure 22.3 The Policy Community

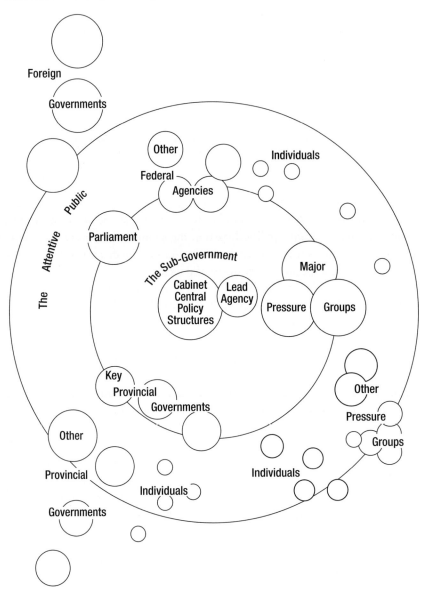

In the rest of Part Four, we examine the informal and formal–legal institutions and their role or function in a modern democratic process.

Questions for Discussion

1. How would you conceptualize the process of politics?

2. What are some of the advantages of taking a systemic or structural approach to politics?

3. What are some of the advantages of taking a policy or "problem" approach to politics?

Internet Links

1. *Canadian Public Policy:* **http://economics.ca/cpp.** Canada's leading academic, peer-refereed journal for the study of public policy.

2. Institute for Research on Public Policy (IRPP), *Policy Options:* **www.irpp.org.** Publishes shorter, less technical articles than *Canadian Public Policy.*

3. C.D. Howe Institute: **www.cdhowe.org.** One of Canada's leading public-policy think tanks.

Further Reading

Almond, Gabriel A., and G. Bingham Powell, Jr. *Comparative Politics—A Developmental Approach: System, Process and Policy.* 2nd ed. Boston: Little, Brown, 1978.

Andrain, Charles F. *Comparative Political Systems: Policy Performance and Social Change.* Armonk, NY: M. E. Sharpe, 1994.

Bertalanffy, Ludwig von. *General System Theory.* New York: George Braziller, 1968.

Birkland, Thomas A. *An Introduction to the Policy Process: Theories, Concepts, and Models of Public Policy Making.* 2nd ed. Armonk, NY: M. E. Sharpe Inc., 2005.

Brooks, Stephen, and Lydia Miljan. *Public Policy in Canada: An Introduction.* 4th ed. Toronto: Oxford University Press, 2003.

Campbell, Robert M., Michael Howlett, and Leslie A. Pal. *The Real World of Canadian Politics: Cases in Process and Policy.* 4th ed. Peterborough, ON: Broadview Press, 2004.

Cummings, Thomas G., ed. *Systems Theory for Organization Development.* Chichester, UK: John Wiley & Sons, 1980.

Doern, G. Bruce, ed. *How Ottawa Spends: 2002–2003.* Toronto: Oxford University Press, 2002.

———. *How Ottawa Spends: 2005–2006.* Montreal: McGill–Queen's University Press, 2005.

Doern, G. Bruce, and Richard W. Phidd. *Canadian Public Policy: Ideas, Structure, Process.* 2nd ed. Scarborough, ON: Nelson Canada, 1992.

Doern, G. Bruce, Leslie A. Pal, and Brian W. Tomlin. *Border Crossings: The Internationalization of Canadian Public Policy.* Toronto: Oxford University Press, 1996.

Dunn, William N. *Public Policy Analysis: An Introduction.* 2nd ed. Englewood Cliffs, NJ: Prentice-Hall, 1994.

Easton, David. *The Analysis of Political Structures.* New York: Routledge, 1990.

———. *A Systems Analysis of Political Life.* New York: Wiley, 1965.

Homer-Dixon, Thomas. *The Ingenuity Gap: How Can We Solve the Problems of the Future.* Toronto: Alfred A. Knopf, 2000.

Howlett, Michael, and M. Ramesh. *Studying Public Policy: Policy Cycles and Policy Subsystems.* 2nd ed. Toronto: Oxford University Press, 2003.

Lilleker, Darren G. *Key Concepts in Political Communication.* London: Sage, 2006.

March, James G., and Johan P. Olson. *Democratic Governance.* New York: Free Press, 1995.

———. *Rediscovering Institutions: The Organizational Basis of Politics.* New York: Free Press, 1989.

Pal, Leslie A. *Beyond Policy Analysis: Public Issue Management in Turbulent Times.* 3rd ed. Scarborough, ON: Thomson Nelson, 2006.

Peters, B. Guy. *Institutional Theory in Political Science: The "New Institutionalism."* London and New York: Continuum, 1999.

Savoie, Donald J. *Breaking the Bargain: Public Servants, Ministers, and Parliament.* Toronto: University of Toronto Press, 2003.

Shapiro, Ian. *Rethinking Political Institutions: The Art of the State.* New York: New York University Press, 2006.

Steinmo, Sven, Kathleen Thelan, and Frank Longstreth. *Structuring Politics: Historical Institutionalism in Comparative Analysis.* Cambridge: Cambridge University Press, 1992.

Stone, Deborah A. *Policy Paradox and Political Reason.* New York: HarperCollins, 1988.

CHAPTER 23

Political Parties, Interest Groups, and Social Movements: The Organization of Interests

Political parties, interest groups, and social movements are vital parts of the political process. Each provides a function essential to the conversion stage of the political process (refer to Figure 22.2). Political parties try to capture the reins of power of government; they want to control the institutions of government by winning a majority in elections. Interest groups, on the other hand, attempt to influence governments; they try to persuade public officials to enact legislation in their or the public's interest. Like interest groups, social movements attempt to influence governments but they go beyond this in attempting to bring about some type of wider social change. In this chapter, political parties, interest groups, and social movements will be discussed separately.

POLITICAL PARTIES

Political parties are an essential feature of politics in the modern age of mass participation. In liberal–democratic systems, they help to keep governments accountable to public opinion. Even in autocratic systems of government, they help the government maintain its hold on power. In either case, political parties are an important link between government and the people.

Political parties are a rather recent phenomenon, having evolved with the extension of the franchise. In the eighteenth century, the Tories and Whigs dominated the British Parliament as political clubs of the upper class. They had little in the way of strong connections with the general population. But as the Reform Acts of 1832, 1867, and 1884 extended suffrage to most adult males, these clubs were transformed to accommodate the influx of voters, and the Conservative and Liberal Parties were formed. The tendency toward greater mass participation continued with the development of the Labour Party in the late nineteenth century as a party of the working class. By the

1930s, it had replaced the Liberals as the principal competitor to the Conservatives, leaving the Liberals a third and minor party in the British system. As reforms expanded the electorate in liberal democracies, political parties were viewed as the primary political organization facilitating mass politics. Political parties not only were the vehicle through which individuals could become involved in politics, but also were considered the primary institutions shaping public policy.

A political party performs so many tasks in the political process that it is difficult to establish a simple definition. However, Joseph LaPalombara's working definition can serve as a point of departure:

> A political party is a formal organization whose self-conscious, primary purpose is to place and maintain in public office persons who will control, alone or in coalition, the machinery of government.[1]

These organizations are not usually part of the formal–legal machinery of government. In most Western nations, they do not derive power from a constitution. Any power they have depends on how the electorate responds in elections. However, there is an increasing tendency in many countries for political parties to be drawn into the formal sphere of government. In Canada, for instance, donations to parties are eligible for tax credits, while party finances are regulated by government and subject to disclosure laws. Their very success as informal institutions is pushing them toward formal–legal status.

The Roles of Political Parties

The first and most important goal of the political party in a democratic system is electoral success. An election win entitles the party to dominate the governmental machinery and perhaps enact some of the proposals to which it is committed. Electoral success short of outright victory may enable it to participate in a coalition government and thus achieve at least some of its aims.

A number of other roles complement the primary objective of winning power. A political party is the mechanism by which candidates are chosen to run for public office. A person may choose to run as an independent, but almost all successful candidates for public office are members of an organized party. A related role is to influence voters during campaigns. A great deal of the work of a party organization involves trying to get voters to support its candidates.

At the governmental level, the members elected with the support of the party put forward and pass legislative proposals in the assembly. Obviously, in a parliamentary body of 308 members (Canada) or 646 members (United Kingdom), there must be some organization. The cabinet of the governing party determines which legislative proposals are to be considered, drafted, debated, and (the governing party hopes) passed.

The party also acts as an intermediary between elected members and the public; that is, between people and their government. While the bulk of party activity occurs at election time, this continuous interchange between people and government can be an important function of the party.

Finally, the political party provides a training ground for political leaders. The party ranks are a pool from which political leaders are recruited. Party workers in constituency organizations often choose to run for office; if elected, they may work their way up from the back benches to a ministerial post. In Canada, however, there has been some tendency in recent decades for leaders of the major national parties to be brought in "sideways," as it were. Pierre Trudeau was a university professor and journalist before being invited into the cabinet and was chosen leader after only three years in Parliament. Brian Mulroney had long been a Conservative activist and insider, but had never held an elected office before becoming a Conservative leader. John Turner came back from political retirement to lead the Liberals, a feat that Jean Chrétien repeated in 1990. Paul Martin, however, became prime minister after serving ten years as finance minister in Jean Chrétien's government, so his success came very much from the inside.

Political leadership means building conditions. For example, in the 2000 and 2004 elections, president George W. Bush pulled together a winning coalition of conservative Republicans, large business interests, and fundamentalist Christians in the southern, mid-western, and northern industrial states. In 2008, Barack Obama mobilized moderate Democrats as well as black and Hispanic voters, and was able to make inroads in the south (Florida, North Carolina, and Virginia), the mid-west (Iowa, Colorado, New Mexico, and Nevada), and in Ohio. This aggregation of specific and regional interests enabled Obama to win the presidency over John McCain.

Another important function of the democratic political party is the aggregation of interests. Various groups make a great many demands on government, and it is never possible for a government to meet all of them, mainly because many of the demands are mutually incompatible. For example, organized consumer groups will demand that import quotas on shoes be abolished, while manufacturers will demand that those quotas be made more restrictive. The political party is a forum at which conflicting interests may be at least partially reconciled, where compromises can be reached and then bundled into a program that most party supporters can accept.

In autocratic systems, the party also aggregates demands to some extent, although because of the lack of political freedom this must be done behind the scenes. Specialists in Soviet politics often suggested that the monolithic façade of the Communist Party concealed squabbling factions representing such interests as the military and agriculture. More obvious is the totalitarian party's function of promoting support for the regime. The party is the government's instrument for enhancing popular acceptance of its policies. To this end, the party coordinates publicity in the mass media, organizes meetings and demonstrations, and carries out persuasion through its cells in workplaces.

It must be remembered that we are speaking of political parties in general. Not all parties perform all of the above roles, and the roles may be played in different ways. For example, the role of political parties in the Canadian system has changed over time. They remain the primary vehicle through which politicians are recruited, and they continue to mobilize the electorate at election time. But their function has changed in the area of policy formation. Most policy proposals come from the political executive— the prime minister and other cabinet ministers and their personal advisers—or from the permanent administration. The work of developing policy proposals is not so much the effort of the party faithful as it is of the senior people working for members of cabinet, some of whom may not even belong to the party organization. Thus, while local, regional, provincial, and national party organizations meet and make policy recommendations to the party leadership, the policy proposals that emerge from the government may not reflect opinions at the grassroots level of the party. This is why most analysts now agree that the role of political parties in the legislative process has declined and that the executive and bureaucracy are now more influential. (More on this issue in Chapter 27.)

Because no two parties function in the same way, it is necessary to have a scheme of classification. Without pretending to be definitive, the following typology captures some of the main types: pragmatic, ideological, interest, personal, and movement parties.

The Pragmatic Party

One of the more common party types in Western society is the **pragmatic party.** The dictionary defines *pragmatism* as a "philosophy that evaluates assertions solely by their practical consequences and bearing on human interests."[2] In other words, a pragmatist's actions are less likely to be driven by a set of basic principles and doctrine than by a concern for the consequences of those actions. The pragmatic political party gears its campaign promises not to beliefs founded on doctrine, but to programs that it believes have the greatest appeal to the public. It is thus open to the criticism of having no principles and of moving with the wind, and its programs sometimes appear to reflect nothing more than a cynical desire for power.

The mass parties in the Anglo-American tradition are generally classified as pragmatic: Conservatives and Labour in Great Britain, Conservatives and Liberals in Canada, Republicans and Democrats in the United States. The pragmatism of such parties always generates confusion about where they stand. Brian Mulroney's Conservatives, for example, were attacked by voices on the left for pursuing a "right-wing, neoconservative" agenda; yet organizations on the right, such as the Fraser Institute and the National Citizens Coalition, condemned Mulroney for failing to implement a conservative agenda. Pragmatic parties sometimes appear more ideological—as the British Conservatives did under Margaret Thatcher—but this usually reflects not so much a fundamental change in the party as the temporary ascendancy of one faction within it. With the passage of time, the party usually reverts to a more pragmatic and less ideological stance, as happened when John Major replaced Thatcher as leader.

When pragmatic parties compete head to head, they characteristically make overlapping proposals, even to the extent of borrowing each other's ideas. For example, the proposal for a comprehensive Free Trade Agreement with the United States arose from a royal commission appointed by the Liberal government of Pierre Trudeau and chaired by Donald Macdonald, a former Liberal cabinet minister. Brian Mulroney opposed the idea when he was running for the leadership of the Conservatives, but later adopted it as the most important policy initiative of his first term in office. The Liberals strenuously opposed the Free Trade Agreement while it was being negotiated, but Jean Chrétien's government gave it final approval for implementation.

This mutual borrowing is not confined to particular policies; it also extends to broader party positions. Between the 1950s and the 1970s, the welfare state and government interventionism were dominant ideas, and the pragmatic parties of the right had to accept them or face electoral extinction. "We are all Keynesians now," said Republican Richard Nixon when he was president of the United States. But during the 1980s and 1990s, when the fiscal difficulties of the welfare state led to the revival of conservatism, the pragmatic parties of the left had to come to terms with privatization, deregulation, and balanced budgets. Bill Clinton was elected president in 1992 and re-elected in 1996 in part because he acknowledged the importance of traditional conservative objectives such as reducing the deficit, tightening up welfare programs, and enhancing business competitiveness; indeed, he claimed to be more able than President George H. W. Bush (1988–92) to attain these ends, albeit using different means. Tony Blair's Labour Party regained power in the British election of 1997 in part by promising to leave Margaret Thatcher's reforms undisturbed (see World View 17.1 in Chapter 17).

The Ideological Party

The **ideological party,** in contrast, emphasizes ideological purity more than the immediate attainment of power. Party doctrine takes precedence over electoral success. Such parties are criticized, of course, for their inflexibility. Often they put doctrine before the wishes of the voters, convinced that in time voters will come around to their way of thinking. The Communist Party is a good example of an ideological party, as are socialist parties and even some social democratic parties. On the right, some conservative parties are as doctrinaire as any on the left.

The New Democratic Party is the most ideological of the traditional Canadian parties. As a party of the left, its major policy commitments have focused on social rights (e.g., opposition to the privatization of health care) and economic rights (e.g., review NAFTA to achieve fairer trade). The Reform Party (1987–2000) was understood by most observers to be an ideological party of the right, in that it also presented a simple, doctrinaire program: balance the federal budget, reduce taxes and government spending, abolish official bilingualism, introduce recall legislation, and so on. More careful observers, however, noted that Reform positions were often phrased with a "calculated ambiguity" suggesting a pragmatic party in waiting.[3]

When the Reform Party merged itself into the Canadian Alliance in 2000, it abandoned or watered down a number of its more radical positions, thus taking further steps toward becoming a pragmatic party; and that process was completed in 2003 when Reform merged with the Progressive Conservatives to form the Conservative Party of Canada.

When pragmatic parties adopt policies that are very similar, they run the risk that new parties may appeal to voters who perceive the pragmatic parties as no longer standing for anything. In Canada, Brian Mulroney's success at adopting many positions previously associated with the Liberals (bilingualism, multiculturalism, employment equity) led many ideological conservatives to defect from the Progressive Conservatives in favour of the Reform Party, which offered a more consistent ideological stance. The Reform Party, however, found its potential limited because it was perceived by many voters as excessively ideological, leading to its reunion with the Progressive Conservatives in 2003. The point is not that pragmatic parties are good and ideological parties are bad, or vice versa; it is that each type of party offers something different to voters and may fail or succeed under various sets of circumstances.

The Interest Party

Another type of party is the **interest party.** Here we find people converting their interest group into a full-fledged political party that runs candidates and attempts to obtain power. Such a group feels that it can best achieve its ends by acting as a party rather than trying to influence existing parties, but its narrow basis of support makes it hard for it to win control of the state. In Australia, the National Party (previously known as the Country Party) began as a farmers' party. There have also been peasants' parties in Eastern Europe and Latin America. In Scandinavia, industrialists have formed conservative parties. Around the world, Green parties have developed from environmental movements when they became convinced of the need to have political parties win seats in legislatures to fight for environmental issues from within rather than outside government. In Canada, the Green Party was established in 1983 and in the 2006 and 2008 general elections, that party earned 4.5 percent and 6.8 percent respectively of the national vote. While not an insignificant share, it was not high enough to win a seat in the House of Commons.

There is vigorous debate about the merits of pragmatic, ideological, and interest parties. Some believe that pragmatic parties contribute to the stability of the political system—that they cover the waterfront, so to speak, in their response to demands made by groups in society. These parties endeavour to include something for everyone in their platforms. They appeal to diverse groups—employers and labour unions, farmers and consumers, conservationists and developers. Many people see pragmatic parties as mechanisms for aggregating interests and mending the fault lines in a pluralistic society.

Those who advocate the virtues of interest and ideological parties make their arguments from the standpoint of representation. They are quite critical of pragmatic parties, suggesting that by making broad appeals to all groups such parties dilute their platforms so that in the end they represent no one. This is the position taken by Maurice Duverger, a noted authority on political parties, whose comparative work is still basic in the field.[4] An interest or ideological party, according to this view, can cater its platform to a specific interest or to a group with a defined ideology. Political parties of this type are able to offer voters a clear choice, and elected members have a responsibility to a specific clientele. But what is made up in representation could be lost in stability. The advocates of pragmatic parties suggest that interest and ideological parties tend to intensify cleavages in society rather than reconcile them. Moreover, when these parties are unwilling to compromise at the legislative level little is accomplished, and governmental instability and inaction may well result.

In fact, both pragmatic parties and interest or ideological parties have shown themselves capable of aggregating interests and reconciling conflicts. In the Anglo-American model of pragmatic parties, the resolution of conflicts takes place within the party. Labour, business, and agricultural organizations come to some sort of compromise with the government of the day, which is almost always formed by a single party. In contrast, in democracies where coalition governments of ideological or interest parties are the norm, interest reconciliation takes place among parties. Parties do not have to surrender their principles internally, but they have to make compromises to keep a coalition cabinet in power. This illustrates the general principle that the necessary functions of the political process may be accomplished in quite different ways in different systems. Any successful political system must resolve conflicts of interest among different social groups; but this task can be carried out within parties, among parties, or by other institutions in the governmental process. The method may not matter very much as long as the job gets done. The advantage of approaching politics as a process is that one becomes sensitive to relationships of this type and learns to look at institutions not in isolation but rather as they relate to other institutions.

The Personal Party

Another type of party is the **personal party,** which is founded around a single, influential political leader. After World War II, supporters of Charles de Gaulle formed the Gaullist Party, which became the strongest political force in France after de Gaulle established the Fifth Republic in 1958. With the support of this party, called the Union for the Defence of the Republic (UDR), de Gaulle was elected president in 1958 and 1965. The Gaullists, under a variety of party names, survived the General's retirement in 1969 and today represent a coalition of moderate conservatives. Juan Perón of Argentina also developed a political party from his personal following. His supporters elected him president in 1946 and 1951. Perón, however, was removed from office after a *coup d'état* in 1955. The Peronistas were the main force behind the election of President Carlos Menem in 1989 and 1995, reinforcing the fact that personal parties need not die with their founders.

Personal parties have been common in the Third World, particularly in Africa. Jomo Kenyatta of Kenya was one of the chief architects of KANU—the Kenya African National Union. KANU provided a base of support for Kenyatta, who attempted to use the party to integrate Kenya's many tribal groups. Kenyatta died in 1978, but his party has remained a dominant force in Kenya. For years Robert Mugabe of Zimbabwe dreamed of establishing his Zimbabwe African National Union–Patriotic Front (ZANU–PF) as the single party under which racial and ethnic groups would be united. This was accomplished in December 1987 and he was re-elected president in 1990, 1996, and 2002. In the 2008 election, however, Morgan Tsvangirai, leader of the Movement for Democratic Change (MDC), earned a sufficient number of votes to force a runoff election for the presidency. Mugabe won the runoff when Tsvangirai withdrew, accusing the government of mounting a campaign of violence against his supporters.

All these examples show that the personal party, like the other types of parties, is not an entirely clear-cut category. All parties have leaders who are usually quite prominent even in a thoroughly democratic party; and even the most dominating leader has to have an organization to be effective. Thus parties that may be considered personal vehicles at the outset often evolve into long-lasting pragmatic, ideological, or interest parties.

The Movement Party

A **movement party** is a political movement that evolves into a party apparatus. A movement is a union of people that aims at a profound social change, such as national independence, but does not itself aspire to govern. A movement sometimes is converted into a party when the prestige it gains by achieving its goals makes it a logical choice to become the government. The Congress Party in India is a good example. The Indian National Congress, organized in 1885, became the instrument by which Indians sought independence from Great Britain. The party became the focus of nationalist feeling throughout India and mobilized popular pressure against the British. After achieving independence in 1947, it became the dominant political force in the federal Parliament, a position that it long maintained, although it slipped a good deal during the 1990s. In Canada, the Bloc Québécois could be considered a movement party. Its only real program is the sovereignty of Quebec. If it ever achieves this goal, it will probably break up into ideological factions. In the meantime, it uses the House of Commons as a forum for promoting the independence of Quebec. For a list of other movement parties throughout Canadian history, see Canadian Focus 23.1.

Political Party Systems

Political party systems also influence the manner in which parties carry out their roles. There are basically three types of party systems: one-party, two-party, and multiparty.

Canadian Focus 23.1

New Political Parties in Canada

For a very long period of time, the two regions of Canada most dissatisfied with the status quo in Canada have been Quebec and the West. It is not surprising, then, that these two regions, so different in other ways, have both given rise to a long series of political parties challenging the constitutional order in fundamental ways. Below are lists of the main parties created in these two regions. The symbol P means provincial party, F means a federal party, and F+P indicates that the party operated at both levels.

New Political Parties Founded in Western Canada

Provincial Rights Party (P)	1905
Non-Partisan League (P)	1916
Progressives (including United Farmers' parties) (F+P)	1919
Co-operative Commonwealth Federation (F+P)	1932
Social Credit (F+P)	1935
Social Credit Party of British Columbia (P)	1952
Western Canada Concept (F+P)	1980
Western Canada Federation (F+P)	1980
Confederation of Regions (F+P)	1983
Reform Party of Canada (F)	1987
Reform Party of British Columbia (P)	1989
National Party (F)	1992
Progressive Democratic Alliance of British Columbia (P)	1993
Saskatchewan Party (P)	1997
British Columbia Unity Party (P)	2001
Alberta Alliance (P)	2002
Wildrose Alliance Party (P)	2008

New Political Parties Founded in Quebec

Parti National (P)	1885
Nationalist League (as political party) (F)	1911
Action Libérale Nationale (P)	1934
Union Nationale (P)	1935
Union des Electeurs (F+P)	1939
Bloc Populaire Canadien (F+P)	1942
Ralliement des Créditistes (F)	1957
Parti Québécois (P)	1968
Ralliement Créditiste du Québec (P)	1970
Equality Party (P)	1989
Bloc Québécois (F)	1990
Action Démocratique du Québec (P)	1994
Québéc Solidaire (P)	2006

The One-Party System

This type includes true **single-party systems** and **one-party-dominant systems.** In the former, there is only one party in the political system, and no political alternative is legally tolerated. The former Communist Party of the Soviet Union, whose leading role was guaranteed in the Constitution, was the classic example. Where political leaders are building a utopian order according to an ideological blueprint, political opposition becomes heresy. Under such conditions any political alternative is prohibited.

In a one-party-dominant state, a single political party dominates the political process without the official support of the state. While a number of minor parties offer political alternatives, the electorate usually votes overwhelmingly for the dominant party. The Institutionalized Revolutionary Party (PRI) of Mexico was an example until the 2000 elections. After the Mexican Revolution began in 1910, a fierce struggle occurred during which many leaders, such as Pancho Villa and Emiliano Zapata, fought to gain control of the national government. Plutarco Calles consolidated power in the late 1920s and developed a party organization that in time emerged as the PRI. Even today the party claims to stand as a symbol of the ongoing revolution. Its critics suggest that the party is more institutionalized than revolutionary. The PRI maintained power by clever use of the state apparatus, especially through patronage and corruption. Electoral reforms initiated under President Ernesto Zedillo (1994–2000) played a role in the victory of the National Action Party under the leadership of Vicente Fox in 2000.

Finally, there are times when one party dominates without in any way using the state machinery to support its position. For whatever reason, voters seem content with a single party for long periods of time. The Democrats dominated the American South for a century after the Civil War. In Canada, the province of Alberta has had the curious habit of endorsing one party for long periods, then suddenly turning to another. Since 1905, no party in Alberta having once formed a government and then lost an election has ever returned to power. The result has been a sequence of one-party-dominant situations rather than sustained competition between two or more credible contenders. This assertion was reinforced in 2008 when the Progressive Conservatives won their eleventh straight election since 1971.

Canadian federal politics also entered a one-party-dominant phase with the 1993 election, which persisted through the elections of 1997 and 2000. The Liberals were the only party able to elect MPs in all regions of the country, while each of the other parties had a much narrower geographic and demographic base. The Bloc Québécois appealed only to francophones in Quebec. The Reform Party and its successor, the Canadian Alliance, were strong in the West but unable to win appreciable numbers of seats elsewhere. The NDP had pockets of support in inner-city ridings, in strongholds of organized labour, and since 1997 in Atlantic Canada. However, the merger of the Progressive Conservatives and the Canadian Alliance in 2003 moved the system back to the two-party-plus system that dominated Canadian federal politics throughout most of the twentieth century.

The Two-Party System

A **two-party system** exists when two parties are credible contenders for power and either is capable of winning any election. The United Kingdom and the United States are commonly cited as illustrations, but neither is literally a two-party system. In Britain, the Conservatives and Labour have been challenged by the Liberal Democrats, plus several regional parties operating in Scotland, Wales, and Northern Ireland. In the American election of 1992, Ross Perot, an independent candidate for president, received 19 percent of the popular vote, although he did not get any electoral votes. Perot then transformed his movement into a more conventional political party, borrowing the name Reform Party from Canada. When he ran for president again in 1996, however, he received only 9 percent of the popular vote and again failed to win any votes in the Electoral College. In 2000, Ralph Nader ran for the Green Party and received only about 3 percent of the popular vote and no Electoral College votes. However, it has been argued that Nader's candidacy was significant. The approximately 100,000 voters he took in Florida might have tipped the balance in favour of Al Gore. This is an example of how even a minor third party may influence a close political race. (For further discussion of this disputed election, see Chapter 25.)

In Britain and the United States there have been many third parties, but they have rarely gained enough popular support to threaten the two major parties. Thus, when we speak of a two-party system, we mean that victory at the polls is likely to go to the Conservatives or Labour (or to the Democrats or Republicans), even though other parties may also contest the election. In systems where third parties receive a significant but minor share of the vote, it might be more accurate to call these systems **two-party-plus systems,** as some observers do.

Germany furnishes an example of two-party-plus politics. The Christian Democrats and Social Democrats there are so evenly matched at the polls that the small Free Democratic Party, the Left, and/or Greens can determine who will govern by throwing their parliamentary weight to one side or the other. The current government, however, is a "grand coalition" between the Christian Democrats and the Social Democrats, the two major parties.

Canada was close to a strict two-party system in the first 50 years of Confederation. From 1867 to 1917, only the Conservatives and Liberals mattered in federal politics. But from 1921 onward, there have always been more than two parties represented in the House of Commons. The Progressives were the first successful third party, followed by Social Credit and the CCF, which both entered the House of Commons in 1935. The CCF continues in the form of the NDP, while more recently we saw the rise of the Bloc Québécois and the Reform Party/Canadian Alliance.

The election of 2004 saw a return to the classic two-party-plus configuration of Canadian federal politics. A close race to the end, the Liberals won only a minority government, with 37 percent of the popular vote and 135 seats; the Conservatives became the Official Opposition with 30 percent of the vote and 99 seats. The 2006 election confirmed the return to the two-party-plus system, only with the Conservatives forming a minority government (with 36 percent of the vote and 124 seats) and the Liberals the official opposition (with 30 percent of the vote and 103 seats). The NDP and Bloc Québécois were never a threat to win, but each secured an important niche in Parliament (29 seats for the NDP, 51 for the BQ). After the 2008 election, the number of seats won by the political parties were: Conservatives 143; Liberals 76; NDP 37; Bloc 50; and Independents 2.

The two-party system is widely praised as a source of political stability, especially in parliamentary systems, in which the cabinet must maintain the confidence of an elected assembly. A two-party system is likely to yield majority governments that can hold office for a respectable length of time. Less convincing is the common argument that a two-party system serves the interests of voters by offering them a clear choice between two responsible aspirants to power. Parties in two-party systems are often highly pragmatic, so that for long periods of time their platforms may greatly resemble each other, giving voters little real choice. American and Canadian politics are like this at most elections. This is not to say that the two-party system is necessarily any worse than the multiparty alternative—only that it is not as obviously superior as newspaper editorials in the Anglo-American democracies often maintain.

The Multiparty System

In a **multiparty system,** three or more political parties have a realistic chance of participating in government. In most cases, the parties are either interest parties or ideological parties, which consider the interests of their supporters their first priority. Sweden is a multiparty system. From left to right on the political spectrum, one could find seven political parties represented in the Riksdag (parliament) after the 2006 election: Left, Greens, Social Democrats, Centre, Christian Democrats, Liberals, and Moderates. The Left Party is the residue of the old Communist Party and is supported by workers; the Greens, as their name implies, are an expression of the environmentalist movement; the Social Democrats are a pragmatic socialist party; the Centre is an agrarian party with some urban support; Christian Democrats advocate Christian values; the Liberals represent professionals and intellectuals; the Moderates represent free-enterprise financial and business interests.

Cabinet instability sometimes occurs in parliamentary systems in which there are many parties. When representatives are drawn from a number of parties, majority governments are difficult to come by, and coalition governments may become the norm. Where the parties in a coalition government hold to principle and refuse to compromise, governments tend to change frequently. This was the case in the Fourth Republic of France in the 1950s, which saw 13 governments in one period of 18 months. The same is true of Italy, which has averaged about one government a year since the end of World War II.

However, in political science generalizations seldom apply without exceptions. Instability does not occur in all multiparty systems. The multiparty systems of Denmark, Norway, and Sweden, for example, have usually produced durable coalitions that cannot be characterized as unstable. The difference has an interesting and logical explanation. Italy and France at various times had large extremist parties of both the left and the right. Because some of these parties were fundamentally opposed to the constitution, they were not acceptable coalition partners, which restricted the number of possible coalitions. Under such conditions, when a working partnership among parties breaks down there may be no alternative to re-establishing it, except perhaps by replacing the cabinet. The result is a game of political musical chairs in which cabinets succeed each other with monotonous regularity. In contrast, the Scandinavian countries do not have large extremist parties. All important parties are acceptable coalition partners, so there is more room to manoeuvre and create durable coalitions.

Assessing Political Parties

Political parties developed in concert with the extension of the franchise and they have helped to legitimize mass democracy. But this does not mean that all political parties are mass organizations with every voter holding a membership; on the contrary, in most Western societies the actual number of party members is very small. In Canada, fewer than 5 percent of voters belong to any federal or provincial party. Moreover, most of those who do are in the middle and upper-middle income brackets, are relatively well educated, and generally feel they have something at stake in the political process. For this reason, political parties have been criticized as representing not the masses but the social and economic elite in society. Indeed, when one examines a sociological profile of party activists, the criticism may seem valid. Oligarchies of a kind do run political parties.

This point was made early in the century by Roberto Michels in his classic work *Political Parties*. Michels argued that even the parties that talked the most about democracy, such as the social democratic parties of his day, inevitably fell under the control of small, self-perpetuating elites. He went so far as to state that an "iron law of oligarchy" represented the real truth about democracy.[5]

However, the charge of elitism conveys the idea of a group closed off from the rest of society by restricted membership; this is not really the case with political parties in most Western democracies. While there may be only a few militants, and they may represent the upper echelons of society, the doors of party organizations are not closed. On the contrary, anyone who pays the nominal membership fee is welcomed with open arms, and anyone who volunteers for party work is quickly inundated with tasks. The ranks of political parties may be filled by a few middle-class activists because they are the ones who choose to become involved. Many people simply may not have an interest in the mundane tasks that accompany political party membership. In most cases, the individual reward or payoff for party work is relatively small when measured against the effort involved.

In another sense, parties are elitist. Modern political competition depends heavily on public relations, advertising, polling, and fundraising—the so-called "black arts" of politics. These tasks require special skills and connections possessed by only a few insiders. While there may be many ordinary people serving as foot soldiers in the trenches of political warfare, the commanders and strategists are well-paid, well-connected people possessing unusual skills. This makes it difficult for the rank and file to feel they have any impact on policy directions of the party.

Be that as it may, we are seeing a remarkable proliferation of new political parties in Western Europe and North America. On the left, the main entrants are the "Green" parties, which represent environmentalism as a rising political issue. There are also a number of "new" socialist parties, which are actually recycled versions of older communist parties. On the right, the picture is even more complex. New "populist" conservative parties emerged recently in several countries; for example, the New Democracy in Sweden and the Reform Party/Canadian Alliance in Canada had temporary but important life spans. These parties tended to be market-oriented, to advocate direct democracy, to be opposed to large-scale immigration, and to be rather antagonistic to corporations, trade unions, government bureaucracies, and other large organizations. Further to the right are nationalistic, even racist, parties like the National Front of Jean Le Pen in France, the Republicans in Germany, and the Freedom Party in Austria.

At one level, these new parties are responding to emerging issues. Green parties are responding to environmental concerns; populist conservative parties are driven by the fiscal problems of the welfare state; and nationalist–racist parties represent a backlash against the flood of refugees and other immigrants into Western Europe. But at another level, this does not explain why the established parties have not responded adequately to these new issues, as they have to other emerging issues in previous decades.

Without pretending to give a complete explanation of why so many new parties have arisen in so many countries in recent decades, we would draw attention to one factor that is surely involved, namely the rise of post-materialism as discussed in Chapter 5. Voters influenced by the post-materialist political culture are more concerned about self-expression and less willing to defer to the compromises engineered by political brokers. This may point toward the emergence of new political parties catering to the demands of a more diverse, opinionated, and fractious electorate. However, with the success of the Liberals and, more recently, the new Conservative Party here in Canada (since 1993), the Labour Party in the United Kingdom (since 1997), and in the United States Republicans (2000–2008) and Democrats (2008–), that is assuming both Republican and Democratic Parties are pragmatic, it appears that pragmatic, centre parties remain the key to electoral success, at least in the Anglo-American world.

INTEREST GROUPS

In addition to political parties, the articulation of interests is also undertaken by particular social groups, usually called interest groups. An **interest group** is defined as "any organization that seeks to influence government policy, but not to govern."[6] It represents people who band together to accomplish specific objectives. Because interest groups exert political pressure to achieve their ends, they may also be called pressure

In 2003, the Progressive Conservative Party of Canada merged with the Canadian Alliance. The cartoon, showing PC leader Peter MacKay and Alliance leader Stephen Harper, poses the question—widely asked at the time—whether the two parties could be successfully merged.
© Graeme MacKay/Artizans.com

groups. Obviously, not all groups are political; people may organize for any number of reasons. There are social groups such as bridge and dance clubs, sports clubs, community associations, and professional organizations. Most of these voluntary organizations will never become involved in politics; however, if they do, they become interest groups in the political process. As such, they facilitate popular participation in politics. By coordinating political activities, they offer individuals an opportunity to become involved in the complex process of politics. Politics is an endless cycle because there are always new demands, generated by a variety of interests, with which government must deal.

Unlike political parties, interest groups do not seek to control the entire machinery of government; they seek merely to influence the political process with the goal of achieving certain legislative or policy ends. Interest groups may work with political parties and may even become affiliated with them—as in the relationship between the New Democratic Party (NDP) and some, but not all, member unions of the Canadian Labour Congress (CLC). Generally, however, parties and interest groups are conceptually distinct, even if their activities sometimes overlap.

Interest groups can be categorized according to the degree to which the benefits that they seek largely benefit their own members (i.e., selective benefits) or the wider community more generally (i.e., diffuse benefits). While the distinction is not watertight and is sometimes subjectively determined, it is important nonetheless to understand that not all interest groups are motivated by self-interest.[7]

The function of an interest group in politics is to articulate the interest of its members with the goal of changing laws and influencing policies. Interest groups seek to achieve their ends by persuading public officials. Land developers may try to influence a city council's decisions on planning and zoning; labour unions may try to persuade the provincial cabinet to amend collective-bargaining legislation; conservation organizations may seek to influence public policies relating to national or provincial parks. Interest groups also address themselves to public opinion; in the Canadian election of 1988, business, labour, and other groups all spoke out vigorously about free trade, although the business community, led by the Canadian Council of Chief Executives (formally the Business Council on National Issues) and the Canadian Manufacturers' Association, had much more money to spend on advertising. In all such cases, citizens with a common goal band together in an effort to shape legislation that they believe affects their lives.

In the second half of the twentieth century, one of the great developments in the political process in Western democracies was the proliferation of organized interest groups. Before World War II, organized interest groups were relatively few in number and consisted chiefly of economic producer groups with a specific focus: business and industrial associations, labour unions, farmers' associations, and the organized professions, such as doctors, lawyers, and teachers. Because groups had to operate with whatever resources they could collect from their members, those representing a well-to-do clientele tended to be the most effective.

The present-day picture is radically different. First, there are now many more politically active groups. Second, there are politically effective groups representing not only traditional producers but also diverse consumer interests (consumer associations, environmental protection groups), as well as a host of moral, cultural, and symbolic causes. Social movements arise (discussed at greater length further on) and organizations are created in rapid succession; witness the way in which the original ethno-linguistic liberation movements of the 1960s (black civil rights in the United States, bilingualism in Canada) have been followed by feminist, gay liberation, and animal-rights movements. Each of these movements has stimulated the growth of a number of organized interest groups to formulate and express distinct political views in the contemporary political process.

Many reasons are suggested as causes for interest-group proliferation. Here we can mention only a few factors. One is the expansion of formal education. More people now have the skills required to run an organization—public speaking, keeping minutes and financial records, doing research on political issues, writing and submitting briefs to public officials. Another is the ongoing revolution in transportation and communication, which has dramatically lowered the costs of building and maintaining a national organization. Modern communication technology, especially fax machines, cell-phones, and e-mail, makes possible the creation of organizations that could not have existed 50 years ago. The same technology has also revolutionized fundraising methods. Even relatively small groups can raise significant amounts of money through telephone solicitation, direct mail driven by computerized lists of target recipients, and credit-card donations on the Internet. Finally, with the declining role of political parties as formulators of public policy, individuals may be more inclined to associate and work for interest groups supporting causes with which they identify because they are perceived to be more effective. This trend is especially true of recent generations (see Figure 23.1).

Ottawa is not the only Canadian city to witness the proliferation of interest groups. In provincial capitals and even at the municipal level, interest groups have become a key part of the political process. Many community or neighbourhood associations are politically active when city councils consider by-laws or otherwise make decisions that have an impact on their section of the city. With governments becoming more involved in all facets of social life, more groups are trying to influence legislation. And many citizens are participating in these groups. According to a recent study undertaken in the United States, almost half of the respondents (48 percent) reported being affiliated with an interest group that took a stand on a political issue.[8] A number of

Figure 23.1 Attitudes on the Most Effective Way to Work for Change by Age Group, Canada, 2000 Strengthening Canadian Democracy Survey

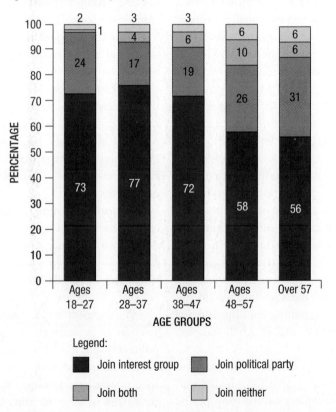

Source: Adapted from Brenda O'Neill, "Generational Patterns in the Political Opinions and Behaviours of Canadians," Policy Matters 2001, 2(5), p. 14. Used with permission of the Institute for Research on Public Policy, www.irpp.com

political scientists have argued that interest groups provide an important opportunity for political participation; participating in an interest group not only provides members with an opportunity for acquiring civic skills and knowledge, but also can provide the "glue" that makes for stronger communities (in political science terminology, this glue is referred to as *social capital*).[9]

A standard typology for classifying interest groups is the fourfold division of **anomic, associational, institutional,** and **nonassociational groups.**[10] For more detail, see Concept Box 23.1 on interest group typology.

A number of issues arise when considering just how interest groups work as part of the political process. For example, an important theoretical analysis by Mancur Olson

---

Concept Box 23.1

Interest Group Typology

Anomic Groups. Spontaneous groups formed by citizens concerned about a specific issue. They usually disband after resolution of the single issue.

Example: Friends of the Calgary General Hospital Society (FCGHS)

After 1994, the Government of Alberta closed three hospitals in Calgary, all of which were in the downtown core. The last closure, the Calgary General Hospital, caused considerable controversy. A group formed to protest the closure, arguing that the downtown needed a full-service hospital. The group continued for a while after demolition of the hospital, taking the government to court on the grounds that the land was set aside for purposes of a hospital and therefore should not be used for anything else; but it faded away after its judicial challenge was unsuccessful.

Associational Groups. Formal organizations set up to articulate the interests of their members over a long period of time.

Examples: Canadian Labour Congress, Canadian Manufacturers and Exporters, Canadian Medical Association

Associational groups are established to further the interests of their members or the public interest. They usually charge their membership a fee and use the proceeds to support a permanent staff to conduct the business of the organization. Most of the large associational groups have representatives in provincial capitals and Ottawa to lobby for their organization.

Institutional Groups. Organizations closely associated with government that act internally to influence public decisions.

Examples: Canadian Union of Public Employees, National Council of Veterans' Associations of Canada.

While people in these groups are part of government and in theory politically neutral, they have interests to articulate and seek specific goals. Like associational groups, they have the advantage of large memberships, permanent organizations, and continuity.

Concept Box 23.1

There are certain associational groups that, according to this classification, might almost be labelled "institutional" because of their close association with governments. Such ties are usually financial. Aboriginal associations are examples, as are francophone and anglophone minority-language associations and multicultural ethnic societies. All such groups receive substantial financial support from the federal government, from departments such as Indian and Northern Affairs, and Canadian Heritage. This funding is often crucial to their existence.

Non-Associational Groups. Unorganized groups made up of individuals who perceive a common identity on the basis of culture, religion, or some other distinctive quality.

Examples: Youth, Catholics, Westerners, Maritimers

Non-associational groups lack formal organizations designed for political activity even though often they are considered as if they were organized. The term *latent groups* captures the significance of these people—at any time, given the right issue, they could mobilize and possibly become a political force. For that reason, politicians take the interests of such groups into account.

suggests that the costs in time and money of organizing for political action often outweigh the benefits that an individual can expect to gain by lobbying, especially when the potential benefits are diffuse.[11] This is another aspect of the free-rider problem discussed in Chapter 10. Why should I spend my time working, for example, in an environmental association when the benefits of cleaner air and water will be enjoyed by all who live in the community, whether or not they contribute to the movement? It might be rational for me to contribute my time and money if I could be sure that others would do likewise, but how can I obtain that guarantee?

One answer is that when a group is already organized for other reasons, its incremental costs of entry into the political system may be much lower. A group may also provide nonpolitical benefits, such as the recreational activities sponsored by the Sierra Club.[12] In both these ways, pre-existing associations have an advantage in undertaking pressure-group activity. The prediction that pre-existing associations such as labour unions and professional associations should be formidable lobbyists seems to be borne out empirically.

Government support of interest groups first became important in Canada as part of Pierre Trudeau's "Just Society." The rationale for it was that Aboriginal peoples, women, and ethnic and linguistic minorities were disadvantaged or even oppressed groups that could not hope to compete on equal terms in the political marketplace. It was thought that giving them financial assistance to form interest groups would enable them to exert political pressure for economic and social reforms and thereby improve their position over the long run. Public support of interest groups was thus a logical corollary of reform liberalism. The public funding of interest groups has declined significantly, however, beginning with the Mulroney government in the 1980s.[13]

It is perhaps surprising that such federally funded interest groups often became the severest critics of federal policy, sometimes in unexpected ways. For example, the National Action Committee on the Status of Women actively opposed most of the initiatives of the Mulroney government, including the FTA and NAFTA, the Charlottetown Accord, and many changes in social policy. But if one considers that such groups received funding because of their relative disadvantage and oppression, then their criticisms are perhaps easier to understand.

Public funding of interest groups raises a number of questions. While the funding provides some groups with the only possibility for participating effectively in the political system, it can also compromise their ability to protect the interests of their members. Government funding also means that certain interests are provided the means with which to organize while others are not; government, in effect, can directly determine which marginalized interests are voiced and heard through its funding decisions. If, however, one accepts that not all interests are equally capable of mobilizing, then public funding remains an important mechanism for ensuring the articulation of a diversity of interests.

Political Consultants and Lobbying

The expansion of interest-group activity has given rise to a new profession, that of the **political consultant.**[14] Consultants often are former politicians, public servants, or military officers who see the opportunity to put their expertise to work in the private sector. For a fee, they keep clients informed of new developments within government and advise them on how to pursue their goals effectively. After consultants have been retired from the public service long enough to avoid charges of conflict of interest, they may also engage in lobbying.

The term **lobbying** is derived from the old practice of individuals and groups buttonholing MPs in the lobby of the British House of Commons. The practice now involves many different methods for influencing decisions: arranging an interview with a cabinet member, submitting a brief to a royal commission or parliamentary committee hearing, writing letters to elected representatives, advertising in the media to generate public pressure over an issue, and offering gifts of various kinds to public officials. In every case, the objective is the same: to influence governors and the public so that they will be favourably disposed to the interest group's position on an issue.

Lobbying has become an accepted part of today's political process. In 2006–07, 9,656 lobbyists were registered under Canada's federal Lobbying Act.[15] While the term carries certain derogatory connotations, many public officials admit that they depend on lobbyists as a source of information. Typically, elected officials depend on members of the administration or bureaucracy to supply the facts they require to make a political decision. But the administration has its own views and biases, or may not have all the information pertinent to a decision; as a result, resorting to lobbyists for a range of views has become a recognized part of politics. In this sense, interest-group lobbying can be seen as a positive part of politics, in that it counters the entrenched views of bureaucrats or cabinet members.

The focus of lobbying depends on the institutional arrangements of government. In the United States, where Congress is a more autonomous body and is not controlled by party discipline, lobbyists concentrate on swaying the minds of individual representatives and senators. Such a strategy would have little payoff in Canada, or in other parliamentary systems in which elected representatives must vote according to party discipline. In the parliamentary milieu, the ultimate goal is to influence members of cabinet and the senior advisers of the prime minister. In practice, however, these people are extremely difficult to reach, so Canadian lobbyists do much of their work with the civil servants who offer advice to politicians over the long term. And in countries like the United States and Canada, where judicial review is an important factor in the political process, interest groups may also devote resources to sponsoring litigation.

Determinants of Influence

An important question is why some groups are more influential in their lobbying than others. What makes an interest group powerful? A number of factors have been suggested: the size and cohesion of the group; its wealth, organizational abilities, and leadership; and the nature of the issue at hand. For a further discussion, see Concept Box 23.2 on determinants of interest-group influence.

Interest groups tend to be particularly influential when several of these factors coincide. Provincial medical associations are an example. While their members are few in relation to the larger society, they are cohesive because their members share a common education and body of professional practices. They have great financial resources as well as excellent leaders and organizational capabilities. All this has made them effective lobbyists on the political scene.

Interest Groups and the Political System

Let us make some general observations about the place of interest groups in contemporary liberal democracies. First, there is a correlation between interest-group activity and the guarantee of political freedom in a society. Without constitutional guarantees of free speech, a free press, and the right to assemble, the political activities of interest groups would be seriously jeopardized. Governments seldom cherish criticism, and a good portion of an interest group's activities involves criticizing proposed or existing laws and policies. Without immunity from reprisal, there would be considerably less enthusiasm

Concept Box 23.2

Determinants of Interest-Group Influence

Numbers. The size of the group cannot help but count in democratic politics. Legislators listen when a group represents a large membership. Numbers, however, do not tell the whole story.

Cohesion. To be effective, members of a group must act cohesively. Organized labour, for example, is one of the largest groups in Canada, and if its members voted as a bloc they could carry many ridings. While labour organizations often endorse political party candidates, the members usually vote across the party spectrum.

Organizational Skills. Effective groups maximize the use of human resources and have the ability to translate emotion into action. No matter how strongly individuals feel about an issue, ad hoc and sporadic complaints may be ineffective. Coordinating individual responses under an effective organization is more likely to have an impact on public policy.

Financial Support. It costs money to set up an organization, monitor government decisions, and engage in lobbying. The main sources of support are large contributions by corporations or unions, small contributions by grassroots members, grants from foundations, and subsidies from government. Interest groups vary greatly in how they combine these sources of revenue, but none can function without money.

Leadership. Good leadership can mobilize concerned individuals and make a difference by inspiring coordinated action on the part of the group.

Nature of Issue. The issue must have significant appeal to legislators and to the public, or there is little chance of obtaining results in politics. Over time, however, appeal for an issue can develop. For example, when the antismoking movement began in the 1970s, it seemed to have little chance of success. More than half of North American adults smoked; and not only was smoking in public taken for granted, it was on the increase. There was already substantial medical evidence about the harmful effects of smoking, but it had made little impact on the public consciousness. Then, as part of wider trends involving diet, fitness, health, and the environment, the medical evidence began to register, public opinion began to turn against smoking, and antismoking groups became highly successful lobbyists, achieving higher taxes on tobacco products, limitations on tobacco advertising, and restrictions on smoking in public places.

for this type of public participation. Even in our own relatively free society, governments are sometimes accused of withholding vital information and even using intimidation.

Second, interest-group activity may be good "therapy" in the participatory society. While all groups cannot achieve all their ends in the political process, most of them are successful at least occasionally. The theory of group politics suggests in part that successful participation in the political process through interest-group activity reinforces confidence in the system. Group politics thus has the potential to enhance the legitimacy of the system in the minds of citizens. To deny groups an opportunity to participate in politics would be to undermine this perceived legitimacy.

The increase in the activity of interest groups is a fact, but it is also a fact that only a small number of people become activists in interest-group politics. Are non-participants—those not affiliated with an interest group—excluded from the benefits of public decisions? Certainly to some extent, but perhaps not entirely, because the unorganized still have the potential to organize and therefore constitute latent interests.[16] In other words, when public officials distribute benefits through the political process, they cannot afford to bypass unorganized interests totally, because the unorganized are voters and have the potential to become organized into effective groups.

Political freedom has nurtured a great deal of interest-group activity, with the benefits described above; yet there are ways in which interest groups may damage the community. For one thing, interest-group activity is closely interwoven with a distributive approach to politics in which political activity represents an exchange: voters render their support (votes) to politicians, and politicians in turn enact programs and policies for the benefit of those groups that support them. Although this may reflect much that occurs in the politics of liberal democracy, it is hard to view it without concern. Liberal democracy as a form of government rests ultimately on the notion that these are universal laws that apply equally to all citizens. It is this general equality before the law that justifies equal political rights for all citizens. But aggressive interest-group activity may easily become a pursuit of special privileges, which is inimical to equality before the law. Manufacturers of certain products lobby for protective tariffs to prevent consumers from buying cheaper foreign products. Organized labour uses collective-bargaining legislation to win benefits denied to the rest of the workforce. Organized farmers use their political power to get government to set up marketing boards to raise prices in their favour. As one special-interest group succeeds in its objectives, other interests may be stimulated to organize themselves for entry into the lobbying contest. If this process continues over many decades, a society of equality before the law can transform itself into a society of entrenched privilege, with each interest group jealously defending its special prerogatives.

A related phenomenon is the tendency to politicize issues. Once groups learn that they can use government to their particular advantage, they tend to begin looking for political rather than economic or social solutions to problems. For example, owners of declining industries, faced with severe competition from foreign producers, may seek protective tariffs and quotas rather than new outlets for their capital. Similarly, the workers in such industries may pressure government to protect their jobs by propping up or even nationalizing faltering companies. What were once economic matters decided in the marketplace can become political issues decided by a preponderance of power. Politicization can jeopardize the fundamental liberal concept of the limited state by injecting government into more and more realms of social activity. If each group single-mindedly pursues its own interests, all groups together may bring about a general situation that none of them would ever have chosen in the first place.

The Dilemma of Interest-Group Politics

Interest-group politics can be seen positively as part of the tendency toward democratization in modern society. The increase in the number of effective interest groups has likely produced a more level playing field in politics. As more people participate in politics, the number of interest groups grows accordingly. Environmental and anti-globalization groups are current examples of different segments of the population organizing around new political issues.

But interest-group politics also has a negative aspect. The playing field in the competition of interest groups is not perfectly level. Some have greater financial resources or better access to the levers of power and therefore get more than their fair share of benefits. Others, like business groups, occupy a privileged position relative to other groups in pluralist societies, and governments are generally more responsive to their interests than to other groups.[17] This reflects the overall importance of the economy on the political agenda rather than anything more sinister but highlights the fact that structural factors can limit the effectiveness of certain groups.

Yet imagining modern participatory politics without interest groups is difficult. So, to curb the possibilities of unfairness in the operations of interest groups, there has been a growing tendency toward public regulation of interest-group activity, including public identification as well as tighter definitions of conflict of interest on the part of politicians and civil servants.

Such problems cause some analysts to see interest-group politics as a long-term threat to liberal democracy. Legislators at all levels of government have voiced the concern that powerful lobbying by special interests can dominate the process for distributing public goods and services. Mancur Olson suggests that small but cohesive organizations with a single purpose have a great capacity for influencing public officials. Because the goals of these groups are usually self-centred, they may create economic inefficiency for the larger society.

Political thinkers at the dawn of the democratic era were acutely aware of these problems. Rousseau went as far as wishing to outlaw organized groups.[18] His view was that individuals could exercise their political responsibilities in the spirit of what he called the "general will"—that is, the good of the whole community—but that the formation of groups fostered a selfish spirit of particular advantage.

Rousseau's diagnosis was undoubtedly shrewd, but his remedy of banning private associations was extreme and perhaps totalitarian in its implications. James Madison suggested a more moderate approach in *The Federalist,* where he discussed interest groups (then called **factions**).[19] Madison realized that factions could not be banned without destroying liberty itself. His remedy (which Rousseau had also accepted as a second-best solution) was to promote the existence of a great number and variety of factions, so as to maintain an approximate balance or equilibrium among them. This fundamentally defensive strategy is based on the hope that a drive for special privilege by one group will generate contrary political pressure from other groups that stand to be adversely affected.

SOCIAL MOVEMENTS

While interest groups continue to play an important role in political systems, social movements have become increasingly important political actors. Interest groups are often elements of social movements but movements encompass more than these traditional political organizations. Social movements are identified by their form (relatively unorganized and fluid); goals (sweeping political, social, and cultural change); structure (non-hierarchical and participatory); and techniques (often non-traditional, including protests—both legal and illegal—and boycotts).[20] An interest group is a hierarchical organization working to influence public policy on issues of concern to its members; **social movements** are loose organizations of groups and individuals working to bring about wholesale change by influencing multiple actors, including governments, business, and individuals. For social movements, the objective is to change more than public policy and legislation, but also political priorities, social values, and individual values and behaviour. And the focus often extends beyond national borders towards transnational actors.

Social movements are not a recent phenomenon, but contemporary movements can be distinguished from earlier ones. "Old" social movements include agrarian, labour, and religious reform movements, spurred in part by the processes of industrialization and urbanization. Examples of "new" social movements, on the other hand, include those focusing on the environment, women's equality, peace, and, most recently, anti-globalization. In line with post-materialism, new social movements focus on issues of identity and non-material goals rather than on questions of redistribution and class. The 1960s are normally identified as the years during which new social movements appeared. Societal changes taking place at that time furnish part of the explanation for their rise, including increased secularization, access to higher education, and the availability of the birth control pill. In 1970, for example, in one of the first examples of national feminist protests, Canadian women organized an abortion caravan, which travelled from Vancouver to Ottawa and ended with demonstrators chaining themselves to the gallery in the House of Commons, to protest amendments made a year earlier to Section 251 of the Criminal Code dealing with abortion.

Political parties frequently emerged from old social movements—the CCF, the British Labour Party, and Christian Democratic parties in a number of Latin American countries. The same is true of new social movements; for example, Green parties have grown out of environmental movements in many countries, including Canada. And as support for the cause grows, existing political parties attempt to adopt the programs of new social movements as part of their party policy.

Social movements often develop from grassroots efforts directed at a particular issue. Interest groups can develop from the efforts, or existing organizations can join in the effort. Mentioned earlier, the Sierra Club lobbies the American government on a number of environmental issues, including the building of dams and carbon emissions. These organizations can also be involved in activities besides lobbying and advocacy such as direct action (e.g., Earth First! employs tree sits and illegal tree spiking in its conservation efforts), conducting research to better understand issues (e.g., Earthwatch supports scientific research around the world to assist sustainability), and changing public attitudes (e.g., the Friends of Nature encourages green tourism to develop an increased love and understanding of nature). Importantly, movements also include unorganized individuals whose behaviour and attitudes reflect the goals of the movement (e.g., the many individuals who use blue boxes to collect recyclables).

The fluid and relatively unorganized nature of social movements means that while there is general agreement on goals (the transformation of community and society), there is often much less agreement on how best to pursue them. Some of the organizations and individuals within a movement may seek change by working with governments to influence policies and legislation (sometimes referred to as "mainstreaming" or "large-P" politics). Others will argue that working with governments can lead to co-optation by requiring that the organizational goals be compromised to some degree to win concessions, an option they flatly reject; instead, their position is one of disengagement or a focus on "small-p" politics. Some will argue that actions should always and everywhere be legal, in part to ensure that public support for the movement remains strong; others argue that the slow pace of change and the consequences of non-action demand the use of illegal means to raise awareness and increase the speed of change. And yet others will adopt a mix of positions, their pragmatic positions responding to changing circumstances.[21]

Anti-globalization protestors provide a current example of a new social movement. They have organized demonstrations, sometimes violent ones, in cities around the world to oppose what they see as the anti-democratic practices of economic globalization. Maude Barlow's Council of Canadians is an important interest group in Canada taking this position. Proponents of globalization argue that reduced trade restrictions will stimulate the economies of all countries, especially the industrializing, transitional democracies, and that this economic growth will in turn enhance democratization. The forces of anti-globalization counter with three points: the process of globalization is undemocratic because discussions on its particulars are closed to the public; the economic growth experienced in industrializing, transitional democracies is uneven, creating great disparities of wealth; and the lack of a regulatory process leads to environmental degradation and poor working conditions.[22]

The anti-globalization movement presents an important example of contemporary interest mobilization: it is transnational; fights for increased citizen access to decision-making processes; focuses on the media, corporations, and international trade organizations in addition to states; and combines the use of "old" techniques (e.g., demonstrations and protests) with new mechanisms for mobilization (e.g., cellphones, text messaging, and the Internet).[23] Many major political issues of the past and present, such as feminism, gay and lesbian rights, and environmentalism, started with the noisy protests of relatively small numbers of people and went on from there to enter the political mainstream.

Questions for Discussion

1. Which political party comes closest to your political positions on issues? Which political issues do you consider to be priorities?

2. When (if ever) is illegal political protest defensible?

3. Are interest groups and social movements a response to increasing political complexity or do they unnecessarily complicate politics?

Internet Links

1. Liberal Party of Canada: **www.liberal.ca**

2. Conservative Party of Canada: **www.conservative.ca**

3. New Democratic Party: **www.ndp.ca**

4. United States Democratic National Committee (DNC): **www.democrats.org**

5. United States Republican National Committee (RNC): **www.rnc.org**

6. Canadian Labour Congress (CLC): **http://canadianlabour.ca**

7. Canadian Council of Chief Executives: **www.ceocouncil.ca**

8. The Global Greens Charter, a statement of the values and principles of Green parties and movements: **www.global.greens.org.au/charter.htm**

9. Greenpeace: **www.greenpeace.org/international**

10. National Organization for Women: **www.now.org**

11. Assembly of First Nations: **www.afn.ca**

Further Reading

INTEREST GROUPS AND SOCIAL MOVEMENTS

Baumgartner, Frank R., and Beth L. Leech, *Basic Interests: The Importance of Groups in Politics and Political Science*, Princeton, NJ: Princeton University Press, 1998.

Berry, Jeffrey M. *The Interest Group Society*. 3rd ed. New York: HarperCollins, 1997.

Chong, Dennis. *Collective Action and the Civil Rights Movement*. Chicago: University of Chicago Press, 1991.

Coleman, William, and Grace Skogstad. *Policy Communities and Public Policy in Canada: A Structural Approach.* Mississauga, ON: Copp Clark Pitman, 1990.

Dalton, Russell J., and Manfred Kuechler, eds. *Challenging the Political Order: New Social and Political Movements in Western Democracies.* New York: Oxford University Press, 1990.

Duverger, Maurice. *Party Politics and Pressure Groups: A Comparative Introduction.* New York: Thomas Y. Crowell, 1972.

Finkle, Peter, et al. *Federal Government Relations with Interest Groups: A Reconsideration.* Ottawa: Supply and Services Canada, 1994.

Hein, Gregory. *Interest Group Litigation and Canadian Democracy.* Montreal: Institute for Research in Public Policy, 2000.

Kingdon, John W. *Agendas, Alternatives and Public Policies.* 2nd ed. New York: HarperCollins, 1995.

Kwavnick, David. *Organized Labour and Pressure Politics: The Canadian Labour Congress 1956–1968.* Montreal and Kingston: McGill–Queen's University Press, 1972.

McAdam, Doug, John D. McCarthy, and Mayer N. Zald, eds. *Comparative Perspectives on Social Movements: Political Opportunities, Mobilizing Structures, and Cultural Framings.* New York: Cambridge University Press, 1996.

Montpetit, Eric. *Misplaced Distrust: Policy Networks and the Environment in France, The United States and Canada.* Vancouver: University of British Columbia Press, 2003.

Olson, Mancur. *The Logic of Collective Action.* Rev. ed. Cambridge, MA: Harvard University Press, 1971.

Petracca, Mark P., cd. *The Politics of Interests: Interest Groups Transformed.* Boulder, CO: Westview Press, 1992.

Pross, Paul A. *Governing Under Pressure.* Toronto: Institute of Public Administration of Canada, 1982.

———. *Group Politics and Public Policy.* 2nd ed. Toronto: Oxford University Press, 1992.

———, ed. *Pressure Group Behavior in Canadian Politics.* Toronto: McGraw-Hill Ryerson, 1975.

Sawatsky, John. *The Insiders: Government, Business, and the Lobbyists.* Toronto: McClelland & Stewart, 1987.

Seidle, F. Leslie, ed. *Interest Groups and Elections in Canada.* Royal Commission on Electoral Reform and Party Financing, vol. 2. Toronto: Dundurn Press, 1991.

Smith, Miriam, ed. *Group Politics and Social Movements in Canada.* Peterborough, ON: Broadview, 2008.

———. *A Civil Society? Collective Actors in Canadian Political Life.* Peterborough, ON: Broadview, 2005.

Tarrow, Sidney. *Power in Movement: Social Movements, Collective Action, and Politics.* New York: Cambridge University Press, 1994.

Truman, David B. *The Governmental Process.* New York: Knopf, 1958.

Verba, Sidney, Kay Lehman Schlozman, and Henry E. Brady. *Voice and Equality: Civic Voluntarism in American Politics.* Cambridge: Harvard University Press, 1995.

Walker, Jack L., Jr. *Mobilizing Interest Groups in America: Patrons, Professions, and Social Movements.* Ann Arbor: University of Michigan Press, 1991.

Wright, John R. *Interest Groups and Congress: Lobbying, Contributions, and Influence.* Boston: Allyn and Bacon, 1996.

Young, Lisa, and Joanna Everitt. *Advocacy Groups.* Vancouver: University of British Columbia Press, 2004.

POLITICAL PARTIES

Ajzenstat, Janet, and Peter J. Smith, eds. *Canada's Origins: Liberal, Tory, or Republican?* Ottawa: Carleton University Press, 1995.

Archer, Keith, and Alan Whitehorn. *Canadian Trade Unions and the New Democratic Party.* Kingston: Industrial Relations Centre, 1993.

Bashevkin, Sylvia B. *Toeing the Lines: Women and Party Politics in English Canada.* 2nd ed. Toronto: Oxford University Press, 1993.

Bickerton, James, Alain-G. Gagnon, and Patrick J. Smith. *Ties That Bind: Parties and Voters in Canada.* Toronto: Oxford University Press, 1999.

Brodie, M. Janine, and Jane Jenson. *Crisis, Challenge and Change: Party and Class in Canada, Revisited.* Rev. ed. Ottawa: Carleton University Press, 1988.

Campbell, Colin, and William Christian. *Parties, Leaders, and Ideologies in Canada.* McGraw-Hill Ryerson, 1996.

Carty, R. Kenneth, et al., eds. *Leaders and Parties in Canadian Politics: Experiences of the Provinces.* Toronto: Harcourt Brace Jovanovich, 1991.

Carty, R. Kenneth, William Cross, and Lisa Young. *Rebuilding Canadian Party Politics.* Vancouver: University of British Columbia Press, 2000.

Christian, William, and Colin Campbell. *Political Parties and Ideologies in Canada.* 3rd ed. Toronto: McGraw-Hill Ryerson, 1990.

Courtney, Johon. *Do Conventions Matter? Choosing National Party Leaders in Canada.* Toronto: Macmillan, 1995.

Cross, William. *Political Parties.* Vancouver: University of British Columbia Press, 2004.

Dalton, Russell J., and Martin P. Wattenberg. *Parties without Partisans: Political Change in Advanced Industrial Democracies.* Oxford: Oxford University Press, 2000.

Duverger, Maurice. *Political Parties.* 3rd ed. New York: Wiley, 1978.

Flanagan, Tom. *Waiting for the Wave: The Reform Party and Preston Manning.* Toronto: Stoddart, 1995.

Gagnon, Alain-G., and A. Brian Tanguay, eds. *Canadian Parties in Transition.* 3rd ed. Peterborough, ON: Broadview, 2007.

Ingle, Stephen. *The British Party System: An Introduction.* London: Routledge, 2008.

Katz, Richard S. *A Theory of Parties and Electoral Systems.* Baltimore: Johns Hopkins University Press, 1980.

Klingemann, Hans-Dieter, Richard I. Hofferbert, and Ian Budge. *Parties, Policies, and Democracies.* Boulder, CO: Westview Press, 1994.

Laver, Michael, and Norman Schofield. *Multiparty Government: The Politics of Coalition in Europe.* New York: Oxford University Press, 1990.

Mair, Peter. "Comparing Party Systems," in Lawrence LeDuc, Richard G. Niemi, and Pippa Norris, eds. *Comparing Democracies 2: New Challenges in the Study of Elections and Voting.* London: Sage Publications, 2003.

Michels, Robert. *Political Parties.* New York: Free Press, 1962. First published in 1911.

Paterson, William E., and Alastair H. Thomas, eds. *Social Democratic Parties in Western Europe.* London: Croom Helm, 1977.

Piven, Frances Fox, ed. *Labor Parties in Postindustrial Societies.* Cambridge: Polity Press, 1991.

Rose, Richard. *Do Parties Make a Difference?* 2nd ed. London: Macmillan, 1984.

Rose, Richard, and Neil Munro. *Elections and Parties in New European Democracies.* 2nd ed. Washington, DC: CQ Press, 2009.

Sáez, Manuel Alca ntara. *Politicians and Politics in Latin America.* Boulder, CO: Lynne Reiner, 2008.

Sartori, Giovanni. *Parties and Party Systems: A Framework for Analysis.* Colchester: ECPR, 2005.

Sayers, Anthony M. *Parties, Candidates, and Constituency Campaigns in Canadian Elections.* Vancouver: University of British Columbia Press, 1999.

Seidle, Leslie F., ed. *Comparative Issues in Party and Election Finance in Canada.* Royal Commission on Electoral Reform and Party Financing, vol. 4. Toronto: Dundurn Press, 1991.

———. *Issues in Party and Election Finance in Canada.* Royal Commission on Electoral Reform and Party Financing, vol. 5. Toronto: Dundurn Press, 1991.

———. *Provincial Party and Election Finance in Canada.* Royal Commission on Electoral Reform and Party Financing, vol. 3. Toronto: Dundurn Press, 1991.

Thorburn, Hugh G., and Alan Whitehorn, ed. *Party Politics in Canada.* 8th ed. Scarborough, ON: Prentice Hall Canada, 2000.

Ware, Alan. *Political Parties and Party Systems.* Oxford and New York: Oxford University Press, 1996.

Wearing, Joseph. *Strained Relations: Canadian Parties and Voters.* Toronto: McClelland & Stewart, 1988.

Webb, Paul, David Farrell, and Ian Holliday, eds. *Political Parties in Advanced Industrial Democracies.* Oxford: Oxford, 2002.

Young, Walter D. *Democracy and Discontent: Progressivism, Socialism and Social Credit in the Canadian West.* 2nd ed. Toronto: McGraw-Hill Ryerson, 1978.

CHAPTER 24

Communications Media

Communications media include all means of transmitting, exchanging, and receiving communication. In the modern world these media include traditional print media such as newspapers, magazines, pamphlets, books, and direct mail, but also more modern electronic forms such as radio, television, cellphones, iPods and MP3 players, DVDs, and the Internet. The media are not political institutions in the same way as political parties, interest groups, and social movements, which have an overt political purpose—that is, to influence or control government. The media's purpose is to inform or entertain. However, the media have such vast influence on the political process that we must consider them an integral part of it. They are vital transmission channels for both articulating demands and expressing support. Communications media are particularly important if democratic government is to be meaningful, for they provide much of the information by which citizens evaluate their governments and assess political options.

Most people involved in newspapers, radio, and television would deny that their work is political in a partisan sense. Their job, so they claim, involves reporting facts, political events, and circumstances without political bias. Whether or not bias exists, the media are political institutions, not necessarily in partisan terms, but as important two-way links between people and government. News outlets broadcast election results as the votes are counted, allowing voters to feel that they are part of the process. In addition, the media provide the basis for public discussion of issues. They not only report political events, but also provide the means for individuals, groups, and government to state positions that can be aired before the public.

We often take the political importance of the media for granted. However, it must be remembered that newspapers have existed for slightly more than two centuries, and the electronic media are even more recent. Representative government, having been established before the age of mass media, was originally based on face-to-face contact between representatives and their electors, who were few in number. Voters personally knew their representatives, and the election was held by a show of hands at a public meeting of electors convened for that purpose. Rival candidates would be present at this meeting to speak before the vote was taken. This method of election persisted well into the nineteenth century, until democratic extension of the franchise so expanded the electorate that it became impossible for representatives and electors to know each other personally. The introduction of the secret ballot made the electoral process more anonymous and impersonal, so that images conveyed by the mass media have now almost entirely replaced direct human contact. The consequences for democratic government are complex and cannot be fully discussed here, but it is clear that representative democracy as we know it could not possibly exist without the mass media.

Political communication through the media takes many forms. On one side, governments use the media to transmit information to the public. A prime minister or president may call a press conference or choose to address a national audience via radio or television. The press agents of important ministers make news releases available on particular issues. Governments employ websites as a way of informing people of public hearings or petitions for rezoning. Some of this flow of information is purely factual, but much of it contains implicit or explicit pleas for support of government policy. The flow of information also moves in the opposite direction. While a letter to the editor of a newspaper remains a possibility for voicing support or opposition to specific policies, a direct e-mail to an MP or MLA is now also an option.

Where political information was once relatively limited in its accessibility, it is now readily available. Most homes today include a number of electronic devices including televisions, radios, and computers that provide unlimited access to around-the-clock news sources. As such, it is hard to imagine that in 1950 only half of American homes included a television set. Today, that share has grown to more than 98 percent.[1] Recent statistics also suggest that over 70 percent of Americans use the Internet, which provides a channel of convergence for all other media.[2]

This growth in access has been matched by growth in the number of news sources. Gone are the days when news was available only in 30-minute television slots a few times a day on a handful of stations or in one's morning newspaper. An array of television channels, including 24-hour news channels such as CNN, CBC Newsworld, and CTV Newsnet, and an unlimited number of news sources on the Internet, including BBC News and automated news aggregators such as Google News, provide access to a wealth of political information from around the world. Add to this the number of the world's newspapers now available online and the vast number of podcasts available for downloading, and the sheer quantity of available political information is truly staggering.

Not all are convinced, however, that the changes have been positive. Television news coverage has been criticized for having "dumbed-down" content to too great an extent. According to David Taras, "television news stories are so visual, so sensational, so fixated on personalities, so fast-moving, so fleeting, and so intent on entertaining that they give viewers almost nothing tangible to hold on to."[3] Others argue that the abundance of information has created a type of overload, with few citizens able to process it.[4]

A positive aspect of the growth of the electronic media, and in particular the Internet, is the ability it affords citizens to become producers as well as consumers of information.[5] Today's citizens have a number of options at their disposal for communicating their opinions on issues: websites, blogs, chat rooms, wikis, video-sharing websites such as YouTube.com, and social networking sites such as MySpace.com and Facebook.com. Each provides users with the possibility of sharing information, and for creating networks and "virtual communities." The importance of such technology as a mobilizing tool for new social movements was identified earlier (see Chapter 23). But it also opens up multiple opportunities not only for communicating with the "commons" but also for individual citizen engagement.

CAMPAIGNS AND THE MEDIA

Political parties and election campaigns have been particularly affected by developments in the communications media. In all industrial democracies, electoral politics is now conducted primarily in the media. One result of this has been the rise to prominence in political parties of communications consultants, who are now indispensable. Four types of activities deserve particular mention.

The first is public relations, as managed by the so-called "spin doctors" whose job is to release news stories to, and answer questions from, print and electronic reporters. Insiders refer to the world of daily news coverage as the **unpaid media.** Every day there is a tremendous volume of potential free publicity in the form of political news coverage, and political leaders have to ensure that their activities are represented as favourably as possible. Amateurism in this enterprise can be dangerous, since reporters are quick to pounce on any error or misstatement. Thus all major parties now place great emphasis on "quick response" and "damage control" to reduce the negative effects of poorly worded statements.

A special form of unpaid media, and one that is having an increasing effect on political campaigns, is the televised debate among party leaders. In 1984 the debate resulted in the decisive turn from the Liberals to the Conservatives when Brian Mulroney effectively attacked John Turner over patronage appointments. Performing well in the debate, however, may yield only a transitory benefit. In 1988 Turner "won" the debate by focusing on free trade, producing a large but temporary spike in support for the Liberals, but the Conservatives were able to regain the lost ground. In 2004, Conservative leader Stephen Harper was generally thought to have performed best in the English-language debate, and support for his party peaked in the days thereafter; but, as in 1988, the other main party, in this case the Liberals, was able to counterattack and went on to win more seats than the Conservatives. In any case, the main purpose of the debate is not to produce better arguments overall but to generate powerful short stretches of political theatre that can be played over and over on news programs and be incorporated into advertising. To make sure they generate the right sound bites, leaders prepare for days with their professional advisers.

The second great branch of media politics is the world of **paid media,** or advertising. Political parties advertise in all media during election campaigns, but television now gets the lion's share of expenditures. As in the realm of unpaid media, professionals have come to dominate. Political advertising campaigns are prepared by advertising executives who lend their services to political parties out of a mixture of motives, such as ideology, personal friendship and loyalty, and the hope of future patronage contracts. Ads are carefully tested in focus groups before they are run, and their performance is monitored equally carefully. If they do not seem to be working, they are pulled and replaced.

In spite of this research and development process, disastrous mistakes can occur. Late in the 1993 election campaign, the Conservatives started to run television ads attacking Jean Chrétien's leadership ability. The ads featured close-up pictures of Chrétien that drew attention to the fact that one side of his mouth is partially paralyzed. When the ads had been tested, members of the focus groups had not perceived them as making fun of Chrétien's disability; but the ads had this effect on the public at large when they were broadcast, and the Conservatives had to pull them amid great embarrassment. A more ambiguous episode occurred with the Reform Party's 1997 attack ad, in which the ability of "Quebec-based" political leaders to deal with the issue of Quebec separatism was questioned. The ad seemed to have increased Reform's support in the West but had a neutral, or even negative, effect in Ontario. Since the ad was intended to bring about the long-awaited Reform breakthrough in Ontario, it could be considered a failure. But its effect in the West was Reform's increase to 60 parliamentary seats from 52 in 1993, and the cementing of its status by becoming the Official Opposition.

How leaders are portrayed by the media can have significant consequences. In 1974, a newspaper photo of Canadian Progressive Conservative leader Robert Stanfield fumbling a football was seen by many to epitomize the state of the party's compaign. The response to a 1992 photo of a bare-shouldered Kim Campbell was less clear-cut.

(left) The Canadian Press (Doug Ball); (right) © Barbara Woodley/Labatt Breweries of Canada/Library and Archives Canada/PA-186869. Source: Woodley, Barbara, *Portraits: Canadian Women in Focus*. Toronto: Doubleday Canada. © 1992, Image 64. Used with permission of Barbara Woodley.

The third activity that has become indispensable to modern politics is public-opinion polling. With the development of survey techniques and computer analysis, it is now possible to get fast and accurate information about the views of the public on any issue. Both public relations and advertising are now driven by polling data, and pollsters have become key figures in most parties' campaign management committees. The goal of such committees is to produce a seamless interface between the party's and politicians' activities as reported in the news and the themes that are repeated in the paid advertising, while at the same time addressing concerns that polling has discovered among the voters. An important development in polling technology is the rolling or **tracking poll,** which most parties now use during campaigns. The pollster surveys a small new sample every night and averages those data with the results of (usually) the preceding two nights' surveys. The aggregate is large enough to be statistically reliable, and the averaging smooths out day-to-day fluctuations. Those in charge of the campaign get a report every morning and can change course if it suggests that things are not going well.

The Internet is also becoming an important medium of political communication. All parties and candidates now maintain websites, which they use for fundraising, enlisting volunteers, and publishing information that they want to place before voters. The 2008 U.S. presidential election showed the contemporary importance of the Internet in politics (see Figure 24.1). Forty percent of Americans went to the Internet for news and information on the campaign in the spring of 2008, compared to only 16 percent in the spring of 2000.[6] The greatest change is the viewing of online videos related to the campaign and in the use of social networking sites for engaging in political activity, particularly by younger voters.[7]

Some observers are concerned about the overwhelming importance of the media and related technology in contemporary public life, fearing that it makes politics too professionalized, expensive, and manipulative. However, the result of the 1992 referendum campaign shows that money, technology, and professionalism do not always win. The Charlottetown Accord was supported by the three major federal parties, who put some of their best strategists, spin doctors, pollsters, and advertisers at the disposal of the Yes committee. Money was also no problem; the Yes committee had more than $7 million to spend, far more than the No side. And polls taken when the Accord was announced made it seem almost certain to pass; it was trailing only slightly in Quebec and leading by large margins in all the other provinces.

The only well-funded opponent of the Accord was the No committee in Quebec, which received about $2 million of public money under Quebec law and which could draw on the considerable expertise of the Parti Québécois machine. Outside Quebec there was only an uncoordinated assortment of poorly funded opponents. The players on the No side had to proceed without tracking polls, focus groups, and the other elements of contemporary technology. The Referendum Act did give both sides equal access to a certain amount of free advertising time on radio and television; but against the professionally produced and tested Yes ads, the No ads looked as if they had been made with a camcorder in someone's basement.

Figure 24.1 Internet Use in the 2008 U.S. Election by Age Groups, Spring 2008

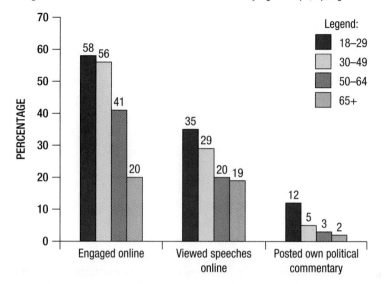

Note: Online engagement includes using the Internet, e-mail, or text messaging to get news or exchange views about the race among all adults surveyed. Viewed speeches online and Posted own political commentary are within the last few months and includes only those respondents who are Internet users.

Source: Adapted from Pew Internet & America Life Project, "The internet and the 2008 election," Pew Internet & American Life Project, June 15, 2008. pp. 5 and 10.

It appeared to be a hopelessly unequal contest, and yet technology and money lost decisively because there were certain parts of the Accord, such as the guarantee of 25 percent of House of Commons seats for Quebec, that were very difficult to defend in the rest of Canada. Sophisticated use of the media is obviously an asset to political parties, and they will continue to strive for technological mastery; but the referendum campaign suggests that there are always limitations on what can be achieved.

Priming and Agenda-Setting

Besides playing a large—and increasingly larger—role in political campaigns, the media actively participate in the day-to-day dissemination of political information, opinion, and symbolism. To some extent, they do this openly in editorials, where they take explicit stands on various issues. However, people have minds of their own and are not necessarily persuaded by editorials. More important than editorials is the "objective" task of factual news reporting. Reporters strive for objectivity, but like the rest of us they work within intellectual and emotional constraints of which they may not be fully aware. Probably more profound in its effects than personal bias is the media's internal logic. We do not need to subscribe fully to Marshall McLuhan's famous dictum that "the medium is the message" to see that news reporting has certain basic and sometimes conflicting requirements. While appearing to be accurate and objective, it must also be concise, interesting, and even entertaining. If it is too detailed, complex, or subtle, it will lose its mass audience. The audience will also evaporate if news reporting is too far at variance with the fundamental values and opinions of the political culture.

One way for journalists to reconcile these various demands is to focus on conflict. Arguments, debates, fights, strikes, boycotts, wars, and revolutions are far more exciting to report than cooperation, agreement, consensus, and quiet compromise. There is, therefore, an understandable tendency for almost all news to be recast according to a conflict model. Journalists play a great role in setting up conflicts by choosing the authorities whose conflicting opinions they cite. They also heighten conflicts by actively seeking out controversial opinions on matters on which there is in fact a high degree of consensus. However, none of this is to say that journalists possess sinister powers of persuasion. Repeated studies of the effects of the mass media on opinion have shown that people tend to pick out reported facts that reinforce their deeply held beliefs. There is no guarantee that even deliberately slanted stories would have the desired effect on their audience.

But if news reporting does not change people's opinions in a direct way, it plays an extremely important role in **agenda-setting.**[8] Attention is a scarce resource; people cannot think about everything at once. The media do not tell people what to think, but they may tell people what to think *about.*[9] And this is of the highest importance in politics, because interest groups, parties, and ideologists often differ profoundly in their assessment of what constitutes a problem worth thinking about. By the late 1980s, Canadian conservatives had come to regard the then-burgeoning federal deficit as the country's most serious problem, while social democrats and reform liberals assigned it a lower priority. It was not, therefore, a politically neutral act when the Canadian media started to run stories about the deficit in the early months of 1989. In the very act of reporting the government's budget plans, they were helping establish an agenda for public discussion.

The role of the media in setting the agenda will vary with the type of issue in question. The importance of some issues, like inflation and unemployment, is less likely to be driven by the media because they are ones that the public is confronted with directly, through their pocketbooks. Yet the prominence of other issues— AIDS and crime, for example—is more susceptible to media effects. The importance that the public attaches to such issues is more likely to be driven by media coverage, because fewer people experience them directly and they seem relatively easy to understand.[10]

A concept related to agenda-setting is **priming,** which "brings to the top of one's head certain pieces of information that then shape one's opinion on a specific issue."[11] Because political events and personalities are always too complicated to be reported in their totality, journalists must be selective in the portraits they present. Inevitably, they produce stereotypical images by attaching key words to names. For example, it was a matter of considerable political importance whether those who opposed the Sandinista government in Nicaragua were "U.S.–backed contras" or "Nicaraguan freedom fighters," and whether American President Ronald Reagan's proposed system of defence against ballistic missiles was called "Strategic Defence Initiative" or "Star Wars." The labels employed to describe political events or policies are part of the information that the public uses to evaluate them. In the same vein, is Dr. Henry Morgentaler best described as an "abortionist" or an "advocate for women's rights"? Even though reporters usually refrain from open editorializing, the way they prime their messages has an effect upon public opinion.

Those who engage in politics are quite aware of the ways in which the media actively create rather than passively report news, so they do their best to manipulate the media. Mass public demonstrations that are supposed to be spontaneous expressions of demand or support are often carefully staged events that depend on the cooperation of the mass media. Organizers invite newspaper and television reporters well in advance. A study of the American news media reports that in the 1960s, when there were many demonstrations against the Vietnam War, "experienced organizers scheduled demonstrations to fit the schedules of camera crews."[12]

Reporters come to such events because mass demonstrations provide an interesting subject. They take photographs and film footage of the most rousing events: the singing, dramatic speeches, shouts of affirmation, violent clashes with police. They hold interviews with the leading demonstrators, which gives the latter a chance to communicate their prepared messages to the public. When it is all over, newspapers and television stations present to the public the news of an event in which the mass media themselves were the most important participants.

The media also shape political reality through their investigative or watchdog activities. With the help of the opposition, reporters often uncover inconvenient facts that governments or powerful interest groups would like to suppress. The most famous example of this activity is, of course, the Watergate affair, when American reporters uncovered the misdeeds of officials in Richard Nixon's administration. As a result of their efforts, Nixon was forced to resign in 1974. This episode elevated the media to new heights of prestige.

This investigative role is less highly developed in Canada than it is in the United States and Great Britain. One reason is the state of Canadian media law. Laws requiring governments and public corporations to disclose information are so weak in this country that journalists often resort to American sources to discover information about Canada. Also, libel laws are so strong that the rich and powerful can effectively use the legal system to discourage reporters from pursuing controversial stories.[13] Another layer of silence arises in the judicial system itself. There is a strong Canadian tradition, enforced by judicial findings of contempt of court, that limits media discussion of cases before the courts. This allows the rich and the powerful to avoid disclosure by launching a libel action and dragging it out for years, during which time the information usually loses its relevance to political action.

Influence, Ownership, and Control

Most of the media are well skilled at continuously reporting a flow of news, but do not involve themselves in a thorough analysis of issues. In many countries, therefore, one or two newspapers have emerged as particularly important in politics because they provide both good coverage and sharp analysis. In Britain, almost everyone involved in government or seriously observing it reads the *Times,* the *Guardian,* or the *Independent.* Letters to the editors of these papers are often carefully thought-out statements written by important people and meant to be read by other important people. The papers in general serve as a handy means of communication among the political elite of the country. In France, *Le Monde* and *Le Figaro* are read in the same way. In the United States, the *New York Times* and the *Washington Post* have this position in national politics, although many other papers are of regional importance. For years Canada did not really have an equivalent, except for *Le Devoir* in Quebec; however, in English Canada, the Toronto-based *Globe and Mail,* using satellite technology, was the first to stake a claim to be a national newspaper. Now, the *National Post* has challenged the *Globe's* claim. Both newspapers can be purchased in every province and territory, and are engaged in a bitter struggle for subscribers. The absence until recent years of a truly national newspaper in Canada may have contributed to the fragmentation of Canadian political culture. Politicians and leaders in other walks of life in different parts of the country often lacked a common frame of reference and fund of information, which might have been supplied in part if they were reading the same paper.

The Print Media

The print media—newspapers, magazines, publishing houses—took shape in the eighteenth and nineteenth centuries, before the socialist idea of state ownership had become influential. These media receive government subsidies in some countries; however, in the Western world they remain almost entirely in private hands and are run as profit-making businesses. Governments do not license or otherwise regulate them, except for enforcing laws against libel, pornography, false advertising, and so on. Underlying this arrangement is the classical liberal philosophy that holds that the public good is best served through the competition of private actors following their own interests. Newspapers, magazines, and books constitute a mass market of profit-seeking interests in the field of ideas, information, and entertainment.

Does competition among newspapers still contribute to an open marketplace of ideas? On the one hand, the number of local, independently owned and operated newspapers declined drastically throughout the twentieth century, so that today corporations and large chains are the rule. On the other hand, these large companies can compete with each other across Canada. Hence, one might argue that readers have more effective choice than ever. Someone wanting to pick up a daily newspaper on the streets of Toronto can choose among the *Globe and Mail, National Post, Toronto Sun,* and *Toronto Star.* Each of these newspapers offers a distinctive product serving a different market niche and espousing different political sympathies. There is also a choice among the two national and two local dailies in Vancouver, Edmonton, Calgary, Winnipeg, and Ottawa. Readers in Montreal have an even greater range of options because of the competitive coexistence of French and English newspapers. It seems that the world of Canadian newspapers is more vigorously competitive than ever, even if the competitors are large corporations rather than local proprietors. On the other side—and there is always another side to political questions—fierce competition among newspapers may lead to staff cuts and more reliance on advertising to maintain profits. There may be intense competition to attract readers, but less emphasis on quality, scope, and depth of reporting.

The Electronic Media

The electronic media, born as they were in the twentieth century, when public ownership was becoming a powerful idea, have been involved with government almost from the start. There are technical aspects of broadcasting that invite public regulation. A radio or television signal is a public good, available to anyone with an antenna and a receiver. Broadcasters can seriously interfere with competitors' transmissions unless they respect the concept of reserved frequencies. In many European countries—for example, England, France, and Germany—radio and television are dominated by public corporations. Private enterprise is permitted, but only in a secondary role. In the United States private ownership is the rule, but—unlike the print media—the electronic media are subject to government licensing. Canada combines both models. There are publicly owned English and French networks of radio and television stations (such as the CBC, Radio-Canada, and some smaller provincial networks), but they do not dominate the market, which consists mostly of privately owned, governmentally licensed stations. Advocates of public ownership say that a network supported by taxes rather than advertising revenue is able to offer news and public affairs in greater depth—an argument that surely has some merit. Perhaps there is something to be said for the Canadian arrangement, which provides the benefits of a subsidized, nonprofit system but does not give government a predominant role in the electronic media.

In Canada, electronic media enterprises are increasing rapidly, and ownership of them is becoming concentrated in a few large corporations. CanWest Global Communications Corp. includes Global Television and E! as well as 26 specialty television networks; the *National Post* and 10 other city-based daily newspapers; and several properties in the Canada.com network. CTVglobemedia is another multimedia company that includes a number of television stations in addition to the large CTV television network, the *Globe and Mail* newspaper, and the CHUM radio division. Quebecor is a major provider of television in Quebec and parts of New Brunswick (Vidéotron) and newspapers across the country (through Sun Media and Osprey Media). The most significant development here is the rise of large communications corporations combining newspapers, radio and television, and Internet service providers—a phenomenon often called "convergence." The Canadian Radio-television and Telecommunications Commission (CRTC), which regulates media in Canada, recently imposed new rules on media ownership: a market share cap that restricts broadcasting assets to no more than 45 percent of Canada's total viewing hours.[14] The change limits the degree to which both CTVglobemedia and CanWest can purchase additional cable channels.

Not everyone is happy with convergence and other new developments in media ownership and operation. David Taras, a political scientist at the University of Calgary who specializes in the study of Canadian media, offers a comprehensive critique. Taras argues that the current media universe is depriving citizens "of the vital information they need to make decisions about their communities and their lives."[15] He builds his argument on five contemporary developments: corporate convergence in the communications industry; fragmentation in the media, illustrated in the "500 channel universe" and the Internet; the relative decline of publicly owned broadcasting in the industry; a decline in the quality of journalism, including a heavy reliance on the rebroadcasting of American programs; and the dominance of right-wing perspectives in the Canadian media. He concludes: "The Canadian public is being betrayed by those who care much more about lining their pockets than about the survival of a distinct Canadian culture or serving the needs of citizens."[16] For more on the implications of media development, see World View 24.1.

Outside the liberal democracies, almost all mass media, whether print or electronic, are owned or controlled by the state. In totalitarian systems, the mass media are quite simply an instrument used by the state to transform society. Communication with the masses is considered too important to be left to independent organizations in society, so state control is total.

Authoritarian states also supervise the mass media, but not quite to the same extent: their chief concern is usually to ensure that the government is not criticized in public. Criticism may result in the imprisonment or exile of writers or the closing of newspapers, journals, and radio and TV stations. Independent units of the media may exist and operate as long as their political reporting is neutral or complimentary to the government. In both totalitarian and authoritarian systems, the media are viewed more as means of generating support for the regime than as means of articulating demands by the public, or serving as an independent source of information. As the late Forbes Burnham, former dictator of Guyana, said in 1975, the media must become "an agency for pushing the development of the nation in the context of Government policy."[17]

However, the pace of technological advancement is now making it increasingly difficult for any kind of government to maintain monopolistic control over what is reported in the country. Satellite dishes, camcorders, cellphones, and the Internet are now available almost everywhere in the world, making it harder for anyone to control the flow of information. Terrorist movements, such as the Revolutionary Armed Forces of Colombia (FARC), maintain their own computerized "hit list," which they use when seeking opponents at roadblocks. Hostage takers with cellphones can broadcast their demands around the world. A bystander holding a camcorder or mobile phone can videotape examples of police brutality, as in the famous Rodney King affair in Los Angeles. And both rebels and government forces now release videocassettes of themselves torturing and executing their opponents as a way of intimidating others. The new technology can be a tool for whoever wishes to use it.

World View 24.1

Speeding Up the News Cycle

The so-called "new media"—24-hour news stations, cellphones, personal computers, e-mail, and the Internet—have had a remarkable impact on the way political news is reported. The main effect has been to speed up the cycle. When politicians issue a news release, the text is now posted electronically on an Internet site. In a matter of minutes, reporters can download it into their own computers and cell-phones and send it to other politicians for comment and rebuttal. Everyone in the media and politics carries a cell-phones and a portable e-mail device, so reporters and politicians can contact each other directly for immediate commentary. Reporters no longer have to fight their way through layers of office staff in order to obtain an interview.

The past statements and position papers of all important political figures are now stored somewhere on the Internet or in a reporter's personal computer files, so it is becoming harder to get away with inconsistencies or changes in interpretation. Newspapers and broadcast media maintain Web pages that are updated continuously throughout the day and night. This, together with the existence of 24-hours broadcasters such as CNN and CBC Newsworld, means that new stories can break almost anytime, day or night. Politicians' denials and rebuttals are themselves denied and rebutted almost as quickly as they are uttered.

The joint impact of these technological developments has been to create a more competitive, harried world of media politics. Political leaders and parties have had to tighten up their organizations to cope with the faster pace of reporting and greater volume of information. The frantic pressure to file leaves reporters less time for reflection and discussion. All of us get more information faster, but are we really any wiser?

Questions for Discussion

1. How has the Internet changed politics? How has it changed liberal democracy?

2. Does ownership in the communications industry really matter?

3. What do you like and dislike about the media in Canada today?

Internet Links

1. Minister of Canadian Heritage: **www.pch.gc.ca.**

2. CTVglobemedia: **www.ctvglobemedia.com.**

3. CanWest Global Communications: **www.canwestglobal.com.**

4. *The Globe and Mail:* **www.globeandmail.ca.**

5. *National Post:* **www.nationalpost.com.**

6. The Institute for Politics, Democracy & the Internet at George Washington University: **www.ipdi.org.**

7. Pew Internet & American Life Project: **www.pewinternet.org.**

Further Reading

Alexander, Cynthia, and Les Pal, eds. *Digital Democracy: Policy and Politics in the Wired World.* Don Mills: Oxford University Press, 1998.

Bain, George. *Gotcha! How the Media Distort the News.* Toronto: Key Porter, 1994.

Baker, William, and George Dessart. *Down the Tube: An Inside Account of the Failure of American Television.* New York: Basic Books, 1998.

Barney, Darren. *Communication Technology.* Vancouver: University of British Columbia Press, 2005.

Bender, David L., and Bereno Leone, eds. *The Mass Media: Opposing Viewpoints.* San Diego, CA: Greenhaven Press, Inc., 1988.

Braun, Stefan. *Democracy Off Balance: Freedom of Expression and Hate Propaganda Law in Canada.* Toronto: University of Toronto Press, 2004.

Capella, Joseph, and Kathleen Hall Jamieson. *Spiral of Cynicism: The Press and the Public Good.* New York: Oxford University Press, 1997.

Cobb, Chris. *Ego and Ink: The Inside Story of Canada's National Newspaper War.* Toronto: McClelland & Stewart, 2004.

Cook, Timothy. *Governing with the News: The News Media as a Political Institution.* Chicago: University of Chicago Press, 1998.

Curran, James, and Jean Seaton. *Power without Responsibility: The Press, Broadcasting and New Media in Britain.* 6th ed. London: Routledge, 2003.

Fletcher, Frederick J., ed. *Election Broadcasting in Canada.* Royal Commission on Electoral Reform and Party Financing, vol. 21. Toronto: Dundurn Press, 1991.

———. *Media and Voters in Election Campaigns.* Royal Commission on Electoral Reform and Party Financing, vol. 18. Toronto: Dundurn Press, 1991.

———. *Media, Elections, and Democracy.* Royal Commission on Electoral Reform and Party Financing, vol. 19. Toronto: Dundurn Press, 1991.

———. *Reporting and the Campaign: Election Coverage in Canada.* Royal Commission on Electoral Reform and Party Financing, vol. 22. Toronto: Dundurn Press, 1991.

Fraser, Matthew. *Free-for-All: The Struggle for Dominance on the Digital Frontier.* Toronto: Stoddart, 1999.

Hackett, Robert A., and Yuezhi Zhao. *Sustaining Democracy? Journalism and the Politics of Objectivity*. Toronto: Garamond, 1997.

Holmes, H., and David Taras, eds. *Seeing Ourselves: Media Power and Policy in Canada*. Toronto: Harcourt Brace Jovanovich, 1992.

Iyengar, Shanto. *Is Anyone Responsible? How Television Frames Political Issues*. Chicago: University of Chicago Press, 1991.

Iyengar, Shanto, and Donald R. Kinder. *News That Matters: Television and American Opinion*. Chicago: University of Chicago Press, 1987.

Jamieson, Kathleen Hall, ed. *The Media and Politics*. Thousand Oaks, CA: Sage, 1996.

Kingdon, John W. *Agendas, Alternatives, and Public Policies*. 2nd ed. New York: HarperCollins, 1995.

Kuhn, Raymond. *Politics and the Media in Britain*. New York: Palgrave Macmillan, 2007.

Lachapelle, Guy. *Polls and the Media in Canadian Elections*. Royal Commission on Electoral Reform and Party Financing, vol. 16. Toronto: Dundurn Press, 1991.

Levine, Allan Gerald. *Scrum Wars: The Prime Ministers and the Media*. Toronto: Dundurn Press, 1993.

Lorimer, Rowland, Mike Gasher, and David Skinner. *Mass Communication in Canada*. 6th ed. Don Mills, ON: Oxford University Press, 2008.

Miljan, Lydia, and Barry Cooper. *Hidden Agendas: How Journalists Influence the News*. Vancouver: University of British Columbia Press, 2003.

Norris, Pippa. *Digital Divide: Civic Engagement, Information Poverty, and the Internet Worldwide*. London: Cambridge University Press, 2001.

Page, Benjamin. *Who Deliberates? Mass Media in Modern Democracy*. Chicago: University of Chicago Press, 1996.

Purvis, Hoyt. *The Media, Politics, and Government*. Toronto: Thomson Nelson, 2001.

Rosenstiel, Tom. *Strange Bedfellows: How Television and the Presidential Candidates Changed American Politics, 1992*. New York: Hyperion Press, 1993.

Taras, David. *The Newsmakers*. Scarborough, ON: Nelson Canada, 1990.

———. *Power and Betrayal in the Canadian Media*. 2nd ed. Peterborough, ON: Broadview Press, 2001.

Turpin, Jennifer E. *Reinventing the Soviet Self: Media and Social Change in the Former Soviet Union*. Westport, CT: Praeger, 1995.

West, Darrell M. *Air Wars: Television Advertising in Election Campaigns*. 4th ed. Washington, DC: Congressional Quarterly Press, 2005.

CHAPTER 25
Elections and Electoral Systems

The process of electing public officials is central to liberal democracy. Elections provide a way of changing rulers without resorting to bloodshed—no small accomplishment in itself, although hereditary selection has achieved the same thing. More profoundly, competitive political elections are the basis of democratic legitimacy. Elections have been defined as the "formal expression of preferences by the governed, which are then aggregated and transformed into a collective decision about who will govern—who should stay in office, who should be thrown out, who should replace those who have been thrown out."[1] But the responsibilities of those choosing governments do not end at the ballot box; the opportunity to participate in choosing rulers confers on the participants an obligation to obey the laws made by those who are chosen. Citizens are presumed to consent to laws to the extent that they have participated in choosing the lawmakers (see Figure 25.1). Disagreement with the substance of lawmakers' decisions is not normally sufficient reason for disobedience, because an opportunity (i.e., another election) will soon arise to vote for other lawmakers who are willing to alter the disliked rule or policy. Of course, if an elected government repeatedly ignores the will of most citizens on issues of vital concern, it is likely to provoke mass demonstrations and even violent protest. In any case, the replacement of traditional with legal authority resulted in the collapse of traditional theories of obligation based on the will of God or on inherited position; democratic elections provide an alternative theory of obligation that is compatible with the legal concept of authority.

In the political process, elections are best interpreted as a form of voter reaction. Because elected governors must answer to the public in a future election, the assumption is that they will rule responsively. Elected officials want to be re-elected and ought therefore to enact laws and policies that meet current desires. As the philosopher John Plamenatz put it, "Elections are important not only for what happens at them but also for what happens because of them."[2]

In a simpler world, public officials might be elected with a mandate to do certain things and thus implement popular desires in a direct and unambiguous way. If that were the case, elections could be considered a mechanism for articulating demands. However, elections are rather inefficient mechanisms for determining the policy preferences of the electorate because elections are about more than just one policy: they involve multiple policies on multiple issues, parties, candidates, and leaders. Elections

Figure 25.1 Elections Legitimize

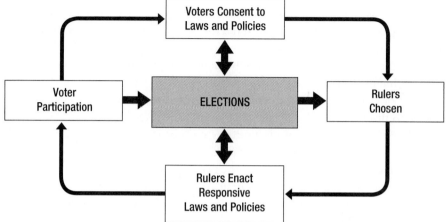

LIBERAL–DEMOCRATIC GOVERNMENT

are more like a judgment of the record of those in office, whose actual performance may have had little to do with the promises they made when elected, given unanticipated events or changes in economic forces. If voters generally like what has happened, they can vote for a continuation; if not, they can vote for a change, without being quite sure what the alternative will be. In this way elections are an ingenious mechanism for coping with an uncertain and ever-changing future. Elected rulers are allowed periods of creativity during which they seek to cope with the unexpected problems that are always presenting themselves; afterward, the voters decide whether they will be allowed to continue their efforts. Dealing with dilemmas gradually as they appear provides greater flexibility than trying to work out far in advance the answers to problems that may never arise in their expected form. The greatest strength of liberal democracy may well be the sophistication of its institutions that link the rulers and the ruled. Among these, elections are paramount.

For elections to provide this link a number of conditions must be present.[3] First, elections must occur at regular intervals and under free and fair conditions. Usually their frequency is specified in a constitution and ranges from every two years (the House of Representatives in the United States) to every seven years (the president of France). The point is that elections must be institutionalized so that a head of government cannot arbitrarily cancel or postpone them in order to rule indefinitely. They must be regular and reasonably frequent if they are to be effective in a democratic system. As voters evaluate political outputs, they may decide to choose new governors. If that opportunity is taken away, the democratic system loses its grounds for legitimacy. Free and fair elections are those that allow voters to cast their ballots secretly and safely—without violence or intimidation—and with sufficient information to make informed choices. They also guarantee that cast ballots are counted and reported honestly.

Second, there must be wide opportunity for all to run for office so that voters have a genuine choice across candidates and parties. If restrictions are placed on who can run for office, elections cannot be democratic. There has been a great deal of discussion about whether elections in one-party systems might be considered democratic. If the process for selecting candidates is rigid, and if this process is controlled by a small party elite, there is little competition for public office and little choice for voters. However, some argue that the one-party system can be democratic if there is competition among factions within the party. If the party nomination process is relatively open, there may be a choice of candidates. But the choice in this case is made by party members, not all voters, so this process is democratic only in a very restricted sense.

Third, the limits on universal adult suffrage must be minimal; practically all adults should have the right to participate in the selection of those who will govern. The legitimacy of a democracy rests on the participation of voters in elections. Restricting the franchise to a select group of voters limits the degree to which those who govern can respond to the desires of the masses. Various devices have been used to limit mass participation. Under the property franchise, for example, an individual was required to own assets of a certain value before being allowed to vote. Poll taxes, which had to be paid as a prerequisite for voting, also limited participation by the poor. More recently, age and residency requirements have been manipulated to influence voter turnout, and literacy requirements are still used in many developing nations to restrict full participation in elections. This is especially true where educational opportunities are limited. Until after World War I, women's right to vote was restricted. As discussed earlier, the long-term trend of liberal democracy has been to erase or minimize all such restrictions.

Finally, there must be a high degree of political freedom. If freedom of speech or of the press is limited, the electoral campaign cannot function as it must, and voters are unable to make fully informed decisions. The rights to express political ideas and critiques, to form independent associations and groups, and to receive political information from independent sources are essential to ensuring that elections provide an effective accountability mechanism. Restrictions on political freedom inhibit the role of the electoral process in democratic systems.

In autocratic governments, elections have little or nothing to do with the give-and-take between rulers and the ruled; rather, they are means of mobilizing support for the regime. Voters ratify lists of selected candidates and often are penalized for not participating in the election. Token opposition is sometimes permitted by authoritarian regimes when they have a firm grip on the government, as a way of enhancing the external legitimacy of the electoral result. This mobilization of support for the government also attaches legitimacy to elections in liberal democracies. National elections are quasi-sacred occasions during which the participants reaffirm their commitment to constitutional procedures. This comparison of liberal–democratic with authoritarian and totalitarian elections again shows how seemingly similar institutions can perform quite different functions in different systems.

An election is a complex procedure, and countries use many different methods to conduct elections. A bewildering variety of electoral systems have been tried at one time or another. Below, we describe some of the more common types and point out a few of the consequences of each type for the democratic process.

Students of physics may have encountered the Heisenberg uncertainty principle, which states that it is impossible to measure simultaneously the velocity and position of a subatomic particle. The very act of measuring the speed will affect the position, and vice versa, so that complete information is impossible to attain. Recent work has shown the existence of a somewhat analogous situation in the use of electoral procedures in democratic politics. It turns out that the result obtained from an election depends in a very fundamental sense upon the method that is employed. There is no "will of the people" independent of the instrument chosen to measure it. The way votes are counted has a profound effect on the outcome. According to David M. Farrell,

> . . . depending on how the [electoral] system is designed it may be easier or harder for particular politicians to win seats; it may be easier or harder for particular parties to gain representation in parliament; it may be more or less likely that one party can form a government on its own.[4]

Political scientists are aware now more than ever that the choice of electoral procedures is a crucial variable in political systems.

ELECTORAL SYSTEMS

Electoral systems involve the set of rules that deal specifically with the process of turning votes into seats: how many votes a citizens will have, and whether they will vote for candidates, political party, or both; how the ballots will be counted; and how the counts will be translated into seats. On election night, these rules establish what happens after the polls have closed and the number of seats won by each political party.

Electoral systems involve a number of rules that can be combined in multiple ways; the result is that no two electoral systems function in quite the same manner. This complexity can be managed, however, by categorizing them into three broad types: plurality/majority; proportional; and mixed systems (see Concept Box 25.1). Plurality/majority systems place importance on ensuring that the governing party holds a majority of seats, a criterion that can help to provide for strong and stable governments. Proportional systems, on the other hand, place more weight on ensuring the **proportionality** of electoral results—the percentage of votes that each party earns should correspond closely to the percentage of seats it is awarded in the legislature. The distortion in the seat-to-vote ratio under Canada's electoral system has been one of the incentives for considering electoral reform, a topic revisited further on in the chapter. Finally, mixed systems attempt to minimize the problems associated with each of the plurality/majority and proportional systems by combining them into a hybrid form.

Concept Box 25.1

Typology of Electoral Systems

Category	Dominant Types	Description	Examples
Plurality/Majority		*Employs single member districts; individual candidates are elected; emphasis on creation of stable, majority governments.*	
	Single-Member Plurality (SMP)	Candidate with the most votes in a district wins the seat.	Canada (legislative), United Kingdom (legislative), United States (legislative)
	Majority–Runoff	Candidate must win a majority of votes to win the election. If not obtained on first ballot, the two leading candidates compete in a second round of balloting.	Brazil (presidential), France (presidential), Portugal (presidential)
	Majority–Plurality	Candidate must win a majority of votes to win the election. If not obtained on first ballot, candidate with a plurality of votes in second round wins the seat.	France (legislative), Mexico (presidential)
	Alternative Vote (AV)	Voters rank their preferences across the candidates on one ballot. Majority of first preferences required to win seat. If not obtained, second preferences of the bottom candidate are reallocated to remaining candidates. Process continues until a majority of first preferences is obtained.	Australia (legislative), Ireland (presidential)
Proportional		*Employs multi-member districts; seats are distributed to parties; employs various formulas for allocating seats within districts (e.g. largest remainder and highest average methods); employs thresholds (i.e. minimum percentage of votes required to be allocated a seat); voters face closed (no choice of candidates) or open (choice of candidate) lists. Emphasis on proportionality of election results.*	
	List: Single or Multiple Multi-Member Districts	Voters cast a ballot for a party's list of candidates. Percentage of votes won by a party determines the number of seats that party wins.	Argentina (legislative), Israel (legislative), Netherlands (legislative), South Africa (legislative)

Concept Box 25.1

Category	Dominant Types	Description	Examples
	Single Transferable Vote (STV)	Voters rank preferences for candidates across all parties. Candidates whose number of first preferences meets a minimum quota are elected. Remaining seats are filled by transferring the unallocated votes of winning candidates and those of the weakest candidates.	Australia (legislative), Ireland (legislative)
Mixed		***Combines elements of plurality/majority and proportional systems.***	
	Corrective	Two tiers of members across the country, some elected by PR and some by plurality/majority. Voters are allocated two votes: one for a party (PR) and one for a candidate (plurality/majority). Distribution of seats occurs so as to correct any distortion in proportionality introduced by the plurality/majority allocation.	Germany (legislative), New Zealand (legislative)
	Superposition or Parallel	Same as in the Corrective system except that the distribution of seats occurs independently in each tier.	Japan (legislative), South Korea (legislative)

Source: Adapted from André Blais and Louis Massicotte, "Electoral Systems." Reproduced by permission of SAGE Publications, London, Los Angeles, New Delhi and Singapore from L. LeDuc, R.G. Niemi and P. Norris, eds., *Comparing Democracies 2* Copyright © Sage Publications, 2003, pp.40–69.

PLURALITY/MAJORITY SYSTEMS

The Single-Member-Plurality System

The **single-member-plurality system (SMP),** popularly known as "first past the post," is familiar from its use in Britain, Canada, and the United States. One candidate is elected in each **constituency**—that is, in each geographical district that has a representative—and each voter has one vote to cast. This vote is cast for individual candidates rather than a party and the winning candidate is the one who receives a plurality of valid ballots—that is, more votes than any other candidate. If there are only two candidates, the winner automatically gets a majority; but if there are several candidates who split the vote fairly evenly, the winner's plurality may be far less than a majority.

The SMP method is a natural partner to the two-party system because it does not distort electoral results when there are only two candidates. In that case, a plurality is also a majority, and the democratic criterion of majority rule is unambiguously satisfied. However, when social cleavages are such that a two-party system cannot be maintained, SMP can have peculiar and even distorting consequences. In the 1996 British Columbia election, for example, the Liberals led in the popular vote (42 percent), the NDP came second (39 percent), and the provincial Reform Party finished third overall (9 percent). Yet the NDP took a majority of seats (39 out of 75, or 52 percent) and thus formed the government, even though the Liberals won substantially more votes. The Liberals got their numbers by running up big majorities in Vancouver suburbs; but in many rural ridings they split the right-wing vote with the Reform Party, allowing the NDP to "come up the middle" and win the seat with a plurality.

In SMP systems, a single seat in each constituency means that votes cast for unsuccessful candidates are "wasted" in that there is no seat rewarded for the votes obtained. As a result, the relationship between votes and seats often can be very disproportional, as happened in New Brunswick in 1987 and in British Columbia in 2001 (see Table 25.1). A party finishing second in every constituency and earning 25 percent of the national vote can fail to gain a single seat in the legislature in spite of a having earned a significant level of popular support. As shown in Table 25.2 using data from the 2006 election, voters in a constituency can be divided fairly evenly among two or three political parties but, because SMP allows only a single winner, the losing parties

Table 25.1

N.B. (1987) and B.C. (2001) Provincial Elections

	Percentage of Popular Vote	Seats	Percentage of Seats	Seat-to-Vote Ratio
N.B. 1987				
Liberals	60.4	58	100	1.66
PC	28.6	0	0	0
NDP	10.6	0	0	0
B.C. 2001				
Liberals	57.6	77	97.5	1.69
NDP	21.5	2	2.5	0.12
Greens	12.3	0	0	0

Note: The seat-to-vote ratio is calculated by dividing the percentage of seats won by the percentage of votes earned; values greater than 1 indicate the party was over-rewarded and values less than 1 that it was under-rewarded.

Table 25.2

Winner-Take-All Effects of SMP: Three Ridings, 2006 Federal Election

	Liberals	New Democrats	Conservatives
Brant	36.9%*	21.3%	36.0%
Fleetwood–Port Kells	31.6%	25.2%	33.5%*
South Shore–St. Margaret's	28.4%	28.5%	36.8%*
(*denotes winner*)			

get no results for the support they have garnered. In the constituency of Brant, the candidate that finished second earned 36 percent of the popular vote, less than 1 percentage point away from the winner, and yet earned no reward for this showing. The reality of "wasted votes" under SMP has been argued to "favour" a two-party system by reducing the number of parties with seats in the legislature and by pushing voters to support larger parties to avoid throwing their vote away.[5]

In general, SMP penalizes parties that earn a solid but small percentage of the vote share. The NDP at the federal level in Canada is a good example; in the 2004 and 2006 elections, the party earned 15.7 and 17.5 percent of the national vote but was allocated only 6.2 and 9.4 percent of legislative seats. The one exception to this relates to parties that are regionally concentrated, such as the Bloc Québécois at the federal level in Canada. It is thus almost a general law of politics that no new party can break into a system based on SMP voting unless it achieves territorial concentration.

SMP also magnifies relatively small shifts in the popular vote. In a two-party system, an increase in a party's popular vote from 50 to 60 percent of the total will produce a landslide in parliamentary seats; and if there are three or more competitive parties, anything over 45 percent for one will probably produce a landslide. For example, between 1980 and 1984 the popular vote for the federal Conservatives went from 37.4 to 49.96 percent, while the same party's seats increased from 103 of 282 (36.5 percent) to 211 of 282 (74.8 percent). Such results may be particularly drastic in multiparty situations, in which fragmentation of the opposition can give the governing party an artificially and enormously inflated strength in the elected assembly. And in some cases, such as the 1987 New Brunswick election shown in Table 25.1, they can lead to a complete lack of opposition in the legislature.

Particularly in ethnically segmented societies, the first-past-the-post method can lead to the permanent underrepresentation of minorities, given the winner-take-all nature of the system. During the years of the Stormont Parliament, the Catholics of Northern Ireland constituted about one-third of the population, but they never came close to winning one-third of the seats in the assembly. This result was reinforced by the use of **gerrymandering**[6]—that is, deliberately drawing constituencies so as to favour one side, in this case the Protestant majority, over the other. Blocks of Catholic voters were divided up so as to form permanent minorities within Protestant-dominated constituencies, thus restricting their ability to elect sympathetic candidates. Such longstanding underrepresentation can destroy the legitimacy of government in the minds of the aggrieved minority. Countries such as Canada and Great Britain have given responsibility for electoral redistricting to non-partisan bodies in order to reduce the likelihood of gerrymandering. Plurality/majority systems, including SMP, have also been linked to the underrepresentation of women in legislatures; the ability to nominate only one candidate per constituency appears to lower the overall chances that a woman will be chosen to run for a party.[7]

Because of these many difficulties, SMP has been falling out of favour over the last hundred years. It was originally used quite widely, but among the world's stable industrial democracies it is now used only in Great Britain, the United States, and Canada. The last time New Zealand used it was 1992, after which voters decided in a referendum to replace it with the form of proportional representation known as mixed-member-proportional (see below). Yet SMP is a relatively simple electoral system that has a tendency to produce single-party majority governments (hence strong and stable governments), and which maintains a clear link between the legislator and his or her constituency.

Majority Systems

Like SMP, majority systems employ single-member constituencies but "raise the bar" in requiring that the winning candidate earn a majority rather than a plurality of valid votes. There are various ways of meeting this requirement. The **majority–runoff system** is favoured in countries that directly elect their president, such as France. In French presidential elections, two rounds of voting take place on two separate dates. The first round of voting is exactly like that held under SMP. If no candidate receives a majority of votes in the first round, however, only the candidates with the highest and second highest number of votes run in the second round, which takes place two weeks later. By reducing the number of candidates to two, a majority of votes for the winner is virtually guaranteed. This system is often used to choose both candidates and party leaders at conventions in Canada and the United States, except that voting takes place over a much shorter time period and only one candidate, the one with the least votes, is dropped from each successive ballot. Ensuring that the ultimate winner has a majority of the votes helps to preserve party unity; to have a leader chosen by less than a majority would be to invite dissension within the party.

The **majority–plurality system** proceeds much like the runoff system except that to win on the second ballot a candidate needs only a plurality of valid votes cast. In French legislative elections, candidates who fail to receive a minimum percentage of votes on the first ballot are dropped from the second; this requirement increases the likelihood but does not guarantee that the winning candidate will have won a majority of votes.[8]

Another variant of plurality/majority systems is the **alternative (or preferential) vote system** (AV), which attempts to capture information not only about voters' first choices but also about their second, third, and further choices. Electors are given a form on which they rank candidates in order of preference. If only two candidates are running, this system operates just like SMP. But when there are three or more candidates, the picture changes radically. Voters' first preferences are tabulated on the first count. If no one has a majority, the candidate with the least number of first-preference votes is dropped and a second count is taken. The eliminated candidate's votes are distributed to the other candidates according to the second preferences expressed on those ballots. The process continues until a majority is reached. The objective of the system is similar to that of a runoff: to ensure that the victor has majority support. The difference is that the alternative vote system collects the necessary information in advance and thus dispenses with further rounds of balloting. In a sense, it is a condensed runoff system.

The alternative vote system is used at present in elections for the Australian House of Representatives. Alberta, British Columbia, and Manitoba have also experimented with it at various times in the past. For instance, it was introduced in British Columbia in 1952 by the Liberals in order to hurt the CCF, whose fortunes were then on the rise. It was widely assumed that the Liberals and Conservatives would be each other's second choice, so that CCF candidates would do poorly on the second count. To everyone's surprise, the next election was won by the new Social Credit Party, which no one had considered a serious contender for power. Perhaps the lesson is that electoral methods, like all political institutions, should be based on general principles rather than opportunistic attempts to help or harm a specific party.

In practice, AV, like the runoff system, allows parties to retain a separate existence while forming coalitions with each other for electoral advantage. In Australia, the Liberal Party and the National (previously Country) Party have maintained a working coalition for decades, and together they dominate the conservative side of the ideological spectrum. The electoral system favours their coalition because a conservative-minded voter who tilts toward one party or the other can rank the Liberal (or National) candidate first and the National (or Liberal) candidate second. At some point in the vote-counting process, the trailing candidate will be dropped, but those votes will be transferred rather than wasted. As a voter on the right, you can vote for your favourite party without fearing that you will "split the right-wing vote" and thus help to elect a left-wing candidate. The same logic would apply on the left, but thus far the large Labour Party has been able to go it alone without a coalition partner.

Proportional Representation Systems

Plurality/majority systems have as one of their goals the creation of stable, strong governments. **Proportional representation (PR)** systems, on the other hand, strive to ensure proportionality; that is, they seek to reward parties with a percentage of seats in the legislature that reflects the percentage of votes earned in the election. To do so requires multimember constituencies, for a single seat cannot be divided between two or more parties.

John Stuart Mill was the first important political thinker to popularize proportional representation. He thought that the first-past-the-post system, which was then widely used, gave too much power to the triumphant majority, which might then abuse the rights of minorities. As he explained in *Considerations on Representative Government,* he preferred proportional representation precisely because it would ensure that various minorities would be represented:

> Because the majority ought to prevail over the minority, must the majority have all the votes, the minority none? Is it necessary that the minority should not even be heard? In a really equal democracy, every or any section would be represented, not disproportionately, but proportionately.[9]

There are two main forms of proportional representation: the *list system* and the much less common *single-transferable-vote* (STV) system (sometimes called the Hare system after its inventor, Thomas Hare). Both have the same aim: to ensure that representatives are elected in numbers proportional to the share of votes that their parties receive in the balloting.

THE LIST SYSTEM

The **list system** is the easier of the two to grasp. The elector votes not for individuals but for parties. Each party has a list of as many candidates as there are seats to be awarded. If a party gets x percent of the popular vote, then the top x percent of its list is declared elected. This system gives great power to the party leaders, who in most cases determine the candidates' positions on the list. Being high on the list of a major party is tantamount to election; being low on the list of any party is tantamount to defeat. Minimum thresholds are usually adopted in such systems to keep splinter parties from gaining seats, such as the German requirement of obtaining a minimum of 5 percent of the list vote in order to be awarded any seats at all. The higher this threshold, the less proportional the election results, as smaller parties are under-rewarded.

The purest examples of the list system in practice are found in Israel and the Netherlands. In each case, the entire country is treated as a single constituency and there is a very low threshold (around 1 percent of the vote) for obtaining representation in the legislature. The result is a faithful translation of popular vote into the proportion of parliamentary seats, as well as a proliferation of parties and a permanent situation of coalition government. Variations from this list system can move the electoral results away from the goal of proportionality. Imposing thresholds, referred to above, is one variation. Another is the district magnitude, or number of seats awarded in each constituency. As this number falls, so does the likelihood of proportionality. Variations in the ballot structure affect the control provided to voters over parties in the selection of candidates. The open ballot structure allows voters to allocate their votes to candidates within party lists; the closed ballot structure allows them only to select a party and leaves candidate selection entirely in the parties' hands.

List systems require the use of electoral formulas for determining seat allocation after the election has taken place. Although a number of variations exist in their use, the two main formulas are the largest remainder and the highest average. The first employs a quota, most often the total vote count divided by the number of seats to be allocated, to allocate seats. If a party's vote count exceeds the quota, it is allocated a seat and the quota removed from its total vote count. This allocation continues until no party's vote count exceeds the quota, at which point the remaining seats are allocated to the parties with the "largest remainders." The second formula—both more common and more complicated—divides each party's vote count by a series of divisors (the simplest being 1, 2, 3, 4, and so on) to produce a set of average votes. The "highest average" is allocated to the first seat; the second highest average is allocated to the second seat, and so on until all the seats are allocated. Variations in these formulas affect the system's proportionality. Importantly, not all PR systems are more proportional than plurality/ majority systems. The list system is widely used, with various modifications, in many European and Latin countries, and in a number of newer African democracies.

SINGLE-TRANSFERABLE-VOTE SYSTEM

The **single-transferable-vote (STV) system** of proportional representation is best understood as an extension of the alternative or preferential ballot from single-member to multimember constituencies. Electors vote for individuals rather than party lists, but they do so preferentially; that is, by ranking the candidates in their order of choice. Thus the proportionality of PR systems is combined with increased voter choice and constituency representation. A formula establishes the quota of votes required to win, and each victor's surplus votes are transferred according to lower preferences. The following formula has often been used:

$$[\text{Total number of valid ballots}/(\text{Number of seats} + 1)] + 1 = \text{Quota}$$

In a constituency with four seats and 100,000 valid ballots cast, the quota would be calculated as follows:

$$[100,000/(4 + 1)] + 1 = 20,001$$

Any candidate receiving 20,001 or more first preferences would be elected immediately. The remaining positions would be filled by counting procedures that take account of second and lower preferences. These procedures are complex, but the basic idea is that votes are transferred both from below and from above. From below, they are transferred as candidates with the fewer first preferences are dropped. From above, they are transferred from candidates who have met the quota, since these candidates will usually have surplus votes to be distributed among other candidates. STV produces a more or less proportional result without providing the party leadership with the extraordinary power given it by the list system.

Proportional representation tends to promote the existence of small parties, although proliferation of parties can be controlled by the use of thresholds. It is not necessary to come anywhere close to a majority to attract voters, as in a first-past-the-post situation. A party only has to be able to retain the support of its loyalists. Thus, proportional representation tends to encourage relatively small or medium-sized interest or ideological parties—for example, Catholic parties, farmers' parties, workers' parties, environmentalist parties. Such alignments can be stable over long periods of time, and this can create a distribution of representatives in the assembly that changes very little from election to election. This is the contemporary situation in many European states.

When the distribution of support is stable, and when no single party commands a majority, the result must be prolonged coalition government. This in itself is not a bad thing, though it is alien to the British tradition. It can work well, as it has in most Scandinavian countries; but in cases such as Italy, from the late 1940s until the fall of communism, when the presence of large extremist parties severely limited the choice of coalition partners, the result was cabinet instability.

Proportional representation has often been attacked for encouraging the proliferation of parties, thus balkanizing politics and making majority government impossible. The criticism is not without force. But it is often true that social cleavages exist that will produce a multiparty system regardless of the electoral method. In these circumstances, proportional representation is a way of keeping civil peace by allowing all significant minorities to feel represented. A first-past-the-post system might extinguish the smaller parties and leave certain minorities permanently underrepresented.

MIXED SYSTEMS

One type of electoral system has saw tremendous growth in the 1990s: the mixed electoral system. Such systems combine the proportionality of PR systems with the constituency representation of single-member districts, but in a simpler system than STV. The two dominant types of mixed systems are the corrective and superposition. Germany provides an example of the corrective system (called the **mixed member proportional system,** or MMP). On election day the voters cast two ballots, one for a local candidate running in a territorial constituency and the other for a national list of candidates put forward by a political party. The winner of each constituency seat is determined by SMP. After the local constituency winners are known, members from the lists are added to the territorial members in the numbers needed to ensure proportionality based on the percentage of votes cast for each party on the national list ballot. For a look at the corrective system in action, see World View 25.1. The superposition system is similar to the corrective except that the list seats are awarded independently of those awarded in the districts. This results in reduced proportionality in the system.

World View 25.1

New Zealand and MMP

In 1992, the New Zealand Government, on the advice of the Royal Commission on the Electoral System, held a non-binding referendum on changing the electoral process. Significant support was registered for changing the first-past-the-post system to something else. In 1993, a binding referendum on various options was held and 53.9 percent of voters supported the option of a mixed-member proportional (MMP or corrective system) while AV and STV received a much smaller degree of support. The National Party government then enacted the change, which applied in the 1996 election.

Parliament is elected for three years, and political parties must elect one electorate member or receive 5 percent of the party (list) vote nationally to receive their proportion of seats allocated. Under MMP, each eligible voter has two votes—a vote for an individual running in a constituency (called an electorate vote) and another vote for a political party (called a party vote). In the most recent election of 20085, there were 70 constituency seats (of which 7 were set aside for Maori voters) and 52 list seats, for a total of 122. Results of the 2008 general election were:

Party	% of Party Votes	% of Electorate Votes	Electorate Seats (General, Maori)	Party Seats	Total Seats
National Party	44.9	46.6	41,0	17	58
Labour Party	34.0	35.2	19,2	22	43
Green Party	6.7	5.6	0,0	9	9
Maori Party	2.4	3.3	0,5	0	5
ACT New Zealand	3.7	3.0	1,0	4	5
United Future NZ	0.9	1.1	1,0	0	1
Jim Anderton's Progressive	0.9	1.1	1,0	0	1
TOTALS			63,7	52	122

Note: Election results available at http://2008.electionresults.govt.nz/

(*continued*)

World View 25.1 (*continued*)

After direct and list seats are combined, each party's seat total in parliament is very close to its proportion of the party preference vote. MMP obviously creates a greater balance between the popular vote and seats in parliament than is the case with the SMP system. However, these results also mean an end to single-party-majority government. The previous government in New Zealand was a minority coalition between Labour and Jim Anderton's Progressive Coalition, which together held 51 of 121 seats. Agreements were entered into with New Zealand First and United Future to provide support to the coalition on confidence and supply motions; in exchange, the leaders of these two parties were given cabinet portfolios although they did not sit in cabinet. In 2008, the National Party has chosen to lead a minority government with confidence support from the ACT, United Future and Māori Parties. This trade-off between proportionality and majority government is a common feature of PR electoral systems.

ELECTORAL REFORM IN CANADA

New Zealand's move to MMP from SMP was part of a larger trend toward reform of electoral systems in the 1990s. Conventional wisdom has argued that electoral reform is very unlikely, given that it requires the willingness of governments composed of political parties that have benefitted from the existing systems to bring about that reform. But significant electoral reform in New Zealand, Japan, and Italy suggests that conventional wisdom may have it wrong. One of the reasons for the increased likelihood of reform is the "democratic deficit" in advanced democracies; the term refers to a widespread belief that democratic institutions are failing to adequately articulate and defend the interests of most citizens.

Canada has not been immune to the trend toward electoral reform. To date, five provinces have seriously considered the possibility of moving away from SMP, employing some very novel mechanisms in the process.[10] British Columbia, for example, employed a citizens' assembly to examine and make a recommendation in 2004; composed of 80 men and 80 women randomly chosen from among each of the province's electoral districts as well as two Aboriginal members, the group met regularly for close to a year, learning about electoral systems and then deliberating on whether to shift from SMP. The first of its kind around the world, the assembly recommended adopting STV because it would increase proportionality, provide direct constituency representation, and maximize voter choice. The choice was put to the citizens of B.C. in a referendum in 2005 but fell just short of meeting the requirements for adoption. A second referendum is scheduled for 2009 to revisit the question. In 2006 an Ontario citizens' assembly also recommended a shift away from SMP toward a corrective mixed system similar to that in New Zealand. This proposal was also defeated in a province-wide referendum in October 2007. New Brunswick, Prince Edward Island, and Quebec employed traditional commissions composed of several appointed members to examine the question of electoral reform. Each commission recommended moving away from SMP toward a corrective mixed system, but to date no changes have been implemented. Although no formal move to examine the question of electoral reform has occurred at the federal level, there has been increasing pressure to do just that.

The key concerns that these forums have raised about SMP include its lack of proportionality, and especially its over-rewarding of seats to parties with a plurality of votes; the problem of wasted votes; its tendency to reward regionally concentrated parties, which reinforces regional divisions; and the system's role in the continuing underrepresentation of women, Aboriginal peoples, and minority groups. The importance attached to voter choice and constituency representation explains the favouring of mixed systems as the alternative of choice. List systems would move too far away from the current system of providing a representative tied to a relative small constituency and would strengthen parties by providing them with the ability to set lists of candidates at elections.

ELECTIONS: WHO VOTES AND WHY

Attempting to explain why people vote the way they do is an integral part of political science. For years there existed an underlying assumption that democracies relied upon the participation of an informed citizenry. It was assumed that when citizens went into the voting booth they made rational choices based on knowledge about issues. However, modern survey research methods, first used on a large scale in the 1940s, have shown that people make voting decisions for a whole variety of reasons, some of which appear rational and some of which may seem irrational. Factors such as religion, class, ideology, party identification, region, education, and gender have been shown to play a role in shaping voting choices.

In an article entitled "The Not So Simple Act of Voting," Russell J. Dalton and Martin P. Wattenberg trace the development of voting studies, primarily in the United States.[11] Voting studies typically employ opinion surveys, most often conducted over the telephone, with a representative sample of the voting population. The questions include answers that will reveal demographic information such as age, gender, place of residence, income, and so on, as well as questions about the party normally supported by the respondent (known as party identification), their beliefs and values, and voting behaviour. From early voting studies in the 1950s and 1960s, the authors identify three approaches to voting behaviour. The sociological approach focuses on socio-demographic characteristics such as ethnicity and gender for explaining voting decisions. Our backgrounds play a role in shaping our values and priorities, and our social groups provide important political cues and reference points for evaluating our political preferences. The psychological approach emphasizes attitudes and beliefs as causal factors, but emphasizes the importance of short-term factors in the vote decision, in particular party identification, issue opinions, and candidate evaluations. The campaign period is also considered an important element in voting behaviour in that it provides the material from which evaluations and attitudes stem. The rational-choice approach, deriving from Anthony Downs's *An Economic Theory of Democracy,* assumes voters evaluate party promises and governmental performance and make their choices accordingly. Contemporary political scientists usually draw on all three approaches for an integrated causal model of voting behaviour.

In 1993 Elisabeth Gidengil conducted a similar review of voting research in Canada in her article "A Quarter Century of Canadian National Election Studies."[12] The initial tendency among Canadian studies was to follow the sociological and the psychological approaches. The sociological approach, in her words, focused on "the role of societal cleavages in explaining voter choice"; the cleavages included "region, religion, ethnicity, subjective social class, community size, age, and gender."[13] The psychological approach focused on "reactions to change in the political landscape—the personalities and the salient issues."[14] In other words, reaction to candidates and issues shapes political choices. And of course party identification, or *partisanship,* also provided the "lens" through which candidates and issues were perceived. Gidengil noted that regionalism and strong party identification emerged as important variables in early Canadian studies, whereas the American system makes the personality of candidates more important. She concluded that to further advance voting studies, "we need to start thinking of the competing traditions of voting research not as rivals but as complementary."[15]

In an analysis of the 2000 Canadian election, Blais et al. developed a model describing the "variables" that explain vote choice (Figure 25.2). The variables closest to the vote decision are those that are closest in time to it; leader evaluations, for example, will have a direct impact on vote decisions but are likely to take place some time during the election campaign when voters get a chance to assess party leaders. Variables further away from the vote decision are more distant in time from it; the greater the distance, the more likely it is that the variable will work indirectly through more proximate factors in shaping the vote choice. Party identification, for example, is likely to shape how voters evaluate party leaders and thus indirectly influence their vote decision. While the model provides a clear picture of the many factors that can influence vote decisions, the authors also point out that individual elections are likely to cue individual elements of the model differently. Some elections may emphasize the importance of issue positions for the vote calculus; opinion on free trade, for example, was an important determinant of voting in the 1988 election. In other elections, evaluations of government performance may play a leading role.

Figure 25.2 The Multi-Stage Explanatory Model

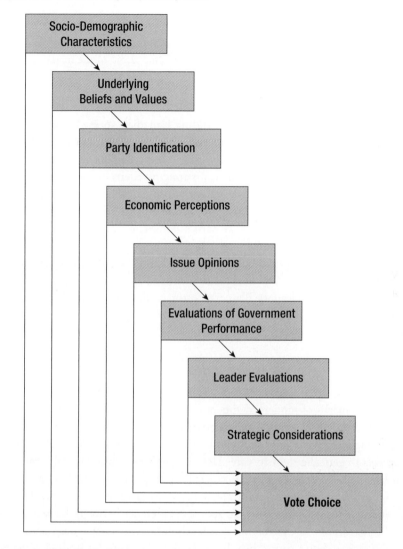

Source: André Blais, Elisabeth Gidengil, Richard Nadeau, and Neil Nevitee, *Anatomy of a Liberal Victory: Making Sense of the Vote in the 2000 Canadian Election* (Peterborough: Broadview, 2002), p. 84. Copyright © 2002 by André Blais, et al. Reprinted by permission of University of Toronto Press Higher Education Division.

Evaluation of survey data collected at the time of the 2000 Canadian election suggests that four sets of factors were especially important in shaping how Canadians voted. First, socio-demographic characteristics, including region, religion, ethnicity, gender, and community type (i.e., urban versus rural), cannot be ignored. Canadian politics has long had a regional and religious dimension; ethnicity, gender, and community type are more recent additions to the voting calculus. Second, values and beliefs are another important part of the voting story in Canada. According to the authors:

> Our results indicate that the main ideological divide, in Canada as elsewhere, concerns orientations towards markets. Those who believe in the virtue of the market tend to support right-wing parties, and those who are more sceptical about market values, tend to vote for center or left-wing parties.[16]

The third important factor in understanding Canadian voting behaviour is partisanship. Conventional academic wisdom has argued that Canadian voters have "flexible" partisan loyalties that play relatively little role in shaping their vote choices.[17] Blais et al. suggest that while the number of strong partisans in Canada may be comparatively low, they nevertheless play an important role in shaping electoral outcomes. More than half of those with a partisan loyalty identified with the Liberal party in 2000, a fact that helps to explain that party's dominance at the time. It also helps to explain the importance of some of the socio-demographic factors outlined above; certain groups, including certain ethnic minorities and Catholics, have longstanding loyalties to the Liberal party. The final factor identified as playing an important role in the vote choice is political leaders. Blais et al. estimate that one in five Canadians voted the way they did because of how they felt about party leaders.

TURNOUT

One of the hallmarks of modern democratic systems is the opportunity for all adult citizens to participate in choosing their governors. This political right was a fundamental principle that fired the hearts and minds of our ancestors, some of whom went to the streets to gain the right to vote. However, in many contemporary nation-states that qualify as liberal democracies, the voter turnout rate is far from 100 percent.

In Figure 25.3, election turnout rates since 1980 are plotted for Canada and the United States. One immediately sees an apparent difference between the two countries; prior to 2000, turnout in Canada was usually about 10 to 15 percentage points higher than in the United States. Since then, however, increased turnout in the United States has closed that gap. Indeed, by 2008, turnout in the United States had surpassed that in Canada. Importantly, the gap in turnout between the two countries is an actual one; turnout figures in Figure 25.3 for both countries are calculated by dividing the number of voters by the number of eligible voters (in Canada, those on the permanent voters' list; in the United States, the voting age population minus non-citizens, ineligible felons, and overseas citizens who are ineligible to vote). Turnout figures in the United States were previously calculated by dividing the number of voters by the number of adult citizens eligible, a practice that artificially deflated the turnout rate. How the turnout rate in the United States is calculated remains a contested issue among political scientists.[18]

Figure 25.3 Voter Turnout Percentages in Canadian Federal and U.S. Presidential Elections, 1980–2008

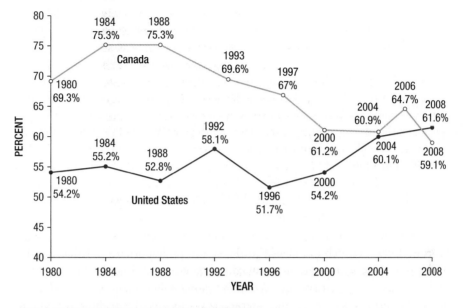

Note: Percentages calculated using number of eligible voters.

Sources: John R. Colombo, ed. *The Canadian Global Almanac,* 1997 (Toronto: Macmillan Canada, 1997), p. 181; *Globe and Mail,* June 4, 1997, p. A6; *Facts on File,* 56: 2918, Nov. 7, 1996, p. 812; *Facts on File,* 60: 3130, Nov. 30, 2000, p. 918; Infoplease.com, June 20, 2001.

According to the Institute for Democracy and Electoral Assistance, voter turnout rates in Canada and the United States are relatively low by world standards for elections since 1945.[19] Compared with 172 other states, Canada ranks 77th and the United States 139th overall, with average turnout rates of 68.4 and 48.3 percent, respectively. Top spot goes to Italy with an overall average turnout of 92.5 percent; Mali comes in last with an average turnout rate of 21.7 percent. If we evaluate regions of the world, Western Europe has the highest average turnout and South and Central America the lowest, but regional trends do not appear to be directly related to overall wealth. The Middle East and Asia, for example, come in as the regions with the 4th and 5th highest turnout levels while North America ranks 6th overall.

The most important question arising from these figures is why citizens in a democracy today would choose to not exercise their franchise. Some may not vote because they are satisfied with what is going on and so do not bother, having decided not to let elections get in the way of their busy lives. If that is the case, there may not be much to worry about. But others may not vote because of **political alienation;** that is, they feel estranged from the process or they have become quite cynical about it. These feelings often are driven by a sense that voters are not effective in the process; if voting is unlikely to make a difference to the political outcome, then why bother? If this is the situation, democracy may be in danger of losing its essential popular support.

In a number of countries, including Canada and the United States, young people are becoming less likely to vote. A recent estimate suggests that in federal elections in Canada, only about 20 to 25 percent of those in the 18 to 24 age group have turned out to cast their ballots on election day. There is no evidence that young people are particularly alienated from the system; they simply do not vote. The reasons for this trend are not entirely clear. Age has always been connected to voter turnout; life cycle explanations point out that as young people age they take on increasing responsibilities such as parenthood and mortgages that increase their stake in political outcomes and thus increase their likelihood of participating. Recent research, however, suggests that the transition to adulthood has been extended over a long period of time. On average, young people today spend more years in school and wait much longer to marry, have children, and enter stable employment. Participation in politics is probably part of adopting a full adult role. If this line of thought is correct, people in their late teens and twenties who do not now vote will probably do so when they reach their thirties and forties. Other research has identified the increasing importance of education for voter turnout; those without a university education are much less likely to vote than those with a degree. Some have argued that increasing political complexity and access to political information through the Internet serves to overwhelm those without an advanced education. If this line of thought is correct, these voters are unlikely to begin voting as they age.

Beyond a question of attitudes, which vary greatly from one country to another, political scientists have learned a lot about factors that contribute to higher turnout rates everywhere. Below are a few of the findings:

- Voters are less likely to vote when it is troublesome to do so. Bad weather can reduce turnout, as can inconvenient registration systems like the American one.

- Within any particular country, older citizens and those with higher education and income are more likely to vote.

- Exciting, closely contested elections tend to increase turnout as people are more likely to believe that their vote will make difference.

- People are more likely to vote in national elections than in local ones. Turnout in Canadian municipal elections is usually well below 50 percent.

- People get tired of having to vote if they are too often asked to do so. Switzerland and the United States, which hold frequent elections and referendums, have low turnout rates.

- Proportional representation tends to be associated with higher turnout rates. Under SMP, many voters feel their ballot is "wasted"; and because they know their preferred candidate has no chance of winning, they do not bother to turn out. This helps to explain why Canada and the United States, two of the few democracies that still use SMP, have relatively low turnout levels.

Questions for Discussion

1. Would you support a shift away from SMP? What would be your main reasons for advocating electoral reform?

2. Do you vote? Why or why not? Do you think that this will change in the future?

3. What institutional reform would you advocate to address the democratic deficit in Canada?

Internet Links

1. International Foundation for Election Systems: **www.ifes.org.**

2. International IDEA (Institute for Democracy and Electoral Assistance): **www.idea.int.**

3. New Zealand Government, Parliament: **www.parliament.nz/en-NZ.**

4. Administration and Cost of Elections: **www.aceproject.org.** An encyclopedia of everything you could possibly want to know about electoral systems and the administration of elections around the world.

5. Elections Canada: **www.elections.ca.**

Further Reading

Bakvis, Herman. *Voter Turnout in Canada.* Royal Commission on Electoral Reform and Party Financing, vol. 15. Toronto: Dundurn Press, 1991.

Bell, David V. J., and Frederick J. Fletcher, eds. *Reaching the Voter: Constituency Campaigning in Canada.* Royal Commission on Electoral Reform and Party Financing, vol. 20. Toronto: Dundurn Press, 1991.

Blais, André, Elisabeth Gidengil, Richard Nadeau, and Neil Nevitte. *Anatomy of a Liberal Victory: Making Sense of the Vote in the 2000 Canadian Election.* Peterborough, ON: Broadview Press, 2002.

Boston, Jonathan, et al., eds. *Left Turn: The New Zealand Election of 1999.* Wellington: Victoria University Press, 2000.

Brennan, Geoffrey, and Loren E. Lomasky. *Democracy and Decision: The Pure Theory of Electoral Preference.* Cambridge: Cambridge University Press, 1993.

Cassidy, Michael, ed. *Democratic Rights and Electoral Reform in Canada.* Royal Commission on Electoral Reform and Party Financing, vol. 10. Toronto: Dundurn Press, 1991.

Clarke, Harold D., Jane Jensen, Lawrence LeDuc, and Jon H. Pammett. *Absent Mandate: Canadian Electoral Politics in an Era of Restructuring.* 3rd ed. Vancouver: Gage, 1996.

————. *Political Choice in Canada.* Toronto: McGraw-Hill Ryerson, 1979.

Conway, M. Margaret, Gertrude A. Steuernagel, and David W. Ahern. *Women and Political Participation: Cultural Change in the Political Arena.* 2nd ed. Washington, DC: CQ Press, 2005.

Courtney, John C. *Elections.* Vancouver: University of British Columbia Press, 2004.

Courtney, John C., et al., eds. *Drawing Boundaries: Legislatures, Courts and Electoral Values.* Saskatoon: Fifth House, 1992.

Dalton, Russell J. *Citizen Politics: Public Opinion and Political Parties in Advanced Industrial Democracies.* 4th ed. Washington, DC: CQ Press, 2006.

Dalton, Russell J., and Martin P. Wattenberg. "The Not So Simple Act of Voting." In Ada W. Finifter, ed. *Political Science: The State of the Discipline II.* Washington, DC: The American Political Science Association, 1993.

Dalton, Russell J., et al. *Electoral Change in Advanced Industrial Democracies: Realignment or Dealignment?* Princeton, NJ: Princeton University Press, 1984.

Everitt, Joanna, and Brenda O'Neill, eds. *Citizen Politics: Research and Theory in Canadian Political Behaviour.* Don Mills, ON: Oxford, 2002.

Farrell, David M. *Electoral Systems: A Comparative Introduction.* New York: Palgrave, 2001.

Gidengil, Elisabeth. "Canada Votes: A Quarter Century of Canadian National Election Studies," *Canadian Journal of Political Science 25* (June 1992).

Ginsburg, Benjamin, and Alan Stone, eds. *Do Elections Matter?* Armank, NY: M. E. Sharpe, 1993.

Harrop, Martin, and William L. Miller. *Elections and Voters: A Comparative Introduction.* London: MacMillan, 1987.

Johnston, Richard, et al. *Letting the People Decide: Dynamics of a Canadian Election.* Montreal: McGill–Queen's University Press, 1992.

Kavanagh, Dennis, ed. *Electoral Politics.* Oxford: Clarendon Press, 1992.

Law Commission of Canada. *Voting Counts: Electoral Reform for Canada.* Ottawa: Her Majesty the Queen in Right of Canada, represented by the Minister of Public Works and Government Services, 2004.

LeDuc, Lawrence. *The Politics of Direct Democracy.* Peterborough, ON: Broadview Press, 2003.

LeDuc, Lawrence, Richard G. Niemi, and Pippa Norris, eds. *Comparing Democracies 2: New Challenges in the Study of Elections and Voting.* Thousand Oaks, CA: Sage, 2002.

Lijphart, Arend. *Electoral Systems and Party Systems: A Study of Twenty-Seven Democracies.* Oxford: Oxford University Press, 1994.

Loenen, Nick. *Citizenship and Democracy: A Case for Proportional Representation.* Toronto: Dundurn, 1997.

Lyons, W. E. *One Man—One Vote.* Toronto: McGraw-Hill Ryerson, 1970.

Miller, Raymond, ed. *New Zealand Politics in Transition.* Auckland: Oxford University Press, 1997.

Milner, Henry, ed. *Making Every Vote Count: Reassessing Canada's Electoral System.* Peterborough, ON: Broadview Press, 1999.

———. *Steps Toward Making Every Vote Count: Electoral System Reform in Canada and Its Provinces.* Peterborough, ON: Broadview Press, 2004.

Nevitte, Neil, André Blais, Elisabeth Gidengil, and Richard Nadeau. *Unsteady State: The 1997 Canadian Federal Election.* Toronto: Oxford University Press, 2000.

Norris, Pippa. *Democratic Phoenix: Reinventing Political Activism.* Cambridge: Cambridge University Press, 2002.

Parry, Geraint, et al. *Political Participation and Democracy in Britain.* Cambridge: Cambridge University Press, 1992.

Pierce, Roy. *Choosing the Chief: Presidential Elections in France and the United States.* Ann Arbor: University of Michigan Press, 1995.

Posado-Carbo, Eduardo. *Elections Before Democracy: The History of Elections in Europe and Latin America.* New York: St. Martin's Press, 1996.

Reeve, Andrew, and Alan Ware. *Electoral Systems: A Comparative and Theoretical Introduction.* London: Routledge, 1992.

Rose, Richard, ed. *Electoral Participation.* Beverly Hills, CA: Sage, 1980.

Seidle, Leslie F., ed. *Comparative Issues in Party and Election Finance.* Royal Commission on Electoral Reform and Party Financing, vol. 4. Toronto: Dundurn Press, 1991.

———. *Issues in Party and Election Finance in Canada.* Royal Commission on Electoral Reform and Party Financing, vol. 5. Toronto: Dundurn Press, 1991.

———. *Provincial Party and Election Finance in Canada.* Royal Commission on Electoral Reform and Party Financing, vol. 3. Toronto: Dundurn Press, 1991.

Shugart, Matthew Soberg, and Martin P. Wattenberg, eds. *Mixed-Member Electoral Systems.* Toronto: Oxford University Press, 2003.

Small, David, ed. *Drawing the Map: Equality and Efficacy of the Vote: Canadian Electoral Boundary Reform.* Royal Commission on Electoral Reform and Party Financing, vol. 11. Toronto: Dundurn Press, 1991.

Tremblay, Manon, and Linda Trimble. *Women and Electoral Politics in Canada.* Toronto: Oxford University Press, 2003.

Verba, Sidney, Norman H. Nie, and Jae-On Kim. *Participation and Political Equality: A Seven Nation Comparison.* Cambridge: Cambridge University Press, 1978.

Wayne, Stephen J. *The Road to the White House 1996: The Politics of Presidential Elections.* New York: St. Martin's Press, 1996.

———. *The Road to the White House 2000: The Politics of Presidential Elections.* 6th ed. New York: St. Martin's Press, 2000.

———. *The Road to the White House 2004: The Politics of Presidential Elections.* 7th ed. Toronto: Thomson Nelson, 2004.

Wearing, Joseph, ed. *The Ballot and Its Message: Voting in Canada.* Toronto: Copp Clark Pitman, 1991.

White, Stephen. *How Russia Votes.* Chatham, NJ: Chatham House, 1997.

CHAPTER 26

Representative Assemblies

The preceding three chapters focused on citizen participation as a part of the political process. Citizens in a democracy can participate by becoming involved in interest groups that try to influence politics; joining political parties that select candidates to run for public office and develop policies; electing representatives to the legislature; and using the communication media as a source of information about government and politics.

The following four chapters focus on the managerial side of the political process, describing how government officials—some elected, some appointed, some hired—manage the public business of a society. These officials include legislators who make laws and policies, members of the executive who organize the legislative process and who supervise the administrators, and judges who adjudicate disputes arising over laws and policies of the government.

According to liberal–democratic theory, the representative assembly should be the central institution for converting political inputs into outputs. Through the mechanism of elections, the sovereign people have delegated to the assembly their power to rule—that is, to make decisions about public business. In the political system, these decisions constitute conversion. Conversion that takes place in the elected assembly meets the standard of democratic legitimacy because it is performed by representatives of the people.

This ideal, which gives central importance to the assembly, must be heavily qualified in reality, because a great deal of decision making also occurs in the executive and judicial branches of government and this decision making is often beyond the effective control and supervision of the assembly. However, we will discuss the assembly first because of its special importance in the theory of liberal democracy.

The most visible function of the democratic assembly is to legislate. This is so true that a representative assembly is commonly referred to as a **legislature.** This terminology is misleading, however, for two reasons: modern assemblies do much more than legislate; and in parliamentary systems, they do not effectively control the content of legislation—such control is in the hands of the executive, at least when there is a stable majority government. In the parliamentary system, as described in Chapter 20, the assembly's role is now mostly to discuss and publicize measures drafted by the executive, while party discipline ensures that the outcome of voting is seldom in doubt. A well-known book on the Parliament of Canada describes the situation in these terms:

Four essential functions of parliament in the Canadian system are: first, to make a government, that is, to establish a legitimate government through the electoral process; second, to make a government work, that is, to give the government the authority, funds, and other resources necessary for governing the country; third, to make a government behave, that is, to be a watchdog over the government; and fourth, to make an alternative government, that is, to enable the opposition to present its case to the public and become a credible choice for replacing the party in power. Parliamentary activities of legislating and policy-making are largely aspects of the function of making a government work, and parliament's role in them is not now, nor has it ever been, the dominant one.[1]

The assembly ensures that the executive branch carries out the business of government: that laws are enforced, taxes collected, roads paved, and so forth. The assembly cannot itself perform such tasks, but it can cause them to be performed, investigate the performance, and debate the results. In the parliamentary system, responsible government is the chief mechanism by which the assembly retains some control over the business of government. The highest executive officers of the state must be members of the assembly, must be answerable to their colleagues in the assembly for the conduct of business, and must retain the confidence of a working majority. Members of the assembly may ask questions of the executive, request disclosure of documents, and even conduct special investigations into governmental business. Assemblies in presidential systems do not have such intimate ties with the executive, but they possess other powers of control, such as the power to alter budgets. In various ways, all democratic assemblies seek to influence the administration of public business.

Other functions of the assembly can be more briefly described. One is local representation, which has two aspects. At the collective level, representatives speak in the assembly for the interests of their constituents. Representatives from Newfoundland and Labrador and coastal British Columbia take a special interest in fisheries, those from Saskatchewan have to be vitally concerned with the Wheat Board, and so on. At the individual level, elected representatives, with the aid of their paid staff, spend a great deal of time acting as virtual ombudsmen for the voters in their constituencies. When citizens experience problems with government services—anything from pension cheques to passports—they may ask their representatives to intervene on their behalf.

Still another function is to provide opposition. Members of the assembly who are not on the government's side of the house criticize policies and programs so that governments cannot sweep issues or incidents under the rug. The organized opposition within the assembly may also be ready to offer an alternative government if necessary, so that changes in power can take place without a period of confusion. This is part of the genius of liberal democracy, to make opposition a part of the system of government rather than drive it outside government. It recognizes that, in a world where everyone's knowledge is limited and everyone is fallible, public opinion benefits by institutionalizing a clash of perspectives.

An assembly plays two additional roles. It educates the public in the sense that its debates and discussions draw the public's attention to certain issues. And it also socializes the public, because as it attempts to wrestle with public problems, it can stimulate the formation of public opinions, attitudes, and beliefs about the nature of the governmental process.

As the scope of state activity has expanded in this century, the limitations on what the assembly can accomplish by itself have grown. During the period of classical liberalism, government was relatively small and the assembly could debate most legislation at length and monitor all the administrative activities of the state. But the welfare state has grown so large that this is impossible today. This is why there has been a trend in all countries toward greater responsibility of the executive at the expense of the assembly.

This tendency is particularly noticeable in parliamentary systems. Through party discipline, the modern cabinet exercises a high degree of control over the majority caucus and thus over the assembly as a whole. Under these conditions, individual members of the assembly have little effective control over legislation and particularly over governmental revenues and expenditures. The assembly still links the executive to the electorate, but it has lost much of its power to initiate legislation. This is less true in presidential systems, where the assembly is not so subject to party discipline; but even in the United States, which probably has the most independent assembly among important democracies, political observers have repeatedly commented on how the president's power has grown at the expense of Congress. Recall the discussion in Chapter 20 about the autonomy of Congress in the presidential system.

To grasp the complexity of the Canadian legislative process and the extent to which it is dominated by the executive, consider Figure 26.1. The chart begins with a minister submitting a legislative proposal to cabinet. Probably, this proposal has already been discussed at length within the minister's department. If the proposal survives consideration in a cabinet committee and receives the formal approval of the whole cabinet, it goes for legal drafting by officials of the Department of Justice. It must then be approved by another cabinet committee and again by the whole cabinet. By this time, members of cabinet will have developed firm views about the draft legislation and will not want to see it greatly altered in Parliament.

There are, of course, opportunities for further discussion and amendment in Parliament. The bill must go through floor debate and committee discussion in both the House of Commons and the Senate, and groups affected by the bill can try to get MPs and senators to introduce amendments favourable to their interests. Changes to bills take place, but party discipline generally ensures that these changes are within limits acceptable to the cabinet. The chief power of the opposition is that it can exploit the complexity of the process to create delay and force the government to set priorities on its objectives. A determined government can have virtually anything it wants, but it cannot have everything it wants.

Although that is the usual situation, things can be somewhat different when the government does not have a parliamentary majority. Under those conditions, the government may have to accept that some of its bills may be defeated, amended, or delayed for long periods of time. Its main weapon is to make a bill a matter of confidence, which

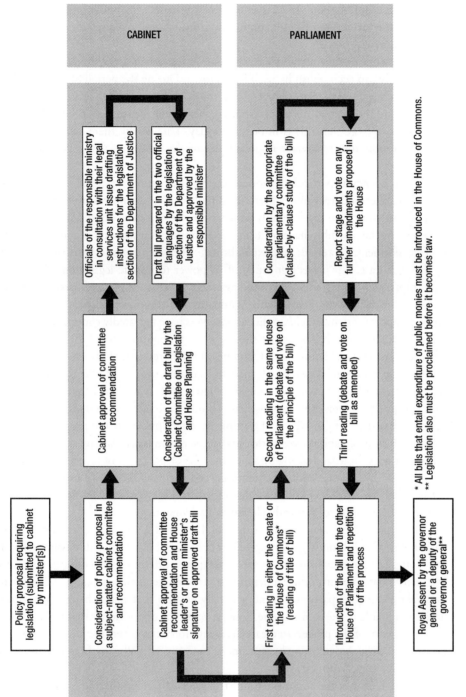

Figure 26.1 Overview of the Legislative Process

means that the opposition will precipitate an election if it defeats that bill. That tactic worked well for the minority Conservative government in Canada in late 2007 and 2008, because the Liberals, fearing they would not do well in a general election, repeatedly abstained on or even voted for government bills, thus enabling them to pass.

The decline of assemblies has long been noted by political scientists but has perhaps not been fully grasped by the public. Many naïve views still exist about how assemblies work. People often visualize the elected assembly as the focal point at which all issues are raised, debated, and voted on. Visitors to Ottawa and to the provincial capitals frequently express disillusionment when they see a single speaker talking to an almost empty House. The fact is that much of the work of the assembly is done elsewhere: in the parliamentary system by cabinet, the bureaucracy, the caucus, and parliamentary committees; in the presidential system by cabinet, the bureaucracy, and congressional committees. Full debates from which significant decisions follow are rare. In many cases, full debates come after most of the wrinkles have been ironed out of legislative proposals and compromises have already been struck. In effect, the assembly is putting its stamp of approval on a bill that has already been subjected to a great deal of discussion and scrutiny; and individual members, by making speeches pro and con, are staking out political turf for possible use in the next election.

It would be impossible for the entire assembly to handle all the intricate details involved in working out a compromise among conflicting interests. This is why the executive is responsible for preparing most of the assembly's business and carrying out the administrative details of bills the assembly passes. But, again, the executive must have the support of a majority of members of the assembly before establishing laws or policies. To that extent, the assembly retains real power in the conversion part of the political process. It remains a check on executive power.

The long-term decline of the assembly relative to the executive arm of government has been accompanied by the decline of bicameralism. Many assemblies today are at least nominally bicameral, as shown by the following list.

Country	Lower House	Upper House
United Kingdom	House of Commons	House of Lords
Canada	House of Commons	Senate
Australia	House of Representatives	Senate
United States	House of Representatives	Senate
Japan	House of Representatives	House of Councillors
Germany	*Bundestag*	*Bundesrat*
France	National Assembly	Senate

Unicameral assemblies are less common but not rare. They exist, for example, in Denmark, Finland, New Zealand, Tanzania, and all the Canadian provinces. Unicameralism is more common in homogeneous societies or in societies where a deliberate attempt is made to avoid fragmenting a government when the society is already divided along cultural, regional, or racial lines.

Most commonly, upper houses have been allowed to atrophy rather than be abolished outright. They do not fit well with either the logic of majoritarian democracy or the machinery of responsible government. The experience of Canada's Parliament, which has seen the Senate decline in both power and prestige, is typical of many countries. Generally speaking, the only upper houses that have been able to retain their vitality are in presidential systems (for example, the United States), or in federal parliamentary systems (for example, Germany). In the former instance, senators are elected by the voters of the states; in the latter, they are appointed by the governments of the *Länder*. In both instances, they are seen to represent important and durable interests of particular regions of the country. This principle, which in the end comes down to protecting the minority rights of different regions, has been able to maintain itself against the democratic legitimacy of majority rule. In contrast, other ways of choosing a second chamber, such as heredity (the House of Lords prior to the latest reforms) or appointment as a reward for service (the contemporary House of Lords, the Canadian Senate) provide those bodies so chosen with little force in a direct conflict with democratically elected lower chambers. However, the expertise of an appointed body can make it a legitimate source of technical amendments to legislation.

These considerations lead directly to the much discussed question of how to reform Canada's Senate. Three main options have been put forward in the constitutional debates of the last 30 years. The first is simply to abolish the Senate. This has long been the official position of the NDP, although individuals in that party have sometimes supported other options. In concise terms, the case for abolishing the Senate is that it does not do anything very important, so we should abolish it and save the cost of running it. The second option is to make the Senate a "House of the Provinces"; that is, to let senators be appointed by provincial cabinets or elected by provincial legislators and let them serve in Ottawa as acknowledged ambassadors of provincial interests. This model, which is loosely based on the German *Bundesrat,* would extend the interstate approach to federalism that has characterized recent Canadian political history, as well as legitimize the growing tendency for provinces to deal with each other and with Ottawa almost as though they were sovereign states. The third option is the "triple-E" proposal, which originated in Alberta and has sometimes received support from other provinces. The second chambers in Australia, Switzerland, and the United States serve as models for this approach. In those countries, each constituent government has the same number of representatives (equal); the members are elected by the people, not by the provincial legislatures (elected); and the second chamber has the same, or almost the same, legislative power as the lower house (effective). The triple-E proposal represents the intrastate model of federalism, in which the interests of the various regions of the country are given effective representation within the machinery of the central government as well as through constituent governments. It has been argued that Canadian federalism has veered too much toward the interstate model and that a triple-E Senate would help to restore this country's intrastate character by establishing a federal institution based on provincial interests.

The Conservative government of Stephen Harper elected in 2006 is committed to what might be called a double-E, rather than a triple-E, approach to Senate reform. Harper wants senators to be elected and to retain their constitutional powers, but he no longer insists that every province should have exactly the same number of senators. The current situation is not stable over the long term because Harper has refused to appoint senators who have not been elected, but only Saskatchewan has joined alberta in adopting an electoral procedure for senators, and meanwhile Harper's own Senate-reform legislation is stalled in Parliament. The membership of the Senate is thus declining as senators individually reach the retirement age of 75 and replacements have been on hold. After the 2008 election, however, Harper indicated that if Senate reform did not materialized in the House, he would begin appointing replacements.

REPRESENTATION

Before continuing this discussion of representative assemblies, we must re-examine the basic concept of representation.[2] The word *representation* has three different meanings, all of which are relevant to political science:

1. A representative may be a symbol—that is, a sign by which something else is known. A flag or national anthem may be said to represent a country.

2. A representative may be an agent who is empowered to act for a principal, as a lawyer represents a client in the courtroom. In a similar sense, city councillors, members of provincial legislative assemblies, and members of parliament are representatives because they are agents who act on behalf of their electors, who are the principals.

3. A person who shares some of the typical characteristics of a group is sometimes said to represent it. At the collective level, a subset of items is said to be a representative sample if it accurately reflects selected characteristics of the population from which it is drawn. For example, feminists have said that the House of Commons is not truly representative of the Canadian people because only about 20 percent of its members are women, although more than half of the adult population is female.

We will not concern ourselves further with representation in the symbolic sense. Our focus will be on the latter two meanings, both of which have a bearing on the way people view the role of representatives. Representation is almost a universal fact of politics. Any system, except the smallest and simplest direct democracy, requires that some people act for others. And questions inevitably arise about whether the agents reflect the salient characteristics of their principals.

Theories of representation are as varied as theories of legitimacy. Autocratic governments of all sorts claim to represent their people in some way that does not need to be tested by competitive elections. We will confine ourselves here to discussing representation in liberal democracies.

There are four different ways in which agents represent those who elect them to a representative assembly. Three concern the individual representatives; the fourth concerns representatives as a collective body. To put it another way, representatives may play any one of four different roles.

Trustee

The role of **trustee** demands that representatives rely on their personal judgment when deciding what is in the best interests of the community as a whole. The people elect them and may refuse to re-elect them if they do not like what they do; but in the meantime the representatives act independently. Edmund Burke gave this theory its classic formulation in 1774 in a speech to the electors of Bristol: "Your representative owes you, not his industry only, but his judgement, and he betrays, instead of serving you, if he sacrifices it to your opinion."[3]

Note that Burke spoke at a time when the right to vote was still extremely limited. Burkean trusteeship is essentially a pre-democratic theory of representation. It gives representatives almost *carte blanche* to carry on the business of government, subject to the sole constraint of facing periodic elections. It does not conceive of democracy as an ongoing process in which the people are actively involved in governing themselves. Interestingly, Burke lost his race for re-election in Bristol in 1780 because he refused to accept instructions from his constituents.

In any event, party discipline in parliamentary systems has largely destroyed trusteeship. Canadian MPs are free to use their own judgment only in rare free votes or in caucus meetings, whose proceedings are confidential. However, cabinet members might be considered trustees to the extent that they deliberate to determine policy positions that are then imposed on backbenchers. City councillors may act as trustees because parties do not normally function at that level in Canada. American representatives may also act as trustees because party discipline in the United States is rather weak.

Delegate

Representatives are **delegates** if they subordinate their own views to those of their constituents and act as instructed by them. Party discipline largely excludes this role, along with that of trustee. But city councillors often act as delegates when they vote in accord with the wishes of their ward on such issues as road location and the granting of building permits. American representatives also sometimes act as delegates. A famous example was Senator William Fulbright from Arkansas: although he privately claimed to be an integrationist, he voted against civil-rights bills because of the wishes of the majority of his constituents. The delegate model is also used in many private associations, such as trade unions, political parties, and churches; in these cases, representatives chosen to attend national conventions go armed with specific instructions. In Canada, the delegate model was revived by the Reform Party, which made a point of claiming that it wanted MPs to be free to vote as their constituents wish; but it slipped from view as Reform mutated into the Canadian Alliance and then merged with the Progressive Conservatives to form the Conservative Party of Canada.

Although the delegate model is attractive to voters in an era when elitism is under attack, there are some major problems in applying it to the running of a large country. Typically, the Parliament of Canada passes dozens of bills every year, sometimes more than one hundred. Is it practical for MPs to find out what voters think about all, or even many, of them? If opinion in a constituency is divided, how would the "majority" be determined? If consultation is required, how should it be organized—town-hall meetings, mail-in ballots, or surveys? And who will interpret the "will" of the constituency? Since there are more than two alternatives on most issues of public policy, a majority within the constituency for any particular position may not result. All in all, MPs would have considerable room to create the appearance of consulting their constituents while in fact predetermining the outcome through manipulation of the process.

Note also that the delegate model requires representatives to pursue the special interests of their constituents, not the general good of the community. This limitation suggests that representatives cannot always be delegates. There are occasions when the general interest must be paramount over sectional concerns and representatives must rise above the wishes of their electors.

Party Member

Representatives who are party members may vote and act only as loyal members of their caucus, following the instructions of the leadership. The underlying assumption is that parties are teams that work together collectively and that people make a choice between these teams when they vote, even though in a legal sense they are voting for individual representatives. Since representatives are team players in this model, they have to vote together in the assembly and be judged on the party's collective record at election time. Party discipline has made this the dominant form of representation in parliamentary systems in the twentieth century. However, it is a lesser feature of American politics and does not apply at all to the nonparty systems found in most municipal governments.

The party model assumes that the policy of the party takes account of the general interest as well as of special interests. In a sense, the party leaders act as trustees, using their own judgment and drawing on their own consciences to determine what is best for the community. Thus, the notion of trusteeship appears somewhere in each of these three models.

The party-member model of representation has become the norm in parliamentary systems, particularly in Canada, where party discipline is stronger than in almost any other democracy; and politicians and political scientists generally accept it as indispensable to responsible government. The public, however, has never really accepted it. At the end of 1992, Canadians were asked in a *Maclean's*/CTV poll to express their opinion about the three main theories of representation by answering the question, "How should your Member of Parliament vote on major issues?"[4] The results showed a huge preference for the delegate theory and only tiny support for the party-member model:

- 71 percent said according to the majority view in his or her own riding;

- 21 percent said according to his or her own conscience and beliefs; and

- 7 percent said according to the policies of his or her political party.

Politicians, of course, are aware of the state of public opinion. The Reform Party tried to capitalize on it by calling on party leaders to allow more free votes in Parliament and on MPs to vote according to the "consensus of the constituency."[5] Many in the other parties have also called for a relaxation of party discipline, but so far nothing much has happened. The brute fact is that the incentives created by the parliamentary system lead inevitably to the party-member model of representation, and the behaviour of MPs will not change without major changes in the system.

University of Dalhousie political scientist Jennifer Smith has argued that reforming the system is more complicated than just abolishing party discipline. The problem with delegate representation in our system is that it will "destabilize" party discipline and responsible government, the genius of the parliamentary process. Party discipline and responsible government are ways of realizing the larger, national interest rather than local interests. Thus, the way to achieve something closer to delegate representation is either to move to a congressional system (which she suggests "is out of the question"), or move to a form of proportional representation (PR). A PR electoral system would enable a closer connection between "like-minded voters" and their representatives.[6] Therefore, one way to improve the parliamentary system might be to change the electoral system.

The Microcosm

Whatever role representatives play, a qualitatively different question is bound to arise: are they similar to those they represent? In other words, do they reflect the characteristics of race, language, religion, gender, class, income, and occupation that are found in the population at large? A common feeling today is that representatives must be similar to their constituents in order to have their best interests at heart. We can call this the **microcosm theory**—the idea that a governing body should be a miniature replica of those it represents. John Adams, the second president of the United States as well as a political philosopher, wrote 200 years ago that the representative assembly "should be in miniature an exact portrait of the people at large. It should think, feel, reason, and act like them."[7]

Obviously, the microcosm theory cannot be applied too literally, for an infinity of characteristics might be considered politically relevant. It is impossible to get a working body of a reasonably small size that will have just the right proportions of all conceivable characteristics. But the theory can be given a more sensible interpretation. While exact proportionality is not important, no significant group of people should be left without a voice. This ties in well with the view of Bernard Crick, discussed in Chapter 1, that politics involves the reconciliation of differences. For example, the precise proportion of French- and English-speaking judges on the Supreme Court of Canada is not critical, but it is important that there be some of each. A more complex example is the Canadian cabinet. In choosing ministers, the prime minister usually tries to select about three-quarters anglophones and one-quarter francophones, including anglophones from inside Quebec and francophones from outside Quebec. In addition, the prime minister wants to have at least one minister from each province, as well as at least token representation for women, ethnic groups, and regions. It is a complicated balancing act with a double purpose: to allow all significant groups to be heard and to convince the population that no sector has been omitted from consideration. Image is as important as reality. For more on this topic, see Canadian Focus 26.1.

Politics is always a matter of trade-offs between competing values. Both representing the whole country in the cabinet and maintaining party unity seem like desirable goals to the prime minister, but pursuing one may interfere with the other. Political leadership requires the ability to manage such inevitable trade-offs and conflicts.

Canadian Focus 26.1

The Fine Art of Composing a Cabinet

On August 14, 2007, Prime Minister Stephen Harper shuffled his cabinet, announcing a new lineup of 32 ministers. Six of them—19 percent—were women. Every province except Prince Edward Island had at least one minister, and the larger provinces had more than one each:

Ontario	10
Quebec	6
Alberta	6
British Columbia	5

The prime minister would probably have liked to appoint someone from every province and territory, as well more women and more members from Quebec, but he was limited by the composition of the Conservative caucus. In the election of 2006, the voters returned only 14 women and 10 Quebeckers as Conservative MPs. No Conservative candidates were elected in Prince Edward Island or any of the northern territories.

In composing a cabinet, a prime minister uses the microcosmic theory of representation within the limitations provided by his caucus, and consistent with the need to appoint cabinet members who have the executive ability to run departments of government. There are always many trade-offs involved in making these choices. After the 2008 election, with increased seats in the House of Commons, particularly in Ontario and British Columbia, Harper had greater flexibility in forming his cabinet.

Although microcosmic representation in the cabinet seems necessary in a pluralistic country like Canada, there can be political costs, as illustrated by the story of Brian Mulroney's first cabinet. Because of the long years of Liberal dominance in Quebec, the 58 Conservative MPs from that province were relatively inexperienced when they came to Ottawa in 1984. Many had not been active in politics before or had been associated with other Quebec parties, such as the Union Nationale or the Parti Québécois. In appointing 11 Quebec ministers to his first cabinet, Mulroney had to draw from a less-experienced pool of talent than is usual and desirable. Several of his original appointments did not turn out well, and a few ministers were forced from the cabinet under embarrassing circumstances. All of this contributed substantially to the Mulroney government's image problems in its first term. But the long-term political consequences of underrepresenting Quebec in the cabinet might have been much worse than the effects of these passing embarrassments.

Stephen Harper faced a similar dilemma after the 2006 election, when the Conservatives elected only 10 MPs from Quebec, most of them with little political experience. He was taking a chance by appointing six Quebeckers to his cabinet; and indeed one of them, Maxime Bernier, was forced to resign in 2008 under embarrassing circumstances—dating a woman with prior connections to biker gangs and organized crime, and leaving confidential cabinet papers at her house.

Another problem with the microcosm theory of representation is that, if pushed hard enough, it can conflict with the ordinary democratic understanding of elected representation. Those with the desired demographic characteristics of race or gender may not nominations and win elections. This conflict has bedevilled recent discussions about how the proportion of women in the House of Commons can be increased. That proportion has been rising, from less than one percent as recently as 1968 to 18 percent after the election of 1993, up to 22% after the election of October 14, 2008, but it is still much less than the percentage of women in the voting-age population (which is greater than 50 percent because, on average, women live longer than men). Leaders can set goals for the proportion of female candidates, but in order to reach these goals, the leader will probably have to appoint women to run in some ridings, thus circumventing the normal process of local nomination races. One can imagine similar problems arising in attempts to fix the gender ratio of elected MPs.

One proposal, however, would at least partially circumvent these difficulties. It has been suggested by the National Action Committee on the Status of Women that single-member constituencies could be turned into dual-member constituencies, and that one member would have to be a woman and the other a man. Voters would have two ballots, one of which they would cast in the women's contest, the other in the men's contest. In this scheme, men and women elected to public office would not just represent their own sex, for each would have been elected by voters of both sexes. In that respect, the proposal would not divide the electorate into opposed camps based on gender. It is true that men would run against only men, and women against only women; but that might not be such a grave drawback when we think of the overall contest as one of party against party, for the candidates of all parties would be equally composed of men and women. A proposal similar to this was advanced for the new territory of Nunavut, but it was defeated in a referendum in the spring of 1997.

Each of the four models of representation has its own strengths and weaknesses. Trustees are a bit removed from popular pressure and can thus take a more independent view. The result of the free vote on capital punishment in the House of Commons was that MPs voted to abolish it, even though public-opinion polls showed that most people wanted to reinstate the death penalty. While the trustee role offers an opportunity for independence, it may also lead to representatives voting their own particular biases. Conversely, a close adherence to public opinion, which is the virtue of the delegate role, may blind representatives to the long-range general interest. Party discipline restricts representatives' initiative, but it tends to produce a more coherent and intelligible set of policies. Local politics often degenerates into a name-recognition or popularity contest because councillors act individually as delegates or trustees but rarely as cohesive, identifiable groups. Finally, the microcosm theory has its own special problem: it can clash with efficiency and even with democracy. The person with the right demographic characteristics of gender, language, region, and ethnicity may not be the most able person for the job, or even the person that the voters would choose if they had a choice.

Perhaps there is no simple solution to these problems. It may be that all the modes of representation are useful in varying circumstances and that each can compensate for the drawbacks of the other three. Regardless of what may be best in some abstract sense, the tendency in parliamentary democracies is clear. The roles of trustee and delegate have declined; the party-member role and the microcosm idea now predominate. These latter two are more compatible with the parliamentary system. Where there is greater opportunity for autonomy in representation is in the presidential–congressional system.

Assessing Representative Assemblies

In theory one might assume representative assemblies to be the cornerstone of democratic government. In practice, however, things are different. In parliamentary systems, and particularly in Canada, members of parliament have their roles limited in two ways. Firstly, the executive dominates the legislative process; the prime minister and the central agencies of the government control the legislative agenda. Secondly, with political party discipline, elected representatives cannot freely represent their constituents. As one critic of the system puts it,

> Democracy teaches that they [members of parliament] receive their authority from the people and are thus the representatives of people. However, parliamentary democracy teaches us that they are instead the representatives of their parties. It is the party that nominates them as candidates, guides them and assists them financially during election campaigns. They are elected under the party banner. The party dictates their behaviour in the House and, in short, structures electoral competition and dominates parliamentary life. There is little room for independent members in this kind of system.[8]

On the other side of the issue, supporters of the existing system of representation argue that executive dominance and party discipline are required to make responsible government work. Representatives in assemblies mirror the people they represent; therefore, any assembly will be divided into factions. The executive, with political party discipline, is then able to craft a legislative agenda that is a compromise in the public interest. These supporters of the representative system argue that the more independent assemblies within the presidential system are torn by faction and often end up in gridlock. Under that process essential legislation may be delayed or never passed.

For the half century that we have been studying and teaching political science, we have been listening to the debate over the proper role of representative assemblies in modern government. It appears to be one of those situations where both sides have something worthwhile to say and the truth, if there is such a thing, lies in a balance of the opposed views.

Questions for Discussion

1. What are two criticisms of parliamentary representative assemblies?

2. What are two criticisms of presidential representative assemblies?

3. Which form of representation—trustee, delegate, or party member—would you prefer that your member of parliament take in representing you? Why?

Internet Links

1. Canadian Parliament: **www.parl.gc.ca.**

2. United States Congress—Senate: **www.senate.gov.**

3. House of Representatives: **www.house.gov.**

4. British Parliament: **www.parliament.uk.**

Further Reading

Arnold, R. Douglas. *The Logic of Congressional Action.* New Haven, CT: Yale University Press, 1990.

Birch, A. H. *Representation.* London: Pall Mall Press, 1971.

Campbell, Colin. *The Canadian Senate: A Lobby from Within.* Toronto: Macmillan, 1978.

Close, David, ed. *Legislatures and the New Democracies in Latin America.* Boulder, CO: Lynne Rienner, 1995.

Docherty, David. *Legislatures.* Vancouver: University of British Columbia Press, 2004.

Fisher, Louis. *The Politics of Shared Power: Congress and the Executive.* 4th ed. College Station, TX: Texas A&M University Press, 1998.

Franks, C. E. S. *The Parliament of Canada.* Toronto: University of Toronto Press, 1987.

Fraser, John A. *The House of Commons at Work.* Montreal: Editions de la Cheneliere, 1993.

Jackson, Robert J., and Michael M. Atkinson. *The Canadian Legislative System.* Rev. ed. Toronto: Macmillan, 1980.

Loewenberg, Gerhard, Peverill Squire, and D. Roderick Kiewiet. *Legislatures: Comparative Perspectives on Representative Assemblies.* Ann Arbor, MI: University of Michigan Press, 2002.

March, James G., and Johan P. Olsen. *Democratic Governance.* New York: Free Press, 1995.

Mezey, M. L., and David M. Olson, eds. *Legislatures in the Policy Process: The Dilemmas of Economic Policy.* Cambridge: Cambridge University Press, 1991.

Norton, Philip, ed. *Legislatures.* Oxford: Oxford University Press, 1990.

Olson, David M. *Democratic Legislative Institutions: A Comparative View.* Armonk, NY: M. E. Sharpe, 1994.

Pitkin, Hanna F. *The Concept of Representation.* Berkeley: University of California Press, 1967.

Remini, Robert Vincent. *The House: The History of the House of Representatives.* New York: HarperCollins, 2006.

Schroedel, Jean Reith. *Congress, the President, and Policymaking: A Historical Analysis.* Armonk, NY: M. E. Sharpe, 1994.

Seidle, F. Leslie, and Louis Massicotte, eds. *Taking Stock of 150 Years of Responsible Government in Canada.* Ottawa: The Canadian Study of Parliament Group, 1999.

Smith, David E. *The Canadian Senate in Bicameral Perspective.* Toronto: University of Toronto Press, 2003.

Strom, Kaare. *Minority Government and Majority Rule.* Cambridge: Cambridge University Press, 1990.

Weaver, R. Kent, and Bert A. Rockman, eds. *Do Institutions Matter? Government Capabilities in the United States and Abroad.* Washington, DC: Brookings Institution, 1993.

White, Randall. *Voice of Region: The Long Journey to Senate Reform in Canada.* Toronto: Dundurn Press, 1990.

CHAPTER 27

The Political Executive

The executive branch of government includes not only highly visible officials, such as the prime minister or president, but also the many anonymous officials who labour in the civil service. We will discuss the latter group in the next chapter under the heading of administration; here we will confine our attention to those at the top of the executive pyramid—those officers of state who are in some sense politically responsible (as opposed to politically neutral, which most public employees are supposed to be). This category includes the head of state, the head of government, and the ministry or cabinet. It also includes the personal advisers and assistants to these officers. We shall refer to all these people as the **political executive.**

THE PARLIAMENTARY EXECUTIVE

We have already discussed the head of state and head of government at some length, but relatively little has been said about other ministers. In Britain, the cabinet is relatively small by Canadian standards; it usually consists of 22 or 23 members.[1] However, the British prime minister also appoints dozens of junior ministers, who have specific responsibilities but do not sit in the cabinet. The whole group, which includes but is not limited to cabinet members, is known as the **ministry.**

In nineteenth-century Canada, Sir John A. Macdonald could make do with a cabinet of 12, and in the late 1940s, Louis St. Laurent's cabinet had only 19 ministers; but membership grew steadily larger with the expansion of the welfare state. Brian Mulroney governed with 39 or 40 ministers in the cabinet, until he reduced the size to 35 in January 1993.

By that time, the size of the Canadian cabinet had become a political issue in its own right. Comparisons with the American cabinet of 16 are perhaps unfair because of other differences between presidential and parliamentary government; all the same, Canada's cabinets of three dozen or more ministers were very large by the standards of other parliamentary systems. Nations such as Great Britain, Australia, France, and Germany got along perfectly well with about two dozen or even fewer ministers (although in some of these cases junior ministers perform executive functions but do not sit in the cabinet).

When Kim Campbell became prime minister in June 1993, she reduced the size of cabinet from 35 to 25. Jean Chrétien initially kept cabinet size at around two dozen, but increased it to 28 after the 1997 election. After the 2000 election, he selected 28 ministers and also appointed another nine "secretaries of state," which are positions equivalent to British junior ministers (ministers of the Crown exercising specific administrative responsibilities and reporting to senior ministers). The secretaries of state are not paid as much as senior ministers, do not have all the perks, and do not normally attend meetings of the full cabinet, though they may participate in cabinet committees. In 2004, Paul Martin appointed 32 ministers and seven junior ministers, or "ministers of state" as they were now called. Stephen Harper in 2008 appointed 27 ministers and 11 secretaries of state. In effect, therefore, the Canadian cabinet is now back to the size it had attained before the modest reduction efforts of the early 1990s.

Canadian cabinets are oversized for political rather than administrative reasons. The extra appointments are made to put MPs from various regions and demographic categories into positions of prominence and to promote and reward members of caucus whom the prime minister wishes to advance because of perceived talent or loyalty.

As Canadian cabinets grew in size under Pierre Trudeau and Brian Mulroney, they almost ceased to function as a whole. The important work was done in cabinet committees and ratified, when necessary, in the increasingly infrequent meetings of the whole cabinet. Each prime minister will set up a different set of cabinet committees, but some structure is indispensable for a body of this size. At the time of publication, the main cabinet committees were Priorities and Planning, Operations, and Treasury Board (this last is required by statute to oversee government spending). In addition, there were several specialized committees for various areas of policy.

The Role of Cabinet

Political executives in a liberal democracy perform much the same tasks as executives in any organization—they manage the business of the enterprise. But this is management on a grand scale. The budget of the federal government is larger than that of the 20 largest Canadian corporations combined.

The political executive has two main functions: to initiate policy proposals for the assembly and to supervise the administration of laws passed by the assembly. The first function is a necessity. A session of Parliament would never end if the entire body had to develop its own policy proposals, debate these proposals, consider amendments, and vote on the final versions. Thus, the executive formulates legislative proposals to be submitted to the entire assembly. In parliamentary systems, of course, the executive goes further and actually controls the deliberations of the assembly, at least when there is a majority government.

Administration of existing laws is also the responsibility of the executive. Ministers run the different departments in their particular areas of responsibility. A minister of agriculture, for example, is responsible for all federal activities that fall under the department of agriculture. This will include keeping trained agricultural agents in the field, running experimental farms, providing loans to farmers in special situations, and keeping statistics on farm production. The same applies to the fisheries, transport, and labour departments, and so on. Each minister, along with the cabinet collectively, is responsible to the House (and ultimately to the people) for the business of a specific administrative department.

It should be noted again that structural differences exist between parliamentary and presidential executives. Because the executive and the legislature in the parliamentary process are fused, all ministers answer to the House for the work of their departments. The institution of Question Period allows backbenchers to pose questions directly to ministers, sometimes putting them under intense political pressure. Steering legislation through the House, and the committees, is the responsibility of the House Leader, who is also a member of the ministry. In the presidential system, the president and cabinet secretaries are not members of the legislative assembly, because these institutions are separated. While the executive formulates policy proposals, it is up to the party leaders and committee chairs to manage the flow of legislation. And since cabinet members do not hold seats in the legislature, they cannot be subjected to routine questioning there; no equivalent to Question Period exists in the presidential system.

The members of the executive also perform symbolic and ceremonial functions, provide party and national political leadership, make government appointments to the judiciary and regulatory agencies, and exercise military power. The expanding role of the political executive has influenced the governmental process in two important ways. First, there has been dramatic growth in the administrative arm of government. Departments, agencies, boards, and commissions have increased in number and size because of the need to carry out more and more administrative responsibilities. This growth is manifested in the size of the civil service at the federal, provincial, and municipal levels. Second, there has developed a very significant organizational tier of advisers to the government. While these advisers are part of the executive, they are separate from the traditional civil service. These personal advisers to the prime minister and the cabinet are important not in terms of numbers, but in terms of their influence on the governmental process.

In Canada, the management of government involves half a dozen so-called **central agencies,** of which four are particularly important: the **Department of Finance;** another government department, the **Treasury Board,** which is supervised by the cabinet committee of the same name; and two staff organizations, the **Prime Minister's Office (PMO)** and the **Privy Council Office (PCO).** All four of these bodies are deeply involved in initiating, implementing, and monitoring policy proposals, and are sometimes called the exclusive club of central agencies.[2]

The Department of Finance is important because the minister of finance, advised by officials from the Department, prepares the annual budget of the federal government. There may be some discussion in cabinet or in cabinet committees; but, under current practice, the minister of finance will make decisions about how much money each department gets. Only the prime minister can give direction to the minister of finance, and that happens very rarely. That is why in the Chrétien government of the 1990s it was Paul Martin, then minister of finance, who received so much credit for moving toward a balanced budget and who would have received the blame if no progress had been made.

Eddie Goldenberg, the long-time policy adviser to Prime Minister Jean Chrétien, explains that decisions over how much to allocate to each department cannot be made by the cabinet collectively. Ministers are simply too caught up in the priorities of their own departments. When ministers spoke at meetings,

> . . . they began their remarks by paying lip service to the importance of fiscal discipline. Then they immediately endorsed a variety of policy ideas, each of which they believed clearly deserved funding by the minister of finance. Unfortunately, the ideas always required the expenditure of billions of dollars of public funds. No one ever suggested cuts to existing programs, or tradeoffs that might make some of their ideas affordable.[3]

Budgetary allocation elevates the minister of finance over all other cabinet members except the prime minister. Several ministers in the Chrétien government learned to their sorrow that they would have to give up cherished spending projects because they could not get Paul Martin's support. Control of the budget is the single most important management tool exercised over the entire range of government activities.

The Treasury Board, which has been separate from the Department of Finance since 1967, is responsible for public administration in general terms. Its minister, known as the President of the Treasury Board, presides over a large bureaucracy, the most important function of which is to provide central control over expenditures. Proposals from departments to spend money must be approved by the Treasury Board, which verifies that they conform to government policy. The Department of Finance prepares the budget and allocates money to the various departments, while the Treasury Board ensures that the money is spent for approved purposes.

The PMO came into its own under Pierre Trudeau and has continued to be important under every prime minister since then. Directed by the prime minister's chief of staff, the PMO includes political operatives as well as advisers on various policy areas. These people are hired and fired by the prime minister and serve without the career security of civil servants. In particular, the prime minister relies on the PMO for political advice that neutral public servants should not be asked to give. The highest appointments in the PMO are usually personal friends or political associates of the prime minister; the junior appointments are usually young people who put in a few years of extremely concentrated work before going on to something more regular (and probably less exciting).

The PCO is a special organization designed to serve the cabinet and cabinet committees. First, a word about the **Privy Council.** It is made up of all present and former cabinet ministers, as well as a few other individuals who have received the special honour of membership. However, the cabinet is the only working part of the Privy Council and acts in its name; the Council as a whole does not meet. R. MacGregor Dawson, a political scientist whose textbook on Canadian government was standard reading for a whole generation, explained it this way:

> The Privy Council . . . performs no functions as a Council, despite the fact that it is
> mentioned a number of times in the British North America Act as an advisory body to
> the Governor. Such functions have been assumed by that small portion of the Council
> which constitutes the Cabinet of the moment.[4]

The PCO, however, is very much alive; as the secretariat to the cabinet, it is responsible for helping that body to manage overall government priorities and coordinating the process by which these priorities are achieved. Cabinet relies on the PCO as a source of advice independent of the permanent departments, which ministers often perceive as captive to tradition and special interests. The PCO can be considered the "control centre" for the government, and its chief executive, the Clerk of the Privy Council, is the head of the whole civil service. Conservative Prime Minister Stephen Harper appointed Kevin Lynch to be the Clerk, even though Lynch had once been deputy minister to Liberal Finance Minister Paul Martin; that illustrates the non-partisan character of the Clerk's position.

These and other central agencies do not themselves provide services to the public; rather, they are instruments by which the prime minister and cabinet attempt to manage the entire public service. The formal lines of responsibility are shown in the accompanying chart.

This structure complements the older direct relationship between the prime minister, the cabinet, and the bureaucracy, and also acts as a counterweight to the growing permanent bureaucracy. At the same time, however, it has led critics to suggest that cabinet ministers and senior bureaucratic officials, such as **deputy ministers** and assistant deputy ministers, have taken a back seat to the prime minister's personal advisers. Critics contend that central agencies have given the prime minister an inordinate amount of power in the legislative arena. With the support of the PMO, PCO, the Treasury Board, and the Finance Department, the prime minister can dominate the process by which public-policy proposals are developed and priorities assigned. The expansion of these organizations reinforces the argument that the collegiality of cabinet government has given way to prime-ministerial government, which is highly focused on the person of the prime minister.

In a study based on extensive interviewing of people who have worked in the Canadian political executive, Donald Savoie concluded:

> Power in the federal government has shifted away from the line ministers and their departments towards the centre, and also, within the centre itself, power has shifted to the prime minister and his senior advisers at both the political and public service levels and away from Cabinet and Cabinet committees.[5]

Savoie described cabinet in that book as essentially a focus group for the prime minister. That is, the prime minister uses cabinet as a sounding board and may listen to the advice that he gets, but does not feel bound by it. More recently, Savoie has gone even further, describing contemporary cabinet government in Canada and the United Kingdom as "court government," in which "effective power now rests with their respective prime ministers and a small group of carefully selected courtiers."[6]

THE PRESIDENTIAL EXECUTIVE

Comparisons are sometimes drawn between the contemporary situation of the prime minister, who has a phalanx of personal advisers in the PMO and PCO, and that of an American president, who has an admittedly much larger staff. The comparison is worrisome in that the president, due to the separation of powers, does not control Congress to the extent that the prime minister controls Parliament. The power of the parliamentary executive is less balanced by an independent legislative assembly.

The executive branch in the United States also is responsible for initiating legislation. The president has some 4,000 staff members who are the organizational network supporting domestic- and foreign-policy initiatives. The president, like the prime minister, is the chief executive officer and is responsible for choosing cabinet secretaries to direct the administrative departments of government, such as agriculture, defence, foreign affairs, and transportation. In addition, the president has two offices that assist in setting the policy direction of the government: the **White House Staff** and the **Executive Office.**

The White House Staff is composed of the personal advisers to the president—the kind of people depicted in the television series *West Wing.* The description by two writers on American politics conveys the flavour of this group:

> It is not accidental that journalists have come to popularize the staff of each president with such names as the "Irish Mafia" (Kennedy), the "Georgia Mafia" (Carter), and the "California Mafia" (Reagan). Every modern president has gathered around himself those people who fought most of the battles with him during his long struggle for ultimate political success. These are his trusted political friends, and their value to him has been proven over time. But this group of trusted cronies is now only the small core of a large personal staff, the White House staff.[7]

Prominent figures in the White House staff of any president include the chief of staff, the communications director, and the special legal counsel. The president's wife (until now

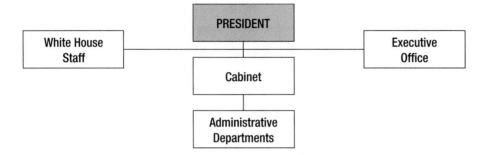

all presidents have been men and almost all have been married) may also be an influential figure. Clinton put his wife, now Secretary of State Hillary Rodham Clinton, in the public eye by appointing her to head a special task force on health care issues. George W. Bush's wife Laura, a teacher and librarian, took a special interest in education and literacy.

The Executive Office is located in the building adjacent to the White House. It comprises a number of agencies that are vital to the president's policymaking role; for example, the Office of Management and Budget, the Council of Economic Advisors, the Office of the United States Trade Representative, and the National Security Council. This latter body, chaired by the president, brings together the secretary of state, secretary of defense, heads of intelligence agencies, and other senior officials concerned with foreign affairs and national security.

The individuals and organizations that make up the executive in the presidential system do not merely initiate policy—they also have the formidable job of selling the policy proposals to Congress. They must get a majority of those voting in both the House of Representatives and the Senate on their side to get the legislation through Congress. This means that much of their work involves finding ways to get members of Congress of whatever party to support their initiatives. This work is part of the dynamic of **logrolling** or **porkbarrelling,** as this kind of politics is sometimes called. "You scratch my back, and I'll scratch yours," says the old proverb. By any name, it involves devising trade-offs that will lead to a majority vote for legislation in Congress. The president may also appeal to the American public, usually on television, if still lacking a majority after working members of Congress in an attempt to persuade Americans to pressure their representatives in the House and the Senate to support his proposed legislation.

RESPONSIBLE GOVERNMENT AND MINISTERIAL RESPONSIBILITY

Returning to the parliamentary system, two mechanisms were traditionally thought to make the assembly the ultimate master of the political executive. Under the principle of responsible government, the cabinet is collectively accountable to the House because the prime minister and the cabinet cannot remain in office without the support of a working majority in the popularly elected branch of the assembly. But we have seen how party discipline has weakened, if not completely destroyed, the meaning of responsible government. Recall the discussion in Chapter 20 about the dominance of the executive in the modern parliamentary system.

The second great check on the political executive was supposed to be the individual responsibility of every minister to the assembly. Most ministers receive a **portfolio** containing one or more departments or agencies (there may also be one or two ministers without a portfolio). Under the doctrine of **ministerial responsibility,** when there is a serious problem in a department, such as dishonesty, mismanagement, or gross incompetence, a minister should offer to resign. This idea developed in the age of smaller government, when it was reasonable to assume that ministers could keep in touch with everything done by the employees of their departments. It is somewhat unrealistic to expect the same today, given the far-flung activities of departments that may have thousands of employees and budgets of billions of dollars. Thus, ministers in Canada today do not usually offer their resignations unless they are personally implicated in a breach of trust, even if the opposition parties demand that they step down.

All recent ministerial resignations under the doctrine of ministerial responsibility have involved personal actions. During Brian Mulroney's first term, eight ministers resigned from cabinet for personal indiscretions. For example, Robert Coates was careless with official documents when he visited a strip bar in West Germany while on an official trip, and Sinclair Stevens did not insulate himself completely enough from his private business affairs. In contrast, Michael Wilson rejected calls for his resignation as finance minister when the 1989 budget was leaked to the press before it was read to the House of Commons. Wilson, supported by the prime minister, said he could not be expected to resign because of an error by an unknown employee far down the chain of command.

The same pattern prevailed during the term of the Liberal government of Jean Chrétien that came to power in 1993. The prime minister accepted the resignation of Sheila Copps because she had publicly promised to resign if the goods and services tax was not repealed; she then won a hastily called by-election and was reappointed to the cabinet. During the Somalia inquiry, David Collenette's position as minister of defence steadily became more untenable as revelations mounted about military misconduct; but, in spite of many calls from the opposition benches for his resignation, he did not resign over this issue. He did resign, however, after newspaper publication of a letter that had gone out with his signature. The letter concerned an immigration problem in his own riding and had nothing at all to do with his ministerial responsibilities. Later Mr. Collenette was brought back into the cabinet as Minister of Transport. In 2005, when Paul Martin was prime minister, Immigration Minister Judy Sgro resigned over charges that she had inappropriately used her personal authority in immigration cases. In 2008, Maxime Bernier resigned as Foreign Minister when Julie Couillard revealed that he had left official documents at her home.

Ministerial responsibility remains, as the aforementioned cases illustrate, but it has lost much of its effectiveness because it is now in practice limited to the minister's personal actions and no longer includes the actions of departmental officials. Nonetheless, the assembly still has the power to inquire, expose, and accuse. Ministers do not wish to appear in a bad light, for even if their jobs are not immediately threatened, their long-term political future could be jeopardized. Thus, most executive functions are tempered by regard for the assembly. In spite of the trend toward executive power, the executive and the assembly remain interdependent. Checks on the executive exist today as they always have. Votes of confidence, the opinions of caucus, and regular elections are only three of these. The power of the executive, while great, is not absolute, and the health of democracy depends on these checks for balancing executive and legislative powers. For more on ministerial responsibility, see Canadian Focus 27.1.

Canadian Focus 27.1

The Problem of Ministerial Responsibility

The sponsorship scandal that arose in 2004 with the auditor general's report raises an important problem with ministerial responsibility. For example, is the head of government, or a cabinet minister, to be held responsible for actions that occur "on their watch" if these actions are deemed to be criminal? In other words, if a civil servant or an appointed adviser of the government is charged with some criminal activity, should the head of government or the minister resign? Former Deputy Prime Minister Sheila Copps touches on the complexity of this issue in trying to explain the actual role of a cabinet minister in conducting the day-to-day business of a government department, in this case Heritage Canada. It is interesting to see her view of the responsibilities of the minister and the deputy minister.

"In fact, a government minister is more like the chairman of the board. The deputy minister is the chief executive officer: All hiring, firing, and day to day operations are managed by the deputy, with the minister giving overall direction. All personnel decisions are handled by the deputy—but when somebody screws up, it's up to the minister to answer publicly for the mistake."

"When I managed Canadian Heritage and crown agencies associated with it, I gave direction for an operation totalling over 25,000 employees. I certainly could not know what was going on in every area under my jurisdiction. Yet by the old-fashioned ministerial code, I was responsible for every mistake made in every part of the department and 18 associated crown agencies. I had to answer in the House of Commons for everything from a Don Cherry rant (courtesy of the CBC) to a salacious Canada Council–funded work called *Bubbles Galore.* It didn't matter that there were thousands of grants given out every year through the Canada Council, and that I had absolutely no say over a single grant. It would have been impossible to explain that I didn't make the decision on grants under my jurisdiction—even though it was the truth."

Source: Excerpt from Sheila Copps, "Don't Believe the Spin on Gomery," *National Post,* February 4, 2005. Used with permission of Hon. Sheila Copps.

Questions for Discussion

1. In the parliamentary system, what has caused power to move to the prime minister?

2. In the presidential system, why was the executive separated from the legislature?

3. Would it be practical in the modern world for cabinet ministers to be required to resign over all mistakes made in their departments?

Internet Links

1. The Office of the Prime Minister, Canada: **www.pm.gc.ca.**

2. The Executive Office of the President of the United States: **www.whitehouse .gov.**

3. The Office of the Prime Minister, United Kingdom: **www.number-10.gov.uk.**

Further Reading

Bakvis, Herman. *Regional Ministers: Power and Influence in the Canadian Cabinet.* Toronto: University of Toronto Press, 1991.

Band, John R., and Richard Fleisher. *The President in the Legislative Arena.* Chicago: University of Chicago Press, 1990.

Burns, James MacGregor. *Leadership.* New York: Harper and Row, 1978.

Campbell, Colin. *Governments under Stress: Political Executives in Washington, London and Ottawa.* Toronto: University of Toronto Press, 1983.

Campbell, Colin, and M. J. Wyszomirski, eds. *Executive Leadership in Anglo-American Systems.* Pittsburgh: University of Pittsburgh Press, 1991.

Davis, James W. *The President and Party Leader.* New York: Greenwood Press, 1992.

Delacourt, Susan. *Juggernaut: Paul Martin's Campaign for Chretien's Crown.* Toronto: McClelland & Stewart, 2003.

Dunn, Christopher J. C. *The Institutionalized Cabinet: Governing the Western Provinces.* Kingston, ON: Institute of Public Administration of Canada, 1995.

Gardner, John William. *On Leadership.* New York: Free Press, 1990.

Goldenberg, Eddie. *The Way It Works: Inside Ottawa.* Toronto: McClelland and Stewart, 2006.

Hennessy, Peter. *Cabinet.* Oxford: Basil Blackwell, 1986.

James, Simon. *British Cabinet Government.* New York: Routledge, 1999.

Keyes, John Mark. *Executive Legislation: Delegated Law Making by the Executive Branch.* Toronto: Butterworths, 1992.

Laver, Michael, and Kenneth A. Shepsle. *Cabinet Ministers and Parliamentary Government.* Cambridge: Cambridge University Press, 1994.

————, eds. *Making and Breaking Governments: Cabinets and Legislatures in Parliamentary Democracies.* New York: Cambridge University Press, 1996.

LeLoup, Lance T. *The President and Congress: Collaboration and Combat in National Policymaking.* Upper Saddle River, NJ: Allyn and Bacon, 1999.

Linz, Juan J., and Arturo Valenzuela. *The Failure of Presidential Democracy.* Baltimore: Johns Hopkins University Press, 1994.

Lynn, Lawrence E., Jr. *Managing the Public's Business: The Job of the Government Executive.* New York: Basic Books, 1981.

Neustadt, Richard E. *Presidential Power and the Modern Presidents: The Politics of Leadership from Roosevelt to Reagan.* New York: Free Press, 1990.

Pal, Leslie, and David Taras, eds. *Prime Ministers and Premiers: Political Leadership and Public Policy in Canada.* Scarborough, ON: Prentice-Hall Canada, 1988.

Punnett, R. M. *Front Bench Opposition: The Role of the Leader of the Opposition, the Shadow Cabinet, and the Shadow Government in British Politics.* London: Heinemann, 1973.

————. *The Prime Minister in Canadian Government and Politics.* Toronto: Macmillan, 1977.

Savoie, Donald J. *Governing from the Centre: The Concentration of Power in Canadian Politics.* Toronto: University of Toronto Press, 1999.

————. *Court Government and the Collapse of Accountability in Canada and the United Kingdom.* Toronto: University of Toronto Press, 2008.

Shapiro, Robert Y., Martha Joynt Kumar, and Lawrence R. Jacobs, eds. *Presidential Power: Forging the Presidency for the Twenty-first Century.* Irvington, NY: Columbia University Press, 2000.

Simpson, Jeffrey. *The Friendly Dictatorship.* Toronto: McClelland & Stewart, 2001.

Smith, David E. *The Invisible Crown: The First Principle of Canadian Government.* Toronto: University of Toronto Press, 1995.

Warwick, Paul. *Government Survival in Parliamentary Democracies.* Cambridge: Cambridge University Press, 1994.

CHAPTER 28
The Administration

The modern state requires a large administrative apparatus to implement its legislation and policies. The assembly and the executive would be powerless without the support of a massive **administration,** a term that is used here interchangeably with bureaucracy. The latter word has acquired many negative connotations relating to delay, inflexibility, and red tape; but it has a particular and indispensable meaning in social science. **Bureaucracy** is a particular kind of social structure for carrying out organized work, a structure that has the following characteristics:

1. The work is divided into impersonal roles or offices that may be filled by different people as the need arises. Bureaucracies always have job descriptions to ensure that the functions of the positions are stable over time.

2. These positions tend to be specialized—another way of saying that there is a high degree of division of labour.

3. This specialization demands a career commitment from employees, because complex roles can be learned only through long experience.

4. Careers are protected by some form of job security or tenure. Usually this means that employees can be dismissed only for designated cause.

5. Positions are filled by **merit recruitment,** which normally means competitive examination. The opposite is recruitment by **political patronage,** which means that jobs are distributed according to kinship, friendship, or personal favour.

6. Ideally, a bureaucracy is supposed to be a neutral instrument in the hands of those who command it; in this regard, it is organized as a hierarchy, with authority flowing from top to bottom.

7. A bureaucracy minimizes the discretion of its employees, who must work within policies and rules laid down by authority. Found in every bureaucracy are an administrative manual, a rule book, a policy manual, and extensive written records; all of these help to make administration regular and predictable.

The bureaucratic form of organization is not confined to government. The Roman Catholic Church and large corporations are examples of private bureaucracies. Although bureaucracies were known in ancient empires such as Rome, Egypt, and

China, they have been perfected and widely used in the West only in recent times. The absolute monarchs of the eighteenth century created bureaucratic armies, but government administration did not become fully bureaucratized until the late nineteenth and early twentieth centuries. The principle of merit recruitment was not really accepted in Canada until passage of the Civil Service Act of 1908.

Bureaucracy has many advantages when it runs smoothly—that is why it has been so widely adopted. Ideally, it exhibits honesty, impartiality, stability, predictability, and competence. It may be short on imagination, innovation, and compassion, but presumably these qualities can be found elsewhere in the political system. In theory, it should be politically neutral, responding to directions from the assembly and the political executive but not itself making political decisions. As we shall see, this last expectation is not wholly realistic: the bureaucracy must be considered an independent element in the conversion phase of the political process, not just a passive adjunct to the political executive. Moreover, because the bureaucracy tends to become the home of many institutional pressure groups that pursue their own interests while also performing public business, it is an important source of demands on the political system.

The bureaucracy has two fundamental roles in the governmental process: it advises the political executive, and it administers the laws and policies enacted by the assembly. Under the first heading, whenever the cabinet wishes to introduce legislation, the preparatory work and the drafting will always be done by civil servants. In its administrative role, the bureaucracy is responsible for such matters as distributing child-benefit cheques and veterans' pensions, staffing customs and immigration offices in Canada and abroad, monitoring environmental conditions, regulating transportation, and performing myriad other tasks in the modern welfare-service state.

TYPES OF STATE AGENCIES

The bureaucratic structure is enormously complex. In the early 1990s, there were about 230,000 core employees in the federal public service, excluding the employees of Crown corporations and uniformed military personnel in the Canadian Forces. The budget cuts made by the Chrétien government in the mid-1990s reduced that total by about 40,000 positions over a period of several years, but growth quickly resumed. The *Ottawa Citizen* reported on November 28, 2004 that the total was very close to 270,000. If one counts the number of people working directly or indirectly for the federal government in departments, agencies, boards, Crown corporations, and the military, the total may be more than 500,000. If one adds provincial and municipal employees, including teachers, nurses, police, and firefighters, the total climbs to around three million people.

Canadian governments have created several kinds of bureaucracies. Most completely under government control is the public service in the narrow sense; this includes the departments and other agencies that are directly supervised by ministers, such as the agriculture and transport departments. Less thoroughly controlled are the many autonomous or semiautonomous boards, commissions, and Crown corporations. It is difficult to generalize about these bodies because their structures and responsibilities vary greatly with the statutes by which they were created. Students will be most familiar with those Crown corporations that are essentially business enterprises owned by the government, such as Canada Post, Via Rail Canada, and the Canadian Broadcasting Corporation. Other boards, commissions, and Crown corporations are more regulatory in character—that is, they do not operate large programs of their own, but monitor and control the activities of others. Examples of regulatory bodies are the Canadian Radio-television and Telecommunications Commission and the Canadian Transport Commission. **Regulatory agencies** attempt to impose public policies on the market without resorting to public ownership.

The term **Crown corporation** is unique to Canada, but public corporations can be found in almost every nation-state. They used to be numerous in Great Britain, where a great wave of nationalization of key resource and transport industries occurred after World War II. Between 1946 and 1951, the Labour government created the National Coal Board, the British Railways Board, the National Bus Company, the National Freight Corporation, the British Gas Corporation, and the British Steel Corporation. Between 1971 and 1977, the government also acquired a number of ailing industries: Rolls Royce, British Leyland, British National Oil Corporation, British Shipbuilders, and British Aerospace. By 1976, nationalized public corporations "accounted for 9.6 percent of GNP and 6.9 percent of employment."[1] But under Margaret Thatcher's privatization policy, almost all of these corporations, as well as many not named here, were sold to owners in the private sector.

Public corporations in the United States are mostly public utilities—for example, electric power companies—managed by independent commissions. These are usually authorized under state law. Amtrak (the national railway-passenger service) and the U.S. Postal Service are two public corporations responsible to the federal government. In all cases, the public corporation, as an alternative to the conventional civil service, is supposed to offer more business flexibility while remaining linked to the political executive.

At the provincial level in Canada, the same distinction exists between the public service in the narrow sense and semi-independent agencies and Crown corporations. For example, most provinces have monopolistic agencies to market alcoholic beverages; from a functional point of view, these are businesses that happen to be owned by government. Provincial governments also own, or have owned in the past, a wide range of businesses such as railways, airlines, natural-resource companies, utilities, and financial institutions. At the provincial and municipal levels, many service agencies have been established by government, and are largely funded by it, but operate more or less autonomously under elected or appointed boards of directors. Public schools, universities, hospitals, and police forces are in this category.

CONTROL OF THE ADMINISTRATION

The basic principle of control of the public service in a parliamentary system is that the bureaucracy is supposed to be responsible to the political executive and through it to the elected assembly. A minister of the Crown heads each department. Quasi-independent agencies and boards, such as the Canadian Human Rights Commission and the National Parole Board, as well as Crown corporations like Via Rail and the Bank of Canada, are not directly under ministerial authority but must report to a minister. If the operations of a commission or Crown corporation do not please the cabinet or the assembly, different personnel may be appointed to leadership positions, or legislation may be introduced to change the body's terms of reference. The underlying principle is hierarchical control and responsibility, modelled on a pyramid of authority delegated from the sovereign.

This political control of bureaucracy in the public sector contrasts with the competitive balance of bureaucracies in the private sector. Private bureaucracies are to some extent a check on each other, as corporations compete for dollars and churches for souls; but what is to restrain the public bureaucrats who wield the authority of the state? When government offers a non-monopolistic public service, competition provides some control, as in the case of the CBC; but most governmental services are monopolistic, so that the competitive model is inapplicable. What remains is the model of authoritative hierarchy and responsibility.

In the British parliamentary tradition, Canada has tried to control the public service by ensuring that it is firmly subordinated to Parliament, as illustrated in Figure 28.1.

Figure 28.1 Subordination of Bureaucracy to Parliament

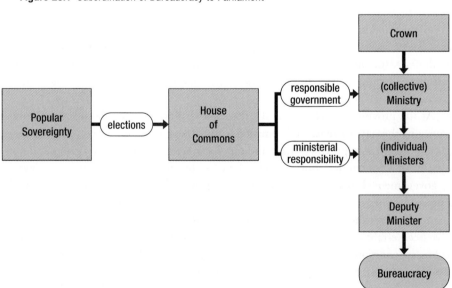

The basis of the Canadian system is that all executive power emanates from the Crown. The Crown acts only through ministers, who in turn are supposed to be accountable to the House of Commons for their actions. These ministers supervise the machinery of government under their respective portfolios and thus share responsibility for the management of the entire public service. The bureaucracy, as a hierarchy, is supposed to respond to direction from above. In this way popular sovereignty is ultimately served and the public service is kept a servant of the people, not its master.

Ministers are politicians, not specialists in the business of their portfolios. They seldom serve in any one position long enough to build up much expertise; in fact, many prime ministers deliberately rotate their ministers to prevent them from becoming too identified with a particular aspect of government. Deputy ministers, in contrast, are not politicians but career civil servants (or, occasionally, administrative experts brought in from the private sector). The prime minister's power to appoint deputy ministers is an important lever for controlling the public service.

Deputy ministers have reached the apex of the bureaucracy; presumably they have been promoted for competence. They run their departments, issuing instructions through assistant deputy ministers down the whole chain of command. They are also supposed to offer advice to their ministers, explaining what is or is not administratively feasible. Because of this huge responsibility, deputy ministers serve at the pleasure of the Crown and can be dismissed at any time; but it is Canadian practice not to fire deputy ministers very often. They may be transferred from one department to another, but they are seldom dismissed unless they have been politically indiscreet. This is in sharp contrast to the American custom, which is for the incoming president to make wholesale changes in the top ranks of the federal civil service.

By the time George W. Bush was inaugurated as president on January 20, 2001, his transition team had been busy finding ideologically and politically suitable people to fill the more than 3,000 appointments he would make. In the United States this "transition" represents a complete housecleaning, and the Republican transition team presented thousands of new faces for appointment. After Mr. Bush was re-elected in 2004 there were some changes within appointees, but the most significant ones occurred at higher levels such as the cabinet. When Barack Obama assumed office in 2009, there was another wholesale house-cleaning.

In the American system, the changeover in personnel goes far beyond the equivalent of the deputy-minister level; it reaches down five or six layers into the bureaucracy. To some extent, the American practice is a survival of the nineteenth-century **spoils system** ("To the winners belong the spoils," President Andrew Jackson is reputed to have said); but it represents more than pure patronage. It is based on the assumption that the political executive—which includes the president and the cabinet—cannot really control the bureaucracy unless it has the support of like-minded administrators at the pinnacle of the civil service. The result is a frank and open politicization of the upper levels of the bureaucracy.

In contrast, Canadian civil servants are supposed to be politically neutral and able to work under a minister of any party. After coming to power in 1984, the new

Conservative government of Brian Mulroney dismissed very few senior civil servants, a surprise after so many years of Liberal government appointments. The new government did, however, initiate an extensive retirement program for senior civil servants as a way of renewing the administration. Similarly, the government of Jean Chrétien in 1993–94 offered generous early retirement incentives, although this was done more to reduce the size of the civil service than to change its political complexion. For his part, Prime Minister Stephen Harper has made a few changes at the deputy minister level, but quietly and gradually so as not to create an impression of political intrusion.

The Canadian model of administrative control assumes that there is a clear distinction between politics and administration. Politics is supposed to be the realm where goals are set and choices are made between options; administration is supposed to be the realm where settled policy is carried into effect. Politics is the business of ministers, and administration is the business of deputy ministers; the latter are clearly subordinate to the former. But this assumption is only partially true. Politicians in power depend on information and expert advice from the public service. These administrative officials, with their knowledge and experience, wield a great deal of power in the political process. This power may overshadow that of elected officials, who are not expected to have technical expertise. Civil servants can make or break legislative proposals. Furthermore, even when legislation is adopted, it will have to be put into effect by the public service. Much may depend on the way a law is put into practice. Modern legislation is only a broad framework; its impact becomes clear only as administrative decisions accumulate.

The British television series *Yes Minister* derived its popularity from the way it portrayed the efforts of Jim Hacker, a new and bumbling minister, to control Sir Humphrey Appleby, his cunning and experienced **permanent secretary** (the British equivalent of a deputy minister). Hacker loses almost all the battles, for many reasons. He cannot deal directly with the civil service but must work through the permanent secretary. Sir Humphrey is far more experienced and knowledgeable about the affairs of the department than is Hacker, and he knows that Hacker is likely to last no more than a year or two at this particular ministry.

We have focused on "controls" because the civil service is an institution that is difficult to manage. In the ideal world, it is designed to serve the people of its society. The goal is to provide public services for citizens of society. However, like any large organization, public or private, it may develop internal goals that do not always square with the ideal goal. These internal goals may be very self-interested, not in the public interest. A police force and prosecutors, for example, may be more interested in a conviction than justice. In the transport department, the goal may be to serve their clientele, not public safety. The department, for example, may have a cozy relationship with airlines or the trucking industry and assist their clients and compromise public safety. Keeping the bureaucracy focused on its ideal goal is a fundamental objective of government.

Many observers of politics fear that too much power is vested in the public service and that it is not as subordinate as it should be to cabinet and Parliament. A number of experiments have been made in an effort to address this issue. As previously mentioned, prime ministers have greatly enlarged their personal staff in the Prime Minister's Office and the cabinet staff in the Privy Council Office with the goal of depending less on the regular public service for advice. The federal House of Commons has appointed an independent **auditor general** to review the annual expenditures of the public service. The Public Accounts Committee of the House, to which the auditor general reports, is chaired by a member of the Opposition, which gives it greater latitude in investigating possible administrative misuse of funds.

The effect of this type of independent audit was very clear in the recent "Adscam" scandal. A report of Auditor General Sheila Fraser exposed administrative laxity in the Chrétien government's sponsorship program, which had tried to combat separatism in Quebec by sponsoring events and public relations campaigns in support of Canadian unity. The auditor general's report showed that much of the program spending was poorly documented and monitored, and some of it seems to have been returned to the Liberal Party in the form of kickbacks.

Over the past 30 years, all provinces except Prince Edward Island have established an ombudsman to deal with complaints from individual citizens who feel that bureaucrats have not treated them properly. Typically, the **ombudsman** does not have the authority to grant relief to a complainant; even so, the power to investigate and expose may be enough to goad the bureaucracy into taking another look at the matter.

These and other reforms may all do something to reduce the power of the public bureaucracy and make it accountable to politicians—and ultimately to the people. Yet it is doubtful whether any true solution to the problem is in sight. The mechanisms of parliamentary control of administration were developed in an era of small government. If people want a service-oriented state that does a great deal for them, they will have to live with a large and powerful bureaucracy, since it is the only means by which such a state can deliver the services people demand of it.

The tendency toward growth in the bureaucracy is equally strong in private and public bureaucracies, but there are stronger countervailing tendencies in the former than in the latter. Business corporations cannot pursue growth to the neglect of profitability; expansion for its own sake will lead to lower rates of return on investment, declining dividends on shares, falling prices on the stock market, and possibly even bankruptcy. The existence of market competition, to the extent that it is effective, is one way to discipline the internal tendencies of the bureaucracy toward expansion for its own sake. Public bureaucracies, which rarely compute profit and loss and usually enjoy a monopoly position, lack this countervailing force. This tendency toward self-aggrandizement must be checked by political resistance—most often a shortage in the public treasury. Because of the internal incentives built into public administration, the political masters of the bureaucracy will continue to receive advice favouring the growth of the welfare-service state.[2] Sir Humphrey Appleby summarized the situation in *Yes Minister:*

> There has to be some way to measure success in the Service. British Leyland [an automobile manufacturer] can measure success by the size of its profits . . . However, the Civil Service does not make profits or losses. Ergo, we measure success by the size of

our staff and our budget. By definition a big department is more successful than a small one.[3]

While large bureaucracies may be a fact of life in modern governments, they nevertheless are a problem. About 25 years ago, the problem came to a head as public spending exceeded public revenues. With the election of Margaret Thatcher (1979), Ronald Reagan (1980), and Brian Mulroney (1984), a philosophical change led to the re-evaluation of the role of the state, and questioned the role of the bureaucracy in delivering public services. The conclusion: governments were trying to do too much and the administrative arm of government was bloated, inefficient, and ineffective. This triggered the downsizing, privatizing, and deregulation of governments and the introduction of reforms in the public service.

Reforms in the public service were extensive and spawned a significant addition to the public administration literature. Two important works include David Osborne and Ted Gaebler, *Reinventing Government*,[4] and Guy Peters and Donald Savoie, eds., *Governance in a Changing Environment*.[5] A full account of these reforms is impossible in this short chapter. We can, however, summarize important features of the movement. The reforms, often referred to collectively as **new public management (NPM),** involve a new paradigm of ideas: "The market . . . has become the paradigm for assessing efficiency in both the private and public sectors. It is a paradigm for a shrinking state on the assumption that a public service ought to be provided only if there is a demand for it."[6]

In Canada, the fiscal crisis of the 1980s and 1990s dictated the necessity of government reforms. These reforms sparked the philosophical debate over the direction of reforms to continue providing services without public spending deficits. This led the Liberal government to initiate the 1993 "Program Review." This program, combined with NPM ideas, shaped changes within the government of Canada. These changes have led to balanced budgets since fiscal year 1997–98, and federal program spending declined to about 12 percent of Canadian GDP in 2001 and subsequent years.[7]

Michael Paquin suggests that "three management practices" are characteristic of the current NPM reforms: strategic management or planning, the quality movement, and process re-engineering. Strategic management involves public administrators bringing "an organization's production of goods and services in line with the demands of clients, beneficiaries, and suppliers." The emphasis on quality "refers to the characteristics of a product or aspects of a service and their conformity to standards." Re-engineering processes means structural changes "to achieve gains in today's critical performances of costs, quality, service, and speed."[8]

Three other changes usually associated with NPM reforms are decentralization, accountability, and evaluation. *Decentralization* involves the "devolution" of decision-making responsibility to lower levels of an organization.[9] According to Paul Thomas, *accountability* means administrators taking personal responsibility: "Under the sway of NPM ideas there is growing insistence that public servants be personally accountable for results, for example, the development and publication of performance indicators."[10]

In addition, *evaluating* the performance of the civil service is an integral part of the reforms; indeed, as one writer puts it, "concern over what constitutes NPM has now given way to an interest in evaluating the managerial revolution."[11]

Over the past two decades NPM reforms have restructured the public service in most Western democracies. Budget cuts and an array of reforms have changed the "traditional core bureaucratic model." Some analysts today argue that the problem now is not a growing bureaucracy but rather the challenge of "revitalizing the public service":

> With the decline of the job-for-life concept, governments need to take advantage of their flexibility to hire, but also to ensure that government is perceived as a dynamic place to work for highly skilled professionals who are comfortable stepping between the public, private, and non-profit sector.[12]

NPM may solve a number of problems in government, but it is not likely to resolve the problem of the role of the state in society. No doubt, in the twenty-second century, people will still be debating that problem in some form.

Questions for Discussion

1. How does the role of public administration differ from that of the political executive?

2. How would you define a Crown corporation?

3. What was the objective of new public management (NPM)?

Internet Links

1. Canada, Departments and Agencies: **www.gc.ca/depts/major/depind_e.html.**

2. Library of Congress: **www.loc.gov.**

3. Brookings Institution: **www.brookings.org.**

Further Reading

Albelda, Randy, and Ann Withorn, eds. *Lost Ground: Welfare Reform, Poverty and Beyond.* Cambridge, MA: South End Press, 2002.

Aucoin, Peter. *The New Public Management: Canada in Comparative Perspective.* Montreal: Institute for Research on Public Policy, 1995.

Barzelay, Michael. *The New Public Management: Improving Research and Policy Dialogue.* Berkeley: University of California Press, 2001.

Bird, Richard M., in collaboration with Meyer W. Bucovetsky and David K. Foot. *The Growth of Public Employment in Canada.* Ottawa: Institute for Research on Public Policy, 1979.

Brooks, Stephen, and Lydia Miljan. *Public Policy in Canada*. 4th ed. Toronto: Oxford University Press, 2003.

Campbell, Colin, and George J. Szablowski. *The Superbureaucrats: Structure and Behavior in Central Agencies*. Toronto: Macmillan, 1979.

Campbell, Robert Malcolm, and Leslie A. Pal. *The Real Worlds of Canadian Politics: Cases in Process and Policy*. 3rd ed. Peterborough, ON: Broadview Press, 1994.

DiIulio, John J., Jr., ed. *Deregulating the Public Service: Can Government Be Improved?* Washington: Brookings Institution, 1994.

Downs, Anthony. *Inside Bureaucracy*. Boston: Little, Brown, 1967.

Dwivedi, O. P., and James Iain Gow. *From Bureaucracy to Public Management: The Administrative Culture of the Government of Canada*. Peterborough, ON: Broadview Press, 1999.

Gormley, William T., and Steven J. Balla. *Bureaucracy and Democracy: Accountability and Performance*. Washington DC: CQ Press, 2003.

Granatstein, J. L. *The Ottawa Men*. Toronto: Oxford University Press, 1982.

Hodgetts, J. E. *The Canadian Public Service: A Physiology of Government 1867–1970*. Toronto: University of Toronto Press, 1973.

Johnson, Cathy Marie. *The Dynamics of Conflict between Bureaucrats and Legislators*. Armonk, NY: M.E. Sharpe, 1993.

Kauffman, Franz-Xavier, ed. *The Public Sector: Challenge for Coordination and Learning*. Berlin: Walter de Gruyter, 1991.

Kernaghan, Kenneth, and David Siegel. *Public Administration in Canada: A Text*. 4th ed. Toronto: Nelson, 1999.

Kingdom, John, ed. *The Civil Service in Liberal Democracies: An International Survey*. London: Routledge, 1990.

Levine, Charles H., et al. *Public Administration: Challenges, Choices and Consequences*. Glenview, IL: Scott, Foresman/Little, Brown Higher Education, 1990.

Morgan, Nicole S. *Implosion: An Analysis of the Growth of the Federal Public Service in Canada, 1945–1975*. Montreal: Institute for Research on Public Policy, 1986.

Osbaldeston, Gordon F. *Keeping Deputy Ministers Accountable*. Toronto: McGraw-Hill Ryerson, 1988.

Osborne, David, and Ted Gaebler. *Reinventing Government: How the Entrepreneurial Spirit Is Transforming the Public Sector*. Reading, MA: Addison-Wesley, 1992.

Paehlke, Robert, and Douglas Torgerson, eds. *Managing Leviathan: Environmental Politics and the Administrative State*. Broadview Press: Peterborough, ON, 1990.

Pal, Leslie A. *How Ottawa Spends 2001–2002: Power in Transition*. Don Mills, ON: Oxford University Press, 2001.

————, ed. *State, Class and Bureaucracy: Canadian Unemployment Insurance and Public Policy*. Kingston, ON: McGill–Queen's University Press, 1988.

Peters, B. Guy. *The Politics of Bureaucracy*. 2nd ed. New York: Longman, 1984.

Peters, B. Guy, and Donald J. Savoie, eds. *Governance in a Changing Environment*. Montreal: McGill–Queen's University Press, 1995.

————. *Governance in the Twenty-first Century: Revitalizing the Public Service*. Montreal: McGill–Queen's University Press, 1998.

————. *Taking Stock: Assessing the Public Sector Reforms*. Montreal: McGill–Queen's University Press, 1998.

Rowat, Donald C., ed. *Public Administration in Developed Democracies: A Comparative Study*. New York: Dekker, 1988.

Savoie, Donald J. *Breaking the Bargain: Public Servants, Ministers, and Parliament*. Toronto: University of Toronto Press, 2003.

————. *The Politics of Public Spending in Canada*. Toronto: University of Toronto Press, 1990.

Taylor, James R., and Elizabeth J. Van Every. *The Vulnerable Fortress: Bureaucratic Organization and Management in the Information Age*. Toronto: University of Toronto Press, 1993.

Vigoda, Eran, ed. *Public Administration: An Interdisciplinary Critical Analysis*. Boca Raton, FL: CRC Press, 2002.

CHAPTER 29

The Judiciary

Although the judicial system was originally intended to be apolitical, it has now become a key part of the political process. After more than 25 years of living with the Charter of Rights and Freedoms, Canadians have grown to see the courts as an integral part of politics. Political actors now view the courts as an alternative (usually the last alternative) to the legislature, the political executive, and the bureaucracy in matters of achieving policy objectives. We will describe some of the less political functions of the judiciary before returning to its role in political decision making.

JUDICIAL STRUCTURES

The rule of law is a cornerstone of civilized life. Institutionalized rules (laws), when applied equally, discourage both public authorities and private individuals from arbitrarily using power. An extension of the rule of law is the court system, where legal disputes are adjudicated. The adjudication of disputes between individuals, between individuals and the state, and between different levels of government within the state takes place within the boundaries of a single country. There are also disputes involving two or more states, and individuals or corporations and other states, which concern breaches of international law. Such disputes may be brought before the International Court of Justice, but the decisions of that body are not binding because no power exists to enforce them; compliance in such cases is voluntary. In this chapter we will not look further at international courts, but will confine ourselves to a discussion of domestic law and court systems.

There is no single model for a system of courts; rather, every country seems to adopt a structure of courts in response to its particular needs. In particular, court systems tend to vary between federal and unitary states. In a unitary system, there is typically a single set of laws passed by the national legislature and a single system of courts administering justice. In a federal system, in which laws are made by different levels of government, there may be more than one tier of courts: federal courts with responsibility for federal laws, and provincial or state courts for provincial or state laws. Moreover, specialized courts may be established to deal with specific laws. For example, tax, labour, family, and juvenile courts can be found in many countries.

Figure 29.1 The American Court System

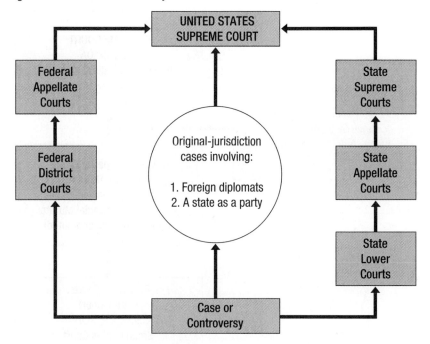

The British courts are an example of court organization in a unitary state. There is a single unified system, and all judges are appointed by the Crown on the advice of the prime minister and/or the Lord Chancellor. The highest court of appeal is the House of Lords, but by custom the whole house does not hear cases. This work is left to a special committee of the Lords with legal expertise. An interesting feature of the British system is that there are separate courts for criminal and civil matters, although appeals from both divisions go ultimately to the Law Lords.

The American system makes an instructive contrast to the British because federalism has had such a strong impact on how American courts are organized. As shown in Figure 29.1, the United States has a dual system of courts. Disputes under federal law go before a system of federal courts. The president appoints federal judges, subject to the advice and consent of the Senate. In addition, each of the 50 states maintains its own system of courts, with a state Supreme Court at the top. There is great diversity among these systems: in some, judges are appointed by the state governor; in others, they are popularly elected. Although federal and state courts are organizationally distinct, they are not completely isolated from each other. For one thing, many cases can go to either federal or state court, because federal and state laws overlap. Kidnapping, for example, is an offence in all states and also becomes a federal crime if state lines are crossed, so that an accused kidnapper may often be tried in either system. Also, the federal Supreme Court exercises appellate jurisdiction over the supreme courts of the states if federal or constitutional questions are involved.

Figure 29.2 The Canadian System

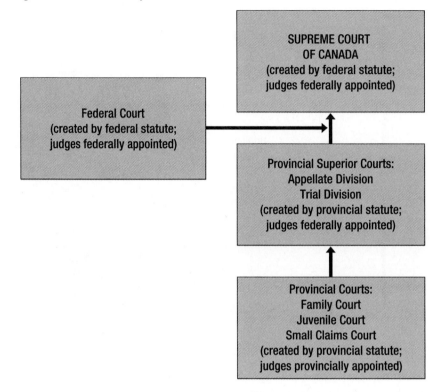

The Canadian arrangement falls between the British and the American. Figure 29.2 shows that the system is fundamentally unified. The Federal Court of Canada deals with certain specialized matters of federal administrative law: claims against the Crown, taxation, customs duties, immigration, and so on. All other cases are heard in the provincially organized courts at one level or another. The provinces maintain their own **provincial courts** for such matters as small claims and minor criminal offences. The judges of the **superior courts** are all appointed by the governor general on the advice of the cabinet. By longstanding practice, the prime minister personally selects the members of the Supreme Court of Canada and the chief justices of the other superior courts, while the minister of justice selects all other federally appointed judges.

Each province organizes its superior courts in a distinctive way. The provinces also provide the support personnel and services required by the courts. Canada's courts are thus a practical compromise between the unitary and federal approaches to court organization. The power of the provinces to organize the provincial and superior courts as they wish recognizes the diversity of local conditions; but the system is pushed toward uniformity of interpretation by the federal power of appointment and by the overall appellate jurisdiction of the Supreme Court of Canada.

The apex of the Canadian court system is the Supreme Court of Canada, which is the highest court of appeal. This does not mean that every appeal will reach the

Supreme Court, for the justices often deny leave to appeal, allowing the decisions of lower courts to stand. The Supreme Court has not always been the highest court of appellate jurisdiction. Before 1949, its decisions could be appealed to the Judicial Committee of the Privy Council in Britain, the highest court of appeal for the British Empire and Commonwealth. The removal of the Judicial Committee's appellate jurisdiction over Canadian cases was another step in Canada's gradual emancipation from British institutions of government.

The Supreme Court is made up of nine justices, of whom one is the chief justice. Three of the justices must be from Quebec, a stipulation that reflects a previously discussed peculiarity in that province's legal system: while other provinces rely on the British common-law tradition, Quebec has its own *code civil* for matters of private law.

INDEPENDENCE AND ACCESS

The professed object of a court system in a liberal democracy is to administer justice equally to all citizens. Unequal treatment before the law constitutes a violation of one of the fundamental principles of liberal democracy. Here we can mention some of the main factors that determine whether equality before the law is realized in practice.

There must be judicial independence from direct political interference; this can be guaranteed in a number of ways. The principle of tenure in office (serving "during good behaviour") ensures that judges cannot be discharged except for violation of law or gross impropriety of conduct. In the United States, Congress is constitutionally barred from lowering judges' salaries while they are in office (although neglecting to grant periodic raises may have the same effect in an inflationary age). In Canada, independent commissions now make recommendations to cabinets on judicial salaries. In spite of such safeguards, politicians may still try to influence judges, either by criticizing them in public or through more subtle private communications. In Canada in the 1970s and 1980s, several ministers had to resign from the federal cabinet after trying to influence judges. Judicial independence, probably the single greatest institutional support of the rule of law, can never be taken for granted.

The courts must be efficient. Cases before the courts must be handled expeditiously. Lives can be ruined if individuals are held in custody for a long period of time awaiting a criminal trial, or if payment of compensation in a civil suit is indefinitely postponed by legal manoeuvres.

Court rulings must be consistent, so that similar punishment is imposed for similar crimes. The sentencing practices of judges have long been debated by law-reform commissions. There is no way to guarantee that judges in Halifax and in Toronto, or even two judges in the same city, will apply the same penalty for similar crimes. Penalties written into the law contain some latitude, and for a good reason: judges usually take account of the particular circumstances surrounding a crime, and their interpretations of the severity of a crime vary greatly. We will undoubtedly never find uniformity when punishing violators of the law, but there must be some common denominator, or, again, the system will be questioned.

A final problem involves the cost of obtaining justice in the court system. Lawyers, especially good ones, are expensive—much too expensive for all except the very wealthy or those with corporate backing. The poor can get free or inexpensive legal services through legal aid; but this helps only the very poor while leaving ordinary people of modest resources facing a legal system that is often far too costly for their use. In practice, lawyers' fees in litigation that goes on for any length of time are usually paid by governments or by other organizations that have deep pockets and are interested in the outcome.

THE JUDICIARY IN THE POLITICAL PROCESS

Canadian courts are strictly neutral in partisan politics, but they still play an important role in the political process. Their decisions about cases sometimes have the same effect as legislative outputs from Parliament, or policy outputs from the executive or bureaucracy, or even amendments to the Constitution. Of course, most cases that come before the courts do not have such sweeping implications; they merely require the application of a known principle of law to a particular situation. But occasionally, there may be no precedent that really applies to the case; or perhaps the dispute hinges on the interpretation of the wording of statutory or constitutional language. In such instances, the court's decision, in that it becomes a precedent for subsequent decisions of other courts, is a source of law just as if a statute were passed or amended.

A good example of the potential importance of statutory construction is furnished by a series of court decisions in Manitoba in the late 1970s and early 1980s that had the effect of abolishing mandatory retirement in that province. The courts held that the way the prohibition of age discrimination in the Manitoba Human Rights Act was worded made it illegal for employers and unions to negotiate contracts with a fixed age of retirement. Public statements from members of the cabinet who brought in the legislation made it clear that they had not intended it to have any effect on retirement plans, but courts construe the words of statutes, not the statements of politicians. The effect was a major change in public policy brought about without any of the normal processes of study by experts and debate in the legislature.[1]

An important example of constitutional interpretation is the celebrated *Persons* case of 1929. Section 24 of the Constitution Act, 1867, allows "qualified persons" to be appointed to the Senate. At the time the Act was passed, "persons" was a technical legal term that generally referred only to adult males. When Prime Minister Mackenzie King wanted to appoint the first woman to the Senate, it was not clear whether the words "qualified persons" included women; but the Judicial Committee of the Privy Council held that women were persons within the meaning of the Act.[2] The case was political in at least two ways: because it changed law and policy to allow women to sit in the Senate, it was virtually the equivalent of a constitutional amendment; and because it signalled a remarkable victory for women as a group, it helped lead to subsequent improvements in their status. In this instance, a judicial decision provided an easier means than formal constitutional amendment for recognizing the emerging social consensus in favour of equal political rights for women.

Another political role of the courts is judicial review. Essentially, judicial review is a court ruling on the constitutionality of legislation or executive action. The concept was mentioned in our earlier discussion of federalism because disputes often arise in federal systems, where legislative powers are granted to different levels of government. Because the distribution of powers is often not entirely clear, or there may be overlapping responsibilities, jurisdictional disputes invariably arise between levels of government.

Judicial review exists in both Canada and the United States, as in most federal systems. However, it has had a different character in the two countries; at least, it did before the adoption of the Canadian Charter of Rights and Freedoms. Before 1982, judicial review in Canada mainly involved the courts deciding which assembly, provincial or federal, possessed legislative power under the Constitution Act, 1867. Having decided which was the appropriate legislature, the Canadian courts seldom used judicial review to challenge legislative wisdom. Also before 1982, there was no Canadian equivalent to a constitutional Bill of Rights placing limits on what any legislature, provincial or federal, could do.[3] The United States has long had such an entrenched document, and it has made American courts more self-confident in ruling legislation *ultra vires*—that is, beyond the constitutional power of a legislature to enact.

The power of the courts to interpret and even set aside legislation, coupled with their relative independence from the assembly and the executive, makes them an attractive alternative for interest groups that lack influence with other decision-making bodies. In the United States, the National Association for the Advancement of Colored People (NAACP) pursued litigation for decades to challenge legal segregation of the races; the case of *Brown v. Board of Education* (1954), in which the Supreme Court held segregated schools to be unconstitutional, is the most famous result of their work. Similar strategies have also paid off in Canada. In Manitoba, the trivial matter of a parking ticket became the case of *Forest v. The Queen,* which led to the ruling that Manitoba, established as an officially bilingual province by the Manitoba Act, 1870, must publish all its statutes in both English and French—an extraordinary victory that the francophone minority of that province could never have won in the legislature.[4]

Interest groups now pursue strategies of litigation as calculatingly as they lobby the assembly for legislation. The four basic steps of such strategic litigation are described in a document produced by the Canadian Advisory Council on the Status of Women:

1. defining a goal in terms of the desired principle of law to be established;

2. plotting how the principle of law can be established from case to case in incremental, logical, and clear steps;

3. selecting winnable cases suitable for each stage taken to achieve the goal; and

4. consolidating wins of each stage by bringing similar cases to create a cluster of cases in support of the principle established.[5]

The most successful practitioner of strategic litigation in Canada has undoubtedly been the feminist Legal Education and Action Fund. LEAF has been associated with most of the major cases involving the legal rights of women in areas such as abortion, employment opportunities, and protection against violence. In some cases, LEAF has actually sponsored the litigation (i.e., paid for legal representation); more frequently, it has **intervened** (i.e., with the permission of the court, it presented its views on the law without actually representing a client). LEAF has also supported research useful in its cause and offered orientation sessions to judges to sensitize them to women's issues.

Aboriginal people are also making sophisticated use of strategic litigation. Two recent cases are particularly significant. The *Delgamuukw* decision (1997) established that aboriginal rights and title had never been extinguished in the province of British Columbia because no land-surrender treaties had been signed there.[6] The province and the federal government are now engaged in a complicated process of negotiation with British Columbia First Nations to sign modern treaties. In 1999, the Supreme Court held in the two *Marshall* decisions that status Indians in Atlantic Canada had a treaty right to fish commercially for eels, and by implication to participate in other fisheries.[7] This ruling touched off violent confrontations between white and Native fishers before the federal government could sort out relative shares in the lucrative lobster fishery.

Strategic litigation dovetails well with the growing activism of courts. **Judicial activism,** defined as the willingness of judges to overturn legislation or executive action, has been a feature of American politics for decades. In the 1930s, the U.S. Supreme Court initially ruled much of Franklin Roosevelt's New Deal legislation unconstitutional. In one period from 1935 to 1937, the court held 12 acts of Congress *ultra vires*. There was then a sudden shift in the court's decisions after the president threatened to "pack" it by expanding its size and appointing members who shared his ideology of reform liberalism. In this instance, judicial activism was a weapon of the ideological right, but it can be used equally to forward the aims of the left.

The U.S. Supreme Court was particularly active between 1954 and 1969, while Earl Warren was chief justice. The Warren court struck down racial segregation, compelled the states to draw constituency lines to approximate "one man, one vote," greatly enhanced the rights of those accused of crimes, outlawed prayer in public schools, and in many other ways wrought unprecedented changes in the social fabric of the United States. When courts begin to decide so many questions of policy, they have plainly become politicized. There is in all of this a difficult question of democratic theory, for judges, after all, are appointed, not elected. Is it compatible with the idea of representative government to have so many questions settled by appointed officials who serve for life and never have to confront the voters?[8]

Since adoption of the Charter of Rights and Freedoms in 1982, the courts have become more "constitutionalized"; that is, many more court cases involve constitutional disputes over the rights of women, immigrants, gays and lesbians, language, and education, as well as the powers of the federal and provincial governments. Alan Cairns even suggests the Charter "is a consciousness-raising instrument that has profoundly changed Canadian constitutional culture." And this prominent place of the Charter in our politics has produced critics who feel it has "shifted more public policy powers to an unelected legal elite," and supporters who feel it "is a progressive change" that has improved "the quality of laws and state actions."[9]

Often we label judges who offer broad interpretations of the constitution as being liberal and judges who narrowly define the constitution as being conservative. In his book *The Judge in a Democracy,* Aharon Barak, a Supreme Court Justice in Israel, explains the problem with using these labels.

> It would be a mistake to define an activist judge as a liberal judge and a restrained judge as a conservative judge. Liberal and conservative are appropriate terms to evaluate the results of the judicial activity. For example, from the turn of the twentieth century until the end of the 1930s, the United States Supreme Court was an activist conservative court that invalidated a number of statutes that sought to recognize individual rights. The Warren Court of the 1970s was an activist liberal court. And today's United States Supreme Court, whose majority is conservative, behaves as an activist court in many areas of law. A liberal judge like Brandeis was viewed as a judge who exercised self restraint; a conservative judge like Scalia is seen as an activist judge. Definitions of activism and self-restraint should therefore address the way judicial discretion is exercised, irrespective of the evaluation of the outcome.

Barak goes on to say that "we should not assume that judges can be divided according to those who are always activists and those who always exercise self-restraint. This absolute approach is inconsistent with a judge's need to act within the framework of his zone of discretion, which at various times will demand more or less activism and more or less self-restraint."[10]

In any case, the Canadian courts are heavily involved in political decision making, and that gives new urgency to debates over how judges, who now have so much decision-making power, should be appointed. The process for appointing judges to the Supreme Court of Canada concentrates power in the hands of the prime minister, leading to calls for reform.

Political scientist Ted Morton has written that "Canada now has an American style Supreme Court with an unreformed British style appointment system."[11] The appointment system is a contentious issue because we straddle two conflicting principles. On the one hand, democracy today requires an independent judiciary that can render objective, unbiased decisions free of interference by legislators. On the other hand, in selecting individuals for the judiciary, we are choosing people who may have been active in partisan politics, and who have discretionary powers as members of the judiciary. As Peter Russell says, "The one clear conclusion to be taken from the accounts of appointing judges . . . is that no matter how the process is constructed it always has a political dimension."[12]

In the United States, the problem is addressed in part by the constitutional requirement that the Senate approve the federal judges nominated by the president. Because of the acknowledged policymaking role of the courts, and particularly of the Supreme Court, it is now commonly accepted that the Senate will interrogate nominees to that body about their political philosophy as well as about their legal competence and personal character. In 1987, the Senate rejected Ronald Reagan's nomination of Robert Bork to the Supreme Court. No one could impugn Bork's character or competence, but the Senate found him to be too conservative. George H. W. Bush's nomination of Clarence Thomas precipitated yet another bitter Senate hearing; Thomas's character and competence were challenged along with his conservative ideology. Ironically, Thomas was confirmed and Bork was not, at least partly because Bork's prolific writings had made his views abundantly clear, whereas Thomas's were less well documented. Whatever one may think of these hearings, they at least draw attention to the political consequences of judicial appointments and bring political factors into the process.

The Canadian tradition has been for superior court judges to be appointed by order in council without any public hearings. In practice, that means selection by the minister of justice for most appointments and by the prime minister for members of the Supreme Court of Canada and for the chief justices of other courts. In 2004, Paul Martin introduced a new wrinkle by allowing a parliamentary committee to review the names of two new appointees to the Supreme Court of Canada. Prime Minister Harper took this farther in 2006 when he appointed Marshall Rothstein to fill a vacancy on the Supreme Court. In that instance, Rothstein appeared in person before a House committee and answered questions from the members. It seems likely that such committee hearings will continue in the future for appointments to the Supreme Court of Canada but not to lower courts.

There is also another form of political balance in Canada, namely Section 33 of the Charter, the **notwithstanding clause.** This clause allows Parliament and the provincial legislatures to enact legislation even if the courts hold it to be in conflict with certain sections of the Charter (Sections 2 and 7–15). This "legislative review of judicial review," as Peter Russell has called it, is a unique way of elevating democratic government over the decisions of unelected judges. However, this tool has not been used very frequently. The fact that the override can be applied only for five years at a time, after which it will expire unless it is passed again by the legislature, creates difficulties for governments seeking to get around a court decision. It might buy a little time to bring in some other legislation, but it is not an attractive long-term solution.

In 1989 Quebec's National Assembly invoked the notwithstanding clause to protect its language legislation from judicial review. This use of Section 33 was subject to the five-year limitation in 33(3). The Supreme Court had held that the law violated freedom of speech inasmuch as it prohibited the posting of commercial signs in languages other than French. In response, Premier Robert Bourassa's government introduced Bill 178 to allow commercial signs inside buildings in languages other than French, as long as French signs were present and at least equally prominent; it then invoked the notwithstanding clause to make sure that this "inside–outside" legislation would not be upset in the courts.

In 1993, Bourassa introduced more permissive legislation, hoping that it would survive judicial challenges so that use of the notwithstanding clause would not be necessary. This illustrates the importance of the five-year limitation. If there had been no such limitation, it would have been easier for the Quebec government to leave Bill 178 on the books; but under Section 33 it was forced to review the matter.

LIFE IN CHARTERLAND

The adoption in 1982 of the Canadian Charter of Rights and Freedoms as part of the Constitution accelerated the growth of judicial activism. The guarantee of individual rights and freedoms now depends on the Constitution and on the courts' protection of the Charter's principles. Constitutional sovereignty has challenged parliamentary sovereignty because the courts can declare laws *ultra vires*, that is, unconstitutional. Parliament, however, can also fight back. If the government, or members of parliament, feel the courts are invading their jurisdiction they can, with popular support, change the constitution. However, as was mentioned in Part One, formally changing the constitution is no easy task. Additionally, Parliament or a provincial legislature may invoke the notwithstanding clause, although this is done only in rare cases. This fundamental change in constitutional law in Canada will by no means work itself out overnight. Individuals and groups are now frequently using the courts to challenge the constitutionality of particular federal and provincial laws.

The reason for adopting the Charter, it was explained to the Canadian public, was to advance toward the ideal of rule of law in a liberal democracy. The Charter would prevent governments, no matter how strong their majority support, from violating the rights of individuals or minorities. While this is undoubtedly true, there is another aspect of the Charter that cannot be overlooked: it involves an extensive transfer of decision-making power from legislatures to the courts.

The rights enunciated in the Charter are necessarily described in such broad language that they become meaningful only through judicial interpretation. To take one example, Section 10 of the Charter reads in part:

> 10. Everyone has the right on arrest or detention . . . (b) to retain and instruct counsel without delay and to be informed of that right.

The *Therens* case, decided in 1985 by the Supreme Court of Canada, hinged on the precise meaning of the word *detention*.[13] After an automobile accident in Moose Jaw, Saskatchewan, Therens was requested by a police officer to come to the police station to take a Breathalyzer test. (To refuse this request is itself a violation of the Criminal Code.) Therens complied and was later prosecuted for driving while impaired. At the trial, Therens's counsel moved for dismissal of the Breathalyzer evidence because the police constable had not informed Therens of his right to retain counsel. The legal question, ultimately decided in the affirmative by the Supreme Court, was whether being asked to go to the police station to give a breath sample amounted to detention.

A related question was whether evidence obtained in violation of Section 10(b) might be introduced anyway. Section 24(2) of the Charter states that "the evidence shall be excluded if it is established that, having regard to all the circumstances, the admission of it in the proceedings would bring the administration of justice into disrepute." Again, the courts were required to interpret abstract words. The Supreme Court upheld the view of the lower courts that to admit such evidence would in fact bring the administration of justice into disrepute.

The point here is not whether the decision was right or wrong, but where decision-making power is located. Parliament, in providing for check-stop procedures under the Criminal Code, had not explicitly said that those requested to "breathe into the box" should be informed of their right to retain counsel. By interpreting the generalized language of the Charter, the courts laid down a new rule, which is just as binding as if it had been legislated by Parliament. See Canadian Focus 29.1 for more on rights.

Canadian Focus 29.1

The Rights Revolution

The growing importance of the courts in Canadian politics is not an isolated phenomenon. In the period since World War II, many other countries have also adopted bills of rights, enlarged the scope of judicial review, and in other ways transferred more decision-making power to courts. Many authors refer to these developments as part of a "rights revolution."

In the 2000 Massey Lectures, the Canadian-born author and now Leader of the Liberal Party Michael Ignatieff developed an interesting thesis on human rights. The "rights revolution," he said, has grown with democracy; in fact, "rights talk" in society "has transformed how we think about ourselves as citizens, as men and women, and as parents" (p. 1). The revolution is making "our democracy more inclusive by incorporating groups and individuals who were marginalized or excluded" (p. 14).

At the same time, attaining human rights is a difficult task, not easy to achieve in the best of democracies. One problem is that we are "enhancing our right to be equal and protecting our right to be different. Trying to do both—that is enhancing equality, while safeguarding difference—is the essential challenge of the rights revolution. . . ." (p. 2).

Thus, the rights revolution does not make democracy any easier. Indeed, it "makes society harder to control, more unruly, more contentious" (p. 6). Nevertheless, there are certainly benefits. Today, "we have learned that the preconditions of order are simple: equal protection under the law, coupled with the capacity for different peoples to behave towards each other not as members of tribes or clans, but as citizens" (p. 141).

See Michael Ignatieff, *The Rights Revolution* (Toronto: The Canadian Broadcasting Corporation and Anansi Press), 2000.

After its proclamation on April 17, 1982, the Charter's effects were at first felt largely in the field of criminal law. Most frequently litigated in the early years were such rights as the right to security against unreasonable search or seizure and the right to counsel. Numerically, the main groups resorting to Charter arguments in the courts were those accused either of driving while impaired or of selling illegal drugs.[14] Because the courts obviously have great expertise in criminal law, the transfer of decision-making power from government and Parliament did not seem problematic. Outside the field of criminal law, only a few early Supreme Court decisions based on the Charter had broad consequences.

This situation, however, has been gradually changing since the proclamation on April 17, 1985, of the **equality rights** section of the Charter, Section 15(1), which reads:

> Every individual is equal before and under the law and has the right to the equal protection and equal benefit of the law without discrimination and, in particular, without discrimination based on race, national or ethnic origin, colour, religion, sex, age or mental or physical disability.

Federal and provincial statute books contain literally thousands of clauses authorizing differential treatment based on the criteria mentioned in Section 15(1). To mention only a few examples: one generally has to be 16 to obtain a driver's licence and 18 to vote; publicly supported athletic competitions are usually divided into classes by sex; physically and mentally disabled children are subject to special treatment of many kinds in the public schools. Proclamation of Section 15 was delayed for three years, from 1982 to 1985, in order to give Parliament and the provincial legislatures time to amend such laws so that they conformed to the Charter; but many of them remain on the books because they seem reasonably justifiable. (Is it really age discrimination to require a minimum age to obtain a driver's licence?) However, now that Section 15 has been proclaimed, the courts are inevitably drawn into deciding whether particular rules or policies are discriminatory.

As mentioned previously, some analysts, such as political scientists Ted Morton and Rainer Knopff, are critical of judicial activism and fear that Canadian democracy will be undermined by too much reliance on the rulings of unelected judges. On the other side of the debate, Peter Hogg, Dean of the Osgoode Hall Law School, and his student Allison Thornton developed a counterargument around the concept of dialogue. In their view, court decisions are seldom final in any practical sense; they almost always leave room for the government of the day to take further action if it wishes. At the extreme, the government can invoke the notwithstanding clause; or, more moderately, it can revise existing statutes or introduce new legislation that will withstand judicial scrutiny. Thus judicial review under the Charter does not mean unchecked judicial supremacy. In the words of Hogg and Thornton:

> A critique of the Charter of Rights based on its supposed usurpation of democratic legitimacy simply cannot be sustained. To be sure, the Supreme Court of Canada is a non-elected, unaccountable group of middle-aged lawyers. To be sure, from time to time the Court strikes down statutes enacted by accountable, representative legislative bodies. But the decisions of the Court almost always leave room for a legislative

Supreme Court of Canada.
Chris Wattie/Reuters/Landov

response, and they usually receive a legislative response. In the end, if the democratic will is there, a legislative way will be found to achieve the objective, albeit with some new safeguards to protect individual rights. Judicial review is not "a veto over the politics of the nation" but rather the beginning of a dialogue on how best to reconcile the individualistic values of the Charter with the accomplishment of social and economic policies enacted for the benefit of the community as a whole.[15]

Because the courts are now so much a part of the political system, students of political science cannot help but hear more of this debate in years to come.

Questions for Discussion

1. Do you think Canadian courts are too activist?

2. Why is judicial independence critical to democracy?

3. What is judicial review and what is its significance in liberal democracies?

Internet Links

1. Supreme Court of Canada: **www.scc-csc.gc.ca.**

2. *Osgoode Hall Law Journal:* **www.ohlj.ca.**

3. *Jurist Canada:* **http://jurist.law.utoronto.ca.**

4. *Lexum:* **www.lexum.umontreal.ca.** Full text of all Supreme Court decisions as well as decisions of some other courts, and various other forms of legal information.

Further Reading

Abraham, Henry J. *The Judicial Process: An Introductory Analysis of the Courts of the United States, England and France.* 5th ed. New York: Oxford University Press, 1986.

Barak, Aharon. *The Judge in a Democracy.* Princeton: Princeton University Press, 2006.

Bogart, W. A. *Courts and Country: The Limits of Litigation and the Social and Political Life of Canada.* Toronto: Oxford University Press, 1994.

Cairns, Alan C. *Disruptions: Constitutional Struggles, from the Charter to Meech Lake.* Toronto: McClelland & Stewart, 1991.

———. *Charter versus Federalism: The Dilemmas of Constitutional Reform.* Montreal: McGill–Queens University Press, 1992.

Geyh, Charles Gardner. *When Courts & Congress Collide: The Struggle for Control of America's Judicial System.* Ann Arbor: University of Michigan Press, 2006.

Horner, Jessie. *Canadian Law and the Canadian Legal System.* Toronto: Pearson Education Canada, 2006.

Horowitz, Donald. *The Courts and Social Policy.* Washington, DC: Brookings Institution, 1977.

Ignatieff, Michael. *The Rights Revolution.* Toronto: The Canadian Broadcasting Corporation and Anansi Press, 2000.

Knopff, Rainer, and F. L. Morton. *The Charter Revolution and the Court Party.* Peterborough, ON: Broadview Press, 2000.

Kulchyski, Peter, ed. *Unjust Relations: Aboriginal Rights in Canadian Courts.* Toronto: Oxford University Press, 1994

Malleson, Kate, and Peter H. Russell, eds. *Appointing Judges in an Age of Judicial Power: Critical Perspectives from around the World.* Toronto: University of Toronto Press, 2006.

Mandel, Michael. *The Charter of Rights and the Legalization of Politics.* Toronto: Thompson, 1994.

Manfredi, Christopher P. *Feminist Activism in the Supreme Court: Legal Mobilization and the Women's Legal Education and Action Fund.* Vancouver: University of British Columbia Press, 2004.

———. *Judicial Power and the Charter: Canada and the Paradox of Liberal Constitutionalism.* Toronto: Oxford University Press, 2000.

Martin, Robert Ivan. *The Most Dangerous Branch: How the Supreme Court of Canada Has Undermined Our Law and Our Democracy.* Montreal and Kingston: McGill–Queen's University Press, 2003.

McCormick, Peter. *Canada's Courts: A Social Scientist's Ground-Breaking Account of the Canadian Judicial System.* Toronto: James Lorimer, 1994.

———. *Supreme at Last: The Evolution of the Supreme Court of Canada.* Toronto: James Lorimer, 2000.

McCormick, Peter, and Ian Greene. *Judges and Judging: Inside the Canadian Judicial System.* Toronto: James Lorimer, 1990.

McWhinney, Edward. *Constitutional Tribunals and Judicial Law-Making.* Dordrecht, Netherlands: Nijhoff, 1986.

———. *Judicial Review in the English-Speaking World.* 3rd ed. Toronto: University of Toronto Press, 1965.

Morton, F. L. *Law, Politics and the Judicial Process in Canada.* 3rd ed. Calgary: University of Calgary Press, 2002.

———. Morgentaler v. Borowski: *Abortion, the Charter, and the Courts.* Toronto: McClelland & Stewart, 1992.

Perry, Michael J. *The Constitution in the Courts: Law or Politics?* New York: Oxford University Press, 1994.

Powers, Stephen, and Stanley Rothman. *The Least Dangerous Branch? Consequences of Judicial Activism.* Westport, CT: Greenwood Publishing Group, 2002.

Roach, Kent. *September 11: Consequences for Canada.* Montreal and Kingston: McGill–Queen's University Press, 2003.

Russell, Peter H. *The Judiciary in Canada: The Third Branch of Government.* Toronto: McGraw-Hill Ryerson, 1987.

Russell, Peter H., and Paul Howe, eds. *Judicial Power and Canadian Democracy.* Montreal: McGill–Queen's University Press, 2001.

Saywell, John T. *The Lawmakers: Judicial Power and the Shaping of Canadian Federalism.* Toronto: University of Toronto Press, 2002.

Shapiro, Martin M. *Courts: A Comparative and Political Analysis.* Chicago: University of Chicago Press, 1981.

Strayer, Barry Lee. *The Canadian Constitution and the Courts.* Rev. ed. Toronto: Butterworths, 1988.

Theberg, Leonard J., ed. *The Judiciary in a Democratic Society.* Lexington, MA: D. C. Heath, 1979.

NOTES

PREFACE

1. E. D. Hirsch, Jr., *The Schools We Need: And Why We Don't Have Them* (New York: Doubleday, 1996), p. 156.

INTRODUCTION

1. David M. Ricci, *The Tragedy of Political Science: Politics, Scholarship, and Democracy* (New Haven: Yale University Press, 1984), pp. 60–61.

2. Alan C. Cairns, "Political Science in Canada and the Americanization Issue," *Canadian Journal of Political Science 8* (1975), p. 196.

3. Thomas Flanagan, *Game Theory and Canadian Politics* (Toronto: University of Toronto Press, 1998).

4. Donald P. Green and Ian Shapiro, *Pathologies of Rational Choice Theory: A Critique of Applications in Political Science* (New Haven: Yale University Press, 1994).

PART 1
CHAPTER 1

1. Edward I. Hall, *The Hidden Dimension* (Garden City, NY: Doubleday Anchor, 1969), pp. 121, 161.

2. A seminal work is Edward O. Wilson, *Sociobiology: The New Synthesis* (Cambridge, MA: Belknap Press of Harvard University Press, 1975). A good synthesis is Bobbi S. Low, *Why Sex Matters: A Darwinian Look at Human Behavior* (Princeton, NJ: Princeton University Press, 2000).

3. Robert Axelrod, *The Evolution of Cooperation* (New York: Basic Books, 1984).

4. Bertrand de Jouvenel, *The Pure Theory of Politics* (New Haven, CT: Yale University Press, 1963), p. 30.

5. J. D. B. Miller, *The Nature of Politics* (Harmondsworth, UK: Penguin, 1965), p. 14.

6. Alan R. Ball, *Modern Politics and Government* (London: Macmillan, 1971), p. 20.

7. Harold D. Lasswell, *Politics: Who Gets What, When, How* (New York: Peter Smith, 1950). First published in 1936.

8. David Easton, *A Systems Analysis of Political Life* (New York: John Wiley and Sons, 1965), p. 21.

9. Jouvenel, *Pure Theory of Politics,* pp. 204–12.

10. Bernard Crick, *In Defence of Politics,* rev. ed. (Chicago: University of Chicago Press, 1972), p. 22.

11. Alexander H. Harcourt and Frans B. M. de Waal, eds., *Coalitions and Alliances in Humans and Other Animals* (Oxford: Oxford University Press, 1992), p. 3.

12. Norman Cohn, *The Pursuit of the Millennium,* rev. ed. (New York: Oxford University Press, 1970).

13. John Gray, *Black Mass: Apocalyptic Religion and the Death of Utopia* (Toronto: Doubleday Canada, 2007).

14. V. I. Lenin, "The State and Revolution," in *Selected Works* (Moscow: Progress Publishers, 1967), vol. 2, p. 345.

15. Marx himself did not use the term "withering away of the state." It was popularized by his collaborator Friedrich Engels. See his "Socialism: Utopian and Scientific," ch. 3, in Karl Marx and Friedrich Engels, *Selected Works* (Moscow: Progress Publishers, 1968), pp. 417–36.

CHAPTER 2

1. Stuart Schram, ed., *The Political Thought of Mao Tse-tung* (New York: Praeger, 1963), p. 209.

2. R. M. MacIver, *The Web of Government,* rev. ed. (New York: Free Press, 1965), p. 64.

3. Carl J. Friedrich, *Man and His Government: An Empirical Theory of Politics* (New York: McGraw-Hill, 1963), p. 225.

4. H. H. Gerth and C. W. Mills, eds. and trans., *From Max Weber* (New York: Oxford University Press, 1950), Part II.

5. Alexis de Tocqueville, *Democracy in America,* Andrew Hacker, ed. (New York: Washington Square Press, 1964), pp. 9–10.

6. Cited in Reinhard Bendix, *Max Weber: An Intellectual Portrait* (Garden City, NY: Doubleday, 1960), p. 88, note 15.

7. Cited in J. G. Ismael and T. Y. Ismael, "Social Change in Islamic Society: The Political Thought of Ayatollah Khomeini," *Social Problems* 27 (1980), p. 614.

8. Gerth and Mills, *From Max Weber,* p. 297.

CHAPTER 3

1. Cited in Jacques Maritain, "The Concept of Sovereignty," in W. J. Stankiewicz, ed., *In Defence of Sovereignty* (New York: Oxford University Press, 1969), pp. 44–46.

2. Jean-Jacques Rousseau, *The Social Contract* (New York: Hafner, 1947), p. 85.

3. Gerth and Mills, *From Max Weber,* p. 78.

4. Robert L. Carneiro, "A Theory of the Origin of the State," *Science 169* (21 August 1970), pp. 733–38; Jared Diamond, *Guns, Germs, and Steel: The Fates of Human Societies* (New York: W. W. Norton, 1997), pp. 265–92.

5. The literature is summarized in Fred H. Wilhoite, Jr., "Political Evolution and Legitimacy: The Biocultural Origins of Hierarchical Organizations," in Elliot White and Joseph Losco, eds., *Biology and Bureaucracy: Public Administration and Public Policy from the Perspective of Evolutionary, Genetic, and Neurobiological Theory* (University Press of America, 1986), pp. 193–231.

6. I Kings 11:3.

7. Rogers Brubaker, *Citizenship and Nationhood in France and Germany* (Cambridge, MA: Harvard University Press, 1992).

CHAPTER 4

1. Cited in Hans Kohn, ed., *Nationalism: Its Meaning and History* (New York: Van Nostrand Reinhold, 1965), p. 1.

2. Louis L. Snyder, *Global Mini-Nationalism: Autonomy or Independence* (Westport, CT: Greenwood Press, 1982).

3. Michael Ignatieff, *Blood and Belonging: Journeys into the New Nationalism* (Toronto: Penguin Books Canada, 1993).

4. Will Kymlicka, *Contemporary Political Philosophy: An Introduction,* 2nd ed. (Oxford: Oxford University Press, 2002), pp. 348–355.

5. Theodore Draper, *The Rediscovery of Black Nationalism* (New York: Viking Press, 1969), ch. 5.

6. Mel Watkins, ed., *Dene Nation: The Colony Within* (Toronto: University of Toronto Press, 1977), p. 3.

7. Menno Boldt and J. Anthony Long, "Tribal Traditions and European–Western Political Ideologies: The Dilemma of Canada's Native Indians," *Canadian Journal of Political Science 17* (1984), pp. 537–53; Thomas Flanagan, "Indian Sovereignty and Nationhood: A Comment on Boldt and Long," *Canadian Journal of Political Science 18* (1985), pp. 367–74.

8. *Renewal: A Twenty-Year Commitment,* vol. 5, Report of the Royal Commission on Aboriginal Peoples (Ottawa: Minister of Supply and Services Canada, 1996), p. 5.

9. Tom Flanagan, "Harper and the N-Word," *Maclean's,* December 11, 2006.

10. Michael Asch, *Home and Native Land* (Toronto: Methuen, 1984), p. 34.

11. P. B. Waite, *The Confederation Debates in the Province of Canada/1865* (Toronto: McClelland & Stewart, 1963), p. 50.

CHAPTER 5

1. Raymond Williams, *Keywords: A Vocabulary of Culture and Society* (Glasgow: Fontana, 1976), p. 76.

2. Thomas Sowell, *The Economics and Politics of Race* (New York: William Morrow, 1983), pp. 47, 49.

3. Richard Simeon and D. J. Elkins, "Provincial Political Cultures in Canada." In *Small Worlds: Provinces and Parties in Canadian Political Life*, eds. D. Elkins and R. Simeon. (Toronto: Methuen, 1980), pp. 31–76.

4. Ailsa Henderson, "Regional Political Cultures in Canada," *Canadian Journal of Political Science/Revue canadienne de science politique 37* (2004), pp. 595–615.

5. Gabriel A. Almond and G. Bingham Powell, Jr., *Comparative Politics: A Developmental Approach* (Boston: Little, Brown, 1966), p. 23.

6. Howard J. Wiarda, "Toward a Framework for the Study of Political Change in the Iberic-Latin Tradition: The Comparative Model," *World Politics 25* (1973), pp. 206–35.

7. For information on the Latin American Public Opinion Project at Vanderbilt University, go to http://www.vanderbilt.edu/lapop/.

8. Edward N. Muller and Mitchell A. Seligson, "Civic Culture and Democracy: The Question of Causal Relationships," *The American Political Science Review 88* (1994), pp. 635–52.

9. Gabriel A. Almond and Sydney Verba, *The Civic Culture: Political Attitudes and Democracy in Five Nations* (Boston: Little, Brown, 1963), ch. 1.

10. Oliver H. Woshinsky, *Explaining Politics: Culture, Institutions and Political Behaviour* (New York: Routledge, 2008).

11. Ronald Inglehart, *Culture Shift in Advanced Industrial Society* (Princeton, NJ: Princeton University Press, 1990). For a summary, see Neil Nevitte, "New Politics," in Mark O. Dickerson, Thomas Flanagan, and Neil Nevitte, eds., *Introductory Readings in Politics and Government,* 4th ed. (Toronto: Nelson Canada, 1991), pp. 145–154.

12. Neil Nevitte, *The Decline of Deference* (Peterborough, ON: Broadview Press, 1996).

13. Robert D. Putnam, *Bowling Alone: The Collapse and Revival of American Community* (London: Simon and Schuster, 2000).

14. Robert Putnam, "*E Pluribus Unum*: Diversity and Community in the Twenty-first Century. The 2006 Johan Skytte Prize Lecture," *Scandanavian Political Studies 30* (2007), pp. 137–74.

15. For background information, see CBC News, "France Riots: Understanding the Violence," November 28, 2007, available online at http://www.cbc.ca/news/background/paris_riots/.

16. Tina Chui, Kelly Tran, and Hélène Maheux, *Immigration in Canada: A Portrait of the Foreign-Born Population, 2006 Census: Findings*, Social and Aboriginal Statistics Division, Statistics Canada, available online at http://www12.statcan.ca/english/census06/analysis/immcit/index.cfm.

17. Ronald Inglehart and Pippa Norris, *Sacred and Secular: Religion and Politics Worldwide* (New York: Cambridge, 2004).

18. Marc Hooghe, "Political Socialization and the Future of Politics," *Acta Politica 39* (2004), pp. 331–41.

19. W. A. Galston, "Political Knowledge, Political Engagement, and Civic Education," *Annual Review of Political Science 4* (2001), p. 217.

20. Sidney Verba, Kay Lehman Schlozman, and Henry E. Brady, *Voice and Equality: Civic Voluntarism in American Politics* (Cambridge, MA: Harvard University Press, 1995).

21. Galston, "Political Knowledge, Political Engagement and Civic Education," pp. 217–34.

22. Dietland Stolle and Marc Hooghe, "The Roots of Social Capital: Attitudinal and Network Mechanisms in the Relation between Youth and Adult Indicators of Social Capital," *Acta Politica 39* (2004), pp. 422–41.

23. Michael X. Delli Carpini, "Gen.com: Youth, Civic Engagement, and the New Information Environment," *Political Communication 17* (2000), pp. 341–49.

CHAPTER 6

1. Exodus 34:27–33.

2. F. A. Hayek, *Law, Legislation and Liberty*, 3 vols. (Chicago: University of Chicago Press, 1973–9), vol. I, p. 81.

3. John Henry Merryman, *The Civil Law Tradition: An Introduction to the Legal Systems of Western Europe and Latin America* (Palo Alto, CA: Stanford University Press, 1969).

4. John E. C. Brierly, "Quebec's Civil Law Codification Viewed and Reviewed," *McGill Law Journal 14* (1968), pp. 521–89.

5. Michelle Falardeau-Ramsay, "The Changing Face of Human Rights in Canada," *Constitutional Forum 4* (1993), p. 64.

6. *R. v. Big M Drug Mart,* [1985] 1 S.C.R. 295.

7. http://www.ipsos-na.com/news/pressrelease.cfm?id=1163, February 15, 2001.

CHAPTER 7

1. Ivor Jennings, *The Law of the Constitution,* 5th ed. (London: University of London Press, 1959), p. 136.

2. Andrew D. Heard, "Recognizing the Variety among Constitutional Conventions," *Canadian Journal of Political Science 22* (1989), pp. 63–82.

3. Rainer Knopff, "Legal Theory and the 'Patriation' Debate," *Queen's Law Journal 7* (1981), p. 54.

4. J. N. Peltason, *Corwin and Peltason's Understanding the Constitution,* 8th ed. (New York: Holt, Rinehart and Winston, 1979), p. 236.

5. *Plessy v. Ferguson,* 163 U.S. 537 (1896).

6. *Brown v. Board of Education,* 437 U.S. 483 (1954).

7. *Marbury v. Madison,* 1 Cranch 137 (1803).

8. Statutes of Quebec, 1990, c. 150, popularly known as Bill 150.

9. Peter Russell, "The Anti-Inflation Case: The Anatomy of a Constitutional Decision," *Canadian Public Administration 20* (1977), pp. 635–65.

10. F. L. Morton, ed., *Law, Politics and the Judicial Process in Canada* (Calgary: University of Calgary Press, 1984), pp. 262–67.

11. J. R. Lucas, *The Principles of Politics* (Oxford: Clarendon Press, 1966), p. 106.

12. Jennings, *The Law of the Constitution,* p. 52.

13. *Roncarelli v. Duplessis,* [1959] S.C.R. 121.

14. *Operation Dismantle v. the Queen,* [1985] 1 S.C.R. 441.

15. Cited in F. A. Hayek, *The Constitution of Liberty* (Chicago: Henry Regnery, 1968), p. 462.

16. Alexander Hamilton, John Jay, and James Madison, *The Federalist* (New York: Modern Library, n.d.), p. 337.

PART 2
CHAPTER 9

1. Lyman Tower Sargent, *Contemporary Political Ideologies,* 4th ed. (Homewood, IL: Dorsey Press, 1978), p. 3.

2. Philip Converse, "The Nature of Belief Systems in Mass Publics," in David Apter, ed., *Ideology and Discontent* (Glencoe, IL: Free Press, 1964), pp. 206–61.

3. Karl Marx, "A Contribution to the Critique of Political Economy" (1859), in Lewis S. Feuer, ed., *Marx and Engels: Basic Writings on Politics and Philosophy* (Garden City, NY: Doubleday, 1959), p. 44.

4. Karl Mannheim, *Ideology and Utopia* (New York: Harcourt, Brace and World, n.d.). First published 1936.

5. Jeremy Bentham, "An Introduction to the Principles of Morals and Legislation" (1789), in Jeremy Bentham and John Stuart Mill, *The Utilitarians* (Garden City, NY: Anchor Books, 1973), p. 73.

6. Karl Marx, "Introduction to the Critique of Hegel's Philosophy of Right" (1843), in T. B. Bottomore, ed., *Karl Marx: Early Writings* (New York: McGraw-Hill, 1963), p. 44.

7. Bill Devall, *Deep Ecology: Living As If Nature Mattered* (Salt Lake City: Peregrine Smith Books, 1985), p. 67.

8. David Caute, *The Left in Europe Since 1789* (New York: McGraw-Hill, 1966), Chapters 1 and 2.

CHAPTER 10

1. Pierre Berton, *The Smug Minority* (Toronto: McClelland & Stewart, 1968), pp. 42–43. Reprinted by permission of McClelland & Stewart.

2. Bertrand de Jouvenel, *Sovereignty: An Inquiry into the Political Good*, trans. J. F. Huntington (Chicago: University of Chicago Press, 1957), pp. 247–59.

3. John H. Schaar, "Equality of Opportunity and Beyond," in J. Roland Pennock and John W. Chapman, eds. *Equality* (New York: Atherton, 1967), p. 242.

4. John Locke, *The Second Treatise of Government* (Indianapolis: Bobbs-Merrill, 1952), p. 5.

5. Ibid., p. 76.

6. Ibid., p. 114.

7. Carl L. Becker, *The Declaration of Independence,* 2nd ed. (New York: Random House, 1942), p. 8.

8. J. Salwyn Schapiro, ed., *Liberalism: Its Meaning and History* (New York: Van Nostrand Reinhold, 1958), p. 129.

9. John Locke, *A Letter Concerning Toleration,* 2nd ed. (Indianapolis: Bobbs-Merrill, 1955), p. 18.

10. Schapiro, *Liberalism,* p. 126.

11. Ibid., p. 129.

12. John Stuart Mill, *On Liberty* (Indianapolis: Bobbs-Merrill, 1956), p. 13.

13. Adam Smith, *The Wealth of Nations* (Chicago: University of Chicago Press, 1976), vol. 1, pp. 477–78.

14. See especially Milton and Rose Friedman, *Free to Choose* (New York: Harcourt Brace Jovanovich, 1970); and Friedrich A. Hayek, *The Constitution of Liberty* (Chicago: University of Chicago Press, 1960).

15. David Hume, *A Treatise of Human Nature* (1739), cited in James Moore, "Hume's Theory of Justice and Property," *Political Studies 24* (1976), p. 108.

16. Friedrich A. Hayek, *Law, Legislation and Liberty* (Chicago: University of Chicago Press, 1973–79), vol. 1, pp. 35–54.

17. Smith, *The Wealth of Nations*, vol. 2, pp. 208–9.

18. The discerning reader will see that the streetlight is a collective good because streets are publicly owned. If the streets were turned over to an entrepreneur who could find an appropriate way of charging for their use, lighting could be furnished as part of the overall service.

19. It is now recognized that many collective goods can be offered in some way in the market. See the essays in Tyler Cowen, ed., *The Theory of Market Failure* (Fairfax, VA: George Mason University Press, 1988).

20. Paul Starr, *Freedom's Power: The True Force of Liberalism* (New York: Basic Books, 2007), p. 3

21. John Stuart Mill, *Principles of Political Economy*, vol. 2 of *The Collected Works of John Stuart Mill* (Toronto: University of Toronto Press, 1965), p. 207.

22. T. H. Green, "Liberal Legislation and Freedom of Contract" (1881), in John R. Rodman, ed., *The Political Theory of T. H. Green* (New York: Appleton-Century-Crofts, 1964), pp. 51–52.

23. F. A. Hayek, ed., *Capitalism and the Historians* (Chicago: University of Chicago Press, 1954).

24. John Kenneth Galbraith, *The New Industrial State* (Boston: Houghton Mifflin, 1967).

25. Neil H. Jacoby, *Corporate Power and Social Responsibility* (New York: Macmillan, 1973), ch. 6.

26. Barry Cooper, Allan Kornberg, and William Mishler, *The Resurgence of Conservatism in Anglo-American Democracies* (Durham, NC: Duke University Press, 1988).

CHAPTER 11

1. Michael Oakeshott, *Rationalism in Politics and Other Essays* (London: Methuen, 1962), p. 169.

2. W. L. Morton, "Canadian Conservatism Now" (1959), in Paul W. Fox, ed., *Politics Canada,* 3rd ed. (Toronto: McGraw-Hill, 1970), p. 233.

3. Edmund Burke, *Reflections on the Revolution in France* (Indianapolis: Liberal Arts Press, 1955), p. 99.

4. Gordon W. Allport, *The Nature of Prejudice* (Reading, MA: Addison-Wesley, 1954), p. 20.

5. Ibid., p. 9.

6. Edmund Burke, "Letter to Sir Hercules Langrische on the Catholics" (1792), cited in Russell Kirk, *The Conservative Mind* (Chicago: Henry Regnery, 1960), p. 99.

7. Burke, *Reflections on the Revolution in France*, p. 110.

8. Kirk, Russell, *The Conservative Mind*, pp. 8–9. Copyright © 1985. All rights reserved. Reprinted by special permission of Regnery Publishing, Inc. Washington, D.C.

9. Clinton Rossiter, "Conservatism," in David L. Sils, ed., *International Encyclopedia of the Social Sciences* (New York: Macmillan and The Free Press, 1968), vol. 3, p. 294.

10. Edmund Burke, "Thoughts and Details on Scarcity" (1795), cited in C. B. Macpherson, *Burke* (Oxford: Oxford University Press, 1980), p. 58.

11. Rod Preece, "The Political Wisdom of Sir John A. Macdonald," *Canadian Journal of Political Science 17* (1984), p. 479.

12. George Grant, *Lament for a Nation: The Defeat of Canadian Nationalism* (Toronto: McClelland & Stewart, 1965), p. 68.

13. Steve H. Hanke, *Privatization and Development* (San Francisco: Institute for Contemporary Studies, 1987), pp. 184–85.

14. N. J. Baxter-Moore, "Ideology or Pragmatism? The Politics and Management of the Mulroney Government's Privatization Programme," *British Journal of Canadian Studies 7* (1992), pp. 290–325.

15. David Frum, *Comeback: Conservatism That Can Win Again* (New York: Doubleday, 2008).

CHAPTER 12

1. Mikhail Heller, *Cogs in the Wheel: The Formation of Soviet Man* (New York: Alfred A. Knopf, 1988). As far as we know, Marx first used the phrase "socialist man" in 1844 in "Economic and Philosophical Manuscripts," in Bottomore, *Karl Marx: Early Writings*, p. 166.

2. Acts of the Apostles 4:32–33.

3. J. L. Talmon, *The Origins of Totalitarian Democracy* (New York: Praeger, 1960), pp. 167–247.

4. John Anthony Scott, ed., *The Defense of Gracchus Babeuf* (New York: Schocken Books, 1972), p. 68. Copyright 1967 by University of Massachusetts Press.

5. Ibid., pp. 62–63.

6. Mark Holloway, *Heavens on Earth: Utopian Communities in America 1680–1880,* 2nd ed. (New York: Dover, 1966).

7. Karl Marx, "Contribution to the Critique of Hegel's Philosophy of Right" (1843), in Bottomore, *Karl Marx: Early Writings,* pp. 58–59.

8. Marx, "Economic and Philosophical Manuscripts" (1844), p. 132.

9. Ibid., p. 124.

10. M. M. Bober, *Karl Marx's Interpretation of History,* 2nd ed. (New York: W. W. Norton, 1965), ch. 12.

11. Friedrich Engels, "Socialism: Utopian and Scientific" (1892), in Karl Marx and Friedrich Engels, *Selected Works* (Moscow: Progress Publishers, 1968), p. 432.

12. Karl Marx and Friedrich Engels, *The Communist Manifesto* (Harmondsworth, UK: Penguin Books, 1967), pp. 104–5.

13. Karl Marx, "Critique of the Gotha Programme" (1875), in Lewis S. Feuer, ed., *Marx and Engels: Basic Writings on Politics and Philosophy* (Garden City, NY: Doubleday, 1959), p. 119.

14. Karl Marx and Friedrich Engels, *The German Ideology* (Moscow: Progress Publishers, 1968), p. 45.

15. On anarchism, see James Joll, *The Anarchists* (London: Methuen, 1964).

16. James Joll, *The Second International* (London: Routledge and Kegan Paul, 1955).

17. Alfred G. Meyer, *Marxism: The Unity of Theory and Practice* (Ann Arbor: University of Michigan Press, 1963), pp. 122–26.

18. Lenin's seminal work on party organization is *What Is to Be Done?* (1902). On democratic centralism see Alfred G. Meyer, *Leninism* (New York: Praeger, 1962), pp. 92–103.

19. Lenin, *Selected Works,* vol. 1, p. 680.

20. Michael S. Cross, ed., *The Decline and Fall of a Good Idea: CCF–NDP Manifestoes 1932–1969* (Toronto: New Hogtown Press, 1974), p. 19.

21. Ibid., pp. 33–42.

22. Quoted in Charlotte Gray, "Designer Socialism," *Saturday Night,* August 1989, p. 8.

23. Cross, *Decline and Fall of a Good Idea,* p. 19.

24. Chrystia Freeland, *Sale of the Century: Russia's Wild Ride from Communism to Capitalism* (Toronto: Doubleday Canada, 2000), p. 326.

25. Gregory C. Chow, "The Integration of China and Other Asian Countries into the World Economy," Mont Pèlerin Society, Vancouver, BC, August 31, 1992.

26. Research Committee of the League for Social Reconstruction, *Social Planning for Canada* (Toronto: University of Toronto Press, 1975). First published in 1935. The League for Social Reconstruction was an intellectual study group, founded in 1932 on the model of the British Fabian Society. It was not, strictly speaking, affiliated with the CCF, but members of the LSR were usually CCF activists.

27. Cross, *Decline and Fall of a Good Idea*, p. 20.

28. The "Waffle Manifesto" (1969), in Cross, *Decline and Fall of a Good Idea*, p. 45.

29. David Lane, *The End of Inequality? Stratification under State Socialism* (Harmondsworth, UK: Penguin, 1971); and Mervyn Matthews, *Privilege in the Soviet Union* (London: George Allen and Unwin, 1978), ch. 2.

30. Charles E. Lindblom, *Politics and Markets: The World's Political–Economic Systems* (New York: Basic Books, 1977). Lindblom adds a third alternative, exhortation, which does not seem to be even close to the other two in long-term effectiveness.

31. See Richard N. Hunt, *The Political Ideas of Marx and Engels* (Pittsburgh: University of Pittsburgh Press, 1974), vol. 1, ch. 9.

32. N. S. Khrushchev, "Report on the Program of the Communist Party of the Soviet Union, October 17, 1961," in *Documents of the 22nd Congress of the CPSU* (New York: Crosscurrents Press, 1961), vol. 2.

CHAPTER 13

1. Aristotle, *Nicomachean Ethics,* 1155a, in Richard McKeon, ed., *The Basic Works of Aristotle* (New York: Random House, 1941), p. 1058.

2. Quoted in Ramsay Cook, ed., *French-Canadian Nationalism: An Anthology* (Toronto: Macmillan, 1969), p. 95.

3. Ibid., p. 98.

4. Seymour Martin Lipset, "Canada and the United States: The Cultural Dimension," in Charles F. Doran and John H. Sigler, eds., *Canada and the United States* (Englewood Cliffs, NJ, and Scarborough, ON: Prentice-Hall, 1985).

5. Letter to Joseph Priestley, June 19, 1802, cited in Saul K. Padover, ed., *Thomas Jefferson and the Foundations of American Freedom* (Princeton, NJ: D. Van Nostrand, 1965), pp. 120–21.

6. Benedict Anderson, *Imagined Communities: Reflections on the Origin and Spread of Nationalism,* 2nd ed. (London: Verso, 1991).

7. Edward A. Tiryakian and Neil Nevitte, "Nationalism and Modernity," in Edward A. Tiryakian and Ronald Rogowski, *New Nationalisms of the Developed West* (Boston: Allen and Unwin, 1985), p. 67.

8. John Stuart Mill, *Considerations on Representative Government* (Chicago: Henry Regnery, 1962), p. 309.

9. Lord Acton, "Nationality" (1862), in Gertrude Himmelfarb, ed., *Essays on Freedom and Power* (New York: The Free Press, 1949), p. 193.

10. Pierre Elliott Trudeau, "The New Treason of the Intellectuals," in *Federalism and the French Canadians* (Toronto: Macmillan, 1968), pp. 177–78.

11. See, for example, C. C. Lingard, *Territorial Government in Canada: The Autonomy Question in the Old North-West Territories* (Toronto: University of Toronto Press, 1946); Lewis Herbert Thomas, *The Struggle for Responsible Government in the Northwest Territories,* 2nd ed. (Toronto: University of Toronto Press, 1978).

12. Frank Cassidy, "Introduction," in Frank Cassidy, ed., *Aboriginal Self-Determination* (Montreal: The Institute for Research on Public Policy, 1991), p. 1.

13. Canada, Indian and Northern Affairs, Communiqué, 3–8304, "Notes Prepared for The Honourable John C. Munro, Minister of Indian Affairs and Northern Development For the Debate in the House of Commons on the Motion to Ratify the Constitutional Accord," Ottawa, 1983, p. 7.

14. Edward McWhinney, *Constitution-Making* (Toronto: University of Toronto Press, 1981), p. 206.

15. Kenneth Woodside, "The Canada–United States Free Trade Agreement," *Canadian Journal of Political Science 22* (1989), pp. 155–70.

16. Hans Kohn, ed., *Nationalism: Its Meaning and History,* 2nd ed. (Princeton, NJ: D. Van Nostrand, 1965).

17. Richard Wagner, "Judaism in Music" (1850), in Hans Kohn, ed., *Nationalism,* p. 165.

18. On the *Protocols,* see Norman Cohn, *Warrant for Genocide,* 2nd ed. (New York: Harper and Row, 1969).

19. An elaborate exposition of "Holocaust revisionism" is Arthur Butz, *The Hoax of the Twentieth Century* (Brighton, UK: Historical Review Press, 1977).

20. Benito Mussolini, "The Doctrine of Fascism" (1932), in Department of Philosophy, University of Colorado, *Readings on Fascism and National Socialism* (Denver: Alan Swallow, n.d.), p. 15.

21. A convenient overview of fascism is Eugen Weber, *Varieties of Fascism* (New York: Van Nostrand Reinhold, 1964).

CHAPTER 14

1. For a summary, see Neil Nevitte, "New Politics," in Dickerson, Flanagan, and Nevitte, *Introductory Readings in Politics and Government,* pp. 161–70.

2. See Brenda O'Neill, "On the Same Wavelength? Feminist Attitudes Across Generations of Canadian Women," in Manon Tremblay and Linda Trimble, *Women and Electoral Politics in Canada* (Don Mills, ON: Oxford, 2003), pp. 178–91.

3. Quoted in Margaret Tims, *Mary Wollstonecraft: A Social Pioneer* (London: Millington, 1976), pp. 135–36.

4. Quoted in Josephine Donovan, *Feminist Theory: The Intellectual Traditions of American Feminism* (New York: Frederick Ungar, 1985), p. 6.

5. John Stuart Mill, *The Subjection of Women,* Sue Mansfield, ed. (Arlington Heights, IL, AHM Publishing, 1980), p. 1.

6. Ibid., p. 5.

7. Ibid., p. 11.

8. Ibid., p. 18.

9. Ibid., p. 26.

10. Ibid., p. 47.

11. Betty Steele, *The Feminist Takeover* (Toronto: Simon & Pierre, 1987), pp. 36–37.

12. Betty Friedan, *The Feminine Mystique,* 2nd ed. (New York: Dell, 1983), p. 15.

13. Ibid., pp. 384–85.

14. Betty Friedan, *The Second Stage* (New York: Summit Books, 1981), p. 16.

15. Ibid., p. 41.

16. Jonathan Beecher and Richard Bienvenu, eds., *The Utopian Vision of Charles Fourier* (Boston: Beacon Press, 1971), p. 195.

17. Robert Owen, *A New View of Society and Other Writings* (London: Dent, 1927), p. 45.

18. Quoted in Donovan, *Feminist Theory,* p. 70.

19. Quoted in ibid., p. 75.

20. Frederick Engels, *The Origin of the Family, Private Property and the State* (New York: International Publishers, 1972), pp. 137–38.

21. Quoted in Donovan, *Feminist Theory,* p. 76.

22. Quoted in ibid., p. 145.

23. Quoted in ibid., p. 144.

24. Quoted in Elaine Storkey, *What's Right with Feminism* (London: SPCK, 1985), p. 94.

25. Quoted in ibid., p. 100.

26. Quoted in Donovan, *Feminist Theory,* p. 146.

27. Quoted in ibid., p. 147.

28. Quoted in ibid., p. 152.

29. Donovan, *Feminist Theory,* p. 147; Storkey, *What's Right with Feminism,* pp. 98–99.

30. See Mary O'Brien, *The Politics of Reproduction* (Boston: Routledge and Kegan Paul, 1981).

31. Roxanne Dunbar, quoted in Donovan, *Feminist Theory,* p. 142.

32. Elisabeth Gidengil, André Blais, Neil Nevitte, and Richard Nadeau, *Citizens* (Vancouver: University of British Columbia Press, 2004), pp. 23–24, 51–54.

33. Ronald Inglehart and Pippa Norris, "The Developmental Theory of the Gender Gap: Women's and Men's Voting Behavior in Global Perspective," *International Political Science Review 21* (October 2000), pp. 441ff.

34. Elisabeth Gidengil, Matthew Hennigar, André Blais, and Neil Nevitte, "Explaining the Gender Gap in Support for the New Right: The Case of Canada," *Comparative Political Studies 38* (December 2005), pp. 1171–95.

35. Elisabeth Gidengil, André Blais, Neil Nevitte, and Richard Nadeau, "Women to the Left? Gender Differences in Political Beliefs and Policy Preferences," in Tremblay and Trimble, *Women and Electoral Politics in Canada,* pp. 140–59.

CHAPTER 15

1. Robyn Eckersley, *Environmentalism and Political Theory: Toward an Ecocentric Approach* (Albany: State University of New York Press, 1992), p. 38.

2. Brundtland Commission Report, *Our Common Future* (United Nations, 1987), quoted in http://geneva-international.org/GVA3/WelcomeKit/Environnement/chap_5.E.html.

3. Quoted in Devall, *Deep Ecology,* p. 70.

4. Quoted in Sylvia LeRoy and Barry Cooper, "Off Limits: How Radical Environmentalists Are Stealing Canada's National Parks," *Fraser Institute Public Policy Sources 45* (2000), p. 12.

5. Quoted in ibid.

6. Tim Flannery, *The Eternal Frontier: An Ecological History of North America and Its Peoples* (New York: Atlantic Monthly Press, 2001), pp. 345–46.

7. Quoted in Eckersley, *Environmentalism and Political Theory,* p. 43.

PART 3
CHAPTER 16

1. Aristotle, *Politics,* iii, 16, in McKeon, *The Basic Works of Aristotle,* p. 1202.

2. Mill, *On Liberty,* p. 7; de Tocqueville, *Democracy in America,* p. 102.

3. Aristotle, *Politics,* iv, 11, p. 1221.

CHAPTER 17

1. Dorothy Pickles, *Democracy* (London: B. T. Batsford, 1970), p. 11.

2. Giovanni Sartori, *The Theory of Democracy Revisited, Part One: The Contemporary Debate* (Chatham, NJ: Chatham House, 1987), p. 6.

3. R. MacGregor Dawson, *The Government of Canada,* 4th ed., rev. by Norman Ward (Toronto: University of Toronto Press, 1963), p. 351.

4. Ibid. p. 351.

5. Terence H. Qualter, *The Election Process in Canada* (Toronto: McGraw-Hill, 1970), p. 9.

6. *Sauvé v. Canada (Chief Electoral Officer),* [2002] 3 S.C.R. 519.

7. The Constitution Act, 1982, ss. 38, 41.

8. Speech of October 11, 1864, in Joseph Pope, ed., *Confederation* (Toronto: Carswell, 1895), p. 58.

9. J. A. O. Larsen, "The Judgment of Antiquity on Democracy," *Classical Philology 49* (1954), pp. 1–14.

10. James Mill, *An Essay on Government* (Indianapolis: Bobbs-Merrill, 1955), p. 66.

11. Ibid, p. 70.

12. Patrick Boyer, *The People's Mandate: Referendums and a More Democratic Canada* (Toronto: Dundurn, 1992), pp. 23–26. See also David Butler and Austin Ranney, eds., *Referendums* (Washington, DC: American Enterprise Institute, 1978).

13. Alvin Rabushka and Pauline Ryan, *The Tax Revolt* (Stanford, CA: Hoover Institution, 1982).

14. Boyer, *The People's Mandate,* pp. 113–16. The argument actually comes from A. V. Dicey.

15. Particulars of the initiative, referendum, and recall can be found in J. A. Corry and Henry J. Abraham, *Elements of Democratic Government,* 4th ed. (New York: Oxford University Press, 1964), pp. 410–22.

16. *Quebec v. Ford,* [1988] 2 S.C.R. 712.

17. Cited in Hayek, *Law, Legislation and Liberty,* vol. 3, p. 1.

18. John Adams, "A Defense of the American Constitutions" (1787), in George A. Peek, ed., *The Political Writings of John Adams* (Indianapolis: Bobbs-Merrill, 1954), p. 148.

19. William A. Galston, "Political Knowledge, Political Engagement and Civic Education," *Annual Review of Political Science 4* (2001), p. 217.

20. Geraint Parry, *Political Elites* (London: George Allen and Unwin, 1969), p. 30.

21. Raymond Aron, "Social Structure and the Ruling Class," *British Journal of Sociology 1* (1950), p. 10, quoted in T. B. Bottomore, *Elites and Society* (Harmondsworth, UK: Penguin, 1966), p. 115.

22. Robert A. Dahl, *A Preface to Democratic Theory* (Chicago: University of Chicago Press), 1956, p. 133.

23. Philippe C. Schmitter, "Still the Century of Corporatism," Philippe C. Schmitter and Gerhard Lehmbruch, eds., *Trends Toward Corporatist Intermediation* (Beverly Hills, CA: Sage Publications, 1979), p. 13.

24. Arend Lijphart, *Democracy in Plural Societies: A Comparative Exploration* (New Haven, CT: Yale University Press, 1977), p. 25.

25. Leo Panitch, "The Development of Corporatism in Liberal Democracies," in Schmitter and Lehmbruch, *Trends Toward Corporatist Intermediation*, pp. 63–94.

26. Gerry Stoker, *Why Politics Matters: Making Democracy Work* (New York: Palgrave, 2006), chapter 1.

27. Russell Dalton, *Citizen Politics: Public Opinion and Political Parties in Advanced Industrial Democracies,* 4th ed. (Washington, DC: CQ Press, 2006), pp. 245–46.

28. Stoker, *Why Politics Matters,* p. 33–34.

CHAPTER 18

1. Samuel P. Huntington, *The Third Wave: Democratization in the Late Twentieth Century* (Norman: University of Oklahoma Press, 1991).

2. Larry Diamond, *Developing Democracy: Toward Consolidation* (Baltimore: The Johns Hopkins University Press, 1999), p. 1.

3. Freedom House, "Freedom in the World, 2000–2001," http://www.freedomhouse.org.

4. Freedom House, "Freedom in the World, 2007 Edition," http://www.freedomhouse.org.

5. Larry Diamond, "Democracy in Retreat," *Foreign Affairs,* March/April 2008, p. 36.

6. Ibid., p. 43.

7. Paul Fairfield, *Why Democracy?* (Albany: State University of New York Press, 2008), p. 91.

8. Peter Frank, "Problems of Democracy in Post Soviet Russia," in Ian Budge and David McKay, eds., *Developing Democracy* (Thousand Oaks, CA: Sage Publications, 1994), pp. 284–5, 290.

9. Andrew Schedler, "Conceptualizing Accountability," in Andrew Schedler, Larry Diamond, and Marc F. Plattner, eds., *The Self-Restraining State Power and Accountability in New Democracies* (Boulder, CO: Lynn Riener, 1999), p. 18.

10. Diamond, *Developing Democracy*, p. 221.

11. Iris Marion Young, "State, Civil Society, and Social Justice," in Ian Shapiro and Casiano Hacker-Cordon, eds., *Democracy's Value* (Cambridge: Cambridge University Press, 1999), p. 153.

12. S. M. Lipset, *Political Man: The Social Basis of Politics* (New York: Doubleday, 1960).

13. World Bank, *World Development Report: 2000/2001* (New York: Oxford University Press, 2001), p. 35.

14. Tatu Vanhanen, *Prospects of Democracy: A Study of 172 Countries* (London: Routledge, 1997), p. 4.

15. Ibid., p. 23.

16. Ibid., p. 99.

17. Amartya Sen, *Development as Freedom* (New York: Anchor Books, 2000), p. 18.

18. Ibid., pp. 36, 144.

19. Ibid., p. 262.

20. Ibid., p. 263.

21. Ibid., p. 295.

22. Hernando de Soto, *The Mystery of Capital* (New York: Basic Books, 2000).

23. Ibid., p. 209.

24. Ibid., p. 5.

25. Ibid., p. 8.

26. Severine Autesserre, "The Trouble with Congo: How Local Disputes Fuel Regional Conflict," *Foreign Affairs,* May/June 2008, p. 94.

27. Ibid.

28. Benazir Bhutto, *Reconciliation: Islam, Democracy and the West* (New York: HarperCollins, 2008), p. 19.

29. Ibid.

30. Ibid., p. 20.

31. Ibid., p.18.

32. Her argument is essentially that radical Islamic "reformers" have hijacked the Muslim religion and that these people are not representative of most Muslims.

33. Joseph Lecler, *Toleration and the Reformation,* vol. 2, tr. by T. L. Westow (New York: Association Press, 1960), p. 3.

34. Daron Acemoglu and James A. Robinson, *Economic Origins of Dictatorship and Democracy* (Cambridge: Cambridge University Press, 2006), p. 224.

35. Ronald Inglehart and Christian Welzel, *Modernization, Cultural Change, and Democracy* (Cambridge: Cambridge University Press, 2005), p. 192–93.

36. Ibid., pp. 219–20.

37. CIA, *The World Factbook 2000,* http://www.ciagov/cia/publications/factbook.

38. For example, Ulrich Beck, *What Is Globalization?* (Cambridge: Polity Press, 2000).

39. Ibid., pp. 20, 42.

40. Howard J. Wiarda, ed., *Comparative Democracy and Democratization* (Toronto: Harcourt College Publishers, 2001), p. 171.

41. Ibid., p. 172.

42. Ibid., pp. 172–3.

CHAPTER 19

1. Freedom House, "Freedom in the World, 2007 Edition," http://www.freedomhouse.org.

2. For a discussion of autocracy see *International Encyclopedia of the Social Sciences* (New York: The Macmillan Company and The Free Press, 1968), vol. 1, pp. 478–80.

3. Aristotle, *Politics*, iv, 10, p. 1219.

4. Baron de Montesquieu, *The Spirit of the Laws* (New York: Hafner, 1949), p. 26.

5. Juan J. Linz, "An Authoritarian Regime: Spain," in Erik Allardt and Stein Rokkan, eds., *Mass Politics: Studies in Political Sociology* (New York: The Free Press, 1970), p. 255.

6. Adam Przeworski, et al., *Democracy and Development: Political Institutions and Well-Being in the World, 1950–1990* (Cambridge: Cambridge University Press, 2000), p. 178.

7. Ibid., p. 271.

8. Giorgio Pini, *The Official Life of Benito Mussolini* (London: Hutchinson, 1939), p. 149.

9. Hannah Arendt, *The Origins of Totalitarianism,* 2nd ed. (New York: World Publishing, 1958), p. 460.

10. Carl J. Friedrich and Zbigniew K. Brzezinski, *Totalitarian Dictatorship and Autocracy,* 2nd ed. (New York: Praeger, 1965); Waldemar Gurian, "The Totalitarian State," *The Review of Politics 40* (1978), pp. 514–27.

11. Arendt, *The Origins of Totalitarianism,* p. 467.

12. Friedrich and Brzezinski, *Totalitarian Dictatorship and Autocracy,* p. 9.

13. Edward McWhinney, *Constitution-Making* (Toronto: University of Toronto Press, 1981), p. 190.

14. Robert Conquest, *The Harvest of Sorrow: Soviet Collectivization and the Terror-Famine* (Edmonton: University of Alberta Press, 1986), p. 306.

15. Schram, *The Political Thought of Mao Tse-tung,* p. 253.

16. Richard Lowenthal, "Beyond Totalitarianism?" in Irving Howe, ed., *1984 Revisited: Totalitarianism in Our Century* (New York: Harper and Row, 1983), pp. 209–67.

17. Robert Jay Lifton, *Revolutionary Immortality* (New York: Random House, 1968), p. 73.

18. McWhinney, *Constitution-Making,* p. 210.

CHAPTER 20

1. Locke, *The Second Treatise of Government,* p. 91.

2. Frank MacKinnon, *The Crown in Canada* (Toronto: McClelland & Stewart, 1976).

3. Constitution Act, 1867, s. 53.

4. Constitution Act, 1867, s. 26.

5. Walter Bagehot, cited in R. MacGregor Dawson and Norman Ward, *The Government of Canada,* 5th ed. (Toronto: University of Toronto Press, 1970), p. 168.

6. C. E. S. Franks, *The Parliament of Canada* (Toronto: University of Toronto Press, 1987), p. 122.

7. Stephen Brooks, *Public Policy in Canada: An Introduction* (Toronto: McClelland & Stewart, 1989), p. 135.

8. Ibid., p. 136.

9. Richard Neustadt, *Presidential Power,* 2nd ed. (New York: Wiley, 1964), p. 42.

10. Stephen Clarkson, *Canada and the Reagan Challenge* (Toronto: James Lorimer, 1982), p. 211.

11. *Congressional Quarterly Almanac 40* (1985), p. 48.

12. Alexander Hamilton, John Jay, and James Madison, *The Federalist, No. 51* (New York: Modern Library, n.d.), p. 337.

13. "Forms of Government," http://en.wikipedia.org/wiki/Forms_of_Government.

CHAPTER 21

1. Canadian Confederation (with a capital C) is an example of federalism. The general term confederation (with a small c) is an abstract concept of political science not particularly associated with Canada.

2. Vernon Bogdanor, *Devolution* (New York: Oxford University Press, 1979), ch. 3.

3. William H. Riker, *Federalism: Origin, Operation, Significance* (Boston: Little, Brown, 1964), p. 2.

4. Garth Stevenson, *Unfulfilled Union: Canadian Federalism and National Unity* (Toronto: Macmillan, 1979), p. 23.

5. Hamilton, Jay, and Madison, *The Federalist,* p. 339.

6. Alan Cairns, "From Interstate to Intrastate Federalism," *Bulletin of Canadian Studies 2* (1979), pp. 13–34.

7. Robert C. Vipond, "From National League of Cities to Garcia: The Framers' Intentions and the Rhetoric of Rights," Conference on Adaptive Federalism, Dartmouth College, June 1989.

8. Roger Gibbins, *Regionalism: Territorial Politics in Canada and the U.S.* (Scarborough, ON: Butterworths, 1982).

9. Discussions of different versions of federalism are found in Alan C. Cairns, *Charter versus Federalism: The Dilemmas of Constitutional Reform* (Montreal: McGill–Queen's University Press, 1992); Guy Laforest, *Trudeau and the End of a Canadian Dream,* tr. Paul Leduc and Michelle Weinroth (Montreal: McGill–Queen's University Press, 1995); Kenneth McRoberts, *Misconceiving Canada: The Struggle for National Unity* (Toronto: Oxford University Press. 1997).

10. Charles Taylor, "The Politics of Recognition," in Amy Gutmann, *Multiculturalism* (Princeton: Princeton University Press, 1994), pp. 38, 52, 61, 64.

11. Laforest, op. cit., pp. 4, 86.

12. Ibid.

13. McRoberts, op. cit., pp. 30, 249.

14. Ibid., pp. 275–76.

PART 4
CHAPTER 22

1. Ludwig von Bertalanffy, *General System Theory* (New York: George Braziller, 1968). James A. Bill and Robert L. Hardgrave, *Comparative Politics: The Quest for Theory* (Columbus, OH: Charles E. Merrill, 1973), ch. 4.

2. Easton, *A Systems Analysis of Political Life,* p. 32.

3. Almond and Powell, *Comparative Politics,* pp. 16–41.

4. William D. Coleman and Grace Skogstad, eds., *Policy Communities and Public Policy in Canada: A Structural Approach* (Mississauga, ON: Copp Clark Pitman, 1990), p. 25.

5. Ibid.

6. Leslie A. Pal, *Public Policy Analysis,* 2nd ed. (Toronto: Nelson Canada, 1992), p. 7.

CHAPTER 23

1. Joseph LaPalombara, *Politics within Nations* (Englewood Cliffs, NJ: Prentice-Hall, 1974), p. 509.

2. *The Canadian Oxford Dictionary* (Toronto: Oxford University Press, 1998), p. 1137.

3. Murray Dobbin, *Preston Manning and the Reform Party* (Toronto: James Lorimer, 1991), p. 215.

4. Maurice Duverger, *Political Parties,* 3rd ed. (New York: Wiley, 1978).

5. Roberto Michels, *Political Parties* (New York: Free Press, 1962; first published 1911).

6. Lisa Young and Joanna Everitt, *Advocacy Groups* (Vancouver: University of British Columbia Press, 2004).

7. Young and Everitt, *Advocacy Groups,* p. 6.

8. Sidney Verba, Kay Lehman Schlozman, and Henry E. Brady, *Voice and Equality: Civic Voluntarism in American Politics* (Cambridge, MA: Harvard University Press, 1995), p. 50.

9. Verba et al., *Voice and Equality;* Jane Mansbridge, "A Deliberative Theory of Interest Representation," in Marc Petracca, ed. *The Politics of Interests* (Boulder, CO: Westview Press, 1992); Robert D. Putnam, *Bowling Alone: The Collapse and Revival of American Community* (New York: Touchstone, 2000).

10. Gabriel A. Almond and James S. Coleman, eds., *The Politics of Developing Nations* (Princeton, NJ: Princeton University Press, 1960), pp. 33–34.

11. Mancur Olson, *The Logic of Collective Action* (Cambridge, MA: Harvard University Press, 1965).

12. Russell Hardin, *Collective Action* (Baltimore: Johns Hopkins University Press, 1982).

13. Young and Everitt, *Advocacy Groups,* p. 79.

14. John Sawatsky, *The Insiders: Government, Business, and the Lobbyists* (Toronto: McClelland & Stewart, 1987).

15. Canada, Office of the Registrar of Lobbyists, *Annual Report, 2006–2007* (Ottawa: Office of the Registrar of Lobbyists, 2007), [online] available at http://dsp-psd.pwgsc.gc.ca/collection_2007/orl-bdl/Iu77-1-1-2007E.pdf.

16. David B. Truman, *The Governmental Process* (New York: Alfred A. Knopf, 1951).

17. Thomas Ferguson, *Golden Rule: The Investment Theory of Political Parties and the Logic of Money-Driven Political Systems* (Chicago: University of Chicago Press, 1995); William D. Coleman, *Business and Politics: A Study of Collective Action* (Kingston and Montreal: McGill–Queen's University Press, 1988).

18. Jean-Jacques Rousseau, *The Social Contract* (New York: Hafner, 1947).

19. Alexander Hamilton, John Jay, and James Madison, *The Federalist* (New York: Modern Library, n.d.).

20. Jacquetta Newman and A. Brian Tanguay, "Crashing the Party: The Politics of Interest Groups and New Social Movements" in Joanna Everitt and Brenda O'Neill, eds. *Citizen Politics: Research and Theory in Canadian Political Behaviour* (Don Mills, ON: Oxford, 2002), pp. 387–412.

21. Miriam Smith, *A Civil Society? Collective Actors in Canadian Political Life* (Peterborough, ON: Broadview, 2005), p. 36.

22. See Russell J. Dalton and Manfred Kuechler, eds. *Challenging the Political Order: New Social and Political Movements in Western Democracies* (New York: Oxford University Press, 1990); John Baylis and Steve Smith, eds., *The Globalization of World Politics: An Introduction to International Relations* (New York: Oxford University Press, 1997); and R. J. Barry Jones, *The World Turned Upside Down? Globalization and the Future of the State* (New York: Manchester University Press, 2000).

23. Smith, *A Civil Society?* p. 78.

CHAPTER 24

1. Television Bureau of Advertising Online, "TV Basics: Television Households." [online] available at http://www.tvb.org/nav/build_frameset.aspx. Accessed on August 6, 2008.

2. Internet World Stats, "Internet Usage and Population Statistics for North America." [online] available at http://www.internetworldstats.com/stats14.htm. Accessed on August 6, 2008.

3. David Taras, *Power and Betrayal in the Canadian Media,* 2nd ed. (Peterborough, ON: Broadview Press, 2001), p. 33.

4. Rusell J. Dalton, *Citizen Politics: Public Opinion and Political Parties in Advanced Industrial Democracies,* 4th ed. (Washington, DC: CQ Press, 2006), pp. 21–22.

5. See Taras, *Power and Betrayal,* pp. 104–106

6. Aaron Smith and Lee Rainie, *The Internet and the 2008 Election* (Washington, DC: Pew Internet and American Life Project, 2008), p. 3.

7. Ibid., pp. 10–11.

8. John W. Kingdon, *Agendas, Alternatives and Public Policies,* 2nd ed. (New York: HarperCollins, 1995).

9. This hypothesis was first stated in Bernard C. Cohen, *The Press and Foreign Policy* (Princeton, NJ: Princeton University Press, 1963), p. 13.

10. Stuart Soroka, *Agenda-Setting Dynamics in Canada* (Vancouver: University of British Columbia Press, 2002).

11. Clyde Wilcox and Barbara Norrander, "Introduction: The Diverse Paths to Understanding Public Opinion," in Barbara Norrander and Clyde Wilcox, eds. *Understanding Public Opinion,* 2nd ed. (Washington, DC: CQ Press, 2002), p. 5.

12. Herbert J. Gans, *Deciding What's News* (New York: Pantheon Books, 1979), p. 88.

13. Kimberley Noble, *Bound and Gagged: Libel Chill and the Right to Publish* (Toronto: HarperCollins, 1992).

14. Grant Robertson, "New Rules to Crimp Broadcast Mergers," *The Globe and Mail,* January 15, 2008. [online] Accessed on August 7, 2008.

15. Taras, *Power and Betrayal,* p. 219.

16. Ibid., p. 195.

17. Rosemary Righter, *Whose News? Politics, the Press and the Third World* (London: Burnett Books, 1978), p. 190.

CHAPTER 25

1. Martin Harrop and William L Miller, *Elections and Voters: A Comparative Introduction* (London: Macmillan Education, 1987), p. 2.

2. John Plamenatz, "Electoral Studies and Democratic Theory," *Political Studies 6* (February 1958), p. 9.

3. Michael Saward, *Democracy* (Cambridge: Polity, 2003), p. 49.

4. David M. Farrell, *Electoral Systems: A Comparative Introduction* (London: Palgrave, 2001), p. 3.

5. Maurice Duverger, *Political Parties: Their Organization and Activity in the Modern State* (London: Methuen, 1954).

6. The term *gerrymander,* which means to draw constituency lines so as to achieve a deliberate result, comes from Elbridge Gerry, governor of Massachusetts in 1812, who tried to favour his party at the time of redistricting. The constituency that he drew looked to some like a salamander, and thus the practice was named. See Farrell, *Electoral Systems,* p. 14.

7. Heather MacIvor, "Women and the Canadian Electoral System," in Manon Tremblay and Linda Trimble, eds., *Women and Electoral Politics in Canada* (Don Mills, ON: Oxford, 2003), pp. 22–36.

8. This minimum is currently set at 12.5 percent of registered voters. See Farrell, *Electoral Systems,* p. 52.

9. Mill, *Considerations on Representative Government,* p. 141.

10. Canada, Parliamentary Information and Research Branch, *Electoral Reform Initiatives in Canadian Provinces* (Ottawa: Library of Parliament, 2007), available online at www.parl.gc.ca/information/library/PRBpubs/prb0417-e.htm.

11. Russell J. Dalton and Martin P. Wattenberg, "The Not So Simple Act of Voting," in Ada W. Finifter, ed., *Political Science: The State of the Discipline II* (Washington, DC: The American Political Science Association, 1993).

12. Elisabeth Gidengil, "Canada Votes: A Quarter Century of Canadian National Election Studies," *Canadian Journal of Political Science 25* (June 1992), pp. 219–48.

13. Ibid., pp. 222 and 234.

14. Ibid., p. 230.

15. Ibid., p. 248.

16. André Blais, Elisabeth Gidengil, Richard Nadeau, and Neil Nevitte, *Anatomy of a Liberal Victory: Making Sense of the Vote in the 2000 Canadian Election* (Peterborough, ON: Broadview, 2002), p. 191.

17. Harold D. Clarke, Jane Jensen, Lawrence LeDuc, and Jon H. Pammett, *Absent Mandate: Canadian Electoral Politics in an Era of Restructuring* (Toronto: Gage, 1996).

18. MacLean, George A. and Brenda O'Neill, eds. *Ideas, Interests and Issues: Readings in Introductory Politics.* Toronto: Pearson Prentice Hall, 2006.

19. Institute for Democracy and Electoral Assistance, *Turnout in the World—Country by Country Performance*, available online at www.idea.int/vt/survey/voter_turnout_pop2.cfm.

CHAPTER 26

1. C. E. S. Franks, *The Parliament of Canada* (Toronto: University of Toronto Press, 1987), pp. 4–5.

2. See, in general, Hanna Pitkin, *The Concept of Representation* (Berkeley: University of California Press, 1967); and A. H. Birch, *Representation* (London: Macmillan, 1971).

3. Edmund Burke, *Burke's Speeches and Letters on American Affairs* (London: E. P. Dutton, 1908), p. 73.

4. *Maclean's,* 4 January 1993, p. 19.

5. Reform Party of Canada, *Principles and Policies,* 1991, p. 39.

6. Jennifer Smith, "Democracy and the Canadian House of Commons at the Millennium," *Canadian Public Administration 42* (Winter 1999), p. 418.

7. Adams, "Thoughts on Government," in *The Political Writings of John Adams,* p. 86.

8. Réjean Pelletier, "Responsible Government: Victory or Defeat for Parliament?" in F. Leslie Seidle and Louis Massicotte, eds., *Taking Stock of 150 Years of Responsible Government in Canada* (Ottawa: The Canadian Study of Parliament Group, 1999), p. 66.

CHAPTER 27

1. Peter Hennessy, *Cabinet* (Oxford: Basil Blackwell, 1986).

2. Donald J. Savoie, *Governing from the Centre: The Concentration of Power in Canadian Politics* (Toronto: University of Toronto Press, 1999), p. 12.

3. Eddie Goldenberg, *The Way It Works: Inside Ottawa* (Toronto: McClelland & Stewart, 2006), p. 107.

4. R. MacGregor Dawson, *The Government of Canada,* 4th ed. (Toronto: University of Toronto Press, 1963), p. 185.

5. Savoie, *Governing from the Centre,* p. 7.

6. Donald J. Savoie, *Court Government and the Collapse of Accountability in Canada and the United Kingdom* (Toronto: University of Toronto Press, 2008).

7. Theodore Lowi and Benjamin Gindsberg, *American Government: Freedom and Power* (New York: W. W. Norton, 1990), p. 273.

CHAPTER 28

1. Colin Leys, *Politics in Britain* (Toronto: University of Toronto Press, 1983), p. 269.

2. William A. Niskanen, Jr., *Bureaucracy and Representative Government* (Chicago: Aldine–Atherton, 1971), pp. 36–42.

3. Jonathan Lynn and Antony Jay, *The Complete Yes Minister* (New York: Harper and Row, 1981), p. 59.

4. David Osborne and Ted Gaebler, *Reinventing Government: How the Entrepreneurial Spirit Is Transforming the Public Sector* (Reading, MA: Addison-Wesley, 1992).

5. B. Guy Peters and Donald J. Savoie, eds., *Governance in a Changing Environment* (Montreal: McGill–Queen's University Press, 1995).

6. Bert A. Rockman, "The Changing Role of the State," in B. Guy Peters and Donald J. Savoie, eds., *Taking Stock: Assessing the Public Sector Reforms* (Montreal: McGill–Queen's University Press, 1998), p. 35.

7. Leslie A. Pal, ed., *How Ottawa Spends 2001–2002: Power in Transition* (Don Mills, ON: Oxford University Press, 2001), p. 319. For updates after 2001, see the federal budgets posted on the Canadian government's website, www.gc.ca.

8. Michael Paquin, "Innovation in Public Sector Management," in Peters and Savoie, *Taking Stock,* pp. 225, 226, 232, 240.

9. John Hart, "Central Agencies and Departments: Empowerment and Coordination," in Peters and Savoie, *Taking Stock,* p. 287.

10. Paul Thomas, "The Changing Nature of Accountability," in Peters and Savoie, *Taking Stock,* p. 381.

11. John Hart, "Central Agencies and Departments," p. 289.

12. Patricia W. Ingraham, B. Guy Peters, and Donald P. Moynihan, "Public Employment and the Future of the Public Service," in B. Guy Peters and Donald J. Savoie, eds., *Governance in the Twenty-first Century: Revitalizing the Public Sector* (Montreal: McGill–Queen's University Press, 2000), p. 420.

CHAPTER 29

1. Thomas Flanagan, "Policy-Making by Exegesis: The Abolition of 'Mandatory Retirement' in Manitoba," *Canadian Public Policy 11* (1985), pp. 40–53.

2. *Edwards et al. v. Attorney General of Canada et al.*, [1930] A.C. 124.

3. Originally, the Bill of Rights applied only to the federal Congress, but the Supreme Court held that it was extended through the Fourteenth Amendment to the state legislatures.

4. [1979] 2 S.C.R. 1032.

5. M. Elizabeth Atcheson, Mary Eberts, and Beth Symes, *Women and Legal Action: Precedents, Resources and Strategies for the Future* (Ottawa: Canadian Advisory Council on the Status of Women, 1984), pp. 166–67.

6. *Delgamuukw v. British Columbia,* [1997] 3 S.C.R. 1010.

7. *R. v. Marshall,* [1993] 3 S.C.R. 456; [1993] 3 S.C.R. 533.

8. See, for example, Theodore J. Lowi, *The End of Liberalism,* 2nd ed. (New York: W. W. Norton, 1979), ch. 11

9. Alan Cairns, *Charter versus Federalism: The Dilemmas of Constitutional Reform* (Montreal: McGill–Queen's University Press, 1992), p. 125.

10. Aharon Barak, *The Judge In A Democracy* (Princeton: Princeton University Press, 2006), pp. 265–66.

11. Ted Morton's chapter is an excellent discussion of attempts at reforming the judicial appointment process.

12. Peter Russell, "Conclusion," in Kate Malleson and Peter Russell, eds., *Appointing Judges in an Age of Judicial Power: Critical Perspectives from around the World* (Toronto: University of Toronto Press, 2006), p. 420.

13. *R. v. Therens,* [1985] 1 S.C.R. 613.

14. F. L. Morton and M. J. Withey, "Charting the Charter, 1982–1985: A Statistical Analysis," *Canadian Human Rights Yearbook,* 1987.

15. Peter W. Hogg and Allison A. Thornton, "The Charter Dialogue Between Courts and Legislatures," *Policy Options* (April 1999).

APPENDIX A

Constitution Act, 1867
(formerly British North America Act, 1867)

Below are a few sections of the Act of particular interest to Canadian students of political science at the introductory level.

. . . .

Preamble

WHEREAS the Provinces of Canada, Nova Scotia and New Brunswick have expressed their Desire to be federally united into One Dominion under the Crown of the United Kingdom of Great Britain and Ireland, with a Constitution similar in Principle to that of the United Kingdom:

And whereas such a Union would conduce to the Welfare of the Provinces and promote the Interests of the British Empire:

And whereas on the Establishment of the Union by Authority of Parliament it is expedient, not only that the Constitution of the Legislative Authority in the Dominion be provided for, but also that the Nature of the Executive Government therein be declared:

And whereas it is expedient that Provision be made for the eventual Admission into the Union of other Parts of British North America:

. . . .

VI. DISTRIBUTION OF LEGISLATIVE POWERS.

Powers of the Parliament

Legislative Authority of Parliament of Canada

91.   It shall be lawful for the Queen, by and with the Advice and Consent of the Senate and House of Commons, to make Laws for the Peace, Order, and good Government of Canada, in relation to all Matters not coming within the Classes of Subjects by this Act assigned exclusively to the Legislatures of the Provinces; and for greater Certainty, but not so as to restrict the Generality of the foregoing Terms of this Section, it is hereby declared that (notwithstanding anything in this Act) the exclusive Legislative Authority of the Parliament of Canada extends to all Matters coming within the Classes of Subjects next herein-after enumerated; that is to say,—

1. The amendment from time to time of the Constitution of Canada, except as regards matters coming within the classes of subjects by this Act assigned exclusively to the Legislatures of the provinces, or as regards

rights or privileges by this or any other Constitutional Act granted or secured to the Legislature or the Government of a province, or to any class of persons with respect to schools or as regards the use of English or the French language or as regards the requirements that there shall be a session of the Parliament of Canada at least once each year, and that no House of Commons shall continue for more than five years from the day of the return of the Writs for choosing the House: provided, however, that a House of Commons may in time of real or apprehended war, invasion or insurrection be continued by the Parliament of Canada if such continuation is not opposed by the votes of more than one-third of the members of such House.

1A. The Public Debt and Property.
2. The regulation of Trade and Commerce.
2A. Unemployment insurance.
3. The raising of Money by any Mode or System of Taxation.
4. The borrowing of Money on the Public Credit.
5. Postal Service.
6. The Census and Statistics.
7. Militia, Military and Naval Service, and Defence.
8. The fixing of and providing for the Salaries and Allowances of Civil and other Officers of the Government of Canada.
9. Beacons, Buoys, Lighthouses, and Sable Island.
10. Navigation and Shipping.
11. Quarantine and the Establishment and Maintenance of Marine Hospitals.
12. Sea Coast and Inland Fisheries.
13. Ferries between a Province and any British or Foreign Country or between Two Provinces.
14. Currency and Coinage.
15. Banking, Incorporation of Banks, and the Issue of Paper Money.
16. Savings Banks.
17. Weights and Measures.
18. Bills of Exchange and Promissory Notes.
19. Interest.
20. Legal Tender.
21. Bankruptcy and Insolvency.
22. Patents of Invention and Discovery.
23. Copyrights.
24. Indians, and Lands reserved for the Indians.
25. Naturalization and Aliens.
26. Marriage and Divorce.
27. The Criminal Law, except the Constitution of Courts of Criminal Jurisdiction, but including the Procedure in Criminal Matters.

28. The Establishment, Maintenance, and Management of Penitentiaries.

29. Such Classes of Subjects as are expressly excepted in the Enumeration of the Classes of Subjects by this Act assigned exclusively to the Legislatures of the Provinces.

And any Matter coming within any of the Classes of Subjects enumerated in this Section shall not be deemed to come within the Class of Matters of a local or private Nature comprised in the Enumeration of the Classes of Subjects by this Act assigned exclusively to the Legislatures of the Provinces.

Exclusive Powers of Provincial Legislatures

Subjects of exclusive Provincial Legislation

92.   In each Province the Legislature may exclusively make Laws in relation to coming within the Classes of Subject next herein-after enumerated; that is to say,—

1. The Amendment from Time to Time, not withstanding anything in this Act, of the Constitution of the Province, except as regards the Office of Lieutenant Governor.

2. Direct Taxation within the Province in order to the raising of a Revenue for Provincial Purposes.

3. The borrowing of Money on the sole Credit of the Province.

4. The Establishment and Tenure of Provincial Offices and the Appointment and Payment of Provincial Officers.

5. The Management and Sale of the Public Lands belonging to the Province and of the Timber and Wood thereon.

6. The Establishment, Maintenance, and Management of Public and Reformatory Prisons in and for the Province.

7. The Establishment, Maintenance, and Management of Hospitals, Asylums, Charities and Eleemosynary Institutions in and for the Province, other than Marine Hospitals.

8. Municipal Institutions in the Province.

9. Shop, Saloon, Tavern, Auctioneer, and other Licences in order to the raising of a Revenue for Provincial, Local, or Municipal Purposes.

10. Local Works and Undertakings other than such as are of the following Classes:—

    (a) Lines of Steam or other Ships, Railways, Canals, Telegraphs, and other Works and Undertakings connecting the Province with any other or others of the Provinces, or extending beyond the Limits of the Province;

    (b) Lines of Steam Ships between the Province and any British or Foreign Country;

    (c) Such Works as, although wholly situate within the Province, are before or after their Execution declared by the Parliament of Canada to be for the general Advantage of Canada or for the Advantage of Two or more of the Provinces.

11. The Incorporation of Companies with Provincial Objects.

12. The Solemnization of Marriage in the Province.

13. Property and Civil Rights in the Province.

14. The Administration of Justice in the Province, including the Constitution, Maintenance, and Organization of Provincial Courts, both of Civil and of Criminal Jurisdiction, and including Procedure in Civil Matters in those Courts.

15. The Imposition of Punishment by Fine, Penalty, or Imprisonment for enforcing any Law of the Province made in relation to any Matter coming within any of the Classes of Subjects enumerated in this Section.

16. Generally all Matters of a merely local or private Nature in the Province.

. . . .

For section 92A, see sections 50 and 51 of the Constitution Act, 1982, in Appendix B in this volume.

. . . .

Education

93.   In and for each Province the Legislature may exclusively make Laws in relation to Education, subject and according to the following Provisions:—

Legislation respecting Education

(1) Nothing in any such Law shall prejudicially affect any Right or Privilege with respect to Denominational Schools which any Class of Persons have by Law in the Province at the Union:

(2) All the Powers, Privileges, and Duties at the Union by Law conferred and imposed in Upper Canada on the Separate Schools and School Trustees of the Queen's Roman Catholic Subjects shall be and the same are hereby extended to the Dissentient Schools of the Queen's Protestant and Roman Catholic Subjects in Quebec:

(3) Where in any Province a System of Separate or Dissentient Schools exists by Law at the Union or is thereafter established by the Legislature of the Province, an Appeal shall lie to the Governor General in Council from any Act or Decision of any Provincial Authority affecting any Right or Privilege of the Protestant or Roman Catholic Minority of the Queen's Subjects in relation to Education:

(4) In case any such Provincial Law as from Time to Time seems to the Governor General in Council requisite for the due Execution of the Provisions of this Section is not made, or in case any Decision of the Governor General in Council on any Appeal under this section is not duly executed by the proper Provincial Authority in that Behalf, then and in every such Case, and as far only as the Circumstances of each Case require, the Parliament of Canada may make remedial Laws for the due Execution of the Provisions of this Section and of any Decision of the Governor-General in Council under this Section.

. . . .

Old Age Pensions

Legislation
respecting old age
pensions and
supplementary
benefits

94A.   The Parliament of Canada may make laws in relation to old age pensions and supplementary benefits, including survivors and disability benefits irrespective of age, but no such law shall affect the operation of any law present or future of a provincial legislature in relation to any such matter.

. . . .

Agriculture and Immigration

Concurrent Power
of Legislation
respecting
Agriculture, etc.

95.   In each Province the Legislature may make Laws in relation to Agriculture in the Province, and to Immigration into the Province, and it is hereby declared that the Parliament of Canada may from Time to Time make Laws in relation to Agriculture in all or any of the Provinces, and to Immigration into all or any of the Provinces; and any Law of the Legislature of a province relative to Agriculture or to Immigration shall have effect in and for the Province as long and as far only as it is not repugnant to any Act of the Parliament of Canada.

. . . .

Use of English and
French Languages

133.   Either the English or the French Language may be used by any Person in the Debates of the Houses of the Parliament of Canada and of the Legislature of Quebec; and both those Languages shall be used in the respective Records and Journals of those Houses; and either of those Languages may be used by any Person or in any Pleading or Process in or issuing from any Court of Canada established under this Act, and in or from all or any of the Courts of Quebec.

The Acts of the Parliament of Canada and of the Legislature of Quebec shall be printed and published in both those languages.

APPENDIX B

Constitution Act, 1982
Schedule B to Canada Act 1982 (U.K.)

PART I

CANADIAN CHARTER OF RIGHTS AND FREEDOMS

Whereas Canada is founded upon principles that recognize the supremacy of God and the rule of law:

Guarantee of Rights and Freedoms

Rights and Freedoms in Canada

1. The *Canadian Charter of Rights and Freedoms* guarantees the rights and freedoms set out in it subject only to such reasonable limits prescribed by law as can be demonstrably justified in a free and democratic society.

Fundamental Freedoms

Fundamental freedoms

2. Everyone has the following fundamental freedoms:
(a) freedom of conscience and religion;
(b) freedom of thought, belief, opinion and expression, including freedom of the press and other media of communication;
(c) freedom of peaceful assembly; and
(d) freedom of association.

Democratic Rights

Democratic rights of citizens

3. Every citizen of Canada has the right to vote in an election of members of the House of Commons or of a legislative assembly and to be qualified for membership therein.

Maximum duration of legislative bodies

4. (1) No House of Commons and no legislative assembly shall continue for longer than five years from the date fixed for the return of the writs at a general election of its members.

Continuation in special circumstances

(2) In time of real or apprehended war, invasion or insurrection, a House of Commons may be continued by Parliament and a legislative assembly may be continued by the legislature beyond five years if such

continuation is not opposed by the votes of more than one-third of the members of the House of Commons or the legislative assembly, as the case may be.

Annual sitting of legislative bodies

5.   There shall be a sitting of Parliament and of each legislature at least once every twelve months.

Mobility Rights

Mobility of citizens

6.   (1) Every citizen of Canada has the right to enter, remain in and leave Canada.

Rights to move and gain livelihood

(2)   Every citizen of Canada and every person who has the status of a permanent resident of Canada has the right

(a)   to move to and take up residence in any province; and

(b)   to pursue the gaining of a livelihood in any province.

Limitation

(3)   The rights specified in subsection (2) are subject to

(a)   any laws or practices of general application in force in a province other than those that discriminate among persons primarily on the basis of province of present or previous residence; and

(b)   any laws providing for reasonable residency requirements as a qualification for the receipt of publicly provided social services.

Affirmative action programs

(4)   Subsections (2) and (3) do not preclude any law, program or activity that has as its object the amelioration in a province of conditions of individuals in that province who are socially or economically disadvantaged if the rate of employment in that province is below the rate of employment in Canada.

Legal Rights

Life, liberty and security of person

7.   Everyone has the right to life, liberty, and security of the person and the right not to be deprived thereof except in accordance with the principles of fundamental justice.

Search or seizure

8.   Everyone has the right to be secure against unreasonable search or seizure.

Detention or imprisonment

9.   Everyone has the right not to be arbitrarily detained or imprisoned.

Arrest or detention

10.   Everyone has the right on arrest or detention

(a)   to be informed promptly of the reasons therefore;

(b)   to retain and instruct counsel without delay and to be informed of that right; and

(c)   to have the validity of the detention determined by way of *habeas corpus* and to be released if the detention is not lawful.

Proceedings in criminal and penal matters

11.   Any person charged with an offence has the right

(a)   to be informed without unreasonable delay of the specific offence;

(b)   to be tried within a reasonable time;

(c)   not to be compelled to be a witness in proceedings against that person in respect of the offence;

(d)   to be presumed innocent until proven guilty according to law in a fair and public hearing by an independent and impartial tribunal;

(e)   not to be denied reasonable bail without just cause;

(f)   except in the case of an offence under military law tried before a military tribunal, to the benefit of trial by jury where the maximum punishment for the offence is imprisonment for five years or a more severe punishment;

(g)   not to be found guilty on account of any act or omission unless, at the time of the act or omission, it constituted an offence under Canadian or international law or was criminal according to the general principles of law recognized by the community of nations;

(h)   if finally acquitted of the offence, not to be tried for it again and, if finally found guilty and punished for the offence, not to be tried or punished for it again; and

(i)   if found guilty of the offence and if the punishment for the offence has been varied between the time of commission and the time of sentencing, to the benefit of the lesser punishment.

Treatment or punishment

12.   Everyone has the right not to be subjected to any cruel and unusual treatment or punishment.

Self-crimination

13.   A witness who testifies in any proceedings has the right not to have any incriminating evidence so given used to incriminate that witness in any other proceedings, except in a prosecution for perjury or for the giving of contradictory evidence.

Interpreter

14.   A party or witness in any proceedings who does not understand or speak the language in which the proceedings are conducted or who is deaf has the right to the assistance of an interpreter.

Equality Rights

Equality before and under law and equal protection and benefit of law

15.   (1) Every individual is equal before and under the law and has the right to the equal protection and equal benefit of the law without discrimination and, in particular, without discrimination based on race, national or ethnic origin, colour, religion, sex, age or mental or physical disability.

Affirmative action programs

(2)   Subsection (1) does not preclude any law, program or activity that has as its object the amelioration of conditions of disadvantaged individuals or groups including those that are disadvantaged because of race, national or ethnic origin, colour, religion, sex, age or mental or physical disability.

Official Languages of Canada

Official languages of Canada

16.   (1) English and French are the official languages of Canada and have equality of status and equal rights and privileges as to their use in all instructions of the Parliament and government of Canada.

Official languages in New Brunswick

(2) English and French are the official languages of New Brunswick and have equality of status and equal rights and privileges as to their use in all institutions of the legislature and government of New Brunswick.

Advancement of status and use

(3) Nothing in this Charter limits the authority of Parliament or a legislature to advance the equality of status or use of English and French.

Proceedings of Parliament

17. (1) Everyone has the right to use English or French in any debates and other proceedings of Parliament.

Proceedings of New Brunswick legislature

(2) Everyone has the right to use English or French in any debates and other proceedings of the legislature of New Brunswick.

Parliamentary statuses and records

18. (1) The statutes, records and journals of Parliament shall be printed and published in English and French and both language versions are equally authoritative.

New Bruswick statutes and records

(2) The statutes, records and journals of the legislature of New Brunswick shall be printed and published in English and French and both language versions are equally authoritative.

Proceedings in courts established by Parliament
Proceedings in New Brunswick courts

19. (1) Either English or French may be used by any person in, or in any pleading in or process issuing from, any court established by Parliament.

(2) Either English or French may be used by any person in, or in any pleading in or process issuing from, any court of New Brunswick.

Communications by public with federal institutions

20. (1) Any member of the public in Canada has the right to communicate with, and to receive available services from, any head or central office of an institution of the Parliament or government of Canada in English or French, and has the same right with respect to any other office of any such institution where

(a) there is a significant demand for communications with and services from that office in such language; or

(b) due to the nature of the office, it is reasonable that communications with and services from that office be available in both English and French.

Communications by public with New Brunswick institutions

(2) Any member of the public in New Brunswick has the right to communicate with, and to receive available services from, any office of an institution of the legislature or government of New Brunswick in English or French.

Continuation of existing constitutional provisions

21. Nothing in sections 16 to 20 abrogates or derogates from any right, privilege or obligation with respect to the English and French languages, or either of them, that exists or is continued by virtue of any other provision of the Constitution of Canada.

Rights and privileges preserved

22. Nothing in sections 16 to 20 abrogates or derogates from any legal or customary right or privilege acquired or enjoyed either before or after the coming into force of this Charter with respect to any language that is not English or French.

Minority Language Educational Rights

Language of
instruction

23.   (1) Citizens of Canada

(a)   whose first language learned and still understood is that of the English or French linguistic minority population of the province in which they reside, or

(b)   who have received their primary school instruction in Canada in English or French and reside in a province where the language in which they received that instruction is the language of the English or French linguistic minority population of the province, have the right to have their children receive primary and secondary school instruction in that language in that province.

Continuity of
language
instruction

(2)   Citizens of Canada of whom any child has received or is receiving primary or secondary school instruction in English or French in Canada, have the right to have all their children receive primary and secondary school instruction in the same language.

Applications where
numbers warrant

(3)   The right of citizens of Canada under subsections (1) and (2) to have their children receive primary and secondary school instruction in the language of the English or French linguistic minority population of a province

(a)   applies wherever in the province the number of children citizens who have such a right is sufficient to warrant the provision to them out of public funds of minority language instruction; and

(b)   includes, where the number of those children so warrants, the right to have them receive that instruction in minority language educational facilities provided out of public funds.

Enforcement

Enforcement of
guaranteed rights
and freedoms

24.   (1) Anyone whose rights or freedoms, as guaranteed by this Charter, have been infringed or denied may apply to a court of competent jurisdiction to obtain such remedy as the court considers appropriate and just in the circumstances.

Exclusion of
evidence bringing
administration of
justice into
disrepute

(2)   Where, in proceedings under subsection (1), a court concludes that evidence was obtained in a manner that infringed or denied any rights or freedoms guaranteed by this Charter, the evidence shall be excluded if it is established that, having regard to all the circumstances, the admission of it in the proceedings would bring the administration of justice into disrepute.

General

Aboriginal rights
and freedoms not
affected by Charter

25.   The guarantee in this Charter of certain rights and freedoms shall not be construed so as to abrogate or derogate from any aboriginal treaty or other rights or freedoms that pertain to the aboriginal peoples of Canada including

(a)   any rights or freedoms that have been recognized by the Royal Proclamation of October 7, 1763; and

(b)   any rights or freedoms that now exist by way of land claims agreements or may be so acquired.[1]

Other rights and freedoms not affected by Charter

26.   The guarantee in this Charter of certain rights and freedoms shall not be construed as denying the existence of any other rights or freedoms that exist in Canada.

Multicultural heritage

27.   This Charter shall be interpreted in a manner consistent with the preservation and enhancement of the multicultural heritage of Canadians.

Rights guaranteed equally to both sexes

28.   Notwithstanding anything in this Charter, the rights and freedoms referred to in it are guaranteed equally to male and female persons.

Rights respecting certain schools preserved

29.   Nothing in this Charter abrogates or derogates from any rights or privileges guaranteed by or under the Constitution of Canada in respect of denomination, separate or dissentient schools.

Application to territories and territorial authorities

30.   A reference in this Charter to a province or to the legislative assembly or legislature of a province shall be deemed to include a reference to the Yukon Territory and the Northwest Territories, or to the appropriate legislative authority thereof, as the case may be.

Legislative powers not extended

31.   Nothing in this Charter extends the legislative powers of any body or authority.

Application of Charter

Application of Charter

32.   (1) This Charter applies

(a)   to the Parliament and government of Canada in respect of all matters within the authority of Parliament including all matters relating to the Yukon Territory and Northwest Territories; and

(b)   to the legislature and government of each province in respect of all matters within the authority of the legislature of each province.

Exception

(2)   Notwithstanding subsection (1), section 15 shall not have effect until three years after this section comes into force.

Exception where express declaration

33.   (1) Parliament or the legislature of a province may expressly declare in an Act of Parliament or of the legislature, as the case may be, that the Act or a provision thereof shall operate notwithstanding a provision in section 2 or sections 7 to 15 of this Charter.

Operation of exception

(2)   An Act or a provision of an Act in respect of which a declaration made under this section is in effect shall have such operation as it would have but for the provision of this Charter referred to in the declaration.

Five year limitation

(3)   A declaration made under subsection (1) shall cease to have effect five years after it comes into force or on such earlier date as may be specified in the declaration.

Re-enactment

(4)   Parliament or the legislature of a province may re-enact a declaration made under subsection (1).

Five year limitation

(5)   Subsection (3) applies in respect of a re-enactment made under subsection (4).

Citation

Citation

34. This Part may be cited as the *Canadian Charter of Rights and Freedoms.*

PART II

RIGHTS OF THE ABORIGINAL PEOPLES OF CANADA

Recognition of existing aboriginal and treaty rights
Definition of "aboriginal peoples of Canada" Land claims agreement

35. (1) The existing aboriginal and treaty rights of the aboriginal peoples of Canada are hereby recognized and affirmed.

(2)   In this Act, "aboriginal peoples of Canada" includes the Indian, Inuit and Métis peoples of Canada.

(3)   For greater certainty, in subsection (1) "treaty rights" includes rights that now exist by way of land claims agreements or may be so acquired.

Aboriginal and treaty rights are guaranteed equally to both sexes

(4)   Notwithstanding any other provision of this Act, the aboriginal and treaty rights referred to in subsection (1) are guaranteed equally to male and female persons.[2]

Commitment to participation in constitutional conference

35.1 The government of Canada and the provincial governments are committed to the principle that, before any amendment is made to Class 24 of section 91 of the "Constitution Act, 1867," to section 25 of this Act or to this Part,

(a)   a constitutional conference that includes in its agenda an item relating to the proposed amendment, composed of the Prime Minister of Canada and the first ministers of the provinces, will be convened by the Prime Minister of Canada; and

(b)   the Prime Minister of Canada will invite representatives of the aboriginal peoples of Canada to participate in the discussion on that item.[3]

PART III

EQUALIZATION AND REGIONAL DISPARITIES

Commitment to promote equal opportunities

36. (1) Without altering the legislative authority of Parliament or of the provincial legislatures, or the rights of any of them with respect to the exercise of their legislative authority, Parliament and the legislatures, together with the government of Canada and the provincial governments, are committed to

(a)   promoting equal opportunities for the well-being of Canadians;

(b)   furthering economic development to reduce disparity in opportunities; and

(c)   providing essential public services of reasonable quality to all Canadians.

Commitment respecting public services

(2)   Parliament and the government of Canada are committed to the principle of making equalization payments to ensure that provincial governments have sufficient revenues to provide reasonably comparable levels of public services at reasonably comparable levels of taxation.

PART IV

CONSTITUTIONAL CONFERENCE

Constitutional
conference

37.   (1) A constitutional conference composed of the Prime Minister of Canada and the first ministers of the provinces shall be convened by the Prime Minister of Canada within one year after this Part comes into force.

Participation of
aboriginal peoples

(2)   The conference convened under subsection (1) shall have included in its agenda an item respecting constitutional matters that directly affect the aboriginal peoples of Canada, including the identification and definition of the rights of those peoples to be included in the Constitution of Canada, and the Prime Minister of Canada shall invite representatives of those peoples to participate in the discussions on that item.

Participation of
territories

(3)   The Prime Minister of Canada shall invite elected representatives of the governments of the Yukon Territory and the Northwest Territories to participate in the discussion on any item on the agenda of the conference convened under subsection (1) that, in the opinion of the Prime Minister, directly affects the Yukon Territory and the Northwest Territories.

PART IV.1

CONSTITUTIONAL CONFERENCES

Constitutional
conferences

37.1   (1) In addition to the conference convened in March 1983, at least two constitutional conferences composed of the Prime Minister of Canada and the first ministers of the provinces shall be convened by the Prime Minister of Canada, the first within three years after April 17, 1982 and the second within five years after that date.

Participation of
aboriginal peoples

(2)   Each conference convened under subsection (1) shall have included in its agenda constitutional matters that directly affect the aboriginal peoples of Canada, and the Prime Minister of Canada shall invite representatives of those peoples to participate in the discussions on those matters.

Participation of
territories

(3)   The Prime Minister of Canada shall invite elected representatives of the governments of the Yukon Territory and the Northwest Territories to participate in the discussions on any item on the agenda of a conference convened under subsection (1) that, in the opinion of the Prime Minister, directly affects the Yukon Territory and the Northwest Territories.

Subsection 35(1)
not affected

(4)   Nothing in this section shall be construed so as to derogate from subsection 35(1).[4]

PART V

PROCEDURE FOR AMENDING CONSTITUTION OF CANADA

General procedure
for amending
Constitution of
Canada

38.   (1) An amendment to the Constitution of Canada may be made by proclamation issued by the Governor General under the Great Seal of Canada where so authorized by

(a)   resolutions of the Senate and House of Commons; and

(b) resolutions of the legislative assemblies of at least two-thirds of the provinces that have, in the aggregate, according to the then latest general census, at least fifty per cent of the population of all the provinces.

Majority of members

(2) An amendment made under subsection (1) that derogates from the legislative powers, the proprietary rights or any other rights or privileges of the legislature or government of a province shall require a resolution supported by a majority of the members of each of the Senate, the House of Commons and the legislative assemblies required under subsection (1).

Expression of dissent

(3) An amendment referred to in subsection (2) shall not have effect in a province the legislative assembly of which has expressed its dissent thereto by resolution supported by a majority of its members prior to the issue of the proclamation to which the amendment relates unless that legislative assembly, subsequently, by resolution supported by a majority of its members, revokes its dissent and authorizes the amendment.

Revocation of dissent

(4) A resolution of dissent made for the purposes of subsection (3) may be revoked at any time before or after the issue of the proclamation to which it relates.

Restriction on proclamation

39. (1) A proclamation shall not be issued under subsection 38(1) before the expiration of one year from the adoption of the resolution initiating the amendment procedure thereunder, unless the legislative assembly of each province has previously adopted a resolution of assent or dissent.

Idem

(2) A proclamation shall not be issued under subsection 38(1) after the expiration of three years from the adoption of the resolution initiating the amendment procedure thereunder.

Compensation

40. Where an amendment is made under subsection 38(1) that transfers provincial legislative powers relating to education or other cultural matters from provincial legislatures to Parliament, Canada shall provide reasonable compensation to any province to which the amendment does not apply.

Amendment by unanimous consent

41. An amendment to the Constitution of Canada in relation to the following matters may be made by proclamation issued by the Governor General under the Great Seal of Canada only where authorized by resolutions of the Senate and House of Commons and of the legislative assembly of each province:

(a) the office of the Queen, the Governor General and the Lieutenant Governor of a province;

(b) the right of a province to a number of members in the House of Commons not less than the number of Senators by which the province is entitled to be represented at the time this Part comes into force;

(c) subject to section 43, the use of the English or the French language;

(d) the composition of the Supreme Court of Canada; and

(e) an amendment to this Part.

Amendment by general procedure

42. (1) An amendment to the Constitution of Canada in relation to the following matters may be made only in accordance with subsection 38(1):

(a)   the principle of proportionate representation of the provinces in the House of Commons prescribed by the Constitution of Canada;

(b)   the powers of the Senate and the method of selecting Senators;

(c)   the number of members by which a province is entitled to be represented in the Senate and the residence qualifications of Senators;

(d)   subject to paragraph 41(d), the Supreme Court of Canada;

(e)   the extension of existing provinces into the territories; and

(f)   notwithstanding any other law of practice, the establishment of new provinces.

Exception

(2)   Subsections 38(2) to (4) do not apply in respect of amendments in relation to matters referred to in subsection (1).

Amendment of provisions relating to some but not all provinces

43.   An amendment to the Constitution of Canada in relation to any provision that applies to one or more, but not all, provinces, including

(a)   any alteration to boundaries between provinces, and

(b)   any amendment to any provision that relates to the use of the English or the French language within a province, may be made by proclamation issued by the Governor General under the Great Seal of Canada only where so authorized by resolutions of the Senate and House of Commons and of the legislative assembly of each province to which the amendment applies.

Amendments by Parliament

44.   Subject to sections 41 and 42, Parliament may exclusively make laws amending the Constitution of Canada in relation to the executive government of Canada or the Senate and House of Commons.

Amendments by provincial legislatures

45.   Subject to section 41, the legislature of each province may exclusively make laws amending the constitution of the province.

Initiation of amendment procedures

46.   (1) The procedures for amendment under sections 38, 41, 42 and 43 may be initiated either by the Senate or the House of Commons or by the legislative assembly of a province.

Revocation of authorization

(2)   A resolution of assent made for the purposes of this Part may be revoked at any time before the issue of a proclamation authorized by it.

Amendments without Senate resolution

47.   (1) An amendment to the Constitution of Canada made by proclamation under section 38, 41, 42 or 43 may be made without a resolution of the Senate authorizing the issue of the proclamation if, within one hundred and eighty days after the adoption by the House of Commons of a resolution authorizing its issue, the Senate has not adopted such a resolution and if, at any time after the expiration of that period, the House of Commons again adopts the resolution.

Computation of period

(2)   Any period when Parliament is prorogued or dissolved shall not be counted in computing the one hundred and eighty day period referred to in subsection (1).

Advice to issue proclamation

48.   The Queen's Privy Council for Canada shall advise the Governor General to issue a proclamation under this Part forthwith on the adoption of the resolutions required for an amendment made by proclamation under this Part.

Constitutional
conference

49. A constitutional conference composed of the Prime Minister of Canada and the first ministers of the provinces shall be convened by the Prime Minister of Canada within fifteen years after this Part comes into force to review the provisions of this Part.

PART VI

AMENDMENT TO THE CONSTITUTION ACT, 1867

Amendment to
Constitution
Act, 1867

50. The Constitution Act, 1867 (formerly named the British North America Act, 1867) is amended by adding thereto, immediately after section 92 thereof, the following heading and section:

*"Non-Renewable Natural Resources, Forestry Resources
and Electrical Energy*

Laws respecting
non-renewable
natural resources,
forestry resources
and electrical energy

92A. (1) In each province, the legislature may exclusively make laws in relation to

(a) exploration for non-renewable natural resources in the province;

(b) development, conservation and management of non-renewable natural resources and forestry resources in the province, including laws in relation to the rate of primary production therefrom; and

(c) development, conservation and management of sites and facilities in the province for the generation and production of electrical energy.

Export from
provinces of
resources

(2) In each province, the legislature may make laws in relation to the export from the province to another part of Canada of the primary production from non-renewable natural resources and forestry resources in the province and the production from facilities in the province for the generation of electrical energy, but such laws may not authorize or provide for discrimination in prices or in supplies exported to another part of Canada.

Authority of
Parliament

(3) Nothing in subsection (2) derogates from the authority of Parliament to enact laws in relation to the matters referred to in that subsection and, where such a law of Parliament and a law of a province conflict, the law of Parliament prevails to the extent of the conflict.

Taxation of
resources

(4) In each province, the legislature may make laws in relation to the raising of money by any mode or system of taxation in respect of

(a) non-renewable natural resources and forestry resources in the province and the primary production therefrom, and

(b) sites and facilities in the province for the generation of electrical energy and the production therefrom, whether or not production is exported in whole or in part from the province, but such laws may not authorize or provide for taxation that differentiates between production exported to another part of Canada and production not exported from the province.

"Primary production"

(5)   The expression "primary production" has the meaning assigned by the Sixth Schedule.

Existing powers or rights

(6)   Nothing in subsections (10) to (5) derogates from any powers or rights that a legislature or government of a province had immediately before the coming into fore of this section."

Idem

51.   The said Act is further amended by adding thereto the following Schedule:

"THE SIXTH SCHEDULE

Primary Production from Non-Renewable Natural Resources
and Forestry Resources

1.   For the purposes of section 92A of this Act,

(a)   production from a non-renewable natural resource is primary production therefrom if

(i)   it is in the form in which it exists upon its recovery or severance from its natural state, or

(ii)   it is a product resulting from processing or refining the resource, and is not a manufactured product or a product resulting fro refining crude oil, refining upgraded heavy crude oil, refining gases or liquids derived from coal or refining a synthetic equivalent of crude oil; and

(b)   production from a forestry resource is primary production therefrom if it consists of sawlogs, poles, lumber, wood chips, sawdust or any other primary wood product, or wood pulp, and is not a product manufactured from wood."

PART VII
GENERAL

Primacy of Constitutional of Canada

52.   (1) The Constitution of Canada is the supreme law of Canada, and any law that is inconsistent with the provisions of the Constitution is, to the extent of the inconsistency, of no force or effect.

Constitution of Canada

(2)   The Constitution of Canada includes

(a)   The Canada Act 1982, including this Act;

(b)   the Acts and orders referred to in the schedule; and

(c)   any amendment to any Act or order referred to in paragraph (a) or (b).

Amendments to Constitution of Canada

(3)   Amendments to the Constitution of Canada shall be made only in accordance with the authority contained in the Constitution of Canada.

Repeals and new names

53.   (1) The enactments referred to in Column I of the schedule are hereby repealed or amended to the extent indicated in Column II thereof and, unless repealed, shall continue as law in Canada under the names set out in Column III thereof.

Consequential amendments

(2) Every enactment, except the *Canada Act 1982,* that refers to an enactment referred to in the schedule by the name in Column I thereof is hereby amended by substituting for that name the corresponding name in Column III thereof, and any British North America Act not referred to in the schedule may be cited as the *Constitution Act* followed by the year and number, if any, of it enactment.

Repeal and consequential amendments

54. Part IV is repealed on the day that is one year after this Part comes into force and this section may be repealed and this Act renumbered, consequentially upon the repeal of Part IV and this section, by proclamation issued by the Governor General under the Great Seal of Canada.

Repeal of Part IV.1 and this section French version of Constitution of Canada

54.1 Part IV.1 and this section are repealed on April 18, 1987.[5]

55. A French version of the portions of the Constitution of Canada referred to in the schedule shall be prepared by the Minister of Justice of Canada as expeditiously as possible and, when any portion thereof sufficient to warrant action being taken has been so prepared, it shall be put forward for enactment by proclamation issued by the Governor General under the Great Seal of Canada pursuant to the procedure then applicable to an amendment of the same provisions of the Constitution of Canada.

English and French version of certain constitutional texts

56. Where any portion of the Constitution of Canada has been or is enacted in English and French or where a French version of any portion of the Constitution is enacted pursuant to section 55, the English and French versions of that portion of the Constitution are equally authoritative.

English and French versions of this Act Commencement

57. The English and French versions of this Act are equally authoritative.

58. Subject to section 59, this Act shall come into force on a day to be fixed by proclamation issued by the Queen or the Governor General under the Great Seal of Canada.

Commencement of paragraph 23(1)(a) in respect of Quebec

59. (1) Paragraph 23(1)(a) shall come into force in respect of Quebec on a day to be fixed by proclamation issued by the Queen or the Governor General under the Great Seal of Canada.

Authorization of Quebec

(2) A proclamation under subsection (1) shall be issued only where authorized by the legislative assembly or government of Quebec.

Repeal of this section

(3) This section may be repealed on the day paragraph 23(1)(a) comes into force in respect of Quebec and this Act amended and renumbered, consequentially upon the repeal of this section, by proclamation issued by the Queen or the Governor General under the Great Seal of Canada.

Short title and citations

60. This Act may be cited as the *Constitution Act,* 1982, and the Constitution Acts 1867 to 1975 (No. 2) and this Act may be cited together as the *Constitution Acts, 1867 to 1982.*

61.   A reference to the *"Constitution Acts, 1867 to 1982"* shall be deemed to include a reference to the *"Constitution Amendment Proclamation, 1983."*[6]

For an online version of Appendices A and B, plus the SCHEDULE to the Constitution Act, 1982: Modernization of the Constitution, visit the text's website at **www.intropolitics8e.nelson.com.**

---

[1]Paragraph 25(b) was repealed and the present paragraph 25(b) was substituted by the Constitution Amendment Proclamation, 1983.

[2]Subsections (3) and (4) of s. 35 were added by the Constitution Amendment Proclamation, 1983.

[3]Section 35.1 was added by the Constitution Amendment Proclamation, 1983.

[4]Part IV.1, consisting of s. 37.1, was added by the Constitution Amendment Proclamation, 1983.

[5]Section 54.1 was added by the Constitution Amendment Proclamation, 1983.

[6]Section 61 was added by the Constitution Amendment Proclamation, 1983.

GLOSSARY

(Numbers in parentheses refer to the chapter(s) containing the main discussion of the term.)

aboriginal (or indigenous) peoples Inhabitants of the Americas prior to the arrival of European settlers. (4)

ad hoc committees Legislative committees appointed for special, temporary purposes, such as to investigate a problem before the government prepares legislation on the subject. (20)

administration The organized apparatus of the state for the preparation and implementation of legislation and policies, also called the bureaucracy. (28)

agenda-setting Controlling the focus of attention by establishing the issues for public discussion. (24)

anarchism A political ideology characterized by the belief that order will result from mutual cooperation in the absence of a higher, coercive authority. (20)

anarchist One who advocates anarchy. Also refers to the followers of Mikhail Bakunin, who opposed Marx's focus on the state. (12)

anarchy Order resulting from mutual coordination in the absence of a higher, coercive authority. (8)

animal liberation A movement that proposes to ban hunting, the raising of domestic livestock for food and other economic purposes, and the use of animals in laboratory experiments. (15)

anomic group Spontaneously formed interest group with concern over a specific issue. (23)

aristocracy A form of government in which a minority rules under the law. (16)

associational group Formally organized group that articulates the interests of its members over long periods of time. (23)

asymmetrical federalism A federal system of government in which powers are unevenly divided among provinces (i.e., some provinces have greater responsibilities or more autonomy than others). (21)

auditor general An official of Parliament whose staff audits the expenditures of government departments and who provides an annual report on selected programs. (28)

authoritarianism A system of government in which leaders are not subjected to the test of free elections. (19)

authority A form of power based on agreement regarding the right to issue commands and make decisions. (2)

autocracy An arbitrary system of government unconstrained by the rule of law and the consent of the governed. (19)

autonomy A state of independence from outside control. (17)

backbencher Members of parliament on the government side who sit on the back benches and are not in cabinet, or those similarly distant from shadow-cabinet posts in opposition parties. (20)

behavioural revolution The introduction of more empirical, especially quantitative, analysis into the study of government and politics. (Introduction)

bicameralism A system of government in which the legislature is divided into two chambers, an upper and a lower house. (17)

bilateral procedure A procedure for amending certain sections of the Canadian constitution in which approval is required only from Parliament plus the legislature(s) of the province(s) affected by the amendment. (7)

bill A piece of legislation under consideration by a legislative body. (20)

binational state Two nations coexisting within one state. (4)

bipolar system An international system in which there are two dominant states. (8)

bourgeoisie A Marxist term referring to those who own the means of production. (12)

bureaucracy A type of administration characterized by specialization, professionalism, and security of tenure. (28)

by-laws Legal enactments, such as parking regulations or zoning ordinances, passed by local government under provincial authority. (6)

cabinet solidarity The convention by which all members of cabinet support government policy and do not criticize it or each other in public. (20)

Canadian politics The study of federal, provincial, and municipal politics in Canada. (Introduction)

caucus A meeting of legislators of any one party to discuss parliamentary strategy and party policy. (20)

central agencies Government agencies such as the PMO, the PCO, the Treasury Board, and the Finance Department that have certain coordinating functions across the whole federal public service. (27)

charismatic authority Authority based on the admiration of personal qualities of an individual. (2)

checks and balances A system of government in which power is divided among the executive, legislative, and judicial branches of government, and these powers check and balance each other. (20)

citizenship Legal membership in the state. (3)

civic nation (nationalism) A national identity based on loyalty to the state rather than on ethnic factors. (4)

civil society The network of self-generating, autonomous social organizations bound by shared rules. (18)

classical liberalism A liberal ideology entailing a minimal role for government in order to maximize individual freedom. (10)

coalition An alliance between two or more political units in response to opposing forces. (1)

coalition government A parliamentary government in which the cabinet is composed of members of more than one party. (20)

code A comprehensive set of interrelated rules intended reduce uncertainty in interpretation of the law by systematizing and making explicit legal precedents. (6)

code civil The unique system of civil law used in Quebec. (6)

coercion A form of power based on forced compliance through fear and intimidation. (2)

collective defence organization An alliance among states against external threats. (8)

collective (public) goods Goods and services enjoyed in common and not divisible among individuals. (10)

collective security A commitment by a number of states to join in an alliance against member states that threaten the peace. (8)

Cominform "Communist Information Bureau," an international communist organization formed after World War II. (12)

Comintern "Communist International"; also known as the Third International, the communist international organization between the two World Wars. (12)

common law The accumulation of judicial precedents as the basis for court decisions. (6)

communications (mass) media A general term for all modern means of conveying information. (24)

communism A political ideology characterized by a belief in eliminating exploitation through public ownership and central planning of the economy. (12)

communist   One who advocates communism. (12)

comparative politics   An area of political study concerned with the relative similarities and differences among political systems. (Introduction)

concurrent majority   Approval by a majority vote in two or more bodies, such as two houses of parliament or multiple provincial legislatures. (17)

confederation   A federal system of government in which sovereign constituent governments create a central government but the balance of power remains with constituent governments. (21)

confidence   Support for the government by the majority of the members of (usually) the lower house of parliament. (20)

consent of the governed   People's acceptance of the form of government under which they live. (10)

conservationism   The attempt to manage natural resources in order to maximize benefits over a long period of time. (15)

conservatism   A political ideology generally characterized by a belief in individualism and minimal government intervention in the economy and society; also a belief in the virtue of the status quo and general acceptance of traditional morality. (11)

consociationalism   A form of democracy in which harmony in segmented societies is maintained through the distinctive roles of elites, the autonomy of organized interests, and a balance of power among these interests. (17)

constituency   An electoral district with a body of electors who vote for a representative in an elected assembly. (25)

constitution   The fundamental rules and principles by which a state is organized. (7)

constitutional democracy   See *liberal democracy*.

constitutionalism   The belief that governments will defer to the rules and principles enshrined in a constitution and uphold the rule of law. (7)

constructive vote of confidence   A system in which the majority in the lower house can bring down the government, but not until that majority approves another government (e.g., in Germany). (20)

convention   A practice or custom followed by those in government, although not explicitly written in the constitution or in legislation. (7)

corporatism   The organization of liberal democracies in such a way that the state is the dominant force in society and the activities of all interests in society are subordinate to that force. (17)

coup d'état   A quick, forcible, and unconstitutional change of government, often by a faction within the military or the ruling party. (19)

Crown corporations   Corporations owned by the government that assume a structure similar to that of a private company and that operate semi-independently of the cabinet. (28)

culture   The pattern of beliefs and behaviour of a people, including the place of the family, the role of religion, and the influence of economics and politics. (5)

custom   A generally accepted practice or behaviour developed over time. (6)

customary law   Rules of conduct developed over time and enforceable in court. (6)

debt (public)   See *public debt*.

deep ecology   A form of environmentalism holding that nature and the natural order should be valued over individual human happiness. (15)

deficit   In international trade, occurs when the value of a state's imports is more than the value of its exports. (11)

delegate   A representative role in which the individual subordinates his or her views to those of his or her constituents. (26)

democracy   In the original sense of the term, a system of government in which the majority rules without legal restraint. Compare *liberal democracy*. (16)

democratic centralism The concentration of power in the leadership of the Communist Party, which in theory acts in the interests of the people. (12)

Department of Finance The government department that has overall responsibility for the government's finances and its role in the economy. (27)

deputy minister A Canadian public servant who heads a government department, manages the department, and advises the minister. (27)

deregulation A government policy designed to remove regulations on market activity. (11)

despotism An individual ruling through fear without regard to law and not answerable to the people. (19)

devolution A system of government in which the sovereign central government devolves (delegates) power to regional governments, subject to its overriding control. (21)

dictatorship of the proletariat A revolutionary seizure of power by the "vanguard" of society, the communist party, which then rules in the name of the working class. (12)

diplomacy A system of formal, regularized communication that allows states to peacefully conduct their business with each other. (8)

direct democracy A system of government based on public decisions made by citizens meeting in an assembly or voting by ballot. (17)

disallowance A power given to the federal government in the Constitution Act, 1867, under which the cabinet can nullify any provincial law, even though it has received royal assent from the lieutenant governor of the province. (21)

discretion The flexibility afforded government to decide something within the broader framework of rules. (7)

distributive laws Laws designed to distribute public goods and services to individuals in society. (22)

downsizing Reduction of the size and scope of government. (11)

doxa Greek word for an opinion that may be at least partly true but cannot be fully expounded. (9)

economic conservatism See *fiscal conservatism.*

Electoral College The body that formally chooses the president of the United States. (20)

elite A small group of people with a disproportionate amount of public decision-making power. (17)

empirical Political analysis based on factual and observable data in contrast to thoughts or ideas. (Introduction)

environmentalism A family of ideologies in which human damage to the natural world is the central concern. (15)

episteme Greek word for knowledge that can be demonstrated by logical argument from first principles. (9)

equality of opportunity The equalization of life chances for all individuals in society, regardless of economic position. (10)

equality of result The equalization of outcomes of social and economic processes. (10)

equality of right Application of the law in the same way to all. (10)

equality rights A section of the Charter of Rights and Freedoms (s.15) that prohibits governments from discriminating against certain categories of people. (29)

ethnic group A subgroup within a nation based on objective factors of common ancestry, language, religion, customs, and so on. (4)

ethnic nation (nationalism) A national identity based on objective factors of common ancestry, language, religion, customs, and so on. (4)

executive Person or persons responsible for managing the business array of government. (20)

executive federalism A federal process directed by extensive federal–provincial interaction at the level of first ministers, departmental ministers, and deputy ministers. (21)

Executive Office The Executive Office of the President is made up of White House offices and agencies that help develop and implement the policy and programs of the president. (27)

extractive laws   Laws designed to collect taxes to pay for governing society. (22)

faction   An association of individuals organized for the purpose of influencing government actions favourable to their interests, now known as *interest groups*. (23)

failed state   A state suffering from conflict, political instability, economic collapse, the inability to provide services to its people, or some combination of these factors. (8)

fascism   An extreme form of nationalism that played on fears of communism and rejected individual freedom, liberal individualism, democracy, and limitations on the state. (13)

federalism   A system of government in which sovereignty is divided between a central government and several provincial or state governments. (21)

feminism   The belief that society is disadvantageous to women, systematically depriving them of individual choice, political power, economic opportunity, and intellectual recognition. (14)

First International   A loose association of socialist parties and labour unions in Western Europe, organized in 1864. (12)

fiscal (economic) conservatism   A variety of modern conservatism that emphasizes property rights and open markets rather than traditional morality. (11)

fiscal policy   Policy related to government spending. (10)

formal–legal institutions   Institutions that are explicitly created by a constitution. (22)

fragment theory   A theory (proposed by Louis Hartz) according to which colonial societies such as Canada originated as fragments of the larger European society and have remained marked throughout their history by the conditions of their origin. (5)

fragmented culture   Political culture where there is a high degree of citizen engagement, but little agreement on the rules of the game. Disagreements, disunity and violence often lead to instability in such cultures. (5)

free-market environmentalism   The view that environmental problems are best solved by property rights and markets. (15)

free riders   Those who enjoy a collective good without helping to pay for it. (10)

free vote   A legislative vote in which members are not required to toe the party line. (20)

functions   Special activities or purposes that *structures* serve in the political process; for example, interest groups to articulate interests. (22)

gender gap   A difference between men and women in political behaviour, such as voting for different parties. (14)

General Agreement on Tariffs and Trade   See *World Trade Organization*.

general procedure   A procedure for amending the Canadian constitution requiring the approval of Parliament plus the legislatures of two-thirds of the provinces having among them at least half of the population of the provinces. (7)

gerrymander   Manipulating constituency boundaries for partisan election purposes. (25)

globalization   The processes and consequences of increasing the scope of exchange in goods and services, money, people, and ideas. (8)

government   A specialized group of individuals, institutions, and agencies that make and enforce public decisions. (1)

Green   Political parties or movements dedicated to environmental protection. (15)

habit   A personal rule of conduct. (6)

head of government   The person in effective charge of the executive branch of government; the prime minister in a parliamentary system. (20)

head of state   An individual who represents the state but does not exercise political power; the Queen in Great Britain and Canada. (20)

human rights   Rights thought to belong to all people simply because they are human beings. (6)

human welfare ecology   Offshoot of conservation movement that addresses the value of the environment to human health and happiness. (15)

ideological party   A type of political party that emphasizes ideological purity over the attainment of power. (23)

ideology A system of beliefs and values that explains society and prescribes the role of government. (9)

immigrants Individuals who have voluntarily moved to another country. (4)

indigenous peoples *See aboriginal peoples.* (4)

influence A form of power based on the ability to persuade others to pursue a desired objective. (2)

informal institution Institutions that are an integral part of the political process, but that are not established by a constitution. (22)

initiative The initiation of legislative action on a particular issue by way of a voters' petition. (17)

institutional group A group that is closely associated with some part of the government and that acts internally to influence public decisions. (23)

interest party A political party with a single interest or purpose, such as the Green Party. (23)

interest (pressure) group Organizations whose members act together to influence public policy in order to promote their common interest. (23)

International Bank for Reconstruction and Development (World Bank) An organization that provides international aid to developing states. (8)

international law The body of rules governing the relationships of states with each other. (8)

international legal persons Those entities (at the present time, only states are included) having full power to act under international law. (8)

International Monetary Fund An international organization created to stabilize of national currencies throughout the world. (8)

international order The combination of major actors, rules, mechanisms, and understandings that manage the coexistence and interdependence of states. (8)

international organization An organization composed of states, non-government organizations (NGOs), and/or other international actors. (8)

international regimes The pattern of regular cooperation governed by implicit and explicit expectations between two or more states. (8)

international relations An area of political study concerned with the interaction of independent states. (Introduction)

intervention In a court case, the presentation of a view on the law without representing one of the parties in the litigation. (29)

irredentism Nationalistic desire to recover lost territory adjacent to the boundaries of the state. (13)

item veto The power of some American state governors to veto particular components of a bill rather than reject the entire legislation; not available to the President. (20)

judicial activism The willingness and inclination of judges to overturn legislation or executive action. (29)

Judicial Committee of the Privy Council (JCPC) Highest appellate court for the British Empire; functioned as Canada's final court of appeal until 1949. (21)

judicial review The power of the courts to declare legislation unconstitutional (*ultra vires*). (3, 20)

judiciary The branch of government with the power to resolve legal conflicts that arise between citizens, between citizens and governments, or between levels of government. (20)

junta A Spanish word meaning a group of individuals forming a government, especially after a revolution or *coup d'état.* (17)

jus sanguinis A Latin phrase meaning literally "right of blood." It is used to describe legal systems that grant citizenship automatically to the children of citizens no matter where they are born. (3)

jus soli A Latin phrase meaning literally "right of place." It is used to describe legal systems that grant citizenship automatically to all those born within state territory. (3)

laissez-faire The nonintervention of the state in the economy. (Introduction, 10)

law Enforceable rules of conduct. (6)

legal authority System of authority based on general rules rather than inheritance or personal qualities. (2)

legislation Consciously formulated and deliberately constructed law. (6)

legislative The branch of government responsible for making laws for society. (20)

legislature A representative assembly responsible for making laws for society. (26)

legitimacy Belief in the "rightness" of rule. (2)

liberal democracy A system of government characterized by universal adult suffrage, political equality, majority rule, and constitutionalism. (17)

liberal feminism The advocacy of equal rights between men and women. (14)

liberalism 1. A family of ideologies that emphasizes individual freedom, a limited state, constitutionalism, and the rule of law. (10) 2. In international politics, a theory of relations between states that stresses the rule of law. (8)

libertarianism A contemporary ideology that advocates maximum individual freedom in all spheres of life, social as well as economic. (11)

limited government A state restricted in its exercise of power by the constitution and the rule of law. (10)

limited state See *limited government.*

list system A form of proportional representation in which the elector votes not for individuals but for parties, which have lists of candidates running for office. (25)

lobbying Activities of interest groups aimed at influencing governors and the public to achieve favourable policy decisions. (23)

logrolling The act of vote trading among legislators in the process of getting legislation passed. (20, 27)

Magna Carta **(Great Charter)** A document signed by King John in 1215, conceding that the king is subject to law. (7)

majority Fifty percent plus one of those voting. Also called "simple majority." (17)

majority-plurality system An electoral system in which there are two rounds of voting. Candidates who do not achieve some minimum proportion of votes on the first ballot are dropped from the second. On the second ballot, the winning candidate only needs a plurality of valid votes cast. (25)

majority-runoff system An electoral system in which there are two rounds of voting. The first round of voting is held as in an SMP system. If no candidate earns a majority of votes in that round, the two candidates with the with the highest vote totals advance to the next round, where the winner is guaranteed to have had the support of the majority. (25)

majority government A parliamentary government in which the party in power has more than 50 percent of the seats in the legislature. (20)

materialist The term used by Ronald Inglehart to describe those who are motivated primarily by personal and economic security; cf. *post-materialist.* (5)

merit recruitment A system of hiring public servants on the basis of qualifications rather than on party preference or personal connections. (28)

microcosm theory The idea that a governing body should be a miniature replica of the society it represents. (26)

ministerial responsibility The principle that cabinet ministers are individually responsible to the House of Commons for everything that happens in their department. (27)

ministry The entire group of MPs appointed by the prime minister to specific executive responsibilities. (27)

minority government A parliamentary government in which the government party has less than 50 percent of the seats in the legislature. (20)

mixed economy An economy based on both private and public (government-controlled) enterprises. (12)

mixed-member-proportional (MMP) system Electoral system in which voters cast two ballots, one for a local candidate running in a territorial constituency (first past the post) and the other for a list of candidates put forward by a political party (list system). (25)

modernization In politics, the replacement of traditional authority with legal authority. (2) In economics, the term refers to the adoption of markets and sophisticated technology in place of barter and subsistence production.

monarchy Form of government in which a single person rules under the law. (16)

monetary policy Governmental control over the supply of money. (10)

monism Exclusive emphasis on a single principle or interest. (19)

movement party A type of political party that emerges from a political movement, such as a national liberation movement. (23)

multinational state Three or more nations coexisting under one sovereign government. (4)

multiparty system A party system in which there are three or more major contenders for power. (23)

multipolar system An international involving several states. (8)

nation Individuals whose common identity creates a psychological bond and a political community. (4)

nationalism The feeling of loyalty and attachment to one's nation or nation-state, and strong support for its interests. (13)

nation-state A state with a single predominant national identity. (4)

natural authority Authority based on spontaneous deference to an individual's knowledge or social position. (2)

naturalization The process of acquiring citizenship not by birth but by grant from the state. (3)

natural law Rules of conduct binding by virtue of human rationality alone. (6)

neoconservatism An American ideological term referring to certain conservative thinkers who were originally leftists; in Canada, usually an anti-American term of abuse. (11)

neo-fascist Term used to describe contemporary anti-democratic, racist parties of the far right. (13)

New Public Management A recent approach to public administration emphasizing efficiency and accountability to the public. (28)

nonassociational (latent) group A group that lacks formal organization but has the potential for mobilizing politically. (23)

non-governmental organization (NGO) A not-for-profit organization that is not associated with a government. (8)

normative Political analysis based on values, commitments, and ideas. (Introduction)

notwithstanding clause Section 33 of the Charter of Rights and Freedoms, which allows federal or provincial legislatures to pass laws that may violate certain sections of the Charter. (29)

Official Opposition In a parliamentary system, the largest of the opposition parties, given a special role to play in the legislative process. (20)

oligarchy A form of government in which a minority rules outside the law. (16)

ombudsman An official with the power to investigate complaints against government administration. (28)

one-party-dominant system A party system in which there are political alternatives but a single political party dominates the political process as a result of the overwhelming support of the electorate. (23)

opposition Those members of parliament who are not part of the government of the day. (20)

order-in-council In the British parliamentary tradition, a decision by cabinet that carries legal force. (6)

parliamentary sovereignty The supreme authority of parliament to make or repeal laws. (3)

parochial culture A type of political culture that emphasizes local grievances and benefits rather than broad concerns of the entire society or nation. (5)

participatory culture A type of political culture that emphasizes individuals actively playing a role in national politics. (5)

party discipline   The convention that all MPs within any party vote together, as predetermined in the party caucus and enforced by the party whip. (20)

patriarchy   The domination of society by men. (14)

peacekeeping   The interposition of lightly armed military forces between combatants who have agreed to stop fighting. (8)

permanent secretary   The British equivalent of a Canadian deputy minister. (28)

personal freedom   The absence of coercion in various aspects of life. (10)

personal party   A type of political party founded around a single, overwhelmingly influential political leader. (23)

philosopher-king   Plato's view of the ideal individual who rules in the common interest and is directed by wisdom and virtue rather than the constraint of law. (16)

planning   Production and allocation of resources determined by a central authority. (12)

plebiscite   Another term for an advisory referendum. (17)

pluralism   The open competition of political interests. (17)

plurality   A voting decision based on assigning victory to the largest number of votes, not necessarily a majority. (17)

policy community   The network of individuals and organizations deeply involved in a particular area of public policy. (22)

polis   Greek city-state. (1)

political alienation   The sense of estrangement from political power. (25)

political consultant   A professional adviser who puts his or her political expertise to work in the private and public sectors. (23)

political culture   Attitudes, values, beliefs, and orientations that individuals in a society hold regarding their political system. (5)

political economy   The study of the involvement of the state in the economy. (Introduction)

political executive   The politically accountable heads of government. (27)

political party   An organized group that makes nominations and contests elections in the hope of gaining control of government. (23)

political patronage   Government appointments made as a payoff for loyal partisan activity. (28)

political philosophy   An area of political study based on historical, reflective, and conceptual methods. (Introduction)

political police   Police force reporting directly to a political leader who uses it for political control rather than law enforcement. (19)

political process   The interaction of organized political structures in making and administering public decisions for a society. (22)

political science   The systematic study of government and politics. (Introduction)

political socialization   The process by which political culture is transmitted from generation to generation. (5)

politics   A process of conflict resolution in which support is mobilized and maintained for collective action. (1)

polity   A form of government characterized by popular sovereignty but exercised within a constitutional framework to prevent the oppression of the minority by the majority rule. (16)

polyarchy   Robert Dahl's term for pluralist forms of liberal democracy, in which many different interests complete. (17)

popular sovereignty   Supreme authority residing in the consent of the people. (3)

porkbarrelling   Using governmental power to do favours for particular groups or constituencies in return for promises of political support. (27)

portfolio   The administrative responsibility carried by a minister, usually some combination of departments and other agencies. (27)

post-materialism   The shift in values since the late 1940s from public order and material prosperity to self-fulfillment. (5, 14)

post-materialist   The term used by Ronald Inglehart to describe those who are motivated primarily by self-fulfillment and self-expression. (5)

power The ability to get other individuals to do as one wants them to do. (2)

pragmatic party A type of political party concerned primarily with winning elections. (23)

precedent A previous judicial case used as an example for deciding the case at hand. (6)

preferential (alternative) ballot Electoral system in which voters rank the candidates. (25)

prerogative The residual powers of the Crown that can be exercised at its own discretion. (7)

Prime Minister's Office (PMO) Support staff appointed by the prime minister to carry out political functions. (27)

priming The selective portrayal of political events and personalities by the media, which in turn affects public opinion. (24)

primus inter pares Latin phrase meaning "first among equals." (20)

private law Laws controlling relations between individuals. (6)

private member A member of parliament who is not in the cabinet. (20)

private member's bill Public bill introduced in the legislature by a member who is not in the cabinet. (20)

privatization The sale of government-owned assets or activities to the private sector. (11)

Privy Council A ceremonial body made up of all present and former cabinet ministers. (27)

Privy Council Office (PCO) A governmental department that supports the prime minister, cabinet, and cabinet committees in devising government policy. (27)

proclamation The announcement of the official date a new law will take effect. (20)

progressive tax A tax rate that increases as the amount of one's income increases. (10)

proletariat A Marxist term referring to those who sell their labour to the bourgeoisie; the working class. (12)

property franchise (suffrage) The requirement that citizens own a stipulated amount of property to receive the right to vote. (10)

proportional representation (PR) An electoral system in which the share of seats won closely matches the share of popular votes received. (25)

proportional tax A tax rate that is the same for everyone. (10)

proportionality This term refers to how closely the percentage of seats awarded to a party corresponds with the percentage of votes earned. Where these percentages match closely, the results are considered to be proportional. (25)

provincial courts Courts created by provincial statute, staffed by judges appointed by the province to deal with matters such as small claims and minor criminal offences. (29)

public authority Authority based on institutional office-holding. (2)

public debt The accumulated sum owed by the government to its creditors. (11)

public law Laws controlling the relations between the state and individuals in society. (6)

qualified majority The raising of the simple majority requirement of "50 percent plus one" to a higher level, in order to protect the rights of minorities. (17)

race A group of individuals differentiated through distinct physical characteristics and common ancestry. (4)

radical feminism A belief that men and women constitute "sexual classes" and that women's subordinate status is the result of a system that is controlled by men. (14)

readings First, second, and third readings representing the introduction, debate, and approval of proposed bills in the legislative chambers. (20)

realism A theory of international relations that holds that struggles are resolved on the basis of power of conflicting parties. (8)

recall The ability of voters in a constituency to remove their elected representative from office by means of a petition. (17)

redistribution The process of reallocating wealth and income to achieve an economic or social objective. (10)

Red Tory   A conservative with collectivist leanings. (11)

referendum   A decision on policy proposals by a direct vote of the electorate. (17)

reform liberalism   A liberal ideology that advocates a larger role for the state in providing equality of opportunity. (10)

regressive tax   A tax that weighs more heavily on those with low incomes. (10)

regulations   Legal enactments made by a minister, department, or agency acting under legislative authority. (6)

regulative laws   Laws that control individual and organizational behaviour. (22)

regulatory agencies   Government agencies established to administer laws in certain fields; for example, the Canadian Human Rights Commission. (28)

rehabilitation   A function of law enforcement that encourages a change in conduct that will prevent lawbreaking in the future. (6)

report stage   The stage in the legislative process after the second reading when the House debates the committee's report on a proposed bill. (20)

representative democracy   A system of government based on the election of decision makers by the people. (17)

reservation   Mechanism by which the lieutenant governor of a province can refuse royal assent to a bill and refer it to the federal cabinet for a decision. (21)

residual powers   Those powers in a federal system of government not explicitly allocated in a constitution. (21)

responsible government   A form of parliamentary democracy in which the political executive must retain the confidence of a majority of the elected legislature or assembly, and must resign or request an election if defeated on a vote of non-confidence. (20)

restitution   A function of law enforcement that provides compensation to those who have been harmed by rule breakers. (6)

restraint   A function of law enforcement that instills fear in those who cannot be swayed by influence or authority. (6)

retribution   A function of law enforcement that results in the punishment of those who violate the norms of society. (6)

royal assent   The approval of a bill by the Crown. (20)

rule of law   Belief that all actions, of individuals and governments, are subject to an institutionalized set of rules and regulations. (7)

runoff system   An electoral system in which additional rounds of balloting are held (with trailing candidates dropped) until a candidate receives a majority of the votes cast. (25)

scientific socialism   The term Marx and Engels used to stress that their ideology was based on an analysis of class conflict. (12)

Second International   The organization of socialist and labour parties in Europe, with the absence of anarchists, established in 1889. (12)

security dilemma   The spiral of preparations and tensions that emerges when the protective actions of one state lead to countermeasures by another state. (8)

self-government   The right of members of a group to control their own collective affairs. (13)

semi-presidential system   A system of governance that combines features of both parliamentary and presidential systems, with a strong popularly elected president as well as a prime minister responsible to a parliament. (20)

separation of powers   The separation of powers between executive, legislative, and judicial branches of government. (20)

shadow cabinet   The cohesive group of specialized critics in the Official Opposition party. (20)

single-member-plurality (SMP) system   An electoral system in which the candidate with the most votes wins, even though that win may not represent 50 percent plus one of the votes. (25)

single-party system   A party system in which there is only one party, and no political alternatives are legally tolerated. (23)

single-transferable-vote (STV) system   A form of proportional representation in which electors vote for individuals rather than party lists, but they do so by ranking the candidates in their order of choice. (25)

social conservatives Conservatives who advocate the restraint of individual desire for the common good. (11)

social democrats Socialists emphasizing popular consent, peaceful change, political pluralism, and constitutional government. (12)

socialism A leftist political ideology that emphasizes the principle of equality and usually prescribes a large role for government to intervene in society and the economy via taxation, regulation, redistribution, and public ownership. (12)

social justice The equalization of wealth and income to reach a more desirable outcome. (10)

society A self-sufficient group of individuals living together under common rules of conduct. (1)

sovereign The highest or supreme political authority. (3)

sovereignty Internally, refers to he highest governmental authority in a territorial state; externally, refers to independence from control by other states. (3)

special (ad hoc) committee Legislative committees appointed for special, temporary purposes, such as to investigate a problem before the government prepares legislation on the subject. (20)

spoils system The assumption that, after successfully winning an election, the political executive is entitled to appoint large numbers of supporters to the bureaucracy. (28)

spontaneous order The pattern of mutual coordination that emerges as individuals pursue their own interests in society. (10)

standing committee Legislative committees that are set up permanently and parallel government functions. (20)

stare decisis The legal principle that precedents are binding on similar subsequent cases; the basis of the common-law system. (6)

state Combination of people, territory, and sovereign government. (3)

stateless society A society without a sovereign government. (1)

statism The heavy intervention of the state in societal affairs, especially in the economic system. (19)

statute A specific piece of legislation. (6)

structuralism A theory of international relations that stresses the impact of world economic structures on the political, social, cultural, and economic systems of countries. (8)

structure In social-science jargon, an organization or an organized pattern of behaviour. Compare *function*. (22)

subject culture Political culture emphasizing obedience to authority. (5)

substate nation An ethnic group that could potentially have developed into a sovereign nation had they not been outnumbered by waves of new settlers. (4)

suffragism A political movement by women to obtain the right to vote. (14)

superior courts In Canada, courts organized by provincial statute and staffed by judges appointed by the federal government. (29)

sustainable development Environmentalist view that economic development should not outstrip available natural resources. (15)

symbolic laws Laws designed to create special meaning for society, such as the adoption of a national anthem. (22)

syndicalism A variation of socialism in which the workers own or control the factory or workplace. (12)

Third International Worldwide association of communist parties, established in 1921. (12)

totalitarianism A modern form of despotic rule in which the state undertakes to remake society according to an ideological design. (19)

traditional authority Authority based on birthright and custom. (2)

Treasury Board A cabinet committee and government department whose primary responsibility is to oversee government spending. (27)

tribe A community of people tied together by a myth of common ancestry. (4)

trustee A representative who acts independently in deciding what is in the best interests of his or her constituents. (26)

two-party-plus system A party system in which there are two major contenders for power of approximately equal strength plus one or more minor parties able to win seats but not to control the government. (23)

two-party system A party system in which there are two credible contenders for power and either is capable of winning any election. (23)

typology A broad classification scheme of governmental systems. (16)

tyranny A form of government in which one person rules arbitrarily. (16)

ultra vires Term used to describe an action that exceeds the conferred constitutional powers of the actor. Literally, "beyond the power." (29)

unanimity A decision rule in which any action must be approved by all participants. (17)

unanimous procedure A procedure for amending the Canadian constitution in which approval from Parliament plus the legislatures of all provinces is required. (7)

unipolar system An international system with only one dominant state. (8)

unitary system A system of government in which a single sovereign government rules the country. (21)

unwritten constitution An uncodified constitution established through traditional practice. (7)

utopian socialism Early-nineteenth-century socialism based on a universal appeal to reason. (12)

veto The authorized power of a president to reject legislation passed by Congress. (20)

violence The use of physical force or power as a means of achieving ends. (2)

vote of censure A motion of non-confidence requiring the prime minister and the cabinet to resign. (20)

welfare state The provision for redistributed benefits such as education and health services by the state. (10)

Westphalian system A system of government named for the Treaty of Westphalia (1648), which marked the recognition of the modern, sovereign state as the chief unit of international relations. (8)

White House Staff Special advisers to the U.S. president; part of the Executive Office and similar to the Canadian Prime Minister's Office. (27)

wilderness preservationism A form of environmentalism positing the intrinsic importance of wilderness for humankind. (15)

World Trade Organization An international organization created to provide the ground rules for international trade and commerce. (8)

Zionism Jewish nationalist movement advocating establishment of a Jewish nation-state. (13)

Index